CURRENT CONCEPTS
IN TRANSGENDER
IDENTITY

GARLAND GAY AND LESBIAN STUDIES
VOLUME 11
GARLAND REFERENCE LIBRARY OF SOCIAL SCIENCE
VOLUME 976

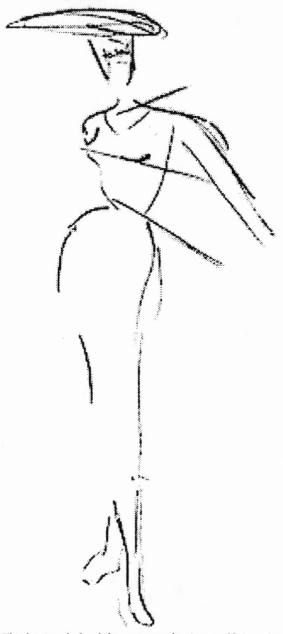

Frontispiece: This drawing of a female by a transsexual patient, age 32, is reprinted from Transsexualism and Sex Reassignment *(R. Green and J. Money, eds. Baltimore: Johns Hopkins University Press). It illustrates an article entitled "Psychological Testing of Male Transsexuals: A Brief Report of Results from the Wechsler Adult Intelligence Scale, the Thematic Apperception Test, and the House-Tree-Person Test" by Ruth Rae Doorbar. Reprinted from* Transsexualism and Sex Reassignment *by permission of Johns Hopkins University Press.*

CURRENT CONCEPTS IN TRANSGENDER IDENTITY

EDITED BY
DALLAS DENNY

GARLAND PUBLISHING, INC.
A MEMBER OF THE TAYLOR & FRANCIS GROUP
NEW YORK AND LONDON
1998

Library of Congress Cataloging-in-Publication Data

Current concepts in transgender identity / edited by Dallas Denny.
        p.   cm. — (Garland reference library of social science ; vol. 976)
(Garland gay and lesbian studies ; vol. 11)
   Includes index.
   ISBN 0-8153-1793-X (alk. paper)
   1. Transsexualism.   2. Gender identity.   I. Denny, Dallas, 1949–
II. Series: Garland reference library of social science ; v. 976.   III. Series:
Garland reference library of social science. Garland gay and lesbian studies ;
vol. 11.
HQ77.9.C87   1998
305.9'066—DC21   97-25972
                                                      CIP

Printed on acid-free, 250-year-life paper
Manufactured in the United States of America

Contents

TABLES

Illustrations

riod and unable to tell, by the way she felt, that her period was coming. The facial hair and her history suggest that she had pre-existing anovulatory androgen excess before beginning testosterone therapy.

Acknowledgments

I would like to thank Dr. Phyllis Korper and Dr. Richard Wallis, my editors at Garland Publishing, for giving me the green light on this project. I would like to thank the authors of the various chapters for their patience when I might have been unclear about exactly what I wanted; they came through marvelously. I'm very proud of each and every one of them. I would especially like to thank Dr. Richard Green, Dr. John Money, and Dr. Ira Pauly for contributing to this work. They have remained active in the study of gender and sex issues in the more than twenty-five years since *Transsexualism and Sex Reassignment* was published, and have made important empirical and theoretical contributions to the literature.

Preface

I am a woman of transsexual experience. That is a revelation that I did not make in my previous book for Garland Publishing, but one I am proud to make now.

For many years, the stigma attached to transsexualism would have prevented me from making such a statement. Indeed, had I acknowledged my transsexualism, or had my transsexual status been known to others, I would have been unable to contribute to the transgender and transsexual literature in any meaningful way. The stigma associated with being transsexual in American society would have silenced me.

That is no longer true. Just as it is impossible to imagine the study of black history without the contributions of black scholars, or the study of homosexuality devoid of the writings of gay men and lesbians, it has become impossible for there to be meaningful study of transsexualism or cross-dressing without input from those who have been directly affected. Walter Williams (1995) has called such people "living experts."*

I am happy and proud to claim my status as a living expert.

Dallas Denny

*Williams, W. (1995). "Two spirit people." Paper presented at the First International Congress on Gender, Cross Dressing, and Sex Issues. Van Nuys, CA: February 23–26, 1995.

Introduction

In 1969, seventeen years after the news of Christine Jorgensen's "sex change" shocked the world, the first collaborative textbook on transsexualism, *Transsexualism and Sex Reassignment*, edited by Richard Green and John Money, was published by the Johns Hopkins University Press. Just as Dr. Harry Benjamin's monograph, *The Transsexualism Phenomenon*, had been three years earlier, *Transsexualism and Sex Reassignment* (or *T&SR*, as I will call it throughout these pages) was a quantum leap forward in the study and treatment of persons who were uncomfortable with their gender of assignment.

Dr. Money, preeminent in his field, and Dr. Green, who was rapidly becoming so, assembled a team of authors who examined transsexualism from a variety of perspectives: historical and mythological, legal, social, psychological, and medical. Articles included not only descriptions of surgical procedures and hormonal regimens, but also discussions of etiology, neurological correlates, and social adjustment after sex reassignment. Many of the chapter authors went on to publish extensively in the field, and many continue to be active today. Of those authors, Dr. Green, Dr. Money, and Dr. Ira Pauly have been good enough to contribute chapters to this book.

The interdisciplinary approach of *T&SR* has been used several times since 1969, most notably in books with a clinical focus (Steiner, 1985; Walters & Ross, 1986; Blanchard & Steiner, 1990; and Bockting & Coleman, 1992), and in conference proceedings (cf. Laub & Gandy, 1973; Wheale, 1992), but increasingly in social critiques (Epstein & Straub, 1992) and anthropology (Herdt, 1994). All of these books have been remarkable in their own right. But what has been lacking has been a work with a larger scope—one which attempts to integrate issues of treatment into the larger perspective that has been made available by those who have worked outside the clinical setting and by transgendered and transsexual persons themselves.

This work is an attempt to do just that. I had initially hoped to subtitle it "A New Synthesis," but in my opinion it is yet too early for that synthesis to occur—or perhaps I should say that I am not yet able to offer such a synthesis.

Current Concepts in Transgender Identity covers a variety of topics by authors with widely varying viewpoints. Moreover, the underlying conceptual and theoretical frameworks from which the authors write vary dramatically, ranging from medical constructions of transsexualism to the emerging transgender view, in which being transgendered is not a pathology but a gift.

Current Concepts does not cover all of the topics of importance. I would have liked to have included, for instance, chapters on chest reconstruction and metadoioplasty (a masculinizing genital-surgery procedure) in female-to-male persons, and chapters on religion and legal issues—but Einsteinian limitations (you know, space and time) made it impossible to do all I wanted. However, if by putting a variety of innovative and even controversial ideas together under one cover I will have helped to lay the groundwork for a synthesis to come about, this book will more than have served its purpose.

REFERENCES

Benjamin, H. (1966). *The transsexual phenomenon*. New York: Julian Press.

Blanchard, R., & Steiner, B. eds. (1990). *Clinical management of gender identity disorders in children and adults*. Washington, DC: American Psychiatric Press.

Bockting, W., & Coleman, E. eds. (1992). *Gender dysphoria: Interdisciplinary approaches in clinical management*. New York: Haworth Press.

Epstein, J., & Straub, K. eds. (1992). *Body guards: The cultural politics of gender ambiguity*. New York: Chapman & Hall.

Green, R., & Money, J. eds. (1969). *Transsexualism and sex reassignment*. Baltimore, MD: Johns Hopkins University Press.

Herdt, G. ed. (1994). *Third sex, third gender*. New York: Zone Books.

Laub, D.R., & Gandy, P. eds. (1973) *Gender dysphoria syndrome: Proceedings of the Second International Symposium on Gender Dysphoria Syndrome*. Berkeley: Stanford University.

Steiner, B., ed. (1985). *Gender dysphoria: Development, research, management*. New York; Plenum Press.

Walters, W.A.W., & Ross, M.W. eds. (1986). *Transsexualism and sex reassignment*. New York: Oxford University Press.

Wheale, J., ed. (1992). *Counselling gender dysphoria: Proceedings of a national conference held at the Arcade Hotel, Birmingham, 15 February 1992*. Cornwall & Devon; The Accredited Training Centre for Cornwall & Devon.

PART I
TOWARD A NEW SYNTHESIS

I   MYTHOLOGICAL, HISTORICAL, AND CROSS-CULTURAL ASPECTS OF TRANSSEXUALISM*

Richard Green

Descriptions from classical mythology, classical history, Renaissance, and nineteenth-century history plus cultural anthropology point to the long-standing and widespread pervasiveness of the transsexual phenomenon.

The term "transsexual," being of comparatively recent origin, cannot be found in historical sources. Therefore, many inferences must be made in interpreting reference material. Even specific mention of "change of sex" may only imply a "change of dress" or the practice of genital homosexuality, the fuller assumption of the individual of cross-gender identity not being apparent. In the following references, the criterion of cross-gender identity appears to be met.

MYTHOLOGY AND DEMONOLOGY

In Greek mythology the transsexual influence is dramatized in the designation of Venus Castina as the goddess who responded with sympathy and understanding to the yearnings of feminine souls locked up in male bodies (Bulliet, 1928).

Specific myths of sex change, not only as a result of desire, but also as a form of punishment, appear frequently. For example, Tiresias, a Thebian soothsayer, is reported to have been walking on Mt. Cylene when he came upon two snakes coupling. He killed the female, and for this act was changed into a woman. Later, after coming to look favorably on his new form and testifying that women's pleasure during intercourse was ten to man's one, he was changed back into a man—again as punishment (Leach, 1949).[1]

---

*This chapter has not been reprinted for more than 25 years. It first appeared in Harry Benjamin's 1966 monograph, *The Transsexual Phenomenon*, and subsequently appeared in *Transsexualism and Sex Reassignment* (Green & Money, 1969). Although it was written more than 30 years ago, it holds up very well. It is reprinted with permission of the Johns Hopkins University Press and Dr. Richard Green.

Another mythical account concerns the Scythians, whose rear guard pillaged the temple of Venus at Ascelon. The goddess is alleged to have been so enraged that she made women of the plunderers, and further decreed that their posterity should be similarly affected (Herodotus, cited by Krafft-Ebing, 1931). Hippocrates, describing among the Scythians "No-men" who resembled eunuchs, wrote, "they not only follow women's occupations, but show feminine inclinations and behave as women. The natives ascribe the cause to a deity. . . ." (Hippocrates, cited by Hammond, 1887). Still another account deals with the ancient kingdom, Phrygia, where the priests of the god Attis, the consort of Cybelle the Earth Mother, were obliged to castrate themselves. This was in deference to Attis, who was alleged to have emasculated himself under a pine tree. The priests were said (following castration) to become transvestites and perform women's tasks. Some of the priests were believed to have gone beyond testicular castration and completely removed their external male genitalia (Spencer, 1946).

The previously noted Tiresias myth parallels a related folk tale of East Indian lore. According to legend in the *Mahabharata,* a king was transformed into a woman by bathing in a magic river. As a woman, he bore a hundred sons, whom he sent to share his kingdom with the hundred sons he had as a man. Later, he refused to be changed back into a man because the former king felt that "a woman takes more pleasure in the act of love than does a man." Contrary to the fate of Tiresias, the transformed king was granted his wish (Leach, 1949).

Not only were the gods empowered with the ability to change one's sex, but change of sex was performed on both human and beast by witchcraft and by the intervention of demons. Witches were claimed to be the possessors of drugs that had the capacity to reverse the sex of the taker.[2] Some said that males could be transformed into females and females into males, but it was also argued that the sex change worked only in one direction. Thus it was declared that the devil could make males of females, but could not transform men into women, because it is the method of nature to add on rather than to take away. In *Malleus Maleficarum* ("Hammer Against Witches"), published in 1489, the book which served as the source of "treatment" of the insane for nearly three hundred years, an eyewitness accounting was reported of a girl changed into a boy by the devil, in Rome (Masters, 1962).

CLASSICAL HISTORY

Accounts exist from the legacy of ancient Greece and Rome of those grossly discontent with their gender role. Philo, the Jewish philosopher of Alexandria, wrote, "Expending every possible care on their outward adornment, they are not ashamed even to employ every device to change artificially their nature as men into women. . . . Some of them . . . craving a complete transformation into women, they have amputated their generative members" (Masters, unpublished).

The Roman poet Manilus wrote: "These [persons] will ever be giving thought to their bedizement and becoming appearance; to curl the hair and lay it in waving ripples . . . to polish the shaggy limbs. . . . Yeah! and to hate the very sight of [themselves as] a man, and long for arms without growth of hair. Woman's robes they wear . . . [their] steps broken to an effeminate gait. . . ." (Masters, unpublished).

A satirical description written of some Romans has been translated:

> But why
> Are they waiting? Isn't it now high
> time for them to try
> The Phrygian fashion to make
> the job complete . . .
> Take a knife and lop off that
> superfluous piece of meat?
>
> —Juvenal, translated by Creekmore, 1963

Even among the histories of Roman emperors are reported instances of "change of sex." One of the earliest sex-conversion operations may have been performed at the behest of the infamous Emperor Nero. Allegedly, Nero, during a fit of rage, kicked his pregnant wife in the abdomen, killing her. Filled with remorse, he attempted to find someone whose face resembled that of his slain wife. Closest to filling the order was a young male ex-slave, Sporum. Nero then is reported to have ordered his surgeons to transform the ex-slave into a woman. Following the "conversion," the two were formally married.

Another Roman emperor, Heliogabalus, is reported to have been formally married to a powerful slave and to have taken up the tasks of a wife following the marriage. He is described as having been "delighted to be called the mistress, the wife, the Queen of Hierocles" (Bulliet, 1928), and is said to have offered half the Roman Empire to the physician who could equip him with female genitalia (Benjamin & Masters, 1964).

Interposed between the era of the Roman Empire and Europe of the sixteenth century is a perhaps apocryphal, but still extraordinary accounting of ninth-century Rome. This concerns a figure known as Pope John VIII. The report goes that this person, nominated as successor to Pope Leo IV in

855, was, in fact, a woman. In an accounting published with the approval of Pope Julius III, it was stated that "she gave birth to a baby and died, together with her offspring, in the presence of a large number of spectators" (De Savitsch, 1958).

French history of the sixteenth to the eighteenth century contributed a number of public transsexual figures. Moreover, at this time the term of reference to the sovereign was "Sa Majeste," which means literally, "Her Majesty." The feminine gender was used, initially, in deference to King Henry III of France, who wished to be considered a woman. It is reported that once, during February, 1577, Sa Majeste made his point strongly felt by appearing before the Deputies "dressed as a woman, with a long pearl necklace and low cut dress . . ." (De Savitsch, 1958).

Among the notable Frenchmen of the seventeenth century, the Abbe de Choisy, also known as François Timoleon, has left for posterity a vivid firsthand description of a strong cross-gender wish. During his infancy and early youth, his mother had attired him completely as a girl. At 18 this practice continued and his waist was then "encircled with tight-fitting corsets which made his loins, hips and bust more prominent." As an adult, for five months, he played comedy as a girl and reported, "Everybody was deceived; I had lovers to whom I granted small favors."

At 32 he became Ambassador of Louis XIV to Siam. Regarding his gender identity he wrote: "I thought myself really and truly a woman. I have tried to find out how such a strange pleasure came to me, and I take it to be this way. It is an attribute of God to be loved and adored, and man—so far as his weak nature will permit—has the same ambition, and it is beauty which creates love, and beauty is generally woman's portion. . . . I have heard someone near me whisper, 'There is a pretty woman.' I have felt a pleasure so great that it is beyond all comparison. Ambition, riches, even love cannot equal it. . . ." (Bulliet, 1928; De Savitsch, 1958; Gilbert, 1926).

One of the most famous examples of cross-gender behavior in history is the Chevalier d'Eon, whose name became the eponym "eonism." He is reported to have made his debut into history in woman's garb as the rival of Madame de Pompadour as a pretty new mistress for Louis XV. When his secret was made known to the King, the latter capitalized on his initial mistake by turning the Chevalier into a trusted diplomat. On one occasion, in 1755, he went to Russia on a secret mission disguised as the niece of the King's accredited agent, and the following year returned to Russia as a man to complete the mission. Following the death of Louis XV he lived permanently as a woman. There was great uncertainty in England, where he spent his final years, as to whether his true morphologic sex was male or whether the periods in male attire were not, in fact, the periods of impersonation. When he died, the Chevalier d'Eon had lived 49 years as a man and 34 years as a woman (Bulliet, 1928; De Savitsch, 1958; Gilbert, 1926).

Another case of interest was l'Abbe d'Entragues, who attempted to replicate feminine facial beauty "pale and interesting" by undergoing frequent facial bleedings (De Savitsch, 1958). One last pertinent abbe was Becarelli, a false messiah, who claimed to be able to command the services of the Holy Ghost and boasted of possessing a drug which could "change sex." While physical sex was not changed, men who took the drug temporarily believed themselves transformed into women and women thought themselves transformed into men (Masters, 1962).

Finally, a person who through the whole of her adult life had been known as Mlle. Jenny Savalette de Lange died at Versailles in 1858 and was discovered to be a man. During his lifetime he had managed to get a substitute birth certificate, designating himself female, was engaged to men six times, and was given a thousand francs a year pension by the King of France with a free apartment at the Chateau of Versailles (De Savitsch, 1958).

The following brief case histories reported by physicians bring the historical European review to the close of the nineteenth century. Bloch described a person of the mid-nineteenth century "who from doing feminine tasks [sewing and knitting] at the bidding of his mother became completely effeminate, plucked his beard, put up his hair, padded his breast and hips, and behaved in every respect as a woman. . . . He called himself Frederica. . . . He managed to deceive [men] so completely that they [unwittingly] performed coitus in anum with him" (Bloch, 1933). Krafft-Ebing reported this firsthand account by a patient: "I feel like a woman in a man's form. . . . I feel the penis as clitoris, the urethra as urethra and vaginal orifice, which always feels a little wet, even when it is actually dry, the scrotum as labia majora. In short I always feel the vulva. . . . Small as my nipples are, they demand room. . . . Of what use is female pleasure, when one does not conceive? . . ." (Krafft-Ebing, 1931).

America, too, had its examples of prominent cross-gender identified persons. The first colonial governor of New York, Lord Cornbury, arrived in the New World from England in full woman's dress and so appeared during his time in office. And, a century later, during the Civil War, Mary Walker became the first American woman to be commissioned an Army surgeon and the only woman expressly granted Congressional permission to wear man's clothing (Brown, 1961).

American Indians

Anthropologic studies of peoples from many areas of the world furnish varied material on cross-gender behavior and identity.

During the first quarter of the century, exhaustive data were gathered on traditional practices among several tribes of North American Indians. "In nearly every part of the continent there seem to have been, since ancient times, men dressing themselves in the clothes and performing the functions of women. . . ." (Westermarck, 1917).

Among the Yuman Indians there existed a group of males called the *elxa* who were considered to have suffered a "change of spirit" as a result of dreams which occurred, generally, at the time of puberty. A boy or girl who dreamed too much of any one thing "would suffer a change of sex." Such dreams frequently included the receiving of messages from plants, particularly the arrowseed, which is believed to be liable to change sex itself. One elxa, however, reportedly dreamed of a journey. "This dream implied his future occupation with women's work. When he came out of the dream he put his hand to his mouth and laughed. . . with a woman's voice and his mind was changed from male to female. Other young people noticed this and began to feel towards him as to a woman."

As a small child the female counterpart of elza, the kwe'rhame, were reported to have played with boys' toys. It is alleged that such women never menstruated; their secondary sexual characteristics were underdeveloped, and in some instances were male, perhaps some form of hermaphroditism or virilism (Ford, 1931).

In the Yuman culture it was believed, further, that the Sierra Estrella, a mountain, had a transvestite living inside and that both this mountain and another nearby had the power to "sexually transform men." Signs of such transformation were said to come "early in childhood." Older people were said to know by a boy's actions that he would "change sex." *Berdache* was the term for those who behaved like women (Bulliet, 1928).[3] Berdaches in the Yuman culture married men and had no children of their own. The tribe also included women who passed for men, dressed like men, and married women (Spier, 1933).

Among the Cocopa Indians, males called *e L ha* were those reported to have shown feminine character "from babyhood." As children they were described as talking like girls, seeking the company of girls, and doing things in women's style. Females known as *war'hemeh* played with boys, made bows and arrows, had their noses pierced, and fought in battles. "Young men might love such a girl, but she cared nothing for him, wished only to become a man" (Gifford, 1933).

Among the Mohave Indians, boys who were destined to become shamans (priest-doctors who used magic and mediumistic trances to cure the sick, to divine the hidden, and to control the events that affected the welfare of all people), would "pull back their penis between their legs and then display themselves as women, saying, 'I too am a woman, I am like you are.'"

For those Mohave boys who were to live as women, there was an initiation rite during the tenth or eleventh year of life. "Two women lift the youth and take him outdoors. . . . One puts on a skirt and dances, the youth follows and imitates. . . . The two women give the youth the front and back pieces of his new dress and paint his face. . . ." Such persons spoke, laughed, sat and acted like women. These "alyhas" insisted that their genitals be referred to by female terminology. The female counterpart, "hwane," did not insist that their genitalia be referred to as though they were male.

An alyha, after finding a husband, would begin to imitate menstruation. He would scratch himself between the legs with a stick until blood was drawn. When he would decide to become pregnant, he would cease these "menstruations." Before "delivery" they would drink a bean preparation, which would induce violent stomach pains dubbed "labor pains." Following this would be a defecation designated as a "stillbirth," which would be ceremoniously buried. There would then ensure a period of mourning by both the husband and "wife" (Devereux, 1937).

Available anthropologic sources make brief mention of similar practices in other tribes.

Among the Navaho, persons called *nadl E*, a term used for either transvestites or hermaphrodites, but usually the former, were addressed by the kinship term used for a woman of their relationship and age and were granted the legal status of womanhood (Hill, 1935).

The *i-wa-musp* (man-woman) of the Jukis and other California Indians formed a regular social grade. Dressed as women, they performed women's tasks. When an Indian would show a desire to shirk his manly duties, he would be made to take his position in a circle of fire; then a bow and a "woman-stick" would be offered to him. He would have to make a choice and forever after abide by the choice (Powers, cited by Crawly [sic], 1960).

Finally, among the Pueblo, the following alleged practice was described. A very powerful man, "one of the most virile," was chosen. He was masturbated many times a day and made to ride horseback almost continuously. "Gradually such irritable weakness of the genital organs is engendered that, in riding, great loss of semen is induced. . . . Then atrophy of the testicles and penis sets in, the hair of the beard falls out, the voice loses its depth and compass. . . . Inclinations and disposition become feminine. [This] *mujerado* loses his position in society as a man. . . . his endeavor seems to be to assimilate himself as much as possible to the female sex, and to rid as far as may be of all the attributes, mental and physical, of manhood" (Hammond, 1887).

A former Surgeon-General of the United States Army reported on one such person, "The first thing that attracted my notice was the extraordinary development of the mammary glands, which were as large as those of a child-bearing women. He told me that he had nursed several infants whose mothers had died, and that he had given them plenty of milk from his breasts . . ." (Hammond, 1887).

Peoples other than American Indians

In paleo-Asiatic, ancient Mediterranean, Indian, Oceanic, and African tribes, men who adopted the ways and dress of women enjoyed high esteem as shamans, priests, and sorcerers—all persons whose supernatural powers were feared and revered.

Among the Yakut of aboriginal Siberia there were two categories of shamans, the "white" representing creative, and the "black" destructive forces. The latter tended to behave like women. The hair was parted in the middle like women, they wore iron circles over the coat representing breasts, and along with biologic females were not permitted to live on the right side of the horse-skin in the living quarters (Czaplicka, 1914).

As to the people of Siberia, the change of sex was found chiefly among paleo-Siberians, namely the Chukchee, Koryak, Kamchadeb, and Asiatic Eskimo (Czaplicka, 1914).

Among the Chukchees living near the Arctic Coast, there was reported a special branch of shamanism in which men and women were alleged to undergo a change of sex in part, or even completely. A man who changed his sex was called "soft man being," "similar to a woman," and a "transformed woman." Transformation would take place by tribal command during early youth.

There were various degrees of transformation. In the first stage, the person subjected to it would impersonate a woman only in the manner of braiding and arranging hair. The second stage was marked by the adoption of female dress. The third stage of transformation was more complete. A young man who underwent it left off all pursuits and manners of his sex and took up those of a woman. His pronunciation would change. "At the same time his body alters, if not in its outward appearance, at least in its faculties and forces. The transformed person . . . becomes . . . fond of . . . nursing small children. Generally speaking, he becomes a woman with the appearance of a man." The "soft-man" after a time would take a husband. The "wife" would take care of the house, performing all domestic pursuits and work. Legend had it that some would even acquire the organs of a woman.[4] A transformed woman was described, who donned the dress of a male, adopted the pronunciation of men, provided herself with a gastroc-nemius from the leg of a reindeer, fastened it to a broad leather belt, and "used in the way of masculine private parts" (Bogoras, 1907).

In Madagascar, men described among the Tanala as exhibiting femi-nine traits from birth dressed like women, arranged their hair like women, and pursued feminine occupations. They were known as Sarombavy. Among the Sakalavas of Madagascar, boys who were noted to be delicate and girl-ish in appearance and mannerisms were selected out from their peers and then raised as girls. Madagascans who were treated as female "finally . . . regard themselves as completely feminine. . . . The autosuggestion goes so far that they quite forget their true sex. . . . They are exempt from military service" (Bloch, 1933).

In some Brazilian tribes women were observed who abstained from every womanly occupation and imitated men in everything. They wore their hair in masculine fashion and "would rather allow themselves to be killed than have sexual intercourse with a man. Each of these women had a woman who served her and with whom she was married. . . ." (De Magalhaens, cited by Crawly, 1960; Westermarck, 1917).

A number of Lango men from Uganda, in East Africa, "dress as women, simulate menstruation, and become one of the wives of other males" (Ford & Beach, 1951). Elsewhere in Africa among the Malagasy (men called *ts ecates*), among the Onondatga of the former Southwest German Africa, and among the Kiakite-Sarracolese in the former French Sudan, men assumed the dress, attitude, and manners of women (Crawly, 1960). Among the Araucanians of Chile there were reported male and female sorcerers. The male sorcerers were required to forsake their sex (Bloch, 1933).

Sir James Frazer wrote in *The Golden Bough*: "[There is] a custom widely spread among savages in accordance with which some men dress as women and act as women throughout their life. . . . Often they are dedicated and trained to their vocation from childhood" (Frazer, 1955). They were reported to be found among the Sea Dyaks of Borneo, the Bugis of South Celebes, and the Patagonians of South America. In the Kingdom of the Congo, there was described a sacrificial priest who commonly dressed as a woman, and glorified in the title of grandmother. "To the savage mind, the donning of another's dress is more than a token. . . . it completes identity. . . ." (Crawly, 1960). Among the Zulus, change of sex (by disguise) was a method of changing or averting bad luck. In the Konkan (India) it was usual to bore the nose of a son as soon as he was born to turn him into a girl (Joshi, cited by Crawly, 1960).

Of the Aleutians, boys—if they were very handsome—would be brought up entirely in the manner of girls (*shupans*), and instructed in the arts women use to please men; their beards would be carefully plucked out as soon as they would appear. They would wear ornaments of glass beads upon their legs and arms and bind and cut their hair in the manner of women (Langsdorf, cited by Crawly, 1960). Arriving at ten or fifteen, they were married to some wealthy man (Westermarck, 1917). It was further reported that sometimes if the parents had wished for a daughter and were disappointed by having a son, they would make the newborn into an "akhnutchik" or shupan (Bloch, 1933).

More recently, in mid-twentieth-century India, the city of Lucknow witnessed a great many eunuchs turning up at the polls and joining the line of female voters. The eunuchs, who were dressed in female garments, were reported to have been "amazed" at finding themselves listed as male voters. "Only after the insistence of the police officers . . . did they bow to the law. . . . These eunuchs, though they resist further surgery to make them more female, have their male genitalia amputated, and the pubic area reshaped to give it the look of the female vagina." The event is celebrated by a grand feast restricted to eunuchs (Siddigui & Rehman, 1963).

SUMMARY

The phenomenon of lifelong, extensive cross-gender identification, now known as transsexualism, is not new to either our culture or our time. Numerous descriptions from classical mythology, classical history, Renaissance, and nineteenth-century history, plus many sources of cultural anthropology, point to the long-standing and widespread pervasiveness of the transsexual phenomenon.

NOTES

1. To see snakes coupling is still considered unlucky in Southern India, the theory being that the witness will be punished with homosexuality (Graves, 1955).

2. Reference will be made later to an eighteen-century abbe who claimed to possess a similar drug.

3. *Berdache* derives from the Spanish, *bardaja* meaning a "kept boy," and *bardashe* from the French; also Italian, *barascia*; Arabian, *bardaj* (a slave), and Persian, *bardah*. The berdache may be variously regarded as (1) a sex-changed person; (2) a man-woman; or (3) a person who is neither man nor woman (Masters,

unpublished). (Because the word *berdache* is now considered to be pejorative, trans-gendered Native North Americans are now known as two-spirit people.—ed.)

4. The change of sex was usually accompanied by future shamanism; indeed, nearly all the shamans were former delinquents of their sex (Westermarck, 1917).

REFERENCES

Benjamin, H. (1966). *The transsexual phenomenon.* New York: Julian Press.

Benjamin, H., & Masters, R. (1964). A new kind of prostitute. *Sexology, 30,* 446–448.

Bloch, I. (1933). *Anthropological studies on the strange sexual practices of all races and all ages.* New York: Anthropological Press.

Bogoras, W. (1907). The Chukchee religion. *Memoirs of the American Museum of Natural History, 11.* Leiden: E.J. Brill.

Brown, D.G. (1961). Transvestism and sex-role inversion. In A. Ellis and A. Abarbanel (Eds.), *Encyclopedia of Sexual Behavior.* New York: Hawthorne.

Bulliet, C.J. (1928). *Venus Castina: Famous female impersonators, celestial and human.* New York: Covici, Friede. Reprinted in 1956 by Bonanza Books and in 1987 by the Human Outreach & Achievement Institute, 405 Western Avenue, Ste. 345, South Portland, ME 04106.

Crawly, E. (1960). *The mystic rose.* New York: Meridian Books.

Creekmore, H., tr. 1963. *The satires of Juvenal.* New York: Mentor.

Czaplicka, M. (1914). *Aboriginal Siberia.* Oxford: Clarendon Press.

De Magalhaens, G.P. (n.d.). *Histoire de la provine de Sancta Cruz, que nous nommons ordinairement le Brizil,* cited in E. Crawly, *The mystic rose.*

De Savitsch, E. (1958). *Homosexuality, transvestism, and change of sex.* London: William Heinemann Medical Books.

Devereux, G. (1937). Institutionalized homosexuality of the Mohave Indians. *Human Biology, 9,* 498–527.

Ford, C. (1931). *University of California publications in American archaeology and ethnology,* Vol. 31.

Ford, C.S., & Beach, F.A. (1951). *Patterns of sexual behavior.* New York: W.W. Norton.

Frazer, J.G. (1955). *The golden bough: A study in magic and religion.* London: Macmillan.

Gifford, E. (1933). *The Cocopa.* University of California Publications in American Archaeology and Ethnology, Vol. 31.

Gilbert, O.P. (1926). *Men in women's guise.* (R.B. Douglas, trans.) New York: Bretano. Reprinted in 1932 in London by John Lane the Bodley Head.

Graves, R. (1955). *The Greek myths.* Baltimore: Penguin Books.

Green, R., & Money, J. (Eds.). (1969). *Transsexualism and sex reassignment.* Baltimore, MD: Johns Hopkins University Press.

Hammond, W. (1887). *Sexual impotence in the male and female.* Detroit: George S. Davis.

Herodotus. (n.d.). Cited in Krafft-Ebing, R., *Psychopathia sexualis.*

Hill, W.W. (1935). The status of the hermaphrodite and transvestite in Navaho culture. *American Anthropologist, 37,* 273–278.

Hippocrates. (n.d.). *Air, water and environment,* cited in Hammond, W., *Sexual impotence in the male and female.*

Joshi, P. (1886–1889). On the evil eye in the Konkan. *Journal of Anthropology and Sociology, 1,* 123, cited by E. Crawly, *The mystic rose.*

Krafft-Ebing, R. (1931). *Psychopathia sexualis.* Brooklyn: Physicians and Surgeons Book Co.

Langsdorf, G. (n.d.). *Voyages and travels in various parts of the world during the years 1803–7,* cited in Crawly, *The mystic rose.*

Leach, M. (Ed.). (1949). *Funk and Wagnall's standard dictionary of folklore, mythology, and legend.* New York: Funk & Wagnall's.

Masters, R.E.L. (1962). *Eros and evil.* New York: The Julian Press.

Powers, S. (n.d.). *Tribes of California 1877,* cited in Crawly, E., *The mystic rose.*

Siddiugi, T., & Rehman, M. (1963). Eunuchs of India and Pakistan. *Sexology, 29,* 824–826.

Spencer, R. (1946). The cultural aspects of eunuchism. *CIBA Symposia, 8,* 147.

Spier, L. (1933). *Yuman tribes of the Gila River.* Chicago: University of Chicago Press.

Westermarck, E. (1917). *The origin and development of the moral ideas,* Vol. 2. London: Macmillan.

2 Transsexualism

Historical Perspectives, 1952 to Present

Bonnie Bullough

Vern L. Bullough

The year 1952 was an important turning point in the history of transsexualism because it was the year in which Christine Jorgensen had surgery that was somewhat sensationally described as changing her from a man to a woman. Hers was not the first genital surgery, nor did it make her into a female—but it was the publicity, and not the reality, which counted. In fact, removal of penis and testes has an old history, and eunuchs have an ancient historical tradition. In the twentieth century, advances in surgical technique and the development of anesthesia had allowed surgeons to better shape ambiguous genitalia in the case of hermaphrodites, and during World War I and World War II, there had even been attempts to reconstruct penises on those wounded in the war. Some surgeons had gone further and attempted to help those who wanted to change their sexual identity, as they did with the Danish painter Einar Wegener, who became Lili Elbe in the 1930s (Hoyer, 1933), and Robert Cowell, a World War II flyer who became Roberta Cowell before Jorgensen had the surgery (Cowell, 1954). However, none achieved the notoriety that Jorgensen did.

The events surrounding the Jorgensen surgery started in 1950, when George Jorgensen approached Christian Hamburger, a Copenhagen surgeon, complaining of severe depression brought on by what might now be called gender dysphoria. He felt himself to be a woman and was convinced that he could not continue his life as a man (Hamburger, Sturup, & Dahl-Iversen, 1953). Nature had simply made a cruel mistake in giving him a male body. He told Hamburger that he had acquired a set of female clothes, secretly put them on, and shaved his pubic hair to shape it more like that of a female. More importantly, his work as a laboratory technician had given him access to supplies of estrogen, which had begun to be commercially produced, and which he had for a time administered to himself.

After a physical and psychiatric evaluation by Dr. Hamburger and his associates, the medical team decided to administer much larger doses of female hormones than Jorgensen had given himself (parenteral estrogen was used). The estrogen changed the shape of Jorgensen's body to one with more feminine contours, while his behavior, gait, and voice became more feminine—although some of this undoubtedly occurred because of his efforts to be more feminine, and not because of direct action of the hormones. His beard became sparse, and electrolysis was used to further remove facial hair. Hamburger and his colleagues, using the theories of the time, diagnosed the case as one of genuine transvestism, and differentiated it from two other types of transvestism: the fetishist, who as a consequence of a neurotic obsession concentrated on one or more articles of dress, thereby developing an interest in cross-dressing; and the homosexual man of the passive type who desired to dress in women's clothing.

The patient was castrated under provisions of the Danish Sterilization and Castration Act of 1935, which allowed castration when the patient's sexuality made him likely to commit crimes, or when it involved mental disturbances to a considerable degree.[1] In 1952, Jorgensen expressed a further desire to have the last visible remains of his detested male sex organs removed, so his penis was amputated one year after his castration had been carried out. This made him technically a castrated man whose penis had been removed. No attempt was made at that time to construct a vagina or other female sex organs.

Hamburger and his colleagues reported the case in the *Journal of the American Medical Association* the following year, pointing out that although they had not actually changed the sex of their patient, since his chromosomal sex would remain the same as it had been, they had relieved his distress by creating the external illusion of a sex change (Hamburger, et al., 1953). Though the removal of the testes undoubtedly assisted in the feminization, it was the ability to use the relatively recently isolated female hormones that made Jorgensen's case different from earlier cases.

Because Jorgensen could pass convincingly as a woman, her case marked a turning point, as she herself leaked news of her surgery to the press. Seizing the opportunity, Jorgensen sold her story to journalists from the Hearst newspapers, went on the stage, and later wrote an autobiography (Jorgensen, 1967). She had what today would be called a firestorm of publicity, and this led other persons, primarily men who felt themselves to be similarly afflicted, to consider surgery. Hamburger reported that he and his colleagues received a total of 465 letters from interested individuals (Hamburger, 1953).

Although Hamburger had called the condition "genuine transvestism" to distinguish it from other types of cross-dressing, the label transsexualism soon evolved. In a paper read before the Society for the Scientific Study of Sex in 1963, Harry Benjamin, the leading American figure in the field, indicated that for the past ten years he had been using the term "transsexualism" in his lectures to describe the phenomenon (Benjamin, 1963). It was, however, a term not unique to him. Benjamin later attributed the first use of the term to David O. Cauldwell, who had written an article for *Sexology* in 1949 describing a case of "psychopathia transsexualis," in which a girl wanted to be a man (Cauldwell, 1949).[2] Daniel G. Brown had also used the term (Brown, 1958), and in 1910 Hirschfeld had referred to one of his patients as a "psychic transsexual" (Hirschfeld, 1991).

Thus the diagnostic category, transsexualism, was not the result of a theoretical breakthrough. Rather, it appeared on the scene as the result of publicity that surrounded the use of surgical and hormonal treatment for a feeling of dysphoria related to gender identity, and the surgery which was done was called sex reassignment surgery (SRS), although it was always known that the surgery did not change the chromosomal sex.

In a sense, transsexualism was a socially constructed phenomenon. Ordinarily a diagnosis is made independent of the planned treatment, but in the case of transsexualism, the treatment became the diagnosis. However, even as a socially constructed phenomenon, transsexualism is a very real entity. The illusion of gender may in fact be the real thing, rather than some technical factor such as chromosomal sex.

Benjamin believed that transsexualism was one manifestation of what had been called transvestism. He divided male transvestites into three major types. The first group included transvestites who led reasonably normal lives, most of whom were heterosexual men who could appease their feelings of gender role disharmony and enjoy erotic satisfaction from cross-dressing. Though these patients might display neurotic symptoms, they were seldom seen by doctors, since their clash was with society and the law. The second group were more emotionally disturbed, and they benefitted from psychological guidance and new endocrine therapy made possible by the discovery of hormones. The third type of transvestism was identical with transsexualism, which was interpreted as representing a disturbance of the normal sex and gender role orientation. Such individuals wanted to be full-scale women and have a male sex partner. The condition could present as fully developed transsexualism from the beginning, or it might gradually appear after shorter or longer periods of transvestism. However, the transsexual was much less interested in the symbol of female attire. He wanted to be a woman and function as a woman. Transsexuals, Benjamin noted, were very often unhappy people. Benjamin also recognized transsexualism in women, although women did not fit into his format for classifying transvestism as the organizing framework for transsexualism (Benjamin, 1966). Women posed a different kind of development.

By 1963, Benjamin had seen 200 transvestites and others, 125 of whom he diagnosed as being transsexual, including 108 men and 17 women. In most patients, the onset was described as being "As early as I can remember." Benjamin remained puzzled by the etiology. A moderate sexual underdevelopment was present in 30 percent of the patients, as had been the case with Jorgensen, but the chromatin tests all conformed to the anatomic sex. Since the etiology of transsexualism remained puzzling, it was usually attributed to unfavorable conditioning. Benjamin found evidence of this in 21 percent of the cases, but he could identify no causal sequence in at least half of the cases. This led him to speculate about such factors as "imprinting," a type of early learning well-documented in young birds, with some baby birds bonding to the first moving object they see, even if it is not from their own species, or even another bird (Lorenz, 1965). Benjamin wondered if imprinting somehow took place among humans, with transsexual patients being imprinted with the wrong gender. Finally, he speculated about prenatal exposure to hormones. What led him to this thought was the hypogonadism he had noted in 28 out of the first 91 patients (said to have also been present in Jorgensen), even though he could detect no current hormonal abnormalities (Benjamin, 1964). Motivations for surgery for men included:

1. the sex motive (men who love heterosexual men and want to have vaginas for sexual intercourse with them)
2. unhappiness with their gender
3. a marked feminine appearance
4. legal problems related to cross-dressing.

The operation for males consisted of either castration or drawing the testicles into the abdomen, the amputation of the penis, and plastic surgery to create a vagina-like opening. Benjamin did a follow-up study of 40 men; most of the time, the outcome of the operation was satisfactory.

The few females he saw (the ratio at that time was six males to every female) presented with a somewhat different pattern. Most of the females had been "tomboys" from earliest childhood. Conditioning could be identified as an etiological factor in only two of the 17 female patients he saw. Physical examination usually revealed a more or less distinct hypogonadism.

Absence of menstruation or a very scanty menses and a late menarche was reported by nine patients. Quite consistently, the female-to-male transsexuals wanted the male role, to marry and become husbands.

Benjamin held that the administration of hormones was an important part of the management of transsexuals: estrogen for men, and androgen for women. Treatment was with androgen (testosterone), which created male hair growth, deepening of the voice, growth of the clitoris, and sometimes acne. Of the 17 female patients he saw, 6 had endocrine treatment only, while 9 had various operative procedures.

Benjamin concluded that in the case of transsexualism, since the mind cannot be adjusted to the body, the adaptation of the body to the mind seems not only permissible but indicated (Benjamin, 1964).

HORMONAL RESEARCH AND THE DEVELOPMENT OF SYNTHETIC HORMONES

Note that this article emphasizes the importance of the development of hormonal therapy in transsexual treatment, something that is often overlooked in general accounts, perhaps because the surgery is the more dramatic element in the process of sex reassignment. In our mind, hormones are more important than the surgery in successful transition, although it might not seem so to the individual involved.

Basic research identifying the sex hormones had started early in the twentieth century, and in 1929 the female hormone estrone was isolated simultaneously by two researchers in the United States, Edgar Allen and Edward A. Doisy, and by Adolph Butenandt in Germany. Other Americans, George W. Corner and his student William M. Allen, succeeded in isolating progesterone in 1930, and shortly afterwards, a second estrogen factor was isolated in pregnant women's urine. The isolation of these substances greatly increased the scientific knowledge about the reproductive process and secondary sex characteristics, and even made hormonal therapy theoretically possible, although in actuality hormones were prohibitively expensive because they could be obtained only from animal sources and required massive numbers of animals to get enough for one treatment (Bullough, 1994, p. 128–129).

The possibility of hormonal therapy became economically feasible when synthetic hormones were developed. A key figure in this development was Russel Marker, a maverick scientist who became interested in the sex steroids in 1935 while working at Pennsylvania State College with grants furnished by Parke Davis. He became convinced that the easiest and cheapest way to make sex steroids was from plant materials, particularly plants of the lily family, which contained sapogenins. He went to Mexico and collected specimens of every known plant of this family, and by 1943, had produced synthetic progesterone and even developed a process for converting it into testosterone (Bullough, 1994, pp. 190–194).

Sponsored by the Syntex company, Carl Djerassi, in 1952, followed up on Marker's research and produced a commercially feasible process for synthesizing orally active analogues of progesterone (Bullough, 1994, p. 195). The commercial development of other steroids followed. This body of hormonal research made it possible to treat Jorgensen with estrogen in 1952, (albeit the expensive animal product), as well as the more economically feasible treatment of the transsexuals who followed with synthetic products. Interestingly, the work of Djerassi made both transsexualism and the birth-control pill a reality.

THE DEVELOPMENT OF THE GENDER-IDENTITY CENTERS

Many of those seeking surgery were referred to Harry Benjamin, who provided hormonal treatment and support while he carried out the difficult task of finding surgeons to do the sex-reassignment surgery. This situation changed with support from the Erickson Foundation, which was established by Reed Erickson, an early female-to-male transsexual. The Johns Hopkins Gender Identity Clinic was established in 1965, partly with Erickson Foundation funds, and performed their first sex-reassignment surgery (SRS) in 1966. Soon after that, gender-identity programs were established at Minnesota, Stanford, Oregon, Case Western Reserve, and the Clarke Institute in Toronto. Interdisciplinary teams including psychiatrists, psychologists, and surgeons were formed to diagnose and treat transsexuals (Pauly, 1985). These centers were very influential in the development of the scientific understanding of the concept of gender (Pauly & Edgerton, 1986). The funds from the Erickson Foundation and other grants not only provided for a psychiatrist or psychologist on the team, but furnished support for research related to transsexualism.

In this same era, the federal government increased its support of basic research in medical schools, and though no federal money was given for transsexual surgery, the new money proved important in changing the nature of research into issues related to transsexualism. For most of the twentieth century, research into gender-related issues had been only a sideline for busy psychiatrists who collected case histories, and as time provided, tried to analyze them and search for meaning. However, the new generation of researchers, financed by private or public grant funds, had a much better understanding of modern research methods than the earlier generations of physician researchers, and could specialize in particular areas such as the influence of hormones on behavior. Those scientists who became part of the gender-identity teams helped not only bring about a better understanding of transsexualism, but of a variety of related conditions.

DIAGNOSTIC CRITERIA

As experience with the condition accumulated, the consensus as to the diagnosis of transsexualism focused on a longstanding preference for the role of the opposite sex. The term "gender dysphoria" was often used to indicate the extreme position held by the transsexual patients who were found to be much more distressed by their gender identity than were transvestites. In addition, the transsexuals who presented for surgery were often anxious and depressed, had attempted suicide, and reported a generally unhappy childhood (Stinson, 1972; Derogatis, Meyer, & Vazquez, 1978; Strassberg, et al., 1979; Uddenberg, Walinder, & Hojerback, 1979). Many of them believed that they already belonged to the opposite sex. Many, but not all, were homosexual in orientation when they presented for treatment, which meant that SRS might have been a means for them to become heterosexual (Freund, Steiner, & Chan, 1982). In some centers, in fact, a homosexual orientation was an early requirement for SRS, but as evidence accumulated, it became clear that some postoperative persons changed their sexual preference and that not all transsexuals, regardless of background, became heterosexual. This requirement was then dropped as a necessary condition (Bentler, 1976; Freund, Steiner & Chan, 1982; Steiner, 1985).

The early transsexual population was made up primarily of men who sought to become women, but the ratio has changed over time to about four men to one woman, with the Swedish data showing a ratio of one to one (McCauley & Ehrhardt, 1977; Pauly, 1985; Walinder, Lundstrom, Ross, & Thuwe, 1979).

THE TREATMENT PROCESS

The comprehensive workup that is done at the gender-identity clinics starts with careful observations, interviews, and psychological testing. If the diagnosis is transsexualism, the testing phase is followed by a period of living in the opposite gender. There is widespread agreement that this real-life test may be the most important evaluative process, since it allows the clients to see the real advantages and disadvantages of the role they seek (Money, 1969). They can see that changing sex roles does not solve many of life's problems and that sometimes the new role has disadvantages which may not have been obvious. For example, some male-to-female transsexuals are unaware of the wage discrimination against women, which they will share if they change sex. A test of living in the opposite gender role for at least one year is considered crucial, and two years is better. Androgen (testosterone) is given to female-to-male patients and female hormones (estrogen and progesterone) are given to male-to-female patients (Money, 1969).

The surgery for male-to-female transsexuals includes a bilateral orchiectomy (excision of the testicles) and, following a technique developed by surgeon Georges Burou in Casablanca, an inversion of the penis to form a vagina. Breast augmentation is sometimes performed. Sometimes other surgery is done to change the size of the nose, shave the larynx, or otherwise change the body contour. SRS for female-to-male clients is more complex, and involves a series of operations in which the ovaries, fallopian tubes, uterus, and breast tissue are removed. Some female-to-male patients stop at this point and do not have a penis constructed because the techniques for phalloplasty are not yet well developed. There are, however, recent improvements using metadoioplasty, a technique which augments the clitoris. Sometimes skin is grafted from the arm or some other part of the body to form a penis which can be permanently stiffened by using bone tissue. It is not yet possible to construct a penis which the female-to-male can use both to urinate in a standing position and for sexual activities. Many female-to-males, unhappy with the thought of multiple surgeries with a problematic outcome, make do with prostheses (Denny, 1991).

In 1980 the term "transsexualism" was recognized as an illness in the *Diagnostic and Statistical Manual of Mental Disorders,* an official publication of the American Psychiatric Association (DSM III, 1980). The definition was revised and simplified in 1987, focusing on feelings of persistent discomfort and a sense of inappropriateness about one's assigned sex (DSM III-R, p. 765). The 1994 edition of the DSM has omitted transsexualism as a diagnosis and uses "gender-identity disorder" in its place to cover all conditions in which there is a strong and persistent cross-gender identification. The diagnosis is not made if the individual has a concurrent physical intersex condition (DSM IV, pp. 532–538).

Because the transsexual is so often distressed with his or her current body, Lindgren and Pauly developed a thirty-item "Body-Image Scale," which they found helpful in differentiating transsexuals from transvestites and homosexual persons (Lindgren & Pauly, 1975; Pauly & Lindgren, 1976). The scale measures the level of dissatisfaction with various body parts, including the genital organs, the breasts, the facial hair, and so on. After surgery, there is a significant decrease in the level of dissatisfaction among transsexuals, but not among homosexuals.

As the definitions have become more formalized, screening out homosexual men who want to escape the stigma of their same-sex erotic orientation has been regarded as an increasing problem for people who run the gender-identity clinics. It is a commentary on our society that some people feel less of a stigma about being transsexual than they do about being homosexual (Ross, Rogers, & McCulloch, 1978). One reason for the exclusion, however, is that so many of those trying to escape a homosexual labeling were so often disappointed by the outcome of the surgery (Blanchard, 1985). Diagnosis of transsexualism, however, is complex, and many differences remain about who is or is not transsexual. One of the major problems in diagnosing stems from the active underground grapevine which exists in the transsexual community and which trains potential SRS clients on the correct responses to psychiatrists and other health-care providers (Billings & Urban, 1982; Blanchard, 1985).

Dissatisfaction among some of those who had undergone SRS led a group of professionals in the field to establish the Harry Benjamin International Gender Dysphoria Association. The members drew up a document in 1979 outlining standards of care for the hormonal and surgical reassignment of gender dysphoric persons. The standards and the principles explaining the standards are 12 pages long in mimeographed form. Excerpts (with editing to preserve space) are presented here:

1.   Hormonal and/or surgical sex-reassignment (SRS) on demand is contraindicated.
2.   Hormonal and SRS (genital and nongenital) must be preceded by a firm recommendation for such procedures made by a psychiatrist or psychologist.
3.   The psychiatrist or psychologist who makes the recommendation for SRS shall have known the patient in a psychotherapeutic relationship for at least 3 months.
4.   A period of 3 months during which the patient lives full-time in the social role of the other sex shall precede hormonal therapy.
5.   Six months in the other sex role should elapse before nongenital SRS (surgery to the face, hip etc.).
6.   Genital SRS shall be preceded by at least 12 months in the social role of the genetically other sex.
7.   If a good case can be made for an improvement in functioning, a diagnosis of schizophrenia does not necessarily preclude SRS.
8.   The recommending psychiatrist or psychologist will seek peer review for the recommendation for SRS.
9.   The surgeon performing the SRS is guilty of professional misconduct if he or she does not receive written recommendations of the

procedure from two behavioral scientists, at least one of whom is a psychiatrist.

10. The physician prescribing hormonal treatment must warn the patient of the potential side effects and monitor the patient with appropriate blood-chemistry studies.

11. A urological examination will be done prior to SRS.

12. Fees will be reasonable.

—Walker, et al., 1979

The standards at many clinics are more difficult to meet than those outlined in the *Standards of Care*. The Clarke Institute in Toronto also requires the patient be physically healthy, gainfully employed, not psychotic, not mentally retarded, not married, and document a minimum of two years living in the opposite gender role, including one year without hormonal treatment (Steiner, 1985; Blanchard & Steiner, 1990). Some clients find the standards beyond their reach or they resent the long psychological workup when they want only surgery. They argue that the gender-identity clinics are paternalistic and research-minded, and that the standards can be very expensive, since SRS is often not covered by insurance. Other transgendered persons, faced with long, expensive physical and psychological workups and a desperate desire for surgery, have turned to forged documents authorizing the procedures (AEGIS, 1993). Consequently, in spite of efforts by the Harry Benjamin Foundation and other groups to control the field by setting official standards, much of the SRS is done by individual surgeons rather than the official centers.

For many years in the 1960s and 1970s, the largest volume of SRS in any one place was done by Georges Burou of Casablanca in Morocco. He was a skilled surgeon who is credited with the development of the surgical technique for SRS on male-to-female clients that is now used almost universally. This technique involves using penile tissue to create a functional vaginal wall. Before his innovation, attempts to create a vagina using intestines or other tissue had not been particularly successful, and many of the early male-to-female subjects went without this aspect of the surgery (Steiner, 1985). A major specialist in male-to-female surgery has been Stanley Biber, a Colorado surgeon who has done SRS for more than 3000 clients. His reputation in the transsexual community is good, and his large volume has allowed him to develop his surgical skill. He does a much less elaborate workup than is done at the gender-identity centers, and struggles to keep his fees reasonable. He receives many queries from potential female-to-male patients, but does SRS for them only rarely because the technology is not yet well developed (Pierce, 1989). Biber is now at retirement age, but he has trained a young surgeon to take his place.

EVALUATION OF OUTCOMES

In 1979, the Johns Hopkins hospital announced that it was discontinuing SRS. Although there were probably a variety of reasons for that decision, a study done by the head of the clinic, Jon Meyer, and his secretary, Donna Reter, was given as the official reason for the decision (Stall, 1979). Meyer and Reter (1979) reported that in 1971 a follow-up study was started on 100 transsexual patients, 34 of whom had surgery, and 66 of whom had not. All had applied to the Gender Identity Clinic and been evaluated. Twenty-four had SRS at Johns Hopkins, and ten elsewhere. The 66 patients who did not have surgery had either changed their mind or were turned down for surgery. Some had gone through trial periods living in the role before surgery, and some had not. Only 50 percent of the sample could be located for the follow-up study, mostly those who had surgery. The fact that so many could not be located, however, does not mean that they did not have the surgery elsewhere; they had, however, cut their ties with the university. One female-to-male patient who had difficulty with a poorly constructed phallus asked to have it removed, but did not ask for any other changes. No other operative patient indicated they wanted to have their surgery undone. However, a scale of adjustment was constructed measuring frequency of address change, job and educational level, marriage adjustment, and frequency of psychiatric contact. The operative patients did not score significantly better on the scale than the unoperated patients, who had gone through a variety of experiences including psychotherapy, hormonal treatment, cross-living, or none of the above. On the strength of these findings, the authors concluded that SRS offered no objective advantages (Meyer & Reter, 1979).

It was clear that this research was fraught with methodological flaws. Most of the other follow-up studies found better results (Fleming, Steinman, & Bocknek, 1980; Docter, 1988). In 1968, Ira Pauly, utilizing data then available, had reported a generally favorable outcome from SRS (Pauly, 1968). In 1981, after the Meyer report, Pauly did a meta-analysis of the literature covering follow-up studies and still found generally favorable results. The data were based upon 11 studies involving male-to-female patients, and eight for female-to-males. Of the 283 male-to-female patients included, results were satisfactory for 71 percent of the sample, uncertain for 18 percent, unsatisfactory for 8 percent, and 2 percent had committed suicide. Among the 83 female-to-male patients, the satisfactory rate was 81 percent, while 13 percent were uncertain, and 5 percent reported dissatisfaction. There were no suicides among the F-M group (Pauly, 1981).

In 1981, Lundström reviewed Pauly's work, added cases located by Lundström, and concluded that an unsatisfactory result occurs in 10–15 percent of the SRS patients. Increasing age and social instability correlated with unsatisfactory results. Secondary transsexuals (patients who wanted surgery because they were homosexual or were transvestites) had a higher frequency of unsatisfactory results (Lundström, Pauly, & Walinder, 1984). Lundström and his group commented:

> We conclude that sex reassignment surgery is the treatment of choice for carefully evaluated, genuine, primary transsexuals. SRS should not be offered patients with secondary gender dysphoria, those with unstable past histories, and patients over the age of 35. It is clear that the decision to offer SRS does not negate the clear indication for supportive psychotherapy before and after SRS.

In 1986, Lindemalm presented data on a smaller number of clients (13), but the study covered long years of follow up—6 to 25 years, with a median of 12 years. Clients were followed by the staff of the Psychiatric Clinic at the Karolinski Hospital in Stockholm, Sweden. Surgical outcomes were generally disappointing, with only one-third of the patients reporting a functioning vagina. (Apparently the technique developed by Burou was not used in Sweden). The overall sexual adjustment was about the same after surgery as before. In spite of the surgery and the hormonal treatment, most retained their libido. Psychosocial adjustment showed a slight improvement after surgery. One patient officially requested a reversal and went back to living as a man before any attempt had been made to construct a vagina. Another three people were judged as showing varying degrees of repentance. The study team emphasized the fact that they did not allow the doctor who had endorsed the study in the first place to do the follow-up and thus judge the level of repentance. It was interesting to note that the repentant people were, however, reasonably well-adjusted (Lindemalm, Korlin, & Uddenberg, 1986).

An evaluation of SRS was requested by the Netherlands Gender Center Foundation to see whether the surgery that had been done in the Netherlands was effective in terms of alleviating or abolishing the gender dysphoria which had driven patients to seek the procedure. The study of 36 female-to-male transsexuals and 105 male-to-female transsexuals was done by Abraham Kuiper and Peggy Cohen-Kettenis, using detailed interviews. The majority of the persons interviewed reported being happy or very happy, and if they did report feelings of dysphoria, it was not related to their gender identity. This contrasted significantly with their sense of unhappiness before the surgery. Detailed data about suicide attempts were gathered from 21 female-to-males and 72 male-to-females, with 19 percent of the former and 24 percent of the latter reporting suicide attempts before treatment started, and only two suicide attempts in each group after treatment started. Given the depth of unhappiness suggested by the suicide data, the authors found the current level of happiness impressive. However, the authors offer a note of caution and point out that it is possible that once the process of SRS has started, the level of commitment it demands is very significant, resulting in a tendency for people to try to reduce the level of cognitive dissonance rather than admit that it was all in vain (Kuiper & Cohen-Kettenis, 1988).

In 1990, Richard Green and Davis Fleming reviewed eleven follow-up studies published between 1979 and 1989; included were 130 reassignments from female to male and 220 reassignments from male to female. The findings were consistent with the earlier composite reviews. Reassignment from female to male was reported as satisfactory 97 percent of the time, with 3 percent reported as unsatisfactory. More problems emerged with the male-to-female group, with 87 percent having a satisfactory outcome and 13 percent unsatisfactory. The criteria for a satisfactory outcome varied widely, but not regretting the decision to have surgery seemed to be a criterion shared by the various researchers (Green & Fleming, 1990).

To Whom Does the Body Belong?

The fact that the two best surgeons in the field have operated outside the respectable university gender-identity clinics raises a question as to who should make the decision about diagnosis and treatment. At the beginning of the century, the diagnosis of transvestism and all related departures from the norms of behavior in the sexual realm belonged to the psychiatrists. They saw all deviations from narrowly constructed norms as psychological illness, and they were in charge of treating it with psychotherapy or other treatment modalities. They made up elaborate (and rather hostile) diagnostic categories for these deviations, which remain, in somewhat more polite language, in the *Diagnostic and Statistical Manual of Mental Disorders,* which came out in its fourth edition in 1994.

The Jorgensen experience challenged the psychiatric hegemony in the field by bringing in surgeons and endocrinologists as new experts. Orthodox psychiatrists were distressed by this threat to their monopoly of judging and treating sexual behaviors. This distress was well-expressed by two letters to the editor of the *Journal of the American Medical Association* following Hamburger's report of the Jorgensen surgery. A New York psychiatrist, G.H. Weideman, criticized Hamburger for not doing a more thorough psychological workup and for treating the patient with surgery rather than psychotherapy. He argued:

> It is true that reports on the treatment of transvestites are scarce in the psychoanalytic and psychiatric literature. This is due to the extreme reluctance of transvestites as well as of other sexual deviates to undergo any treatment that would remove the perversion and deprive them of their perverse gratifications. The difficulty of getting the patient into psychiatric treatment should not lead us to compliance with the patient's demands, which are based on his sexual perversion.
>
> —Wiedeman, 1953

A letter from Mortimer Ostow criticized both Hamburger and his patient, arguing that the only thing that would have helped Jorgensen was "intensive, prolonged, classic psychotherapy" (Ostow, 1953). In 1974, Ostow published a report of the research activities of a group of eight analysts who met every month over the years to share their experiences working with clients. They did not recognize transsexualism, but defined transvestism as a perversion caused by early childhood experiences resulting in anxiety—primarily castration anxiety, which could be treated only by psychoanalysis (Ostow, 1974).

Joost A.M. Meerloo argued that transsexuals were usually transvestites who for some neurotic or psychotic reason wanted a change-of-sex status, and that the physicians who participated in the SRS process were collaborating with the patients' psychosis (Meerloo, 1967). Similarly, Charles Socarides, in a report based on one "transsexual" patient, held that transsexuals were homosexuals who recast their identity; they did so in order to alleviate their guilt and to ward off paranoic psychosis, which they feared would result if they were to engage in homosexuality in a true anatomical sense (1970). While these criticisms may have been partly valid, they are tainted with self-interest, and suggest a fear of losing total power over an important client population.

As time passed, the criticism from the psychiatric community decreased. Possibly this is because the field of psychiatry broadened to include other approaches to therapy, or the dedicated Freudians died or rethought their opposition. However, their power was still formidable, as suggested by their prominent place in the Standards of Care.

The development of SRS did not, however, empower the client; it simply shifted the power to the team made up of surgeons, psychiatrists, and psychologists. This raises the question as to who should make the decision as to whether an individual should have SRS. Is it the highly trained medical and psychological team, or is it the individual? A few years ago, the question would not have been asked, but the consumer movement puts a new light on the question. SRS is plastic surgery, yet in the major centers, the requirements make it seem to be much more. Is it the mystical power of the sex organs, with all of their magical and religious connotations, that make the decision so fraught with meaning that plastic surgery for a nose does not have? In addition, the elaborate rules of the treatment centers are always based on the knowledge and assumptions of the time. For example, the early rule that patients must present as homosexuals was based on an assumption that the same sexual orientation would remain after surgery (and thus patients would magically become heterosexual and "respectable"). This assumption was false. Some people change their sexual orientation after surgery, and some do not. In fact, the whole question of the relationship between sexual orientation and gender is much more complex than it seemed earlier (see Devor's chapter 16 in this book).

In an article in *Social Problems*, Billings and Urban argued that transsexualism is not a diagnosis that exists in the real world; rather, it was a socially constructed reality created by medicine. They accused physicians of inventing the idea, and the Erickson Foundation of selling it:

> Transsexual therapy, legitimated by the terminology of disease, pushes patients toward an alluring world of artificial vaginas and penises rather than toward self-understanding and sexual politics. Sexual fulfillment and gender-role comfort are portrayed as commodities available through medicine.
>
> —Billings & Urban, 1982

Janice G. Raymond agreed that SRS was an invention of the medical-psychiatric complex, which developed a surgical approach to a moral and political issue. This avoidance of the real issues helped reinforce the current sex stereotypes. She believes that instead of operating on people who want to live a less stereotyped sex role, we should support their right to broaden their horizons (Raymond, 1979).

Holly Devor located and interviewed fifteen women who had lived at least part of their lives as men, yet only three had considered SRS, and none of them had gone through with it. She calls this process of living a partial male role "gender blending." Devor perceives the current norms of gender as paternalistic and discriminatory, and argues that gender blending is a strategy which women can use to get some of the advantages ordinarily reserved to men (Devor, 1989).

The ethnographic study by Anne Bolin carefully documents the difficult paths walked by her subjects as they went through the SRS process. Her definition of SRS as a rite of passage is thought-provoking, suggesting that the society should be able to devise a less traumatic rite of passage (Bolin, 1988).

There is also criticism of SRS from clients or would-be clients who would like to see more thoughtful treatment from health-care providers rather than abolishing the treatment. In an article in *Chrysalis Quarterly,* Dallas Denny criticized the university-affiliated gender clinics for failing to be patient-oriented, pointing out that since none of them could handle the large numbers of patients who came to them after 1952, they tended to choose the people they wanted for research and turn the others away. This was distressing to the would-be patients, and it probably distorted the research. Denny (1992) summarizes this problem as follows:

> The clinics viewed sex reassignment as a last-ditch effort to save those with whom other therapies and interventions had failed. Those who were accepted for treatment were usually prostitutes, those with substance abuse problems, sociopaths, those who were schizophrenic, those who were profoundly depressed or suicidal, and others who were considered "hopeless"—i.e., likely to die anyway. It was a classic misapplication of the triage method, with those most likely to benefit from the intervention being turned away, and the terminal cases receiving treatment.

Denny has now established an information clearinghouse that is independent of the medical establishment: the American Educational Gender Information Service (AEGIS). In a recent document published by AEGIS, Denny reviewed the transsexual process with all its attendant difficulties, so that people who are considering the surgery can understand the many problems involved in changing sex (Denny, 1990).

Another reasonable alternative to sex-change surgery for the transgendered individual is to simply cross-dress and live permanently in the opposite sex role. Others have advocated this in the past, but the idea may now grow more influential as it becomes more legally possible. Recent data suggest that this is in fact happening, and it is coming from the gender community, the clients themselves, rather than the medical professions. More people are opting to simply change their lifestyle without surgery to accommodate their sexual identity.

In a new study of 360 men who cross-dress, Bullough and Bullough found that 7.6 percent of the group are living full-time as women without benefit of surgery (Bullough & Bullough, 1997). Many do this with the aid of hormones, which may well become the major treatment modality for sexual dysphoria instead of surgery.

NOTES

1. Danish Sterilization and Castration, Act No. 176, May 11, 1935, and the earlier Danish Sterilization Act No. 130, June 1, 1929. There were similar laws in Norway, Sweden, Holland, and certain parts of Switzerland. Citation is from Hamburger, et al., 1953.
2. Cauldwell developed the term further in two booklets (Cauldwell 1950, 1951).

REFERENCES

American Educational Gender Information Service, Inc. (AEGIS). (1993). Medical Advisory Bulletin: Beware of forged or inappropriate documentation for sex reassignment procedures. Atlanta, GA: AEGIS.

(1980). *Diagnostic and statistical manual of mental disorders*. DSM III. Washington, DC: American Psychiatric Association.

(1987). *Diagnostic and statistical manual of mental disorders*. DSM III-R. Washington, DC: American Psychiatric Association.

(1994). *Diagnostic and statistical manual of mental disorders*. DSM IV. Washington, DC: American Psychiatric Association.

Benjamin, H. (1963). Clinical aspects of transsexualism in the male and female. Paper presented at the Sixth Annual Conference of the Society for the Scientific Study of Sex, New York City, 2 November, 1963.

Benjamin, H. (1964). Nature and management of transsexualism with a report on 31 operated cases. *Western Journal of Surgery, Obstetrics, and Gynecology, 72*, 105–111.

Benjamin, H. (1966). *The transsexual phenomenon*. New York: The Julian Press.

Bentler, P.M. (1976). A typology of transsexualism: Gender identity theory and data. *Archives of Sexual Behavior, 5*(6), 567–584.

Billings, D.B., & Urban, T. (1982). The socio-medical construction of transsexualism: An interpretation and critique. *Social Problems, 29*(3), 266–282.

Blanchard, R. (1985). Gender dysphoria and gender reorientation. In B.M. Steiner (Ed.), *Gender dysphoria: Development, research, management*, 365–392. New York: Plenum Press.

Blanchard, R., & Steiner, B. (1990). *Clinical management of gender identity disorders in children and adults*. Washington, DC: American Psychiatric Press.

Bolin, A. (1988). *In search of Eve: Transsexual rites of passage*. South Hadley, MA: Bergin & Garvey Publishers, Inc.

Bradley, S.J., Blanchard, R., Coates, S., Green, R., Levine, S.B., Meyer-Bahlburg, H.F.L., Pauly, I.B., & Zucker, K.J. (1991). Interim report of the DSM-IV subcommittee on gender identity disorders. *Archives of Sexual Behavior, 20*(4), 333–343.

Brown, D.G. (1958). Inversion and homosexuality. *American Journal of Orthopsychiatry, 28*(2), 424–429.

Bullough, B., & Bullough, V.L. (1997). Men who cross dress: A survey of 357 male cross dressers. In B. Bullough & V.L. Bullough (Eds.), *Gender Blending*, 174–188. Buffalo, NY: Prometheus Books.

Bullough, V.L. (1994). *Science in the bedroom*. New York: Basic Books.

Cauldwell, D.O. (1949). Psychopathia transexualis. *Sexology, 16*, 274–280.

Cauldwell, D.O. (1950). *Questions and answers on the sex life and sexual problems of transvestites: An exhaustive, revealing, surprising, informative, educational, entertaining and even shocking encyclopedic compilation of seldom-suspected facts*. Girard, KS: E. Haldeman-Julius, Publishers.

Cauldwell, D.O. (1951). *Sex transmutation . . . Can one's sex be changed?* Girard, KS: E. Haldeman-Julius, Publishers.

Cowell, R. (1954). *Roberta Cowell's Story*. Melbourne: William Heinemann Ltd.

Denny, D. (1992). The politics of diagnosis and a diagnosis of politics: The university-affiliated gender clinics, and how they failed to meet the needs of transsexual people. *Chrysalis Quarterly, 1*(3), 9–20.

Denny, D. (1990). *Deciding what to do about your gender dysphoria: Some considerations for those who are thinking about sex reassignment*. Decatur, GA: AEGIS. Available from American Educational Gender Information Service, Inc., P.O. Box 33724, Decatur, GA 30033.

Denny, D. (1991, June). Female-to-male reassignment surgery in the '90s. *Our Sorority*, 42–44.

Derogatis, L.R., Meyer, J.K., & Vazquez, N. (1978). A psychological profile of the transsexual: I. The male. *Journal of Nervous and Mental Disease, 166*(4), 234–254.

Devor, H. (1989). *Gender blending: Confronting the limits of duality*. Bloomington: Indiana University Press.

Devor, H. (1993). Toward a taxonomy of gendered sexuality. *Journal of Psychology & Human Sexuality, 6*, 23–55.

Docter, R. (1988). *Transvestites and transsexuals*. New York: Plenum Press.

Fleming, M., Steinman, C., & Bocknek, G. (1980). Methodological problems in assessing sex-reassignment: A reply to Meyer and Reter. *Archives of Sexual Behavior, 9*(5), 451–456.

Freund, K., Steiner, B., & Chan, S. (1982). Two types of cross-gender identity. *Archives of Sexual Behavior, 11*, 49–63.

Green, R., & Fleming, D.T. (1990). Transsexual surgery follow-up: Status in the 1990s. In J. Bancroft, C.M. Davis, & D. Weinstein (Eds.), *Annual Review of Sex Research*, 163–174. Society for the Scientific Study of Sex, P.O. Box 208, Mount Vernon, IA.

Hamburger, C. (1953). The desire for change of sex as shown by personal letters from 465 men and women. *Acta Endocrinologica, 14*, 361–375.

Hamburger, C., Sturup, G.K., & Dahl-Iversen, E. (1953). Transvestism: Hormonal, psychiatric, and surgical treatment. *Journal of the American Medical Association, 12*(6), 391–396.

Hirschfeld, M. (1991). *Transvestites: The erotic drive to cross dress* (Translated from the 1910 German edition by Michael A. Lombardi-Nash). Buffalo, NY: Prometheus Books.

Hoyer, N. (1933). *Man into woman: An authentic record of a change of sex. The true story of the miraculous transformation of the Danish painter, Einar Wegener (Andreas Sparrer)*. New York: E.P. Dutton & Co. Reprinted in 1953 in New York by Popular Library.

Jorgensen, C. (1967). *Christine Jorgensen: A personal autobiography*. New York: Paul S. Ericksson, Inc. Reprinted in 1968 by Bantam Books.

Kuiper, A.J., & Cohen-Kettenis, P.T. (1988). Sex reassignment surgery: A study of 141 Dutch transsexuals. *Archives of Sexual Behavior, 17*(5), 439–457.

Lindemalm, G., Korlin, D., & Uddenberg, N. (1986). Long-term follow-up of "sex change" in 13 male-to-female transsexuals. *Archives of Sexual Behavior, 15*(3), 187–210.

Lindgren, T.W., & Pauly, I.B. (1975). A body image scale for evaluating transsexuals. *Archives of Sexual Behavior, 4*(6), 639–656.

Lorenz, C. (1965). *Evolution and modification of behavior.* Chicago: University of Chicago Press.

Lundström, B., Pauly, I., & Walinder, J. (1984). Outcome of sex reassignment surgery. *Acta Psychiatrica Scandinavica, 70*(4), 289–294.

McCauley, E. & Ehrhardt, A.A. (1977). Role expectations and definition: A comparison of female transsexuals and lesbians. *Journal of Homosexuality, 3*(2), 137–147.

Meerloo, J.A.M. (1967). Letter to the editor: Change of sex and collaboration with the psychosis. *American Journal of Psychiatry, 124*(2), 263–264.

Meyer, J.K., & Reter, D. (1979). Sex reassignment: Follow-up. *Archives of General Psychiatry, 36*(9), 1010–1015.

Money, J. (1969). Sex reassignment as related to hermaphroditism and transsexualism. In R. Green & J. Money (Eds.), *Transsexualism and sex reassignment,* pp. 91–113. Baltimore: The Johns Hopkins University Press.

Ostow, M. (1953). Transvestism. Letter to the editor. *Journal of the American Medical Association, 152*(16), 1553.

Ostow, M. (Ed.), with Gillmor, M.H. (1974). *Sexual deviation: Psychoanalytic insights.* New York: Quadrangle/New York Times Book Co.

Pauly, I. (1968). The current status of the change of sex operation. *Journal of Nervous and Mental Disease, 147*(5), 460–471.

Pauly, I. (1981). Outcome of sex reassignment surgery for transsexuals. *Australian and New Zealand Journal of Psychiatry, 15*(1), 45–51.

Pauly, I. (1985). Gender identity disorders. In M. Farber (Ed.), *Human sexuality: Psychosexual effects of disease,* pp. 295–316. New York: Macmillan Publishing Company.

Pauly, I., & Edgerton, M.T. (1986). The gender identity movement: A growing surgical-psychiatric liaison. *Archives of Sexual Behavior, 15*(4), 315–329.

Pauly, I., & Lindgren, T.W. (1976). Body image and gender identity. *Journal of Homosexuality, 2*(2), 133–142.

Pierce, W. (1989). Interview with Dr. Biber. *Rites of Passage: A Magazine for Female-to-Male Transsexuals and Crossdressers.*

Raymond, J. (1979). *The transsexual empire: The making of the she-male.* Boston: Beacon Press.

Ross, M.W., Rogers, L.J., & McCulloch, H. (1978). Stigma, sex and society: A new look at gender differentiation and sexual variation. *Journal of Homosexuality, 3*(4), 315–330.

Socarides, C.W. (1970). A psychoanalytic study of the desire for sexual transformation ("transsexualism"): The plaster-of-Paris man. *International Journal of Psycho-Analysis, 51*(3), 341–349.

Stall, B. (1979, 16 August). Sex change surgery value questioned. *Los Angeles Times,* Pt. 1, 20.

Steiner, B.W. (1985). The management of patients with gender disorders. In B.W. Steiner (Ed.), *Gender dysphoria: Development, research, management,* pp. 325–350. New York: Plenum Press.

Stinson, B. (1972). A study of twelve applicants for transsexual surgery. *Ohio State Medical Journal, 68*(3), 245–249.

Strassberg, D.S., Roback, H., Cunningham, J., McKee, E., & Larson, P. (1979). Psychopathology in self-identified female-to-male transsexuals, homosexuals, and heterosexuals. *Archives of Sexual Behavior, 8*(6), 491–496.

Uddenberg, N., Walinder, J., & Hojerback, T. (1979). Parental contact in male and female transsexuals. *Acta Psychiatrica Scandinavica, 60*(1), 113–120.

Walinder, J., Lundstrom, B., Ross, M., & Thuwe, I. (1979). Transsexualism: Incidence, prevalence and sex ratio: Comments on three different studies. In *Proceedings of the 6th International Gender Dysphoria Association.* Coronado, CA.

Walker, P.A., Berger, J.C., Green, R., Laub, D.L., Reynolds, C.L., Jr., & Wollman, L. (1979). *Standards of care: The hormonal and surgical sex reassignment of gender dysphoric persons.* Galveston, TX: The University of Texas Medical Branch.

Wiedeman, G.H. (1953). Letter to the editor. *Journal of the American Medical Association, 152*(12), 1167.

3 BLACK TELEPHONES, WHITE REFRIGERATORS

RETHINKING CHRISTINE JORGENSEN

Dallas Denny

The opening shot of the 1985 film, "What Sex Am I?" features a black-and-white newsreel from 1953. A slim, blonde woman, stylish in a mink coat and matching pillbox hat, disembarks from an airplane to face hordes of reporters, jostling for position, trying to get a quote or a photograph. She looks frail and feminine, the very opposite of the male uniformed Scandinavian Airlines pilots at the bottom of the ramp. At the press conference which follows, facing a phalanx of microphones, she protests in a slightly throaty voice, "I think it's too much."

It really *was* too much. This woman had traveled to Europe in pursuit of physical congruity and personal happiness. She found that happiness, but she staggered the world by bringing into question long-held and oft-cherished notions about the immutability of sex and gender.

What was extraordinary was that this woman, whose name was Christine Jorgensen, had, as one punster put it, gone abroad and come back a broad. Once, she had been a man named George Jorgensen. She was returning to the United States after an extended stay in Denmark, where she had received feminizing hormonal treatments and surgery, and where she had forever given up George's ostensible manhood for a new name and role as Christine.[1]

George Jorgensen, Jr., was born in Manhattan on Memorial Day, 1926, to a family of Scandinavian ancestry. He was a quiet, shy boy with a feminine manner, and grew up to be a painfully self-conscious young man who, at the age of 19, found himself in the US Army in October 1945. He was honorably discharged sixteen months later, after a bout of pneumonia.

While in the service, Jorgensen had compared himself to the other men in his unit. Where they were strong and hearty and ruggedly masculine, he weighed 98 pounds and was feminine in appearance and demeanor. He wondered whether he might be homosexual (he had found himself emotionally attracted to several of his close male friends, but was unattracted to women); eventually, he decided that his emotions were more those of a woman than of a gay man.

> I couldn't condemn them, but I also knew that I certainly couldn't become like them. It was a thing deeply alien to my religious attitudes and the highly magnified and immature moralistic views that I entertained at the time.
>
> —Jorgensen, 1967, p. 33

Jorgensen had a lifelong interest in photography. He set out for Hollywood in 1947, hoping to land a job in the film industry. After an unsuccessful year, he returned home and used his GI-bill benefits to attend Mohawk College and then the Progressive School of Photography in New Haven, Connecticut. He continued to be haunted by his feeling of being different, and began to wonder whether his femininity was caused by an endocrine condition.

It was in his reading about experiments in which female chicks were masculinized and roosters were revitalized by administration of the newly synthesized sex hormones that Jorgensen first conceived of the notion that perhaps his "imbalance" could be corrected. But he was not interested in becoming more like "normal" males. When he found himself in front of an endocrinologist, he asked if perhaps it was his genitals, rather than his feminine appearance, which was the mistake. The doctor responded by referring him to a psychiatrist, who proposed that Jorgensen begin psychoanalysis to rid himself of his "feminine inclinations."

George Jorgensen was looking for a miracle, but none were to be found. So he made one himself: first, by submerging himself in textbooks and scientific papers; and then by going to a drugstore where he persuaded a pharmacist to give him a prescription for ethinyl estradiol (an estrogen); and finally by saving his pennies for a journey to Denmark, where doctors were experimenting with sex hormones.

Shortly after his arrival in Copenhagen, Jorgensen persuaded the endocrinologist Christian Hamburger to use him as a human guinea pig for a program of feminization that included hormones, electrolysis, resocialization, and, eventually, genital surgery.

The effect of sex hormones is gradual, but powerful, as anyone who has gone through puberty can attest. Jorgensen's appearance began to change, at first subtly. Eventually the physical change became profound.

Jorgensen began to dress as a woman, going out in public to socialize and work on her favorite project, a color travel film. She took the name Christine, the feminine version of Christian, in honor of the man who had granted her access to the treatments which she had so desperately desired.

When the time to return to the United States grew near, Jorgensen wrote her parents to inform them of her circumstances. The family was understandably shocked and confused, but to their credit, sent a telegram telling her that they loved her more than ever.

In November 1952, as Jorgensen lay in a hospital bed, recovering from her second operation (penectomy), and contemplating her impending return to the US, someone—never identified by name in her autobiography—leaked the fact of her medical treatments to the press. The story broke on the first of December, in headlines 'round the world: "Ex-GI Becomes Blonde Beauty"; "Bronx GI Becomes a Woman"; "Dear Mum and Dad, Son Wrote, I Have Now Become Your Daughter."

If Jorgensen's life had suddenly turned upside-down, the earth had certainly wobbled a bit on its axis. Sex, which had been considered to be constant and enduring, was suddenly capable of being changed. As I write this, 43 years after the Jorgensen headlines and more than 6 years after her death, many of us, transsexual and nontranssexual alike, are still struggling with the Pandora's box opened by this one human being who chose to call herself Christine.

It was not until Jorgensen's return to the United States that the world got to see just what she looked like. And the difference between the shy young man with protruding ears who had left for Denmark in 1950 and the confident woman in mink in 1953 was astounding. Thin and stylish, and reasonably pretty, there was nothing about her other than the headlines and a few old photos to suggest that she had not always been a woman. In a world in which refrigerators were white, telephones were black, boys were boys and girls were girls, and there were few shades of gray in between, her physical appearance confirmed that she had indeed been "changed." The reporters had been impressed that a team of surgeons could bring about such a transformation, and wrote their stories as if that had been so. Having been already blessed by the scientists with such marvels as hydromatic transmissions and atom bombs, the average American believed that all of life's little problems, including George Jorgensen's, could be fixed by a simple application of technology. Certainly, this woman had, as the press suggested, been created out of whole cloth by the doctors.

Cut to a modern 1950s all-electric kitchen. White appliances have the same rounded curves as the family Buick, which is visible through the curtained window. Mom is at the stove, wearing a checked apron and a big smile. Dad, with pipe and paper, sits at the table. Sis, her hair in pigtails, wearing penny loafers, and Junior, with butch cut and freckles, are helping themselves from a selection which contains the Five Basic Fifties Food Groups (cholesterol, fat, refined sugar, red meat, and iodized salt).

Spot, his head tilted to one side, watches Dad with fascination as he (Dad, not Spot) says, "Say, now, look at this. Seems those darn scientists have turned a man into a woman."

"That's nice, dear," Mom replies.

Junior hides his interest by making a disgusting noise.

"Gee, Dad," says Sis, "That's great!"

"It was bound to happen," pronounces Dad. "If they can split the atom, it stands to reason they can do something reasonably simple like this."

"Do you think it hurt?" asks Sis.

Of course, even as Americans were simultaneously fascinated and repelled by the thought of Jorgensen's surgery, it was not the unseen surgery site that made her seem a woman to them, but her physical presentation; she was for all practical purposes indistinguishable from other women her age. She looked like a woman, moved like a woman, sounded like a woman, and no doubt smelled like a woman. Surely it was those darn scientists, who, by putting things in and taking things out and shaking things all about, had turned the jug-eared George into the Scandinavian princess Christine, had transformed a man into a woman.

But of course, that was not true.

Jorgensen was not the first transsexual person, nor even the first to be sexually reassigned.[2] Hers was simply the first case to capture the attention and imagination of the press. To the world, she was a symbol and a celebrity, and she paid a high price for her notoriety.

In terms of the medical treatments she had received, Jorgensen's sex reassignment (a term not yet coined) had consisted of hormonal therapy and two surgical procedures: castration (removal of the testicles) and penectomy (removal of the penis). Her medical team was unwilling to go any further. Later, she would quietly have yet a third procedure, vaginoplasty, in which a vaginal cavity was created in the Barbie-Doll-like groin that Dahl-Iversen, her Danish surgeon, had given her. But if her operations were what constituted her "sex change" in the popular imagination, it was the feminization caused by female hormones and electrolysis which shouted "woman" to the millions who were, courtesy of the media, onlookers. Her surgery sites were invisible, but that smooth face, those blonde curls, those slim hands were right out there in the wind for everyone to see. If Christine Jorgensen was something less than a woman, it was not because of her appearance or demeanor, but only because of the particulars of a past which had been laid open by journalists as deftly as Dahl-Iversen had once laid open her male parts with a scalpel. Christine was a new sort of person, a woman who had not always been a woman, a human being who had not been content with her biology and had, by damn, done something about it.

So let's get this straight: Christine Jorgensen had not been "made into a woman" by her surgeons. She had no vagina: she had simply had her male organs removed and undergone a course of female hormones and electrolysis. Many men have these operations or take female hormones for medical reasons, such as prostrate or penile cancer, others lack facial hair, yet they do not consider themselves women, nor are they considered women by others. But Jorgensen, even if many Americans could not bring themselves to regard her as a woman, was obviously something and someone very different from a man, and someone very like a woman—and for almost everyone, the difference was somehow viscerally rooted (no pun intended) in what had been done "down there."

But it was not physicians who had actually accomplished Jorgensen's sex reassignment. No lancet, no hormone tablet can make a woman of a man, or a man from a woman.[3] It was Jorgensen herself who was the driving force in her own sex reassignment. Certainly the medical procedures helped by giving her a body which matched her voice and deportment, but the doctors had not suddenly said, "Hey! I have an idea. Let's see if we can turn a man into a woman!" and gone in search of a willing victim. No, the entire thing was Christine's idea. As she has documented in her autobiography, she learned of the experimental work being done in Denmark with hormones and surgery, and went there to check into it. She had set an impossible-sounding goal for herself—becoming a woman—and when she identified a possible way to realize that goal, she took advantage of it—and it worked!

It was the sheer force of her will which set the process in motion, persuading reluctant physicians to undertake such a novel set of treatments. Although she did not wield the scalpel, Christine Jorgensen did her own sex change, moving into the female role with confidence and aplomb.

Although the sensibilities of the 1950s now seem distant and more than a bit quaint, Jorgensen's sex reassignment was in fact a prime example of the intersection of the human condition and modern technology. Pills synthesized in laboratories or made from the urine of pregnant farm animals (as are some brands of female hormones), plastic-surgery techniques which were originally developed to correct deformities and repair disfigurements, doctors from Denmark—these were merely the tools Jorgensen used to orchestrate the metamorphosis she sought. She managed to conceive of the possibility of changing her sex, figure out that she would need medical help in order to do so, and recruit physicians to give her that help. She was the project manager of a bold social experiment which lasted until 1989, when she died of pancreatic cancer. And it was a successful experiment. Her last public act was to assure the world that she had no regrets about what she had done.

Christine Jorgensen was not only a medical pioneer, but a social pioneer and a role model for a people who had up until then been invisible in our society. She showed the way to tens of thousands of others like herself. With no socialization or training in womanhood, she put on her high heels and went out into the world to slay dragons. She lived with dignity and died with dignity, a spokeswoman for transsexualism, a pioneer, a woman.

I realize that many people still consider Christine Jorgensen an anomaly, a curiosity, a freak, neither fish nor fowl, but I have a better word for her: woman. She was a woman, pure and simple. A transsexual woman. And what a woman. What determination she showed. What resolve, to go against convention, to journey into unknown territory as certainly as had Dr. Livingston a century before her. What nerve it must have taken to face rooms full of shouting, jostling journalists while wearing clothing which would have gotten George into a lot of trouble. What courage, to hold her head high in the face of criticism about who she was and what she had done, to ignore with good grace the tasteless jokes that were made about her, the social snubs, the derogatory headlines, the names she was called to her face and in print.[4] Few of us would have had such fortitude—certainly least of all, her more vocal critics. She was a woman of fierce resolve, and wondrous determination—and yet, to many Americans, she was, and is, not so much a pioneer as a joke, a subject for ridicule. What does that tell us about ourselves?

Because she was a pioneer, Christine Jorgensen was a favorite target of the media. From the time of her return to the United States, and even after her death, she had no privacy. She was, to the American public, the first person in the world who had had a sex change, and to the news media which had made her such, she was a defenseless, if not entirely reluctant, target.

Every milestone in her life was chronicled by reporters, often in articles riddled with puns and double entendres. Every mention of transsexualism would send reporters to her house to ask her opinion. Any hope she might have had of leading a private life was shattered.

This lack of privacy contributed to the fact that she never married, for any husband or even lover of hers was fair game also. Her attempt to get a marriage license caused such a media furor that she and her fiancé mutually decided to let the matter of marriage drop. Only a man with the same quiet good grace and determination could have stood up to the pressure—and such men are not easy to find. And so, Jorgensen remained single, living a life for which she was on the one hand vilified by preachers and politicians and stand-up comedians, and on the other hand honored and admired and acclaimed. Hers could not have been an easy life. Certainly, it was a lonely one, and a wearing one—which may account for rumors that she became an alcoholic in her later years. And if she did drink too much, who could blame her?

The press' treatment of Jorgensen began a longstanding tradition of treating transsexual persons as something less than human. But Christine's relationship to the press was a curious one. The news media made her into a celebrity, something to which she was not completely averse. In her autobiography, she writes at length about the travel film she had made and her desire to show it. Eventually, she did. She also found herself appearing in nightclubs on four continents and acting in the occasional play.

Although Jorgensen eventually became an adequate performer, it was her status as an instant celebrity which resulted in job offers; indeed, they began rolling in on the very day her story first broke. Many people had a voyeuristic desire to see this miracle woman of modern science, and promoters were not blind to it. Her stage career was a moderate success, eventually dying out more because her performances were of less-than-stellar quality than because interest in her transsexualism waned.

In her autobiography, Jorgensen maintains that she eventually discovered the identity of the person who tipped off the press. The thought has crossed my mind that perhaps she blew the whistle on herself. Perhaps, while she was pondering how to go about obtaining a change of sex, formulating her fantastic plan, she considered what she might do afterwards. Certainly, she was proud of her travel film and wished for its promotion and success. Certainly, she had learned the bitter lesson in her earlier journey to Hollywood that doors in the entertainment world would not automatically open. Certainly, it must have occurred to her that her most special quality was not her photographic skills, but her gender status. Certainly, she later took advantage of that status to build a career in show business. Surely she must have known what a hot property she could become with one phone call. And apparently, she made that phone call. Bullough and Bullough, who knew Jorgensen, report in their chapter in this book that she leaked the news to the press.

We'll probably never know exactly what role Jorgensen had in her own "outing," but one thing is for sure: an awkward, maladjusted man named George became a woman who was poised and confident in the face of harassment and an incredible media feeding frenzy.

Christine Jorgensen's 1953 return to the United States was a major cultural landmark, as profoundly impacting in its own way as the launching of Sputnik or the erection of the Berlin wall. It changed the way the world thought about sex and gender; about men and women; about maleness and femaleness. For the first time, binary notions of gender were challenged.[5]

Today, more than 40 years post-Jorgensen, there is discourse on gender on a variety of fronts. This is reflected in a seemingly endless coverage of gender-bending in news, movies, literature, and television; in endless message-passing on the Internet, in examination and re-examination of what gender is and what it means; and in this book. The world has changed, and continues to change, as gender roles are challenged and deconstructed by academicians, historians, anthropologists, sociologists, by gay and lesbian academicians, and by transgendered scholars.

That's quite an accomplishment for one ex-GI from the Bronx.

NOTES

1. Jorgensen's story was simplified and sensationalized by the press, but is told in her own words in her autobiography, *Christine Jorgensen: A Personal Autobiography*, which was published in hardback in 1967 by Paul S. Ericksson, Inc. and in paperback the next year by Bantam. Many of the details of her life, as related in this chapter, were taken from her book. While out of print, it can occasionally be found at second-hand bookstores, and should be available through interlibrary loan.

2. Jorgensen had both predecessors and contemporaries. Roberta Cowell was a contemporary. She caught the attention of the British press, just as Jorgensen had the American press. Cowell's past as a race-car driver and RAF fighter pilot made for a good story. Like Jorgensen, she made an attractive woman. Her autobiography, *Roberta Cowell's Story*, is out of print.

Jorgensen's predecessors lived in a time when hormonal therapy and surgical manipulations of the genitalia were not possible. Many nonetheless lived and died as members of the other gender, undiscovered until their deaths. A recent examination of official records by Dekker and van de Pol (1989) revealed the existence of hundreds of Dutch females who lived as men during the Middle Ages.

As Bullough (1994) has noted, it was the synthesis of human sex hormones in the 1940s rather than the availability of genital surgery which made sex reassignment possible. But attempts were made to turn women into men and men into women by surgical means. In a 1931 paper in the German medical journal *Zeitschrift Sexualwissenschaft*, Abraham reported on two genital alterations. But for a more accessible (though still out-of-print account) see Neils Hoyer's hauntingly written *Man into Woman,* which documents the social and surgical conversion of the Danish painter Einar Wegener (Andreas Sparrer) into Lili Elbe.

3. I've noted elsewhere that if you were to go and find Clint Eastwood and convince a doctor to do "the operation," he would not wake up to be a woman. He would wake up to be a very pissed Clint Eastwood. Womanhood and manhood are not achieved in the operating room, but in the ways in which men and women live their lives.

4. Occasionally, Jorgensen would defend herself; see Anon., n.d. (A newspaper clipping exists, but its source and date are unknown.) Spiro Agnew once called Senator Charles E. Goddell "The Christine Jorgensen of the Republican Party." Jorgensen sent him a telegram, asking him to apologize. Considering Agnew's character (or, rather, lack thereof), he almost certainly did not.

5. If she changed the world for nontranssexual people, Jorgensen had an even more profound effect on people who were like her. Her story galvanized many transsexual men and women into seeking the same sort of medical treatment. In 1953, Christian Hamburger published a paper in which he described receiving 465 letters from men and women, desperately begging for a "sex change." Neither he, nor anyone else, was prepared to oblige them.

Many more didn't write, but carried the image of Christine Jorgensen around in their minds and hearts for years or decades before coming to terms with their own transsexualism. I have in my files a number of accounts from transsexual persons, describing their reaction when they heard the news in November 1952. Some were too ashamed to even buy the newspaper with the headlines. Others bought it, read it with trembling hands, and threw it away for fear that they would be discovered with it and their own transsexualism would become immediately transparent. One person, then a man and now a woman, describes how, when she heard the news, she had to hold onto a lamppost; her world was shaken that much.

Like Christine, I crossed the Atlantic in search of congruity. Unlike her, I did not change my social role while overseas. I was already functioning as a woman. But we both faced the same knife. Fortunately, only one of us had to face the reporters.

REFERENCES

Abraham, F. (1931). Genitalumwandlung an zwei maennlichen transvestiten (Genital alteration in two male transvestites). *Zeitschrift Sexualwissenschaft, 18,* 223–226.

Anonymous. (1952, 1 December). Ex-GI becomes blonde beauty. *New York Daily News,* 1.

Anonymous. (1952, 2 December). Dear Mum and Dad, son wrote, I've now become your daughter. *The Daily Mirror.*

Anonymous. (n.d., 10 October). Miss Jorgensen asks Agnew for apology. (n.p.).

Bullough, V. (1994). Preface. In D. Denny (Ed.), *Gender dysphoria: A guide to research.* New York: Garland.

Bullough, B., & Bullough, V. (1996). Transsexualism: Historical Perspectives, 1952 to Present. In D. Denny (Ed.), *Current concepts in transgender identity: Towards a new synthesis.* New York: Garland Publications.

Cowell, R. (1954). *Roberta Cowell's story.* London: William Heinemann, Ltd. Reprinted (1955), New York: Lion Library.

Dekker, R.J., & van de Pol, L.C. (1989). *The tradition of female transvestism in early modern Europe.* New York: St. Martin's Press.

Hamburger, C. (1953). The desire for change of sex as shown by personal letters from 465 men and women. *Acta Endocrinologica, 14,* 361–375.

Hamburger, C., Sturup, G.K., & Dahl-Iversen, E. (1953). Transvestism: Hormonal, psychiatric, and surgical treatment. *Journal of the American Medical Association, 12*(6), 391–396.

Hoyer, N. (1933). *Man into woman: An authentic record of a change of sex. The true story of the miraculous transformation of the Danish painter, Einar Wegener (Andreas Sparrer)*. New York: E.P. Dutton & Co. Reprinted in 1953 in New York by Popular Library.

Jorgensen, C. (1967). *Christine Jorgensen: A personal autobiography*. New York: Paul S. Ericksson, Inc. Reprinted in 1968 by Bantam Books.

What sex am I? (1985). Film, Lee Grant, Dir. Home Box Office.

4 GENDER AND GENITALS

CONSTRUCTS OF SEX AND GENDER*

Ruth Hubbard

The ways scientists conceptualize nature, the questions they ask about it, and the answers they accept as plausible or true are inevitably grounded in the beliefs they share with the wider culture of which they are a part. The resulting preconceptions and biases, though often unconscious and unacknowledged, are usually most blatant in relation to questions that involve the interplay of biology and society, hence to most questions to do with human biology and medicine. They are especially prevalent, but also particularly well concealed, when it comes to our understandings of sex and gender, since in Western societies sex and sex differences are linchpins of the way we conceptualize ourselves and our culture.

Beginning in the 1970s, however, a number of scholars and activists have tried to achieve fuller insight into the way the social and biological sciences have constructed sex and gender. In these discussions, it is still usual to draw a distinction between these two terms. In general, sex—whether we are male or female, women or men—is defined in terms of chromosomes (XX or XY), gonads (ovaries or testes), and genitals (the presence of a vagina or a penis—or, rather, merely the presence or absence of a penis). Gender, specified as masculine or feminine, denotes the psychosocial attributes and behaviors people develop as a result of what society expects of them depending on whether they were born female or male. However, as Kessler and McKenna and Barbara Fried have pointed out, the concepts of sex and gender are often overlapping and blurred, not only in ordinary speech but also in the scientific literature (Kessler & McKenna, 1978; Fried, 1982). Thus, note that Money and Ehrhardt's classic *Man and Woman, Boy and Girl,* which popularized the distinction between the terms "sex" and "gender," confuses them in the subtitle—*Differentiation and Dimorphism of*

*An earlier version of this article was published in *Social Text, 14* (1–2), 157–165.

Gender Identity from Conception to Maturity—since, surely, conception is too early to speak of "gender identity" (Money & Ehrhardt, 1972).

Not all languages have two words comparable to sex and gender. The fact that both terms are in common use in English may have encouraged American scientists to try to assign a different word to the biological aspects of sex difference and to their psychosocial manifestations. But, as with all attempts to sort "nature" from "nurture," the resulting muddle is more than linguistic. The point is that many manifestations we decide to designate as natural are shaped, or at least affected, by cultural factors, while biology—genes, hormones, and such—affects manifestations we choose to attribute to nurture. Furthermore, in general, what we attribute to nature is no more immune from change than what we attribute to socialization.[1] And, in our technological and medicalized era, supposed biological factors often are easier to manipulate than are the forces thought to reflect cultural institutions and traditions or deeply held beliefs. Despite these caveats, I shall, in what follows, accept the conventional, though blurry, distinction between sex and gender.

Sex is usually assigned when an infant is born by looking to see whether it has a penis. If it does, it's a boy; if it doesn't, it's a girl. Gender develops over time and the lore generally accepted in the social science and medical literature is that, for psychic health and to develop a coherent gender identity, children should know that they are a girl or a boy by the time their language abilities are at the appropriate stage, so by about age two or two and a half.

Embedded and unquestioned in this developmental formulation from sex to gender is the binary paradigm that, biologically speaking, there are only two kinds of people—women and men—so, two sexes and that people who belong to one or the other, through socialization and experience, come to emphasize the characteristics appropriate to the corresponding gender. Let us now look at this situation in greater detail.

When it comes to sex, the Western assumption that there are only two sexes probably derives from our culture's close coupling between sex and procreation. That coupling, if it does not grow out of the teachings of Western religions, is surely reinforced by them. Yet, this binary concept does not reflect biological reality. The biologist Anne Fausto-Sterling estimates that approximately one or two percent of children are born with mixed or ambiguous sex characteristics, though, for obvious reasons, it is difficult to be sure of the numbers. Such ambiguities can involve frank hermaphroditism—an infant born either with one ovary and one testis or with so-called ovotestes, organs that contain a mix of both kinds of tissues. They can also involve inconsistencies between chromosomal and gonadal or genital sex.

For example, the tissues of some children born with XY chromosomes, who as embryos develop testes, do not differentiate in the usual way in response to the hormones their testes produce. Though "male" according to their chromosomes and gonads, these children develop a vagina. In medical parlance, they are said to have "androgen insensitivity" and since they are born looking like girls, they are usually assigned and reared as females. Depending on the kind of medical care they encounter, no one may notice that they have (undescended) testes or anything else unusual until puberty, when they do not begin to menstruate at the expected time. They may, however, develop breasts, since their testes and adrenals secrete sufficient amounts of the necessary hormones.

In an analogous variation, some XX (so, "female") embryos have what is called adrenogenital syndrome, which means that their adrenals secrete excessive amounts of so-called male hormones or androgens.[2] Though as embryos they develop ovaries, their uterus, vagina, and labia may or may not develop as usual, and their clitoris may be enlarged to the point that it looks like a penis. At birth, such children may be "mistaken" for boys or considered ambiguous as regards their sex. The existence of various intermediate forms has led Anne Fausto-Sterling to refer to "the five sexes," though there are likely to be more (Fausto-Sterling, 1993).

Other types of intermediate forms exist. For example, in several villages in the Dominican Republic a certain number of children who are chromosomally XY and develop embryonic testes (so, "male") manifest a genetic variation in which the transformation of their testosterone into dihydrotestosterone (DHT) is impeded. Since DHT is the form of testosterone that ordinarily masculinizes the external genitalia in XY embryos, these children are born looking like girls and are therefore socialized like girls. However, at puberty their testosterone shows its effects: their testes descend into what have hitherto been thought to be their labia, their voice deepens, and their clitoris is transformed into a penis. The US biomedical scientists who first described this situation reported that, though these children have been raised as females, most of them accept their transformation and have it accepted by their society. They change not only their sex, but their gender identity. In other words, they become biological and social males (Imperato-McGinley, et al., 1979).

In fact, there is a good deal of debate about this situation. The original team of US scientists seems to have been entirely unaware of their own enculturation in the binary paradigms of sex and gender and apparently did not ask any questions about how the people among whom this phenomenon occurs thought about sex differences, the immutability of sex, or the relationship between sex and gender.

The fact is that the villagers have special terms for these individuals. They call them *guevedoche* (balls at twelve) or *machihembra* (male female). This suggests that they do not regard such persons as either female or male, but as a third category, a third sex. The attempt to describe the Dominican Republic system in terms of our own binary sex/gender systems has been criticized by the anthropologist Gilbert Herdt (Herdt, 1994). He notes that unfortunately the lack of self-awareness of the biomedical researchers may have distorted the Dominican villagers' viewpoint sufficiently to make it impossible to reconstruct the way they conceptualized this situation before the American researchers arrived on the scene and how they coded it in terms of either sex or gender, if this distinction is at all valid in their setting.

A hermaphroditism of the same biological origin has also been described among several peoples in New Guinea who clearly make room for a third sex in addition to male and female. However, Gilbert Herdt points out that the Sambia, which is the group he has observed most closely, make every effort to detect the condition, which they call *kwolu-aatmwol* or *turnimman* (turns into a man), at birth. If they do, though the infant may look "female" and be coded as a kwolu-aatmwol or third-sex person, he is reared as male from the start. On occasion, an especially talented *kwolu-aatmwol* is honored as a shaman or war leader, but most are looked upon as "a sad and mysterious quirk of nature" (Herdt, 1994, p. 436). However, Herdt emphasizes that where there are options beyond that of male or female, there are ways of incorporating differences into identities which are obscured by our own medicalized system.

Other examples of the acceptance of more than two sexes have long been described among Native Americans, especially the Navahos and Zunis, where a person can be *nadle* or *berdache* (as it was called by the French colonizers), in which case they have a special status and function as neither male nor female. It is not clear to what extent *berdache* have been biological hermaphrodites or transvestites and cross-dressers. The point is that, either way, they are accepted as a third sex. This is true also of the *hijras* in India, who are considered neither man nor woman in their sex or gender identity and are able to function as a third group.

In our own culture, in the old days, people who were obviously intermediate in their anatomy or physiological functions had closeted lives whenever possible. If their indeterminate status became known, they lived more or less miserable lives because intermediate forms are not accepted in the West. In the last few decades, in conformity with the binary paradigm, medical interventions have been developed to try to "correct" the genitals of infants who manifest any form of sex ambiguity.

I do not want to pass judgment about whether and to what extent such medical "solutions" benefit the individuals in question. Given the intense social pressure that sex be binary, so that people must be male *or* female, only very unusual parents would choose not to "repair" their child's genital or other sex ambiguities if physicians assure them that it can be done. But, finally, some people who as children experienced such repairs are beginning to speak out against them.[3]

A rule that appears to operate in such medical sex reconstructions—or rather constructions—is to concentrate on the appearance of the external genitalia and to make them look as unequivocally male or female as possible. Since chromosomal and gonadal sex are thus pushed into the background and it is more difficult to construct a credible-looking penis than vagina (which is fashioned as a blunt pouch or tube), this means that the majority of children born with ambiguous genitals are turned into girls. Some effort is made to accommodate parents' wishes for a boy, but given the choice of a "real girl" or an "ambiguous boy," most parents will opt for the former.

Another rule is for the physicians to emphasize that, from the start, the infant has been of the sex they have decided to assign it to. The ambiguity is made to appear as a minor mistake of nature that modern medical methods can readily right. Therefore, the physicians try to determine as quickly as possible which sex assignment is technically most feasible and to stick with that decision. If they must revise their assessment, every effort is made to say that the baby all along was the sex to which it is being definitively assigned and that the physicians initially made a mistake. The goal is to make the parents feel sure of their child's intrinsic male- or femaleness as soon as possible so that they can act on this conviction in the way they raise her or him from earliest infancy (Kessler, 1990).

In this way, as Suzanne Kessler points out, "the belief that gender consists of two exclusive types is maintained and perpetuated by the medical community in the face of incontrovertible physical evidence that this is not mandated by biology" (Kessler, 1990, p. 25). In other words, our gender dichotomy does not flow "naturally" from the biological dichotomy of the two sexes. The absolute dichotomy of the sexes into males and females, women and men, is itself socially constructed and the fact that we insist on sex being binary and permanent for life feeds into the notion that, for people to be "normal," their gender must also be binary and must match their genital sex. Where ambiguities exist, whatever their nature, the external genitalia are taken to be what counts for gender socialization and development.

Kessler and McKenna summarize the situation this way:

> Scientists construct dimorphism where there is continuity. Hormones, behavior, physical characteristics, developmental processes, chromosomes, psychological qualities have all been fitted into [sex or] gender dichotomous categories. Scientific knowledge does not inform the answer to "what makes a person either a man or a woman?" Rather it justifies (and appears to give grounds for) the already existing knowledge that a person is either a woman or a man and that there is no problem in differentiating between the two. Biological, psychological, and social differences do not lead to our seeing two genders. Our seeing two genders leads to the "discovery" of biological, psychological, and social differences. (p. 163)

If, as we have seen, sex differences are not all that clear-cut, the situation is even more confused when it comes to gender. We admit in our everyday language that both males and females can be more or less feminine or masculine. And we know from experience that most of us play with gender, or "play gender." The degree of our masculinity and femininity is not fixed for life, but changes over time and in different social situations. As we construct our persona and revise it at different times, we allow ourselves more or less leeway in the way we express gender. Our culture not only accepts, but admires and enjoys, the ambiguities embodied in a Marlene Dietrich or Greta Garbo as well as the deliberate "gender-bending" of Grace Jones, David Bowie, k.d. lang, the Rolling Stones, or Madonna, to name but a few examples. Movies and the theater celebrate cross-dressing and many people, without ever identifying as "transvestites," enjoy cross-dressing, and do it with verve, even if only at parties and "for fun." Unisex used to appall when it appeared in the 1960s, but now is an accepted part of our culture and it and cross-dressing provide so-to-speak legitimate outlets for our desire, or need, to allow our imagination to roam in the realm of sex and gender.

Lately, however, a more radical change has occurred as transgender theorists and activists have begun to insist that the binary model is hopelessly flawed and needs to be abandoned. They argue not only for an increased fluidity, but want to have gender unhooked from genitals and speak of a "rainbow" of gender. There is no good reason, they say, why the accident of being born with a penis or a vagina should prevent one from fully experiencing what it is like to live the life of either a woman or a man (Bornstein, 1994; Rothblatt, 1995).

Not surprisingly, transgender activists and theorists want to have their decisions about gender demedicalized and hence to abolish psychiatric categories such as "gender identity disorders" or "gender dysphoria." At the same time, many of them want to ease access to hormones and surgery so as to make it less difficult for people to transform their anatomies in ways that blur their sex/gender or change it outright.

Some, but not all, of the present-day transgender theorists are what used to be called transsexuals, though they prefer the term "transgendered" or "transperson." However, there is a substantial difference between modern transpersons and classical transsexuals, who by-and-large repudiated the genitals with which they were born and spoke of themselves as men "imprisoned in the body of a woman" or the other way around. Until recently, except for a few public transsexuals such as Jan Morris or Renée Richards, most transsexuals hid the fact that they were living a different sex from the one into which they were born, and invented personal histories to go with their transformed bodies. ("When I was a little girl, my mother used to . . ."; or "In high school, my girlfriends and I . . .") But as transpersons have come out of the closet, they have acknowledged their life stories and are exploring the personal, political, and theoretical implications of their transformations. As a result, both the theory and the situation have changed.

Accounts by or about the newer transgenderists place less emphasis on actual surgical transformations of the genitals than used to be true, and concentrate more on other satisfactions associated with becoming a transperson. Martine Rothblatt and Kate Bornstein say they never rejected the (male) genitals with which they were born and are not especially focused on the genital aspects of their transformation. Rothblatt writes: "I learned how one's genitals are not the same as one's sex. And I experienced sex as a vast continuum of personality possibilities, a frontier still scarcely explored after thousands of years of human development" (Rothblatt, 1995, p. 164). She looks forward to the use of computer technology for "cybersex," where people can "try on genders and . . .pave the way . . .[to] being liberated from single birth-determined sex" (Rothblatt, 1995, p. 153).

Janice Raymond's erstwhile claim—that male-to-female transsexuals merely reinforce gender stereotypes and represent the furthest reach in men's appropriation of women's bodies—no longer fits the bill, if it ever did. Sandy Stone, a transsexual whom Janice Raymond chose to attack by name in the

1970s, writes in 1991: "Besides the obvious complicity of [earlier autobio-graphical accounts by male-to-female transsexuals] in a Western white male definition of performative gender, the authors also reinforce a binary, op-positional mode of gender identification. They go from being unambiguous men, albeit unhappy men, to unambiguous women. There is no territory between" (Stone, 1991, p. 286). Her article is an attempt to address gender ambiguity in a positive fashion.

As a result of the greater openness, the demographics have begun to look different. The fact that most of the earlier public transsexuals had been born male gave the appearance that many fewer born women than men wanted to change their sex. Now about the same number of women and men approach medical providers about a sex change (Bloom, 1994). And among the female-to-male transpersons, for whom the techniques of genital recon-struction are fairly inadequate, genitals are assigned even lower priority. In her *New Yorker* profile of female-to-male transpersons, Amy Bloom quotes some of them as suggesting that the surgeons seem to be keener on the sur-gery than the clients are. They joke about preferring to save their money for travel, a condominium, and other ways to enjoy life. Neither do they insist on a rigid gender identity. Here is one of the transpersons who spoke with Bloom: "The gender issue isn't at the center of my life. Male, female—I don't even understand that anymore. And I find . . .it doesn't matter much" (Bloom, 1994, p. 40).

How different this is from "Agnes," one of the earliest transsexu-als, whom Harold Garfinkel interviewed for several years during her sex change, beginning in 1958. Agnes was disgusted by her penis and her existence revolved around getting rid of the hated object and acquiring a surgically constructed and heterosexually serviceable vagina (Garfinkel, 1967).

To the extent that transgenderism is becoming just another way in which people construct a gender identity and gender transformations become more acceptable and easier to achieve, the changes need no longer involve the agonies experienced by people who had to overcome society's and their own sense that they were disgusting freaks. At the same time, surgical trans-formations, though still important, are becoming more optional and less central to the transgender experience. As people can come out of the closet, they find it easier to think about what they really need or want, and some-times that is a public persona (or range of personae) rather than a more pri-vate, genital transformation.

The question for social and natural scientists to ponder is how to rec-oncile these newer ways of looking on sex and gender with the barrage of sex-differences research that claims to "prove" that there are clear-cut differences between women's and men's learning styles, mathematical abilities, brain structures and functions, and so on.

To understand both the motivation and the results of this research, we have to bear in mind that, as I suggested earlier, most Western scientists come to sex-differences research imbued with the binary male/female model. Indeed, if they did not accept this model, they probably would not choose to focus their research around sex differences. If this binary model is their theoretical starting point, the scientists must begin their investigations by identifying the significant attributes that distinguish the two groups. When they find (as they must) that women and men overlap so widely as to be virtually indistinguishable on a specific criterion, they must go on to look for other criteria and to concentrate on whatever differences they unearth. Small wonder they come to highlight characteristics that fit in with their difference-paradigm, while ignoring the overlaps that contradict it. And so, the dichotomization into two and only two sexes or genders gets superimposed on a heterogeneous mix of bodies, feelings, and minds.

As far as medical "sex-change" interventions are concerned, just as pediatricians, confronted with a "sex-ambiguous" newborn, frame the situation in terms of the question "will we be more successful in producing a girl or a boy," so psychiatrists and surgeons look at their adult clients through the binary spectacles of "can we bring the psyche into conformity with the genitals this person was born with or had we better alter the genitals." Neither situation leaves room for a middle ground. Faced with genital or gender ambiguities, the professionals see only males or females. By contrast and largely under the influence of feminist theorizing about sex and gender, transgenderists have begun to see the distortions introduced by the insistence on such a polarity and to color in the rainbow between male and female.

The time is ripe for physicians and scientists also to remove their binary spectacles and, rather than explore what it means to be "male" or "female," look into what it means to be neither or both, which is what most of us are. All of us, female or male, are very much alike and also very different from each other. Major scientific distortions have resulted from ignoring similarities and overlaps in the effort to group differences by sex or gender. A paradigm that stresses fluidity will generate quite different questions and hence come up with different descriptions and analyses than those derived from the binary view. Social and natural scientists need to move on and explore the implications of the emerging paradigm of a continuum or rainbow for the study of sex and gender.

NOTES

1. For a more detailed discussion, see especially the Introduction and Chapter 9 in R. Hubbard, *The Politics of Women's Biology* (New Brunswick, NJ: Rutgers University Press, 1990).

2. For a discussion of the history of the concept of sex-specific, so "male" and "female," hormones from its origin around the turn of the century to its demise by the 1940s, see Nelly Oudshoorn, "Endocrinologists and the Conceptualization of Sex, 1920–1940," *Journal of the History of Biology* 23 (1990), 163–186.

3. For some personal statements, see *Hermaphrodites with Attitude,* Spring 1995, published by the Intersex Society of North America, P.O. Box 31791, San Francisco, CA 94131.

REFERENCES

Bloom, A. (1994, 18 July). The body lies. *The New Yorker,* 38–49.

Bornstein, K. (1994). *Gender outlaw: On men, women, and the rest of us.* New York: Routledge.

Fausto-Sterling, A. (1993, March/April). The five sexes: Why male and female are not enough. *The Sciences,* 20–24.

Fried, B. (1982). Boys will be boys will be boys: The language of sex and gender. In R. Hubbard, M.S. Henifin, & B. Fried (Eds.), *Biological woman: The convenient myth.* Cambridge, MA: Schenkman Publishing Co.

Garfinkel, H. (1967). *Studies in ethnomethodology.* Englewood Cliffs, NJ: Prentice-Hall.

Herdt, G. (1994). Mistaken sex: Culture, biology and the third sex in New Guinea. In G. Herdt (Ed.), *Third sex, third gender: Essays from anthropology and social history,* pp. 419–445. New York: Zone Books.

Imperato-McGinley J., et al. (1979). Androgens and the evolution of male gender identity among male pseudohermaphrodites with 5–alpha reductase deficiency. *New England Journal of Medicine, 300,* 1235–1236.

Kessler, S.J. (1990). The medical construction of gender: Case management of intersexed infants. *Signs, 16,* 3–26.

Kessler, S.J., & McKenna, W. (1978). *Gender: An ethnomethodological approach.* Chicago: University of Chicago Press.

Money, J., & Ehrhardt, A.A. (1972). *Man & woman, boy & girl: The differentiation and dimorphism of gender identity from conception to maturity.* Baltimore, MD: Johns Hopkins University Press.

Raymond, J. (1979). *The transsexual empire: The making of the she-male.* Boston, MA: Beacon Press. Reissued in 1994 with a new introduction by Teacher's College Press, New York.

Rothblatt, M. (1995). *The apartheid of sex: A manifesto on the freedom of gender.* New York: Crown Publishers.

Stone, S. (1992). The empire strikes back: A posttranssexual manifesto. In J. Epstein & C. Straub (Eds.), *Body guards: The cultural politics of gender ambiguity,* pp. 280–304. New York: Chapman and Hall.

5 THE TRANSGENDER PARADIGM SHIFT TOWARD FREE EXPRESSION

Holly Boswell

Until this decade of the 1990s, the emerging transgender community consisted of three recognizable components: transsexuals, cross-dressers (usually heterosexual), and drag kings and queens. While the need to challenge culturally imposed stereotypes remains just as strong today, these three models have proven to be far from sufficient to describe the true range of transgender expression, ironically reinforcing the myth that there are only two genders, as defined by most contemporary assimilationist cultures. More and more people are not confining themselves to familiar territory and well-known labels like transsexual, cross-dresser, and drag, but are moving into new and unexplored space (Boswell, 1991).

In the cases of transsexualism and cross-dressing, notions of femininity and masculinity are for the most part thoroughly emulated—even to the point of radical surgery for transsexual people. The transgenderist, as defined by Virginia Prince, is usually no different than the nonoperative transsexual, who expresses only one of two genders. Even in our "either/or" culture, this is still risky business, often involving the loss of marriages, children, parents, family, friends, and livelihood. Such is the depth of the quest for selfhood, struggling to survive against social stigmatization and rejection (Goffman, 1963).

What we are now beginning to experience is a newly blossoming—yet anciently rooted—way of being that defies and transcends the fallacious linkage between biological sex and gender expression. While biological sex manifests most noticably between our legs, the complexity of sexual and gender expression originates between our ears. Even so, the concept of sex itself must be challenged as an artificial construct (Rothblatt, 1995), especially in view of recurrent hermaphroditism and a host of other persistent psycho/social deviations from so-called male or female characteristics. Sex, in spite of how we have been conditioned to perceive it, is far from black or white, and is as much a state of mind—distinct from anatomy—as the outward expression we call gender. It is time to move beyond the bipolar masculine/feminine model of sex and gender based solely on anatomy. Manifesting our true humanity has much more to do with the rainbow of possibilities emanating from within our hearts, minds, and spirits.

It is important to recognize that this new paradigm of gender is coming from, and is finally being articulated by, the very people who are living it. For us, the experience comes first, then our conceptual explanation of it—unlike the academic approach of postulating a hypothesis which must then be proven. Many of us have become living proof of transgender reality. Some of us have been the willing subjects of research, but we are also recognizing the need to assert our own voices.

We are discovering how difficult it is to describe to others what it is like to be transgendered. We have been amazed that, despite our elaborate explanations, no one can ever quite understand our experience of transgender, until we realize that neither have we ever understood what it is to be a man or a woman (Bornstein, 1994). We seem to be neither, or maybe both, yet ultimately only ourselves. So, is transgender simply a result of being more honest with oneself and resistant to socialization, or is it chromosomally or hormonally induced, or better described as spirit taking precedence over form? All we know is that we can no longer live any other way, and so we move on and discover many others who share our experience.

The word "transgender" describes much more than crossing between the poles of masculinity and femininity. It more aptly refers to the transgressing of gender norms, or being freely gendered, or transcending gender altogether in order to become more fully human. To deny part of our humanity (the so-called masculine or feminine aspects) is to lock in and shut down a beautiful part of one's true self. It takes extra energy to do this, but that energy can be freed and manifest by asserting the truth of one's being, despite the risks (Stone, 1976).

Ultimately, transgender has to do with reinventing and realizing oneself more fully outside of the current system of gender (Williams, 1995). There are probably as many genders as there are people (Rothblatt, 1995). Gender may be nothing more than a personal matrix of personality traits.

In fact, once the concept of gender is freed from various cultural and biological expectations of sex, the terms "masculine" and "feminine" become so relative that they are virtually meaningless. The Bem Sex-Role Inventory (Bem, 1974) lists 200 personality characteristics such as: analytical, gentle, independent, sympathetic, idealistic, and worldly. It is understood that each culture assigns different groupings of traits to each anatomical sex and leaves some in a neutral category. No trait is intrinsically masculine or feminine, though a few are more commonly attributable. As a culture evolves, it defines and redefines which traits are appropriate for each sex through the contrived linkage of anatomy with gender (Bem, 1993). But imagine a nonpolarized culture without this linkage, where each person would be free to explore and express their own unique set of traits. So much human potential could be unleashed that both the individual and the culture as a whole might self-actualize en masse.

Psychologists have come to acknowledge that androgyny is a healthier gender model for self-actualization and fulfillment than either of the binary genders (Bem, 1977). This entails a process of transcending social conditioning in order to more fully become ourselves. Jung's process of individuation, with its reconciliation of animus and anima, leads to "wholeness"—a word that is related to health and holiness (Jung, 1981). If most people were more honest about it, they would probably find themselves somewhere in the middle of the bell-shaped curve of gender distribution rather than the "Rambo-Bimbo extremes" (Parker, 1995).

So while many people have androgynous potential, the traditions of alternative gender expression involve a minority within which these tendencies are much more pronounced. These are the profoundly transgendered, who have real difficulty conforming to polarized codes of gender, and whose gender identities stray far beyond the normal expectations of their biological sex. This has always been so (Dragoin, 1995; Feinberg, 1996).

Despite advances in hormonal and surgical procedures, many of us are choosing to customize the program to suit our individual self-definitions and expression (MacKenzie, 1994). This hearkens back to the many "two-spirit" traditions throughout human history and enlivens a growing awareness among transgendered people that "passing" (Goffman, 1963) is becoming passé. Only within the last few decades have transgendered people become so seduced by the ability to assimilate, made possible by recent hormonal and surgical advances, that they would deny their transgender spirit and lock themselves into the closet of assimilation (Feinberg, n.d.). This has relieved society of its responsibility to recognize more than two genders. All of us—transgendered and otherwise—continue to live under the constant "tyranny of passing" (Williams, 1985), of questioning our sense of belonging against self-worth. Are we living up to the societal roles and expectations that are imposed on us? Are we accepted and valued by others? How much should we care? How much societal rejection can we endure to achieve honest self-expression before we are undermined or destroyed in the process?

Diverse manifestations of transgender, however, are certainly not new. We have existed throughout history all over the planet (Dragoin, 1995; Roscoe, 1994; Williams, 1986). We are a normal, recurring expression of human nature. As Lakota shaman Lame Deer explained, "To us a man is what nature, or his dreams, makes him. We accept him for what he wants to be. That's up to him" (Fire & Erdoes, 1972, pp. 117, 149).

Various cultures in the past have honored our unique ability to make special contributions to society as shamans, spiritual leaders, visionaries, healers, mediators, counselors, storytellers, and teachers. Within these value systems, weeds don't exist. Every being has its sacred purpose, and none is to be wasted (Swifthawk, 1992). Anthropologists are continually unearthing more evidence of such multifarious traditions as the two-spirit person in native North America (Roscoe, 1988, 1990; Williams, 1986), shamans in Siberia and the Arctic (Bogoras, 1907), *hijras* in India (Nanda, 1989, 1994), *xanith* in the Middle East (Wikan, 1977), *gallae* in the Roman Empire (Roscoe, 1994), certain Druid priestesses in Old Europe (Boswell, 1993), the *mahu* of Polynesia (Besnier, 1994), one-breasted Amazons (Wheelright, 1979), and many more. Ancient Goddess religions, and other natural spiritual world-views, respected men and women as equals, regarded Nature as divine, revered diversity, and loved all manifestations of life. But since the replacement of Mother Nature with God the Father (about 5000 years ago), the constructs of gender have been defined more narrowly and rigidly to suit the purposes of those in control of each particular society (Stone, 1976).

So what impact does all this have on the transgender community, and all of us as human beings? Because of Western civilization's emphasis on materialism and its inherently polarized value system, most transgendered people have been manifesting as their assumed opposite, either through cross-dressing or sex-reassignment surgery. This is often motivated more by a need to assimilate than a quest toward truly becoming oneself, which would otherwise support the notion of gender as the many-splendored thing it ought to be. Whereas cross-dressing may vicariously lead to gender insights, and transsexualism is redundant for those who see their gender/anatomy variance as a problem, the newly emerging paradigm of gender will lead to a potent activation of healthy and renewable alternative gender expression.

Yes, the paradigm of transgender—perhaps all gender—is shifting. Never before have we had so many options, yet chosen to manifest—despite our culture—as our true selves. We are choosing to define ourselves outside of our cultures, and virtually outside of the very system of gender that has been imposed upon us. Transgendered people are redefining gender.

For perhaps another generation or so, this will no doubt be perceived as a radical course by the prevailing cultural consciousness, but it will increasingly be embraced on a personal level as the simple, honest human expression of nature that it ultimately is. Gender liberation is a crucial key to human evolution, promoting the idea that we should strive to be whole-gendered, cultivating all our gender traits to meet the critical challenges of our time.

Is this not a timely universal message, emanating deeply from within our collective consciousness? Are we not connected by our "continuous common humanity" (Bolin, 1994), in exploring fully what it is to be ourselves—infinitely unique, yet united by the undeniable commonality of our human experience? This is the very bridge of transgender: connecting the myth of polarity into a whole, healing the illusions of our separateness, and celebrating the diversity of what it is to be fully human.

The mass media, especially cinema—after television talk shows ad nauseam—seems to be acknowledging the revelatory human truth of transgender. This needs little documentation here, as examples are pervasive. Professional care-givers are gradually becoming more educated about the breadth and depth of transgender phenomena, and how they might more appropriately help their transgendered clients. This is happening at the grass-roots level, and even more extensively at events like the First International Congress on Gender, Cross Dressing, and Sex Issues, which was held in February 1995 in Van Nuys, California, and was the first scientific conference at which transgender credentials were as important as academic credentials (Denny, 1995). There has also been an increasing influx of updated, cutting-edge educational programming at certain annual transgender conferences, such as Southern Comfort, and the annual meetings of the International Foundation for Gender Education and the International Conference on Transgender Law and Employment Policy.

With all this newly emerging awareness comes new resolve among transgendered people to be honest, to be "out," to endeavor to educate, to be politically active, to support young people joining our ranks with new issues, to venture into the cyberspace of "virtual gender," and to gather into our own circles for the intimate, spiritual processing of who we are truly becoming (Boswell, 1994). All this is very exciting, and ought to help serve as a catalyst to inspire the rest of humanity. Becoming truly oneself, on any level, is a most beautiful and worthwhile process. Yet how few actually venture into this territory?

Transgendered people can serve as a bridge to help others find their own way. As avid students make the best teachers, we are living advocates for the profound experience of exploring one's true humanity—nothing less. And as we are each in need of healing ourselves on this essential level, we may then be able to hope for a world that reflects the dazzling rainbow of our immense wholeness, along with our long-sought harmony, and the true beauty of our natural grace as fully human beings.

REFERENCES

Bem, S.L. (1974). The measurement of psychological androgyny. *Journal of Consulting and Clinical Psychology, 42*(2), 155–162.

Bem, S.L. (1977). Psychological androgyny. In A.G. Sargent (Ed.), *Beyond sex roles,* pp. 319–324. St. Paul, MN: West Publishing.

Bem, S.L. (1993). *The lenses of gender.* New Haven: Yale University Press.

Besnier, N. (1994). Polynesian gender liminality through time and space. In G. Herdt (Ed.), *Third sex, third gender: Essays from anthropology and social history,* pp. 285–328. New York: Zone Books.

Bogoras, W. (1907). The Chukchee religion. *Memoirs of the American Museum of Natural History, 11.* Leiden: E.J. Brill.

Bolin, A. (1994). Transcending and transgendering: Male-to-female transsexuals, dichotomy, and diversity. In G. Herdt (Ed.), *Third sex, third gender: Essays from anthropology and social history,* pp. 447–485. New York: Zone Publishing.

Bornstein, K. (1994). *Gender outlaw: On men, women and the rest of us.* New York: Routledge.

Boswell, H. (1991). The transgender alternative. *Chrysalis Quarterly, 1*(2), 29–31.

Boswell, H. (1993). The eleven hundred maidens of Brittica. *Chrysalis Quarterly, 1*(6), 29–30.

Boswell, H. (1994). New berdache circling. *TV-TS Tapestry, 1*(68), 36–38.

Denny, D. (1995). Transgender: Some historical, cross-cultural, and modern-day models and methods of coping & treatment. Workshop presented at the International Congress on Gender, Cross Dressing, and Sex Issues, Van Nuys, CA, 24–26 February, 1995.

Dragoin, W. (1995). The gynemimetic shaman: Evolutionary origins of male sexual inversion and associated talent? Paper presented at the International Congress on Gender, Cross Dressing, and Sex Issues, Van Nuys, CA, 24–26 February, 1995.

Feinberg, L. (1996). *Transgender warriors: Making history from Joan of Arc to Ru Paul.* Boston: Beacon Press.

Feinberg, L. (n.d.) *Transgender liberation: A movement whose time has come.* World View Forum, 55 W 17th St., 5th Floor, New York, NY 10011.

Fire, J., & Erdoes, R. (1972) *Lame Deer, seeker of visions.* New York: Simon & Schuster.

Gabriel, D.A. (1995). Interview with the transsexual vampire: Sandy Stone's dark rift. *TransSisters, 1*(8), cover, 14–27.

Goffman, E. (1963). *Stigma: Notes on the management of spoiled identity.* Englewood Cliffs, NJ: Prentice-Hall.

Jung, E. (1981). *Animus & Anima.* Dallas, TX: Spring Publishers.

MacKenzie, G.O. (1994). *Transgender nation.* Bowling Green, OH: Bowling Green University Popular Press.

Nanda, S. (1989). *Neither man nor woman: The Hijras of India.* Belmont, CA: Wadsworth Publishing.

Nanda, S. (1994). Hijras: An alternative sex and gender role in India. In G. Herdt (Ed.), *Third sex, third gender: Essays from anthropology and social history,* pp. 373–418. New York: Zone Books.

Parker, W.S. (1995). An abdication of power: A transgendered perspective. Paper presented at the First International Congress on Gender, Cross Dressing, and Sex Issues, Van Nuys, CA, 24–26, February, 1995.

Roscoe, W. (Ed.). (1988). *Living the spirit: A gay American Indian anthology.* New York: St. Martin's Press.

Roscoe, W. (1991). *The Zuni man-woman.* Albuquerque: University of New Mexico Press.

Roscoe, W. (1994). Priests of the goddess: Gender transgression in the Ancient World. Presented at the 109th Annual Meeting of the American Historical Association, San Francisco, CA.

Rothblatt, M. (1995). *The apartheid of sex: A manifesto on the freedom of gender.* NY: Crown Publishers.

Stone, M. (1976). *When God was a woman.* New York: Harcourt Brace Jovanovich.

Swifthawk, R. (1992). We have a duty to the earth. *Chrysalis Quarterly,* 1(6), 48–49.

Wheelright, J. (1979). *Amazons and military maids: Women who dressed as men in pursuit of life, liberty, and happiness.* Unwin: Pandora Press.

Wikan, U. (1977). Man becomes woman: Transsexualism in Oman as a key to gender roles. *Man,* 12(2), 304–319.

Williams, C. (1985). *TGIC Newsletter* (Albany, NY).

Williams, C. (1995, March-April). Why transgender? *Gender Quest* (Asheville, NC).

Williams, W.L. (1986). *The spirit and the flesh: Sexual diversity in American Indian culture.* Boston: Beacon Press.

6 TRANSCENDING AND TRANSGENDERING

MALE-TO-FEMALE TRANSSEXUALS, DICHOTOMY, AND DIVERSITY*

Anne Bolin

Fluidity and discontinuity are central to the reality in which we live.
—Mary Catherine Bateson, 1989, p. 13

The *berdache* traditions documented globally have captured the anthropological imagination as testimony to the complexity and diversity of gender, offering serious challenges to scientific paradigms that conflate sex and gender. This complexity is reiterated in Euro-American gender variance among those who have come to identify themselves as preoperative, postoperative, and nonsurgical transsexuals, as well as male and female cross-dressers and transvestites.

These individuals form a transgender community that is in the process of creating not just a third gender but the possibility of numerous genders and multiple social identities. As such, they challenge the dominant American gender paradigm with its emphasis on reproduction and the biological sexual body as the sine qua non of gender identity and role. As a political movement, the transgender community views gender and sex systems as relativistic structures imposed by society and by the privileged controllers of individual bodies, the medical professions. The transgenderist is disquieting to the established gender systems and unsettles the boundaries of bipolarity and opposition in the gender schema by suggesting a continuum of masculinity and femininity, renouncing gender as aligned with genitals, body, social status and/or role. Transgenderism reiterates what the cross-cultural record reveals, the independence of gender traits embodied in a Western biocentric model of sex.

---

*This chapter was previously published with the same title in G. Herdt (Ed.), *Third Sex, Third Gender: Essays from Anthropology and Social History,* pp. 447–485. New York: Zone Books, 1994. Reprinted with permission.

The purpose of this essay is to contribute to the deconstruction of the Euro-American gender paradigm by focusing on cultural change in gender-variant social identities with particular attention to the male-to-female transsexual. Gender-variant identities are analyzed as derivative yet transgressive of the wider gender schema. Ethnographic data from my research on male-to-female transsexual and male transvestite identities are provided as historical background to this undertaking as they situate the social construction of gender-variant identities of approximately 10 years ago (data were collected from 1979 to 1981).[1] The question of cultural change in the social construction of the male-to-female transsexual identity is examined on the basis of information collected in 1992. Three sociocultural factors influencing this change are subsequently identified, followed by a discussion of their implications for the Euro-American gender paradigm (see Bolin, 1987a, 1987b, 1988a, 1992a, and 1992b).

PARAMETERS AND METHODS

Several caveats are in order at the start. Because the ethnographic effort is labor intensive, there are limits placed on the parameters of research.[2] This essay concerns only those individuals born with the appearance of male genitals who are assigned and raised as males but who are gender transposed to varying degrees. The research and consulting population includes males who identify themselves as male-to-female transsexuals, cross-dressers (the term preferred by those in the transgender culture over transvestite) and those who label themselves "transgenderists." Member ("native") language usage is followed in referring to this community.[3]

Although physiological females are indeed part of the transgender community, this study does not include female gender variation. Unfortunately, this exclusion inadvertently contributes to the silence of female-to-male preoperative, postoperative, and nonsurgical transsexuals, female transvestites, and "masculine"-appearing lesbians. In this regard, Jason Cromwell suggests that the invisibility of female-to-male transsexuals is directly related to the Western gender paradigm, just as the visibility and privileging of male-to-female postoperative transsexuals is dominant in clinical discourses.[4] As will be discussed, this paradigm is a biocentric one emphasizing the physiological insignias of gender.

My methodology is primarily qualitative. The ethnographic scope of this research spans 10 years and includes investigation of male-to-female transsexualism and transgenderism locally, regionally, and nationally. For 2 years I immersed myself in the daily lives of male-to-female transsexuals and, to a lesser degree, those of male cross-dressing consultants (Bolin, 1988a, pp. 32–39). In 1992, I interviewed transgendered individuals using formal and informal methods, including content analysis of an open-ended in-depth questionnaire as well as discourse analysis of various transgender community newsletters, brochures, and other texts (Bolin, 1988a, pp. 32–39). In addition, I attended and collected data at two national conferences for the transgender community, the "National Transgender Annual Meetings" (a fictive name) and a well-known and much-celebrated annual international event, the Fantasia Fair. This approach allowed for an in-depth focus on diversity.[5]

MALE-TO-FEMALE TRANSSEXUALS AND MALE TRANSVESTITES: DICHOTOMIZING DIVERSITY

In 1982 I concluded the intensive participant-observation phase of my research in the Berdache Society, a grass-roots organization of male-to-female transsexuals and male transvestites. My inquiry followed male-to-female transsexuals as they separated themselves from their former male lives after they found the social identity of transsexual and began a process of transformation that included hormonal treatment and psychotherapy, ideally culminating in sex-conversion surgery. Their transformation had the char-

TABLE 6.1. Schematic Representation of Becoming

Stages	Inside	Outside		
	Personal Identity Transformation	Social Identity Transformation	Phenotypic Transformation	Rite of Transformation
1	Gender confusion and/or self-concept that one is more like girls than boys	Occupying male role, secretly dressing as a female	Male	
2	Transsexual primary identity, subidentity as woman	Dressing as woman more and more, dual role occupancy, passing in public, self-consciousness	Male, but feminization from hormonal reassignment	Separation and transition, liminality, disorder
3	Primary identity as woman, transsexual subidentity	Dual role occupancy, anticipating full-time status as woman, successful passing, less self-consciousness	Hormonal reassignment, increasing feminization and feminized	Separation and transition, liminality, out of disorder
4	Primary identity as woman, rejection of transsexual identity, a natural woman	Full-time status as woman (successful passing rejects notion of passing), role performance as woman, natural and unselfconsciousness	Increasing feminization and feminized, anticipates, and undergoes, surgical construction of vagina	Incorporation, normalcy, and order

acteristics of a rite of passage in which men "became" women; their "becoming" involved the transmutation of personal identity, social identity, and physiology. This approach suggested that transsexuals did not begin their transition with fully crystallized feminine personal identities, as is widely reported in the medical literature, but rather gradually acquired a feminine identity. Their transformation is summarized in Table 6.1.

The Berdache Society and the networks it spawned played a critical role in the creation of a transsexual identity among its members. This was in part enhanced by the approximately 25 self-identified heterosexual male transvestites (the term they used at the time to describe themselves) whose participation in the Berdache Society contributed to its identity-brokering functions by providing an identity counterpoint. Effecting the construction of the identity was information available in the popular media, newsletters, and magazines of various male-to-female transsexual and male transvestite organizations, as well as the professional medical-psychological literature At the time of my fieldwork, there were only three gender options (social identities) available for physical males who cross-dressed among the group I worked with: the surgically oriented male-to-female transsexual, the male transvestite, and the gay female impersonator/cross-dresser.

Transsexuals distinguished themselves from gay female impersonators and male transvestites. Gay female impersonators represented one kind of inside-outside dichotomy; the male is inside, beneath the outside sartorial system of female. The inner or "real" self is male and the social self is an illusion of presentation (Newton, 1972, pp. 338–339). Transsexuals viewed themselves as the only authentic participants in the inside-outside dilemma, perceiving gay female impersonators as engaged in parody and play, "camping it up" with gender identity and role (Sontag, 1970, pp. 277–278). Transsexuals established a party line that polarized male-to-female transsexuals and gay female impersonators. In contrast to gay cross-dressers, the transsexual was not engaging in an illusion or an impersonation but rather in a true expression of a feminine gender identity. By extension, male-to-female transsexuals regarded themselves as heterosexual if erotically attracted to males, lesbian if attracted to women, and bisexual if attracted to both. According to my informants, gay men did not understand the critical difference between gay female impersonators and male-to-female transsexuals.

Because gay cross-dressers were eliminated from the Berdache Society, male-to-female transsexualism and male transvestism emerged as two discrete social identity options with clearly defined attributes, associated lifestyles and coping strategies. Male-to-female transsexuals defined themselves by a bottom-line criterion of desire for hormonal reassignment and surgery, privileging their status within the Berdache Society. If one was not absolutely committed to having the surgery, then one was de facto, a transvestite. Transvestites were delineated as heterosexual men (men attracted to women) who had the urge to cross-dress, but were not "really" women. If these individuals had a feminine identity, the reasoning went, they would be pursuing surgery—with no apologies.

While male-to-female transsexuals regarded these identities as qualitatively discrete, many transvestites did not agree. For them it was a distinction of degree rather than kind. However, the transsexual dichotomization came to dominate the Berdache Society in various subtle yet clearly visible ways. Newcomers were presented with only two mutually exclusive possibilities for experiencing cross-dressing. If one was transsexual, then pursuit of hormones and surgery accompanied one's transition. Desire for bodily reassignment became a mark of authenticity to male-to-female transsexuals. Identifying someone as "TS," member argot for male-to-female transsexual, or "TV," member argot for a male transvestite, provided members with a script for relating to one another: what topics would be of interest, how they could be helpful, what common ground existed, associating outside the group meetings, and so on. Members of the Berdache Society were more comfortable interacting with others who clearly identified themselves as either TV or TS. Neophytes were made aware of this expectation and learned that it facilitated their incorporation into the group.

DISCOURSES OF DESTINY: CONSTRUCTIONS OF THE TRANSSEXUAL IDENTITY

The previous discussion has focused on the social organization of gender-variant identities among a group of transsexuals and transvestites. In this section, I take the position that the social construction of these gender-variant identities reproduces the Euro-American gender paradigm. Furthermore, the biological bias of this paradigm has framed the emergence of the transsexual identity both as a clinical entity and as a member-constructed and member-experienced identity. Because gender is conflated with biological sex, it is no surprise that the transsexual identity has emerged as a medicalized one. This may be understood as part of a more generalized trend in which bodies, physiological sex and reproduction have been co-opted by the clinical sectors (Foucault, 1988; Gallagher & Laquer, 1987; Bordo, 1989, 1990, pp. 83–112). In this context, I emphasize the medicalization of the transsexual identity as a social-historical discourse reifying gender as biological. I then analyze the transsexual identity as it is constructed by the members of the Berdache Society. While the native construction reproduces the biologized and medicalized one in many ways, it is also resistant. This rebellion against the dominant gender schema is an important ideological element of the social changes in the cultural shaping of gender-variant identities presented in the final section of this essay.

MEDICALIZATION AND SOCIAL REPRODUCTION

The late 1960s spawned an era that may be characterized as the flourishing of the physiologically altered preoperative and postsurgical transsexual. During the 1970s and early 1980s more than forty North American gender clinics, many affiliated with medical schools and universities, were offering programs leading to surgical reassignment (Denny, 1992). Male-to-female transsexualism was given form by such growing medicalization.

From its inception, the transsexual identity sustained the Western paradigm that the sexes are oppositional and differences in behavior, temperament, character, emotions, and sexual orientation are constituted in biological polarity. This opposition is represented by the genitals, the symbols of reproductive differences and the primary basis for assigning biological sex. "Gender attribution is, for the most part, genital attribution," write Suzanne J. Kessler and Wendy McKenna (1978, p. 153). However, despite the power of genitals in assigning sex, late-twentieth-century medicine has produced increasingly sophisticated methods for determining biological sex and identifying "invisible" physiological components such as chromosomes, hormones, internal gonads, and reproductive structures. It is ironic that, the more scientific and complex the determinants of biological sex become, the less they can be relied on to indicate gender. The androgen insensitivity syndrome in women illustrates the preeminence of genitals in assigning and attributing sex, despite the presence of contradictory biological evidence (Kessler & McKenna, 1978, pp. 142–55).

Androgen insensitivity syndrome (or testicular feminization syndrome) is a sex anomaly in which genital women are found to be chromosomal males with male levels of circulating testosterone (Money & Ehrhardt, 1972, pp. 109–110). They are, however, bodily females as a consequence of an inherited inability to utilize their own testosterone. Because they are born with a vagina, they are generally identified and raised as girls (Money & Ehrhardt, 1972; Lemonick, 1992, p. 65). This anomaly, among others, clearly points to the segmentation of sex from gender and the complexity of determining sex from biology. Despite the bolstered scientific effort to locate the determinants of sex, it is no wonder that genitals emerge as a safer and seemingly more stable biological insignia than that which cannot be seen, the internal and invisible parameters such as cells and hormones. In the final analysis, genital reductionism is the template for the medical construction of the transsexual identity, since that which cannot be seen is not essential in the construction of identities and for individuals.

In the Western paradigm women are people with vaginas; therefore, if a man believes himself to be a woman, then he must look the part, down to the genitals. This paradigm has no room for the social woman with male genitals as is found elsewhere in the world (Bolin, 1987b; Roscoe, 1991a; Williams, 1986). Male-to-female transsexual surgery underscores the Euro-American principles of gender that are regarded as natural and inevitable: that is, that there are only two sexes and that these are inviolable and are determined by genitalia (Kessler & McKenna, 1978, p. 4). These principles are articulated in a legal postsurgical policy in which the male-to-female transsexual may be issued a new birth certificate or the existing one is altered to reflect the new status. This new gender status is justified on biological grounds that the postsurgical male-to-female transsexual is a genital and bodily woman. This articulates with heterosexuality as a central component in the polarity of gender (Weston, 1991). Male-to-female transsexuals are thus required to divorce their spouses before a surgeon may perform the conversion operation. Failing to do so would create a situation of legal lesbian marriage.

It is important to note that transsexualism, as a historical phenomenon, was defined by the development of two important medical technologies that made possible innovative alterations of the male body: hormonal-reassignment therapies and sex-reassignment surgery. These treatments circumscribed the medical creation of male-to-female transsexualism. The newly developing field of endocrinology in the 1920s played an important part in the medicalization of transsexualism. However, Vern Bullough notes that the significance of this field has been neglected in the history of transsexualism (Bullough, 1992). It was during this era that Harry Benjamin, recognized as the parent of the discipline of transsexualism, first treated a male client experimentally with ProgynonRX (an estrogenic hormone) and was successful in promoting breast growth.[6] Although the first male-to-female transsexual surgical procedures may have been those performed on "Lili Elbe" in the 1920s, it was not until 1953 that the male-to-female transsexual identity first gained widespread recognition through the work of Christian Hamburger, George Sturup, and E. Dahl-Iverson, who made public the surgical conversion of George Jorgensen into the now-famous Christine (Benjamin, 1966, pp. 3, 14).

Surgical conversion and hormonal reassignment have come to dominate the medical designation and psychological diagnosis of transsexualism. An individual is judged to be transsexual on the basis of a cross-sex identity that is manifested by a sustained desire for surgery (Green & Money, 1969). Although Benjamin proposed early on that male-to-female trans-sexualism and male transvestism represented a continuum and were really "symptoms or syndromes of the same underlying psychopathological con-ditions, that of sex or gender role disorientation and indecision," he still prioritized the desire for physical changes as the critical factor that distin-guished the two syndromes (Benjamin, 1966, pp. 17–22). In Benjamin's model, fully developed transsexualism was diagnosed by the quest for sur-gery and the wish to live as a female, while the male transvestite "is con-tented with cross-dressing alone" (Benjamin, 1966, p. 22).

Both the surgical conversion of transsexuals and hormonal manage-ment reproduce the biological imperative of the Euro-American gender ide-ology. For example, among the variety of hormonal management regimens available to transsexuals, two primary strategies have dominated. One strat-egy involved daily and/or regular intake of a consistent hormonal dosage. The other approach is one in which transsexuals are given a hormonal regi-men in which estrogen, with or without progesterone, is cycled in order to stimulate the fluctuation in estrogen in the woman's reproductive cycle. In a study of twenty gender clinics, five were found to subscribe to a cycling program of three weeks of daily intake of estrogen, followed by a week with-out hormonal therapy (Meyer, et al., n.d.). One endocrinologist in my area of research endorsed a program of two weeks of oral estrogens, followed by seven to ten days of a progestational agent in conjunction with estrogen, and finally a week free of hormones. Because there is evidence (although very controversial) that fluctuations in hormones may have side-effects, I asked the endocrinologist how cycling might affect male-to-female transsexuals. He acknowledged the possibility of fluid retention and mood fluctuations but suggested that these could be treated with the interventions, such as di-uretics, used to treat premenstrual syndrome in women.

This cycling regimen may be viewed as a discourse that defines the "normal" woman as a reproductive one. Despite male-to-female transsexual infertility, this approach duplicates the menstruating woman's hormonal system. Such a regimen is based on a model of biological coherence between hormones, genitals, and the salience of reproduction in medical accounts of women's biology (Martin, 1989).

Transsexuals: Biological Reproduction and Rebellion

Transsexuals in the Berdache Society were culturally active in constituting their own self-definition. Nevertheless, this self-image was refracted through the medical construction. As previously discussed, this was embodied in surgical and hormonal reassignment. A few examples of transsexual discourses from my research follow to illustrate the impact of medicalization and the imperialism of biology in asserting gender (Bolin, 1988a, 1992c).

In support of the surgical solution was an "origin" story and ideology that male-to-female transsexuals were individuals on whom nature had played a cruel joke—they were females trapped in male bodies. Through surgery they were destined to escape their stigmatized status, unlike male transvestites, who would remain men in women's clothing. In this sense, conformity with the prevailing biocentric gender schema privileged male-to-female transsexuals through the potential to achieve "normalcy" and authenticity through genital and hormonal conversion. This belief facilitated the development of a personal identity as female rather than transsexual, a status that would eventually be discarded and replaced with the sense of lived "womanness" made surgically and legally legitimate.

Transsexual distinctions between male-to-female transsexuals and transvestites were girded by this model of potential transsexual authenticity and completeness as women. For transsexuals, the distinction between the two populations was a qualitative one based on the desire to become completely "natural," to have the surgery along with hormonal reassignment. The result was a biologically created female who was physiologically and cognitively concordant. As described in the words of one transsexual: "Because of my transsexualism I have suffered, but I have also learned many wonderful things about life and the human spirit. I have learned to accept my condition and to love myself. I think of myself as a woman whose condition can be corrected through surgery" (Bolin, 1988a, p. 15).

From the transsexual's standpoint, being a male-to-female transsexual was only a temporary condition. Transsexualism was an identity to be outgrown as one eventually became a "whole" woman. Physical feminization was an important part of this process of personal and social identity transformation. Transsexual humor and folklore often played on the "natural" differences between transvestites and transsexuals. Transsexuals teased one another with remarks such as "Jane [a transsexual] certainly passes well for a TV." Although there were a number of transvestites who passed as well as the transsexuals, the transsexual sentiment was that they were destined to be superior at passing because they were, after all, women inside who had the added advantage of hormonal therapy. This was carried even further in the comment of one transsexual, who joked: "I can always tell when one of the TVs has visited because the toilet seat is always left up." Finally, the biological elitism of the transsexual was expressed by one who stated: "TVs will always be sick men."

As mentioned previously, it is important to note that transvestites did not view the difference between themselves and transsexuals as a qualitative one, but rather one of degree. From the transvestite's standpoint, there was a great deal more diversity among people who were male transvestites than was acknowledged by the member dichotomy of TV and TS. They regarded gender-variant identities as much more fluid and plural than did the transsexuals. They did not, for the most part, see transvestites and transsexuals as two distinct and static identities. In fact, they frequently stated that the context of a person's life was essential in determining how cross-dressing or one's "feminine" side was expressed. For example, how a man was situated in terms of career, family, and age could make all the difference in whether he identified himself as TV or would actually take the step and begin taking hormones. One transvestite who was recently divorced with grown children stated, "I can make this change [begin taking female hormones] now where I couldn't before with the kids around and my wife against it." For some transvestites, life context was regarded as the feature that distinguished the two gender-variant identities, while for others the distinction was just a matter of degree of desire.

Transvestite members generally viewed gender-variant identities as shifting and nonunitary. For transvestites multiple motivations and psychic complexity characterized their lives. Some transvestites liked to cross-dress because it had an erotic element, yet others were driven by public passing as an exciting and risk-taking adventure. Many transvestites shared the view that cross-dressing provided relief from the stress of the male role. In such a way, cross-dressing allowed them to reveal a "feminine" inner side of themselves that they could not express as men. This was not unlike the transsexual self-view of an inner female self trapped in a male body. Despite this evidence, transsexuals maintained a view of distinctiveness based on motivation for surgical and hormonal reassignment. For transsexuals, any reason *not* to pursue biological alteration was just an excuse and indicative of transvestite status.

Transsexuals relied on biological paradigms to enhance the meaning of their process of transformation as well. As they went through transition, the period of changing gender through the use of hormones, electrolysis, intensifying passing efforts in public and the like, they regarded themselves as in a neo-puberty. Hormonal changes in the body were a central defining feature of this period. Their bodies were changing just "as" a genetic woman's had (Bolin, 1992c). This distinguished them from male transvestites and gay cross-dressers who were impersonators of women, both ersatz females. Their puberty was modeled on "natural" maturation, an authentic or "real" woman's experience. The development of the female body shape (despite the penis) eventually led transsexuals to reject the notion of passing and ultimately their transsexualism, for their outward appearance was aligning with their "true" inner selves, women. Transsexuals did not regard permanent nonsurgical status as an option. There were no voices for choices at this time, unless one wanted to acknowledge that one was not "really" transsexual but rather transvestite. Transsexuals themselves were legitimized by the hope and desire for surgical conversion (Bolin, 1988a, pp. 106–120).

While male-to-female transsexuals supported a premise that equated biology with social gender through the quest for surgery and genital legitimacy, they offered a nascent challenge to biological reductionism that gained impetus over the course of the next decade. As a social identity, transsexualism posits the analytic independence of the four gender markers—sex, gender identity, gender role or social identity (including behaviors and appearance), and sexual orientation—that are embedded in the Western gender schema as taken-for-granted premises and regarded in a number of scientific discourses as "naturally" linked. Such categories of classification involve a binary gender paradigm that reverberates with the ideological underpinning of heterocentrism.

Male-to-female transsexuals rebelled openly and verbally against the underlying heterocentrism of the dominant gender paradigm. While supporting the polarization of genders on the basis of genitals and body, transsexuals were quite adamant about segregating gender identity and sexual orientation as discrete, subverting the conflation of femininity and heterosexual eroticism. For the male-to female transsexual, heterosexual eroticism was designated by an erotic attraction to physical males, while a lesbian erotic orientation was defined by attraction to physical females. A review of the professional literature revealed that heterosexuality was frequently cited as an intrinsic attribute and defining feature of transsexualism. Data from my research population on sexual orientation indicated far more diversity in sexual preference than was commonly reported in the literature. Of my sample, only one person was exclusively heterosexual, three of the six exclusive lesbians were living with women who themselves were not self-identified as lesbian, one bisexual was living with a self-identified lesbian,[7] and two male-to-female transsexuals were living with one another. This diversity contradicts a paradigm that equates gender identity with sexual preference. Lesbian or bisexual preoperative male-to-female transsexuals challenged the "natural" equation of gender identity, genitals, appearance, and heterosexual orientation, by presenting a rainbow of possible arrangements of these attributes.

In reiterating Western biologized gender through surgical reassignment, male-to-female transsexualism endorses a formula for gender constitution in which social woman is equated with genital woman. In addition, Berdache Society transsexuals proffered a categorization scheme in which transsexuals were polarized as "protowomen," and transvestites as men who dressed as women, a model that also sustained gender as genitally based. Yet transsexualism also offered a challenge to the biological basis of gender and consequently provided the opportunity for change from a polarized system in which transsexuals and transvestites were dichotomized as variant women and men, respectively, into one in which a continuum and multiplicity of social identities were recognized and encouraged. Through recent research, it has become apparent that there has been movement in which people of various gender-transposed identities have come to organize themselves as part of a greater community, a larger in-group, facing similar concerns of stigmatization, acceptance, treatment, and so on. This recognition of similarity fostered by a growing political awareness of gender organizations has facilitated the burgeoning of new gender options, such as the "transgenderist." "Transgenderist" is a community term denoting kinship among those with gender-variant identities. It supplants the dichotomy of transsexual and transvestite with a concept of continuity.[8] Additionally, it highlights a growing acceptance over the past decade of nonsurgical options for physical males wishing to live as women. An emerging sense of collectivity has propelled the recognition of the multiplicity of gender-variant identities including transsexualism and transvestism but exceeding these as well. This sense of collective interests is important for understanding cultural-historical change in gender identities and in clarifying the relationship of individual experience to the social construction of gender variance.

Diversity in the personal identity of the male-to-female transsexual and male transvestite populations has been an important source of change in the social construction of identities over the last ten years. Heterogeneity in personal gender identity was the raw material for the creation of pluralism in social identities. Although diversity of gender identity was found among both transsexuals and transvestites in terms of personal identity, it was masked by a Berdache Society polarization into the two social identities of transvestite and transsexual, a distinction that was also supported by clinical segregation (American Psychiatric Association, 1980). Underlying this dichotomy was a continuum of gender identities among those whom I researched. It included a pantheon of personal motives involved in wearing women's apparel described earlier: as sexual arousal, to relieve tension generated by male role strain, to express a "feminine" component of the personality and, for the surgically oriented, as a vehicle to express a cross-sex identity. This continuum of identities was artificially severed by the classificatory criterion of an extreme desire for physiological alteration by male-to-female transsexuals. Over time, the expression of heterogeneity in the subjective experience of individuals has been given voice in the social construction of gender variance. The polarization of transsexuals as women and transvestites as men is currently in a process of ideological revision in which continuity is emphasized and the dominant Western gender paradigm is challenged rather than cloned.

Pluralism in gender variation is both cause and consequence of at least three sociocultural influences intersecting with diversity in personal gender identity. These are (1) the closing of university-affiliated gender clinics (Denny, 1992), (2) the grass-roots organizational adoption of a political agenda, and (3) social alternatives to embodiments of femininity as somatic frailty.[9]

THE CLOSING OF UNIVERSITY-AFFILIATED GENDER CLINICS

The Berdache Society polarization of transvestite and transsexual was embodied in the surgical conversion of male-to-female transsexuals. Segregation emerged as a praxis within gender clinics where only the most extreme cases of cross-sex identity qualified for the surgery. According to Dallas Denny (1992):

> The clinics subscribed to "man trapped in a woman's body" notions of transsexualism (and vice versa) [just as did Berdache Society transsexuals]. Transsexual people were considered to be homogenous. Those men who had not played with dolls in childhood, who did not report feeling like a girl from the earliest age, or who had any history of enthusiasm or success at masculine activities were in trouble (p. 13).

> The directors and staff of the clinics tended to view SRS [sex reassignment surgery] as essential for satisfactory adjustment in the new gender. They did not seem to realize that it is possible to live as a woman or a man without the expected genitalia. . . . Those who were not accepted for SRS were not offered hormonal therapy. . . . Those who were not offered services were often told that they were not transsexual (p. 17).

75

Denny warns that this is not an indictment of all gender clinics or of the surgery itself but that it does reflect the experience of thousands of transsexual men and women. A number of social rationales conspired to perpetuate this situation (Denny, 1992). By carefully controlling clients, the clinical personnel, particularly surgeons, was protected from possible malpractice litigation in the case of patients with regrets (Bolin, 1988a, pp. 51–52). In addition, rigid "entrance" requirements for clinics ensured small populations so that intensive follow-up as well as research was possible (Denny, 1992).

Just as clinics were partially responsible for the dichotomization of gender-variant identities through promoting the sex-reassignment surgery, their widespread closing in the 1980s facilitated sociocultural mutation in the social construction of transsexual and transvestite identities. The termination of the Johns Hopkins Gender Clinic as a result of political rifts in the professional treatment community was subsequently followed by the closing of University-affiliated clinics throughout the United States. Only about a dozen gender clinics remain and these are notably unaffiliated with the research interests of academia and are consequently more client centered (Denny, 1992). Client-centered gender clinics may contribute to greater flexibility in the expression of gender identities. The research agenda of university-sponsored treatment programs may well have biased the selection of the male-to-female transsexual clinic population through the use of extreme and stereotypical entrance criteria, thereby denying treatment to more divergent individuals.

Sharon, a 50-year-old postoperative transsexual, provides a classic profile of the male-to-female transsexual who would be considered a likely candidate for surgery in the traditional gender clinics.

> When I was a child my favorite pastime was playing dress-up. When I told people I wanted to be a girl, no one listened, or told me I could not because I was a boy. . . . In 1953, the Christine Jorgensen story became headlines. It confirmed my belief that I could be a female. . . . In 1954, I began to experience erotic sensations while dressed [as a woman]. I considered this to be negative. I did not understand the sensations, and an erection destroyed the appearance I wished to achieve. . . . 1962 was the first year I admitted to myself that I was not a man, and never would be. I was a "God knows what," with a male anatomy. By 1979 my life-long dream was to be a legal and functional female.

In contrast, client-centered programs cater to the diverse interests and personal goals inherent in gender-variant peoples and populations, allowing for a pluralism in the expression of gender identities. The following three examples represent variations and revisions of the traditional dichotomy. These voices would not have been heard 10 years ago. Without the availability of categories extending beyond and between transsexual and transvestite, such individuals have suffered great confusion and emotional stress over where to fit in. Joan, born a male 39 years ago, offers another view of transsexualism:

> I'm a transsexual. I'm different from many in that I do not, at this time at least, feel a need to "fade into" society and hide my past. Rather, I have come out to all around me, family, friends and co-workers. . . . I am not yet living as a woman full time, but I am just starting a part-time job where I'll be doing a . . . job as Joan. On my regular job (three days a week), I'm still Jerry. . . . I don't really believe that I'm a "woman trapped in a man's body." I'm not sure what I am, only that making this transition is more important to me than anything else in my life.

Karen, who waited until forty-five to pursue full female attire, expresses self-identity in this way:

> To use the more common terminology, I would say I am transgendered. I cross-dress but not for sexual display or attraction. There is a feeling that is feminine, pretty, and desirable. Yet, I don't change as a "person." My gestures and walk are compatible with a feminine appearance, but not exaggerated, my voice unchanged. I don't consider myself a different person, just another visage or aspect of the same person. My friends that observe me in both modes would substantiate this. In addition, passing is of no concern to me. I don't really "do outreach" or "in your face" but only subject myself to situations in which people are aware of my maleness.
>
> At times I prefer feminine gestures and expressions, but more often masculine responses. When societal binarism insists I choose one pole or the other, I choose masculine. I have been raised as a male, my sexual anatomy is male, etc. Nonetheless, I insist that I am "ambigenderal." I claim all gender space, if you will, and exist within this spectrum at different points at different times.

Pat expresses both a male and female self:

I currently maintain a full-time androgynous persona, eliciting as many "ma'ams" as I do "sir" responses. My goal is to be free to present myself full female all the time, while still expressing a healthy degree of androgyny. Living as a woman gives me a much fuller range of expression than as a man. In time, I may feel more comfortable confronting the world with the unabashed ambiguity of total androgyny.

Public recognition and legitimacy of alternatives encourages multiple treatment options and the opportunity for the continued decoupling of gender and sex.

Grass-Roots Organization, Political Action, and Transgenderism

While there is not universal agreement on the term "transgendered," there is an emerging generic semantic that is inclusive of all people who cross-dress. It includes those who self-identify as male-to-female transsexuals, male transvestites, cross-dressers, and those who lie between the traditional identity of transsexual (as someone seeking hormonal and sex-reassignment surgery) and the male transvestite.

The transgender community is viewed here as a reflection of the expanding political concerns of the individuals involved who wanted a voice in treatment, in defining themselves, and in offering activities, conferences, support groups and other events to further their interests and needs as a growing community. The social construction of identities has become the property of a community with a political agenda. Among the organizations I have investigated, efforts have been made to embrace diversity and recognize similarity amidst the disparity. This may be regarded as a pan-gender trend reflected in the creation and public use of a new category, transgenderism.

"Transgenderist" may be used in a very specific sense to include persons such as nonsurgical or even presurgical male-to-female transsexuals who want to live permanently as female (*A Gender Glossary,* n.d.; Lynn, 1988). According to Merissa Sherrill Lynn of the International Foundation for Gender Education (IFGE), "Most people who consider themselves to be transgenderists do not want or need sexual reassignment surgery, and do not identify with 'transvestite'" (Lynn, n.d.). These individuals are also described as

persons who change gender roles, but [who] do not plan to have reassignment surgery. They have alternatively been defined as persons who steer a middle course, living with the physical traits of both genders. Transgenderists may alter their anatomy with hormones or surgery, but they may purposefully retain many of the characteristics of the gender to which they were originally assigned. Many lead part-time lives in both genders; most cultivate an androgynous appearance.

—Denny, 1991

Transgenderism may therefore include the self-proclaimed androgyne, the individual who wishes to express both male and female identification through sartorial and bodily symbols of gender, appearing as a blend, sometimes of one gender more than the other. Ariadne Kane, Director of the Human Achievement and Outreach Institute, has promoted this approach as an option for individuals. Kane has a variety of personal expressions of "felt" gender that vary from day to day or even within the day, and uses cultural symbols of gender to reveal inner felt dimensions of gender.

Throughout my earlier research in the Berdache Society, nonsurgical male-to-female transsexuals remained invisible; I knew only one individual locally who, although claiming to be a transsexual, was going to live as a woman without having the sex-change surgery. Recently, I located a number of similar individuals with no great effort. The implications of this field research are substantiated by various other indicators as well, for example, community journals, newsletters, and literature. It seems there has been a "coming out of the closet" of those who regard themselves as nonsurgically inclined and hence transgenderists. This transgender social identity most likely includes a number of people who in the past would have considered themselves transvestites. Current transgenderism would likely incorporate people like the male transvestites of the Berdache Society who in my earlier research did not see the distinction between themselves and male-to-female transsexuals. Other candidates likely to self-identify as transgenderists are those who would have been rejected from the gender clinics.

"The Transgender Alternative," an article that appeared in the journals of two of the major organizations for the gender community, offers an excellent definition of this identity (Boswell, 1991, p. 29). This article discussed nonsurgical solutions by a self-identified transgenderist, Holly Boswell:

> When a transsexual sister of mine observed that "so many of us simply stall out and fail to achieve our goals of sex reassignment surgery," I felt compelled to question her premise: "Maybe a lot of these people

who apparently stall out have found a more comfortable and appropriate middle ground. Maybe there are not so many transsexual people after all." Cross-dressers may also have a sense of this, yet be equally unsure of this middle ground.

The middle ground I am referring to is transgenderism. I realize this term (heretofore vague) also encompasses the entire spectrum: cross-dresser to transsexual person. But for the purpose of this article . . . I shall attempt to define transgender as a viable option between cross-dresser and transsexual person, which also happens to have a firm foundation in the ancient tradition of androgyny.

Boswell promotes transgenderism as an alternative that may include transvestite men who cross-dress, nonsurgical male-to-female transsexuals who live as women full-time but choose not to have the surgery but who may or may not take female hormones, and even androgynes, persons who blend genders and do not try to pass. According to Boswell "S/he is, perhaps an harbinger of our future" (Boswell, 1991, pp. 30–31).

The revisioning of gendered identities is reflected in national organizations for the transgender community such as the International Foundation for Gender Education and the American Educational Gender Information Service, two prominent organizations with political agendas. Such organizations have focused on bringing the diverse members of the transgender community together and providing information as well as influencing treatment issues such as classification in the *Diagnostic and Statistical Manual of Mental Disorders* (DSM III-R), a document widely used by therapeutic professionals in the mental illness classification and diagnosis of clients, including those with gender identity "disorders" (American Psychiatric Association, 1987).

A decade ago, organizations kept a low profile and focused on service to their particular gender identity group. The focus was inward and it lacked a political emphasis. In contrast, today the Congress of Representatives, an umbrella organization that encompasses all the transgender community organizations and groups in the United States, provides a community-based approach that emphasizes serving the needs of the various organizations and extant gender constituencies. This national network is a vehicle for the further blending and expansion of identity borders. Each organization has a representative in this Congress:

Despite its rough beginning, the Congress of Representatives is ready to offer a forum for extensive dialogue between support group reps. . . . As we open ourselves to the ideas of others, let's keep in mind that these "labels" (CD [cross-dresser], TG [transgenderist], TS, etc.) need not be divisive. They're just a shorthand expression of individuality. . . .

Because the gender community was first organized mostly by members of focused [closed] groups, there has been a troubling lack of cohesiveness that has resulted in polarization [between TS's and heterosexual CD's]. With the new trend of open support groups, that foundation [of commonality] can be strengthened. And as open support groups begin to nurture more columns of non-hetero CD's, TG's, female-to-male TS's, androgynes, etc., we may achieve a structure that can support a roof. With the spirit of unity and inclusiveness that is promoted by open minds, open hearts, and open groups, we may indeed create the temple of a community we can all call home.

—Boswell, n.d.

Ideally, the interests of no single group are privileged and the political focus can be kept on common concerns rather than differences. This realignment illustrates the shifting of identities as part of a strategy for empowerment and extends from the national level to the local level. It is expressed in support groups such as the Southern Janus Alliance, "which is open to people dealing with all gender issues: androgyny, cross dressing, transgenderism and transsexualism."

This recent strategy contrasts rather sharply with the early efforts of the Berdache Society. The male-to-female transsexual members who came to dominate the governing of Berdache Society felt that the less people knew about them the better. There was a consensus among both transsexuals and transvestites that education of the public at large could only result in making it more difficult for them to pass. The primary concerns of transsexuals centered on areas of contact, such as the medical and psychological sectors, the legal profession, and significant others (who were also of concern to transvestites). Challenging media stereotypes was regarded as an impossible task, necessitating "outing" themselves as transsexuals or transvestites. The specific needs of the transvestite population were overshadowed by those of the transsexual group. The transvestite members were satisfied at that time with support, information, and opportunities to cross-dress.

Sharon (a male-to-female transsexual) described the formation of an organization not unlike the Berdache Society in the Northeast in 1979 known as the Ephemeral Center, a pseudonym. By the fall of 1981, she reports,

A few cracks began to show up in my idealism . . . to form an organization that would provide community such as housing, a strong financial base, a self-supporting organization by and for the community of TS's and TV's—a community for unity that would be an international organization with a political agenda. . . . The second generation of Ephemeral Center members had arrived, and they did not share my vision. For the most part, they were satisfied with the status quo, and were resistant to change . . . [By 1982] the third generation had arrived and the resistance to change . . . became worse than ever.

In 1986, Sharon's goals were finally achieved, and with the help of friends the Ephemeral Center was renamed and reconstituted as an international organization dedicated to bringing the diverse segments of the community together. Sharon organized the first international convention in 1987 for the entire gender community. This organization and convention served as an important model for fusing plurality. According to Sharon:

This convention was the first time any effort was made . . . to bring our community's leaders together to tend to the business of our community as a whole. It was our community's first real convention. . . . I emerged as a leader just at the time our community was ripe to become a community, and society was ripe to allow that to happen.

The open organizations of today now seem to aim at integrating the interests of all the transgendered constituency. In the words of one organization advertising for a conference:

Our intention is to bring our people and our friends together so we can learn how to better understand each other's needs and issues, learn how to respect each other's differences, . . . and to work together for the benefit of all. The convention also exists to reach out to the general public, to help them better understand our issues, and to respect us as positive, constructive and contributing members of society and as human beings.

The agenda of valuing and respect has advanced the possibility of a permanent rather than temporary transsexual social identity, an "out" transvestism and a pride in one's past social history as gender-variant people. It is akin to a new kind of ethnicity. In this regard, Lydia, a middle-age postoperative transsexual, argues that:

Transsexual people must learn to come out. The closet for them is as real as it is for gay men and lesbians. But transsexualism has two closets. . . . That's where people go after their transitions to deny their pasts and their transsexualism. It makes them vulnerable to outing, just as it does the gay and lesbian community. In the past, there was little choice but to go into the closet at the end of the rainbow, for public identity as a transsexual person meant media attention, ridicule, loss of employment and employability, and even physical danger. As times have changed, it has become possible to have a public identity as transsexual and still have a reasonably normal life. The most important result of this is that it enables transsexuals to provide feedback about the treatment process.

Political efforts also include destigmatizing transvestism by divesting it of its association with fetishism and "sexual perversion." In this regard Tracy, a self-identified transvestite comments:

Those of us who are transvestic and/or transgendered—but not transsexual—are most unhappy with the DSM III-R classification. There "we" are listed as transvestic fetishists, right there with the sado-masochists, . . . child molesters and . . . aggressive butt-rubbers. Considering we don't "do" anything to anybody, especially a nonconsenting person, the inclusion with this group makes us furious. We are summarily dismissed as deviants rather than variants in Western society.

The alternative is to be transsexual or gender dysphoric—i.e., GIDAANT, gender identity disorder of adolescence and adulthood, nontranssexual type. Now is that a mouthful? An obviously exaggerated attempt to force people into a category. George Orwell would be delighted.

When identities go public and become the domain of organizations as image managers, then efforts at normalization will effect presentation of self and social construction of gender identities (Goffman, 1963, 1967). For example, one organization that hosts a weekend of mingling and public cross-dressing stated in their brochure:

we are going to enforce our dress and behavior policies. . . . Evidently there are a few uninformed who think hotels allow "real" women dressed as hookers to "troll" the lobby . . . *please* (for all our sakes) use the same taste in *attire* you would want your sister, mother, or your dad, (if he's one of us) to use. People in _____ have very definite ideas about what a *lady* should look like . . . help us convince them we are no different from the average woman in style of dress.

Despite the recent political agenda supporting diversity, this policy represents a continuing conservative trend that discourages variant gender-identity presentations. It seems evident in this case that androgyny would not be welcomed either. Nor is it implied here that divisions within the transgender community and the privileging of surgically oriented transsexuals no longer occur. For example, the New Woman's Caucus, an organization for male-to-female transsexuals, offers a special conference for the postsurgical transsexual population. The caucus recognizes the surgery as an "unambiguous rite of passage, which separates the *seeker* from the *changed*" (Second Annual New Woman's Conference, 1992). Lee, a postoperative male-to-female transsexual, has described herself this way: "I am a new woman. My identity is that of a female—mentally, spiritually, physically, legally, and socially." Because Lee works for a nationally self-supporting transgender organization employing members of the transgender community, she has represented the traditional dichotomy of transsexual and transvestite in a unique way:

> My problem now [since her recent surgery] is a little different than it has been . . . now I'm a female and still have to work with men. The only real difference between me and any other woman is most of the men I have to work with wear dresses [i.e., are male transvestites and transgenderists].

Lisa, a self-identified transvestite remarked to me that the breach between transsexuals and transvestites still continues amidst the change:

> Fetishistic TV's are generally closeted, or use prostitutes, but have no interest in organization or socialization. The TS community often protests that the TG's are not "real women" because there is no surgical orientation to their goals. For me, it is difficult to understand these divisive attitudes. Without tolerance or acceptance of gays, there is no tolerance of the cross-dresser, and the TS is considered a freak.

While division does continue to exist, the efforts of the national organizations have led to significant progress (Boswell, n.d.). For example, one postoperative male-to-female transsexual asserted that "the greatest change is the ever increasing willingness of different groups and people to respect other people's differences and work together for the benefit of all. We're growing up." Another individual acknowledged that "one of the biggest changes I have seen in the transgender community is you no longer have to fit in a box. You do not have to be 'TS' or 'TV.' It is okay to be transgendered. You can now lay anywhere on the spectrum from non-gendered to full transsexual."

It is not surprising that the cross-cultural record and anthropology's relativism have been included in the social construction of gender-variant identities by the organizational gatekeepers of the gender community. At both the gender community conferences I attended, symposia were organized that included historical and cross-cultural aspects of cross-dressing. This emphasis has continued as an interest of various organizations throughout the United States where anthropologists and historians are called on to present evidence of "traditions" of cross-dressing. At the National Transgender Annual Meetings, a community-based conference, I was invited as an anthropologist to present cross-cultural evidence of cross-dressing. Members of the audience were most interested in two topics: the kinds of data that identified the *berdache* as a high-status position and the question of how *berdache* are conceptualized as third or alternative genders mitigating against clinical typologies (Bolin, 1988b).

It was apparent that various audience members were familiar with the recent anthropological works on this subject such as Serena Nanda's (1989) study of the hijras of India, Will Roscoe's (1991a) *The Zuni Man-Woman* and Walter L. Williams' (1986) research on the Native American *berdache*. All were mentioned by members of the audience at both the national gender community conferences I attended.

Based on this recent foray and my previous experience, I've concluded that the plethora of anthropological works on the subject of gender variation have an eager market outside of academia. At the National Transgender Annual Meetings, a handout written by Wendy Parker was distributed entitled "Historical Facts of Interest to the Gender Community," containing two full pages of citations demonstrating (1) events and individuals involving the acceptance and tolerance of cross-dressing, for example, "1530 A.D.—Spanish explorer Cabeza de Vaca documents seeing 'soft and feminine' men doing 'womens' work among Florida Indian tribes. First observation of Indian *Berdache* by Western culture"; (2) events and explanations exploring the reasons cross-dressing was discriminated against, for example, "1200s—The beginning of church/state campaign against gender and sexual variations begin during Medieval period of Crusades. Brought in from Persia, sexual relations with young feminized boys was considered an accepted Islamic practice and therefore considered 'heresy' as it was a 'pagan' ritual"; (3) information concerning important figures in the history of cross-dressing, including the "invention" of various clinical terminologies, for example, "1900—Julian Eltinge becomes big hit on Broadway performing in drag. Becomes America's first successful female impersonator"; and (4) important events in the organization of cross-dressing, for example, "1976—Ariadne Kane founds the Outreach Institute and begins the first Fantasia Fair. This major cross-dressers convention has been given yearly uninterrupted to today."

Anthropological as well as historical data are reinterpreted as part of the "roots" and developing empowerment of the transgender community. Interestingly, what seems to be happening is an integration and valuing of the anthropological concept of relativism, the recognition that culture is an important component in the construction of gender ideologies, identities, and status. Cross-historical and cross-cultural education allows individuals, regardless of their self-identity, to employ this information as a "neutralization technique" or disclaimer. Because relativism is a "reflection on the process of interpretation itself," for transgender people it facilitates the re-creation and re-invention of themselves as a gender community (Marcus & Fischer, 1986).

This recently developing unity seems to be expanding to include the gay community, which has been previously excluded as a separate subculture based on oppression of sexuality rather than gender identity. Both the transgender community and the gay community have shared a serendipitous interest in cross-cultural material.[10] According to Midnight Sun, "cross-cultural material is often used to support claims about contemporary Western homosexuality" (Sun, 1988). In *Living the Spirit: A Gay American Indian Anthology*, gay Native Americans have also found their roots in *berdache* traditions just as transsexuals and transvestites. By being Other and seeking roots with Otherness, transgendered people and gay men and women can transform their status momentarily or more deeply. By using the *berdache* as a model, the transgender community and homosexual community become active participants in reshaping their culture and in finding affiliation where division existed (Roscoe, 1991a, p. 3).[11]

Such reconceptualizations are not just labeling theory in action but a complex process of revisioning. It may be likened to Roscoe's concept of lesbian and gay "cultur-ing"—defined as "the negotiation and formulation of homosexual desire into cultural forms and social identities" (Roscoe, 1991b). The transgender community is perhaps involved in a project of gender "cultur-ing," creating new forms and seeing new relationships in social forms as identities. Diversity in personal identities are re-presented as social constructions through formal organizations that, in turn, affect personal identity by providing more flexibility in the ideological system of gender.

FEMININITY, EMBODIMENT, AND SOCIAL CHANGE

The growing transgender community has also been influenced by changes and challenges to embodiments of femininity. Conventional femininity in the late twentieth century is in a process of redefinition socially, economically, and, especially important to this essay, somatically, as feminine fragility is contested by an empowered athletic soma. Women's bodies have undergone radical revision from the nineteenth-century hourglass and corsetted ideal to the very thin silhouette of the 1960s (Bolin, 1991, 1992d).

The 1980s and 1990s have brought alternative somatic models for women. While the slenderness of the 1960s has continued to prevail, a world-wide movement toward health and fitness has resulted in a revised feminine body ideal that includes toned muscles and taut physiques (Bolin, 1992d, p. 87). Women bodybuilders' stout muscles, previously relegated as a trait reserved for men, have begun to undermine biocentric ideologies and equations of muscularity and manliness. Rachel McLish and Cory Everson have helped to usher in a new femininity that has subverted prevalent images of frailty. Feminism has opened new embodiments of womanhood that offer greater flexibility in appearance and somatic contours (Duff & Hong, 1984). Since bodies in the Western gender paradigm were regarded as "naturally" constituted contours, this has implications for the social mapping of transgenderism. There may be backlashes against somatic revisioning, but it nevertheless continues to undermine biological sex as the determinant of bodily form.

Women bodybuilders in particular and other women athletes in general, have contested the male equation of muscularity, strength, and masculinity embedded in biologistic readings of bodies. The new muscular soma of women reinscribes other changes in women's position socially and economically. Women athletes' physiques may even appear androgynous. Sports like track, long-distance running, heptathlon and triathlon, mountain climbing, and bodybuilding create new embodiments of femininity and defy the traditional soma of woman as soft and curvaceous. Women athletes have added significant muscularity and leanness, advancing a new contour that has little body fat and few curves (Bolin, 1992d, 1992e).

Have such widespread changes in the feminine body and its implicit query to biology inspired changes in the transgender community? Has the broadening of body "shapes" and images for women perhaps influenced requests for surgery by making passing easier? Will the more androgynous woman's image and changes in gender roles contribute to a lessening of male cross-gender identification? While these questions cannot be answered at this time, it may be assumed that the relaxing of bodily gender rules and the undermining of the biological paradigm since the 1960s has undoubtedly contributed to the trend towards a transgender community and the creation of nonsurgical transsexuals. Such transformations of the female body erode constructs of behaviors and bodies as natural by creating the possibility for a social woman with a penis.

The androgynous-appearing soma of some women athletes combines symbols of masculinity and femininity on a physical level. It could be argued that this external mixing of gender cues may also imply and reflect an internal blending of emotional, characterological, and behavioral propensities previously segregated by gender (Bolin, 1992d; Klein, in press). The approach of Kathy, a petite middle-aged cross-dresser, to womanhood resonates such a blend of neo-femininity in which assertiveness is combined with an empowered body image:

> The women I have always found attractive and try to emulate are assertive, self-sufficient, and emotionally and physically strong. This body type and personality type have become increasingly accepted. The image I portray is essentially that of an alert, athletic, highly trained female bodybuilder. Acceptance by society of this type of woman has benefitted me greatly. Ten years ago, there were no female body types such as mine thought to be attractive. Cory Everson, Florence Griffith Joyner, and others have broken new ground.

Lois, a 45-year-old preoperative transsexual, reiterates this new femininity:

> These changes in the wider societal gender roles have had an effect. I found that in today's society a woman can do anything she wants. This means I did not have to give up my interest in economics or engineering. These changes meant that I did not have to be Susie Homemaker if I did not want to. Also, these changes have made it easier for me to do a transition and pass. Being six feet tall and having big bones made for one big girl. In the past you would have stuck out like a sore thumb, but today there are a lot of big girls and also you don't have to be a Barbie doll in order to pass as a woman.

Ten years ago male-to-female transsexualism supported the binary gender schema by dividing gender-dysphoric into men and women where transvestites were considered "sick" or pathological men and transsexuals were women on whom nature had erred. In contrast, the recently emerging transgender identity offers an account of gender as a social product by giving one the option of living as a woman or a "blend" without surgical reassignment. The transgenderist may or may not feminize, some appear androgynously, and others pass. The possible permutations within transgenderism are innumerable and lay bare the point that gender is not biology but is socially produced. Moreover, female gender identity as lived by male-to-female transsexuals, transgenderists, and women, is not necessarily framed or limited by an attraction to men. Transsexuals have contested this blatantly. Gender identity operated independently, thereby subverting the biocentric paradigm in which gender identity is "naturally" cojoined with heterosexuality.

In an analysis of the content of brochures and flyers from a number of support groups, it was common to find groups not limited to particular gender identity advertise, for example, "a safe and caring atmosphere that is open to anyone male or female, gay, straight, bisexual or asexual, who wishes to explore their gender issues," or "a new club for cross dressers is [now] open to all CD's, regardless of sexual preference(s), . . . No Gay and/ or Bi-men unless CD." Sexual orientation as a critical characteristic for identification is thus dismissed; or as one preoperative transsexual stated, "When you're transsexual, every sex is the opposite sex." This view repeals the idea of polarity inherent in the biocentric model of gender, and it signifies sexuality as an unruly and potentially malleable construct that is independent of identity.

It is in the arena of sexual orientation where the unrealized potential for a third gender may be found. Out of deconstructed gender polarity arises the possibility of a social woman with a penis. This woman embraces the ineffable by eroding the coherence of heterosexuality and biological gender. The polyvocality of sexual and gender potentialities are illustrated by the following four examples in which the complexity and decoupling of physiological sex, gender identity, and sexuality are explored.

Sharon is a 50-year-old physiological male and lives as a transsexually inclined female:

> Although I'm capable of performing sexually as a male, I must fantasize myself as a women in order to do so. I'm basically asexual. Sex is not and never has been important. I've never really felt sexually

attracted to anyone, male or female. However, my preference for sexual partners has always been female.

Roland, 40 years old, was born a physiological female and offers another narrative in which sexual orientation is destabilized.

I'm a female-to-male in transition on his way to becoming his true self—*male*. I am presently living with a post-op male-to-female [transsexual] who is my significant other. She is very successful—a professional woman. We plan to marry. [In my thirties,] I began to sexually awaken—I had numerous lesbian relationships and kept it [transsexualism] hidden. . . . Most of my time has been spent in the gay community, as a lesbian, where transsexualism is rarely understood or accepted.

Clare, a 46-year-old male-to-female transsexual who has been taking female hormones for the last two years, also recorded a sexual history that defies the gender schema of heterosexuality. Clare has been involved with a bisexual man for twelve years:

[My partner's] primary orientation is homosexual. He fell in love with my male person. I have been, until recently, a reluctant lover for him because I'm not gay. . . . Two years ago he [left the country for employment] and when he returned, my body had undergone changes, considerable breast development, I'd removed the hair from my chest and legs. As I had feared, his passion for making love with me has waned, yet our bond of love is as strong as before. It's interesting how my desire for him has changed. I now crave his touch whereas before I did not. . . . Our love transcends our physical relationship which has become the stuff of bad fiction. When he was wildly hot for me, I was hesitant. Now, the roles are reversed. We laugh about it, though the pain of loss on both sides is real. . . . [He said] he was amazed upon seeing Clare for the first time. He said he found himself treating me differently, being more gentle with me.

Jane, a late-thirtyish transgenderist, lives as a woman with "her" wife, Mary. They were married when Jane was John, and over the course of time John has become feminized with hormones, electrolysis, and hairstyle. Although this has caused problems in the marriage, Mary has continued to try and accept these changes. John is still able to engage in penile intercourse, as the hormones have not as yet interfered with the capacity for erection, although this will eventually happen. This case illustrates how Western gender terminology, which is so reliant on biological insignias, becomes incoherent when the genitalism of the gender paradigm is revoked. From her perspective, Jane has a lesbian relationship with her wife (Mary). Yet she also uses her penis for pleasure. Mary does not identify as a lesbian, although she maintains love and attraction for Jane, whom she regards as the same person she fell in love with, although this person has changed physically. Mary regards herself as heterosexual in orientation, although she defines sexual intimacy with her spouse Jane as somewhere between lesbian and heterosexual.

The rules for construction of heterosexuality as "natural" in the gender equation are impugned by these cases. In the Western paradigm, gender operates as "the central organizing principle of sexuality" and sexual orientation exists only in relationship to gender and physiology (Kimmel, 1990). "Males are expected to be *men*: tough, strong behavior is not enough unless they are also attracted to women as sexual partners. Thus, heterosexuality is a major component of 'normal' gender expression" (Irvine, 1990, p. 231). When sexuality can no longer signify heterosexuality because biology no longer signifies gender, the disjunction of sex as reproduction is played out and the gender paradigm is unsettled.

CONCLUSION

In earlier research I analyzed the transformation of the male-to-female transsexual as a journey from gender disorder order. The surgically oriented male-to-female transsexual rendered invisible the instability of gender through their quest for sex-reassignment surgery. A decade later, as a result of several sociocultural factors previously described, transgenderism subverted rather than sustained the Euro-American gender paradigm. Transgenderism perpetrated the disassembling of gender. According to Jason Cromwell, "To acknowledge the validity of 'men with vaginas' (and 'women with penises') would be to admit that men as well as women could resist and thus, subvert the social order, by approximating the 'other' but never fully becoming the 'other'" (Cromwell, 1991, pp. 16–17).

The transgenderist harbors great potential to deactivate gender or to create in the future the possibility of "supernumerary" genders as social categories no longer based on biology (Martin & Voorhies, 1975, p. 84). The surgically oriented male-to-female transsexual has confirmed the independence of sexual orientation and gender identity through bisexual and lesbian orientations. The transgenderist has pushed the parameters of the gender paradigm even further by disputing the entire concept of consistency between sexual orientation and gender. If, indeed, "the paradigm that there are two genders founded on two biological sexes began to predominate in Western culture only in the early eighteenth century," (Trumbach, 1991, p. 112) then perhaps the task of twenty-first-century scholars will be to deconstruct the social history of a trigender paradigm whose awakenings began in the 1990s.

NOTES

1. I want to give special thanks and appreciation to Gilbert Herdt for his invaluable and incisive comments and helpful suggestions for this chapter from its inception and throughout its revision. I am extremely grateful to Vern and Bonnie Bullough for their careful reading, thorough and insightful critique, and graciousness in helping me. Unfortunately, their landmark book, *Cross-Dressing, Sex and Gender* (Philadelphia, University of Pennsylvania Press, 1993), was not available at the time of this writing. I am indebted to Tom Henricks, who provided me with his expertise on developing my research methodology, as well as intellectual engagement and supportive guidance. Many thanks to Linda Martindale for her excellence in manuscript preparation and her editorial skills.

2. Although I refer to such groups as male-to-female transsexuals, male transvestites, and transgenderists, this should not be construed as a statement of representativeness but merely as a literary convenience. My findings were based on a limited population using a snowball sampling technique. While generalization was sacrificed, I feel I have helped make visible the diversity within the transgender community by the detail and substance provided by ethnographic and textual materials.

3. A number of member terms are used to generally denote that group of people whose genitals, status, appearance, and behaviors are not in congruence with the Western schema that mandates an essential relationship between sex and gender (i.e., genitalia, status, appearance, and gender role). Some refer to the "transgender community," or more cursively, "the gender community." Ariadne Kane, Director of the Human Achievement and Outreach Institute, prefers the term "the paraculture" to include alternative life-styles of individuals who cross-dress. While gay cross-dressers or female impersonators are not usually included as transgenderists, this is not invariable. In addition, sexual eroticism varies among those identified as transgenderists as well.

4. Jason Cromwell continues by stating that female-to-male transsexuals "by not altering their bodies through surgery (or only moderately so). . . . can be dismissed as 'masculine women'" (Cromwell, 1991, p. 38). See also Cromwell, n.d., and Devor, 1989. Outside of Cromwell's work, there is a dearth of sociocultural studies on female-to-male transgendered people. Vern Bullough and Bonnie Bullough's (personal communication) broad historical perspective identifies cross-dressing as primarily a phenomenon among women with male cross-dressing as only a very recent phenomenon.

5. This approach is in the genre of interpretive anthropology, defined as a covering label for a diverse set of reflections on both the practice of ethnography and the concept of culture. It includes a view of culture as negotiated meanings that can be "read" (or analyzed) as a text by the ethnographer and "read" and "decoded" by the natives. See Marcus & Fischer, 1986; Geertz, 1972, 1986; and Turner, 1967, 1974.

6. Harry Benjamin subsequently founded the Harry Benjamin International Gender Dysphoria Association, an organization for professionals with gender-dysphoric clients, i.e., people requesting hormonal and surgical reassignment (see Berger et al., 1980). Benjamin published the first medical article on the subject as well as organized the first symposium at the Association for the Advancement of Psychotherapy in 1953 (see Benjamin, 1969).

7. This is the description of Sasha, a presurgical male-to-female transsexual, hormonally reassigned as female who was in a sexual relationship with a self-identified lesbian.

8. Although "transgenderist" has a generic quality and may be used to include both biological males and females, my discussion continues to focus on gender variance among physiological males.

9. This is not to suggest that these are the only three social influences shaping twentieth-century gender-variant identities. Vern and Bonnie Bullough emphasize the great contribution of Virginia Prince in constructing the current transvestite identity and that as other individuals gain ascendance more options will be made available other than the classic married heterosexual transvestite. In addition, the Bulloughs explore in their recent book *Cross-Dressing, Sex, and Gender* the importance of homophobia in shaping cross-gendered identities, particularly that occurring from within the gender community (personal communication).

10. Evidence of this pattern is found in a variety of sources. For example, Wendy Parker makes reference to the 1969 Stonewall resistance by "street queens" among her list of dates in "Historical Facts of Interest to the Gender Community," thereby recognizing a commonality between "street queens" and transgenderists. According to one consultant, efforts at integrating the gay community into transgender community conferences have begun with invitations to various local gay communities in the host city. In fact, the Human Achievement and Outreach Institute incorporated two gay interns working at the 1992 Fantasia Fair. The two interns spoke about an effort by their regional gay community center to be more incorporative and less stigmatizing of the "drag queen" community. They took their role as interns very seriously in terms of wanting to learn more about the diversity of cross-dressing. These two young men regarded themselves as quite different from gay female impersonators whose cross-dressing was performance oriented. They viewed themselves as part of a new younger generation of cross-dressers in the gay community. While gay camp allows for contrasting expressions of gender (see Sontag, 1970), the interns' presentation lacked the contrasts and the hyperglamorous attributes. Like many but certainly not all of the cross-dressers at the Fantasia Fair, the interns dressed so as to pass. This represents a new construction of an identity within the gay community that blends attributes of heterosexual cross-dressing with gay female impersonation.

11. For the purposes of this analysis, the issue of whether the *berdache* can be framed in Western terms, e.g., homosexuality and transsexualism, is not relevant. What is important are the uses made of the berdache by the diverse constituencies in the gender community and the gay and lesbian communities.

REFERENCES

American Psychiatric Association. (1980). *Diagnostic and statistical manual of mental disorders.* DSM III. Washington, DC: American Psychiatric Association.

American Psychiatric Association. (1987). *Diagnostic and statistical manual of mental disorders.* DSM III-R. Washington, DC: American Psychiatric Association.

Bateson, M.C. (1989). *Composing a life.* New York: Penguin Group.

Benjamin, H. (1966). *The transsexual phenomenon: A scientific report on transsexualism and sex conversion in the human male and female.* New York: Julian Press.

Berger, J.C., et al. (1980). *Standards of care: The hormonal and surgical sex reassignment of gender dysphoric persons.* Galveston, TX: The Harry Benjamin International Gender Dysphoria Association.

Bolin, A. (1987a). Transsexuals and caretakers: A study of power and deceit in intergroup relations. *City and Society, 1*(2), 64–79.

Bolin, A. (1987b, September–October). Transsexualism and the limits of traditional analysis. *American Behavioral Scientist, 31*(1), 41.

Bolin, A. (1988a). *In search of Eve: Transsexual rites of passage*. South Hadley, MA: Bergin & Garvey Publishers, Inc.

Bolin, A. (1988b). The splendor of gender: Socio-cultural contributions to gender variance. Address delivered to the Second Annual Oklahoma Conference of the Society for the Scientific Study of Sex, Edmond, OK, 30 September–1 October, 1988.

Bolin, A. (1991). Flex appeal: Women, body image and identity. Paper presented at the Annual Meeting of the American Anthropological Association, Chicago, 20–24 November, 1991.

Bolin, A. (1992a). Gender subjectivism in the construction of transsexualism. *Chrysalis Quarterly, 1*(3), 22–26, 39.

Bolin, A. (1992b). Review of H. Devor, *Gender blending: Confronting the limits of duality. Journal of the History of Sexuality, 2*(2).

Bolin, A. (1992c). A transsexual coming of age: The cultural construction of adolescence. In T.L. Whitehead & B. Reid (Eds.), *Gender constructs and social issues*. Urbana: University of Illinois Press.

Bolin, A. (1992d). Flex appeal, food, and fat: Competitive body building, gender and diet. *Play and Culture, 5*(4).

Bolin, A. (1992e). Vandalized vanity: Feminine physiques betrayed and portrayed. In Frances E. Mascia-Less & P. Sharpe (Eds.), *Tattoo, torture, mutilation, and adornment: The denaturalization of the body in culture and text*. Albany: State University of New York Press.

Bordo, S.R. (1989). The body and the reproduction of femininity: A feminist appropriation of Foucault. In A.M. Jagger & S.R. Bordo (Eds.), *Gender/Body/Knowledge: Feminist reconstructions of being and knowing*. New Brunswick, NJ: Rutgers University Press.

Bordo, S.R. (1990). Reading the slender body. In S.R. Bordo, *Body/Politics: Woman and the discourses of science*. New York: Routledge.

Boswell, H. (1991). The transgender alternative. *Chrysalis Quarterly, 1*(2), 29–31.

Boswell, H. (n.d.). Getting it together. *Tapestry, 63*, 45–46.

Bullough, V. (1992). Crossdressing: Crossgender, perceptions, ideals, and realities. Paper presented at the Fantasia Fair, Cape Cod, MA, 18 October, 1992.

Bullough, V., & Bullough, B. (1993). *Cross-dressing, sex, and gender*. Philadelphia: University of Pennsylvania Press.

Cromwell, J. (1991). Talking about without talking about: The use of protective language among transvestites and transsexuals. Paper presented at the annual meeting of the American Anthropological Association, Chicago, IL: 20–24 November, 1991.

Cromwell, J. (n.d.). Fearful others: The construction of female gender variance. Paper presented for the University of Washington, Seattle, WA: Kenneth Payne Student Prize.

Denny, D. (1991). *Dealing with your feelings*. AEGIS Transition Series. Decatur, GA: American Educational Gender Information Service, Inc., p. 6.

Denny, D. (1992). The politics of diagnosis and a diagnosis of politics. *Chrysalis Quarterly, 1*(3), 9–20.

Devor, H. (1989). *Gender blending: Confronting the limits of duality*. Bloomington: Indiana University Press.

Duff, R.W., & Hong, L.K. (1984). Self-images of women body-builders. *Sociology of Sport Journal, 1*(4).

Foucault, M. (1988). Technologies of the self. In L.B. Martin, et al. (Eds.), *Technologies of the self: A seminar with Michel Foucault*. Amherst: University of Massachusetts Press.

Gallagher, C., & Laquer, T. (1987). *The making of the modern body*. Berkeley and Los Angeles: University of California Press.

Geertz, C. (1972). Deep play: Notes on the Balinese cockfight. In C. Geertz (Ed.), *Myth, symbol, and culture*. New York: Norton.

Geertz, C. (1986). Making experience, authoring selves. In V.W. Turner & E.M. Bruner (Eds.), *The anthropology of experience*. Urbana: University of Illinois Press.

A gender glossary. (n.d.). South Portland, ME: Human Outreach and Achievement Institute.

Goffman, I. (1963). *Stigma: Notes on the management of a spoiled identity.* Englewood Cliffs, NJ: Prentice-Hall.

Goffman, I. (1967). *Interaction ritual.* Garden City, NY: Doubleday.

Green R., & Money, J. (Eds.). (1969). *Transsexualism and sex reassignment.* Baltimore, MD: Johns Hopkins University Press.

Irvine, J.M. (1990). *Disorders of desire: Sex and gender in modern American sexology.* Philadelphia: Temple University Press.

Kessler, S.J., & McKenna, W. (1978). *Gender: An ethnomethodological approach.* New York: John Wiley & Sons. Reprinted in 1985 by The University of Chicago Press.

Kimmel, M. (1990). After fifteen years: The impact of the sociology of masculinity on the masculinity of sociology. In J. Hearn & D. Morgan (Eds.), *Men, masculinities and social theory,* p. 99. Boston: Unwin Hymin.

Klein, A. (in press). Body double: Ethnography meets post-modernism in the gym. In *Little big men: Gender construction and bodybuilding subculture.* Albany: State University of New York Press.

Lemonick, M.D. (1992, 24 February). Genetic tests under fire. *Time, 139*(8), 65.

Lynn, M.S. (1988). Definitions of terms used in the transvestite-transsexual community. *Tapestry,* 51.

Lynn, M.S. (n.d.). Definitions of terms commonly used in the transvestite/transsexual community. Wayland, MA: IFGE Educational Resources Committee, p. 9.

Marcus, G.E., & Fischer, M.M. (1986). *Anthropology as cultural critique: An experimental moment in the human sciences,* pp. 25 and 38. Chicago: University of Chicago Press.

Martin, E. (1989). The cultural construction of gendered bodies: Biology and metaphors of production and destruction. *Ethnos, 54,* 3–4.

Martin, M.K., & Voorhies, B. (1975). *Female of the species.* New York: Columbia University Press.

Meyer, W.J., III, Walker, P.A., & Suplee, Z.R. (1981). A survey of transsexual hormone treatment in 20 gender treatment centres. *Journal of Sex Research, 17,* 344–349.

Money, J., & Ehrhardt, A.A. (1972). *Man and woman, boy and girl: The differentiation and dimorphism of gender identity from conception to maturity.* Baltimore, MD: The Johns Hopkins University Press.

Nanda, S. (1989). The Hijras of India: Cultural and individual dimensions of an institutionalized third gender role. *Journal of Homosexuality, Special Issue: Anthropology and homosexual behavior, 11*(3–4), 35–54.

Newton, E. (1972). *Mother camp: Female impersonation in America.* Englewood Cliffs, NJ: Prentice-Hall.

The Second Annual New Woman's Conference. (1992). North Berwick, ME: The New Woman Caucus.

Roscoe, W. (1990). *The Zuni man-woman.* Albuquerque: University of New Mexico Press.

Roscoe, W. (1991b). Writing gay and lesbian culture(s): An impossible possibility. Paper presented at the Annual Meeting of the American Anthropological Association, Chicago, 20–24 November, 1991.

Shapiro, J. (1991). Transsexualism: Reflections on the persistence of gender and the mutability of sex. In J. Epstein & K. Straub (Eds.), *Body guards: The cultural politics of gender ambiguity,* pp. 248–279. New York: Routledge.

Sontag, S. (1970). Notes on camp. In S. Sontag, *Against interpretation and other essays.* New York: Dell.

Sun, Midnight. (1988). Sex/gender systems in native North America. In W. Roscoe (Ed.), *Living the spirit: A gay American Indian anthology,* p. 33. New York: St. Martin's Press.

Trumbach, R. (1992). London's Sapphists: From three sexes to four genders in the making of modern culture. In J. Epstein & K. Straub (Eds.), *Body guards: The cultural politics of gender ambiguity.* New York: Chapman and Hall.

Turner, V. (1967). *The forest of symbols; Aspects of Ndembu ritual.* Ithaca, NY: Cornell University Press.

Turner, V. (1972). *Dramas, fields, and metaphors: Symbolic action in human society.* Ithaca, NY: Cornell University Press.

Weston, K. (1991). *Families we choose: Lesbians, gays, kinship between men, between women.* New York: Columbia University Press.

Williams, W. (1986). *The spirit and the flesh: Sexual diversity in American Indian culture.* Boston: Beacon Press.

Blending Genders

Contributions to the Emerging Field
of Transgender Studies*

Richard Ekins

Dave King

*The naming or identifying of things is, then, a continual problem, never
really over and done with.*
—Anselm Strauss, *Mirrors and Masks,* 1977, p. 25

When we both (independently) began research in this area in the latter half
of the 1970s, the term "gender dysphoria" had been in use for some time.
In the United Kingdom, however, transsexualism and transvestism were in
more common use. Even now, more than 20 years on, transvestism and
transsexualism have not been expunged from the literature (Bockting &
Coleman, 1992b). The history of these terms and their conceptions has now
been fairly well documented (King, 1981, 1993).

At the time of the Second World War, "transvestism" had become the
preferred term and was used, across the literature, broadly enough to encompass those wishing to change sex through to the "automonosexual" fetishistic cross-dresser. With the wider availability of sex-reassignment procedures in the 1950s and 1960s, a term was required to specify those
"transvestites" who wished for and were suitable for such procedures. In
such cases, Benjamin's "transsexual" became the preferred term. It was not
until the late 1960s that the terms "transvestite" and "transsexual" and their
differentiation became standard throughout the literature.

No sooner had this happened, however, than these terms were being
superseded by the idea of "gender dysphoria" (Fisk, 1973). Although sometimes used synonymously with transsexualism, gender dysphoria represents
more than a change of terminology. The problem was that transsexualism

---

*An earlier version of this chapter was originally presented at the 14th Harry Ben-
jamin International Gender Dysphoria Symposium, Kloster Irsee, Germany, 7–10 September, 1995.

was too specific—it detailed a condition which only the patients' own accounts could demonstrate, and it specified a type of treatment (sex-reassignment surgery) (Fisk, 1973). Gender dysphoria is, by contrast, a very general descriptive term for a symptom. To say that a patient suffers from gender dysphoria is as noncommittal as saying a patient suffers from back pain or headaches. Further diagnosis and treatment is firmly retained in professional hands.

All of these terms have limitations for research from a sociological point of view. In the first place they presume pathology—things have gone wrong. We do not wish to deny the pain of those struggling with issues surrounding their gender identity, but social problems are not necessarily sociologists' problems. As Peter Berger (1963, pp. 49–50) put it:

> the sociological problem is not so much why some things "go wrong" . . . but how the whole system works in the first place . . . the fundamental sociological problem is not crime but the law, not divorce but marriage . . .

Secondly, they typically refer to a narrow range of cross-dressing/sex-changing phenomena—those which come to the attention of the medical profession. Other phenomena which might be of interest to the sociologist such as, for example, androgynous fashions in youth culture, are excluded. Either that or they are reduced—as anthropological and historical instances of cross-dressing and/or sex-changing often are—to mere examples of the modern condition. Whilst this may be satisfactory from a medical perspective, for the sociologist it removes from sight what may be radically different social characteristics.

Thirdly, when medical practitioners study transsexualism, for instance, they study the characteristics of those labelled with this condition. As sociologists, we may do the same, but we are also interested in looking at the behaviour of those medical practitioners, social workers, speech therapists, and others who, from a sociological point of view, are also part of what transsexualism means in our society.

From time to time we have therefore sought to use other terms such as "gender reversal," "gender mobility," and "gender migration." Others have written of "gender crossing" (Whitehead, 1981; Shapiro, 1991). When one of us (Ekins) founded the Trans-Gender Archive in 1986, that title was chosen to reflect the wide base of the archive, indicating that it was not confined to material relating to medical conditions. The term "transgender" has now come to have a number of connotations. It can refer to "any kind of dress and/or behaviour interpreted as 'transgressing' gender roles" (Raymond, 1994, xxv). It has been used more narrowly within the subculture as an umbrella term uniting transvestites and transsexuals as the "transgender community." More narrowly still, it has been used to refer to those who live full-time in the "opposite" gender but without surgery (Rudd, 1989, p. 134).

In the mid-1980s, the term "gender blender" could be found in the mass media. "Gender blending" was first used in an academic context by Devor to refer to females who "have clear female identities and know themselves to be women concurrently with gender presentations that often do not successfully communicate these facts to others" (1987, p. 12). Used in a much broader way, we think that the concept of a process of blending gender is a useful one. Blending has two basic meanings—to mix or combine, and to harmonise. The use of this term points to something important about what is going on. It also allows us to pursue our concerns with those who—in both senses—attempt to, or succeed in, blending various aspects of the culturally established components of gender, either in respect of themselves (e.g., transvestites, transsexuals, or whatever) or in respect of others (e.g., medicine, the mass media).

Gender is attributed to social actors by self and others (Kessler & McKenna, 1978), and is a fundamental element in the everyday presentation of self (Goffman, 1976; Cahill, 1989). Once a gender attribution has been made, expectations follow that an actor will display the "correct" blend of such things as dress and demeanour, sex-object choice, occupation, leisure-time activities, and so on. In theory, the whole of social life could be dichotomised by gender, but in practice, a lot of "incorrect" elements are allowed into the blend, particularly on an occasional and trivial level. More sustained and more fundamental blending of the elements themselves threaten the gender categories themselves. In most cultures this is problematic, although some authors argue that in some societies such as that of the North American Indians, a third gender category exists (Kessler & McKenna, 1978; Herdt, 1994). Connell (1987, p. 76) argues that some transsexuals who live openly as such in contemporary society may be seen in similar ways, as a "third" gender category.

Gender blending in the first sense—the mixing of various aspects of male and female gender—has been seen in contemporary industrial societies as a pathological phenomenon, properly apprehended within a medical discourse, or as a source of amusement to be conceptualised as entertainment. Gender blending in the second sense of harmonisation is, arguably, a psychological and cultural imperative. Thus, in their accounts, individuals seek to bring harmony to otherwise disparate elements (Ekins, 1993; King, 1993). Medical and other interventions in cases of transsexualism or intersexuality seek to harmonise gender identity, gender role, social status, the body, and so on. Media representations of transsexualism can be seen to be mainly concerned with the symbolic maintenance of the gender dichotomy (Pearce, 1981; Silverstone, 1982).

We have divided the remainder of this chapter into five parts. In each part, we comment on the major developments and current areas focused on by social scientists, and consider their implications for transgender studies.

Experiencing Gender Blending

A sociological approach certainly does not mean that individual experiences are of no interest. On the contrary, we both subscribe to a sociological tradition which emphasises a respect for and an intimate appreciation of the lives of the people we study. That is not to say that we simply report the lives of others, but it does mean that our analysis cannot be imposed from outside without regard to the way in which society's members make sense of their own lives. One of the sociologist's tasks is to relate individual experiences and biography to their historical and social context.

Prior to the categorisation and medicalisation of sexual "perversions" in the latter half of the nineteenth century, gender blending could be written about in terms of simple descriptions of enjoyable experience and preferred behaviour (Farrer, 1987, 1994). Medicalisation, however, brought with it new "pathologies," and the emergence of new identities. Increasingly, gender-blending experiences and behaviours were made sense of in terms of the categories of "science," most notably those of the "transvestite" and the "transsexual."

A concept that is widely used in sociological writings as a means of imposing an analytic order on experiences, actions, and identities over time is that of career (Abrams, 1982; Ekins, 1993, 1997). Its value lies in its incorporation of the ideas of movement, of development, of becoming, and of personal history. Furthermore, as Goffman (1961, p. 119) points out, it "allows one to move back and forth between the personal and the public, between the self and significant society," and is, therefore, peculiarly sociological. Ekins' use of the methodology of grounded theory leads him to reconceptualise the research arena of male cross-dressing and sex-changing in terms of the basic social process (Glaser, 1978) of "male femaling" (Ekins, 1993, 1997). His analysis considers the major modes of male femaling within a phased ideal-typical career path of the "male femaler" and indicates oscillations between the major facets of sex, sexuality, and gender frequently confronted in each phase. This approach enables the proper respect to be paid to the processual and emergent nature of much cross-dressing and sex-changing phenomena. In particular, the approach facilitates an exploration of neglected interrelations between sex, sexuality, and gender, with reference to the differing modes of femaling; to the categorisations of "transvestite" and "transsexual"; and to the constitution of "femaling" self and world as variously sexed, sexualised, and gendered.

In the past—and this is probably still true for most—the actions and emotions involved in gender blending have been confusing and often distressing. Adopting an identity which makes sense of things—"finding oneself," as it is sometimes put—can therefore be immensely liberating. As April Ashley put it, "You cannot imagine the comfort of knowing that one is *something,* and not merely monstrous" (Fallowell & Ashley, 1982, p. 76). Those whom we interviewed in the late 1970s and 1980s and into the 1990s did not doubt the existence of a special group of people characterised by a condition to which the terms "transvestite" and "transsexual" had some reference, despite doubts about their own or others' "correct" identity and despite some controversy over the central characteristics of the conditions. There were a number of aspects to this claimed identity or condition.

Firstly, it was endowed with a reality and a centrality which was denied to other aspects of their existence which by contrast, would be described as "not real," "an act," or peripheral to the "real self." In many cases, this real self was also a purely private self or one which only a small number of others were aware of. In some cases, the private "real" self had become harmonised with public identity through "changing sex."

Secondly, transvestism and transsexualism were seen as pervasive aspects of self. They were described as a part of the actor's nature of which they were "always" aware. In some cases, this pervasiveness also extended to actual effects on the person's lifestyle, for example, influencing choice of job or house, spending patterns, and, of course, in the case of some transsexuals, resulting in an almost total change of lifestyle and public identity.

A third aspect of this state of being, perhaps readily inferred from the foregoing, is the assumption of its permanence. Although some recalled believing at some time in the past that it was or could be temporary, perhaps conceptualising it as something which they would "grow out of," or which could be removed by therapy of some kind, at the time they were interviewed most were convinced that transvestism or transsexualism had been and would always be a central feature of their existence.

Finally, as an inherent and integral part of their nature, transvestism and transsexualism were seen as something over which they had little or no control. Whether childhood experiences or biological anomalies were cited as the cause, the emergence of their natures was not seen to be dependent on their own volition, and neither could it be effectively or permanently brought under their own control. Most informants reported periods of fighting "it," without any lasting success.

Their identities also contained a strand which related to conventional gender identities. Male transvestites might talk of expressing their feminine selves, and male-to-female transsexuals might see their quest for surgery as bringing their bodies into line with their gender identity as women. Transvestite and transsexual identities only made/make sense in relation to the conventional gender dichotomy.

These identities were also hidden identities. The male transsexual and the male transvestite in public seek to pass as women—not to be read as a transsexual or transvestite.

However, in the mid-1990s it appears that more people are experiencing gender blending in new ways and are devising new forms of identity. In contrast to the transsexual and transvestite identities, what is increasingly seen as the transgender identity breaks down the gender dichotomy by mixing and matching its characteristics in any combination. It is also a more open identity in that transgenderists may be perceived as neither male nor female. Pushed further, the idea of permanent, core identities and the idea of gender itself disappear. The emphasis today, at least in some parts of the literature, is on transience, fluidity, and performance. In Kate Bornstein's *Gender Outlaw,* she talks about "the ability to freely and knowingly become one or many of a limitless number of genders for any length of time, at any rate of change. Gender fluidity recognizes no borders or rules of gender. A fluid identity," she continues, "is one way to solve problems with boundaries. As a person's identity keeps shifting, so do individual borders and boundaries. It's hard to cross a boundary that keeps moving" (1994, p. 52; also quoted by Whittle, 1996). In this writing, however, the experiences and behaviours are made sense of in terms of the deconstructions of postmodernist cultural theory rather than from the standpoint of the experiences of cross-dressers and sex-changers themselves. In consequence, these writings have yet to make a substantial impact on the subjective experience of the vast majority of gender blenders. In that gender fluidity recognises no borders or "laws" of gender, the claim is to live "outside of gender" (Devor, 1987; Whittle, 1996) as "gender outlaws." Whether this can be sustained remains to be seen.

THE SOCIAL ORGANISATION OF GENDER BLENDING

Under certain conditions, subcultures or communities develop around shared spheres of activity. When that sphere of activity is considered deviant and is thus both unexpected and without moral sanction, there are additional pressures toward subcultural or communal formulations. When an activity is deviant, engaging in it carries additional problems such as those concerning access, secrecy, and guilt. A subculture can thus be seen to provide solutions to some of these problems. Deviant activities, to varying degrees, provoke a hostile response from others. Such condemnation can further contribute to the emergence of subcultural forms by reinforcing, alienating, and segregating deviant groups (Plummer, 1975).

The men who wrote to various publications about their experiences of wearing female clothing in the later years of the last century and the early years of this century (see Farrer, 1987, 1994) appear, in the main, to have pursued their activities in isolation from other men who were similarly engaged. There is some evidence that around this time a number of informal networks of cross-dressers were emerging, but it was not until the 1960s that these became more formalised and extensive (King, 1993, chapter 5). The male femalers who provided the material on which Richard Ekins' analysis (1993, 1997) is based had available a wide range of organisations and settings in which to pursue their activities along with others in similar situations. By contrast, there has been little available to the "female maler," who has often been forced to carve a small niche in the world of the male femaler. This is reflected in the literature, which is almost exclusively concerned with male femalers. In that literature we can discern two types of community.

The first type of community covers a range of small communities which seem to be centrally concerned with doing rather than being, with celebrating and enjoying the artistic possibilities and the pleasures of cross-dressing and its associated sexual and other activities. In some cases, such communities may be occupational ones concerned with, for example, prostitution (Perkins, 1983) or female impersonation (Newton, 1979). Some may be geographically located in those areas associated with deviant sexuality which are to be found in most large cities—Soho in London, King's Cross in Sydney, the Tenderloin in San Francisco.

The members of these communities are full-time "outsiders," living out their gender "deviance" in "deviant" ways—stripping, engaging in prostitution, performing as female impersonators in bars and nightclubs (Driscoll, 1971; Kando, 1973). They may also be involved in drug use or petty theft. This type of community is not consciously organised as such, although particular aspects of it will obviously require organisation of some kind. It depends primarily on face-to-face contact; it is not literate, in the sense that its members are concerned more with enjoyment, expression, or practice than analysis or remote communication. The "outpourings" of such a culture are in the form and language of art—for example, the photograph (Goldin, Armstrong & Keller, 1993; Kay, 1976; Kirk & Heath, 1984; Berg, 1982; Mark, 1982; Newman, 1984) and the novel (Rechy, 1964; Marlowe, 1965).

The second type of community is that described by Feinbloom (1976), Talamini (1982), and Woodhouse (1989). This is not delineated by a geographical area, and its members are not full-time "outsiders." They come together because they feel they share a common problem, one which is often hidden from the members of the other social worlds within which the major part of their lives is lived. If and when their lives do become organised around their gender deviance, this happens still within "respectable" worlds, not the "underworld" of prostitution or stripping. This community is more centrally concerned with individual being or identity. It has been consciously engineered in relation to the terms supplied by modern medicine. It is a literate community, since one of its central characteristics is the production of written accounts of its aims, its policies, and its activities. It does not depend on face-to-face contact (although this does, of course, take place), since membership depends not on doing but on identity. It is possible to live in remote parts, never meet another member, yet to feel a part of a community to which one is linked by the written word. Such a community is thus less locally based than the first type and its potential membership much larger. It forms a national and even international network of those who identify with the terms "transvestite" or "transsexual."

During the 1990s, but with roots reaching back earlier, some changes have taken place. The two types of communities mentioned above continue, but currently commentators have drawn attention to a number of changes.

First is the emergence of a greater diversity of transgendered people not conforming simply to the transvestite/transsexual patterns and associations created to cater for them. As Whittle puts it, "There is now a plethora of groups catering for a significant level of diversity in cross-gendered behaviour (1996; see also Bolin, 1994, and in this volume).

Secondly, at the same time as there is an acknowledgement of diversity, there also appears to be developing a greater sense of unity. So writers now comment on the "transgender community," and this is sometimes seen to extend into the gay community (see MacKenzie, 1994; Whittle, 1996).

Third is the greater visibility of transgendered people as a permanent status or "third sex." Formerly, the transsexual ideal was to disappear into the other gender and to be known simply as a man or a woman. Transvestites typically pursued their activities in solitude or in safe, private venues (Bolin, 1994, and this volume; MacKenzie, 1994).

Fourth is the greater involvement of transgenderists in gender and sexual politics both in the practical and theoretical senses. This has become possible as a result of the changes detailed above and also as a result of the changing view of the political significance of transgenderism (Bolin, 1994, and this volume; MacKenzie, 1994). The influence of writers such as Janice Raymond effectively silenced transgenderists for many years, as it did other groups whose behaviours or views were not seen as politically correct (Whittle, 1996).

The Medicalisation of Gender Blending

What ethnomethodologists call the "natural attitude" toward gender (Garfinkel, 1967, pp. 122–128; Kessler & McKenna, 1978, pp. 113–114) assumes that all human beings will belong to one of two discrete categories permanently determined on the basis of biological ("naturally" given) sex characteristics. Congruence is expected both within and between a person's sex and gender. Congruence is also expected between these two areas and a persons' sexuality with the "default" assumption being probably—even in the 1990s—that this will be heterosexual. These are expectations in both cognitive (this is how things are) and normative (this is how things should be) senses.

Any breach of these expectations is therefore a potential threat to this aspect of what constitutes our reality. In the face of threats such as these, societies

> develop a conceptual machinery to account for such deviations and to maintain the realities thus challenged. This requires a body of knowledge that includes a theory of deviance, a diagnostic apparatus, and a conceptual system for the "cure of souls."
> —Berger & Luckmann, 1966, p. 131.

In contemporary industrial societies, the institution of medicine has assumed or been given the task of maintaining this aspect of our reality, just as many phenomena have become "medicalised" (Conrad & Schneider, 1980). The innocence with which the men discussed by Peter Farrer (1987, 1994) pursued their activities is now no longer possible. Medicine has provided us with a language through which the activities of such men are apprehended as pathologies which can be diagnosed, treated, and perhaps ultimately prevented. So now, medical perspectives stand out as the culturally major lens through which gender blending may be viewed in our society. Other perspectives must take medical perspectives into account, whether they ultimately incorporate, extend, or reject them.

The history of medical intervention in this area has stretched over little more than a hundred years. This history discloses much controversy over the nature of "transvestism" and "transsexualism," and particularly over the appropriate methods of dealing with the latter. Since the late 1940s, when the endocrinological and surgical means to "change sex" became widely available, transsexualism has dominated the literature with some practitioners advocating physical or psychological methods directed at removal of the transsexual's "pathological" wishes and desires, and others being willing to facilitate a "change of sex" in what are regarded as appropriate cases. Both approaches can be regarded as seeking to restore harmony in a situation of discord. Both are, in different ways (and this is also true of the patients who seek out the practitioners of these approaches) seeking to ensure that identity, social status, and biology "match." The end result is that the binary structure of gender is maintained.

The dominant medical position is that transsexualism is a "given" disorder which has been discovered. Several critics from outside the profession (Birrell & Cole, 1990; Eichler, 1980; Raymond, 1979; Sagarin, 1978) and some within it (Socarides, 1969, 1977; Szasz, 1980) have argued in contrast that transsexualism has been invented. The medical conception of transsexualism is, it is claimed, an illusion, a fabrication whose explanation must therefore be sought in terms other than the putative "thing" itself. Once conjured up, legitimated, and disseminated, this illusion has real social consequences through the actions of members of the medical profession, "transsexuals" themselves, and other members of society, all of whom have been seduced into believing in it. The invention of transsexualism is said to serve the interests of men and patriarchal society (Raymond, 1979) or capitalism (Billings & Urban, 1982) or both, depending on whose account you read. Whilst we certainly would not deny the need for a critical/skeptical stance towards medical or any other categories, we have argued elsewhere (King, 1987, 1993) that the arguments of Raymond, Billings and Urban, and others are flawed and do not accord with empirical reality.

In what ways has medical practice changed during the 1980s and into the 1990s? What transsexuals wanted, in the past, was to slip invisibly into the other gender—to assimilate. Transvestites wanted to be "cured" if they came to the medical profession, or, if they were comfortable with the idea, they wanted to be able to cross-dress without being seen to do so: to remain in private settings, or to pass in public. With regard to transsexuals, medicine either helped them to cross over completely or remain where they were. Much the same was true with regard to the medical approach to intersexual conditions: patients had to be one or the other; they could not remain in-between (Fausto-Sterling, 1993). Fausto-Sterling suggests that maybe we should accept what she calls sexual multiplicity instead of shoehorning people into one or the other of the two available sexes. We know of at least one group of intersexual people who are now campaigning for just that—the Intersex Society of North America. Something similar seems to be occurring in the transgender field. Bolin (1994, and this volume), for example, argues that one factor which facilitated the emergence of a transgender category was what she calls "the widespread closure of university-affiliated gender clinics in the 1980s." Such clinics, in selecting patients for sex-reassignment surgery, had enforced the segregation of transvestites and transsexuals and the latter's conformity to conventional sex/gender dichotomies. The reduction in the number of such clinics, she argues, left a small number of non–university-affiliated "client-centered" clinics which contributed to "greater flexibility in the expression of gender identities" (Bolin, 1994, p. 463, and this volume).

This apparent shift in power may perhaps be reflected in Bockting and Coleman's use of the term gender-dysphoria "client" rather than patient. Such clients, they claim, "often have a more ambiguous gender identity and are more ambivalent about a gender-role transition than they initially admit (1992a, p. 143). Their treatment program allows their clients, they say, to "discover and express their unique identity" (1992a, p. 143) and "allows for individuals to identify as neither man or woman, but as someone whose identity transcends the culturally sanctioned dichotomy (1992a, p. 144).

Gender Blending and the Media

The medical and psychological literature dealing with cross-dressing and sex-changing is probably larger than the prevalence of these phenomena would lead one to expect (Hoenig, 1985). The coverage of these topics by the mass media is probably even greater again, and certainly reaches a wider audience than does the medical and psychological literature.

The terrain covered by the media is not the same as that covered by medical practice. There is some overlap, but media interest does not begin or end with the medical categories of transvestism or transsexualism. Transgressing the boundaries between the categories of male and female, in whatever way, seems to be always of interest to the media. However, medicine has become the culturally major lens through which gender blending is viewed in modern Western societies. So, whilst the media do not simply reproduce medical knowledge, this perspective has had a major impact on the media treatment of gender blending.

As one moves out from the few medical and psychological specialists in "gender identity disorders"—through specialists in other psychosexual areas, psychiatrists and other medical professionals—to lay members of society, it becomes probable that "knowledge" of cross-dressing and sex-changing is framed less and less by the medical literature and more and more by the mass media. There are grounds, then, for regarding the media as potentially having the greater influence on the conceptions of these phenomena held by the general public, the largest part of the medical profession, and many of those who themselves cross-dress or sex-change.

Given the secrecy that is imposed on those whose gender or sexuality falls outside the mainstream, it is not surprising that the media play an important role in helping them to gain a degree of understanding—"assembling their stories"—as Plummer calls it (1994). In the stories of transsexuals in particular, encounters with media reports occur frequently and are accorded some significance. Mark Rees, a female-to-male transsexual, describes the impact a newspaper article had on him:

> In 1969, four years after my WRNS' discharge, I chanced to see an article in *The Times* of London which described the condition of transsexualism. It was a moment of enlightenment; at last it all fitted into place. I was transsexual.
>
> —Rees, 1996

Such writers credit media reports with a profound effect on their understanding of themselves. In the reports, they find clarification of puzzling thoughts, feelings, and behaviour; they find the suggestion of a possible solution to their problems; and some even find enough practical information to begin to reach that solution.

This is not a state of affairs that is welcomed by some writers. Sagarin (1978), Raymond (1979, 1994), and Billings and Urban (1982), who have been critical of the role of medicine in relation to transsexualism, have argued (complained?) that the American media, pushed by a greedy medical profession and self-interested transsexual groups, have induced us to believe that transsexualism is a legitimate medical condition which can best be managed by sex reassignment. However, as we have argued elsewhere (King, 1987, 1993), in Britain, the media present a more complex picture of changing sex and cross-dressing, one which does not simply reproduce medical perspectives, and one which is not universally favourable.

In addition to encouraging positive attitudes toward transsexualism and changing sex, Billings and Urban (1982), Birrell and Cole (1990), and

Raymond (1979) argue that one of the wider consequences of the media dissemination of current conceptions of and responses to gender dysphoria is, by affirming the link between sex and gender, a reinforcement of an oppressive gender system. In a similar vein, Garber (1992) argues, with regard to the discussion of the motives of Billy Tipton, a jazz musician known as a man, but who was discovered upon his death to have a female body, that "such normalization reinstates the binary (male/female)" and "recuperates social and sexual norms" (Garber, 1992, p. 69).

It is not possible to disagree: behind all the various press, television, and radio reports of cross-dressing and sex-changing, and informing all the novels, films, and stage plays which deal with these themes, there is a necessary backdrop—a system of two gender categories, based on sex and distinguished by "appropriate" dress, mannerisms, and many other characteristics. The "self-evidence" of this system is what gives the media content any point at all. Only on this basis can the producer and consumer make sense of it. However, this is true of all media content, and not only that fraction which is concerned with gender blending in some way.

What may now perhaps be thought of as the traditional mass media, the press and television in particular, continue to present us with personal stories and scandals, much as they have done since the 1950s. Alongside this, though, are occasional new themes. Thus, a recent British documentary looked at the idea of a "third sex" (QED, BBC1, 1994). The press and television, in the form of teletext, has also come to provide us with "contact services," and gender blenders are to be found there. The telephone has come to take on new roles in the late 1980s and 1990s. Like the press and teletext, the telephone has, with the development of "chat lines" provided new methods of contact for gender blenders. Pre-recorded material may be accessed for medical advice and other information as well as pornography (Ekins, 1996). An interesting question is whether such ways of making contact with others are superseding or supplementing the organised groupings. The latter, though, are beginning to make use of the growing availability of computer networks.

GENDER BLENDING AND GENDER POLITICS

Until the late 1960s, to write of the political aspects of gender blending would have made little sense. However, with the second wave of feminism and a new focus on the myriad dimensions of gender, it became possible to conceive of ways in which the apparently private practices of cross-dressing and sex-changing could have political significance.

In the era of the Gay Liberation Front in the early 1970s, "it seemed to many homosexuals that a new day was dawning, ushering in an era of spontaneity, openness, and liberation (Weeks, 1977, p. 185). In retrospect, it seems that what was initially the transvestite/transsexual community emerged too late to benefit greatly from the period of "liberation." By 1974, the end of the gay-liberation period, cross-dressers and sex-changers were only just struggling to reach the position from which their gay counterparts had begun. Whilst there were some small groupings which showed a willingness to engage with these issues being raised by the gay and women's movements, the importance of these radical groupings, like those of the more conservative ones, probably lay in their provision of a means whereby gender blenders could come together and forge identities as transvestites and transsexuals.

In the mid-1970s, the largest and most influential organisations for transvestites and transsexuals were the American Foundation for Full Personality Expression (FPE) and its many offshoots, such as the British Beaumont Society (King, 1993) or the Australian Seahorse Club, all of which were criticised by sections of the gay and women's movements as well as by other transvestites and transsexuals (Brake, 1976; Weeks, 1977, pp. 224–225). These organisations were attacked for their failure to engage openly in sexual politics; for their low-profile "closed closet" form; for their support of conventional norms and structures such as marriage and the family; for their portrayal, in the image of women portrayed by members and in their publications, of traditional sexual stereotypes; and for their attempt to normalise transvestism by excluding from or denying the presence within their membership of, for example, transsexuals, homosexuals, or fetishists.

Despite a few dissenting views such as those of Brake, who, in an article originally given as a conference paper in 1974, noted that transsexuals and transvestites whose "oppression is similar to that experienced by gay men and all women" (1976, p. 187) could be perceived as "revolutionaries who publicly challenge the notion of ascribed gender" (Brake, 1976, p. 188), the prevailing view came to be that cross-dressing and sex-changing were conservative, reinforcing traditional gender roles and (in the case of transsexualism), reinforcing the link between gender and biology.

By the end of the 1970s, transsexualism was seen by some writers to have increasing political significance. Raymond (1979, 1994) is the best-known exponent of these views. She argues that transsexuals are among the victims of patriarchal society and its definitions of masculinity and femininity. By creating transsexualism and treating it by means of sex change, the political and social sources of the "transsexuals'" suffering are obscured. Instead, transsexualism is conceptualised as an individual problem for which an individual solution is devised. By means of this illegitimate medicalisation, then, the "real" problem remains unaddressed. Medicalisation also serves to "domesticate the revolutionary potential of transsexuals" who are "deprived of an alternative framework in which to view the problem" (p. 124).

Raymond also sees other reasons for the creation of transsexualism and sex-change surgery. She places these alongside "other male interventionist technologies such as cloning, test-tube fertilisation, and sex selection" as an "attempt to wrest from women, the power inherent in female biology" (p. xvi) or "an attempt to replace biological women" (p. 140). She also sees "gender identity clinics" where transsexuals are "treated" as prototypical "sex-role control centers" (p. 136). Thus, transsexualism is not merely another example of the pervasive effects of patriarchal attitudes—it actually constitutes an attack on women. "Transsexualism constitutes a sociopolitical program that is undercutting the movement to eradicate sex role stereotyping and oppression in this culture" (p. 5). Views such as this were used, for many years, to legitimate violence toward transsexuals and effectively silence the production of any dissenting views within the academy.

In contrast, crossing the gender border is now seen by some as subversive, transgressive. Recently, Garber (1992, p. 17), for example, has argued that "transvestism is a space of possibility structuring and confounding culture: the disruptive element that intervenes, not just a category crisis of male and female, but a crisis of category itself." Similarly, Anne Bolin (1994, p. 485, and this volume) argues that the transgenderist "harbors great potential to deactivate gender or to create in the future the possibility of 'supernumerary' genders as social categories no longer based on biology." This is because of its "decoupling of physiological sex, gender identity, and sexuality" (p. 483).

CONCLUSION

Gender blending is not a static phenomenon which remains unchanged as we look at it from different perspectives. At times, the perspectives we use can have a major impact on its nature, as many writers have argued the medical gaze has had. Moreover, as a social and cultural practice, it changes as a result of other dynamics. Over the past 10–15 years, gender blending has become more complex and diverse. It has also been subjected to some reassessments and new interpretations of its political significance. For some, the issue of transsexualism has been largely superseded by debates over transgenderism or what has been called "sexuality's newest cutting edge" (Raymond, 1994, xxv). In particular, gender blending has achieved a position of prominence in a number of recent contributions to cultural studies and in what has come to be known as "queer theory." This, according to

Segal (1994, p. 188) "seeks to transcend and erode the central binary divisions of male/female, heterosexual/homosexual in the construction of modern sexualities."

Once this move is made, however, the tension in the umbrella term "gender blending" becomes apparent. As Plummer (1996) points out, "Gender blending . . . might imply that a core gender exists that can be mixed, merged, and matched." On the other hand, it might refer to those "'blenders' who transcend, transgress, and threaten," with a view to living "beyond gender." In each of the areas we have considered, we have traced a shift from the former to the latter. This shift, as we might expect, is difficult to discern in the conservative areas of medicalisation and the mass media, and most obvious in the radical political and cultural literature. The status of the shift is perhaps most problematic in the areas of "experiencing" and social organisation.

We have found the term "gender blending" useful to organise our thoughts on some key areas in the emerging field of transgender studies. The particular advantage of the term is that it enables a polyvalent stance to be taken on the study of both those who themselves gender blend, and those who blend the gender of others. In particular, the concept of "blending genders" allows for a sensitive treatment of individuals who are attempting to harmonise gender, and it opens up for enquiry the medical profession's attempt to do likewise.

ACKNOWLEDGMENT

Our thanks to Wendy Saunderson, whose rigorous suggestions and support provided invaluable assistance.

REFERENCES

Abrams, P. (1982). *Historical sociology.* Shepton Mallet: Open Books.

Berg, A. (1982). *Creatures.* Paris: Pink Star Editions.

Berger, P. (1963). *Invitation to sociology: A humanistic perspective.* Harmondsworth, UK: Penguin.

Berger, P., & Luckmann, T. (1966). *The social construction of reality: A treatise in the sociology of knowledge.* Garden City, NY: Doubleday.

Billings, D.B., & Urban, T. (1982). The socio-medical construction of transsexualism: An interpretation and critique. *Social Problems, 29*(3), 266–282.

Birrell, S., & Cole, C.L. (1990). Double fault: Renee Richards and the construction and naturalization of difference. *Sociology of Sport Journal, 7*(1), 1–21.

Bockting, W.O., & Coleman, E. (1992a). A comprehensive approach to the treatment of gender dysphoria. In W.O. Bockting & E. Coleman (Eds.), *Gender dysphoria: Interdisciplinary approaches to clinical management,* pp. 131–155. New York: Haworth.

Bockting, W.O., & E. Coleman, E. (Eds.). (1992b). *Gender dysphoria: Interdisciplinary approaches to clinical management.* New York: Haworth.

Bolin, A. (1994). Transcending and transgendering: Male-to-female transsexuals, dichotomy, and diversity. In G. Herdt (Ed.), *Third sex, third gender: Essays from anthropology and social history,* pp. 447–485. New York: Zone Publishing.

Bornstein, K. (1994). *Gender outlaw: On men, women, and the rest of us.* New York: Routledge.

Brake, M. (1976). I may be a queer, but at least I am a man: Male hegemony and ascribed versus achieved gender. In D.L. Barker & S. Allen (Eds.), *Sexual divisions in society: Process and change.* London: Tavistock.

Cahill, S.E. (1989). Fashioning males and females: Appearance and the social reproduction of gender. *Symbolic Interactionism, 12*(2), 281–298.

Connell, R.W. (1987). *Gender and power.* Oxford: Blackwell.

Conrad, P., & Schneider, J.W. (1980). *Deviance and medicalisation.* London: C.V. Mosby.

Devor, H. (1987). Gender blending females: Women and sometimes men. *American Behavioral Scientist, 31*(1), 12–39.

Devor, H. (1989). *Gender blending: Confronting the limits of duality.* Bloomington: Indiana University Press.

Driscoll, J.P. (1971). Transsexuals. *Transaction,* Special Supplement, *8*(5–6), 28–37, 66, 68.

Eichler, M. (1980). *The double standard: A feminist critique of feminist social science.* London: Croom Helm.

Ekins, R. (1993). On male femaling: A grounded theory approach to cross-dressing and sex-changing. *Sociological Review, 41*(1), 1–29.

Ekins, R. (1996). Male femaling, telephone sex, and the case of intimacy scripts. In R. Ekins & D. King (Eds.), *Blending genders: Social aspects of cross-dressing and sex-changing.* London: Routledge.

Ekins, R. (1997). *Male femaling: A grounded theory approach to cross-dressing and sex-changing.* London: Routledge.

Epstein, J., & Straub, K. (Eds.). (1992). *Body guards: The cultural politics of gender ambiguity.* New York: Chapman & Hall.

Fallowell, D., & Ashley, A. (1982). *April Ashley's odyssey.* London: Jonathan Cape.

Farrer, P. (Ed.). (1987). *Men in petticoats: A selection of letters from Victorian newspapers.* Liverpool: Karn Publications.

Farrer, P. (1994). *Borrowed plumes: Letters from Edwardian newspapers on male crossdressing.* Liverpool: Karn Publications.

Fausto-Sterling, A. (1993, March/April). The five sexes: Why male and female are not enough. *The Sciences,* 20–25.

Feinbloom, D. (1976). *Transvestites and transsexuals: Mixed views.* New York: Delacorte Press.

Fisk, N. (1973). Gender dysphoria syndrome (the how, what and why of a disease). In D. Laub & P. Gandy (Eds.), *Proceedings of the Second Interdisciplinary Symposium on Gender Dysphoria Syndrome,* pp. 7–14. Palo Alto, CA: Stanford University Medical Center.

Garber, M. (1992). *Vested interests: Cross-dressing and cultural anxiety.* New York: Routledge.

Garfinkel, H. (1967). *Studies in ethnomethodology.* Englewood Cliffs, NJ: Prentice-Hall.

Glaser, B. (1978). *Theoretical sensitivity: Advances in the methodology of grounded theory.* Mill Valley, CA: Sociology Press.

Goffman, E. (1961). *Asylums: Essays on the social situation of mental patients and other inmates.* New York: Doubleday.

Goffman, E. (1976). *Gender advertisements.* New York: Harper Colophon.

Goldin, N. (with Armstrong, D., & Keller, W.). (1993). *The other side.* New York: Scalo Press.

Herdt, G. (Ed.). (1994). *Third sex, third gender: Essays from anthropology and social history.* New York: Zone Books.

Hoenig, J. (1985). Transsexualism in the arts. In B.M. Steiner (Ed.), *Gender dysphoria: Development, research, management*, pp. 411–416. New York: Plenum Press.

I.C.S.T.I.S. (1993). *The Independent Committee for the Supervision of Standards of Telephone Information Services: Activity report*. [U.K.]

Kando, T. (1973). *Sex change: The achievement of gender identity among feminized transsexuals*. Springfield, IL: Charles C. Thomas, Publishers.

Kay, B. (1976). *The other women*. London: Matthews Miller Dunbar.

Kessler, S.J., & McKenna, W. (1978). *Gender: An ethnomethodological approach*. New York: John Wiley & Sons. Reprinted in 1985 by The University of Chicago Press.

King, D. (1981). Gender confusions: Psychological and psychiatric conceptions of transvestism and transsexualism. In K. Plummer (Ed.), *The making of the modern homosexual*. London: Hutchinson.

King, D. (1987). Social constructionism and medical knowledge: The case of transsexualism. *Sociology of Health and Illness, 9*(4), 352–377.

King, D. (1993). *The transvestite and the transsexual: Public categories and private identities*. Brookfield, VT: Ashgate Publishing Co.

Kirk, K., & Heath, E. (1984). *Men in frocks*. London: GMP Publishers, Ltd.

MacKenzie, G.O. (1994). *Transgender nation*. Bowling Green, OH: Bowling Green University Popular Press.

Mark, M.W. (1982). *Falkland Road*. London: Thames & Hudson.

Marlowe, K. (1965). *Mr. Madam: Confessions of a male madam*. Los Angeles: Sherbourne Press.

Newman, B. (1984). *The ultimate angels*. London: Hutchinson.

Newton, E. (1979). *Mother camp: Female impersonators in America*. Chicago: University of Chicago Press.

Pearce, F. (1981). The British press and the "placing" of male homosexuality. In S. Cohen & J. Young (Eds.), *The manufacture of news: Deviance, social problems, and the mass media*. London: Constable.

Perkins, R. (1983). *The drag queen scene: Transsexuals in King's Cross*. Hemel Hempstead: Allen & Unwin.

Plummer, K. (1975). *Sexual stigma: An interactionist account*. London: Routledge & Kegan Paul.

Plummer, K. (1994). *Telling sexual stories: Power, change, and social worlds*. London: Routledge.

Plummer, K. (1996). Foreword. In R. Ekins & D. King (Eds.), *Blending genders: Social aspects of cross-dressing and sex-changing*. London: Routledge.

Raymond, J. (1979). *The transsexual empire: The making of the she-male*. Boston: Beacon Press.

Raymond, J. (1994). *The transsexual empire: The making of the she-male* (2nd Ed.). New York: Teacher's College Press.

Rechy, J. (1964). *City of night*. London: MacGibbon & Kee.

Rees, M. (1996). Becoming a man: The personal account of a female-to-male transsexual. In R. Ekins & D. King (Eds.), *Blending genders: Social aspects of cross-dressing and sex-changing*. London: Routledge.

Rudd, P. (1989). *My husband wears my clothes: Crossdressing from the perspective of a wife*. Katy, TX: PM Publishers.

Sagarin, E. (1978). Transsexualism: Legitimation, amplification, and exploitation of deviance by scientists and mass media. In C. Winck (Ed.), *Deviance and mass media*. Beverly Hills, CA: Sage.

Segal, L. (1994). *Straight sex: The politics of pleasure*. London: Virago.

Shapiro, J. (1991). Transsexualism: Reflections on the persistence of gender and the mutability of sex. In J. Epstein and K. Straub (Eds.), *Body guards: The cultural politics of gender ambiguity*. New York: Routledge.

Silverstone, R. (1982). A structure for a modern myth: Television and the transsexual. *Semiotica, 49*(1–2), 95–138.

Socarides, C.W. (1969). The desire for sexual transformation: A psychiatric evaluation of transsexualism. *American Journal of Psychiatry, 125*(10), 1419–1425.

Socarides, C.W. (1977). *Beyond sexual freedom.* New York: Quadrangle Books/New York Times Book Company.

Strauss, A.L. (1977). *Mirrors and masks.* London: Martin Robertson.

Szasz, T. (1980). *Sex: Facts, fraud, and follies.* Oxford: Blackwell.

Talamini, J.T. (1982). *Boys will be girls: The hidden world of the heterosexual male transvestite.* Lanham, MD: University Press of America, Inc.

Third sex. (1994, 24 March). (Television program). QED, BBC1, UK.

Weeks, J. (1977). *Coming out: Homosexual politics in Britain from the 19th century to the present.* London: Quartet Books.

Whitehead, H. (1981). The bow and the burden strap: A new look at institutionalized homosexuality in native North Americans. In: S. Ortner & H. Whitehead (Eds.), *Sexual meanings: The cultural construction of gender and sexuality,* pp. 80–115. Cambridge, MA: Cambridge University Press.

Whittle, S. (1996). Gender fucking or fucking gender? Current cultural contributions to theories of gender blending. In R. Ekins & D. King (Eds.), *Blending genders: Social aspects of cross-dressing and sex-changing.* London: Routledge.

Woodhouse, A. (1989) *Fantastic women: Sex, gender and transvestism.* Basingstoke: Macmillan Education.

8 FEARFUL OTHERS

MEDICO-PSYCHOLOGICAL CONSTRUCTIONS OF FEMALE-TO-MALE TRANSGENDERISM

Jason Cromwell

> *To date, the literature reflects the male-female discrepancy in the sex ratio*
> *of this population and consequently a much greater body of information is*
> *available on male-to-female transsexuals.*[1]
>
> —Bolin, 1988, p. 3

> *(I will consider female-to-male transsexuals in another paper.)*
> —Stone, 1991, p. 284

> *Transvestism in women . . . is so rare it is almost nonexistent.*
> —Stoller, 1982, p. 99

> *[F]emale-to-male transsexuals . . . are a relatively homogeneous group.*
> —Steiner, 1985, p. 3

The above are only a few examples of the marginal treatment of female-to-male transsexuals and female transvestites.[2] Perhaps, at least in the vast literature concerning transsexuals, transvestites, and gender variance in general, Janice Raymond is correct in her estimation that female-to-male transsexuals are "tokens" designed to validate transsexualism as a human phenomenon (1979, p. xxi).

In many societies women, children, racial and ethnic minorities, gender and sexual minorities are constructed as "Others" by those in power. Individuals become a group or a class of people: all women are . . . children are . . . certain races are. . . . Like the epigraphs selected for this paper, such statements deny the lived experiences of individuals. Experiences are denied as a result of the discourses which construct them. Transvestism and transsexualism are constructed from a male perspective and are about male gender variance.

Analogous to early sexologists' construction of female sexuality in general and lesbianism in particular, female gender diversity has been viewed through male-focused lenses. But as women, whether feminists or not, have illustrated, the constructed discourses create/d a paradox of individuals' lived experiences.

> The paradox of a being that is at once captive and absent in discourse, constantly spoken of but itself inaudible or inexpressible, displayed as spectacle and still unrepresented or unrepresentable, invisible yet constituted as the object and the guarantee of vision; a being whose existence and specificity are simultaneously asserted and denied, negated and controlled. . . .
>
> —De Lauretis, 1990, p. 115

Although Teresa De Lauretis' statement is addressing the "non-being of woman" it is applicable to the paradox of female gender diversity.

My purpose in this paper is to examine the paradoxes and to critique the dominant discourses concerning female gender variance. My critique will focus on the construction of the medical/mental illness model of medico-psychological discourses, which, with its assumptions and biases, fails to account for the heterogeneity of female gender diversity.

Sandy Stone notes that polyvocality is needed to develop "a deeper analytical language for transsexual theory" (Stone, 1991, p. 29). Thus, my critique is delineated by providing multiple voices—mine, as an anthropologist and as an FTM who has worked with transsexuals and transvestites for eight years, and voices from the individuals themselves. The individuals' voices have come from conversations, letters, and the responses to a questionnaire I designed and distributed through *FTM*, the newsletter of FTM International, a support organization for female-to-male transsexual people and female transvestites.[3] The voices are used here in most cases as a contrast to medico-psychological discourses about transvestism and transsexualism. My selection of voices reveals two of my assumptions: first is my belief that because transvestites and transsexuals do not conform to gender stereotypes, they are constructed as pathological; and second, that for many individuals, crossing the gender borders is normal, not pathological.

The imposition of the dominant order does not end with the biophysically ambiguous. Despite individual variations, the sex/gender order imposes standards of normalcy on each and every one of us, thus

. . . the cultural norm is always the arbiter of what is "appropriate," "natural," and, ultimately, "good." There is an unarticulated assumption that men should be stereotypically masculine, women stereotypically feminine, and both heterosexually oriented. Deviations from this standard of normality are received with varying degrees of tolerance. . . .

—Irvine, 1990, p. 237

The assumptions noted above by Irvine are very clearly articulated.

When I first started living as a man, an older male-to-female transsexual told me that if I wanted to succeed as a man, I needed to quit crossing my legs at the knees; I should never say words like "cute"; I should only wear somber clothes: no reds, purples, flowery prints and the like; and I should get a man's job like carpentry, engineering, or mechanics.

—27-year-old teacher of disabled children

I'm tired of having to present strictly conventional male signals or behavior, even if these go against the grain. How many men of my generation prefer long hair and aren't questioned as I am? Or are downright unhealthy, like stuffing all feelings or taking a sexist attitude toward women?

—37-year-old artist

The messages for conformity to stereotypic behaviors bombard us, transsexual and nontranssexual alike, from everywhere.

FEARFUL OTHERS

Carroll Smith-Rosenberg comprehends that "the fearful project onto the bodies of those they have named social misfits their own desire for social control" (Smith-Rosenberg, 1989, p. 103). Thus, in the early nineteenth century, the female individual who rejected the traditional female role by cross-dressing would be constructed by sexologists as an "unstable, incoherent subject, the embodiment of disorder, the fearful Other" (Smith-Rosenberg, 1989, p. 110). Smith-Rosenberg points out that the focus of early studies by sexologists was on behaviors and physical appearances (p. 113). This focus on appearances and behaviors is germane to the present medico-psychological discourses. Although Smith-Rosenberg's discussion is limited to a specific historical period in Western culture, it still remains that those individuals who do not conform to the sexed/gendered order are feared by many people.

Fearful Others are feared precisely because observers do not have control over the signs of sex and gender. In other words, without being aware of it, observers can be "fooled" by outward signs.

> I consider myself androgynous and I intentionally dress ambiguously. It doesn't matter how people perceive me. If I'm taken as a man then I'm a man. If I'm taken as a woman then I'm a woman. I'm comfortable either way and I like to play with people's perceptions.
>
> —27-year-old software engineer

While some individuals are comfortable with their ambiguity, and even play with it, there are frequently costs for non-conformity, for being a fearful Other. One cost is ridicule:

> I was always called a freak and tomboy—among other things—by my family.
>
> —Letter

An extreme cost is brutal violence.

> I got jumped at a straight bar. They called me lesbian and kept saying stuff. I tried to ignore it; left the bar and went to my truck. Two women and two men jumped me, using a crowbar. My friends came over to my truck to see why I hadn't followed them. They found me lying next to my truck with blood covering my face. One of my friends went into the bar to call an ambulance and the cops, but they wouldn't let her. They told her to just let me die. I now have scars from 22 stitches in my forehead, 13 in my jaw and 7 in my skull.
>
> —Letter

Although the above-cited individual perceives himself as a man, his observers perceived him as a lesbian. For some men and women, lesbians are feared because they are a threat to the heterosexual order. Both behavior and sexual identity are linked to gender in most people's minds. Social norms insist that men are males with masculine behaviors and a sexual preference for women; women are females with feminine behaviors and a sexual preference for men (Irvine, 1990). Gay men, lesbians, transvestites, transsexuals, and others who live in gender borderlands[4] challenge the traditional concepts of maleness, femaleness, masculinity, and femininity, and, as such, they become fearful Others.[5] Because those on the gender borderlands challenge traditional concepts, many societies try to eliminate them out of internalized fear of "being different, being other, and therefore lesser, therefore subhuman, in-human, non-human" (Anzaldúa, 1987, p. 18).

Like gay men and lesbians, individuals (whether they identify as transvestite, transsexual, transgender, androgynous, gender blender, gender bender, or none of these) who do not affirm the primary categories of gender are feared, and consequently, they are ignored, disavowed, discounted, discredited, and frequently accused of not being "real," i.e., not a "true" person.

> Having experienced being both a man, and although many years ago, a woman, I'm often asked "How does it feel to be a man? How does it feel to be a woman?" My response, always, is "I don't know"— what I do know is what it is like to be treated like a woman and what it is like to be treated like a man. What I feel like is a person who mostly identifies as a man but I recognize the femaleness of my self. Specifically, I can't divorce myself from the femaleness of certain parts of my body. More generally, I can't deny that some of my behaviors, manners, and even some of my thinking has been criticized (by others) as being female.
>
> —39-year-old graphics designer

Identity must be "analyzed from the inside and the outside, from the point of view of self-concept and of social identity" (MacCormack & Draper, 1989, p. 149). Self-concept is the conscious or subconscious image the individual has of her/himself. Social identity is a person's status within his/her social groupings (MacCormack & Draper, 1989). However, social identity and self-concept are not always congruent.

> I'm a practicing lesbian of 12 years. I'm very open and I consider myself, out of "the old ways," an aggressive "butch" woman. I admire and am only attracted to women. But I don't want to be one [a woman] any more. I didn't want to be one *very* young in life. I want to become a man, more strongly now than ever. I am also in a position in my life where I'm happier than I've ever been and I have a wonderful female lover who supports me in my desire [emphasis in original].
>
> —32-year-old letter writer

The letter writer's social identity is that of a lesbian. Less clearly articulated is her/his self-concept as a man. Once she/he is living as a man, the social identity of lesbian will be dropped, and that of man added. Some transgendered females have found lesbian communities to be relatively tolerant of their masculine identities and behaviors.

> I lived for a number of years as a lesbian. Even though I never really felt totally comfortable within the lesbian community my masculinity was tolerated by most lesbians. I'm attracted to women but sex has always been difficult and sometimes its nearly impossible because what most lesbians want is another woman. I've been considered a stone butch. I'm pretty good at satisfying my lover but I never let her touch me. You see, I don't really think of myself as a woman or for that matter as a lesbian. I've always thought of myself as a man. Whether or not I'll ever live as a man is another question.
>
> —40-year-old mail carrier

Outside of surgical contexts, it is difficult for some individuals to determine where "mannish" lesbian (Newton, 1984) ends and female-to-male transsexual or female transgender begins.[6] Ultimately, we must leave the describing and the labeling to the individual her/himself.

MAKING FEMALE GENDER VARIANCE INVISIBLE: HE BECOMES SHE

What becomes of the individual who does not describe or label him/herself, but goes about quietly living? What becomes of the individuals who do not have surgery, but live their lives as men?

> When I went to publish the Jack Garland story the straight presses said it was a gay story. The gay presses said it was a woman's story. The women's presses said it was a man's story.
>
> —Lou Sullivan (personal communication, 1989)

Why was there such confusion over a simple biography? Because, like so many before him and so many since, Jack Garland was a female-bodied individual who lived life as a man—i.e., his social identity and self-concept was that of a man. Lou Sullivan persisted and finally found a publisher for his biography of Jack Garland. But had he not, one voice, one story would have been lost. How many voices, stories have been lost? How many voices, subtly and not so subtly, have been silenced? In a previous paper of mine (1991) concerning transsexuals and transvestites, in which I gave voice to female-to-male transsexuals, one of the readers commented: "this seems a bit female-to-male centric." Another felt it was "awfully" so. I do not believe either reader *intended* to silence the voice, but such comments might have resulted in or led to silence. The silencing of voices takes many forms. For instance, an article by anthropologist Anne Bolin was rejected by a sociology journal with a comment that "the author must be a transsexual" (Bolin, personal communication, 1992). Similarly, an article in a newsletter for transvestites and transsexuals criticized individuals who go public either in print or on talk shows, stating, "In my opinion the release of this type of information serves no practical purposes, nor any reasonable service to the public" (Julie G., 1991, p. 3). The silencing of voices contributes to the construction of binary oppositional sexed/gendered discourses and effectively obfuscates the rich potential of multiple voices found in individual lived experiences (cf., Stone, 1991, pp. 295–297). Silencing of voices also leads to inappropriate labeling of individual's lives.

Is it appropriate to use such phrases as "passing women," or even "transsexual" when referring to female-bodied individuals who live their lives as men? In a move away from the labels "passing women" and "transsexual," I have chosen the term "female-bodied men." This term resulted from conversations with female transvestites, female-to-male transsexuals, and those individuals who felt they were somewhere between categories (i.e., transgendered people). Female-bodied man is akin to "man with a vagina." As such, "female-bodied" recognizes that the individual had a female body, i.e., biologically, the individual's genitalia, chromosomes, and basic phenotype (although the latter varies among individuals) is that of a female. The designation "man" recognizes that the individual lived (or is living) as a man. Female-bodied men are also those individuals who acknowledge that their bodies are those of biological females but who do not identify as either a female transvestite or a female-to-male transsexual.

At the end of the play, "T.S./Crossing" the narrator asks the audience:

What happens when Terry Smith dies? When his soul has left his body? Will you insist that he may have lived his life as a man, but died a woman?

—Finque, 1989

The phenomenon of transgendered people, or female-bodied men is an excellent example of the sociocultural essentializing of the (sexed) body. The "discovery" of female-bodied men leads to interesting linguistic and sociocultural results. For example, some writers footnote the life of Billy

Tipton as a woman who passed as a man in order to play saxophone at a time when women could not play instruments in jazz bands (see Faderman, 1991; Tyler, 1989; and Herrmann, 1991).

> I get so angry when I hear people call Tipton "she" or "her." After 50 years of living as a man, you'd think it was obvious that there was more to it than just playing the saxophone. Give me a break, he was a man in every way.
>
> —36-year-old engineer

In part, the anger that female transgendered people feel when female-bodied men are claimed by some women centers on the certainty that the very same women would have ignored or excluded Billy Tipton and Jack Garland (and others like them) as a part of women's and lesbian culture while Tipton and Garland were alive.

It is erroneous to assume that Tipton lived his life as a man simply to play saxophone. Furthermore, the assumption that Tipton passed as a man in order to play jazz saxophone obscures the history of women as jazz musicians,[7] as well as obscuring the fact that Tipton did not try to join an existing all-male band, but rather formed his own group (*People Weekly,* 1992, 24 February).[8] It is also erroneous to assume that all females who "passed" as men were merely "passing women" as a means to economic survival or as a "cover" for lesbianism.[9] Some were, indeed, female-bodied men.

> Has love had anything to do with my present mode of living? Such a question to ask!
>
> —Jack Garland, cited in Sullivan, 1990, p. 154

For Jack Garland, the notion was ridiculous that he "passed" as a man in order to have sexual relationships with women; in fact, he did not have any intimate relations with women (Sullivan, 1990). In Sullivan's well-documented biography of Garland, it is clear that Garland's motivation for living as a man was his consciousness of being a man (Sullivan, 1990).

It is interesting that neither men nor women claim Christine Jorgensen, Renée Richards, and others as part of their history. They are considered separate, part of transsexuals' history. Female-to-male transgendered persons, whether they have self-identified as transsexuals, transvestites, or passing women, are invalidated and dispossessed of a history because they have a biological female body. The recent death of Billy Tipton and the switch in pronouns concerning his life is an excellent example of how female gender variance is rendered invisible.

> I don't care what anyone says, people like Tipton, Garland, [Charley] Parkhurst, [Charley] Wilson, any one who lived the better part of their life as men were men. When women claim them as women they steal our history, my history is taken away from me.
>
> —34-year-old law lecturer

Why then, do some claim the Tiptons and Garlands as part of women's history? (see Tyler, 1989; Faderman, 1991; Herrmann, 1991). Is the claim an essentialist argument? Is it because female transvestites and female transgendered people are the embodiment of the fearful Other, that they are rejected as men and claimed as women? The answers to these questions lie in the paradoxes of the individuals who possess a female-body, but live as men.

Some theorists claim that male-to-female transgendered individuals move down the social hierarchy and that the reverse is true for female-to-male transgendered (Irvine, 1990; Shapiro, 1991). While, indeed, female-bodied individuals who live as men may elevate their status to that of men and it may be more acceptable to advance upward, it only lasts until the "discovery" that the man has or has had a female body. Once the discovery is made, then the man is again less-than-a-man. Like Billy Tipton, he becomes she.[10] By insisting on the body as the essential signifier of sex, and subsequently gender, the switch in pronouns from "he" to "she" reifies sex/gender as two, and only two. Anyone who steps outside of the sex/gender order is perceived as dangerous, and consequently, threatening. Female-to-male transgendered individuals are often threatening to some men vis-à-vis defining what it means to be a man. If female-bodied men can be "men with vaginas," then men who believe that their penis is what makes a man a man must rethink what it is to be a man or reject the "man with a vagina." To acknowledge the validity of "men with vaginas" (and "women with penises") would be to admit that men as well as women could resist and thus, subvert the social order, by approximating the "other" but never fully becoming the "other."

MEDICO-PSYCHOLOGICAL DISCOURSE CONSTRUCTS THE "WRONG BODY"

One of the paradoxes of transsexual discourse is the notion of having a "wrong body." Many individuals believe they are in the wrong body.

When a man *is* a man *in every way* (except) the lower part of his body, *he is trapped,* and I mean *trapped,* in a woman's body [emphasis in original].

—Letter

For many transsexuals, once the "wrong body" is surgically altered they no longer consider themselves to be transsexual.

About the question of whether or not I consider myself a transsexual. I don't but . . . that is what I would be classified as by a health professional.

—21-year-old college student

I was a transsexual. Now I'm just a man.

—50-year-old printer

Their "wrong body" (a biophysical entity *of* sex), now corrected, becomes a gendered body of "woman" or "man." Such individuals are insisting on the right to declare a gender, thus overruling and subverting society's biological designation of sex.

In the preceding paragraphs, I emphasized two phrases: "wrong body" and "surgical correction." My intent here is two-fold: first, to problematize the very definition which has come to embody the transsexual syndrome (i.e., "the wrong body" [Stone, 1991, p. 297]); and second, to go one step further and problematize the concept of "surgical correction."

For whom is the body "wrong" and for whom is the surgery "corrective"?[11] As Stone (1991, p. 297) notes:

in pursuit of differential diagnosis a question sometimes asked of a prospective transsexual is "Suppose that you could be a man [or woman] in every way except for your genitals; would you be content?" There are several possible answers, but only one is clinically correct.

The "correct" answer, of course, is "No, I would not be content." Because to answer "yes" or "maybe" is to be rendered a diagnosis, at best, of nontranssexual, at worst, of pathology, for, as Judith Shapiro comments, "Transsexuals' fixation on having the right genitals is *clearly less pathological* than if they were to insist that they are *women with penises* or *men with vaginas*" (1991, p. 260 [emphasis mine]). To conceive of oneself as either a "woman with a penis" or a "man with a vagina" is considered pathological because "under the binary phallocratic founding myth by which Western bodies and subjects are authorized, only one body per gendered subject is 'right.' All other bodies are wrong" (Stone, 1991, p. 297). That is, according to the imposed order, one can only be one or the other, not both, and certainly not neither, regardless of choice. However, the order does not prevent individuals from challenging and thus subverting the order.

> If I didn't have the label transsexual I'd probably think of myself as a man with a female body. I belong to neither sex, yet I'm both: I have a beard and a deep voice, I've had a mastectomy but I still have a vagina. I don't have a problem with that, neither does my wife, but society does.
>
> —26-year-old sales representative

"Wrong body" is an inadequate description of an individual's experience of their body not being a part of their "self." The experience of the lived body is incongruous with the lived experience of the mind. The insider within the body does not recognize the outside of the body as belonging to the insider within. Such attempts to describe this phenomenon, because of the limitations of the language available to describe the experience, seemingly lead back to "wrong body" as the only possible description. A language which cannot accurately hear or adequately interpret the individual experience of transsexualism results in the discourse of the "wrong body." In part, the answer, then, to the question for whom is the body "wrong" and for whom is the surgery "corrective" is embedded in the sexed/gendered ideology of what constitutes femaleness and maleness (or woman and man) within Western societies.

"WHAT IS A TRANSSEXUAL?"

So many people seem unable to grasp the concept that transsexuals have not, or only superficially so, ever identified with their bodies. It seems unfathomable in so many people's minds that an individual can be born with one body and identify as a person with a different body—that is, that a person born with a male body can identify as a woman, or vice-versa.

> Sure I was born female. But I don't know what it is to be a woman, or for that matter, what it is to be a girl. While it's true I was raised female, I don't know what it *is* to be female. I practiced and put on a

face that the world saw as being female. But locked inside was a child (I say child, because there is no concrete image of either a boy or a girl), who knew that irrespective of how I was treated I was *not* what everyone thought [emphasis in original].

—22-year-old artist/writer

It is also difficult for many to understand that individuals can identify as "men with vaginas" or "women with penises."[12]

I consider myself a *man* (social gender) who happens to be *female* (biological sex). [emphasis in original]

—31-year-old private investigator

Marjorie Garber asks

But what *is* a transsexual? Is he or she a member of one sex "trapped" in the other's body? Or someone who has taken hormones and undergone other somatic changes to more closely resemble the gender into which he (or she) was not born? More pertinent to this inquiry, does a transsexual *change subjects?* Or just bodies—or body parts? [emphasis in original]

—Garber, 1989, p. 15

These are essentialist questions which equate gender with genitals. Diana Fuss defines essentialism "as a belief in the real, true essence of things, the invariable and fixed properties which define the 'whatness' of a given entity" (Fuss, 1989, p. xi). While Garber argues that transvestites and transsexuals essentialize their genitalia (1989, p. 143), she essentializes their entire being, imposing the order: men are born with male bodies; women are born with female bodies. Underlying Garber's question of whether or not transsexuals are changing subjects is a mistaken belief that transsexuals identify as either a male or a female subject in the first place.

I've been accused of "betraying womanhood." How can I betray something I've never identified with?

—33-year-old office manager

For most female-to-male transgendered individuals, there is no shift from conceiving of oneself as (fe)male to that of a man. What needs to be understood is that the individual has never identified as female, but rather has always identified as male. In spite of messages from family, peers, and society in general, and in spite of biological evidence (genitalia) to the contrary, most female-to-male transgendered people have always had a self-concept of themselves as male. Their self-image and belief is that they are boys who will grow up to be men.

> When I was young, I did not think of my body and my mind as belonging to two very different people. My name, if shortened (which I preferred) could be androgynous. It was easy to believe that I was as I saw myself. But when I reached puberty, the girl-turning-woman caught up with my image of the boy-turning-man.
> —John Taylor (cited in Taylor & Taylor, 1983, p. 13)

What shifts once transition is initiated is the social identity, i.e., how others perceive them. Even if surgery was not available, many female-to-male transgendered individuals would live out their lives as best as they could as men.

> I am able to pass as a male 98 percent of the time just as I am. I am 6 foot, 150 pounds, have a deep baritone voice, look and pass as male. With all of this in my favor, I see no reason at this time to invest money and health issues into hormones and surgery. If I could change my name legally, it would probably be all that I would need to live out my life as male. Perhaps if treatment were safer and cheaper, I would invest in transition as an option.
> —33-year-old special-education teacher

Medico-psychological and transsexual discourses to the contrary, for many individuals, surgery is not the final or ultimate destination. Some individuals chose not to have surgery and live their lives as "women with penises" or as "men with vaginas."

THE CONSTRUCTION OF GENDER VARIANCE: FEMALE-TO-MALE TRANSSEXUALISM

In the following two sections I will explore two elements of the discourses that have constructed transvestism and transsexualism, both of which are contained in this paper's epigrams: i.e., the disproportion of male-to-female transsexuals to female-to-male transsexuals and the nonexistence of female transvestites. The answer to how these discourses have become "truths" is rooted in the definitions of transvestism and transsexualism, as well as a sexed/gendered ideology whose mechanisms attempt to cure gender-variant males and ignore gender-variant females.

In the introduction to *Gender Dysphoria: Development, Research, Management,* Betty Steiner states

> The essential features of the disorder [transsexualism] are stated to be a persistent sense of discomfort and inappropriateness about one's anatomic sex and a persistent wish to be rid of one's genitals and to live as a member of the other sex.
> —American Psychiatric Association, 1980, pp. 261–262

> The preceding definition is all one really needs to approach the literature on female-to-male transsexuals, who are a relatively homogeneous group. Male gender patients, on the other hand, present with a wide range of clinical signs and symptoms, and it is mainly in regard to gender-disturbed males that authors vary in their terminology.
> —Steiner, 1985, p. 3

It is because female-to-male transsexuals are treated by medico-psychological practitioners as a homogeneous group that there appears to be disproportion in numbers. By assuming that female-to-male transsexuals are homogeneous, clinics are able to ignore and disregard the wide range of signs that individuals may exhibit.

In what ways are female-to-male transsexuals constructed as a homogeneous group? In the following discussion, I will outline three stereotypes found in medico-psychological discourses concerning female-to-male transsexuals: their androgyny, their heterosexuality, and their obsession with having penises. Some of the individuals' voices will confirm these stereotypes, but others will contradict them.

ANDROGYNY STEREOTYPE

> Compared to other groups, female-to-male transsexuals are more androgynous. That is, female-to-male transsexuals are more flexible in their behaviors and are comfortable expressing a range of behaviors.
> —Fleming, MacGowan, & Salt, 1984, p. 52

> I feel all men and women (whether genetic or transsexual) have elements or aspects of both, male and female. I have feminine aspects which do *not* embarrass me at all! [emphasis in original]
> —39-year-old disability-rights activist

While some female-to-male transsexuals are flexible and have a large repertoire of behaviors, others strongly adhere to masculine stereotypes.

> I have known since age 14 that I was masculine except biological. For almost 15 years I have dressed masculine and lived masculine. I look very masculine. Some people probably consider me very macho, you know, a tough guy. They're right. I certainly dress the part and most of the time I act it.
>
> —35-year-old mechanic

Heterosexuality Stereotype

> Female-to-male transsexuals "form stable and enduring intimate sexual relationships with biological women. These female-to-male transsexuals and their partners considered their relationships heterosexual."
>
> —Fleming, MacGowan, & Costos, 1985, pp. 47–48

But, not all female-to-male transsexuals agree, even when married to or partnered with women.

> I'd have to say my sexuality shifts—mostly I identify as bisexual—sometimes I think of myself as a gay married man—but I never think of myself as straight.
>
> —40-year-old commercial photographer

Steiner goes so far as to state that "all transsexual biological females are homosexual in erotic object choice" (1985, p. 353). In less confusing words, the erotic choices of all female-to-male transsexuals are females. Again this is an example of the essentializing of the (sexed) body. If the individual did not self-identify as a man and chooses women as sexual partners, then she would indeed have a homosexual erotic choice. However, when an individual self-identifies as a man and chooses women as sexual partners, then his erotic choice is heterosexual. But some individuals contradict the heterosexual stereotype.

> What I really want is a sexual relationship with a gay man, as a gay man. One clinic told me that I could not possibly live as a gay man since gay men were primarily interested in large penises and were not sexually aroused when shown photos of female-to-male surgeries.
>
> —Lou Sullivan, 1989, pp. 69–70

While the biases of medico-psychological practitioners toward heterosexuality is being challenged by transsexuals and some practitioners (see Pauly, n.d.; Bockting 1987; Coleman & Bockting, 1988), homophobia still prevails. In an interesting homophobic twist, the medico-psychological discourse has stated female-to-male transsexuals "deny that they are homosexual and avoid homosexual women, except occasionally as nonsexual acquaintances" (Stoller, 1982, p. 48).[13] As discussed earlier, some female-to-male transsexuals do live as lesbians prior to living as men.

> I can't remember ever being happy about being female. I can't remember being happy but for the two years that I was involved in a homosexual relationship. That happiness was not in the sexual aspect, but of being the "man" and of being with people who accepted me as I was. I *don't* consider myself gay. I only consider myself "straight" with a woman's body structure [emphasis in original].
>
> —Letter

OBSESSED WITH HAVING PENISES STEREOTYPE

> Female-to-male transsexuals are obsessed with ridding themselves of their breasts, internal female organs, and "with the idea of having a penis."
> —Lothstein, 1983, p. 13; cf., Steiner, 1985, p. 353)

Numerous studies have documented that almost all female-to-male transsexuals have mastectomies and that the majority have had hysterectomies (e.g., Fleming, MacGowan, & Costos, 1985; Fleming, Costos, & MacGowan 1984).

> I am content with my choice to change and if I had to do it all again—I certainly would. But I don't feel whole because of my lack of "genitals" and don't feel comfortable even thinking of initiating sex with someone.
>
> —Letter

But not everyone wants or feels obsessed by the need for a penis.

> When you ask me if I am a transsexual I have to pause—because although I take hormones, have had a mastectomy and a hysterectomy—I don't intend to have any more surgery. I'm comfortable and

happy where I am. I present as a man in my life but I have no problem with having a vagina.

—29-year-old parts salesperson

For others, surgery is a possibility but by no means a necessity nor an obsession.

I'm living full-time as a man now. I feel comfortable at the stage I'm at. Depending on finances, priorities, and the degree of medical risk I'm willing to take once, and if, I can afford these further procedures (hysterectomy and genital surgery) I will decide whether or not to have them done; they are not necessary at this point, as I see it.

—38-year-old office clerk

Like everyone else, female-to-male transsexuals are heterogeneous. But because many female-to-male transsexuals do not conform to the homogeneous portrait of gender clinics, they are ignored or discounted.

The medico-psychological discourses construction of female-to-male transsexuals as homogeneous is not the only reason they are ignored or discounted. Garber lists a number of reasons why female-to-male transsexuals have been neglected: (1) the gender-identity clinics were set up to service males; (2) the majority of applicants were male; (3) most researchers were male with their male bias intact; (4) social pressures ease female-to-male transsexuals' ability to live as men without surgery (it is considered natural or normal for women to want to be or live as men); and (5) a traditional latitude for men expressing dysfunction (Garber, 1989, pp. 146–147). These five reasons are, indeed, among the reasons female-to-male transsexuals have been neglected, but I believe there are deeper reasons.

Leslie Lothstein (1983, p. 14) unwittingly poses the reasons as a series of questions:

Why is there so much resistance to learning about female transsexualism? Is there something inherent in the female transsexual's quest that silences our curiosity? Does the female transsexual's psyche arouse something dreadful within each of us that says "hands off"? Have male researchers ignored the topic because they view a woman's desire to become a man as natural, and therefore a trivial phenomenon to investigate? Or have male researchers ignored this aspect of female sexuality, just as they have ignored other problems of female sexuality, because of their homocentrism?

The answer to Lothstein's last two questions is an emphatic "yes" (and quite similar to Garber's reasons). Both questions are answered by a "yes" because of male researchers' homocentrism. First, because the desire to become men is viewed as natural,[14] female-to-male transsexualism is trivialized. Although, as I will discuss below, there are limitations to the degree with which female-to-male transsexuals can become men. Second, because researchers have focused on males, females have been neglected in all research areas, and it should come as no surprise that female-to-male transsexuals are neglected also. The more telling questions are Lothstein's first three. There is resistance to learning about female-to-male transsexuals because their "quest" does arouse something "dreadful" in male researchers' "psyches." Garber pinpoints the "dreadful" when she states, "What lies behind some of the resistance to or neglect of the female-to-male transsexuals is, I think, a sneaking feeling that it should not be so easy to 'construct' a 'man'—which is to say, a male body" (Garber, 1989, p. 147). The body part is, in fact, easy (i.e., hormones will provide all of the secondary sex characteristics, but the "ultimate/absolute insignia of maleness, the penis" (Garber, 1989, p. 142) is supposedly not so easy to construct).

> Throughout his slide presentation, every time he [the surgeon] said "penis" he changed it to "phallus" immediately. It was clear to me that he doesn't make penises—he makes phalluses. I wouldn't let him touch me. And it's not just his attitude. Did you see the scars that he leaves?
> —32-year-old convention attendee

Underlying the switch in terms by the surgeon is a belief that surgery can construct only a poor facsimile of a penis, but never a "real one."[15] Only "real" men can possess "real" penises. Garber (1989) states the latter as

> In sex reassignment surgery there remains an implicit privileging of the phallus, a sense that a "real one" can't be made, but only born. The (predominantly male) surgeons who do such reconstructive surgery have made individual advances in technique, but the culture does not yet strongly support the construction of "real men" by this route[16] (p. 149).

It is common knowledge among female-to-male transsexuals that surgeons do not create "real" penises.

> I've said for years that surgeons can't and won't construct a "real penis" simply because to do so would be a threat to their definition

of what it is to be male. If female bodies can have penises made then what does being a man mean? What we need is a female-to-male transsexual to become a surgeon. Then the surgery will improve because he won't be threatened.

—23-year-old medical student

One reason that many transgendered people are not having surgery is "resistance" to a system that dictates that one has to be either a man or a woman. There is also "resistance" to stereotypes of maleness and femaleness as well as heterosexuality as a requirement for qualification for surgery.

I live very successfully as a man. Surgery just isn't a priority right now. I don't think it ever will be. But not having surgery doesn't keep me from being sexual. I enjoy sex with gay men as well as lesbians, anyone who identifies themselves as queer. I'm a queer bigendered person.

—30-year-old restaurant manager

More and more transsexuals are coming forward who do not invest in their genitalia as signifiers of their womanliness or manliness. Perhaps an alternate explanation is the recognition, as well as questioning on the part of many individuals, that genitals do not signify gender.

What most men don't realize is that having a penis isn't what makes them a man.

—23-year-old lab technician

Through networking and the sharing of the discourses about them, many transsexuals are resisting the imposed order that dictates they have to be either a man or a woman. For those who choose not to give into the order, their self-definition does not have to include society's "ultimate insignias."

If people cannot accept me (only [a] few know) and some haven't, too bad. I no longer feel a need to try to be accepted. I am me and that's who I will be the rest of *my* life. I like this saying (song): "It's only a wee-wee so what's the fuss, its only a wee-wee so what's the big deal . . . there's better things to discuss" [emphasis in original].

—31-year-old custodian

Of course, Robert Stoller and others would argue that they are not "real" or "true" transsexuals. But many individuals do not care how the dominant discourses attempt to construct them and the validity of their lives.

> I've spent my life hidden behind my culture's version of truth and a constant cycle of self-betrayal masked by achievement. I've discovered that we are not the badges we wear, nor the burdens we bear.
>
> —Letter

THE CONSTRUCTION OF GENDER VARIANCE: FEMALE TRANSVESTISM

While the dominant discourses attempt to homogenize the existence of female-to-male transsexuals, they also deny the existence of female transvestites. In their recent book entitled *The Tradition of Female Transvestism in Early Modern Europe,* Rudolf Dekker and Lotte van der Pol state that female transvestism has not existed since the end of the nineteenth century (1989, pp. 102–103). As explanations for the lack of transvestism among women since the nineteenth century, Dekker and van der Pol offer the following: the closing gap between men and women as well as cultural tolerance of women wearing men's clothing. It is not clear in their argument whether or not their analysis is limited to their geographic area. However, if their analysis is not limited in this way, they are grossly inaccurate, for, at least in England and the United States, the tradition has not ended, but rather has been made invisible.[17]

In part, the tradition became invisible due to the sexologists' limiting definition of transvestism. According to Stoller, the most prolific writer on the subject, a transvestite is a heterosexual male who dresses as a woman and is erotically aroused by dressing in women's clothing (Stoller, 1975).

> I do not remember ever wanting to wear "girls" clothes. But my mother was in control and I had to wear what she bought. As I got older, I had more choice—or really more power to make decisions about what I would wear. I gradually added more and more men's clothes to my wardrobe. At the age of 30, I remember taking my dresses, shoes, purses, etc. and depositing them in a dumpster. I wore women's slacks and very tailored blouses to work. Finally, at the age of about 33 or 34, I began wearing men's clothes 100 percent of the time. I did not meet another woman like myself until just a few months ago.
>
> —42-year-old systems analyst

As noted in the epigraphs of this paper, Stoller considers transvestism in females extremely rare. He argues that where there is an absence of eroticism in the female individual who dresses as a man, it is because "she" is really a transsexual (Stoller, 1968, p. 195; cited in Garber 1989, pp. 143–144).[18] Many female transvestites do not dress for erotic purposes, nor did (or do) they consider themselves to be or identify themselves as men (cf. Devor, 1989).

> I daily wear men's clothing, but I only dress fully to pass less than once a month.
>
> —20-year-old college student

While for some female transvestites, cross-dressing behavior is only a small part of their lives, for others it is a significant part.

> When I tell people I feel more comfortable in men's clothing, I don't mean physical comfort (anyone who has ever properly worn a men's tie knows it is not physically comfortable). When I wear men's clothing I feel a deep sense of satisfaction. I feel very right, emotionally. I feel free. I like what I see when I look at myself in the mirror.
>
> —Bernstein, 1991, p. 5

While Stoller's definition excludes females, it also excludes males (both heterosexual and homosexual) who cross-dress for reasons other than eroticism. Feinbloom more generously defines transvestism as involving a person who cross-dresses, regardless of their sex or gender (Feinbloom, 1976). Based on many years of working with transvestites, not only do I agree with Feinbloom's broader definition, but so do the majority of transvestites I know. Given the limitation of Stoller's definition, there are very few male transvestites, which leaves the majority of men who cross-dress with no definition or label for their behavior. Steiner (1985, p. 5) notes that

> In the lay vocabulary, the term *transvestism* most often means the simple act of cross-dressing; hence, laymen [sic] sometimes refer to cross-dressing homosexual males as transvestites. Nowadays, few sexologists use the term transvestism to mean simply cross-dressing. Sexologists, oddly enough, have never gotten around to inventing a dignified label for cross-dressing nontranssexual homosexuals, and so are sometimes reduced to referring, in their scholarly works, to "drag queens." [emphasis in original][19]

While this definition (drag queen) is more helpful than Stoller's, it is less useful than Feinbloom's. It is less useful because, like the majority of medico-psychological discourse, it focuses on male gender variance, to the exclusion of female transvestism. The danger of limited definitions is that they can create confusion for women who dress as men (and vice versa).

The following letter writer is just one example of many who have been confused by the lack of a definition for their behavior or confused by ambiguous or restrictive definitions.

> Recently, I saw a talk show where they were talking about having changed their sex. This isn't what I want but I don't know where else to turn. I feel so confused. When I get home from work I like to change into men's clothes. Sometimes it's just jeans and t-shirt. But other times I wear jockey shorts, t-shirt, suit and tie, everything else men wear. I bind my breasts and stuff rolled up socks in my shorts. When I feel like I really look like a man I go out. I don't try to pick up anybody, male or female. I just like to go out that way. Is something wrong with me? Am I sick? Am I a transsexual?
>
> —First letter

> I can't tell you how relieved I was to read your letter. I've heard about and read about men who wore women's clothes but I've never heard of women wearing men's clothes.
>
> —Second letter

Another danger of limited definitions of transvestism is found in Marjorie Garber's essay "Spare Parts: The Surgical Construction of Gender." Garber cites Stoller as a recognized authority on transvestite and transsexual issues. In using such an authority, Garber and others are doing the very thing that feminists protested so loudly about in the beginnings of the women's movement—that is, that men were speaking for women's experiences—men claiming to know what women were or should be. Until Anne Bolin (1988) and Sandy Stone (1991), at the academic level, no one had written about the experiences of transvestites and transsexuals other than "eminent authorities" such as Stoller and Lothstein.[20] Both Bolin and Stone write about either the male transvestite and/or male-to-female transsexual experiences.

While Garber sees "these apparently marginal and aberrant cases, that of the transvestite and the transsexual" as viable for both defining and problematizing the concept of "male subjectivity" (Garber, 1989, p. 143), I disagree. While male transvestites do retain a male identity, male-to-female transsexuals do not. Furthermore, although male transvestites retain a male identity, it is not, as Stoller purports, an eroticized identity focused on the retention of their penises. Stoller's so-called mechanisms of transvestism are phallocratic posturings of eroticism which may be the experiences of a few male transvestites, but are by no means the experiences of the majority of male transvestites, nor are they the experiences of female transvestites.

CONCLUSION

In order to understand the fear that is invoked by the existence of fearful Others we must ask, as Mary Douglas proposes: "who is the dangerous actor? who is endangered? what is the dangerous act?" (Douglas, 1973, 132; cited in Smith-Rosenberg, 1989, p. 105). For my discussion here, the dangerous actors are female-bodied individuals (as well as all other transgendered people, male and/or female) who do not become one or the other but instead choose a middle ground. The endangered are men, especially, but it seems that some women feel endangered also, particularly those who invest in the maintenance of sexed/gendered structures. The dangerous act, as stated in response to the first question, is that of living as the "other" gender with little or no surgical "correction." This action may be seen as endangering because the observer does not have control over how the sexed body is signified as a gendered being; i.e., the observer can be "fooled" by the outward signs of gender. Thus the dangerous actor is capable of revealing the arbitrary relationship between the signifier and the signified; capable of reconstructing the notion of sexed/gendered bodies as "naturally" gendered and sexed (cf., Butler, 1990, p. 123). The dangerous act is especially dangerous to the discourses that maintain the *status quo* of sexed/gendered differences. To live as men (or women) with partial or entirely female (or male) bodies may mean that ultimately there is no, or little, difference. The act is also dangerous because it is a resistance to and a subversion of the dominant ideologies. It is resistance and subversion because the individual has "declared . . . *self*hood and [a] *will*fulness against the determination of biology" (Smith-Rosenberg, 1989, p. 105 [emphasis in original]).

Critics view transsexuals and transvestites, on the one hand, as representatives of "a challenge to traditional notions of maleness and femaleness" (Irvine, 1990), and on the other hand, as seemingly making "the referent ('man' or 'woman') knowable" (Garber, 1989, p. 156). While both of these views may be a possibility, they remain, from at least two sides, an improbability, for, on the one side, the biological and cultural determinists or essentialists, and on the other side, the perpetuators of a mental-illness model (also essentialists) are really the same in that both seek to cure and would rather eradicate than accept (cf., Irvine, 1990). What needs to be understood by both sides is that while having a "wrong body" discourse may lead to a cure for some, it also constructs gender variance as a pathology, a disease for which (and from which) not everyone wants a cure. For many of the individuals given voice throughout this paper:

> There is something about being both male and female, about having an entry into both worlds. Contrary to some psychiatric tenets, half and halfs are not suffering from a confusion of sexual identity, or even from a confusion of gender. What we are suffering from is an absolute despot duality that says we are able to be only one or the other. It claims that human nature is limited and cannot evolve into something better. But I, like other queer people, am two in one body, both male and female.
>
> —Anzaldúa, 1987, p. 19

For individuals who conceive of themselves as "men with vaginas," or as "female-bodied men," or even as "transsexuals" or "transgendered," it is normalcy, not pathology, which leads them to reject the surgeon's knife. Likewise, for individuals who have sex-reassignment surgery, it is normalcy, not pathology, which leads them to the surgeon's knife.

In order to move beyond the dominant discourses, we must ask why critics keep turning to "medical discourses for specificity and distinction, [only] to find, instead a blurring of categories and boundaries" (Garber, 1989, p. 152). Perhaps it is because they have neglected to consult the individuals about whom the discourses are ostensibly written. But the discourses are not really about transsexuals and transvestites; rather they are about the doctors, clinicians, and society's beliefs of what it is to be male or female, transvestite and/or transsexual, neither/nor as well as both/and.

NOTES

1. While this quote does not in itself marginalize female-to-male transsexuals, I use it as an example of the paucity of literature concerning female-to-male transsexuals. As I will argue later on in this chapter, it is because there is so little data on female-to-male transsexuals that the dominant discourses are capable of rendering these individuals marginal.

2. In the dominant discourse transvestites are assumed to be heterosexual males (this will be discussed in detail later). As Bolin has noted, the label "transsexual" implies female-feminine identity (Bolin, 1988, p. 77). Thus, throughout this chapter I will designate transvestites and transsexuals as male transvestites, female transvestites, male-to-female transsexuals, and female-to-male transsexuals. By designating female transvestites and female-to-male transsexuals I am signifying their difference from male transvestites and male-to-female transsexuals. I intend this signification as a move away

from generalizations toward specificity, and the equal marking of females and males.

3. *FTM* is published in San Francisco and distributed to female transvestites and female-to-male transsexuals primarily in the United States, but it is also mailed to individuals in Canada, Europe, Japan, New Zealand, and Australia. Through *FTM*, my questionnaire was mailed to 275 individuals in October 1991. An additional 75 questionnaires were distributed through personal contacts. As of April 1992, I had received over 100 responses. With the exception of eleven from England, all responses have had U.S. postmarks. Results from the questionnaire will be published in a subsequent paper.

4. My concept of gender borderlands is taken from Gloria Anzaldúa (1987).

5. Irvine (1990) makes a similar argument but without the additional conceptualization of fearful Other (see esp. p. 270).

6. My appreciation to Carolyn Allen for re-posing this dilemma and to Sue-Ellen Jacobs for our many discussions concerning the differences between "mannish" lesbians, "mannish" women, female-to-male transsexuals, and female transgendered people. For writings by mannish and/or butch lesbians, see Nestle (1992).

7. See Gossett & Johnson (1980) for a discussion of the history of the all-women bands of the 1940s as well as other female jazz musicians.

8. Some might argue that Tipton formed his own band because of class issues, but, given what is known about his life, this is doubtful. However, class issues are beyond the scope of this chapter.

9. For a similar argument see Garber (1992), esp. pp. 67–71.

10. For examples of this linguistic and social phenomenon see popular media accounts concerning the death of Billy Tipton: Boss (1989); Chin (1989); *Seattle Post Intelligencer* (22 February, 1989; 19 May, 1989). Interestingly, *Time* magazine (1989) did not make a linguistic switch and retained masculine markers in its brief report of Tipton's death. Also of interest is the linguistic and social phenomenon of the retention of feminine pronouns in popular media accounts when the discussion concerns pre-operated male-to-female transsexuals (e.g., *People Weekly,* 24 February, 1992, p. 61).

11. See my paper "Talking About Without Talking About" for a discussion concerning the differences between male-to-female transsexuals and female-to-male transsexuals regarding the "corrective" benefits of surgical sex reassignment. There is a significant difference in attitude toward transsexualism as a "disorder." For example, following a transgender speakout (Seattle, Washington, 29 April, 1992), where a male-to-female transsexual repeatedly used the term "affliction" to describe her transsexualism, one female-to-male transgendered consultant said to me, "I resent people using words like 'afflicted.' I'm not afflicted."

12. It is interesting to note that rather than "men with vaginas," some practitioners use the term "penisless men" (i.e., Steiner, 1985, p. 356). In a Freudian sense (men have penises, women do not), this seems like an underhanded way of labeling female-to-male transsexuals who do not have surgery as really "females" and not men.

13. It is interesting to note that Stoller's etiological factors sound suspiciously like those postulated for lesbianism. A discussion concerning these factors is beyond the scope of this chapter.

14. Both Garber (1989) and Irvine (1990) discuss this point.

15. The medico-psychological establishment is acutely aware that it is not creating penises, hence "neophallus" frequently appears in its discourses (e.g., Steiner, 1985, esp. p. 339).

16. I know of no female surgeons who do sex reassignment surgery.

17. It is interesting to note that, as opposed to Dekker & van der Pol (1989), the San Francisco Lesbian and Gay History Project states that female transvestism started in the 19th century. "The tradition of passing women, begun in the nineteenth century, lives on today, a small but important part of lesbian and women's history" (1989, p. 194).

18. Interestingly, when Stoller (1965, p. 194) discusses an individual who ex-

presses a disinterest in having a penis or the surgery to create one, he places all masculine referents in quotation marks, signifying that the individual's identity as a man is invalid—"he" is really a "she." This devaluing of and judgment upon the individual's self-identity is both phallocentric and Freudian (i.e., the absence of a penis equals female).

19. While I am tempted to comment on the language in this passage, I shall leave it to the reader to surmise the medico-psychological discourses position.

20. It is significant that Bolin's *In Search of Eve* (1988) is regarded by many transsexuals as an accurate and honest interpretation of their lives and the process they must undergo vis-à-vis the medico-psychological caretakers. Even more significant, and probably because it is highly regarded by the transsexual community, Bolin's work is virtually ignored by the medico-psychological discourses and their practitioners. I have yet to see a reference to Bolin's work in any of their publications.

REFERENCES

American Psychiatric Association. (1980). *Diagnostic and statistical manual of mental disorders.* DSM III. Washington, DC: American Psychiatric Association.

Anzaldúa, G. (1987). *Borderlands: La frontera.* San Francisco: Aunt Lute Books.

Bernstein, S. (1991, July). A crossdresser's closet: A different kind of "coming out." *FTM Newsletter, 5.*

Bockting, W. (1987). Homosexual and bisexual identity development in female-to-male transsexuals. Paper presented at the International Scientific Conference "Homosexuality Beyond Disease." 10–12 December, Amsterdam, The Netherlands.

Bolin, A. (1988). *In search of Eve: Transsexual rites of passage.* South Hadley, MA: Bergin & Garvey Publishers.

Boss, K. (1989, 19 March). No rest in peace. *The Seattle Times,* L1, L6.

Butler, J. (1990). *Gender trouble: Feminism and the subversion of identity.* New York: Routledge.

Chin, P. (1989, 20 February). Death discloses Billy Tipton's strange secret: He was a she. *People Weekly.*

Coleman, E., & Bockting, W. (1988). Heterosexual prior to sex reassignment—Homosexual afterwards: A case study of a female-to-male transsexual. *Journal of Psychology and Human Sexuality, 1*(2), 69–82.

Cromwell, J. (in press). Talking about without talking about: The use of protective language among transvestites and transsexuals. In W. Leap (Ed.), *Beyond the lavender lexicon: Authenticity, imagination and appropriation in lesbian and gay languages.* New York: Gordon & Breach.

Dekker, R.M., & Van der Pol, L.C. (1989). *The tradition of female transvestism in Early Modern Europe.* London: Macmillan Press.

De Lauretis, T. (1990). Eccentric subjects: Feminist theory and historical consciousness. *Feminist Studies, 16*(1), 115–150.

Devor, H. (1989). *Gender blending: Confronting the limits of duality.* Bloomington: Indiana University Press.

Douglas, M. (1973). *Natural symbols: Explorations in cosmology.* New York: Pantheon Books.

Faderman, L. (1991). *Odd girls and twilight lovers: A history of lesbian life in twentieth century America.* New York: Penguin Books.

Feinbloom, D. (1976). *Transvestites and transsexuals: Mixed views.* New York: Delacorte Press.

Finque, S. (1989). *T.S./Crossing.* Performed 12–14 January, Seattle, WA.

Fleming, M., Costos, D., & MacGowan, B. (1984). Ego development in female-to-male transsexual couples. *Archives of Sexual Behavior, 13*(6), 581–594.

Fleming, M., MacGowan, B., & Salt, P. (1984). Female-to-male transsexualism and sex roles: Self and spouse ratings on the PAQ. *Archives of Sexual Behavior, 13*(1), 51–57.

Fleming, M., MacGowan, B., & Costos, D. (1985). The dyadic adjustment of female-to-male transsexuals. *Archives of Sexual Behavior, 14*(1), 47–55.

Fuss, D. (1989). *Essentially speaking.* New York: Routledge.

G., Julie. (1991). *Rose City Gender Center Newsletter,* pp. 2–4.

Garber, M. (1989). Spare parts: The surgical construction of gender. *Differences: A Journal of Feminist Cultural Studies, 1*(3), 137–159.

Garber, M. (1991). *Vested interests: Cross-dressing and cultural anxiety.* New York: Routledge.

Gossett, H., & Johnson, C. (1980). Jazz women. *Heresies, 10,* 65–69.

Herrmann, A. (1991). Passing women, performing men. In E. Laurence (Ed.), *The female body: Figures, styles, speculations,* pp. 179–189. Ann Arbor: University of Michigan Press.

Irvine, J.M. (1990). *Disorders of desire: Sex and gender in modern American sexology.* Philadelphia: Temple University Press.

Lothstein, L. (1983). *Female-to-male transsexualism: Historical, clinical, and theoretical issues.* Boston: Routledge & Kegan Paul.

Low, H. (1848). *Sarawak: Its inhabitants and productions.* London: Richard Bentley.

MacCormack, C.P., & Draper, A. (1989). Social and cognitive aspects of female sexuality in Jamaica. In P. Caplan (Ed.), *The cultural construction of sexuality,* 2nd edition, pp. 143–165. London: Routledge.

Nestle, J. (1992). *The persistence of desire: A femme/butch reader.* Boston, MA: Alyson Publications, Inc.

Newton, E. (1984). The mythic mannish lesbian: Radclyffe Hall and the new woman. *Signs: The Journal of Women and Culture in Society, 9*(4), 557–575.

Pauly, I. (n.d.). *Sexual preference of transsexuals.* Unpublished paper. Reno: University of Nevada School of Medicine.

People Weekly. (1992, 24 February). When the bough breaks, 61.

Raymond, J. (1979). *The transsexual empire: The making of the she-male.* Boston: Beacon Press.

San Francisco Lesbian History Project. (1989). "She even chewed tobacco": A pictorial narrative of passing women in America. In M. Duberman, M. Vicinus, & Chauncey, E., (Eds.), *Hidden From history: Reclaiming the gay and lesbian past,* pp. 183–194. New York: New American Library.

Seattle Post Intelligencer. (1989, 22 February). To her adopted sons, she'll always be "Dad."

Shapiro, J. (1991). Transsexualism: Reflections on the persistence of gender and the mutability of sex. In J. Epstein & K. Straub, (Eds.), *Body guards: The cultural politics of gender ambiguity,* pp. 248–279. New York: Routledge.

Smith-Rosenberg, C. (1989). The body politic. In E. Weed, (Ed.), *Coming to terms: Feminism, theory, politics,* pp. 101–121. New York: Routledge.

Steiner, B. (Ed.). (1985). *Gender dysphoria: Development, research, management.* New York: Plenum Press.

Stoller, R.J. (1965). Passing and the continuum of gender identity. In J. Marmor, (Ed.), *Sexual inversion: The multiple roots of homosexuality,* pp.190–210. New York: Basic Books.

Stoller, R.J. (1968). *Sex and gender: On the development of masculinity and femininity,* Vol. 1. New York: Science House.

Stoller, R.J. (1972). Etiological factors in female transsexualism: A first approximation. *Archives of Sexual Behavior, 2*(1), 47–64.

Stoller, R.J. (1975). *Sex and gender: The transsexual experiment,* Vol. 2. New York: Science House.

Stoller, R.J. (1982). Transvestism in women. *Archives of Sexual Behavior, 11*(2), 99–115.

Stone, S. (1991). The empire strikes back: A posttranssexual manifesto. In J. Epstein, & K. Straub (Eds)., *Body guards: The cultural politics of gender ambiguity,* pp. 280–304. New York: Routledge.

Sullivan, L. (1989, 6 June). Sullivan's travels. *The Advocate*, 68–71.

Sullivan, L. (1990). *From female to male: The life of Jack Bee Garland*. Boston, MA: Alyson Publications, Inc.

Taylor, J., & Taylor, M. (1983, Spring). Dear child. *Friendly woman*. Seattle: Friendly Woman Collective, 13.

Time Magazine. (1989, 13 February). A secret song, p. 41.

Tyler, C-A. (1989). The supreme sacrifice? TV, "TV," and the Renée Richards story. *Differences: A Journal of Feminist Cultural Studies, 1*(3), 160–186.

9 FTM

An Emerging Voice

Jamison Green[1]

The phenomenal growth of the grass-roots FTM (Female-to-Male) trans-sexual/transgender community over the past decade cannot be attributed to any one factor or even to a clutch of factors. I'm sure social scientists will have their theories, and perhaps someday it will be possible to look back through the eyes of historians who will interpret events and come reasonably close to the truth. But I am convinced that just as there is no simple etiology for the occurrence of transsexualism that applies to all those individuals who express its symptoms, the postulation of one simple explanation for the rising visibility of FTM transsexuals, transvestites, and transgenderists will undoubtedly generate immediate opposition from both within and without the FTM ranks. In fact, it is often that desire to rebut which I think characterizes marginalized people who are in the process of defining a collective voice.

There are a few living forerunners who have played major roles in building the contemporary FTM community: Jason Cromwell, Steve Dain, Mario Martino (a pseudonym), Jude Patton, Rupert Raj, and Stephen Whittle. A seventh influential figure, now deceased, was Louis G. Sullivan. Each of these men has, in his own way, worked very hard to promote education for and about transsexual men. Before their time, we know of no one who tried to build community or raise the level of visibility for female-bodied people who lived as or became men. Before their time, most female-to-male people lived in secrecy, like Billy Tipton, or in isolation, like Babe Bean (a.k.a. Jack Bee Garland), never drawing other like-minded, like-bodied people to them, never bonding with others for political purposes.[2] They had female bodies and they lived as men without benefit of hormones or surgery, and the repercussions of having their "secret" known were ridicule and various types of abuse. Today's transgendered women and transsexual men are the vanguard of a new movement in gender consciousness, unwilling to live with denial or shame. Of the six living men named above, Jason Cromwell and Stephen Whittle—the youngest at 42—are presently active in transsexual politics. The others have long provided counseling and other types of support services to their brothers, though in low-key, individually oriented ways that do not involve organizational leadership.

Lou Sullivan was perhaps the most outspoken early activist. Infected with the HIV virus (he died of AIDS in March of 1991, just weeks short of his 40th birthday), he was in the unique position of having nothing to lose in dedicating his remaining time to advance the cause of education and freedom from shame for transsexuals. In 1987, he started the quarterly *FTM Newsletter* with his friend Kevin Horowitz, and held three or four meetings each year in the homes of friends. Eventually the attendance grew to average about 16 men, large enough to warrant renting meeting space at trans-friendly churches or restaurants in San Francisco. Sullivan self-published the very useful handbook, *Information for the Female-to-Male Cross-Dresser and Transsexual,* which he distributed by placing small ads in other gender community publications which were targeted mostly for male-to-female people, but where he knew from experience female-to-male people would look for the little information that was available to them. He built his newsletter mailing list from the responses to the ads for his handbook, and from referrals by men who were anxious to help desperate friends realize there were others like them in this world.

Sullivan was in touch with the other six men named above, and with scores of others. He was a prolific letter writer, and treated everyone equally and well, whether his correspondent was a fellow activist or simply an anonymous soul seeking connection with someone else who was travelling along the same—or a similar—path. He was sincerely interested in helping others, and was aware that whether or not one seeks a surgical solution to improve his or her life, one is entitled to support and respect. He knew well the isolation and fear one can experience as a transgendered person, and he wanted to alleviate it.

Perhaps Sullivan's greatest contribution was his willingness to confront the medical/psychological establishment with the fact of his existence: Lou Sullivan identified himself as a gay man at a time when homosexual orientation was an automatic disqualification from transsexual diagnosis and treatment. Sullivan's cogent arguments with several of the leading theoreticians and practitioners in the field led them to recant their previous ideology and to recognize that gender identity and sexual orientation are separate characteristics in any individual, even though these characteristics apparently line up along a sexual orientation axis in most people (Pauly,

1989, 1992). Sullivan never demanded that anyone else be just like him in order to be worthy of respect.

Sullivan actually worked with Jude Patton at the Janus Information Facility in the early 1980s. This organization operated out of San Francisco and was an information resource and referral service for gender questioning people. Many of its assets were inherited from the Erickson Foundation, an early information source on TS issues, which was founded in the 1970s by an independently wealthy FTM named Reed Erickson. Patton moved to Southern California in the mid-1980s, and the organization became J2CP with the assistance of Sister Mary Elizabeth (then named Joanna Clark), and continued to provide information to transsexuals until the early 90s, when J2CP passed its legacy on to the Atlanta-based American Educational Gender Information Service, Inc. Patton now works as a counselor in private practice in the Pacific Northwest.

Mario Martino wrote his autobiography, *Emergence*, published in 1977 by Crown Publishers, and has counseled many FTM people who live in his region. His book was a revelation to many people who had never conceived of the existence of transsexual men, and though it is now out of print, it has had a significant effect on the public grasp of female-to-male issues through the 1980s.

Rupert Raj, a Canadian, counseled FTM people from 1971 to 1990. Between 1978 and 1988 he founded three transsexual support/educational-counseling service organizations, as well as three (now defunct) newsletters from 1978 to 1988: the Foundation for the Advancement of Canadian Transsexuals (FACT) and its *Gender Review: The FACTual Journal;* Metamorphosis Medical Research Foundation, and its *Metamorphosis Magazine;* and Gender Worker (renamed Gender Consultants) and its newsletter, *Gender NetWorker.* He was also active with the International Foundation for Gender Education (IFGE) from 1985 to 1990. He appeared six times on Canadian television shows, and once on the "Sally Jesse Raphael" show in the US. He continues to develop writing projects documenting the experiences of transpeople.

Steve Dain was probably the first widely visible FTM in America. He was a high-school girls' physical-education teacher in the San Francisco Bay Area when he went through his transition in the mid-1970s. His fight to retain his teaching position became front-page news, and he appeared on every major American television talk show of the period. Poised and articulate, Dain was the epitome of the rational spokesman. He appeared in the 1984 HBO film, "What Sex Am I?" along with his friend John G. and John's wife, S. After winning a legal battle for his job, Dain found that many school administrators still found "reasons" not to hire him, and he was forced to develop another career path, even though he had been awarded recognition as "Teacher of the Year." As he rebuilt his life, working in several different fields and eventually returning to school for a Doctor of Chiropractic degree, he offered counseling and support to other FTMs on an ad-hoc basis. He now teaches human sexuality at a community college and operates his own chiropractic clinic.

Jason Cromwell was one of the early organizers (1984) of the Ingersoll Gender Center in Seattle. He has been active in the gender community for many years, developing educational programs and support groups, as well as working with IFGE to broaden its outreach to FTM people. He also serves on the Board of Directors of AEGIS. Cromwell arranged with Sullivan to assume the copyright to his handbook, and Ingersoll Gender Center published the third edition before Sullivan's death. Cromwell is also actively engaged in the academic debate about gender identity. In 1996 he defended his Ph.D. dissertation in anthropology, entitled "Making the Visible Invisible: Constructions of Identities by and about Female-To-Male Transgendered People." He has published papers in several academic journals that increase the visibility of transsexual men, and he served as guest editor of *Chrysalis: The Journal of Transgressive Gender Identities*, Volume 2, No. 2, Summer 1995, which represents the first time an established gender community magazine published by a transsexual woman was devoted entirely to men's issues.

Stephen Whittle (along with Cromwell) is coordinating a Transgender Academic Network, formed in 1994, for people doing research on or about transgender issues. The network keeps its members apprised of work being published in the field, of conferences and other events of interest, and provides an online forum for discussion and exchange of ideas. Whittle resides in England and has been active in advancing the cause of legal and human rights for transsexuals in Europe for over 10 years, as well as providing support and education for FTM people in Great Britain.

From the groundwork laid by these seven men came the foundation of the contemporary FTM movement. Sullivan's *FTM Newsletter* inspired similar efforts in England, Australia, and Japan, as well as other US regions. These efforts spread the word among local populations that remain closeted, or see no need for contact outside their own area, or are unaware of the existence of a larger community. There is often considerable overlap in information among these publications, since a loose network of the editors permits reprinting articles.

A week before Sullivan died, he asked me if I would continue producing his newsletter, and I have done so. In 1991, the mailing list had 275 names; now it numbers over 800, with subscribers in 13 countries. We have published over 37 issues, and the *FTM Newsletter* continues to be the pre-eminent FTM-specific publication in the world, publishing divergent views, new ideas, new images, and responses from and for FTM people.

When Lou Sullivan died, the FTM community of San Francisco took a quantum leap into the present. It was almost as if in the year or two preceding his death everyone was being respectful of Lou, knowing he was ill, not wanting to make demands on him to which he couldn't respond. Sixty people showed up at the next scheduled meeting following his memorial service, and the majority wanted meetings to be monthly instead of quarterly. Factions started to form between heterosexual- and homosexual-identified FTMs, between FTMs who wanted the group to be politically active and those who just wanted to drop in for a while, get information, and go their own way. For a while we designated every third meeting as a "social," where we would just hang out, picnic, or go bowling, but attendance at these events dropped off and we abandoned the scheme. Now we alternate monthly meetings with open informational meetings, and closed support meetings (open only to FTM-identified people), with an average attendance of around 40 people at informationals and 25–30 at support meetings. All over the United States, in Canada, Japan, Australia, western Europe, Scandinavia, even in Greece and Russia, FTM people are meeting and helping each other in numbers never before imagined.

The medical model of an FTM transsexual has long been an independent tomboy-type who is sexually attracted to women and uncomfortable relating to women as a woman (Green, 1974; Fagan, Schmidt, & Wise, 1994). It is common knowledge among people who seek surgical assistance to achieve self-determination that if the doctor wants to hear certain "facts" about your motivation before he will treat you, then you tell the doctor what he wants to hear (Stone, 1991). Doctors have therefore assumed that all FTM transsexuals are attracted to women, and that they are afraid to be homosexual—that is, they are homophobic and cannot accept themselves as lesbians. As long as we have been kept separate from each other, many of us have felt that fitting the medical model was the only way to get treatment.

The medical model attempted to reinforce another aspect of stereotypical gender behavior—that men are uncommunicative. For years, gender clinics and peer support groups alike sponsored rap sessions for transsexuals which were attended mostly by male-to-female (MTF) transitioning people. Because FTM people were not interested in hearing about female hormones and female grooming tips, they stayed away from these groups, prompting professionals to assume that, like other men, transsexual men prefer their independence and don't need support groups. Ironically, the American culture of the late 1980s and 1990s has seen the rise of the mythopoetic men's movement (and other branches of the men's consciousness-raising movement) coinciding with the increase in visibility of transsexual men. While "men's work" has been widely ridiculed, it has had a powerfully positive effect in the lives of countless men as they have learned to listen to and empathize with their own and other mens' emotions and confront their own internalized fears of men. As the stereotype of the strong, silent male is broken down in our society, transsexual men and the medical model mavens have also learned that communication among men does not threaten their independence and that transsexual men will come together or link up to communicate when they realize that they are not alone. For too long, individual transsexual men have come to clinics or support groups only to find themselves more isolated and alone than before when they are told, "We find the men like to go it alone." This reinforces the separateness between men that our cultural stereotype promotes, and simultaneously decreases the personal power of transsexual (not to mention, other) men.

Since we have been in contact with each other for the past several years, and as our network keeps expanding, we find that we are not all alike in our motivations or desires, or in our life experiences. We are as diverse as the larger population, and we are no longer content to sit quietly in the corner while "the experts" determine what to do with us. We want to, and will, have a hand in our own future.

In conforming to the previous medical model, transsexual men have lived largely invisible lives. That is, they have found work, found marriage partners, and lived in relatively stable situations, often keeping their histories secret from their partner's families, their communities, their children, and—in some cases—even their partners. For many, that is how they wish to live, and these men are troubled by the increasing visibility of other transsexual men. Many do not want to be known as transsexual; many feel their past is not relevant, that it's no one's business but their own. Their goal is to live as men, and they're doing just that. Some of these men feel that their lives would be more peaceful if all the activists and media queens would please just go away and not give the general public any idea that transsexuals exist, claiming that some of the people who appear on TV cast such a poor light on transsexuals that they make it more difficult for those who are trying to undergo transition in situations where people know their histories, such as long-term employment situations. But it is not likely that activists will be screened for image appropriateness, especially if one of our stated goals is inclusion and respect for every human being. It is not likely that FTM activism will subside in the near future: not if the state of FTM surgery is to be improved, not if the level of understanding among psychologists about who we are is to increase, not if we are discontent with the lies perpetrated about us, not if we want to obliterate the shame that forces so many of us to avoid treatment or to deny our histories, not if we want to be treated as human beings.

In 1990, Les Nichols and sex artist Annie Sprinkle (assisted by Johnny A., another FTM consciousness raiser and occasional regional support-group leader who has long been a shadowy background figure in the larger community because of his desire to remain out of the public eye) released a video called "Linda/Les and Annie," part sex education, part sex, which showed an abdominal tube phalloplasty being used sexually. Stills from the video also appeared in the February issue of *Hustler* magazine that year. These events created quite a stir in the FTM world: some people were affronted and embarrassed by Les and his mysogynistic attitudes; others spoke out in support of Les and Annie's efforts to educate people and to celebrate sexuality. No matter what one's position was, the FTM cat was out of the proverbial bag. Outside of medical texts and journals, no one else had ever shown pictures of a phalloplasty so publicly. Later that year, journalist Marcy Sheiner's article, "Some Girls Will Be Boys," was published in the March/April 1991 issue of *On Our Backs*, a lesbian sex magazine with a wide North American distribution, and included a tiny photograph of a metadoioplasty. Two of Sheiner's interview subjects, Mickey and Manx, have since gone on to speak in public using their real names: James Green (myself) and Loren Cameron, respectively. In fact, the experience of having his photo in *On Our Backs* inspired Cameron to practice photography in order to demystify the transsexual experience through his own images rather than leaving it to others to objectify transsexual photo subjects.

Prior to this, discussion of transsexualism in the lesbian community had been limited to debate over whether a man could become a woman, especially a lesbian woman. Now some androgynous or butch female-bodied people were beginning to experiment with the notion that they might actually be transsexual, and this led some academics to question whether the lesbian community itself was squeezing butches out, forcing them to become transsexual men (Rubin, 1995). I don't agree with this thesis. I think butch women have always been held in high esteem in the lesbian world: what people reacted against in the 1970s was stereotypical role playing, efforts to form relationships and adopt behaviors that were conservative and ordinary, that did not acknowledge a lesbian-feminist consciousness. If lesbians were anti-butch, Martina Navratilova would be just another great tennis player, another Chris Evert for example, instead of a superstar. If lesbians were anti-butch, they would not want to claim as their own people who might otherwise be identified as transsexual men, such as Billy Tipton (Cromwell, 1994). The line between butch and male is etched by self-definition: Martina identifies as a woman; Billy identified as a man. When a female-bodied person does not self-identify as female, the capacity to hold the status of androgynous or butch no longer exists for them. It was heterosexual feminists, in their effort to distance themselves from the lesbian community, who cast out the butches. Some lesbian feminists may have been caught up in their own ideological confusion and treated some butches disparagingly, and some of these butches may have felt they were (or may have become) transsexual men; but on the whole, the lesbian community has always had a place for a butch woman, and most female-bodied people who identify as women and butch lesbians know that place.

Many of the transsexual men who have come out of the lesbian community in the past 5 or 6 years are men who were once staunch lesbians, with highly evolved feminist consciousnesses. Some were not so butch as others; others were not so feminist as some. Some were active in the lesbian community for over 20 years. It is difficult to dismiss the manifestation of their transsexualism as an inability to accept themselves as lesbians. On the contrary, many of these men would have been happy to accept themselves as lesbians (it's certainly much less expensive than being transsexual) if that didn't mean perpetuating a lie that they had lived with for long enough.

Not all transsexual men come from a lesbian background, nor are they all uniformly attracted to women as their sex partners. I have met and/or corresponded with hundreds of transsexual men from all over the world, many more than the average researcher or therapist ever meets. Since I am not someone they must convince of their legitimacy in order to receive treatment, they don't have any reason to give me false information about their backgrounds or their feelings. Based upon these conversations and correspondences, I can say with some authority that many transsexual men have never been attracted to women, many are bisexual, many are gay-identified, and many have never been involved with women before transition, though they later find themselves attracted to women. I'm sure there are people who honestly do fit the old medical model, and maybe some of them truly are homophobic. But not everyone who says they aren't homosexual is homophobic, even if their morphology is, or was, generally female, even if they are attracted to women.

Because transsexual men come from such widely diverse backgrounds, because they do not share a race, an ideology, or a sexual orientation, developing a real community has been problematic. Our population is scattered throughout the world, and we are not bound in geographic proximity: we can never hope to see each other all at once, which is what has historically conferred community status. Some major cities have transsexual ghettos where drugs and sex are currency, where poor people sometimes find themselves, but transsexual men are not part of these communities in significant numbers. Our community is of a more fluid nature than one conferred by place, or color, or economy. We gather in small numbers at regional conferences geared primarily toward male-to-female transpeople, and at occasional support meetings in major cities. We meet on the Internet and exchange ideas, information, and the stories of our lives. We compare notes on the effects of hormones, the results of surgery, the reactions of family, friends, co-workers, the nuances of relating to women as men, the codes of behavior among men, both gay and straight. We discuss raising children, medical care, legal status, insurance coverage, the politics of obtaining civil and human rights. And some of us publish our ideas and our exchanges so that others may benefit from our experience. We publish in the underground FTM network, in academic journals, on the World Wide Web, and increasingly in the mainstream media. We are appearing in documentaries, in feature films, and on television, and more of us are doing so every year. No longer are our representatives just one or two brave men who have been forced out of hiding; now there are several dozen of us who are active all at once. But what for? What is it we hope to accomplish with this exposure?

In 1994, two major articles about transsexual men appeared in mainstream magazines: the July 18 *New Yorker,* and November *Details.* Each of these pieces was written by a heterosexual woman who had no prior knowledge of our population: Amy Bloom and Emily Yoffe. A third piece, a profile of San Francisco Police Sergeant Stephan (formerly Stephanie) Thorne appeared in the September *Harper's Bazaar,* written by yet another heterosexual woman, Cynthia Gorney, with no prior knowledge of us. Marcy Sheiner had no prior concept of FTM transsexualism before she wrote her piece four years earlier, either. Only two men have written anything serious about transsexual men for the popular press: journalists Curtis Rist *(New York NewsDay* and *New York Magazine),* and Richard M. Levine, who has a book about FTMs in progress. It is interesting to note that when other people write about us, they do so from a particular vantage point. They are able to adopt a stance of incredulity or erudition, and then they can allow the reader to go along on their journey toward benevolent understanding or critical dismissal. Even though these journalists use liberal quotes, very little of the FTM voice is actually heard in these pieces written by others.

Our quotes are usually used to explain or justify ourselves, or otherwise shed light on the writers' observations. Why is it that mostly female journalists are interested in transsexual men? Are males threatened or disdainful? Are they refusing to accept us as men without even having met us, just as women often refuse to accept transsexual women as women? Or are editors just plain uninterested in any transsexualism that does not involve the titillatingly disgusting act of voluntarily removing the sacred phallus?

In 1995, Tony Barreto-Neto, a county deputy sheriff in Florida, founded a national organization for peace officers called TOPS, Transgendered Officers Protect and Serve. TOPS has been present for numerous protests and vigils in support and honor of transpeople across the U.S., and is instrumental in providing support and education for and about transgendered and transsexual people in law enforcement and fire fighting. Deputy Barreto-Neto and I started the loose-knit activist group Transexual Menace Men in early 1996. And there are countless other transmen doing important political work in their own cities, colleges, companies, wherever people gather and inadvertently or overtly oppress us. Several FTM rising stars of note are: Ben Singer, Ken Morris, Alexander Goodrum, Shadow Morton, Marcus Arana, Yoseñio Lewis, and Jacob Hale. There are many more.

Exposure—publicity—is a two-edged sword: it both serves and harms. It can educate, and it can misinform. It can lead to better opportunities, and it can cause some avenues of possibility to recede, recoil, dry up. Those of us who have our egos licked by the soft tongues of media attention must be very careful not to believe that we are more important than anyone else, that our opinion or our vision is more valid. Precisely because our community is scattered, diverse, and usually invisible, it may be that the most effective way to represent it is to say that we don't represent it, to acknowledge that there is no monolithic transsexual or transgendered presence. To do otherwise smacks of oppression, the same oppression that we have long felt from outsiders. Our collective voice, in my mind, is like a chord that, once it has been struck, cries out for recognition of all its component notes, overtones, whether they are harmonic or dissonant.

There are three primary areas in which the FTM voice is growing louder: the academic, the political, and the artistic. In most cases, the men who are actively expressing themselves in these areas are doing so because they are fed up with all the lies that have been perpetrated about whom and what we are. We are fed up with seeing our brothers and sisters suffering abuse due to fear, ignorance, and callous inhumanity. We have had enough of other people speaking for us *as if* we lack the capacity to speak for ourselves.

On the academic front, Jason Cromwell, Stephen Whittle, Thurin Schminke, Jacob Hale, and Henry Rubin are setting precedents. Schminke became the first transsexual man to teach a university class on Transsexualism in Society, at Northern Arizona University in 1994. Rubin earned his Harvard Ph.D. in sociology by studying female-to-male transsexualism as he began his own transition. Hale is the first openly transsexual man to receive tenure—he teaches philosophy at California State University, Northridge. And many more transsexual men have been coming forward to tell their stories in classes on human sexuality, sociology, psychology, and gender studies at colleges and universities in major metropolitan areas. Still other transsexual men who are maintaining their confidentiality are graduating with professional degrees from prestigious schools and going on to practice law, medicine, theology, and engineering; these men will lend their own flavor to the FTM voice. Even though they are in the closet, they still communicate with those of us who are out, and we exchange ideas and inform each other's thinking. These men will carry the consciousness of transition and the consciousness of their early oppression as female-bodied individuals and as transsexual men (two distinctly different oppressions) into their practices, and, if they are enlightened practitioners, they will educate others by example, through their own behavior as men. And numerous others, myself included, lecture about gender and transsexualism in college and university classes across the country.

On the political front, Cromwell acted in an advisory capacity during an effort which culminated in Seattle's adoption of a new definition of sexual orientation in the city's 1986 anti-discrimination ordinances that now includes and protects transgendered and transsexual people. He also lobbied Congress for transgender rights during the 1987 Gay and Lesbian March on Washington. Aaron Davis and attorney Michael Hernandez have been providing the FTM voice to the International Conference on Transgender Law and Employment Policy, an annual proceeding that involves an ongoing effort to educate legal practitioners and legislators, and which in 1995 included presentations from Stephen Whittle, myself, and Armand Hotimsky, a leading transsexual activist from France and president and cofounder of CARTIG, a nonprofit education and advocacy group assisting transsexuals in Europe.

In September 1994, the San Francisco Human Rights Commission issued a report on discrimination against transgendered people that included the most comprehensive public evaluation of the condition of transsexual and transgendered people's lives ever conducted by an American municipality, and the most far-reaching findings and recommendations. I am proud to say that the city contracted with me to write this document, and that its most immediate effect was to spur the city supervisors to pass legislation adding gender identity to the list of protected classes, along with race, religion, color, ancestry, age, sex, sexual orientation, disability, or place of birth. It has also led the Human Rights Commission to organize an educational team of volunteers from the transsexual and wider transgender communities to assist in training the staffs of social service agencies, and has enabled Police Sergeant Stephan Thorne and myself to implement transgender sensitivity training at the San Francisco Police Academy.

Most of the negative response to these developments from the conservative right wing ignored the existence of transsexual men, and focused on the threat of men in dresses becoming child-care workers or food servers. One newspaper even assumed that since Sergeant Thorne is transsexual he would undergo a transition from male to female.

The artistic FTM voice is just beginning to be heard. We've had drag kings and female Elvis impersonators for decades, but the voice of "out" transsexual men is very new. In San Francisco, it started with publication of two stories in the Summer 1991 (#3) issue of *Anything That Moves*: "Meaning To Change," which I wrote about a friend's transition, and "What They See," by Marcy Sheiner, which concerns a woman's feelings about her relationship with a transsexual man.

In 1992, Max Wolf Valerio debuted his FTM-specific poetry and prose at A Different Light bookstore in San Francisco. Both Valerio and I have appeared in documentary films, but even though we were both allowed to speak directly from our own experience, our artistic expression was limited because we were not the directors or the editors. (In fact, there have been several plays and films about FTM characters, but all of these have been interpretations by their authors; if they do include elements of personal experience, the authors have not acknowledged the extent of their affinity with FTM people.)

Leslie Feinberg, also a political activist, published the novel *Stone Butch Blues* in 1993. This book has a bit of an anti-transsexual overtone, but it is a period piece, examining a class and place and time, and as such it reflects the isolation and confusion prevalent in the life of its main character. The book deserves much credit for its chillingly authentic depiction of the brutality and oppression that transgendered people faced in the 1950s and 1960s, and its revelations about the fear and shame that many transsexual and transgendered people still grapple with today. As an openly transgendered person who passes as a male, Feinberg is a staunch advocate of and friend to transsexual and transgendered men and his voice adds to ours. His latest book, *Transgender Warriors* (Feinberg, 1996), is especially effective in communicating about our historical struggle, and has contributed greatly to the growing sense of trans pride.

Also in 1993, Valerio and I read from our creative work at "Over and Out: Dispatches from the Gender Front—Readings/Performances by Openly Transsexual People." The readings, which also included two transsexual women, Susan Stryker and Christine Beatty, were held in conjunction with a photo exhibit "Crossing the Line: Gender Transgressions," sponsored by the Gay and Lesbian Historical Society and financed by money left them by Lou Sullivan expressly for the purpose of public display of gender transgressive images. The exhibit included snapshots and images from the Gay and Lesbian Historical Society's collection. Valerio's memoir of transition, *A Man: The Transsexual Journey of an Agent Provocateur,* is slated for publication in 1998 by William Morrow/Avon.

Loren Cameron, photographer, had his first exhibition in May 1994. His show, "Our Vision, Our Voices," was the first to present high-quality artistic images of transsexuals made by an openly transsexual person. The photos include both portraits and self-protraits, and nudes exposing surgically constructed genitals in nonmedical contexts. The images were accompanied by text obtained in interviews with the subjects. Cameron leapt to critical prominence with surprising vigor: very few emerging artists receive reviews in *ArtWeek* and *Camerawork*, as Cameron did that fall. His work has also been exhibited at several universities, art institutes, and independent galleries in solo and group exhibitions, and selected images have been reproduced in numerous newspapers, magazines, gender-community publications, and academic books and journals. His second major solo exhibit unveiling new work was in May 1995, when his show "Body Alchemy" opened to overflow-capacity crowds. Cameron's openings are major community events, accented by readings from transsexual literary artists, including myself and playwright and performance artist David Harrison representing transsexual men. Cameron's first book of photographs, entitled *Body Alchemy* was released in 1996 from Cleiss Press.

Also in May 1994, Harrison debuted his autobiographical one-man play, *FTM,* which he has gone on to perform in many cities across North America and in Europe. Harrison has also published interviews and essays in various magazines and anthologies, as have Michael Hernandez, Max Valerio, and I. *Dagger: On Butch Women* (1994) is one of the more provocative anthologies that brought the FTM voice to a wider public: two chapters featuring Michael Hernandez, Sky Renfro, and Shadow Morton explode myths and shatter the conventional walls of gender definition.

There are a growing number of highly creative people who are entering the FTM world: graphic artists, painters, writers, photographers, musicians. As they struggle with their personal gender issues, as they become stronger and more self-confident, as they take on the identity of transsexual men and learn that the truth of their whole experience has value in their creative expression, these men will find their voices and add them to ours. They will shock us, reinforce us, delight us, challenge us. In the end, our culture can only be enriched by the texture of transgendered lives.

The emerging voice of FTM transgendered people is serious, observant, reflective. It is laced with humor and rage. We have a great deal to say, and we've been silent for too long. Dan Riley organized the first day-long FTM program associated with an IFGE (International Foundation for Gender Information) conference in March 1990; approximately 15 men attended. On August 18, 19, and 20, 1995, FTM International hosted the first all-FTM conference of the Americas; over 370 people attended the San Francisco event: 75 percent transsexual men, 10 percent transgendered women, and the remainder partners, family members, friends, and therapists and doctors who work with FTMs. Participants came from Canada, Japan, Australia, Germany, and all over the United States. This overwhelmingly successful conference was an historical milestone in the development of the transgender movement. It signalled the rising awareness that people who identify as FTM will not be confined to prescribed behavior roles outlined in theoretical papers published by prejudiced researchers and based upon extremely limited studies. The conference theme, "A Vision of Community," was chosen to help focus participants' awareness that they are not alone in dealing with their gender issues, and that unity is necessary to make improvements in FTMs' lives. During the opening ceremonies, an awestruck Dr. Susan Stryker was heard to remark that she had never seen so many FTMs together at one time. Her listener, Mrs. Thalia Gravel, responded, "No one has ever seen so many FTMs together before. They've never been together before. Ever."

It was very moving for me to see so many men come together, hoping for and dedicating themselves to better lives for transgendered and transsexual people, their partners and their families. I can't help but wonder about men like Billy Tipton, Brandon Teena, and Michael Dillon, men who never knew there was such a thing as community available to them: would they have come to such a conference? Would they have been nourished by such a community? Would they have learned to share the burden of their secret pasts? Would Brandon Teena still be alive had he been able to talk to "elders" in his community about the risks of cross-living and the feelings of rage and betrayal that an "outing" can lead to for uneducated, insecure men? All three of these men were discovered to be female-bodied after their deaths. Brandon Teena was discovered to have a female body shortly before he was murdered, at age 21, for daring to take on a man's role in the rural Nebraska town where he had tried to create a new life. Michael Dillon, the first westerner ordained as a Buddhist monk in Tibet, and the first person to undergo a medically documented surgical sex reassignment—in 1949—died in 1962 at age 47 of unknown causes, possibly malnutrition. He had fled to Tibet following a 1958 press exposé that revealed his transsexual past and shattered his life in England. And Billy Tipton, who lived as a man for over 50 years without hormones or surgery, died at age 74 in 1989. Only his family of origin knew his secret. We have watched as the lesbian community claimed Billy and Brandon as their own, and converted them into women who were victimized by the gender system. We have watched as the mainstream media denied these men their self-definitions and proceeded to define them as they saw fit, as their female bodies. I won't argue that all three of these men were not victims: but they were both victims and heroes. They were heroic because they lived with their convictions about themselves and they did what they knew how to do in order to be themselves. What we can learn from watching all this is that we must declare ourselves; we must own our own destinies and name ourselves, or others—who don't understand—will do it for us. We must learn to recognize the dividing line between honesty and overexposure; we must be able to discern the difference between gratuitous self-absorption and necessary (and appropriate) self-revelation; we must realize that it is possible to come out for transgender and/or transsexual inclusion under basic human and civil rights without identifying oneself as transsexual or transgendered. And we must learn that only by standing up for ourselves can we hope to achieve anything, because no one is going to go out of his or her way for us.

The FTM conference showed that we are coming to grips with our collective responsibility and learning to let go of our collective shame. The emerging FTM voice is only now coming into its adolescence. One day that voice will resonate with power and self-confidence, but not until we have achieved authority over our own lives. That day is coming soon. We have opened the door to our future. We can never again be isolated and mute. And we have only scratched the surface.

NOTES

1. Jamison "James" Green works tirelessly on behalf of the transgender community. Under his leadership, FTM has flourished, becoming an international organization. James has been a strong advocate for FTM concerns throughout the "gender community," raising the realities of the differences between female-to-male and male-to-female transitions, the issues of the inadequacy of surgery for FTMs, and the is-

sues of gender oppression as it affects both men and women, whether heterosexual or homosexual, trans or nontrans. James is a frequent guest lecturer at San Francisco State University, the University of California at Berkeley, Stanford University, Santa Clara University, and other Northern California institutions. He developed the curriculum on transgender sensitivity training that is used at the San Francisco Police Academy and has been adapted for use with other law enforcement agencies. He authored the landmark document "Report on Discrimination Against Transgendered People" for the San Francisco Human Rights Commission, which served as the foundation for the establishment of protective legislation in the City and county of San Francisco, and is being used to assist community groups in many other municipalities. He has appeared in several educational films and on television in the USA, Japan, Germany, and France. He has been honored by the International Foundation for Gender Education with a 1995 Trinity Award for "extraordinary acts of love and courage," with the 1995 Transgender Pioneer Award from the International Conference on Transgender Law and Employment Policy, and with the 1996 Community Leader Award from San Francisco's largest transgender social and support group, ETVC. In August of 1995, he gave the keynote address at the first FTM Conference of the Americas, hosted in San Francisco by FTM International, and attended by 372 registrants. His writing appears in the *FTM Newsletter,* the *San Francisco Bay Times, Anything That Moves, Chrysalis, Transgender Tapestry, CrossTalk,* the *Transsexual News Telegraph,* and the books *Transgender Warriors* by Leslie Feinberg (Beacon Press, 1995), *Bisexuality: The psychology and politics of an invisible minority,* edited by Beth Firestein (Sage, 1996), *Body Alchemy* by Loren Cameron (Cleiss Press, 1996), and *Reclaiming Gender: Essays on transsexuality/ transgressing gender at the fin de siecle* (working title) edited by Kate More, M.A., and Stephen Whittle, Ph.D. (Cassell, in press). He also published a collection of short stories, *Eyes,* (Olive Press, 1976). —editor

2. Babe Bean, a.k.a. Jack Bee Garland, was a female-bodied man who for a time was covered extensively by the press in turn-of-the-century San Francisco. Shortly before his death, Lou Sullivan published his biography of Garland (Sullivan, 1990a). Billy Tipton was a jazz musician of some reknown, who, after his death, was discovered to have a female body.

REFERENCES

Bloom, A. (1994, 17 July). The body lies. *New Yorker,* 38–49.

Cromwell, J. (1994). Default assumptions or the Billy Tipton phenomenon. *FTM Newsletter, 28,* 4–5.

Fagan, P.J., Schmidt, C.W., & Wise, T.N. (1994, 22 & 29 August). Letter to the editor. *The New Yorker.*

Feinberg, L. (1993). *Stone butch blues.* New York: Firebrand Books.

Feinberg, L. (1996). *Transgender warriors.* Boston: Beacon Press.

Gorney, C. (1994, September). A sex-change odyssey: Stephanie Thorne recently realized a lifelong dream: To become the man she always felt she was. Now, as Stephan Thorne, he's finding that his journey has just begun. *Harper's Bazaar,* 410–413, 456–458, 464.

Green, R. (1974). *Sexual identity conflict in children and adults.* New York: Basic Books, Inc. Reprinted in 1975 by Penguin Books.

Martino, M., & Martino, H. (1977). *Emergence: A transsexual autobiography.* New York: Crown Publishers.

Pauly, I.B. (1989). Female to gay male transsexualism. Paper presented at the 11th Harry Benjamin International Gender Dysphoria Association Symposium, Cleveland, OH, 20–23 September.

Pauly, I.B. (1992). Review of L. Sullivan, *From female to male: The life of Jack Bee Garland. Archives of Sexual Behavior,* 21(2), 201–204.

Rubin, H. (1995). Transformations: Emerging female-to-male transsexual identities. Dissertation in sociology. Cambridge, MA: Harvard University.

Stone, S. (1991). The *Empire* strikes back: A posttranssexual manifesto. In J. Epstein & K. Straub (Eds.), *Body guards: The cultural politics of gender ambiguity*, pp. 280–304. New York: Routledge.

Sullivan, L. (1990a). *From female to male: The life of Jack Bee Garland.* Boston, MA: Alyson Publications, Inc.

Sullivan, L. (1990b). *Information for the female-to-male cross-dresser and transsexual.* Seattle, WA: Ingersoll Gender Center.

Yoffe, E. (1994, November). Becoming a man. *Details, 56–58, 60, 62–64.*

10 MULTIPLE PERSONALITY ORDER

AN ALTERNATE PARADIGM FOR UNDERSTANDING CROSS-GENDER EXPERIENCE

William A. Henkin

"Nobody knows as yet what is normal—we only know what is customary."
—Harry Benjamin, as quoted by Christine Jorgensen (1967)

A few months ago, I had a telephone call from a prospective client who was a member of the Educational TV Channel, or ETVC, the San Francisco Bay Area's principal male-to-female (MTF) cross-gender group. The person wanted to know why, considering how important I find Juliette, my own principal femme persona, I was not transsexual. I explained that, important as she is and important as her contributions are to the whole structure of my personality, Juliette does not control a large enough portion of my inner life that she can effectively command my outer life.

Perhaps because I spoke of Juliette so readily as if she were a separate person, the caller asked if I had multiple personalities. I answered that I did, but not the way I thought he meant. I explained that as I understand the process, there's a sort of continuum of dissociation ranging from dissociative identity disorder (what used to be called "multiple personality *disorder*") at one extreme, to what I've come to call "multiple personality *order*" at the other.

MULTIPLE PERSONALITY DISORDER

Classically, someone whose multiple personalities are disordered has "two or more distinct identities or personality states (each with its own relatively enduring pattern of perceiving, relating to, and thinking about the environment and self) . . . at least two of [whom] recurrently take control of the person's behavior" (American Psychiatric Association, 1994, p. 487, Diagnostic Criteria A & B). Classically, too, the individual has an "inability to recall important personal information that is too extensive to be explained by ordinary forgetfulness" (American Psychiatric Association, p. 487, Diagnostic Criterion

C). This form of amnesia is generally experienced as lost time, or as blanks in the person's life that may, for example, cover a year or two in her history, or may cover a particular time of day over a period of months or years, or may cover a particular event or series of events. She might not remember her ninth year, for instance. Or she may have normal recall for most features of being 8 years old: she may remember getting up in the morning and going to school, being in school, and going to bed at night, yet she may *not* remember ever coming home from school in the afternoon.

In addition, although it is not stipulated as a diagnostic criterion, at least one personality generally does not know about the existence of some or all of the others (American Psychiatric Association, 1987, p. 270).[1] As a conservative, church-going adult who wears only tailored clothes and neither smokes nor drinks, the same person may feel bewildered to find a gaudy gown at the foot of her bed one morning, stained with whiskey and smelling of cigarettes, along with a picture of her in the gown on the arm of a disreputable playboy at the bar of a well-known night club.

When someone's multiple personalities are *in* order, he technically may meet the first two diagnostic criteria (A & B) for multiple personality disorder (MPD), but typically his memory is not unusually compromised thereby, and with increasing awareness of the process of his own dissociation, similar to the awareness we all can have of our own processes on a moment-to-moment basis, he experiences *co-consciousness:* the various sides of himself are at least somewhat aware of each other. They may converse with one another, and they can come to align themselves so that the single entity in which they are all contained—the individual—functions as a sort of integrated team, which is not the same as integrating into a single personality.

It is well documented in both the clinical and the popular literature that MPD is a creative survival response to what the individual experiences, usually early on, as some kind of trauma (Ross, 1994; Chase, 1987; Castle and Bechtel, 1989; Coons, 1986; Kluft, 1985; Putnam, 1985; Schreiber, 1973). I used to say dissociation was response to "abuse" instead of to "trauma," but I was persuaded to change my mind by a 30–year-old woman who had been "lovingly" fondled at the age of two or, probably, younger by a close family member, and eventually seduced into a highly sexual love affair that lasted until she was 18. The woman's memory of the experience and her thoughts about it were clearly positive, and despite a high native intelligence she was unable to connect her extensive psychological problems (narcissistic personality disorder, depression, anorexia nervosa, bulimia, kleptomania, body dysmorphic disorder, probable MPD) with these events in her history. But in any case, whether positive or negative, traumatic experiences are overwhelming to some degree: they are traumatic *because* they are too much to accommodate, too much to adapt to, too much to process for someone who has to find a way to deal with more input than she is really equipped to handle.

Though it is generally acknowledged by students of dissociative disorders that alternate personalities "as they are originally developed are involved directly in survival and thus their modes of operation are necessarily severely focused in order to guarantee survival" (Sliker, 1992, p. 31), I am using severe dissociation only as a model here so that we can see in its boldest relief a process I believe is entirely normal. I am not now talking about the multiple personalities of MPD, but rather of the alternate personalities of what I call "multiple personality order," or MPO, whose development is also, though perhaps not equally, a creative survival strategy.

The process of dissociation as I experience it in myself and as I observe it in other people both in and out of the consulting room is so common that phrases in our colloquial language attest to our individual diversity. For example:

> I'm of two minds about this.
> I'm beside myself with anger.
> Why don't you act your age?
> I don't feel like myself today.

Not only our language, but our behavior expresses the most basic forms of dissociation: we do not bring the same personalities to interactions with our parents as we bring to interactions with our children. We do not bring the same personalities to work as we bring to play. We do not bring the same personalities to our spouses as we bring to our golfing buddies, or knitting buddies, or anyone else we pal around with. Perhaps the very fact that we're so different with different people from time to time reflects our *need* to allow our multiple parts to emerge, to breathe, and to grow. If so, our different personalities become problematic only when the process by which they come and go is not conscious or when it is out of control.

Since I am suggesting that we literally live multiple lives at once, it may not be surprising that my remarks are consonant with the explanation of reincarnation provided by the Buddhist scholar Walpola Rahula (1959, p. 34):

> It is a series that continues unbroken, but changes every moment. . .
> It is like a flame that burns through the night: it is not the same flame
> nor is it another. A child grows up to be a man of sixty. Certainly the

man of sixty is not the same as the child of sixty years ago, nor is he another person. Similarly, a person who dies here and is reborn elsewhere is neither the same person nor another. It is the continuity of the same series.

Rahula's words apply equally well to the idea of reincarnation over many lifetimes, to our progress through one lifetime from birth to death, and to what any of us does on any single day.

Since this paper is really about the nature of the self, albeit in a gender framework, I should say a little more about my own self, or selves. First, a story.

Back when I was working in a community mental-health facility with a population described as "severely disturbed," most of my clients came from a county hospital where they had been diagnosed by new residents in psychiatry. Because often the residents were still working out the bugs in their educations, many of my clients carried diagnoses that reflected the residents' current studies better than they reflected my clients' symptoms. For instance, I was told by one resident that when a client he had referred with schizophrenia was getting better she knew that the voices she heard came from inside her head; when she was getting worse she believed the voices were coming from some external medium, like the stove. That was neither the way I'd read the literature, nor was it my experience of the woman, but it was a kind of understanding that contributed to a lot of odd diagnoses.

In any case, for about a third of the year a large number of people would arrive at our door with diagnoses of chronic paranoid schizophrenia. For about a third of the year a similar number would arrive diagnosed with bipolar disorder, and for about a third of the year as many would arrive diagnosed with borderline personality disorder. Some people who stayed in that particular county's system for a while had all three diagnoses earned at different seasons. But if they had been around the system long enough to have a logbook, they generally knew what to say anyway: if they would benefit by hearing voices inside their heads rather than outside, inside was where they'd hear voices.

One young man I remember quite well had just turned eighteen. He was tall, handsome, athletic, and newly diagnosed schizophrenic. While I was chatting with him in the office one evening, he suddenly jumped up and started climbing the wall. Literally. He ran at the wall and ran up 4 or 5 feet before he fell down, then ran up the next wall and fell down again. He quickly became enraged and threatening.

We didn't have any tools to deal with an athletic young man who was out of control in that facility, so I followed protocol and called the police. Two minutes later a couple of officers ran into the house and wrestled the boy to the ground, and as they sat on him and handcuffed him he started to talk in voices. First some loud angry male voice yelled, "Get your fucking hands off me!" Then a young, girlish voice asked, "What's happening? Please tell me what's happening! I don't understand!" Then a child cried and somebody else pled to let him go, and all the while the boy's face was changing right along with his voices.

By this time I had started to read some of the literature about dissociation, and my partner and I had begun to explore our alternate personas together. Sybil had a lot of hands-on experience doing make-overs for transvestites and providing surrogate mommying for infantilists, eliciting the woman within one and the child within the other. Her experience dovetailed with the hypothesis I had generated from my reading and my clinical work.

One afternoon I found myself driving on the freeway in a most unseemly manner. I was speeding, swerving, passing other cars recklessly, and in general endangering myself and dozens of other motorists. Putting to use what I'd been learning, I asked myself who was driving. The image that appeared immediately on my personal little mental television screen was of a terrified little boy about two years old clutching the steering wheel that was too high for him, stretching for the gas pedal that was too low for him, and driving for all he was worth, trying desperately to follow the orders a youngish man about 27 was barking at him from the passenger seat: "Drive here! Go there! Pass that car! Go faster!" The baby, who wanted nothing but to gain the young man's love, was doing his best to obey, but really nothing would satisfy, and I was in fear for my life. "Get in the back seat," I told them both: "I'll drive." And in my mind's eye I saw them both clamber over the seat back as I felt myself take conscious control of the car. The remainder of the journey was made safely, with no upset either internal or external.

When I concluded that the boy in my facility was not schizophrenic but was, rather, a multiple whose internal alignment had cracked under some kind of stress, I also realized that his personalities and mine had some generic similarities. The way multiples are supposed to develop—from severe, unremitting, unavoidable trauma, usually in very early childhood—then seemed to me to be a paradigm for how all personalities develop. For some people who become classically multiple, the trauma was more severe, less remitting, less escapable, than it was for me and perhaps for you, but the structure was the same. After all, even in the very best of families, with the most ideal childhoods, we all had to do things we didn't want to do. We had to go to bed when we didn't want to, learn to use the toilet instead of our diapers, learn to eat our brussels sprouts, okra, or spinach. There was always some kind of nonconsensual domination that was more than a little kid could tolerate.

I am *not* saying that the process of socializing children is bad or wrong, and I am not saying we should have avoided growing up. I am also not saying the development of alternate personas must be a wholly psychological process, or that there might not be a strong genetic or biochemical basis for it: sometimes I am sure there is. I *am* saying that when people are confronted with circumstances that seem to threaten us in some way we cannot accommodate, we tend to split off little facets of ourselves to deal with them until our minds resemble cut gemstones: one heart with many faces.

The personas with whom I spoke in my car were Baby Billy and the Executive, whom I sometimes call the Psychopath. Like Juliette, they had been making their influences felt in my life for decades before I met them. The Executive's need for control, for example, coupled with his barely contained anger, had kept my friends from riding in my car during several volatile periods in my life. The Baby's profound need for acceptance, coupled with his inability to judge other peoples' trustworthiness, had led me into romantic and business liaisons everyone except me could see were doomed. And Juliette had not only added cashmeres and silks to my tweed- and corduroy-filled closet: she had given me an early career in music and helped me to gain and maintain my independence with her serenity and strength.

As time went on I learned to identify a dozen major and perhaps two dozen minor players on my internal stage. Arguably, each began as simply a limited ego state. But as I let them talk to me and to each other they fleshed out into something like satellite personalities around my organizing center. And as they took on lives of their own, they began to inform me about the nature and meaning of my interests, desires, fears, and so forth. The more real they became, therefore, the fuller and more satisfying my whole life became. The more real they became, in a sense, the more real I became.

MULTIPLE PERSONALITY ORDER

Not surprisingly perhaps, one of the first tacit discussions of multiple personality order (tacit because it did not have any such label at the time) came from within the gender community. When Virginia Prince founded the organization that became the Society for the Second Self in the early 1960s, and acknowledged "the woman within" some morphological males, she anticipated by 30 years "the child within" that many people would discover in their quests to recover from childhood trauma. Where Prince and the recovery movement parted company—or, more properly, where they never met—was that she did not accept the conventional psychiatric definitions of her own experience as pathological, even as she sought to understand that experience with the help of psychotherapy. In other words, she was among the very first modern people to recognize the possibility of nonpathological multiplicity, or what Roberto Assagioli called a "pluridimensional conception of the human personality" (Assagioli, 1965).

Docter (1988), Fraser (1991), and others have noted people in the gender communities who talk about their cross-gendered personas as alternate "selves." In her study of transsexualism, Bolin (1988) specifically notes that "[p]ersonal identity is envisaged as a hierarchy of identities such that one identity is primary and others are subidentities around which one organizes the self" (Bolin, 1988, p. 70).

Whether transvestites, transgenderists, transsexuals, gender-benders, or shape-shifters of any sort, many people in the gender paraculture experience themselves somewhat differently in their variant than in their usual gender roles. While at first blush the differences may sometimes seem superficial, upon further examination they often turn out to encompass "relatively enduring pattern[s] of perceiving, relating to, and thinking about the environment and one's self . . . exhibited in a wide range of important social and personal contexts" (American Psychiatric Association, 1987, p. 269).

In other words, we experience all the components needed to satisfy the psychiatric designation of an alternate personality state, replete with variations from our baselines in feeling, thought, memory, posture, belief system, attitude, behavior patterns, and social relationships that are usually associated with a severe dissociative disorder.

Unlike the experience reported by people with Multiple Personality Disorder, however, transgendered persons do not generally forget their customary identities while in their cross-gender personalities; unlike the experience reported by people with depersonalization disorder, transgendered persons rarely feel unreal while in their cross-gender identities; and unlike the experience reported by people with psychogenic amnesia or psychogenic fugue, while in their cross-gender states transgendered persons are ordinarily quite able to recall important personal events of their usual personalities. In other words, despite having a full experience of living in an alternate personality, they satisfy none of the *pathological* hallmarks of dissociation.

I'll come back to alternate personas and gender identity shortly, but I mentioned Baby Billy and the Executive because I don't want to suggest that alternate personas or multiple personalities, whether ordered or disordered, are *only* a matter of gender. The Society for the Second Self evokes by its very name the reality of alternate personalities, but if a man can have an inner woman, as Virginia Prince proposed, or if a woman can have an inner man, as Lou Sullivan asserted correlatively (Sullivan, 1988), and if anyone can have an inner child or even multiple inner children, as some theorists have proposed (Pearson, 1991), why can't one have a sort of whole inner family?

Myth and religion provide intimations that multiple personalities have been common throughout history, since the many goddesses and gods of every pluralistic pantheon can be understood to represent different aspects of their cultures' people. In modern America we can look to Madonna, O.J. Simpson, and other media stars to see reflections of ourselves, as those of us of Western extraction can look to the Greek and Roman traditions with which we're still at least nominally familiar. There it may be easy to see how a person can be dominated by the rational characteristics thought of as Apollonian or the passionate ones we call Dionysian, for example, and still exhibit others relating to the virginal qualities of Artemis, or the sexually seductive ones of Aphrodite.

Both in our New Age and in the Old Ages to which it throws back we can see similar patterns of understanding expressed in tarot, astrology, past-life regression, channelling and spirit guidance, palmistry, and other arenas. Indeed, any discipline that breaks the incorporeal human entity into component parts reflects different aspects of a human personality. In the modern West we've accommodated this process in the psychological tradition, and not only through Freud's concept of the triune mind made up of id, ego, and superego.

Dissociation was a fairly common notion in the West during the nineteenth and early twentieth centuries. It underlay the development of mesmerism, hypnosis, and various other trance-induced cures for mental and emotional problems (Ellenberger, 1970). Around the turn of the last century, Alfred Binet and William James both described cases of multiple personality, and both regarded dissociation as a likely model by which the enigma of the human mind might be understood and studied (Binet, 1886; James, 1980 [1890]).

Jean Charcot, a seminal figure in Freud's development even though they worked together for only 5 months, saw features of dissociation in hysteria, but his mechanical view of the human being would not admit principles of nonphysiological psychology (Ellenberger, 1970). Another of Freud's teachers, Pierre Janet, was among the very first to examine dissociation and wrote about "secondary personalities" alternating with or operating behind what Assagioli calls the "everyday personality" and what I call the "front" personality (Janet, 1889, cited in Assagioli, 1965; Janet, 1907). Some dozen additional cases of multiple personalities were written up in the United States before World War I; in all, some 90 cases of what we would understand today as multiple personality disorder were reported in the *Index Medicus* and *Psychological Abstracts* between 1820 and 1960 (Baldwin, 1984).

Not everything about dissociation was considered pathological a century ago. In the *Principles of Psychology,* James (1980 [1890]) described a hierarchy of selves whose multitude constituted the "empirical me." Soon thereafter, his friend and colleague Boris Sidis became co-author of a textbook on the subject that was more philosophy than medicine (Sidis and Goodheart, 1905). As a boy, Carl Jung was aware of having two personalities, and in his middle years he discovered several more, including a female named Salome (Sliker, 1992). Roberto Assagioli, whose theories of psychosynthesis underlie a great deal of subpersonality work today, claimed that "Everyone has different selves—it is normal" (Allesandro Berti, as quoted in Sliker, 1992, p. 13).

We know that in multiple personality disorder some personalities display allergic reactions to substances that other personalities in the same body do not exhibit. I have seen eye color change from persona to persona, and I have a client whose chiropractor reports that while the male host personality's legs are of unequal length, the legs of his leading female personality are quite even (Berry, 1993).

Despite the interest of his teachers and colleagues, Freud based his work on a model of repression rather than pursue dissociation (Freud, 1955 [1900]). Although first regarded as outrageous and radical, his views soon became psychological orthodoxy, and, as their stature waxed, attention to dissociation waned: there were almost no cases of dissociation or MPD reported in the literature between 1920 and the 1950s. Even though one of the most important psychological texts of its day, William McDougall's *Outline of Abnormal Psychology* (1926), contained references to numerous cases of "coconscious personalities," the dissociative model was already anomalous, fallen into a state of clinical disregard from which it did not begin to emerge for more than 30 years, when two psychiatrists, Corbett Thigpen and Hervey Cleckley, published a popular account of their treatment of an MPD patient as *The Three Faces of Eve* (Thigpen & Cleckley, 1957).

For the next 16 years, isolated reports of multiplicity once again trickled into the professional journals. In 1973 a second popular book, *Sybil* (Schreiber, 1973), alerted the public to this most dramatic dissociative condition. At about the same time, other psychologists began to acknowledge the possibility of MPD, and cases started to be reviewed again in the journals (Baldwin, 1984).

During the middle of the twentieth century, plural identity was explored more by spiritual philosophers than by academically trained psychologists; many saw it as the normative human mode. For example,

> Man is a plural being. When we speak of ourselves ordinarily we speak of "I" . . . [but] There is no such "I," or rather there are hundreds, thousands of little "I's" in every one of us. . . . At one moment it is one "I" that acts, at the next moment it is another "I." It is because the "I's" in ourselves are contradictory that we do not function harmoniously.
>
> —Gurdjieff, 1973, p. 75

> We think that if a man is called Ivan he is always Ivan. Nothing of the kind. Now he is Ivan, in another minute he is Peter, and a minute later he is Nicholas, Sergius, Matthew, Simon. . . . You will be astonished when you realize what a multitude of these Ivans and Nicholases live in one man.
>
> —Ouspensky, 1949, p. 53

Artists, too, began to address the multiple facets of the human being early in the century, though it is hard to imagine that Picasso, Braque, other cubists, or the Dadaists intended such a psychological exegesis consciously. The great acting coach Constantin Stanislavski did intend it, however, as the basis for method acting. In *An Actor Prepares,* published in 1936, Stanislavski writes extensively about the need for an actor to find the essence of any character he is going to play within himself, then to imbue his character with that part of himself on stage. This is, of course, what Marlon Brando and other members of Lee Strassberg's Actor's Theatre became famous for in the 1950s and 1960s, at just the time dissociative psychology began to make its rather theatrical comeback.

The 1920s and 1930s are also the years when Jacob Moreno developed psychodrama, a theatrical approach to psychotherapy which assumes that psychologically the protagonist contains all her antagonists; and the late 1950s and early 1960s are the years when Fritz Perls brought forth Gestalt therapy, many of whose techniques are closely related to psychodrama (Perls, 1969). In "empty chair" work, for example, the client talks to parts of herself imaginatively seated in a chair across from her, then moves over to the formerly empty chair and talks back to the part of herself that she was to begin with. In Gestalt dream work, Perls asserted that the client was everything in a dream: not only all the people, but all the animals and all the objects as well, including the kitchen sink. If you are that kitchen sink in your dream, what do you feel as the sink?

In 1964, Eric Berne, the founder of Transactional Analysis, published a simplified explanation of his theories called *Games People Play*, which became an extremely popular best-seller. In his book, Berne provided dramatic examples, with explanations, of ways two people typically interact when they are expressing three major components of their personalities, demonstrating how those interactions typically emerged as manipulations rather than clear communication. The component parts of the personality, in his model, were the parent, adult, and child; this was not dissimilar from Freud's model using the superego, ego, and id.

Also in the 1960s, Gregory Bateson, Virginia Satir, Jay Haley, and the other members of what came to be known as the Palo Alto group started to work with family systems. One exemplary technique they developed was "family sculpting," in which the client uses human or clay models to display the members of his family, talks about his issues with them, and moves the pieces around to change the outcome of his own story. In this way family sculpting works very much like psychodrama.

The Three Faces of Eve, *Sybil*, and the other developments in clinical psychology brought new attention to multiplicity and dissociation as psychological and pathological experiences. In the 1970s alone, about 50 cases of multiple personality disorder were reported in the clinical literature. By 1980, the DSM III included MPD as a diagnostic category; today, some controversy about the nature of the disorder notwithstanding, thousands of cases have been documented.

In 1895, Freud and Josef Breuer, following Charcot, had identified as hysteria behaviors that might also have been understood as dissociative, and psychiatrists still diagnosed dissociation as a form of hysteria more than 70 years later (DSM II, 1968). By the time dissociation was recategorized as a disorder on its own, it encompassed depersonalization, psychogenic amnesia, psychogenic fugue, and multiple personality (DSM III). In its next revision, the *DSM* acknowledged that MPD may also be present when someone does not exhibit fully rounded personalities, but only exhibits two or more "personality states" or fragments which may or may not be aware of one another, if they are amnestic and aware of having lost time (DSM III-R).

We are closer and closer to acknowledging a form of dissociation that does not meet diagnostic criteria for psychopathology. Certainly that is how the "ladder of selves" may be understood, upon which an individual may locate himself and climb through consciousness, and it is also how Ken Wilber's "Spectrum of Consciousness" may be seen to extend the dissociative model to the whole of human evolution (Wilber, 1980, 1986).

An Alternate Paradigm for Understanding Cross-Gender Experience

As my partner and I developed our concept of alternate personas with ourselves and with each other, we thought we had discovered something new. I remember one evening when I actually encouraged her not to talk about it too much until we could write for publication, because I thought we were onto something really hot with our concept of normal dissociation. It was both a pleasure and a trial, then, to learn that we had reinvented the wheel. It was a trial for the same reasons Columbus would have found it a trial to return to Spain only to learn that 20 or 30 other explorers had already charted and mapped the New World. And it was a pleasure because we now discovered that we had a lot of support for what we were doing, as well as a tradition and a framework against which to measure our work.

Although there are still psychotherapists who do not accept even the concept, let alone the diagnosis, of multiplicity, among others the basic tenets of both customary and unusual dissociation seem to be more common. John Rowan, a British psychologist with a growing American following, bases his work on Assagioli's pioneering theories of psychosynthesis (Rowan, 1990). For more than a decade, Hal and Sidra Stone have been teaching their technique of "voice dialogue," which has very palpable roots in Moreno's and Perls's work (Stone & Stone, 1992). In the late 1980s and early 1990s, Carol Pearson published several books that are concerned with distinguishing different parts of the personality structure in archetypal terms as components of the "Hero's Journey" (Pearson, 1991).

For me, multiple personality order, or alternate personas, is simply normative; it is, for me, common. I have a psychologist friend who does not accept dissociative diagnoses and who for the longest time seemed to me to really have only one personality. He became my test. I'd become convinced that *everyone* had multiple personalities, but every time I saw this man he was exactly the same guy. And I figured if he was the same guy, my notion didn't hold. Then one day, in true California style, I got into a hot tub with him and his wife, and he became a little baby, flapping around in the water with wonder, delight, and abandon. His face opened up, and I could all but hear him burbling "goo," and "gaa." He was a baby who acted just like the grownup, but he was a baby nonetheless, and his transformation freed me to embrace my thesis.

So out in the world, I try to keep in mind that when I'm talking to someone who looks like an adult, I may actually be talking to a child who doesn't know she is a child. When I'm talking to a man, I may actually be talking to the woman within, or when I'm talking to a woman, I may be talking to the man within. I may be talking to a dog or a bird or a bear or, as people sometimes do with me, to a lion. It's *important* to pay attention to whoever is really behind the curtain of the body because otherwise, as Berne demonstrated, communications can get hopelessly bolluxed up.

Sometimes I'll mention alternate personalities to a client and the client will draw a blank; then we'll work in some other direction. Sometimes the client will lay out a whole inner family without any further prompting. I remember telling one man, who had been very sedate for our first few meetings, that I work with these sorts of personas, and he immediately presented three kids, a couple of teenagers, some women, some men, and some animals, and we spent the next large piece of our work together drawing each of his parts and letting them talk back and forth through the drawings.

There's an ongoing debate in parts of the gender community which I encounter particularly with some of my own clients who are exploring transsexuality. The question is, "Where does the man go when the woman takes over?" or "Where does the woman go when the man takes over?" I never want to answer this question for anybody else, but in my own experience and observation nobody disappears. I've never met a persona who died or really vanished, though I have come across some who seem to have gone to sleep.

One of my own, who was sort of the keeper of despair, managed to take a nap 4 years ago and hasn't awakened since. This was a great relief, because once upon a time, when I was very much younger, that persona used to take over for months at a time, and I walked around under a constant black cloud. As I worked with this part of myself, its domination dropped to weeks at a time, then days at a time. My last major experience with it lasted about 8 hours. I watched this persona take over, and I went out in the evening, having spent the entire day in bleak despair, knowing who the persona was but not being able to affect it. I took a walk and ended up on a little beach by San Francisco Bay, sitting on some concrete steps watching the black water and feeling utterly dead. I have no idea how long I sat there; I really didn't care. Eventually I got up and walked home because there was no reason not to: I had no other motivation than that I'd sort of sat there long enough.

Then about 4 years ago, that same persona showed up at an inappropriate time. I was in an erotic situation with my lover, and the persona that was supposed to be present initiated a conversation with the interloper that lasted about 15 minutes. The conversation went approximately like this:

"Do you know you don't belong here?"
"Yes, I know that."
"Are you happy here?"
"No, I'm not happy here."
"Are you ever happy?"
"No."
"Would you like to go someplace else?"
"I don't know and I don't care."
"Where would you like to go?"
"I don't know and I don't care."
"Would you like to go to sleep?"
"Yes."

The end. That personality has certainly stirred in its sleep since then, and I have certainly experienced sorrow, grief, and even intermittent depression since then as well. But though it hasn't returned with its earlier full force, its stirrings let me know it is still a part of me; it didn't disappear.

One of the great breakthroughs I witnessed with a male-to-female transsexual client only weeks before her scheduled sex-reassignment surgery was the reemergence of her full male personality. His appearance allowed her to make peace with her past and to thank him for living the life he had to live, against his will, until she was ready to take over.

In answer to the gender question, "Where does the man go when the woman takes over?" or "Where does the woman go when the man takes over?" I opine that one recedes as the other steps forward, but that neither is or ever was altogether absent or dead. In Billy Milligan's image, one steps into the spotlight and the other steps out (Keyes, 1981).

Going back to the conversation I had with my prospective client, if Juliette were larger in my inner pantheon, if she carried more weight than she does, she'd be out a lot more than she is and merely advising me a lot less. If she were very large, I might have been transsexual and started taking female hormones long ago. As it is, she comes out now and then, and from behind the scenes, she influences all my other parts one way or another. Of course, she conveys considerable insight to the therapist when he works with gender clients.

One of the things Juliette's been best at reminding me about has been the utter normalcy of alternate personalities, including those who cross gender lines. Another is the vital importance of their being accompanied, within the system, by co-consciousness: of being simultaneously self-aware and aware of other personalities, as well as discovering how all the system's parts are aligned so that each one contributes to the purposes of the whole, and the individual doesn't have to suffer the kind of anxiety that results from feeling torn in many directions at once. Just as in "real" life or family systems, this alignment results in teamwork, with every part working toward a common goal, even if all parts don't fully agree with it.

I don't mean, strictly speaking, that everybody has a vote: this is not a matter of democracy. Otherwise I might have a majority minus one on many of my life decisions, leaving me unhappy with everything I did. What we seek is consensus: a weight of support from the people inside agreeing with what the system is doing, while those parts that don't agree, agree to support the team and not to get in the way. When that happens, in my experience, anxiety diminishes, because I'm not being pulled, I'm not being torn in different directions.

In this way, instead of defining cross-gender and other alternate personalities as examples of psychopathology, I find evidence of their original expressions as creative strategies, and as very living testimony to the richness of the human spirit.

ACKNOWLEDGMENTS

I am grateful to Rebecca Auge, Ph.D., and Howard Devore, Ph.D., for their critical evaluations of this paper, and I am profoundly indebted to my partner, Sybil Holiday, with whom I explored my own personas in a deeply experiential fashion, and with whom I worked out some of the concepts presented here.

NOTES

1. Since mine is somewhat too personal and anecdotal to be considered a formal academic paper, I'm going to continue to use the old terminology; I do so not because I prefer the DSM III-R to the DSM IV, and not just because I find the old term more poetic and evocative than the new, but chiefly because the older term more accurately reflects my own experience of the spectrum. Multiple personality disorder, or MPD, is a relatively rare condition. Multiple personality order, on the other hand, or MPO, seems to me to be extremely common.

REFERENCES

American Psychiatric Association. (1968). *Diagnostic and statistical manual of mental disorders*. DSM II. Washington, DC: American Psychiatric Association.

American Psychiatric Association (1980). *Diagnostic and statistical manual of mental disorders,* DSM III. Washington, DC: American Psychiatric Association.

American Psychiatric Association (1987). *Diagnostic and statistical manual of mental disorders,* DSM III-R. Washington, DC: American Psychiatric Association.

American Psychiatric Association (1994). *Diagnostic and statistical manual of mental disorders,* DSM IV. Washington, DC: American Psychiatric Association.

Assagioli, R. (1965). *Psychosynthesis.* New York: Penguin.

Baldwin, L. (1984). *Oneselves: Multiple personalities, 1811–1981.* Jefferson: McFarland.

Berne, E. (1964). *Games people play: The psychology of human relationships.* New York: Grove.

Berry, L. (1993). Personal communication.

Binet, A. (1886). *Alterations of personality.* New York: Appleton & Co.

Bolin, A. (1988). *In search of Eve: Transsexual rites of passage.* New York: Bergin & Garvey Publishers, Inc.

Castle, K. & Bechtel, S. (1989). *Katherine, it's time.* New York: Harper & Row.

Chase, T. (1987). *When Rabbit howls.* New York: Dutton.

Coons, P.M. (1986). Child abuse and multiple personality disorder: Review of the literature and suggestions for treatment. *Child Abuse & Neglect, 10,* 455–462.

Docter, R.F. (1988). *Transvestites and transsexuals: Toward a theory of cross-gender behavior.* London: Plenum Press.

Ellenberger, H. (1970). *The discovery of the unconscious.* Boston: Basic Books.

Fraser, L. (1991). *Classification, assessment and management of gender identity disorders in the adult male: A manual for counselors.* Unpublished doctoral dissertation, University of San Francisco.

Freud, S. (1900 [Reprinted 1955]). *The interpretation of dreams.* New York: Norton.

Gurdjieff, G.I. (1973). *Views from the real world.* New York: Dutton.

James, W. (1890 [Reprinted 1980]). *Principles of psychology.* New York: Dover.

Janet, P. (1889). *L'automatisme psychologique.* Paris: Alcan.

Janet, P. (1907). *The major symptoms of hysterics.* New York: Macmillan.

Jorgensen, C. (1967). *Christine Jorgensen: A personal autobiography.* New York: Erikson.

Keyes, D. (1981). *The minds of Billy Milligan.* New York: Random House.

Kluft, R.P. (Ed.) (1985). *Childhood antecedents of multiple personality.* Washington, DC: American Psychiatric Press.

Kluft, R.P. (1987). An update on multiple personality disorder. *Hospital and Community Psychiatry 38,* 363–373.

McDougall, W. (1926). *Outline of abnormal psychology.* New York: Scribner's.

Ouspensky, P.D. (1949). *In search of the miraculous.* New York: Harcourt Brace & World.

Pearson, C. (1991). *Awakening the heroes within: Twelve archetypes to help us find ourselves and transform our world.* San Francisco: HarperCollins.

Perls, F. (1969). *Gestalt therapy verbatim.* Lafayette, CA: Real People Press.

Putnam, F.W. (1985). Dissociation as a response to extreme trauma. In R.P. Kluft (Ed.), *Childhood antecedents of multiple personality.* Washington, DC: American Psychiatric Press.

Rahula, W. (1959). *What the Buddha taught.* New York: Grove.

Ross, C.A. (1994). *The Osiris complex: Case-studies in multiple personality disorder.* Toronto: University of Toronto Press.

Rowan, J. (1990). *Subpersonalities: The people inside us.* New York: Routledge.

Schreiber, F.R. (1973). *Sybil.* Chicago: Henry Regnery.

Sidis, B., & Goodheart, S.P. (1905). *Multiple personality: An experimental investigation into the nature of human individuality.* New York: Appleton.

Sliker, G. (1992). *Multiple mind: Healing the split in psyche and world.* Boston: Shambhala.

Stanislavski, C. (1936). *An actor prepares.* New York: Theatre Arts Books.

Stone, H., & Stone, S. (1992, March/April). Talking to our selves. *AHP Forum*.

Sullivan, L. (1988). Personal communication.

Thigpen, C.H., & Cleckley, H.M. (1957). *The three faces of Eve*. New York: McGraw-Hill.

Wilber, K. (1980). *The Atman project*. Wheaton, IL: Quest.

Wilber, K. (1986). *Up From Eden*. Boston: Shambhala.

11 ON MALE FEMALING

A GROUNDED THEORY APPROACH TO
CROSS-DRESSING AND SEX-CHANGING*

Richard Ekins

This preliminary report is based on eleven years of qualitative sociological research (Schwartz & Jacobs, 1979) in the United Kingdom with males who either wear the clothes of the opposite sex for the pleasure it gives them (cross-dressers) or who wish to change sex and are actively going about it (sex-changers).

The bulk of the fieldwork was carried out during concentrated periods of research in major British cities between 1980 and 1985—sometimes as a casual participant, sometimes as an overt observer. During this period I accessed all the major subcultural settings—drag balls, pubs and clubs, "transvestite" weekends, private parties, and contact magazine and erotica networks throughout the United Kingdom. Where specific material about individuals is used, it is presented anonymously, and persons concerned were aware at the time of its collection that I was an observer. From 1984 to date, the focus has been on intensive life history work (Plummer, 1983) with selected informants. I have worked with several cross-dressers and sex-changers throughout the entire period of the research. From 1986 to date, I have directed the Trans-Gender Archive, University of Ulster. The Archive is supported by the major "transvestite" and "transsexual" organisations in Britain: The Beaumont Society; the Beaumont Trust; the Transvestite/Transsexual Support Group (UK); the Gender Dysphoria Trust International; and the Gender Trust (UK). It contains a comprehensive collection of material on cross-dressing and sex-changing—the first public collection of its type in the world (Ekins, 1988, 1989, 1990).

Over the eleven-year period, several thousand cross-dressers and sex-

*This chapter originally appeared in *The Sociological Review,* 1993, 41(1), 1–29. See also R. Ekins. (1997). *Male femaling: A grounded theory approach to cross-dressing and sex-changing.* London: Routledge.

changers were observed; several hundred became informants; several scores were followed up over a period of years and were accompanied in the full range of settings—at home, at clinics, at work, at leisure; and several dozen became the subject of detailed life history work which is still continuing. At all stages I discussed my developing thoughts with selected informants and applied my developing ideas in the full range of settings.

I first mapped the various scientific, subcultural and lay conceptualisations and theorisations of cross-dressing and sex-changing phenomena and their interrelations from the standpoint of a sociology of knowledge informed principally by symbolic interactionism (Curtis & Petras, 1970; Blumer, 1969; Ekins, 1978). I then focused on individual and group participation in the social worlds (Strauss, 1978; Unruh, 1979, 1980) of cross-dressers and sex-changers. The mass of observations were ordered in terms of grounded theory, which is the discovery of theory from data systematically obtained and analysed in social research, following the basic methodology set forth in Glaser and Strauss (1967); and expanded in Glaser (1978); Bigus, Hadden, and Glaser (1982), and Strauss (1987).

It is instructive to introduce the paper by distinguishing the grounded-theory approach from others hitherto used in the area. This will serve as both a review of the cognate literature and an introduction to the research methodology which generated the theory and "findings" (Strauss, 1987, pp. 217, 262).

The Medical Model and the Approach from Grounded Theory

The vast majority of work in the area follows "The Medical Model" (Kando, 1973, pp. 139–140). Collection of biographical and in-depth psychological data is followed by classification, diagnosis, and etiological theorising.

Hirschfeld (1991[1910]) collected case histories and then coined the term "transvestite" for cross-dressers, distinguishing them from homosexuals. He stressed that transvestites most typically are heterosexual in overt object choice, though may be homosexual, bisexual, monosexual, or asexual. Benjamin (1966) popularised the term "transsexual" for sex-changers, distinguished transsexuals from transvestites, and obtained hormonal and surgical intervention for them. Person and Ovesey (1974a, 1974b) distinguished primary and secondary transsexuals. Primary transsexuals are seen to have a gender identity at variance with biology from an early age; secondary transsexuals are seen to take a transsexual route after following a career path (Buckner, 1970) more typically associated with transvestites who are seen to cross-dress for sexual gratification or to achieve pleasure associated with the adoption of the opposite gender role. Contemporary stress on the incongruent gender identity of transsexuals is marked by the increasing use of the term "gender dysphoria" to refer to a profound sense of unease or discomfort about one's identity as a male or female, which is felt to be in opposition to one's physical sex (Gender Trust, UK, 1990, p. 2). Koranyi, 1980 (pp. 29–30) gives the flavour:

> While the typical fetishist, transvestite or male homosexual will never give up his pleasure-providing sexual organ, the transsexual, the rare atypical transvestite and the effeminate passive homosexual will gladly exchange his usually low sexual potency for the identification pleasure he gains by the complete surgical transformation. Differentiation within that group of people is sometimes a futile academic exercise, which is why the term gender dysphoria (Stoller, 1973; Fisk, 1974), an intense displeasure with one's own physical and sexual role, was introduced.

Writers and practitioners within the medical model most typically work within biological or psychological perspectives already developed to explain the development of gender identity and sex role more generally. Thus the "pathology" is understood and explained in terms of a favoured biologic, psychoanalytic, social learning or cognitive developmental theory (Kessler & McKenna, 1978, 41–111), with the most prolific writers frequently developing their own particular combination of these traditions (Green, 1974, 1987; Money & Ehrhardt, 1972; Stoller, 1968, 1985).

From the grounded-theory perspective, a number of points stand out. In the first place, the definitions of the situation (Thomas, 1923, p. 14) of cross-dressers and sex-changers themselves (member definitions) are never explored as social constructions of reality (Berger & Luckmann, 1966) with their own legitimacy. In particular, the focus on doctor-patient encounters precludes systematic exploration of the social worlds of cross-dressers and sex-changers outside the clinic and consulting room. Secondly, the terms in which the "pathology" is viewed tend to preclude serious attention being given to radically different formulations. Feminist writers, for instance, have described gender dissatisfaction in terms of sex-role oppression. Thus Raymond (1979, p. 9) writes:

> It is significant that there is no specialized or therapeutic vocabulary of *black dissatisfaction, black discomfort,* or *black dysphoria* that have been institutionalized in black identity clinics. Likewise, it would be rather difficult and somewhat humorous to talk about *sex-role oppression clinics.* What the word *gender* (when used in conjunction with *gender dissatisfaction, gender discomfort,* or *gender dysphoria*)

ultimately achieves is a classification of sex-role oppression as a therapeutic problem, amenable to therapeutic solutions.

Thirdly, and most fundamentally, writers and practitioners working within the medical model inevitably reify existing "taken for granted," "common-sense" notions of sex and gender role appropriate behaviour (Berger & Luckmann, 1966; Kessler & McKenna, 1978). It is not so much that they are unaware of sex- and gender-role stereotyping, rather that their focus of concern on the patient's well-being precludes systematic consideration of their own presuppositions (Greenson, 1966).

Following a grounded-theory methodology inevitably leads to a grounded exploration of these gaps in the medical model. Emergents from doctor-patient encounters are seen as just one species of data amongst others. The researcher using the grounded-theory procedures of "theoretical sampling" and "constant comparisons" (Glaser, 1978, pp. 36–54) is inevitably led to research cross-dressers and sex-changers as they make sense of their situations in work, family, medical, and member settings. He is soon confronted with the complex ways in which various expert, member, and common-sense meanings interrelate. Further, he is led to consider alternative formulations of different experts, members, and lay-folk in terms of their settings, interests, and presuppositions.

CLASSICAL VARIABLE ANALYSIS AND THE APPROACH FROM GROUNDED THEORY

Classical variable analysis is the sociological approach which is most compatible with the medical model in terms of many of its underlying presuppositions. It tends to presuppose the legitimacy of existing sex and gender roles. The "what it is" of cross-dressing and sex-changing is largely taken for granted. There is the same tendency to conflate the rule-violating behaviour with the people who break the rules (Rubington & Weinberg, 1973, pp. 1–10). At the crudest level, work within this tradition simply lists some of the variables associated with the "condition" (Hoenig, Kenna, & Youd, 1970). More usually, it is endeavouring to discover regularities in the patterning of stimuli-and-response that suggest a causal relationship (Walinder, 1967). More sophisticated approaches within this tradition start off with some sociological paradigm, deduce formal hypotheses from it, and then test them (Kando, 1973, pp. 140–142).

From the perspective of grounded theory, the weaknesses of such approaches are many. In addition to the problems raised concerning the medical model, the following points might be made. The variables chosen are divorced from context. Their selection frequently has its origins in the presuppositions of the researcher, not the data. The meanings of the variables are rendered static. The nature of the relationships between variables is not specified. In this sense, nothing is understood or explained (Blumer, 1956). Furthermore, the hypothesis-testing version deduces its hypotheses not from the data but from the paradigm and in consequence closes enquiry. Kando, who has researched sex-changers extensively using a variety of perspectives, writes (1973, p. 141):

> The problem with this procedure is that, since the paradigm only allows for those articulations which the conceptual framework permits, therefore a wide variety of findings is totally beyond its vision. While earlier in the development of the current body of sociological knowledge this paradigm may have provided the necessary articulations to lead researchers in constructive research, an increasing number of sociologists now experience it as an obstacle to the open-minded approach to new phenomena, the possible discovery of new processes and the creative formulation of new questions and new sociological interpretations of behaviour.

Significantly, Kando found classical variable analysis to be particularly inappropriate in the understanding and explanation of sex-changing.

THE CRITICAL TRADITION AND THE APPROACH FROM GROUNDED THEORY

The critical tradition in social theory sees social science as coterminous with ethics and social philosophy (Bernstein, 1976). Through the method of ideology-critique it examines the ideological basis and presuppositions of both scientific and common-sense thought (Billings & Urban, 1982). Contemporary work on cross-dressing and sex-changing within this tradition most frequently has a radical feminist tone (Birrell & Cole, 1990). The particular strength of the approach lies in its ability to reveal societal stereotypes as regards what counts as masculine and feminine and how these are linked with patriarchy, the exploitation of women, and the restriction of human possibility more generally. Raymond's (1979) "transsexual empire" gives the flavour. The possibilities of transsexualism are rooted in sex- and gender-role stereotyping, she argues, but its actuality is the creation of the "trans-sexers": the empire of male medics and paramedics who steer the individual through the change. A trinity of men are seen to dominate the field (Money, Green, and Stoller). The operation is only performed if the client can prove that he can "pass" as a woman. It is "a male supremacist obscenity" (Raymond, 1979).

This approach has considerable merit from the standpoint of grounded theory. Common-sense and scientific definitions of sex- and gender-role–appropriate behaviour are inevitably rendered problematic (Seeley, 1966) by the grounded theorist as he attempts to understand and explain competing constructions of reality in the area. In this regard, the critical tradition marks a considerable sociological advance on the medical model and classical variable analysis. Furthermore, the tradition provides a clear articulation of a radically distinct definition of the situation which constitutes valuable data in its own right. However, as grounded theory and as social science, it is defective. It is a version of "grand theory" which provides a version of data as filtered through an imposed theoretical framework. In the language of grounded theory, it does not "fit and work" adequately (Glaser & Strauss, 1967, pp. 10–11). In particular, the theory is not readily modifiable. Raymond's brief treatment of female-to-male sex-changers (1979, p. 27) is revealing:

> The female-to-constructed-male transsexual is the *token* that saves face for the male "transsexual empire." She is the buffer zone who can be used to promote the universalist argument that transsexualism is a supposed "human" problem, not uniquely restricted to men. She is the living "proof" that some women supposedly want the same thing. However, "proof" wanes when it is observed that women were not the original nor are they the present agents of the process. Nor are the stereotypes of masculinity that a female-to-constructed-male transsexual incarnates products of a female-directed culture. Rather women have been assimilated into the transsexual world, as women are assimilated into other male-defined worlds, institutions and roles, that is, on men's terms and thus as tokens.

For grounded theory, since most of the categories are generated directly from the data, the criteria of fit is automatically met and does not constitute an unsatisfactory struggle of half fits (Glaser, 1978, p. 4).

Significantly, others working within the critical tradition see cross-dressers and sex-changers very differently from Raymond. To Brake (1976), for example, they are mould-breaking sexual radicals with revolutionary potential. Grounded theory enables a detailed look at the features of cross-dressing and sex-changing that provide evidence for these alternative formulations. "Categories are not precious, just captivating. The analyst should readily modify them as successive data may demand. The analyst's goal is to ground the fit of categories as close as he can" (Glaser, 1978, p. 4).

It is the interactionist tradition that looks most promising when the aim is the understanding and explanation of phenomena through detailed analysis of concrete empirical situations. I take this tradition to include those perspectives which focus on the emergence of meanings and social realities within social interaction. This definition would include historical analysis which seeks to show how social constructions have emerged and changed within social interaction over time (King, 1981).

The place of grounded theory within this tradition can best be seen by placing it in the middle of a continuum which moves from ethnography on the one hand, to ethnomethodology on the other. The ethnographic approach relies heavily on description. Newton (1979) researches the world of female impersonators (male entertainers who cross-dress), using descriptive and unstructured methods to "tell it as it is." This is traditional anthropological fieldwork in an urban setting. Certainly, it is not theory. For the grounded theorist, it is not even adequate as preliminary work upon which to base subsequent theorising. Had Newton used the grounded-theory procedures of theoretical sampling and constant comparisons, she would have been led into research settings outside the narrow world of the "drag" artists and their audiences. This, in turn, would have led her to more sophisticated conceptualisations.

Similarly, it is noteworthy that interactionist subcultural studies of cross-dressers and sex-changers and their organisations provide little or no detail of the role of the erotic in either its subjective or social aspects (Sagarin, 1969; Feinbloom, 1976; Talamini, 1982). Grounded-theory data collection and sampling procedures so quickly and frequently lead into this domain that it is presumably only the a priori assumptions, preconceived problems, or personal predilections of these writers that have led to its neglect in these studies.

Insofar as grounded theory is generating theoretical categories which transcend particular examples of data, it can be seen as doing "formal" sociology. In this sense, it is engaged in the same sort of activity as Simmel (Zerubavel, 1980) and Goffman (1963). Goffman has discovered the "form" of stigma situations which is operative whatever the particular "content" of the stigma. However, Goffman does not provide us with an account of the method which leads us to the insight. It is difficult to know to what degree it is grounded and how (Glaser & Strauss, 1967, p. 139). Furthermore, grounded theory will not let us spin webs of insights divorced from the concrete empirical world. They must emerge from the data and be referable back to it in a way that enables explanation and prediction.

The differences with ethnomethodology are more marked. Grounded theory enables the explorations of a substantive area or set of problems having a direct reference and application to a substantive area in a way that ethnomethodology does not. Here, Garfinkel's study of the sex-changing Agnes is pertinent (Garfinkel & Stoller, 1967). Empirical work on Agnes illuminates the "taken for granted" world of "normals" as to common-sense constructions of sex and gender. It also studies "doing gender" as an ongoing accomplishment. This is well-grounded theory. However, following Heap and Roth (1973), I take the particular contribution of ethnomethodology to be its move away from a concern with transsituational phenomena to the question of the phenomenon of transsituationality itself. Ethnomethodology's central problem is "how *members* produce and sustain the sense of objective phenomena taken to exist outside the occasion where that sense is made collectively available" (Heap & Roth, 1973, p. 364). For grounded theory, this takes us too far away from the empirical social worlds of cross-dressers and sex-changers themselves.

MALE FEMALING AS A BASIC SOCIAL PROCESS

"The goal of grounded theory is to generate a theory that accounts for a pattern of behaviour which is relevant and problematic for those involved. The goal is not voluminous description, nor clever verification" (Glaser, 1978, p. 93). The researcher generates substantive codes from the data which conceptualise the empirical substance of the research area. He generates theoretical codes in order to conceptualise how the substantive codes may relate to each other as hypotheses to be integrated into the theory (Glaser, 1978, p. 55). Both are then subsumed under a handful of core categories which have the greatest explanatory power. Codes and categories can, if appropriate, be seen in terms of basic social processes—those staged, patterned, pervasive, and fundamental social processes in the research domain which enable maximum explanatory grip to be obtained on the data (Glaser, 1978, pp. 93–115). Another delimiting function of a core category is its requirement that the analyst focus on one core at a time. To try to write about more than one core category at a time "is to denude each of its powerful theoretical functions" (Glaser, 1978, p. 94).

Within a couple of years of simultaneous data collection, coding, and analysis, I had generated the core category "male femaling." Not long afterwards, it emerged as the single major social process being researched. It was pervasive and fundamental. It was patterned. It occurred over time and went on irrespective of the conditional variation of place. From then on, I found it increasingly illuminating to conceptualise male cross-dressers and sex-changers as males who wish to "female" in various ways, in various contexts, at various times, with various stagings, and with various consequences. The emphasis could be on typing behaviour, not people (Glaser, 1978, p. 69). In particular, this reconceptualisation showed the proper respect for the ambiguous, ambivalent, multicontextual, multidimensional, emergent nature of much cross-dressing and sex-changing phenomena.

The next step was the emergence of three major modes of femaling— "body femaling," "erotic femaling," and "gender femaling." Around this time, I was also trying to make sense of the many very different and confusing scientific, member, and lay definitions of "sex," "sexuality," and "gender" (Gould & Kern-Daniels, 1977; Shively & de Cecco, 1977). I found it useful for conceptual clarity to restrict the term "sex" to the biological and physiological aspects of the division of humans into male and female; "sexuality" to "those matters pertaining to the potential arousability and engorgement of the genitals" (Plummer, 1979, p. 53); and "gender" to the sociocultural correlates of the division of the sexes. A subsidiary theme of comparative analysis then emerged: namely, the exploration of the facets of "body femaling," "erotic femaling," and "gender femaling," and their interrelations in terms of the various facets of "sex," "sexuality," and "gender" that emerged from the data.

For a basic social process to be genuinely processual, it must have a minimum "process out" requirement of two clear, emergent stages which should differentiate and account for variations in problematic patterns of behaviour (Glaser, 1978, p. 97). I found that the staged career paths of male femalers processed out into five major phases: "Beginning Femaling," "Fantasying Femaling," "Doing Femaling," "Constituting Femaling," and "Consolidating Femaling." In terms of grounded theory, these phases are stages in vivo; that is, perceivable by the persons involved, but demarcated by the sociologist for theoretical reasons (Glaser, 1978, p. 98). This led me to construct an ideal-typical career path within which I was able to use the "constant comparative method" (Glaser & Strauss, 1967, pp. 101–115) to explore the interrelations between the three modes of femaling and the interrelations between sex, sexuality, and gender as they developed in individual biographies over time.

BODY FEMALING, EROTIC FEMALING, AND GENDER FEMALING

Male femaling takes place in three major modes: body femaling, erotic femaling, and gender femaling. These are broadly comparable with facets of sex, sexuality, and gender, respectively. However, in the interests of clarity and exposition, it will be helpful, initially, to set forth these modes without reference to their interrelations with each other or their precise interconnectedness with the distinctions made between sex, sexuality, and gender. I emphasize that setting them out in isolation is a focusing strategy. In particular, each illustrative example I give should be read specifically in terms of the respective mode of femaling under consideration. This is because the "same" act, event, object, or dimension will almost certainly have alternative femaling potential. The simple act of cross-dressing, for example, will always be an instance of gender femaling. It may or may not be experienced in terms of erotic femaling; Much of the complexity in the area derives from the multifaceted combinations of the three modes. The male femaler defining homosexual erotic encounters as heterosexual, or heterosexual encounters as lesbian, for instance, is frequently genderizing his sexuality—he may be erotic femaling, as may the male femaler attempting to masturbate in what he perceives to be a female fashion. Both femalings may or may not involve body femaling.

Body Femaling

Body femaling refers to the desires and practices of femalers to female their bodies. This might include desired, actual, or simulated changes in both primary and secondary characteristics of "sex." Thus, it would include chromosomal change (which is not presently possible), gonadal, hormonal, morphological, and neural change, at one level (Money, 1969); and change to facial hair, body hair, scalp hair, vocal chords, skeletal shape and musculature, at another level (Lukas, 1978).

Thus, body femaling may be carried out in a variety of ways. A helpful continuum is that of the degree of permanence. At one end would be the self-styled "new woman" who has undergone treatment and surgery in such a manner that for all practical purposes "she" is now of "her" desired sex. Given a good surgeon and good fortune, the castration, penectomy, and vaginoplasty "she" has undergone will not only convince "her" medically unqualified lover that "she" is a genetic female, but will also allow "her" to pass muster as such at a routine gynecological examination. To date, it is impossible to reverse this operation. At the opposite end of the continuum would be body femaling of the most impermanent type, such as the addition of concealed padding to simulate the female body form. Such impermanent body femaling ranges from the practices of femalers who merely add bird-seed fillings to their bras to those who don elaborate costumes such as artificial "doll-like" bodies.

Overlapping with such practices would be the various procedures of depilation. Here, degrees of visibility may form an important consideration.

Many femalers depilate all those parts of the body that cannot be seen by those observing them as males. Thus, unconcealed parts of forearms are left hirsute. Siobhan shaves "her" arms in the autumn and winter, letting the hair grow in time for the cricket season, when "her" arms will be exposed. Again, eyebrows may be plucked, with varying degrees of obviousness.

A third dimension is that of the degree of progression and accumulation versus oscillation. There are those femalers who follow a steady route to increasing feminization of the body. Others oscillate, going on periodic binges, in preparation for an important function for instance, or for a lover.

Another dimension is the degree of premeditation. Suzie shaves "her" legs every Thursday and does "everything else" every Friday. There are body femalers who execute their feminisation with lingered planning, and others who do it frenetically and impulsively. Again, there are differing degrees of celebration or regret of the permanence, or semipermanence incurred.

Erotic Femaling

Erotic femaling refers to femaling which is intended, or has the effect of arousing sexual desire or excitement. Although the term might be stretched to include femaling intended to arouse, or that does arouse sexual desire or excitement in others, the particular feature of erotic femaling in cross-dressers is that the desire, or excitement, is aroused in the femaler himself by his own femaling, and/or through the awareness of others of his own erotic femaling.

The modes of erotic femaling are boundaried only by what the femaler finds erotic or potentially erotic, by his own ingenuity, and by what he and/ or his culture deem to be associated with the female. Thus it may have to do with the behavioural, the emotional, the cognitive, or the anatomical. In this sense, erotic femaling is the most embracive mode, for any facet of female "sex" and the feminine "gender" when it is adopted by the femaler may be found erotic. At one extreme might be the femaler experiencing what he perceives as a multiple female orgasm, while experiencing himself as female during role-reversed lovemaking. When Cindy has intercourse with "her" wife "she" *is* the female, "her" wife becomes "her" male lover. "Her" wife has the penis, "she" the vagina. At the other extreme might be the casual erotic thought evoked involuntarily by the sight of a woman's magazine in a newsagent, and the fleeting imagining that the femaler is a female casually interested in this object of the world of women.

As regards sensations experienced, these might be placed on continua of focus/diffusion. The range-of-intensity continuum might be exampled by the femaler experiencing intense orgasm following a dressing sequence at one end, whilst at the other end, the femaler might find himself mildly enjoying the sensual feel of his bra strap against his shoulder as he makes the minor movements necessary to eat a meal or drink a cup of coffee. The focus/diffusion feature of erotic femaling may be more or less intense. The eroticism might be experienced over the entire body, inside and out, at one extreme (diffuse eroticism; more or less intense). At another extreme would be the highly focused sensations of pleasure as the femaler experienced a focused genital orgasm implicated in some femaling episode (focused eroticism; intense).

Erotic femaling may be more or less volitional, fantasied, scripted/ritualised, visible, narcissistic, developmental/progressive, and constant object-related. These properties may be illustrated by Suzanne, who on occasion chooses, in private, to initiate a protracted, ritualised erotic script which leads "her" to experience "herself" as "her" femme self, visually and tactually, and who reports the ability to do this as a "breakthrough." Suzanne is erotically femaling in a highly volitional, largely invisible, highly constant object-related (the script), highly scripted/ritualised, highly fantasied, highly narcissistic, highly developmental/progressive fashion. At the other extreme might be Jennifer, who, during an episode of masturbation, fantasies some facet of femaling ritualistically, finds other imagined objects/events emerging involuntarily, shifts from fantasied object/event to fantasied object/event, from one cross-dressing activity to another, until "she" eventually tires of the whole femaling episode and moves on to some non–male-femaling pursuit, which may or may not be related to the erotic.

Gender Femaling

Gender femaling refers to the manifold ways in which femalers adopt the behaviours, emotions, and cognitions socioculturally associated with being female. Gender femaling need not be associated with erotic femaling.

At one somewhat stereotypical extreme would be Betty, a self-styled "transgenderist" who is living "full-time" as a woman. Betty feels "she" has chosen a female gender identity that has developed from a more ambiguous self-concept. "She" has no desire to "cross-over" physically. "She" avoids sexual relationships altogether. "She" does not masturbate. "She" deliberately chooses to work in a "feminine" occupation. "She" spends her evenings in a stereotypically "feminine" fashion—dressmaking. "She" has the "ordinary woman's interest in make-up and making the best of herself" and sees "herself" as passive, nurturant, compliant, and emotional. At the other extreme would be the femaler who ordinarily leads a contented life as a male "in every sense," but periodically enjoys "dressing up" as a woman, although he would feel foolish role-playing feminine mannerisms, or voice intonation, preferring to act "normally" while cross-dressed. Somewhere in the middle of the continuum would be those who enjoy stereotype role playing, such as Ginger (1980, p. 5), who reports:

> I really get into feminine role playing. I like to choose a typical feminine role and then dress and make-up for a stereotype of that kind of girl. I try to also suit my actions, manner, and personality to the role. In the past I've experimented with these various female stereotypes: hooker; chic fashion model; dominatrix; French maid; little girl; slut.

Gender femalers, however, need not follow such obvious stereotypes. Many find them unreal, offensive, or sexist. Insofar as each and every "RG" (real girl) provides a potential role model, it follows that the possibilities are boundless. Thus, many male femalers prefer to develop a middle-of-the-road femme personality they feel is suitable to their age, class, looks, and background. Gail models "herself" on a respected career-woman acquaintance. In this vein, too, are femalers who are particularly complimentary about the "natural TV" (transvestite) who can "pass" in "straight" settings as an RG whilst wearing "little or no make-up, a skirt and top, and some flatties."

Gender femaling may be seen in terms of the time spent doing it, its continuity, and the degree of fine-tunedness to things feminine: some femalers quit gender femaling for years at a time before returning to it; many gender femalers make a study of "beauty know-how." A major dimension is the degree of development of a "femme self" (or selves) with "her" own personality, tastes, and preferences, and its relation to the male self of the femaler. In Ekins (1983, pp. 23–25), I consider the possibilities in terms of "aparting," "fusing," "substituting," and "integrating." Pepper (1982) first tries to keep his developing feminine self at bay ("aparting"). At other times it starts involuntarily "fusing" with his male self. He rejects the options of going "full time" as a woman or sex-changing ("substituting"). His autobiography ends with the "integrating" of his male and female selves "at the feet of the lamas of Tibet, the first glimpses of the ancient mystical secret of the androgynous impulse." Others take less esoteric pathways, but many, like Pepper, come to see the impulse behind gender femaling as being essentially liberating.

MALE FEMALING AND SOME INTERRELATIONS BETWEEN SEX, SEXUALITY, AND GENDER

In the process of femaling, persons (bodies, selves, and identities), actions, events, and objects (clothes and the paraphernalia of femininity) are variously implicated. They are, or become over time, in varying degrees, and with varying degrees of interconnectedness, sex, sexualised, and/or gendered (SSG'd). Thus, for example, in body femaling, the characteristics of the genetic female's (sexed) body are taken on by the genetic male's body, which becomes correspondingly sexed as female. Whereas in erotic femaling the gendered object "petticoat" may be eroticized (sexualised). Again, in gender femaling, the gendered mannerism "sitting down in 'ladylike' fashion" may be adopted by the gender femaler as a facet of his gendered presentation of self (Goffman, 1959, 1976). This is an exceedingly complex business, the components of which may be best illustrated with reference to the major phases in an ideal-typical career path of the male femaler that emerged from my analysis of the staged (Glaser, 1978, pp. 97–100) male femalings of over 200 informants.

PHASE I: BEGINNING FEMALING

In this first phase of femaling, the emphasis is upon initial femaling behaviours—what deviancy theorists would call primary deviance.

An incident of cross-dressing occurs. It might occur by chance. It might be encouraged by others. It might take place in childhood, adolescence, or adulthood. It might be more or less charged with affect. The cross-dressing incident, which I take to include the content and accompanying feelings and cognition, may evoke varying degrees of certainty about its meaning. It could be remembered, re-experienced, or reconstructed as primarily erotic or sexual, especially when originally accompanied by perceived sexual excitement and arousal. It could be remembered, re-experienced, or reconstructed in terms of fascination, sensuousness, mystery, or awe. Further, the experience may be conceptualised in terms of the tactile, the visual, or the olfactory, or any combination of them, and with varying degrees of focus and precision.

Typically, it is the untoward affect that leads to pondering the incident. What is the meaning of this pleasure, mystery, or awe that I experienced? What sort of person am I that I could experience such a thing? In short, what does it all mean? Typically, in the "beginning femaling" phase, the meanings are inchoate. In terms of the interrelations between sex, sexuality, and gender, the feature of this phase is undifferentiation. There is undifferentiation because typically in this phase the untoward incident is dismissed, not taken seriously, or is seen as a temporary aberration, and subtle distinctions are not made. There is also undifferentiation because the individual lacks not only the conceptual wherewithal, but also a sense of purpose, direction, and volition, and, indeed, the means to gain them through interaction with others or relevant literature.

As likely as not, he will simply and inchoately conceive the incident in terms of "something to do with sex." Possibilities include variants of "I wish I was a girl" (inchoate as regards fantasy body femaling versus fantasy/acted-out gender femaling); "I wish these clothes were part of my world. I wish I could be part of this world" (inchoate as regards gender-femaling stress). Where the erotic looks large, beginning femaling might be seen in terms of the sexual (prehistory of erotic femaling), with the relations between the sexual and sex and gender obscure at this stage.

As regards the interrelations between the constitution of self and world as SSG'd, typically, "normality" reinstates itself after the incident. Nevertheless, from thenceforth, the meaning of female objects—clothes, for example—may well be different. In some more or less undifferentiated way, they may be seen as charged, or capable of being charged with affect, which may be built on in a more or less cumulative fashion, pondered on, and invested with new meaning. Likewise, new self-concepts will be rendered more or less negotiable; though typically in this phase the re-involvement within the meaning frames of "normal" everyday life, following the cross-dressing incident, are such as to leave "normal" self-concept and the world more or less intact.

PHASE 2: FANTASYING FEMALING

Fantasying femaling will frequently arise in tandem with "doing femaling" (phase 3), but in this case, the stress is on the elaboration of fantasies involving femaling. The fantasies may be more or less elaborate, scripted, adapted from incidents in "real" life, innovative, and imaginative. They may entail nothing more than fantasying the feel and texture of an imagined petticoat as implicated within a femaling episode (cf., fetishism unrelated to femaling). They might involve an elaborate script in which the boy child is taken shopping by his mother, has chosen for him all sorts of "feminine" finery, and lives "happily ever after" as an accepted girl child in the family.

In terms of sex, sexuality, and gender and their interrelations, a number of possibilities arise. There may be quite unambiguous fantasies of being a girl or woman (fantasy body femaling). A common boyhood variant is "waking up in the morning as a girl." Many femalers who later conceptualise themselves as transsexuals and who are conceptualised as primary transsexuals within the psychiatric-medical literature (Person & Ovesey, 1974a) recall variations on this theme. For others, the fantasy femaling takes on a gender stress. Thoughts of male and female morphology do not arise. Rather, the emphasis is upon romantic fantasies relating to such things as dreamy dresses, ribbons, doll play, and the like. For still others, the emphasis is upon masturbatory fantasy cross-dressing in a range of variations.

There is a tendency in this phase for fantasies initially to cluster around certain themes, which develop only slowly. They may have a body/sex, gender, or erotic/sexual core, which may then be fuelled by one or another mode.

As regards the interrelations between the constitution of self and world as SSG'd, a number of points might be made. As with "beginning femaling," there is a tendency for the meaning frames (Goffman, 1974) of everyday life to reassert themselves when the incident of day-dreaming or masturbation is over. However, in the case of erotic fantasy femaling, gendered objects are increasingly invested with potential affect, to form material for future masturbatory scripts. *Pari passu,* the environment is gaining potential for being increasingly eroticised/sexualised. Alternatively, there may be an increasing fascination with "the world of women" (prehistory of gender femaling leading to gender femaling stress), with varying degrees of volition. As regards self and world, body femalers may become so preoccupied with their fantasying that their self-concepts as males become increasingly under threat; gender femalers, likewise, in more dreamy a fashion. More typically, however, there will be merely what might be termed incipient "dual worlding." An embryonic world will be constituted within which a femaling self and femaling-related objects and practices are emerging; but which at this stage, the fantasying femaler keeps separate from his everyday world, thus keeping the latter more or less "normal" and enabling its development more or less boundaried from this incipient femaling world.

PHASE 3: DOING FEMALING

Although fantasying femaling is frequently accompanied by partial cross-dressing, doing femaling includes more "serious" cross-dressing, and acting out aspects of fantasy body femaling. The body femaler may, for instance, depilate parts of his body periodically. He may experiment with hiding his male genitalia ("tucking"), and producing a simulated vulva. With, or just as likely without, body-femaling variants, the gender femaler may well build up private collections of clothes, jewelry, and accessories. All of these may, or may not, be built into masturbatory routines (erotic femaling), which may become more protracted.

In terms of sex, sexuality, and gender, and their interrelations, it is as though the femaler is developing along clustered lines, without really quite knowing what he is doing. Cross-dressing is likely to play a major part in this phase, whether the clusters follow sex, sexuality, or gender patterns; but typically, the femaler is not sure of the differences or where precisely he stands with regard to them. In this phase, femalers become more knowledgeable about the gendered world of girls and women, about what dresses they like, about styles, and so forth; this, in itself, gives pleasure. Others may place the emphasis upon increasingly elaborate masturbatory routines. Others may become more preoccupied with aspects of their morphology.

As regards the interrelations between the constitution of self and world as SSG'd, this is likely to be the period of particular personal confusion and of vacillation. Not only is the femaler "betwixt and between" two worlds, but he has no clear notion of what he is doing or its likely outcome. His "everyday" meanings in respect of his self and world are increasingly threatened by his increasing "doing femaling," but he is still not advanced in his conceptualisation of what he is doing and what it means. The femaler vacillates, for instance, between cross-dressing episodes, attempts to stop what he is doing, marked symbolically by frequent "purges"—the periodic throwing away of offending collections of clothes, cosmetics, jewelry, and so on.

As "doing femaling" becomes more frequent, the tendency to seek to "explain" it may well become more pressing. The search for meaning is incipient. But unless the femaler chances upon, for example, media coverage of "people like me," or comes across "explanations" by others in scientific texts, he may well continue to think, as many do in this phase, that "I am the only one in the world"; "I am a freak"; "Why I do this I do not know"; "Where will it all end?"

Phase 4: Constituting Femaling

This phase marks the period where the femaler begins to constitute the meanings of his activities in a more serious and sustained way. As femaling experiences and activities are increasing, many femalers are drawn increasingly to "explain" themselves, to "make sense" of themselves and their activities, and to work out where femaling fits with the rest of their lives.

A number of possibilities are typical of this phase. The femaler may seek professional guidance—a "cure"—having constituted himself as, for example, a pervert in need of help. He may in rare cases construct his own definition of the situation without access to literature or subculture. More typically, he will have chanced upon media references to "people called 'transvestites' (or 'transsexuals')," with whom he can identify. Many femalers, either through contact with subcultural literature, or through their reading of the "scientific" literature, begin to constitute a personalized transvestite or transsexual self-concept within a world of femaling, which is defined as they compare themselves with self-proclaimed transvestites and transsexuals they may meet in the subculture. Some definitions of the situation will be adopted "ready-made," as it were. Others are seen as inapplicable. More typically, the newly confronted constitutions are moulded to fit the particular self-concepts and understandings of self and femaling that the femaler has constituted thus far.

It is in this phase that meanings begin to crystallize around particular "namings" (Strauss, 1977, pp. 15–30), often quite discriminating namings having to do with psychiatric-medical conceptualisations as they have been absorbed into the subculture.

Frequently, much thought and careful consideration is directed towards "finding the label that fits." Some come to label themselves as a "true transsexual"; others as a "TV (transvestite) with TS (transsexual) tendencies"; others a "middle-of-the-road transvestite"; while others, as "primarily fetishistic."

Having adopted a label, meanings can now be ordered and understood. Once the femaler has sorted out *what* he is (and this is where the emphasis lies), beginnings can be made towards understanding *who* he is, and towards understanding the meanings of objects to him as variously SSG'd. The emphasis on "constituting femaling" does, however, tend to be on conceptualisations of self and identity. Once the label has been adopted, past identities are typically reinterpreted in the light of the newly discovered "condition." This is especially evident in the context of a consideration of the interrelations between sex, sexuality, and gender, the modes of femaling, and the constitution of self and world as SSG'd. What had been a confusing melange now becomes clear or clearer. Sally comments: "I fought it for years, I realise now that I had been TS (transsexual) all along" (new-found "sex," body femaling identity). Whereas for Annie "it was always a sexual thing. Now I can meet partners and we can 'rub slips' together. I know that's where I'm at" (erotic femaling identity, constructed around the sexual, with residual gender femaling).

The important and influential subcultural variant in which gender, and gender femaling is stressed—in many cases almost to the exclusion of sex, sexuality, body femaling, and erotic femaling—is best seen with reference to the Beaumont Society.

The Beaumont Society is the largest and most well established society for transvestites and "gender-motivated transsexuals" in the United Kingdom (Alice, L100, 1991). It is an association for transvestites and "gender motivated" transsexuals "whose motivation for cross-dressing is primarily of a gender, rather than a sexual, nature" (Beaumont Society Constitution, 1983). In its texts, it conceptualises transvestism in terms of love of the feminine; the transvestite self in terms of "full personality expression." Moreover, the society, through its various activities in promulgating its ideas and in holding "respectable" gender-orientated meetings at "respectable," "straight" venues, provides those identifying with it opportunities for managing the sexual stigma often attached to cross-dressing activities, both by cross-dressers themselves and the general public. Many of my Beaumont Society informants constituted their femaling selves and world in terms of "the Beaumont" and would state publicly that their cross-dressing had nothing whatsoever to do with sex or sexuality. Privately, though, many would say this was not the case.

PHASE 5: CONSOLIDATING FEMALING

This stage marks the period where a more full-blown constitution of femaling self and world is established. This will provide the individual with a more or less comprehensive and coherent framework within which to consolidate or develop his femaling self and world, and will also provide him with the means to relate these systematically to his "everyday," nonfemaling world.

The consolidation may be centered around body femaling, erotic femaling, or gender femaling, with the emphasis upon the corresponding features and facets of sex, sexuality, or gender. Various combinations over time are possible, but typically, having constituted self and world, "consolidating" sees reconstructions of pasts, consolidations of presents, and moves made toward intended futures, clustering around "chosen" foci.

Thus, a consolidating body femaler, having come to see that "really" "she" was transsexual all along (sexed identity), takes stock of "herself," and embarks upon a programme of appropriate body feminisation, which may be seen as culminating in "the op.," now defined in terms of becoming as near as is possible and practicable to what "she" should have been all along. "She" now dresses as a woman, because "she" *is* a woman. Her presentation of self is herself. As Sheila puts it: "Richard, this *is* me!" "She's" not merely expressing parts of "herself," or play acting. Thus, the meanings of what might have been conceptualised in terms of gender or sexuality are now redefined, and may take on different career paths of their own, all, in a sense, as adjuncts to the major focus of "her" femaling. As regards gender issues, "she" develops "her" personal style much as a genetic girl would have done—the difference being that "she" is starting rather late, has to do it rather quickly, and is likely to be hampered by residues of "her" maleness. As regards "her" sexuality, as hormonal treatment continues, "she" loses what male sexuality "she" has, and is, in effect, desexualizing "her" old sexuality concurrent with the construction of a new sex and sexuality.

The erotic femaler, having now consolidated his femaling around the erotic/sexual, may look to new ways to develop his erotic femaling. He may build up collections of subcultural literature and exotic paraphernalia. He may experiment with a view of finding what "turns him on" maximally. He may begin to conceptualise what "turns him on" in a fairly fine-tuned way. His female style may take on sadomasochistic variants which would normally be considered fetishistic and which may take increasingly bizarre forms, for he is not so much interested in the subtleties of femininity as he is with his personal sexual excitations. The role and meaning of body and gender femaling are redefined and clarified accordingly. Serious and sustained body femaling has no appeal at all. It would entail the loss of his eroticism and his pleasure-giving penis. Likewise, orthodox gender femaling may become seen as having prissy, drab, or effete connotations.

Another tack lies in the developing of subcultural contacts that will lead to a conscious celebration of the erotic. Erotic femalers may advertise for partners in subcultural magazines such as *The World of Transvestism* or *Transcript*. They may provide the magazines with photographs, personal details, and accounts of some of their sexual exploits carried out with other "TVs" (transvestites) or "TV punters" (apparent "straights" who fancy and hang around TVs and TSs) met through the magazine. Many erotic femalers build up something of a cult-following through this procedure. Some may get further excitement from being paid for their services. In this case, the erotic femaler gets maximum sexual excitation by becoming the stereotypical female, the "sexy hooker."

Embedded within the social worlds of cross-dressers and sex-changers in Britain are a number of sometimes overlapping and interrelating social circles (Simmel, 1955; Kadushin, 1966) of erotic femalers. Entry into these social circles is often instrumental in consolidating an erotic femaling identity.

The gender femaler, on the other hand, tends to move in the opposite direction. Residual fetishism may erode. Now his fascination with the whole world of the feminine knows no bounds. He wants to look and behave like a "real" woman (as he sees women), not some stereotypical male fantasy of one. This may entail the steady development of his femme self with "her" own personality, tastes, and enthusiasm. Many will model themselves on admired "RGs"; others will study deportment, voice production, fashion, make-up, and the like.

Body femaling and erotic femaling are now redefined in terms of the gender foci. It is not necessarily true that there is no body femaling. In fantasy, there may be much of it. Similarly, the gender femaler may adopt every bit of the sex role paraphernalia his ingenuity can dream up. He may, for instance, insert tampons in his fantasied vagina (rectum), or occasionally "go on the pill." But he does these things "because that is what RGs do," not because he thinks he is one, or is becoming one, or because of any very obvious erotic kick he gets out of doing it ("That wouldn't be feminine").

Typically, his relationship with the erotic is likely to be ambiguous. While there are gender femalers who are asexual, or increasingly become so, and who female for "reasons of tranquility" or even aesthetic reasons, the eroticism is more likely, perhaps, to be attenuated and dispersed and may indeed become increasingly so. We might say eroticism is adjuncted to gender femaling in these cases. For some, with increasing gender fine-tunedness, an ever-increasing number of objects in the world of women become mildly eroticised. But at the same time, their own sexuality becomes increasingly genderized. This can lead to a distaste for sexuality except as expressed in gender form. Sexual intercourse, for example, is fantasied in terms of gender femaling role play. Another possibility is that past gender femalings which were not erotic femalings at the time, come to form material for erotic scripts in subsequent episodes of fantasy femaling.

CONCLUSIONS AND IMPLICATIONS

This paper has been concerned to generate grounded theory in the substantive area of male cross-dressing and sex-changing. Reconceptualisation of the area in terms of the basic social process of male femaling has enabled justice to be done to the processual and emergent nature of much cross-dressing and sex-changing phenomena. It has generated a number of categories which have highlighted facets of male femaling hitherto not studied. In particular, it has examined some of the major possible and neglected shifting interrelations between facets of human sex, sexuality, and gender. Cross-dressers and sex-changers make an excellent case study in the consideration of these issues because of their sensitivity to them.

In reconceptualising the area in terms of the basic social process of male femaling, I inevitably raised a number of important issues that were peripheral to the focus of this paper, but which would profit from further work. Principal amongst these are the following:

1.   The psychiatric-medical literature is marked by disputes as to whether transvestism should properly be considered a sexual or gender anomaly, and whether transvestism and transsexualism should be considered as discrete clinical syndromes. These disputes might well be illuminated if considered in the light of male femaling as a basic social process.

2.   More fundamentally, a major task lies ahead for the researcher who would do full justice to the complexities, consequences, and ramifications of the interrelations in practice between psychiatric-medical conceptualisations and categorisations of cross-dressing and sex-

changing, and those of the male femalers themselves. Male femalers tend to be skeptical of medics and psychiatrists and, indeed, all so-called experts, whilst existing in an umbilical relationship with them. This warrants comprehensive investigation.

3. Of major interest to sociologists might be the exploration of male femaling as a case study in the sociology of secrecy. My theory and "findings" were illustrated with data which suggested that certain femalers come to adopt the label "transvestite" and come to gender female at the expense of overtly celebrating the erotic; whilst others come to adopt the term "transsexual," and then body female, redefining their gender femaling, and underplaying facets of male eroticism to extinction. Both of these routes provide rich material for work on the management of stigma and related issues.

4. Of potential importance and relevance outside the substantive area of male femaling are a number of highly complex issues that need to be explored further. In the process of male femaling, identity, selves, and objects become variously and with varying degrees of interconnectedness sexed, sexualised, and gendered. If any sociology (cf., social anthropology, Herdt, 1981) of sex, sexuality, and gender is to be based upon firm foundations, we need to know much more about this process, both inside and outside the specific area of male femaling.

5. Finally, I would raise another interesting issue. To what extent would our understanding and explanation of the behaviour of all males and females be enhanced by utilization of the sort of conceptual framework proposed in this paper?

ACKNOWLEDGMENTS

The fieldwork upon which this paper is based was enabled by funding from the Faculty of Social and Health Sciences Research Committee, University of Ulster, between 1980 and 1985. I wish to thank the many cross-dressers and sex-changers who have so readily shared their time and thoughts with me, particularly Miss Phaedra Kelly. I also acknowledge the assistance of Dr. Dave King and Dr. Wendy Saunderson.

REFERENCES

Alice, L100. (1991). A history of the Beaumont Society. *Beaumont Bulletin, 23*(3), 37–39.

Beaumont Society. (1983). *Beaumont Society Constitution.* London: Beaumont Society.

Benjamin, H. (1966). *The transsexual phenomenon: A scientific report on transsexualism and sex conversion in the human male and female.* New York: Julian Press.

Berger, P., & Luckmann, T. (1966). *The social construction of reality: A treatise in the sociology of knowledge.* Garden City, NY: Doubleday.

Bernstein, R. (1976). *The restructuring of social and political theory.* Oxford: Basil Blackwell.

Bigus, O., Hadden, S., & Glaser, B. (1982). Basic social processes. In R. Smith & P. Manning (Eds.), *Qualitative methods: Vol. II of a handbook of social science methods.* Cambridge, MA: Ballinger Publishing Co.

Billings, D.B., & Urban, T. (1982). The socio-medical construction of transsexualism: An interpretation and critique. *Social Problems, 29*(3), 266–282.

Birrell, S., & Cole, C.L. (1990). Double fault: Renee Richards and the construction and naturalization of difference. *Sociology of Sport Journal, 7*(1), 1–21.

Blumer, H. (1956). Sociological analysis and the variable. *American Sociological Review, 21,* 683–690.

Blumer, H. (1969). *Symbolic interactionism: Perspective and method.* Englewood Cliffs, NJ: Prentice-Hall.

Brake, M. (1976). I may be a queer, but at least I am a man: Male hegemony and ascribed versus achieved gender. In D.L. Barker & S. Allen (Eds.), *Sexual divisions in society: Process and change.* London: Tavistock.

Buckner, H.T. (1970). The transvestic career path. *Psychiatry, 33*(3), 381–389.

Curtis, J., & Petras, J. (Eds.). (1970). *The sociology of knowledge: A reader.* London: Gerald Duckworth.

Ekins, R. (1978). G.H. Mead: Contributions to a philosophy of sociological knowledge. Ph. D. Dissertation. University of London.

Ekins. R. (1983). The assignment of motives as a problem in the double hermeneutic: The case of transvestism and transsexuality. Paper for the Sociological Association of Ireland Conference, Wexford, Ireland.

Ekins, R. (1988). News from around the world—In their own words. Interview with Dr. Richard Ekins of the Trans-Gender Archive, University of Ulster. *Renaissance News, 1*(5), 4–5 (The Chrysalis Interview).

Ekins, R. (1989). Archive update: Interview with Dr. Richard Ekins of the Trans-Gender Archive, University of Ulster. *Fanfare,* 41, 9–12.

Ekins, R. (1990). Building a trans-gender archive: On the classification and framing of trans-gender knowledge. In A. Purnell (Ed.), *First International Gender Dysphoria Conference Report,* pp. 31–34. London: Beaumont Trust.

Feinbloom, D. (1976). *Transvestites and transsexuals: Mixed views.* New York: Delacorte Publishing Co.

Fisk, N. (1974). Gender dysphoria syndrome: The conceptualization that liberalizes indications for total gender reorientation and implies a broadly based multi-dimensional treatment regimen. *Western Journal of Medicine, 120,* 386–391.

Garfinkel, H., & Stoller, R.J. (1967). Passing and the managed achievement of sex status in an "intersexed" person. In H. Garfinkel (Ed.), *Studies in ethnomethodology,* pp. 116–185. Englewood Cliffs, NJ: Prentice-Hall.

Gender Trust, U.K. (1990). *A guide to transsexualism, transgenderism, and gender dysphoria.*

Ginger. (1980). *Female mimics international,* No. 2.

Glaser, B. (1978). *Theoretical sensitivity: Advances in the methodology of grounded theory.* Mill Valley, CA: Sociology Press.

Glaser, B., & Strauss, A. (1967). *The discovery of grounded theory.* Chicago: Aldine.

Goffman, E. (1959). *The presentation of self in everyday life.* Garden City, NY: Doubleday.

Goffman, E. (1963). *Stigma: Notes on the management of spoiled identity.* Englewood Cliffs, NJ: Prentice-Hall.

Goffman, E. (1974). *Frame analysis: An essay on the organization of experience.* New York: Harper & Row.

Goffman, E. (1976). *Gender advertisements.* New York: Harper Colophon.

Gould, M., & Kern-Daniels, R. (1977). Towards a sociological theory of gender and sex. *The American Sociologist, 12,* 182–189.

Green, R. (1974). *Sexual identity conflict in children and adults.* New York: Basic Books, Inc. Reprinted in 1975 by Penguin Books.

Green, R. (1987). *The "sissy boy" syndrome and the development of homosexuality.* New Haven, CT: Yale University Press.

Greenson, R.R. (1966). A transvestite boy and a hypothesis. *International Journal of Psycho-Analysis, 47*(2), 396–403.

Heap, J., & Roth, P. (1973). On phenomenological sociology. *American Sociological Review, 38,* 354–367.

Herdt, G.H. (1981). *Guardians of the flutes: Idioms of masculinity.* New York: McGraw-Hill.

Hirschfeld, M. (1991[1910]). *Transvestites: The erotic drive to cross-dress.* (Michael A. Lombardi-Nash, translator.) Buffalo, NY: Prometheus Books.

Hoenig, J., Kenna, J.C., & Youd, A. (1970). Social and economic aspects of transsexualism. *British Journal of Psychiatry, 117*(537), 163–172.

Kadushin, C. (1966). The friends and supporters of psychotherapy: On social circles in urban life. *American Sociological Review, 31,* 786–802.

Kando, T. (1973). *Sex change: The achievement of gender identity among feminized transsexuals.* Springfield, IL: Charles C. Thomas, Publishers.

Kessler, S.J., & McKenna, W. (1978). *Gender: An ethnomethodological approach.* New York: John Wiley & Sons. Reprinted in 1985 by The University of Chicago Press.

King, D. (1981). Gender confusions: Psychological and psychiatric conceptions of transvestism and transsexualism. In K. Plummer (Ed.), *The making of the modern homosexual.* London: Hutchinson.

Koranyi, E.K. (1980). *Transsexuality in the male: The spectrum of gender dysphoria.* Springfield, IL: Charles C. Thomas, Publishers.

Lukas, M.J. (1978). *Let me die a woman: The why and how of sex-change operations.* New York: Rearguard Productions.

Money, J. (1969). Sex reassignment as related to hermaphroditism and transsexualism. In R. Green & J. Money (Eds.), *Transsexualism and sex reassignment,* pp. 91–113. Baltimore, MD: Johns Hopkins University Press.

Money, J., & Ehrhardt, A.A. (1972). *Man and woman, boy and girl: The differentiation and dimorphism of gender identity from conception to maturity.* Baltimore, MD: Johns Hopkins University Press. Also (1972). Mentor, New York: New American Library.

Newton, E. (1979). *Mother camp: Female impersonators in America.* Chicago: University of Chicago Press.

Pepper, J. (1982). *A man's tale.* London: Quartet Books.

Person E., & Ovesey, L. (1974a). The transsexual syndrome in males: I. Primary transsexualism. *American Journal of Psychotherapy, 28,* 4–20.

Person, E., & Ovesey, L. (1974b). The transsexual syndrome in males: II. Secondary transsexualism. *American Journal of Psychotherapy, 28,* 174–193.

Plummer, K. (1979). *Symbolic interactionism and sexual differentiation: An empirical investigation.* Final report on Grant HR 5053 to the SSRC.

Plummer, K. (1983). *Documents of life: An introduction to the problems and literature of the humanistic method.* London: Allen & Unwin.

Raymond, J. (1979). *The transsexual empire: The making of the she-male.* Boston: Beacon Press. Reissued in 1994 with a new introduction by Teachers College Press, New York.

Rubington, E., & Weinberg, M. (Eds.). (1973). *Deviance: The interactionist perspective: Texts and readings in the sociology of deviance.* London: Macmillan.

Sagarin, E. (1969). Transvestites and transsexuals: Boys will be girls. In E. Sagarin (Ed.), *Odd man in: Societies of deviants in America.* Chicago: Quadrangle Books.

Schwartz, H., & Jacobs, J. (1979). *Qualitative sociology: A method to the madness.* New York: The Free Press.

Seeley, J. (1966). The "making" and "taking" of problems. *Social Problems, 14,* 382–389.

Shively, M.G., & de Cecco, J. (1977). Components of sexual identity. *Journal of Homosexuality, 3*(1), 41–48.

Simmel, G. (1955). *The web of group affiliations.* New York: The Free Press.

Stoller, R.J. (1968). *Sex and gender: On the development of masculinity and femininity,* Vol. 1. New York: Science House.

Stoller, R.J. (1973). Male transsexualism: Uneasiness. *American Journal of Psychiatry, 130*(5), 536–539.

Stoller, R.J. (1985). *Presentations of gender.* New Haven: Yale University Press.

Strauss, A. (1977). *Mirrors and masks: The search for identity.* London: Martin Robertson.

Strauss, A. (1978). A social world perspective. In N. Denzin (Ed.), *Studies in symbolic interaction.* Vol. 1. Greenwich, CT: JAI Press.

Strauss, A. (1987). *Qualitative analysis for social scientists.* Cambridge: Cambridge University Press.

Talamini, J.T. (1982). *Boys will be girls: The hidden world of the heterosexual male transvestite.* Lanham, MD: University Press of America, Inc.

Thomas, W. (1923). *The unadjusted girl.* Boston: Little Brown.

Unruh, D. (1979). Characteristics and types of participation in social worlds. *Symbolic Interaction, 2,* 115–119.

Unruh, D. (1980). The nature of social worlds. *Pacific Sociological Review, 23,* 271–296.

Walinder, J. (1967). *Transsexualism: A study of forty-three cases.* University of Göteborg, Sweden: Scandinavian University Books.

Zerubavel, E. (1980). If Simmel were a fieldworker: On formal sociological theory and analytical field research. *Symbolic Interaction, 3,* 25–33.

12 A New Concept of Body-Image Syndromes and Gender Identity

John Money

Definition

The concepts of the body image and the body schema are attached in the manner of Siamese twins—different, but merged. Body schema is the older term. It had its origins early in the twentieth century, in the writings of Henry Head on the phenomena of brain lesions and peripheral neuropathology that would alter the representation or schema of one's body and one's body functions in one's brain. These alterations in the brain would, in turn, alter one's personal recognition of one's own body, and of the location and function of its parts and regions.

Whereas in early usage there was a close connection between the body schema in the brain and the body image in personal recognition (Weinstein & Kahn, 1955; Signer, 1987), in later usage the connection loosened, and the terms "body schema" and "body image" became used interchangeably (Schilder, 1950, first edition, 1935).

Eventually, the body image assumed an existence of its own as an intrapsychic construct, independent of the body schema. Thenceforth, the representation of the body image in the brain, though it was not denied, was simply taken for granted. Advances in brain technology might, at some time, allow the body image to be traced to its corresponding representation in the brain schema.

A person's body image may be accurate in the sense of being accepted by other people as being consistent with their conception of that person's bodily appearance and function. By contrast, it may be so inaccurate in the sense of being rejected by other people as being, according to their criteria, a foolish and absurd fixation or delusion. An aberrant body image may be obsessively and tenaciously fixated, so as to be unyielding to rational and critical analysis. It then qualifies as a body image disorder or syndrome, of which the definition is as follows:

Body-image Syndrome: A condition pertaining to one's personal recognition of one's own body, including the location and function of its parts or regions, and characterized by discordancy between what has existed as compared with what presently exists, or between what presently exists as compared with one's projection of how it should be changing or is changing to become.

BODY-IMAGE PSYCHOSIS, NEUROSIS, COSMETICS

The intensity of a body-image syndrome ranges across the entire spectrum from lightweight and benign to heavyweight and malignant. It may be as benign as, for example, to become ornamentally tattooed; or as malignant as, for example, to become a eunuch by genital self-amputation, of which the fortuitous outcome may be to bleed to death.

The most virulent manifestations of a body-image syndrome may be characterized as body-image psychosis. That is to say, it may be classified as psychosis in its own right, and not attributed to some other psychosis, notably schizophrenia or bipolar psychosis. However, a body-image psychosis may share features in common with other psychoses, including psychoses associated with a brain lesion, without being diagnostically identical. Not only is the diagnosis different, but also the treatment and prognosis, insofar as the body-image psychosis is, like a monomania, more likely to be self-contained than psychopathologically diffuse.

This same diagnostic principle applies also to the less virulent manifestations of a body-image syndrome, which may be classified as a body-image neurosis. There is no clear line of demarcation that separates body-image neurosis from body-image psychosis. Demarcation on the criterion of the degree of body-image dysphoria experienced by the patient is contraindicated, insofar as it is impossible to measure subjectively experienced mental states. Moreover, any nosology based on mental states allows diagnosis to rely too much on what may be the capricious judgment, or wrong judgment of the diagnostician. The alternative and more reliable criterion is the degree to which the body-image syndrome incapacitates the patient for the daily routines and responsibilities of living.

The body-image syndromes do not have a place of their own in today's official nosology. The body-image cosmetology syndromes are accorded legitimacy in plastic surgery, and named according to the organ or region on which surgery is performed. The body-image neuroses and psychoses are diversely assigned a psychiatric diagnosis, which may or may not be in the category of somatoform disorder, as a body dysmorphic disorder or dysmorphophobia. It may also be diagnosed as a delusional disorder of the somatic subtype.

The principles of body alteration that apply to all the body-image syndromes, including the sexological ones, are realignment and enhancement, obliteration and relinquishment, and augmentation and amplification. All three principles of alteration are exemplified in the procedures of sex reassignment.

The procedures of sex reassignment were originally developed for the rehabilitation of patients whose natal sex was ambiguous or hermaphroditic and whose body image developed to be discordant with that of the sex in which they had been officially named and registered, and in which they were socially assigned and reared.

In the 1960s, sex reassignment (Benjamin, 1966; Green & Money, 1969) became recognized as an acceptable procedure for people whose natal sex was not ambiguous or hermaphroditic but whose body image nonetheless developed to be discordant with their natal sex. The same term, transsexualism, names not only the syndrome, but also the method of rehabilitation by changing the body to be concordant with the body image.

In the case of the male-to-female transsexual, the body image of the face is feminine and is discordant with that of the actual physiognomy, which in the majority of cases is bearded and has masculine features. The principle of alteration according to which congruence between the femininity of the facial body-image and the actual physiognomy is effected is realignment and enhancement. The method is electrolysis for facial hair removal, administration of female hormones for feminized skin texture, and plastic surgery for changes of the physiognomy—which are not invariably necessary.

The corresponding alterations for the female-to-male transsexual are also of the realignment and enhancement type, but the method is more simple. Treatment with male sex hormone suffices. It produces facial hair, masculine skin texture, and, ultimately, thinning or balding head hair. By enlarging the larynx, it also realigns the voice to conform to the body image—an effortless process unmatched in male-to-female reassignment, which requires vocal retraining.

The principle of obliteration and relinquishment is of paramount importance to the male-to-female transsexual with respect to the external genitals, which are a reproach and an offense to the feminine body image. In a majority of cases, being rid of the offensive male genitals takes precedence over the augmenting and amplifying procedure of vaginoplasty.

In the female-to-male transsexual, the offensive organs are those responsible for menstruation. Their extirpation takes precedence over the augmenting and amplifying procedure of phalloplasty, for which, despite its importance to the patient, there is no completely successful surgical technology.

In female-to-male transsexuals, the obliteration and relinquishment principle applies also to surgical extirpation of the breasts. By contrast in male-to-female transsexuals, it is the principle of augmentation and amplification that applies to the breasts. Hormonally induced breast enlargement (gynecomastia) may fail to match the body image of mammary hyperplasia in some patients, who may then resort to augmentation mammoplasty either by surgery, or by the very dangerous procedure of silicone injections. The latter may also be resorted to for hip enlargement.

The transsexual body image is individually variable with respect to the hierarchical position of the three principles of body alteration on the agenda of sex reassignment. Thus, in a case of male-to-female transexualism in which the principle of realignment and enhancement is hierarchically above relinquishment and obliteration, even an appointment with the hairdresser may take precedence over an admissions appointment for genital reassignment surgery.

In another case, by contrast, in which the obliteration and relinquishment principle is uppermost, the patient may embark on a frantic round of clinic shopping for a surgeon who will extirpate the offending external genital organs on the basis of personal request alone, with no waiting period, and without the delay of a psychologic, psychiatric, or sexologic consultation.

In yet another case, in which the augmentation and amplification principle is uppermost, large breasts may be so high on the agenda that a patient will find a way of meeting the cost of obtaining them, despite failing to meet other medical, surgical, or related rehabilitation expenses.

BIOGRAPHY AND ETIOLOGY

In some cases of sexological body-image syndrome, it is possible to retrieve biographical information sufficient to formulate a psychodynamic connection between the symbolism of the syndrome and the biographical experiences that antedated its onset. For example, in the biography of a girl with the androgen-insensitivity syndrome of male hermaphroditism, the unspeakable stigma of having male chromosomes and testicles may be sealed-off behind a fixation on the stigma of pubic baldness.

To understand the history of a fixation, however, is to understand a temporal, not a causal contingency. A temporal relationship is not synonymous with a causal relationship, and it does not guarantee either an accurate prognosis or a valid form of treatment. Long-term chronological follow-up may, however, show that the natural history of a body-image syndrome is that it resolves and goes into remission. That has proved to be the case in at least some sexological body-image syndromes, hence the value of therapeutic support.

Accurate description and phenomenological definition are the precursors of causal understanding. Phenomenologically, body-image syndromes including those that are sexological, are disorders of recognition. It is under the criterion of recognition that, in the brain and in the mind, the causality of all body-image disorders will eventually be comprehended.

REFERENCES

Benjamin, H. (1966). *The transsexual phenomenon: A scientific report on transsexualism and sex conversion in the human male and female*. New York: Julian Press.

Green, R., & Money, J. (Eds.). (1969). *Transsexualism and sex reassignment*. Baltimore: Johns Hopkins Press.

Schilder, P. (1950). *The image and appearance of the human body: Studies in the constructive energies of the psyche*. Psyche Monographs No. 4. London: Kegan Paul. New York: International Universities Press.

Signer, S.F. (1987). Capgras' syndrome: The delusion of substitution. *Journal of Clinical Psychiatry, 48*, 147–150.

Weinstein, E.A., & Kahn, R.L. (1955). *Denial of illness*. Springfield, IL: Charles C. Thomas.

PART II
RESEARCH AND TREATMENT ISSUES

13 Therapeutic Issues in Working with Transgendered Clients

Barbara F. Anderson

To be clear, let me define some of the words associated with this subject. "Transgender" is an umbrella term describing the community of individuals who believe themselves either to embody the other gender within themselves or be the other gender trapped in the wrong body. These individuals span a continuum from those who have occasional need to express the part of themselves that is gender-dissonant, to those who have an unwavering conviction that their true gender differs from that which is apparent to the world.

The term "cross-dresser" is used to describe a number of individuals, some of whom are transgendered. While not seeking surgical or hormonal modification of their bodies, they do experience a periodic need for cross-gender expression. Nontransgendered individuals who cross-dress may be motivated by a desire to shock, to entertain, to deceive or to achieve erotic arousal. Those who associate cross-dressing with erotic arousal are called transvestic fetishists or transvestites and are not considered truly transgendered. However, over time, some transvestites experience the emergence of cross-gender feelings along with a diminution of associated erotic sensations and may ultimately be revealed as transgendered. Therefore, this work will include the treatment of such individuals within its purview.

"Transsexual" describes those on the other end of the continuum who believe they are really of a gender different from their genetic sex and yearn to bring their body into congruence with their perceived gender.

The *Diagnostic and Statistical Manual of Mental Disorders,* 4th ed. (DSM IV) defines gender-identity disorder as ". . . a strong and persistent cross-gender identification, which is the desire to be, or the insistence that one is, of the other sex. . . . There must also be evidence of persistent discomfort about one's assigned sex or a sense of inappropriateness in the gender role of that sex. . . . [There may be no] concurrent physical intersex condition . . . [and lastly,] there must be distress or impairment in social, occupational, or other important areas of functioning" (1994, pp. 532–33). Another term for these feelings of discomfort, inappropriateness, and distress is "gender dysphoria." Not all transgendered individuals suffer from gender-identity disorder or gender dysphoria, as they do not feel discomfort with their situation, nor experience impaired functioning.

Some transgendered individuals may seek sex reassignment. This is a process which can include any or all of a number of procedures designed to align clients' gender identity and genetic sex in the interest of their psychological and social adjustment. These include legal, hormonal, cosmetic, and genital surgical procedures, as well as vocal training and image consultation. Many clients will seek psychological evaluation and counseling as part of the process.

This brings me to a discussion of psychotherapy of transgendered individuals. It is important to keep in mind that the treatment of gender-identity disorders is a specialized area of psychotherapy, even within the field of sex therapy. Clinicians considering treating a transgendered client should feel secure with regard to their knowledge of this population, experience, and access to supervision. If they lack such expertise, they should refer to a more competent practitioner. It is unprofessional as well as irresponsible to refuse treatment to any client without making a sincere effort to refer them to some accessible resource.

There are many reasons why transgendered people enter psychotherapy. One is to meet the requirements of the medical profession and obtain the procedures they seek. The desire for sex reassignment is a powerful motivator to individuals convinced that only a major physical modification of their body will relieve feelings of gender dysphoria. If clients desire sex reassignment through a program or by an endocrinologist or surgeon who adheres to the Standards of Care (Walker, et al., rev. 1990) developed by the Harry Benjamin International Gender Dysphoria Association (HBIGDA), they will be required to have a psychological evaluation and a period of therapy. To qualify for hormonal or surgical sex reassignment, clients must have psychotherapy for 3 or 6 months respectively, followed by a recommendation for each treatment (4.6.2., Std. 6., p. 8 and 4.8.1., Std. 8, p. 9). In addition, for genital surgery, clients must obtain a second evaluation and recommendation by another therapist (4.7.5., Std. 7).

This is a rather paradoxical situation, for the therapist holds the key to that which the client desires (Feinbloom, 1976), yet the client is expected to be open, honest, and completely self-revealing. One must question whether an atmosphere conducive to the therapeutic process can really occur in such an adversarial circumstance (Bolin, 1988). However, even clients who lack a sincere desire to benefit from treatment, who remain guarded and reserved in therapy, and who have an ulterior motive, can have a positive experience; for in spite of oneself, an individual's curiosity can be piqued, information about one's condition can be absorbed, and insight can develop. At the very least, useful facts about resources can be acquired by the client.

Some clients desire a "case manager" to oversee the process of preparing for a life change which may or may not proceed all the way to sex-reassignment surgery. This includes the therapist making referrals to resources such as endocrinologists, sex-reassignment and cosmetic surgeons, electrologists, attorneys, counselors for family and employment matters, social and educational organizations, and clothing stores friendly to the transgendered community, as well as providing pre- and postoperative support.

Other individuals experience a need to understand or make sense of their behaviors and feelings such as the compulsive desire to cross-dress, hatred of and disgust with their genitals, the belief of being in the wrong body, the idea that they are different from all other people, the conviction of being homosexual, perverted, mentally ill, or sinful. It is in these clients that we see the classic gender-identity disorder as described by the DSM IV. They are often high-risk individuals subject to self-destructive behaviors and will need the best of their psychotherapists' skills and understanding of transgender issues.

Problems with family members around gender concerns and behaviors frequently bring clients into treatment. Who, when, how, and what to to tell about gender-identity concerns are the kinds of issues they raise. Dealing with children and adolescents in the family also presents a challenge to transgendered individuals seeking to find an accommodation between their need for gender expression and their desire to maintain stability in the family constellation. Lastly, negotiating privacy and financial consideration to meet one's need for clothing, medical care, and other requirements specific to the transgendered condition usually emerge in the course of treatment.

On occasion a transgendered individual is sent to a therapist known to have expertise in the area of gender disorders by a family member such as a spouse or parent of a teen or young adult to be "cured." This is not an appropriate expectation in working with these clients, for numerous reports indicate the futility of this pursuit (Pomeroy, 1975; Money & Walker, 1977). Prospects of this being a useful therapeutic experience are contingent upon participation by the referring family member(s) as well as the identified patient. It is an opportunity for the therapist to educate all the participants and demystify the condition of transgenderism.

In the best of outcomes an understanding and respect for the client's feelings and needs will emerge, guilt and blame will dissipate, and familial bonds will remain intact. When a less-than-ideal outcome is achieved, one sees a tacit agreement to sever relations, a decision to maintain only the most superficial contact, or a schism among family members who gravitate into different camps, some in support of and others rejecting the transgendered client. The worst outcome is one in which all participants in therapy calcify their beliefs that the identified patient is perverted, sick, or sinful, that some or all family members are to blame for the transgendered condition, and the only resolution is a "cure." The therapist may feel terribly torn between loyalty to the transgendered client and to the uncomprehending family, all of whom are suffering. If an impasse is reached and family treatment is no longer productive, my belief is that the therapist who specializes in working with the transgendered should remain available to the client while referring the family for continued treatment elsewhere.

Some transgendered individuals anticipate they will need support during the 12 months of full-time cross-living in the gender role of the opposite sex that is required by HBIGDA's Standards of Care as a condition for reassignment surgery (5.2.4., p. 12). Even those who do not plan to proceed through surgery may choose to live and work in the gender role they feel is most authentic for them. Although most clients who have reached this point of commitment to cross-living have experimented with cross-dressing for periods of time and may have "come out" to those closest to them, they may never have worked or socialized with nontransgendered people while cross-dressed. For them, therapy provides encouragement, offers appropriate referral to adjunctive services to improve their appearance, supports them in dealing with social rejection and discrimination on the job, and prepares them to confront harassment in public venues.

Lastly, clients may enter therapy for help with postoperative adjustment. They may have to face medical complications, cosmetic disappointments, and social rejection. To the extent that these clients had competent counseling prior to sex-reassignment surgery, there may be only a minimal need for support and direction to necessary resources. Unfortunately, many transgendered individuals find their way through the maze of medical services, including reassignment surgery, without any counseling, education, or preparation for the postoperative period. Ironically, those individuals who are most likely to avoid the required "roadblocks" of medical and psychological evaluation, psychotherapy, and a period of cross-living, all of which are designed to insure the best postoperative outcome (Bolin, 1988), often suffer the greatest disappointments at the hands of physicians who remain unaccountable to anyone.

Other postoperative clients who seek counseling are those who relocated prior to or following surgery, often "to start a new life." They may encounter all the earlier mentioned postoperative adjustment issues in addition to feeling isolated, estranged, and lonely in an unfamiliar environment. Again, the therapist can be most helpful in a supportive role, furnishing referrals to community organizations and bolstering the client's reality-testing and coping skills.

Many transgendered individuals never enter a therapist's consulting room. They may be blessed with a loving and wise family that supports them through their development of a gender identity with which they can feel comfortable. Or they may just muddle through life utilizing personal resources undiminished by societal and familial taboos. However, those transgendered individuals who do request treatment tend to present with similar symptoms and dysfunctions. Therapeutic issues that arise in this client population are fairly uniform. Depression, low self-esteem, guilt, suicide, substance abuse, and social isolation are the most common. One emotion, shame, and its concomitant behavior, secretiveness, seem to be endemic within transgendered people seeking therapy. While some are able to muster coping defenses such as denial and sublimation, others retreat into depression or act out self-destructively with suicidal behaviors and substance abuse. It is rare to meet a transgendered client who reports entering adulthood with good self-esteem and a sense of competence. Lastly, social isolation seems to be a hallmark of these clients as well. This is especially so of transsexuals, whose sense that their gender role is inappropriate often begins early, and whose childhood cross-gender behaviors may have made them a constant target of rejection and abuse from peers and family. In addition to poor self-esteem, the socially isolated individual does not have the normal childhood and adolescent experiences with peers so important in the accomplishment of necessary developmental milestones. This results in an adult with interpersonal skills fixated at a level far below that of the client's chronological age.

Family relationships are often dysfunctional in the lives of the transgendered clients with whom I have worked. It is tempting to regard the estrangement, enmeshment, domestic violence, skewed loyalties, and isolation in their families of origin as begetting gender-identity problems as well as any other atypical condition. However, despite speculation and case studies by Stoller and others, no research has confirmed any relationship issues as causal of this condition (Stoller, 1967). It is more likely that the presence in a family of an individual with a shame-inducing condition and its behavioral concomitants is a greater contributor to family dysfunction than the reverse.

Family life rarely improves for transgendered clients as they enter adulthood and attempt to form a nuclear family of their own. Some number never even try this, being too shy, socially inept, or isolated. Many do, however, with disastrous consequences. Some hope marriage and children will "cure" them. This may lead to multiple marriages and divorces in the search for the right "medicine." Others confide in their spouse and are met with horror, fear, and rejection. Relationships with children are often disturbed, marked by either self-distancing to protect the children from knowledge of their parent's transgendered condition or estrangement engineered by an angry, frightened spouse. The specific transgendered condition also presents its own difficulties. The cross-dresser is usually more concerned with hiding his activities and keeping his store of makeup and clothing secreted while the transsexual struggles with existential matters such as identity, lifestyle, and body image.

Dealing with substance abuse is a major therapeutic issue in this client population. Because of the pervasive shame and guilt around their feelings and behaviors, alcohol and other drugs become a convenient and accessible means to dull the pain the transgendered feel much of the time. When these individuals present for counseling for gender concerns they must be helped to understand the necessity of addressing their substance-abuse problems as well. Under ideal circumstances, a client would be drug-free for six months before entering counseling, but in the real world we often settle for concurrent treatment of both conditions.

A major therapeutic focus in working with this population is providing accurate and meaningful information about their gender-identity problems. While many other clients can be helped without becoming particularly knowledgable about their condition, in the case of those with gender concerns, who so often are misinformed or totally uninformed about their condition, knowledge is essential. It empowers a group which is largely disenfranchised, it gives words to feelings and needs never spoken of, and lastly, it creates a community of individuals who have been isolated by shame. All the traditional psychological interventions will be wasted without the empowering impact of information about this condition and the many other sufferers who are coping with and resolving gender-identity issues. Additionally, clients need to have ready access to resources which can facilitate their coming to peace with their condition, whether this is a transgender-friendly clothing store, an electrologist or surgeon, or a support group.

Related to the above, but deserving of distinct attention is the issue of helping clients deal with discrimination and victimization on the job, in housing, and in the use of normally gender-segregated public facilities. With increased comfort with their transgendered condition, clients often begin their tentative entry into society-at-large. If they do not have an accurate appreciation of their impact on the social milieu (i.e., how well they pass, whether they are operating in a liberal or conservative climate, etc.), they are apt to be shocked by the response they elicit from others. They need their therapist to mirror their appearance and behavior in a way that they can absorb, reprocess, and modify if necessary. They also need help in facing up to unkindness and unfairness until they develop the skills to avoid these responses from others.

Therapists who treat the transgendered will serve their clients doubly well by devoting a small part of their time advocating for the rights of the transgendered. In doing so, they both contribute to building a more receptive social environment, as well as model behaviors that can help clients enter into a ready-made supportive community of politically active transgendered individuals with a mission in keeping with the clients' goals.

The last issue that must be considered in treating clients with gender concerns are those of health care. Because of the marginal social position many transgendered individuals have occupied, their health may be impaired by drug abuse, sexually transmitted diseases, and other debilitating conditions that have become chronic through inconsistent and indifferent health care. Some clients have experimented with illegally acquired hormones which have compromised their health. Others have mutilated their genitals in a futile effort to rid themselves of the hated reminder of their transgendered condition. Because of employment discrimination, many have had difficulty holding jobs and obtaining health insurance. A therapist can be helpful in finding medical resources that offer respectful and competent health care to a population unused to such quality service.

One of the most challenging therapeutic situations occurs when transsexual clients present with health problems that preclude sex reassignment. These include but are not limited to, severe circulatory or respiratory disorders, diabetes, and AIDS. Such clients need help in finding creative ways to minimize their dysphoria while also dealing with managing medications and facing the consequences of life-threatening illnesses.

In considering the therapeutic process, the first matter to be dealt with is assessment and possible diagnosis. In evaluating whether clients are truly transgendered, a thorough psychosexual history is crucial. Once transgendered status is confirmed, a client needs to be further assessed with regard to whether he or she is a transsexual, cross-dresser, androgyne, transgenderist, or one of several other types of individuals with feelings or behaviors at odds with their assigned gender role. An inquiry into the presence of any physiological or anatomical anomalies should be made in the course of the psychosocial history, and if a question in this regard arises, a medical evaluation should be included in the assessment.

The matter of diagnosis may be a moot question. The 1994 DSM IV does not mention the terms "transgender" or "transsexual," thus removing them from the category of mental disorders. It does describe the diagnostic entity "gender-identity disorder," defined earlier in this paper. To review, it is marked by cross-gender identification, feelings of discomfort and inappropriateness in one's assigned gender role, the absence of a physical intersex condition, and impairment in social, occupational, or other arenas of living.

Because diagnoses can be tools of discrimination, I do my best not to use them. Descriptive statements about a particular individual are far more informative and useful than a formal category subsumed under a group of mental disorders. However, HBIGDA's Standards of Care state that a therapist's recommendation for sex reassignment be based "in part" on the client's match with the criteria for transsexualism found in the then current DSM III-R (4.3.1., Prin. 8, p. 6). Also, many insurance companies require diagnostic categorization in order to reimburse for medical and psychological services. As fewer third-party payers are covering treatment related to sex reassignment, the use of such diagnoses for the purpose of receiving insurance benefits may become obsolete.

Suffice it to say that an assessment leading to the therapist's understanding the nature and cause of the client's distress is of supreme importance. As there are no tests for transgenderism, the ultimate evidence is the client's own experience. The therapist may be most helpful by encouraging clients to reveal their perceptions of their gender condition and responding with reassurance that they are not unique, that their condition is known to medical science, and that it is a manageable one. However, clients presenting with transgenderism may be suffering instead from a mental disorder such as dissociative identity disorder (formerly multiple personality disorder), or delusional disorder. Or they may have a mental disorder concurrent with gender concerns. In such cases, HBIGDA's Standards of Care recommend that the presence of a mental disorder, as distinct from a transgender condition, should take precedence in treatment (4.3.3., Prin. 10, p. 6).

Once transgenderism is confirmed, differentiation must be made between transgendered cross-dressers and transsexuals. Some distinctions between the two are as follows: The former usually describe a high sex drive, frequent masturbation, and episodic cross-dressing, which is accompanied by erotic pleasure and which may be necessary for arousal. Clients are predominantly heterosexual males who describe the onset of behavior as occurring at puberty. Transsexuals often describe low libido, express disgust with their sex organs, frequently consider sex reassignment, and may give a history of genital self-mutilation. Clients may be male or female, hetero-, homo-, or bisexual and usually recall memories of gender confusion and feelings of being different from peers dating back to their third or fourth year of life.

Another aid in distinguishing these categories of individuals is the use of the Benjamin Sex Orientation Scale for male clients. This is a form identifying numerous types of behaviors which can be completed by male clients and which is useful in both assessment and as a trigger for discussion in therapy.

By the time the assessment is completed, it is hoped that the establishment of rapport between counselor and client is in process. Many qualities contribute to this essential aspect of therapy. Most obvious are the general therapy skills of empathy, competence, clear communication, and capacity for optimism. Contributing to rapport in this particular population is the therapist's mastery of solid information about this condition and the ability to convey to the client a sense of comfort with the subject. I offer reassurance that transgenderism is not a sickness, defect, or sin, but is a statistically uncommon condition which, because it is not an illness, is not curable. I stress its manageability and the challenge it presents to the individual and society. When necessary, I also counter and attempt to overcome the client's belief that therapy is useful only to the mentally ill.

As treatment progresses, I attempt to use the therapeutic relationship or transference to help clients examine and modify their relations with others. I share my responses to the client's behavior and wonder if others feel the same way. I encourage reflection, modification of old patterns if they seem nonproductive, experimentation with new behaviors, and exploration of feelings toward me in the service of psychological growth and development of confidence and self-esteem.

Maintenance of neutrality concerning whether sex reassignment is right for the client is both essential yet impossible to maintain within the therapeutic relationship as defined by HBIGDA's Standards of Care (4.6.2., std. 6, p. 8). While the decision must remain the client's, in fact the therapist who adheres to these Standards of Care is encouraged to deny approval under certain conditions. One reason for withholding endorsement for sex reassignment is a client who does not meet the diagnostic criteria for transsexualism as described by the DSM III-R (4.3.1., Prin. 8, p. 6). Another is the presence of a coexisting psychiatric condition (4.3.3., Prin. 10, p. 6).

Additionally, it is required that clients have reached the age of majority (4.14.2., Prin. 29, p. 10), completed the required legal process to change documents to reflect new sexual and gender status (4.13.2., Prin. 26, p. 10), and cross-lived for the prescribed period of time (5.2.4., p. 12). Some of these restrictions are targets of criticism by prominent professionals in the field. Dallas Denny, executive director of AEGIS maintains that ". . . the individual, whatever his or her characteristics, has the right to live as a man or a woman, and should not have to fit anyone's predefined criteria in order to do so. Schizophrenia, MPD, or personality disorders must be considered, but should not affect the decision, except as the desire for sex reassignment might, for instance, be caused [by] and would remit with treatment of the coexistent disorder" (Denny, 1994).

Apart from the requirements of HBIGDA's Standards of Care, some common-sense restrictions come to mind. I would withhold my endorsement for surgery and possibly for hormonal reassignment as well, in situations in which clients lack conviction that sex reassignment is the right choice for them, if they can't demonstrate the ability to accept the limitations of surgery or of immutable physical or cosmetic conditions, or if an addiction exists. Other gender programs have been known to impose very subjective, idiosyncratic conditions on the giving or withholding of permission for procedures, such as client's attractiveness, sex appeal, or ability to pass (Peterson & Dickey, 1995) but I do not concur on any of these criteria.

At this point, I would like to suggest that the way to avoid the ethical conflict facing the therapist who must judge whether the client is to get the desired procedures is for the responsibilities for therapy and endorsement to be divided between two professionals. The protocol for this procedure is explicated in another paper published by the author.

Another aspect of the therapeutic process is the maintenance of an empathic but firm response to manipulative behaviors by clients seeking endorsement for sex reassignment or any other documentation such as that required for financial assistance or disabililty benefits. While manipulative behavior per se is not cause for withholding of permission, when it is used in the service of countering the therapist's best clinical judgment, it must be resisted. I deal with this situation by periodically restating the purpose of therapy and clarifying the reason for my unreadiness to fulfill the client's wishes. Hopefully, this issue will resolve itself, at least with regard to permission for surgical reassignment, when the therapist is relieved of this responsibility and it is shifted to a second evaluator.

Adjusting the focus of therapy for transsexuals and transgendered cross-dressers is another part of the therapy process. Transsexuals involved in electrolysis, hormonal therapy, and cosmetic surgery, and heading toward surgical reassignment require much more concrete information, referral to community resources, and a strong counseling emphasis on reality testing and examination of future expectations than do those who are not. Therapeutic work tends to last longer with this population, a minimum period of six months prior to surgery and then for a continued period of time to solidify postoperative adjustment. Transsexuals who do not opt for reassignment or are not able to consider these procedures due to health or financial constraints may become long-term clients and require years of support to come to peace with their unfulfillable dream of bringing their body and gender into accord. They can be helped to accept that one can cross-live successfully without surgical modification of the body.

Cross-dressers need to work more on learning to articulate their needs to a partner, confining their cross-dressing behaviors to appropriate venues, broadening their ability to achieve sexual pleasure beyond dependence on dressing, and dealing with compulsive behaviors. Couple and family therapy can be very useful in ameliorating the anxiety, guilt, and secretiveness associated with cross-dressing and which fuel the compulsivity of their cross-gendered behaviors. Treatment with these clients is often brief but periodic, recurring when relationship stresses occur, as children mature, or partners enter or leave their lives. As mentioned earlier, some individuals formerly thought to be cross-dressers re-enter therapy with the new awareness that they are in fact transsexual. A reassessment is then indicated, and therapy should continue until newly evolved goals are reached.

This brings me to a discussion of goals of therapy with the transgendered client population. The primary objective is the relief of symptoms and the restoration or creation of a state of psychological homeostasis, allowing the client to live a productive and fulfilling life. A second objective is increased self-awareness and the ability to make an informed decision about the course of one's life. Related to this goal is the development of the capacity to assess, accept, and adapt to the reality of one's situation while continuing to explore appropriate means to modify and improve one's life.

REFERENCES

American Psychiatric Association. (1994). *Diagnostic and statistical manual of mental disorders*. DSM IV. Washington, DC: American Psychiatric Association.
Bolin, A. (1988). *In search of Eve: Transsexual rites of passage*. South Hadley, MA: Bergin & Garvey Publishers, Inc.
Denny, D. (1994). Personal communication.
Feinbloom, D.H. (1976). *Transvestites and transsexuals: Mixed views*. New York: Dell Publishing Co.

Money, J., & Walker, P.A. (1977). Counseling the transsexual. In J. Money & H. Mustaph (Eds.), *Handbook of sexology*, pp. 1289–1301. New York: Elsevier/North Holland Biomedical Press.

Pomeroy, W.B. (1975). The diagnosis and treatment of transvestites and transsexuals. *The Journal of Sex and Marital Therapy, 1*(3), 215–224.

Walker, P.A., et al. (1990) (rev. ed.). *Standards of care: The hormonal and surgical sex reassignment of gender dysphoric persons.* Sonoma, CA: The Harry Benjamin International Gender Dysphoria Association, Inc.

14 TRANSGENDER BEHAVIOR AND DSM IV

Collier M. Cole

Walter J. Meyer III

Transgenderism is a socio-legal-behavioral term referring to individuals who express feelings and behaviors that are discordant with recognized gender, based on anatomic sex. Most commonly, this term includes the following subgroups: transvestites (i.e., males who cross-dress; there is no clinically recognized female counterpart); transsexuals (i.e., individuals, both male and female, who are dissatisfied with their anatomic sex and desire to change to the opposite sex, often living full time in the new role, taking hormones, and pursuing sex-reassignment surgery); and transgenderists (i.e., individuals similar to the transsexual, both male and female, who are dissatisfied with their anatomic sex, often living full time in the desired role and taking hormones, but not desiring sex-reassignment surgery and instead electing what is coming to be called the "nonsurgical option").

While the term "transgenderism" is relatively new, the phenomenon described is well recognized throughout the history of man (Green & Money, 1969). Early efforts to describe transgender behavior have fallen on the field of medicine, likely because this phenomenon involved nonusual or atypical behavioral manifestations of the human condition, and such was considered in the realm of medicine and psychiatry. Hirschfeld (1910), at the turn of the century, was one of the first sexologists to detail cross-dressing behavior; he coined the term "transvestite." Half a century later, Benjamin (1966) studied aspects of transsexualism, culminating in his classic book on the subject. And, in 1980, the Harry Benjamin International Gender Dysphoria Association was formed and Standards of Care were developed to guide professionals in working with transsexual individuals (Walker, et al., 1985). Specifically, the Standards of Care offer minimal criteria for determining how and when to recommend such interventions as hormone therapy and sex-reassignment surgery for those seeking these treatments. Methods for follow-up are provided too. In general, the study of transgender behavior is relatively recent, with most research coming in the last several decades. The conceptualization of such behavior has been based primarily on clinical samples of individuals in distress or who are seeking specific medical therapies. Much of this professional literature portrays transgender individuals as having additional associated psychopathology.

Along this historical pathway, the American Psychiatric Association also recognized this behavioral condition. And, with the current *Diagnostic and Statistical Manual,* 4th edition (DSM IV), two primary types are identified (American Psychiatric Association, 1994). First, transvestic fetishism (formerly "transvestism," also referred to as "heterosexual cross-dressing") is listed under the paraphilias, or sexual deviant behaviors, a category which also includes pedophilia, exhibitionism, voyeurism, and other prominent sex-offending problems. This particular paraphilia involves recurrent fantasies, urges, and behaviors involving cross-dressing (see Table 14.1). While this appears to be predominantly a male phenomena, there is anecdotal information that a female counterpart exists. However, this has not been reported in the clinical literature, probably because society has not concerned itself with women who dress in male clothes.

The second DSM IV classification, gender-identity disorder (formerly "transsexualism," also referred to as "gender dysphoria"), stands alone with its own classification. This phenomenon can be seen in both sexes at various developmental stages, and so can be diagnosed at childhood, adolescence, or adulthood. It involves a strong and consistent cross-gender identification and discomfort with one's anatomic sex, often beginning in the early developmental years and evolving over time to include a desire to alter one's self through hormones and surgery (see Table 14.2).

It is important to note that both transvestic fetishism and gender-iden-

---

TABLE 14.1. DSM IV Criteria for Transvestic Fetishism (Paraphilia)

A.   Over a period of at least 6 months, in a heterosexual male, recurrent intense sexually arousing fantasies, sexual urges, or behaviors involving cross-dressing.

B.   The fantasies, sexual urges, or behaviors cause clinically significant distress or impairment in social, occupational, or other important areas of functioning.

Source: American Psychiatric Association, 1994.

TABLE 14.2. DSM IV Criteria for Gender-Identity Disorder

A. A strong and persistent cross-gender identification (not merely a desire for any perceived cultural advantages of being the other sex). In children, the disturbance is manifested by four (or more) of the following:

1. repeatedly stated desire to be, or insistence that he or she is, the other sex

2. in boys, preference for cross-dressing or simulating female attire; in girls, insistence on wearing only stereotypical masculine clothing

3. strong and persistent preferences for cross-sex roles in make-believe play or persistent fantasies of being the other sex

4. intense desire to participate in the stereotypical games and pastimes of the other sex

5. strong preference for playmates of the other sex

In adolescents and adults, the disturbance is manifested by symptoms such as stated desire to be the other sex, frequent passing as the other sex, desire to live or be treated as the other sex, or the conviction that he or she has the typical feelings and reactions of the other sex.

B. Persistent discomfort with his or her sex or sense of inappropriateness in the gender role of that sex.

In children, the disturbance is manifested by any of the following: in boys, assertion that his penis or testes are disgusting or will disappear or assertion that it would be better not to have a penis, or aversion toward rough-and-tumble play and rejection of male stereotypical toys, games, and activities; in girls, rejection of urinating in a sitting position, assertion that she has or will grow a penis, or assertion that she does not want to grow breasts or menstruate, or marked aversion toward normative feminine clothing.

In adolescents and adults, the disturbance is manifested by symptoms such as preoccupation with getting rid of primary and secondary sex characteristics (e.g., request for hormones, surgery, or other procedures to physically alter sexual characteristics to simulate the other sex) or belief that he or she was born the wrong sex.

C. The disturbance is not concurrent with a physical intersex condition.

D. The disturbance causes clinically significant distress or impairment in social, occupational, or other important areas of functioning.

Source: American Psychiatric Association, 1994.

tity disorder are considered to be mental disorders, per DSM IV, only if one or more of the following conditions are met. These include:

1.   The condition produces distress (i.e., is perceived as painful);
2.   The condition is disabling (i.e., causes impairment in social, occupational, or other areas of life functioning); and/or
3.   The condition represents a danger to oneself, others, or may lead to a loss of freedom.

In spite of the additional clarification regarding these conditions, controversy still surrounds the way transgender behavior is described in DSM IV. For some clients as well as therapists, the APA's diagnostic criteria are too limiting and do not take into account variations that exist which do not fit into the specified categories. Also, some transgender consumers and activists feel that a psychiatric description of this condition is stigmatizing (Raymond, 1994; Gamson, 1995). They point out that transgender behavior should not be viewed as a psychiatric diagnosis, just as homosexuality is not viewed as a psychiatric diagnosis. A recent article in *Esquire* magazine describes the increasingly visible "transgender movement" and the concerns these individuals have about this issue (Taylor, 1995). Yet, the same article points out that those protesting appear to be in the minority, with the vast "silent" majority of transsexuals and transgenderists simply wanting to pursue desired medical therapies, blend into society, and live in quiet anonymity. In reality, there are no epidemiological studies of the true incidence or range of these types of behaviors.

This poses an interesting question: to what extent is transgender behavior psychopathological? Is there some research to suggest that perhaps such behavioral states are not psychiatrically disordered, per se?

Contemporary Research

In a recent work by George R. Brown, M.D., a psychiatrist and gender specialist, the area of transvestism or heterosexual cross-dressing is extensively reviewed (Brown, 1995). He points out that various treatment approaches used to "cure" adults of this behavior (e.g., psychotherapy, aversion techniques, pharmacological agents) have been abysmal failures, with none resulting in permanent behavior change. Rather, most cross-dressers enjoy their behavior, coming to the attention of mental-health professionals only when a crisis arises (e.g., a spouse discovers and will not accept such behavior, feelings of guilt and shame develop associated with cross-dressing). Brown notes that current views of transvestism are based on such clinical cases of individuals in distress. Surveys of large groups of individuals drawn from social and support networks of cross-dressers, however, indicate no sense of distress, but rather self-satisfaction and feelings that such activities are fulfilling and enriching aspects of their adult lives (Docter, 1988). Also, the psychiatric profession views cross-dressing behavior as associated with sexual arousal, often with masturbation accompanying the activity. Yet, the above-mentioned surveys suggest another motivation. For many, the desire to cross-dress, while often starting out with accompanying sexual activity in the early phase, evolves over time until nonerotic pleasure is a predominant motivator (e.g., expressing one's feminine side, providing a sense of calmness and relaxation, being able to network socially with friends around such behavior).

Such observations suggest for many cross-dressers there may not exist a psychiatric disorder, per se. That is, there may be people out there, as yet undetermined in number, who have largely gone unnoticed by mental-health professionals. For these individuals, there would seem to be no significant personal distress or impairment in functioning (e.g., social, vocational) or threat (e.g., to self, others, loss of freedom), hence no need to be described as having a psychiatric problem. From Brown's perspective then, cross-dressing behavior could be seen as compatible with mental health rather than mental illness.

Cole and his colleagues in Galveston have likewise surveyed a primarily transsexual population (Cole, O'Boyle, Emory, & Meyer, 1997). In their study, 435 individuals presenting with a self-diagnosis of transsexualism were evaluated extensively, participating in a minimum 1–2 hour interview and completing a lengthy biographical questionnaire. The areas addressed included hormonal/surgical treatments undertaken, and histories of documented psychiatric problems (i.e., previously diagnosed mental disorders). In addition, a subgroup of individuals completed the MMPI, a standardized personality inventory commonly used in the field of psychiatry.

Of particular note, results suggested that less than 10 percent evidenced problems associated with previously diagnosed mental illness, not inclusive of gender dysphoric concerns. This ten percent figure is noteworthy, according to the authors, as recent estimates from the National Institute of Mental Health (NIMH) regarding the American population in general, suggest that up to 25 percent report having had identifiable psychiatric symptoms suggestive of diagnoses such as anxiety disorders, depression, drug and alcohol abuse, and personality disorders (Weissman & Myers, 1978; Robins, et al., 1984). In light of this, it would appear that the sample studied had an incidence of previously diagnosed mental illness no higher than that found in the general population. The mental-health problems noted in this sample included affective disorders, schizophrenia, and personality disorders.

Additional findings indicated that those completing the MMPI demonstrated profiles that were notably free of psychopathology according to both Axis I (i.e., major clinical syndromes) and Axis II (i.e., personality disorders) criteria as set forth in DSM IV. That is, for the 92 male-to-females (29 percent of the original MTF sample) and 44 female-to-males (38 percent of the original FTM sample) who completed the MMPI, their averaged profiles did not show consistent notable elevations on the clinical scales such as depression, paranoia, schizophrenia, and others. The one scale where significant differences were observed was the Mf scale, a broad measure of masculinity-femininity. Here the profiles of the male-to-female subsample, and to some extent the female-to-male subsample, appeared more "normal" when examined from the perspective of the desired sex rather than the anatomic sex, suggesting better comfort and adaptation in the new gender roles. In summary, this study offered support to the view that transsexualism is usually an isolated diagnosis and not part of any general psychopathological disorder.

It is important to remember that the Cole, et al., findings noted above are not without critics, as some studies have found opposite results. Specifically, Pauly (1990) has noted a significant incidence of mood disorders in gender-dysphoric individuals, and Levine (1989) has reported on notable Axis II pathology in this group (i.e., DSM IV criteria for associated personality disorders). These varied findings suggest a need to conduct further surveys of large groups of transsexuals and transgenderists, addressing issues of self-satisfaction, social-familial problems encountered, and evidence of symptoms suggestive of mental illness.

Those individuals studied by Cole and his colleagues had presented to a gender clinic for medical assistance in achieving their desired goals of successfully living as men or women. Over two-thirds were undergoing hormone reassignment, suggesting a commitment to the real-life process. And virtually all of the individuals were seeking to pursue sex-reassignment surgery, hence the reason for coming to this medical clinic. Only a handful were considering the nonsurgical option (i.e., living as transgenderists, taking hormones of the desired sex, but not wanting to pursue surgery). Such an option, as noted earlier, has been appreciated only recently and has not been extensively studied by gender specialists, who have traditionally viewed hormones with eventual surgery as the appropriate outcome sought by individuals.

TOWARD THE FUTURE

These recent studies suggest that an expanded view of transgender behavior may be in order. Frankly, one should not be surprised in this regard.

After all, knowledge regarding other human conditions has evolved with time and closer examination. This does not rule out the existence of individuals with problems who certainly can benefit from psychiatric intervention, but this may not be a characteristic of the group as a whole. Clearly there is a need for additional empirical research around the variations of transgenderism and possible associated psychiatric illnesses in order to revise understanding of this human condition, as well as ways to intervene and assist where indicated. Perhaps one direction worth considering would be to consolidate all variant subgroups under one classification, transgenderism, thus reflecting the continuum of this human condition and also eliminating one of the major criticisms of cross-dresser groups about being identified as a whole with the paraphilias or "sexual perversions." Also, it should be noted that transgender behavior, per se, may not reflect a psychopathological process unless specific qualifying criteria are met, as detailed previously (e.g., distress, disability, danger).

Since many may elect to pursue the options of hormone therapies and/or surgery, medical involvement in some fashion will likely remain in place. After all, a period of evaluation is practical and judicious when contemplating interventions of this nature. The Benjamin Society's Standards of Care recognize the importance of this fact and were clearly developed to be of benefit to the consumer, professional, and payor of services. No form of medical treatment is simply provided "on demand" without an interactive component between professional and consumer, exploring both potential risks and benefits. For example, if hormone medications were so safe and simple, why does the FDA not assign these to over-the-counter status? Research clearly indicates that there can be risks to this form of treatment, and so medical involvement with follow-up is warranted to ensure safety for the consumer (Meyer, et al., 1986). Another issue to remember too, and a very practical one at that, is pointed out by Pauly (1992), who notes that tremendous gains have been made over the years in getting insurance carriers to recognize transgender behavior as a legitimate, reimbursable expense for a medically recognized condition. With Standards of Care and identified diagnostic criteria, major battles have been won in this regard. In many cases, coverage has gone beyond the medical-surgical expenses to include speech therapy, electrolysis, and other recommended interventions. Eliminating such guidelines could return a consumer's coverage for professional expenses to one's own out-of-pocket capabilities. Instead of trying to eliminate medical involvement, the important point here is that both consumer and professional need to work together and, in cases in which there is not a good match, either should be free to go elsewhere.

So, one should not be quick to downgrade or abandon the current Standards of Care. Along with "clinical judgment" and experience, they serve to help an individual come to understand himself/herself and develop a tailored plan to move toward better adjustment and self-acceptance. They are, however, not written in stone and, indeed, are subject to change as new information comes forth. (Such is a common practice in medicine and psychiatry as various illnesses and behavioral states are revisited and approaches to intervention and management are revised.) The Fourteenth International Symposium on Gender Dysphoria was held in September 1995 in Germany, and similar feelings were expressed by many members present. Specifically, there was a sense that the original Standards may need to be reexamined and updated, for not everyone who presents today with transgenderism neatly fits into the original defining classification (that is, expresses a desire for life-long hormone therapy or adamantly desires surgery) or exhibits additional associated psychiatric symptomology. Instead, based on the authors' experience, there is a genuine mix of individuals who span the full continuum of transgenderism. Many colleagues at the HBIGDA symposium noted the same, expressing the belief that if expectations on the patients were relaxed, that is, they would not be required to fit a classic mold, then perhaps they would feel less threatened by the professionals, provide more truthful information about themselves and their feelings, and likely return for further consultation and help with their gender transformation. There was a sense that rigidity of the current criteria may in fact be isolating some individuals and keeping them away from the professionals out of fear of psychiatric stigmatization or being questioned if they do not follow a standard course of treatment. Also, the Standards may be leading individuals to have surgery who might stop short of those procedures if a hormone-alone option was available and acceptable.

Finally, in view of the research noted previously, efforts must continue toward demystifying and destigmatizing transgenderism. Clearly, inequalities remain, discrimination continues, and society-at-large still sees such behavior on a continuum from amusing to distasteful (Taylor, 1995). Handling this gargantuan challenge will require planning and coordination and time. Attitudes will not change overnight. However, positive steps can be taken, as called for here, with more empirical research on nonclinical groups, with consumer groups meeting with and educating professionals from fields such as medicine, psychiatry, the insurance industry, state and national government, and with tasteful, well-prepared media coverage and documentaries, not of the tabloid variety. Frontal assaults on these typically conservative groups will not work and predictably will reinforce notions that transgender individuals are abnormal or flaky at best. Rather than dictating to these groups, it will be important to have dialog with them.

SUMMARY

Transgenderism is a variation on the human condition and, in light of new thinking and evidence, may not be simply a psychiatric disorder, per se. It appears that individuals can hold down jobs, raise families, establish close relationships, pay taxes, and generally live successfully, with no significant debilitating distress or impairment in functioning or danger to self and others. Additional research is needed to explore and verify these observations. In the meantime, however, much has been accomplished with the development of Standards of Care and a growing group of dedicated professionals from various walks of life who appear committed to working with a group that so often has been treated like the lepers of ancient society. And, efforts must continue to eliminate discrimination and stigmatizing attitudes toward transgender individuals. Rather than simply abandoning and vilifying what has been achieved, attention should be turned to working within the system to educate and improve opportunities for all.

REFERENCES

American Psychiatric Association. (1994). *Diagnostic and statistical manual of mental disorders*. DSM IV. Washington, DC: American Psychiatric Association.

Benjamin, H. (1966). *The transsexual phenomenon: A scientific report on transsexualism and sex conversion in the human male and female*. New York: Julian Press.

Brown, G. (1995). Transvestism. In G. Gabbard (Ed.), *Treatment of psychiatric disorders - DSM-IV Edition*. Washington, DC: APA Press.

Cole, C., O'Boyle, M., Emory, L., & Meyer, W. (1997). Comorbidity of gender dysphoria and other major psychiatric diagnoses. *Archives of Sexual Behavior, 26,* 13–26.

Docter, R.F. (1988). *Transvestites and transsexuals: Toward a theory of cross-gender behavior*. London: Plenum Press.

Gamson, J. (1995). Must identity movements self-destruct? A queer dilemma. *Social Problems, 42,* 390–407.

Green, R., & Money, J. (Eds.). (1969). *Transsexualism and sex reassignment*. Baltimore, MD: Johns Hopkins University Press.

Hirschfeld, M. (1910). *Die transvestiten: Eine untersuchung uber den erotischen verkleidungstrieh*. Berlin: Medicinisher Verlag Alfred Pulvermacher & Co.

Levine, S. (1989). Gender identity disorders of childhood, adolescence, and adulthood. In H. Kaplan, & B. Sadock (Eds.), *Comprehensive textbook of psychiatry,* Vol. 1, 5th ed. Baltimore, MD: William and Wilkins.

Meyer, W., Webb, A., Stuart, C., Finkelstein, J., Lawrence, B., & Walker, P. (1986). Physical and hormonal evaluation of transsexual patients: A longitudinal study. *Archives of Sexual Behavior, 15*(2), 121–138.

Pauly, I. (1990). Gender identity disorders: Evaluation and treatment. *Journal of Sex Education and Therapy, 16,* 2–24.

Pauly, I. (1992). Terminology and classification of gender disorders. In Bockting, W. and Coleman, E. (Eds.), *Gender dysphoria: Interdisciplinary approaches in clinical management*. New York: Haworth Press.

Raymond, J. (1994). The politics of transgender. *Feminism & Psychology, 4,* 628–633.

Robins, L.N., Helzer, J.E., Weissman, M.M., Orvaschel, H., Gruenberg, E., Burke, Jr., J.D., & Regier, D.A. (1984). Lifetime prevalence of specific psychiatric disorders in three sites. *Archives of General Psychiatry, 41,* 949–958.

Taylor, J. (1995, April). The third sex. *Esquire,* pp. 102–114.

Walker, P., Berger, J., Green, R., Laub, D., Reynolds, C., & Wollman, L. (1985). Standards of care: The hormonal and surgical sex reassignment of gender dysphoric persons. *Archives of Sexual Behavior, 14,* 79–90.

Weissman, M.N., & Myers, P.S. (1978). Psychiatric disorders in U.S. urban populations. *American Journal of Psychiatry, 135,* 459–465.

15 GENDER IDENTITY AND SEXUAL ORIENTATION

Ira B. Pauly

Cross-gender behavior has been known since antiquity. However, it was not until the early nineteenth century that a case of cross-gender identity was first described by a German author, Friedreich (1830). Subsequently, German sexologists continued to describe examples of cross-gender identity behavior, using terms like "the contrary sexual feeling," and "metamorphosis sexualis paranoia." This German tradition culminated with the work of Magnus Hirschfeld and the publication of his classic monograph *Die Transvestiten* (1910). The equivalent English term, transvestism, was widely used to describe cases of what is now referred to as "gender dysphoria." Havelock Ellis (1936) coined the terms "sexoesthetic inversion" and "eonism" to describe this condition. D.O. Cauldwell first used the term "transsexualism" in 1949, and this term has been used ever since to describe the most extreme example of gender dysphoria. However, it was not until the famous Christine Jorgensen case received worldwide attention in the press that transsexualism became known to the public and the medical field. Harry Benjamin, an endocrinologist and sexologist from New York, popularized the term "transsexualism" in his writing, which culminated with the publication of his classic monograph *The Transsexual Phenomenon* (1966). Dr. Benjamin was recognized for his leadership and pioneering work in this field by having the International Gender Dysphoria Association named after him. In 1973, the term "gender dysphoria" was coined; this has become a generic term that includes all individuals who suffer from some form of gender discomfort (Laub, 1973; Laub & Fisk, 1974). Finally, the term "gender-identity disorders" (GID) has been used to describe individuals with gender dysphoria since 1980 with the publication of the American Psychiatric Association's *Diagnostic and Statistical Manual,* 3rd edition. This generic term, GID, continues to be the primary designation for this group of disorders (American Psychiatric Association, 1994).

I gave my first presentation on transsexualism at the 1963 annual meeting of the American Psychiatric Association (Pauly, 1963). At that time, very few psychiatrists or other mental-health professionals had significant clinical experience with this dramatic gender-identity syndrome. In the last three decades, what Dr. Milton Edgerton and I have referred to as the "gender-identity movement" (Pauly & Edgerton, 1986) has flourished, and the spectrum of gender-identity disorders are now well recognized and their clinical evaluation and treatment are generally accepted. The inclusion in DSM III (1980) of transsexualism and gender-identity disorders, plus the revision in DSM-III-R in 1987 has secured a legitimate place for these disorders within the mainstream of psychiatry, psychology, and sexology. A work group under the leadership of Dr. Susan Bradley improved the criteria and description of gender-identity disorders and transsexualism for DSM IV (1994).

The success of sex-reassignment surgery is not universally proclaimed, and the justification of sex reassignment has been challenged vigorously (Meyer & Reter, 1979; Stoller, 1982). Standards of care have emerged, and criteria for recommending sex-reassignment surgery are now more stringent than before (Walker, et al., 1985). There has emerged a body of data which concludes that sex-reassignment surgery (SRS) for primary transsexuals (Person & Ovesey, 1974a, 1974b) who have been carefully evaluated and followed for a significant period of time while living full-time in the cross-gender role, carries a far better chance for successful outcome than the reverse (Pauly, 1981, 1985; Pauly & Edgerton, 1986; Steiner, 1985; Lundstrom, 1981; Lundstrom, et al., 1984; Blanchard, et al., 1989; Walinder, Lundstrom, & Thuwe, 1978).

However, of even greater importance than whether SRS for gender-dysphoric individuals is appropriate treatment is what we have begun to understand about the normative developmental process of gender identification. Often in medicine, from studies of extreme pathology, we come to appreciate the more fundamental, basic science of the normal function or developmental process. Certainly, our examination of individuals with such dramatic examples of gender dysphoria as transsexualism has begun to shed light on the development of gender identification. The major contributors to our current understanding of this important and fundamental process have all studied the transsexual, as well as other pathological genetic and hormonal conditions, in arriving at their hypotheses (Stoller, 1968, 1982; Money & Ehrhardt, 1972; Green, 1987; Pauly, 1981, 1985; Pauly & Edgerton, 1986). Developmental psychologists such as Beverly Fagot (1987) have demonstrated that this developmental process is usually established by age 25 months.

Even today, our understanding of how it is that most of us arrive at a reasonably comfortable sense of our maleness or femaleness is far from clear. Likewise, the development of our sexual orientation or preference for sexual partner is only beginning to emerge. It is my hope that my updated summary of the sexual preference of transsexuals may prove useful in illuminating the shadows which have been cast on these important psychobiological phenomenon.

In my work on female-to-male transsexualism published in *The Archives of Sexual Behavior,* I made the following statement:

> It should be emphasized that the previously discussed manifestations of gender role reversal predate the sexual preference aspects now being discussed. Failure to discriminate between the gender and sexual motives of this condition is a source of great confusion. Once one understands and accepts the primary, basic, and life-long gender identification, the secondary sexual-object preference follows automatically . . . by definition all female transsexuals are homosexual, in that these biological females who psychologically reject their femaleness and assume a masculine role are interested in and at one point become involved with females as sexual partners (86 percent). But they are all *heterogenderal*, in that they have always considered themselves to be masculine, if not male, and are accepted by their female partners as male.
>
> —Pauly, 1974, p. 502

This statement, written some 15 years ago, offered an appropriate summary of our understanding of the sexual preference of female-to-male transsexuals up to that time. It was accepted as accurate until subsequent research proved it to be no longer correct. Before and since transsexualism gained entrance into DSM III in 1980, it was generally believed that the male-to-female transsexual was a more heterogenous condition. Benjamin (1966) spoke of the transition from transvestism to transsexualism in men, as did Stoller. Person and Ovesey (1974a, 1974b) distinguished between primary and secondary male-to-female transsexuals, based on the age of onset and defining many of the secondary transsexuals as fetishistic cross-dressers. Blanchard (1985), in collaboration with his colleagues at the Clarke Institute of Psychiatry in Toronto, defined typologies in male-to-female transsexualism and concluded that there are homosexual and heterosexual male-to-female transsexuals, but only homosexual female-to-male transsexuals, thus agreeing with my previous observation (Pauly, 1974). These designations refer, of course, to the preferred sexual choice, based on the transsexual's original biological or genetic status. This view is adopted in DSM III and the designations homosexual, heterosexual, or asexual are recommended as further discriminations.

However, let us complicate this situation further. In 1981, at the 7th International Gender Dysphoria Symposium at Lake Tahoe, William Casey reported on three patients known to him who met the criteria for male-to-female transsexualism and openly admitted that they wished to have their genitalia removed in order to be practicing lesbians. His paper was entitled "Transsexual Lesbians." Betty Steiner (1985) credits Feinbloom, Fleming, Kijewski, and Schulter (1976) with the first mention in the literature of the phenomenon of male-to-female transsexuals who prefer "lesbian" sexual and affectional relationships, as well as a feminist value orientation. Steiner goes on to describe two case vignettes in which exactly the same relationship is sought by postoperative male-to-female transsexuals. Of course, these biological males, now living as women and seeking other women as sexual partners in a lesbian relationship, are still referred to as heterosexual using our DSM III guidelines. By now, many centers are reporting increased numbers of male-to-female transsexuals who adopt a lesbian preference. Although this phenomenon had been rarely described in the literature, it is apparently well known in the gay and transsexual subcultures. Many preoperative male-to-female transsexuals who are applying for SRS are afraid to be candid regarding their lesbian preference, for fear they will not be accepted for SRS.

Current estimates indicate that a much higher percentage of biological males requesting SRS may indeed be interested in homosexual women as partners. Blanchard, Clemmensen, and Steiner (1987) report that for every biological male who wishes to live as a woman and pursue a sexual relationship with a nonhomosexual man, there are 1.4 biological males who, in their lives as women, wish to relate to homosexual women. These latter individuals, for whom DSM III would require a heterosexual designation, were somewhat older at initial contact and may indeed be considered secondary transsexuals, in that their gender dysphoria or reversal started later than is the case of the primary transsexual. From their histories, these "heterosexual" gender-dysphoria individuals reported that their first cross-gender wishes occurred around the same time they first cross-dressed, whereas the "homosexual" group reported that cross-gender wishes preceded cross-dressing by three to four years. Also, a history of fetishistic arousal was acknowledged by over 80 percent of the "heterosexual" males, compared with less than 10 percent of the "homosexual" male gender dysphorics. The pattern of development is such that heterosexual and homosexual gender dysphoria are likely to prove to be etiologically distinct conditions (Blanchard, et al., 1987).

In Blanchard's 1989 publication entitled "The Classification and Labeling of Nonhomosexual Gender Dysphorias," he describes four groups of gender-dysphoric adult males: (1) those attracted to heterosexual males (homosexual); (2) those attracted to homosexual females (heterosexual); (3) those attracted to males and females (bisexual); and (4) those attracted neither to males nor females (for whom he uses the term "analloerotic"). He goes on to demonstrate that there is much similarity among the last three groups (heterosexual, bisexual, and analloerotic) as compared with the first group (homosexual).

1. These nonhomosexual types of male gender dysphorics acknowledge a history of erotic arousal in association with cross-dressing. Only a minority of homosexual gender dysphorics do so.
2. The three nonhomosexual groups were significantly older at initial presentation than the homosexual subjects.
3. All three nonhomosexual subjects reported significantly less childhood femininity than the homosexual group.
4. All three nonhomosexual gender-dysphoric subjects were more likely to have been sexually aroused by the fantasy of having a woman's body (which Blanchard refers to as autogynephilia).
5. All three nonhomosexual groups report more heterosexual experience than do the homosexual subjects.

For these reasons, Blanchard concludes that the classification of male gender dysphoria should simply be divided into homosexual and nonhomosexual types.

The relative percentages of distribution of these four groups of some 212 male gender-dysphoric subjects is shown in Table 15.1.

TABLE 15.1. Sexual Orientation of 212 Male-to-Female Transsexual Subjects

	n	Percent
Homosexual	117	55
Bisexual	58	27
Heterosexual	19	9
Analloerotic	18	9
	212	100

Source: Blanchard, 1989a.

What is surprising to me is the relatively high percentage of bisexual subjects (27 percent), compared with heterosexual subjects (only 9 percent). However, one should be aware that these subjects were chosen from a database of 3,000 subjects who completed a self-administered questionnaire in which they answered positively to the statement that "they had felt like women at all times for at least the past year." It is speculative as to what percentage of the 212 subjects would meet the criteria for transsexualism. However, I know of no other study to date which addresses the relative frequency of the subtypes of male-to-female transsexuals. Whatever the exact distribution turns out to be, it is clear that the sexual orientation of male-to-female transsexuals is a great deal more complex than was originally suspected.

I had reported in 1974 that all female-to-male transsexuals were homosexual (Pauly, 1974). These biological females who were unable to accept their sex of birth and assignment, and who developed a male gender identity, all wished to pursue a relationship with a nonhomosexual woman. Pierce, et al. (1981) confirmed this observation that the wives and/or girlfriends of a group of female-to-male transsexuals whom she studied were all heterosexual woman with no homosexual experience. Both partners to this social and sexual liaison considered themselves to be heterosexual, normal, or straight. This finding was generally accepted and continued to be the case even as late as 1987 when Blanchard, et al. reported that "typologies exist in male-to-female transsexuals, but not in female-to-male transsexuals." By this statement they refer to the observation that there are homosexual and heterosexual male-to-female transsexuals, but only homosexual female-to-male transsexuals. Obviously, there are problems and confusion with these descriptors, not the least of which is the participating partners' perception that their relationship is not gay, but rather heterosexual. This potential source of confusion, or difference of perception, was my rationale for introducing the term "heterogenderal" (Pauly, 1974), thus emphasizing the gender relationship between the two partners, rather than the genetic relationship.

In 1983, Lothstein published a monograph on female-to-male transsexuals. In it, he gave a brief vignette of a female-to-male transsexual, who in the male role, pursued sexual relationships only with gay men. Blanchard, et al. (1987) reported on the Clarke Institute's series of over 80 female-to-male transsexuals, in which there was only one such female-to-male transsexual who reported an exclusive preference for homosexual men as sexual partners. Dorothy Clare, in an unpublished paper which she presented in 1986, describes a similar sexual preference in some 12 gender-dysphoric biological females who pursue relationships with gay men. She refers to this condition as "transhomosexuality," thus introducing a new term. When I discussed this finding at the biannual meeting of the Harry Benjamin International Gender Dysphoria Association in Amsterdam in 1987, the Dutch group of gender-identity professionals had seen 17 female-to-gay-male transexuals in that small country. Similarly, the author gave a presentation on this subject recently, and a reliable gender professional practicing in the Los Angeles area said that he was aware of some eight or ten such individuals. More recently, Dickey and Stephens reported two additional cases of female-to-male transsexuals who are attracted to homosexual men (1995).

Obviously, the statement that all female-to-male transsexuals are homosexuals in their sexual preference can no longer be made, even though it appeared to be correct for over ten years. Like any new phenomenon, once it has been reported, it quickly receives confirmation from other practitioners in the field.

This initial focus on male-to-female transsexuals has an interesting history. Lukianowicz (1959) reported that transsexualism was "an exclusively male" phenomenon. Early on, the male to female ratios were reported as high as 8:1 (Benjamin, 1968). Currently, the more accurate figures suggest a 1:1 male to female ratio (Walinder, et al., 1979). Similarly, we have found that this interesting reversal of the expected preference of transsexuals was thought originally to pertain to males only. What was initially felt to be rare, and therefore reportable, is now representing over 20–30 percent of the new cases in some studies. Again, the female-to-male transsexual was thought *not* to exist—yet within a short time after the first case of female-to-gay-male transexualism was reported, larger numbers came forward. As one of my patients said, "One is reluctant to come forward as representing a new form of perversion." Now that we appreciate that this phenomenon does exist in female gender-dysphoric individuals, the question arises as to whether it is as prevalent as in the male-to-female transsexual. Since many of these male gender-dysphoric individuals are ego-dystonic transvestites, and since this phenomenon (transvestism) is still unreported in females, I would doubt that as high a prevalence will be found in female-to-male transsexuals preferring a gay sexual orientation.

CONCLUSIONS

1. Male-to-female transsexuals choose as their sexual partners:

a.   Heterosexual men; I would describe this relationship as "heterogenderal," whereas DSM III defines this as "homosexual," and DSM IV describes it as "sexually attracted to males";

b.   Homosexual women; I would describe this relationship as "homogenderal," whereas DSM III defines this relationship as "heterosexual," and DSM IV describes it as "sexually attracted to females";

c. Both heterosexual men and homosexual women; I would define this relationship as "bigenderal," and DSM III defines this as "bisexual," and DSM IV describes it as "sexually attracted to both";

d. Attracted to neither men nor women—which Blanchard refers to as "analloerotic," and DSM III defines as "asexual," and DSM IV describes as "sexually attracted to neither."

2. Female-to-male transsexuals choose as their sexual partners:

a. Heterosexual women; I would refer to this relationship as "heterogenderal," whereas DSM III defines it as "homosexual," and DSM IV describes it as "sexually attracted to females."

b. Homosexual men; I would refer to this relationship as "homogenderal," or female-to-gay-male transsexualism; whereas DSM III sees it as "heterosexual," and DSM IV describes it as "sexually attracted to males."

3. Whereas there is a significant percentage (20–30 percent of male-to-female transsexuals whose sexual orientation is for lesbian women, the prevalence of female-to-gay-male transsexualism will probably turn out to be very small. This may be explained by the absence of or extreme rarity of transvestism in females. It appears that many male-to-female transsexuals are compensating for ego-dystonic homosexuality or ego-dystonic transvestism by changing to the opposite sex.

4. The relationship between gender identity and sexual orientation is truly a complex one. Much of the evidence from gender-dysphoric and non–gender-dysphoric subjects suggests that these are independent variables. To wit:

a. Individuals *without* gender-identity problems assume either a heterosexual or homosexual orientation; i.e., there are many homosexual men who are unmistakably masculine and many homosexual women who are unmistakably feminine.

b. This paper demonstrates that individuals with gender dysphoria also develop a sexual orientation for partners of either sex, whether we label this as heterogenderal or homosexual, or the reverse.

c. What is known about the developmental process by which an individual acquires his/her gender identity suggests that this process is established at an earlier time than his/her development of a sexual orientation.

5. On the other hand, Richard Green's work, published in his monograph "The 'sissy boy' syndrome and the development of homosexuality" (1987), demonstrates that some 75 percent of the effeminate boys he followed pro-

spectively met the criteria for gender-identity disorder in childhood, yet became homosexual as adults. Green concludes that ". . . cross-gender boyhood and homosexual manhood are age-appropriate manifestations of the same underlying homosexual developmental process." Since homosexuality is approximately 1000 times more prevalent than transsexualism, I can only assume that if his sample were large enough, some of these effeminate boys would become transsexuals as adults. In fact, one of Green's subjects probably does meet the criteria for transsexualism. It is difficult to explain this correlation without implying some relationship between gender identity and sexual preference, in which case these are dependent variables. On the other hand, 25 percent of these boys did not develop into either homosexuals or transsexuals, but rather developed a heterosexual orientation.

6. The majority of gender-dysphoric individuals applying for SRS fall into the primary-transsexual category. These individuals give a developmental history consistent with DSM IV's classification of gender-identity disorders. These male-to-female transsexuals are most likely to prefer heterosexual men as partners, and their female-to-male transsexual counterparts are most likely to prefer heterosexual women as sexual partners. Less frequently, one encounters individuals with a secondary form of gender dysphoria, who have established a gender identification in childhood which is consistent with their biological sex, but in adolescence make a gender accommodation to their underlying, atypical sexual preference. These so-called ego-dystonic homosexual or transvestic individuals are then able to express their sexual preference without society or themselves viewing this behavior as deviant or abnormal. This division of gender-dysphoric individuals into two distinct groups, primary or secondary, begins to explain why gender identification and sexual orientation appear to be both dependent and independent variables.

7. Obviously, our current information is inadequate to explain 100 percent of the variance. Therefore, we must pursue our research into these fundamental developmental processes until a clearer understanding emerges. This task remains a challenge for those of us involved in research of these fundamental human conditions.

REFERENCES

American Psychiatric Association. (1980). *Diagnostic and statistical manual of mental disorders*. DSM III. Washington, DC: American Psychiatric Association.
American Psychiatric Association. (1987). *Diagnostic and statistical manual of mental disorders*. DSM III-R. Washington, DC: American Psychiatric Association.

American Psychiatric Association. (1994). *Diagnostic and statistical manual of mental disorders*. DSM IV. Washington, DC: American Psychiatric Association.

Benjamin, H. (1953). Transvestism and transsexualism. *International Journal of Sexology, 7*, 12–14.

Benjamin, H. (1966). *The transsexual phenomenon: A scientific report on transsexualism and sex conversion in the human male and female*. New York: Julian Press. Currently available in reprinted form from The Human Outreach & Achievement Institute, 405 Western Avenue, Ste. 345, South Portland, ME 04106.

Benjamin, H. (1968). The transsexual phenomenon. *Transactions of the New York Academy of Sciences, 29*(4), 428–430.

Blanchard, R. (1985). Typology of male-to-female transsexualism. *Archives of Sexual Behavior, 14*(3), 247–261.

Blanchard, R. (1988). Nonhomosexual gender dysphoria. *Journal of Sexual Research, 24*, 188–193.

Blanchard, R. (1989a). The classification and labeling of nonhomosexual gender dysphorias. *Archives of Sexual Behavior, 18*(4), 315–334.

Blanchard, R. (1989b). The concept of autogynephilia and the typology of male gender dysphoria. *Journal of Nervous and Mental Disease, 177*(10), 616–623.

Blanchard, R., Clemmensen, L.H., & Steiner, B.W. (1987). Heterosexual and homosexual gender dysphoria. *Archives of Sexual Behavior, 16*(2), 139–152.

Blanchard, R., Steiner, B.W., Clemmensen, L.H., & Dickey, R. (1989). Prediction of regrets in postoperative transsexuals. *Canadian Journal of Psychiatry, 34*(1), 43–45.

Bradley, S.J., Blanchard, R., Coates, S., Green, R., Levine, S.B., Meyer-Bahlburg, H.F.L., Pauly, I.B., & Zucker, K.J. (1991). Interim report of the DSM-IV Subcommittee on Gender Identity Disorders. *Archives of Sexual Behavior, 20*(4), 333–343.

Cauldwell, D.O. (1949). Psychopathia transexualis. *Sexology, 16*, 274–280.

Clare, D., & Tully, B. (1989). Transhomosexuality, or the dissociation of sexual orientation and sex object choice. *Archives of Sexual Behavior, 18*(6), 531–536.

Coleman, E., & Bockting, W. (1988). "Heterosexual" prior to sex reassignment— "homosexual" afterwards: A case study of a female-to-male transsexual. *Journal of Psychology and Human Sexuality, 1*(2), 69–82.

Coleman, E., Bockting, W., & Gooren, L. (1993). Homosexual and bisexual identity in sex-reassigned female-to-male transsexuals. *Archives of Sexual Behavior, 22*(1), 37–50.

Dickey, R., & Stephens, J. (1995). Female-to-male transsexualism, heterosexual type: Two cases. *Archives of Sexual Behavior, 24*, 439–446.

Ellis, H.H. (1936). *Studies in the psychology of sex: Erotic symbolism, mechanism of detumescence, the psychic state in pregnancy*. Philadelphia: F.A. Davis Co.

Fagot, B. (1987). The development of gender identity. *Proceedings of the 10th Harry Benjamin International Gender Dysphoria Conference*, 9–12 June, 1987, Amsterdam, The Netherlands, p. 68.

Feinbloom, D.H., Fleming, M., Kijewski, V., & Schulter, M.P. (1976). Lesbian/feminist orientation among male-to-female transsexuals. *Journal of Homosexuality, 2*(1), 59–71.

Fisk, N. (1973). Gender dysphoria syndrome (the how, what and why of a disease). In D. Laub & P. Gandy (Eds.), *Proceedings of the Second Interdisciplinary Symposium on Gender Dysphoria Syndrome*, pp. 7–14. Palo Alto, CA: Stanford University Medical Center.

Friedreich, J. (1830). *Versuch eines niterangeschichte der pathologie und therapie des psychischen krankheiten*. Wurzburg.

Green, R. (1987). *The "sissy boy" syndrome and the development of homosexuality*. New Haven, CT: Yale University Press.

Green, R., & Money, J. (Eds.). (1969). *Transsexualism and sex reassignment*. Baltimore, MD: Johns Hopkins University Press.

Hirschfeld, M. (1910). *Die transvestiten: Eine untersuchung uber den erotischen verkleidungstrieh.* Berlin: Medicinisher Verlag Alfred Pulvermacher & Co. (Reprinted in 1991 as *Transvestites: The erotic drive to cross dress.* [Michael A. Lombardi-Nash, translator] Buffalo, NY: Prometheus Books.)

Krafft-Ebing, R. Von. (1877). Uber gewisse anomalien des geschlechtstriebs. *Archiv fur Psychiatrie und Nervenkrankheiten, 7,* 291–312.

Laub, D.R. (1973). Total management and responsibility for transsexual patients. In D. Laub & P. Gandy (Eds.), *Proceedings of the Second Interdisciplinary Symposium on Gender Dysphoria Syndrome,* pp. 208–210. Palo Alto, CA: Stanford University Medical Center.

Laub, D.R., & Fisk, N. (1974). A rehabilitation program for gender dysphoria syndrome by surgical sex change. *Plastic and Reconstructive Surgery, 53*(4), 388–403.

Levine, S.B. (1989). Gender identity disorders of childhood, adolescence, and adulthood. In H.I. Kaplan & B.J. Sadock (Eds.), *Comprehensive textbook of psychiatry,* Vol. 1, 5th ed., pp. 1061–1069. Baltimore: Williams & Wilkins.

Lothstein, L. (1983). *Female-to-male transsexualism: Historical, clinical and theoretical issues.* Boston: Routledge & Kegan Paul.

Lukianowicz, N. (1959). Survey of various aspects of transvestism in the light of our present knowledge. *Journal of Nervous and Mental Disease, 128,* 36–64.

Lundstrom, B. (1981). Gender dysphoria: A social psychiatric follow-up study of 31 cases not accepted for sex reassignment. *Reports from the Department of Psychiatry and Neurochemistry,* St. Jorgens Hospital, University of Goteborg, Sweden.

Lundstrom, B., Pauly, I., & Walinder, J. (1984). Outcome of sex reassignment surgery. *Acta Psychiatrica Scandinavica, 70*(4), 289–294.

Meyer, J.K., & Reter, D. (1979). Sex reassignment: Follow-up. *Archives of General Psychiatry, 36*(9), 1010–1015.

Money, J., and Ehrhardt, A.A. *Man and woman, boy and girl.* Baltimore, MD: Johns Hopkins University Press.

Pauly, I.B. (1963). Female psychosexual inversion: Transsexualism. In *Summaries of the scientific papers of the 119th annual meeting of the American Psychiatric Association.* Washington, DC: American Psychiatric Association.

Pauly, I.B. (1965). Male psychosexual inversion: Transsexualism. A review of 100 cases. *Archives of General Psychiatry, 13,* 172–181.

Pauly, I.B. (1968). The current status of the change of sex operation. *Journal of Nervous and Mental Disease, 147*(5), 460–471.

Pauly, I.B. (1969a). Adult manifestations of male transsexualism. In R. Green & J. Money (Eds.), *Transsexualism and sex reassignment,* pp. 37–58. Baltimore, MD: Johns Hopkins University Press.

Pauly, I.B. (1969b). Adult manifestations of female transsexualism. In R. Green & J. Money (Eds.), *Transsexualism and sex reassignment,* pp. 59–87. Baltimore, MD: Johns Hopkins University Press.

Pauly, I.B. (1974). Female transsexualism: Parts I & II. *Archives of Sexual Behavior, 3*(6), 487–507, 509–525.

Pauly, I.B. (1981). Outcome of sex reassignment surgery for transsexuals. *Australian and New Zealand Journal of Psychiatry, 15*(1), 45–51.

Pauly, I.B. (1985). Gender identity disorders. In M. Farber (Ed.), *Human sexuality: Psychosexual effects of disease,* pp. 295–316. New York: Macmillan Publishing Company.

Pauly, I.B. (1990a). Gender identity disorders: Evaluation and treatment. *Journal of Sex Education and Therapy, 16*(1), 2–24.

Pauly, I.B. (1990b). Gender identity disorders: Update. In F. Bianco & R. Hernandez Serrano (Eds.), *Sexology: An independent field.* Amsterdam: Elsevier.

Pauly, I.B. (1990c). Gender identity and sexual preference: Dependent versus independent variables. In F. Bianco & R. Hernandez Serrano (Eds.), *Sexology: An independent field.* Amsterdam: Elsevier.

Pauly, I.B., & Edgerton, M.T. (1986). The gender identity movement: A growing surgical-psychiatric liaison. *Archives of Sexual Behavior, 15*(4), 315–329.

Person E., & Ovesey, L. (1974a). The transsexual syndrome in males: I. Primary transsexualism. *American Journal of Psychotherapy, 28*, 4–20.

Person, E., & Ovesey, L. (1974b). The transsexual syndrome in males: II. Secondary transsexualism. *American Journal of Psychotherapy, 28*, 174–193.

Pierce, D., Pauly, I., & Matarrazzo, R. (1981). The psychosocial characteristics of the wives and girlfriends of female-to-male transsexuals. *Proceedings of the 7th Harry Benjamin International Gender Dysphoria Conference*, Lake Tahoe, NV, p. 73.

Steiner, B.W. (1985). The management of patients with gender disorders. In B.W. Steiner (Ed.), *Gender dysphoria: Development, research, management*, pp. 325–350. New York: Plenum Press.

Stoller, R.J. (1982). Near miss: "Sex change" treatment and its evaluation. In M.R. Zales (Ed.), *Eating, sleeping, and sexuality*, pp. 258–283. New York: Brunner/ Mazel.

Walinder, J., Lundstrom, B., & Thuwe, I. (1978). Prognostic factors in the assessment of male transsexuals for sex reassignment. *British Journal of Psychiatry, 132,* 16–20.

Walinder, J., Lundstrom, B., Ross, M., & Thuwe, I. (1979). Transsexualism: Incidence, prevalence and sex ratio: Comments on three different studies. In *Proceedings of the 6th International Gender Dysphoria Association*. Coronado, CA.

Walker, P.A., Berger, J.C., Green, R., Laub, D., Reynolds, C., & Wollman, L. (1985). Standards of care: The hormonal and surgical sex reassignment of gender dysphoric persons. *Archives of Sexual Behavior, 14*, 70–90.

Westphal, C. (1870). Die contrare sexualempfindung. *Archives Psychiat. Nervenkrank, 2*, 73–108.

16 SEXUAL-ORIENTATION IDENTITIES, ATTRACTIONS, AND PRACTICES OF FEMALE-TO-MALE TRANSSEXUALS

Holly Devor

The ways in which female-to-male transsexual persons (FTM TSs) form their sexual-orientation identities (SOIDs) remains unclear. An improved understanding of the processes they employ might also further illuminate those used by other, more conventional members of society. I investigated some sexual attractions, practices, and SOIDs of 45 self-identified FTM TSs. The data presented in this article are based on interviews conducted outside any clinical context. Interviewees ranged from those who had not yet initiated their transitions into men to those who were 18 years beyond that point.

I have focused first on the patterns of sexual attractions, sexual practices, and sexual-orientation identities which the participants reported having experienced before they began to live fully as men. I have then compared that information with what they reported about their patterns of sexual attractions, sexual practices, and sexual-orientation identities after their transitions into men.

DEFINITIONS

A number of terms I use have been variously defined by other authors. To avoid confusion, I have provided my definitions.

When I use the word "sex," I refer only to the physiological status of persons as either female or male. There have been many criteria used to define biological sex status. In this discussion, I use genetic sex and morphological sex as determining factors while recognizing that, in cases of some transgendered persons, morphological sex may vary in multiple ways from that which might usually be expected for a person of a particular genetic sex.

When I use the word "gender," I refer only to the social status of persons as women (girls) or men (boys). This distinction is especially important in cases of transgendered individuals whose social persona (or body morphology) may be entirely different from that which their genetic sex would typically suggest.

When I use the term "gender role relational style," I refer roughly to what others call femininity and masculinity. I use this term to emphasize that gender props are not the most important aspect of communicating gender to others; rather, styles of relating to others are among the strongest markers of gender (Devor, 1993).

When I use the words "sexuality" or "sexual orientation," I refer to the patterns of sexual attractions, fantasies, desires, and/or practices of persons. I recognize that fantasies with no desires for actual sexual practice, desires for actual practice, and actual sexual practices often are not congruent or consistent either across a person's lifetime of experience or within particular temporal periods of individuals' lives.

I use the term "sexual attraction" to refer to people's visions of the person(s) and activities which they find sexually stimulating. Such attractions might include both fantasies and desires concerning anything from romance to genital contact. I use the term "sexual fantasies" to refer to those images (generated from whatever source) which persons find sexually stimulating but in which they have no desire actually to engage personally. I use the term "sexual desires" to refer to those activities and persons that one actually desires to experience sexually at some time in the future. "Sexual practice" refers to the sexual activities in which persons actually engage as differentiated from those which might be fantasized or desired but not realized.

The term "identity" refers to a person's acceptance of a sex, gender, or sexual-orientation categorization as descriptive of themselves (Devor, 1993). In this research I have proceeded on the assumptions that (a) genetic sex may, or may not, form the basis of persons' sex identities (e.g., "I may have been born female but I am male now"); (b) sex identity and gender identity may, or may not, match in a normative way (e.g., "I may have a female body, but I am a man"); (c) SOID may be based on any, or all, of the following: the genetic sex, morphological sex, sex identity, gender identity, gender role relational style, sexual fantasies, sexual desires, and sexual practices of oneself or one's partner(s) and/or the SOID of one's partner(s); (d) that any of these identities may change over the course of a lifetime; and that therefore (e) FTM-TS–identified persons may, at various periods of their lives, identify as straight, gay, lesbian, men, or women. These have not always been the assumptions of previous investigators.

I also have made a distinction between sex and gender when I have made sexual-orientation attributions. To do so I have used a classificatory schema based on the concepts of gendered sexuality (Devor, 1993). In that system, "male," "female," "heterosexual," and "homosexual" are terms which are used to refer to people in relationships (actual, desired, fantasized) according to their genetic sexes. "Straight woman and man," "lesbian woman," and "gay man" are terms used to refer to the genders of people in relationships. Terms such as "transsexual" or "crossdresser" are used to clarify situations where sex and gender combinations might initially seem erroneous. All of these are combined to produce attributions of gendered sexuality, or sexual orientation, which have two components, one which refers to genetic and morphological sex (e.g., female-to-male transsexual) and the other which refers to gender (e.g., gay man). The "gender community" loosely includes transsexuals, crossdressers, transgenderists, and their partners; some gay men and lesbian women or sadomasochists also include themselves under its umbrella.

THEORIES OF SEXUAL-ORIENTATION IDENTITY

The problem of defining the sexuality of members of society has been vexing students of human behavior since sexuality began to be used as a basis for identity in the nineteenth century (Weeks, 1989). In recent years, the question of the relationship between biological sex and social gender has become a contentious issue in this discourse. This has been especially highlighted by research about the sexuality of transsexuals and other transgendered people.

Modern systems of classification of sexual orientation are largely built on the original Kinsey model (Kinsey, Pomeroy, & Martin, 1948). More recent authors have questioned the utility of a single continuum and introduced distinctions between physical preference and affectional preference (Shively & De Cecco, 1977), among sexual behaviors, sexual fantasies, and sexual desires (Klein, Sepekoff, & Wolf, 1985), and between sexual orientation as determined on the basis of one's own identity versus what others might think (Cass, 1984; Devor, 1993).

The idea that sexual orientation might be based more on social statuses, such as gender, rather than on biological characteristics, is central to an understanding of the SOIDs of transsexual persons. A shift to more broadly defined questions of the social meanings and political, economic, and social contexts within which relationships take place allows for a more sociologically and historically sensitive rendering of this complex phenomenon (De Cecco & Shively, 1984). Clearly for many members of society, sexual desires, even sexual practices, do not solely determine persons' SOIDs (Lever, Kanouse, Rogers, Carson, & Hertz, 1992).

An historical and a contextual reading of the literature on sexual orientation leads readily to the possibility of the instability, across time and circumstance, of persons' SOIDs or their comfort with those identities (Coleman, 1987). This point is especially important to take into account with persons who may change both their morphological sex and social gender statuses during their lifetimes. Logically, it would follow that transsexual or transgendered persons might also have changing SOIDs, over a course of time, which might be based more heavily on either gender or sex, depending on their particular circumstances.

A number of authors have attempted to incorporate some of these variations on sex and gender as lived by members of the gender community. Pauly (1974) argued that transsexual people should be termed "homo-" or "heterogenderal" rather than "homo-" or "heterosexual" because gender is what is most salient for them. Grimm (1987) proposed a rather complex scheme for classifying gendered human relationships, both erotic and nonerotic, which resulted in 45 different possible combinations of two individuals in relationship to one another.

Pillard and Weinrich (1987) and Weinrich (1988), building on the work of Money (1988), developed a sociobiological model of "gender transpositions" to explain some of the variety in human sexual orientation. In their "periodic table model" they proposed that genetically, hormonally, and environmentally induced variations in degrees of defeminization and masculinization of human brains result in the variety seen in sex, gender, and sexuality. Weinrich (1988) further argued that their model explained differences in women's and men's patterns of sexual attractions. He claimed that women are more likely to fall in love with people initially on the basis of their personalities and later to eroticize their physical characteristics, whereas men are more likely to desire sexual relations with people initially on the basis of their physical characteristics.

Several authors have turned their attention specifically to the question of the classification of the sexual orientations of gender-dysphoric people. The main concern has been whether classifications should be on the basis of sex, usually defined in terms of genetic sex regardless of surgical status, or on the basis of gender identity or presentation. Blanchard (1989) argued in favor of a system based on genetic sex. According to such a system, gender dysphoric persons would be classified as homosexual when attracted to persons of the same genetic sex as themselves. Nonhomosexual persons would be subdivided into heterosexual, bisexual, and analloerotic (defined as "unattracted to male or female partners, but not necessarily devoid of sexual drives or activities" p. 315). The DSM III-R uses a similar system, classifying TSs as heterosexual, homosexual, asexual, and unspecified (American Psychiatric Association, 1987).

Present classificatory systems are unable to capture adequately the subjective experience of posttransition transsexuals who identify and live as gay men or lesbian women. The existence of such people calls into question the utility of systems which classify sexuality on the basis of either genetics or genitalia (Coleman, Bockting, & Gooren, 1993).

The DSM-IV Subcommittee on Gender Dysphorias (Bradley, et al., 1991) has suggested a five-category system which would be more sensitive to the diverse realities of gender-dysphoric persons. Their system would involve five subtypes which specify only the sex of the persons to whom one is attracted, i.e., attracted to females, to males, to both, to neither, and unspecified. The proposed system would add a much-needed mechanism for the recognition of the existence of bisexuality among gender-dysphoric people (Paul, 1983).

But their schema left unaddressed the central issues of social-group membership, either by identity or by attribution. The opportunity to be part of established and recognized groups in society is an important element in the maintenance of both social order and self-esteem. The ability to claim membership in particular, socially recognized sex, gender, and sexual-orientation groups is especially important in the lives of transsexual persons. It seems essential, therefore, that socially meaningful, and clinically useful, ways of understanding SOID be available to transsexual persons and to the clinicians who deal with them.

EMPIRICAL RESEARCH ABOUT THE SEXUALITY OF FTM TSs

Almost all published information about the sexuality of FTM TSs has either been from (auto)biographical or clinical sources. The bulk of it has been about FTM TSs' lives prior to their transitions with a number of follow-up studies providing some information about their lives thereafter. Generally, these reports have either been based on small numbers of FTM TSs who have been seen in therapy by the author(s) of the reports, or they were based on larger clinical samples who have responded to questionnaires. Data from these sources may have been limited by the fact that transsexual persons may present modified or fictional biographies to clinicians if they believe that it will enhance the likelihood of their procuring desired professional services (Bolin, 1988).

Early published reports by Stoller (1972) and Pauly (1974) were significant in establishing the long-standing profile of FTM TSs as exclusively homosexual and heterogenderal people who see themselves as straight men.

In Pauly's view, heterosexual involvements with men were seen as a diversionary tactic, "a flight into heterosexuality as a means of denying homosexuality" (1974, p. 502), despite his data that approximately 50 percent of the 80 FTM TSs covered in the report had dated or had sexual intercourse with men and that 19 percent had married men. Pauly's current views can be found in chapter 15 in this volume.

Several authors during the 1980s continued to assert that FTM TSs were generally attracted to women, but some also began to note that some FTM TSs have had relationships with women which they acknowledged as lesbian rather than as straight. Toward the end of the decade, a few authors began to acknowledge that the occasional FTM TS might have a significant history of attraction to men and that some might view themselves as gay men.

For example, McCauley and Ehrhardt (1980) reported on a survey of 15 FTM TSs who had requested sex-reassignment surgery (SRS) at a US gender clinic. The FTM TSs in their sample were uniformly attracted to women, but only two-thirds of them saw themselves as straight men in relation to their female partners, four had had sexual intercourse with one or more males, and one person had married in a heterosexual relationship.

Lothstein's (1983) report on 53 US FTM TSs focused on debunking some "myths" about FTM TSs, including the idea that all FTM TSs are actually "stigmatized homosexuals" (p. 10). He reported that only half of the 53 FTM TSs in the study saw themselves as straight men in their relations with women. He also noted that half had had some heterosexual experience, nine of whom had been married to men. Similarly, Stuart (1991) reported that 70 percent of the 20 US FTM TSs contacted in her field study said that they had identified as lesbian women and 50 percent had married men while living as women.

Dixen, Maddever, Van Maasdam, and Edwards (1984) reported the results from a 100–item questionnaire administered to 285 applicants for SRS in the 13–year history of another US gender clinic. Their results were similar to those found by other researchers. They reported that although 87 percent of the respondents had had homosexual sexual experience, approximately 50 percent of the FTM TSs they had seen at their clinic had also had heterosexual sexual experience and 11 percent had married men.

Initial reports from researchers at a Canadian gender clinic reiterated the refrain that FTM TSs sexually desire female partners and see themselves as straight. This was reported despite the fact that more than 25 percent had been sexually involved with straight men (Steiner & Bernstein, 1981).

The first published reports of FTM TS gay men started to appear in the late 1980s. Coleman and Bockting (1988) first presented a single case study in which they noted that such FTM TSs found that their transsexualism was disbelieved at US gender clinics if they were honest about their sexual orientation, although European clinics were more flexible in this regard. Clare and Tully (1989) have also discussed FTM TS gay men and suggested the term "transhomosexuality" to describe the phenomenon. Stuart (1991) reported that 10–17 percent of her sample identified as gay men.

Even though reports of only a handful of FTM TS gay men have appeared in the professional literature, this small number has been sufficient to undermine the previous assumption that FTM TSs are uniformly or exclusively heterogenderally oriented. Clearly, many FTM TSs have had heterosexual experience in their pasts, but the accepted professional opinion, until recently, has been that such activity was compensatory rather than a reflection of a preferred sexual orientation. The recognition that some pretransition FTM TSs identify as straight or lesbian women and that some posttransition FTM TSs identify as gay men forces open the question of whether SOID must be linked to either genetic or morphological sex.

It is important to remember that, for many people, SOID is not stable. SOIDs are, in part, built on a foundation of sex and gender identities. These are not static for most transsexual persons. A more complete understanding of female-to-male transsexualism demands more thorough, and nonclinical, investigations of the lives of FTM TSs both before and after their transitions.

Much previously published work on FTM TSs has taken a different approach to the question of sexual orientation than I have done in this report. I have not attempted to establish a single, dominant pattern of sexual or romantic attractions by discounting some, and not other, attractions and practices as irrelevant to persons' SOIDs. Instead, I have taken the view that people enter into relationships with others for a wide variety of reasons which, although they may not reflect their most deeply felt desires, nonetheless constitute valid and valuable reasons for having relations with others. As a result I have not dismissed relationships with men as peripheral to the SOIDs of the participants in this research.

The data presented in this article were gained through in-depth interviews and observation. The interview data were gathered between September 1988 and September 1992 as part of the research for a monograph on FTM TSs (Devor, 1997).

METHOD
Subjects

A total of 46 self-defined FTM TSs were interviewed. They ranged from people who had, at the time of first contact, taken no concrete steps toward becoming men to those who had completed their transition 18 years before their participation in this research. All participants in this study volunteered their time as a result of hearing about this project through public advertisements or networks within the transsexual community. The sample was therefore probably biased toward those people who were less private about their transsexual status, more socially connected to other transsexuals, and more inclined to educate nontranssexual people about FTM TSs. One person declined to be included in the data set after completing one interview. He was unwilling to contribute to research conducted from an explicitly feminist perspective.

Although the participants in this study did not constitute a random sample of all FTMs, they did represent a relatively large and diverse group. They were probably more forthcoming than many FTMs, and the sample surely included a disproportionate number of individuals who had been active as FTM advocates. Some participants had had little or no contact with the therapeutic community in regard to their gender issues. Others had sampled all that gender clinics had to offer and were many years into their new lives.

This study was unusual in that it was conducted under nonclinical social relations by a sociologist who had no gatekeeping powers in the lives of any individuals who participated. As such, it seems reasonable to believe that participants' responses were less tainted by goal-oriented distortions than is usually found in clinically based research. Nonetheless, these data are subject to the usual distortions from which any retrospective account might suffer. The data presented here must be taken with some caution but might also be viewed as providing insights into the lives of FTM TSs from a different perspective than that of previous researchers.

Measures

Data were obtained from responses to a detailed interview schedule which I created specifically for a research project leading to a monograph on FTM TSs (Devor, 1997). General areas of questioning included (a) demographics; (b) gender issues with family members, peers, in schools, and at work; (c) child abuse; (d) sex and romance; (e) physical health and body image; (f) development of gender and transsexual identities; (g) transition experiences; and (h) philosophical questions about sex, gender, and sexuality. In-person interviews were loosely structured to allow participants more freedom to follow their own thoughts to their own conclusions. As a result, in those interviews, topics were not always covered in exactly the same way, and unique information sometimes was recorded. This report pertains primarily to question group (d), although relevant information may have appeared in a variety of places throughout an interview.

I operationalized the beginning of hormone therapy as the point where FTM TSs start their permanent transitions into living as men. I used this marker because (a) I believe that the changes to secondary sex characteristics brought about by testosterone are highly significant in the attribution of gender and sexuality, (b) many FTM TSs begin cross-living with the aid of hormone therapy but before undertaking any surgeries, and (c) many FTM TSs do not complete more extensive surgical sex-change procedures.

Procedure

Announcements describing the project goals and my background were posted in places where transsexuals might congregate, distributed at transsexual support-group meetings, distributed by prominent members of the gender community, and printed in publications which might be read by FTM TSs. Potential participants were asked to contact me directly.

When potential participants made contact, I once again explained the project to them and answered any questions. If potential participants expressed interest in participation, I obtained written consent. Some persons were initially asked to complete two paper/pencil tests, the results of which were used for my doctoral thesis (Devor, 1990).

I interviewed 27 individuals face-to-face and in depth. In four cases, part of the interview was conducted face-to-face and part was self-administered. Another 18 people were mailed copies of the interview questions and either answered the questions in writing or by speaking into a tape recorder. Face-to-face interviews were audiotaped. Eight of the self-administered interviews were quite brief in comparison to the interviews which were conducted in person. All participants completed at least Part I of the interview process; 31 persons also completed Part II. Each part of the interview process, when conducted in person, usually lasted between 2 and 3 hours.

I conducted all face-to-face interviews at a place chosen by each participant. One FTM TS chose to have a male-to-female transsexual friend ask the questions I provided. I am unaware of the conditions under which the other self-interviews were conducted.

Correspondence, face-to-face, and/or telephone contact was maintained with all participants throughout the period of time required to complete the interviews. All names, and any other identifying information, are kept in a locked cabinet, to which I have sole access. I also attended a number of formal and informal gatherings of FTM TSs during the research period. Field notes were taken when I was in attendance in an official capacity as a researcher. Transcribed interview materials and field notes were coded and collated for information about childhood, teen, and adult sexual attractions; sexual practices; and sexual-orientation identities.

RESULTS AND DISCUSSION

Both qualitative and quantitative descriptive data obtained through field research methods are presented in this section. The nature of the data is such that it is more efficient and informative to discuss the results as they are presented.

I begin by describing the demographic profile of the sample. I then report and discuss participants' answers to questions about their (a) sexual attractions and practices before and after transition and (b) sexual-orientation identities before and after transition. I conclude by suggesting a theoretical model of SOID formation.

Demographics

Thirty-eight participants lived in the United States, seven lived in Canada, and one person resided in New Zealand at the time of contact. They ranged in age from 22 to 53 years, with a mean age of 37 years at the time of first contact. All participants had a minimum of a high-school education, with the average being 4 years of postsecondary education. Participants' incomes ranged from a low of welfare support to a high of US $75,000/year. Average income was approximately US $22,600/year. Thirty-eight participants were Caucasians of European heritage; five people were of mixed heritage, two of whom were of Eurasian background, two of Amerindian and European heritage, and one of Polynesian and European heritage. There was one African American participant and one Hispanic American participant.

The mean number of years during which participants had been receiving hormone therapy was 6.5 years; the median was 4.5 years. Six participants had not yet begun hormone therapy, one of whom was reluctant to do so for health reasons. The two people who had been on hormone therapy for the longest period had been receiving treatment for 18 years. Thirty-four persons had undergone either bilateral mastectomies or sufficient breast reduction surgeries to achieve similar results. Twenty-one participants had undergone some form of hysterectomy. Only four persons had undergone phalloplastic surgeries. Another two participants had opted for metoidioplasties (a surgical procedure which allows a hormonally enlarged clitoris to more closely resemble a small penis).

One participant, who had undergone hormone therapy, mastectomy, and hysterectomy, gave no information as to when he began his transition. One other person had begun hormone therapy four years prior to contact with me but had discontinued hormone therapy because of medical complications at that time. This person had reentered a gender program shortly before being interviewed and had recommenced hormone therapy. In this case, as with others who had begun hormone therapy in the same year as their interviews, I counted these participants as having one year of hormone therapy. One participant had used masculinizing hormones for four years and, after discontinuing their use, had temporarily returned to living as a woman. I counted this person as being four years past the beginning of hormone therapy even though a number of years had passed during which this participant lived as a woman.

Some people had breast reductions and hysterectomies performed by surgeons who were unaware of the transsexuality of their patients; some of these operations were ostensibly done for medical or cosmetic reasons unconnected to transsexualism. In most cases, participants who had not yet had mastectomies or hysterectomies intended to do so when they had sufficient funds to pay for them. Participants were more ambivalent about the current state of surgical expertise at phalloplasty and, although all were intrigued by the idea of a fully-functioning penis, only a few said that they were willing to pay the physical or financial price for considerably less than perfect phalloplastic surgery.

Sexual Attractions and Practices with Women

There can be a great range of reasons for wanting to participate in sexual relations with other people, and the FTM TSs who participated in this research project recounted many of them. It should come as no surprise that people who suffer through a profound search for identity, especially when that identity is so entirely entangled in the contours of their sexual body parts, would feel intensely motivated to explore whatever sexual options they perceive as open to them.

Table 16.1 summarizes sexual and romantic attractions of participants. Table 16.2 summarizes sexual practices of participants. Six persons had not yet begun their transitions into men, and so all posttransition data are in reference to the 39 persons who had taken that step by the time of their interviews.

All but one of the participants who reported having been sexually attracted to anyone before transition reported having been attracted to women. This is similar to previous findings. In many cases, the simple fact of these feelings was taken by participants as evidence that they were, or

TABLE 16.1. Sexual and Romantic Attractions of Female-to-Male Transsexuals

Persons Attracted to	n Before	n After
Women or girls	43	35
Straight men	25	01
Gay men	04	11
Women only	19	27
Men only	01	02
Both women & men	24	07
Gay men only	00	02
Women & gay men only	01	06
Women & straight men only	25	00
Neither women nor men	01	02

Note: n before = 45, n after = 39.

TABLE 16.2. Sexual Practices of Female-to-Male Transsexuals

Type of Sexual Practice	n Before	n After
No sexual experience	03	13
With women		
None	05	14
Casual sex only	04	03
Stable relationship	36	22
Through transition	11	11
With straight men		
None	21	39
Casual sex only	16	01
Stable relationship	08	00
Legal marriage	04	00
With gay men		
None	44	34
Casual sex only	01	04
Stable relationship	00	01
Other		
Casual sex with MTF TS	02	02
Stable relationship		
with FTM TS	00	01
with MTF TS	01	01

Note: n before = 45, n after = 39.

should be, men. One participant's story was representative of how they first made this connection:

Q: What's your earliest memory of being male?

A: I remember the first girl I had a crush on; I was in nursery school and her name was Betty Ann. I can remember playing with the boys and they were talking about who they really liked. I said that I liked her and they just jumped all over me, oooh! They said "Well, you can't like another girl; you're a girl." Humh. I didn't want to go back, but I went back and didn't talk to anybody for weeks and weeks because I knew . . . definitely that there was something wrong with me for feeling that way but then there was also another part of me that said "Hey, that's ok because little boys are supposed to like little girls."
[Quotations have been edited for clarity and relevance. All names have been changed.]

For many, such patterns of thinking continued to retain much of their explanatory power in subsequent years.

Almost all participants who reported having been attracted to women were successful in translating those attractions into either casual sexual affairs or more committed relationships. For most, these affairs and relationships in some way validated their identities as men, either by demonstrating to the participants that lesbianism was not satisfying to them, or by allowing them the confirming experience of playing the part of straight men in relation to their female partners.

All of the people who had been attracted to women as adults before beginning their transitions continued to be attracted to women afterward, but 10 of those who had begun transition and were attracted to women had not yet been sexually involved with women as men. They averaged 2.6 years since beginning their transitions. Some of them may have been of a similar mind to the participant who said, "I was going through so many changes I couldn't keep up with them. I didn't really want to get into an intimate involvement with anyone. I wanted to concentrate on myself for a change." It also seems possible that they were reluctant to approach women for sexual contact because they feared that they would be rejected as physically inadequate. These sentiments were quite forcefully put forth by one participant:

This is not fun. Being in the middle. . . . I'm still not getting what I want from my life. In order to get that I need to have the phalloplasty done. It's not fair! All I really want is—I want to have the same damned opportunities that everybody else takes for granted! . . . Even if there was a woman who was all I want, and who said to me "I don't care if you have a penis or not, I love you and I want to have a relationship with you," it's not going to get physical. It's not going to come down to that because it's still the same thing as before.

He, and others like him, were trapped in a conundrum. They would not have sexual relations until they were complete. Medical technology cannot yet make them that way.

Those participants who had been involved in long-term relationships with women were either further into their transitions, or the women with whom they were involved had been in their lives since before they had begun their transitions. Those whose partners had not come through their changes with them were an average of 7.5 years beyond beginning their transitions when they were interviewed. Their first long-term relationship had begun an average of 1.4 years into their lives as men, more than half of them having begun within one year of the beginning of their transitions. Thus, they had started their relationships early in their transitions. They had been willing to risk rejection. It would seem that they were more confident that they might find women who would accept them as men, physically incomplete though they may have felt.

It would seem that the FTM TSs in this sample broke roughly into three types on this issue: (a) those who hesitated to become sexually involved with women because of feelings of inadequacy, (b) those who entered into their transitions with a supportive partner, and (c) those who felt confident enough to start relationships soon after they began their transitions. The first group would seem to be the most committed to an unrealistic expectation of having a complete male body. The second group had the valuable support of a partner who validated their manhood as coming from a noncorporal source within them. The third group would seem to have been satisfied with the camouflage offered by understanding the state of their bodies as a medical condition which was in the process of being "cured." But even for those brave enough to risk initiating sexual relationships, the process was still fraught with anxieties. One participant told this story about the night he first disclosed his condition to the woman he later intended to marry:

I planned out an evening of "I've got to tell you something about myself." . . . I just told her that when I was little I was different. I don't think I used the word transsexual 'til later on in the story. . . . And I just kind of told the story. Afterwards . . . she was pretty quiet. She said, . . . "I need to process this." . . . So, I left that with her, and drove home. . . . It couldn't have been a few minutes later before she called me. . . . I could not believe that someone could actually listen to this story and still accept me and love me. It was a fantasy of unheard of proportions coming true right before my very eyes . . . her space was definitely "I want you to know that . . . I do see you . . . that yes, I am having sex with you. With these parts right here."

It seems from this story, and others like it, that having partners who believe in FTM TSs' manhood and validate it on a sexual level is an important contributing factor in FTM TSs' acceptance of themselves as credible men.

Sexual Attractions and Practices with Straight Men

More than half of the pretransition group also reported having been attracted to straight men. For most, their attractions for men were not as enduring or as deeply felt as their attractions for women. For many, their feelings for men were rooted in a wish to gain social acceptance and to avoid social stigma. Many participants said that their attractions to straight men were either for the purposes of sexual experimentation or for male-buddy types of relations. Some were carried away on adolescent feelings of lust and romance and took what, at the time, appeared to be the easiest route to satisfaction. One participant summed up many of these reasons, and their limitations, when he said:

I think a good portion of it was curiosity. I had a "boyfriend" who I really liked because he played ball . . . and I thought we could be good buddies. But he had other ideas. . . . When he wanted to start playing little sex games and petting I went along with it because I was curious and I was aroused. . . . I didn't enjoy him touching me but I enjoyed touching him and experimenting, just knowing. He wanted to penetrate me and I just went bananas, it freaked me, no way that anybody is going to do that to me.

A couple of people said that they were attracted to men to learn about the sexual or companionate behavior of men for later reference when they themselves became men. For instance, one person had this to say about a single experience of heterosexual intercourse:

> It was more like an observation. This is when I knew I was going to do something about myself, and I wanted to know what sex felt like for women. So . . . that when I had a relationship, I would know what they were feeling. So I would know what works. So, I went and did it, and pretended I was a female. It was pleasurable for me. I got off. There was no love with a man. It was for the sex. I used him.

In adulthood, many had satisfied their curiosity to the point where less than one-third of pretransition participants were still attracted to straight men (five of whom were people who had not previously found straight men attractive). Eight of the participants acted on their attractions to straight men to the extent that they became involved in stable relationships. This finding is within the range reported by previous researchers (Lothstein, 1983; McCauley & Ehrhardt, 1980). Two of the four who did not marry formed their longest relationships with straight men with whom they shared masculine interests and activities. One person's recollections summed up this pattern nicely:

> In order to feel like a woman with a particular man, he had to feel more masculine than I was. . . . Most of them were men I wanted to be like. I have to say, a lot of my men were role models for what I've become today.

The attractions felt to men, in such cases, can best be described as masculine buddy relations with the usual sexual overtones acted upon. For the FTM TSs in such relationships, the buddy aspect tended to be more satisfying than the sexual aspect.

The other two, who had stable nonmarital relationships with men before beginning their transitions, were each unique among those in this sample. One had a stable SOID as a gay man, which was not altered by relationships with straight men. The other was involved in street prostitution and described himself as "sexually compulsive." He had experience with a great deal of casual and impersonal sex with a wide variety of people both before and after commencing his transition. In addition, while still a young teenager, this person had a 3-year "open" relationship with a young adult man whom he described as having "male-to-female tendencies."

Four persons married and had children before beginning their transitions. This is similar to that reported by previous authors. One person, who married twice and had five children, explicitly stated that he had done so in flight from the possibility of being a lesbian woman. Two persons married as a result of unplanned pregnancies at a time in their lives when they had no idea how to prevent such occurrences. One unusual FTM TS, who married and had four children, explained many years of pleasurable sexual involvement with men, saying that "As long as I'm stuck being a damn female, I might as well do the one thing that I like about being female, which is make a lot of babies. And here again, enjoy what you got."

Only one posttransition person continued to find straight men attractive. He was an individual who sought out a great many casual sexual encounters with both men and women. He had impersonal sexual relations with straight men in public places, but he did so as a man himself. (See Table 16.1 for a further description of romantic and sexual attractions before and after FTM TSs' transitions.)

Sexual Attractions and Practices with Gay Men

Only one of the four individuals who found gay men attractive before beginning transition was exclusively interested in male gay men; one other participant was attracted to the gay men's sexual and social world but seemed to be attracted to men's bodies only on the fantasy level. The attractions the rest felt seemed to occur in the context of their eclectic and voracious sexual tastes. Only one person actualized his feelings of sexual attraction for gay men before starting his transition. This person was, at the time of the sexual contact, passing as a male street prostitute without the aid of hormone therapy and identified as a bisexual man. The relative reluctance of pretransition FTM TSs to attempt sexual relations with gay men may have been based on a fear of rejection because of their female genitalia (Blanchard, 1985). One participant, who maintained a SOID as a gay man, said that he had never become involved in a sexual relationship with another gay man because of such fears.

It is intriguing that there was a 275 percent increase in the number of posttransition participants who began to find gay men sexually attractive. The participants who developed an interest in sexual relations with gay men after they themselves had become men tended to be among the furthest into their changes, averaging 10.75 years since beginning their transitions. More significantly, they averaged 7.4 years into their transitions before starting to find men sexually attractive.

The explanations they offered for having developed their attractions for gay men were telling. Clearly, men and masculinity are captivating subjects for FTM TSs. They spend much of their lives searching for their own identities as men and the remainder of their lives learning to live effectively as men. During the first part of the process they may find men attractive in myriad ways, including sexually, but for FTM TSs, the experience of sexual relations with men, while living as women, can be profoundly disconfirming of their fledgling identities as men. After FTM TSs have securely passed over the invisible fuzzy line that divides men from women, they are less vulnerable to being cast as women. I suspect that it is only when they feel solidly established as men that they can begin to indulge their sexual curiosity about men and the most powerful signifier of manhood, the penis, without having it threaten to dislodge their identities as men.

And their curiosity must have been great. Fewer than 20 percent of the participants in this study had ever been involved in stable relationships with men. More than a third had only had occasional casual sexual experiences with men. Almost half had never had any sexual contact with men. Few people could have less intimate knowledge of the sexuality of men than such a group. Yet they became men. At the very time in their lives when they needed to know men as closely as possible, men must have felt like long-lost brothers: the kinship was there, but the day-to-day knowledge was absent. There were many ways open to them to explore the social world of men but only one avenue open to learning about how to act sexually like men.

It seemed that the longer they had been living as men, the more secure their identities as men, the more convinced they were that others in the world saw them as men, the more free they became to admit their curiosity about how men have sex. Of course, after such a journey to become men, the logical way to explore male sexuality would be through interactions with gay men. As one participant put it:

> I've actually done it a lot with gay men. And what I do is I go more to movie theaters and bathrooms. And I've—it's incredible! Oh, my God. It's so wild! It's so amazing! It's such an education! First of all, it's like a very intense male-bonding thing. I cannot describe it. When straight FTMs say to me, "I don't understand how a woman can become a man to be gay," I don't understand how they could not at least explore that. Because it's the ultimate in masculinity. People think faggots are queers; they're fairies. No way. They're more men than anybody, 'cause they're totally homoerotic. How much more masculine can you get? They're not even interested in women. They're just interested in men. It's incredible! I love it! And, of course, it's risky, it's a real adventure. When you're in a totally male environment where

no women are allowed, if you're discovered, I could imagine that could be dangerous.

Exploration, risk, adventure, danger—all stereotypically masculine attributes. An ironic twist, they had become men, they had become relatively secure in their manhood, yet they lacked knowledge of the penis in action. The route to that knowledge was through gay men, who are usually seen by others as less than fully manly, and it carried with it a threat of exposure as still female despite hormone therapy, surgeries, and years of living on the men's side of the gender divide.

But few of them actually acted on these attractions. Fear of AIDS figured prominently in their reasons for not exploring their sexuality with gay men; fidelity in their relationships with women was also mentioned. Perhaps more importantly was the concern some felt about the state of their genitals. One participant, who, as a man without a penis, had been involved with a gay man, eloquently summed up a dilemma faced by FTM TSs who were attracted to gay men:

> When I am with a male the presence of his penis and the lack of mine just makes it that much stronger in my head that I'm missing something. I feel very inadequate and I don't want to see myself as female, and when I'm with a male it's very hard not to. It's hard to see this physical difference and get past that.

Table 16.2 provides additional information about FTM TSs' sexual practices.

Other Sexual Attractions and Practices

The few participants who became sexually involved with pretransition TSs met them in the gender community. One person reported that he and another FTM TS had been involved in a three-year relationship as gay men. That participant later married a male-to-female (MTF) TS. He, and one other person, had also had casual sex with MTF TSs. I only know of one other documented case of a similar type (Huxley, Kenna, & Brandon, 1981), which seems surprising given the reluctance that transsexual people often express about exposing their bodies to possibly unsympathetic others.

The small number of participants who said that they had never engaged in any sexual activity with another person gave reasons similar to those found in other reports, e.g., aversion to female homosexual practices and inability to perform sexually as men (Blanchard, 1990). One-third reported that their first sexual experience with another person was nonconsensual. These data are reported elsewhere (Devor, 1994).

The data about FTM TSs presented in this article illustrate some difficulties with the simplistic use of the categories of sex or gender, or the usual SOID of persons' partners as bases for determinations of sexual orientation. These data also exemplify some creative steps that members of society may take to circumvent difficulties they encounter when trying to position themselves in relation to the dominant gender schema. Table 16.3 represents the reported SOIDs of the FTM TSs. Sixteen people went through more than one SOID before beginning their transitions. One person claimed no SOID as he had never been attracted to anyone. Four of the 39 participants who had begun their transitions changed SOIDs at least once after their transitions began. The important point that these data raise is that SOID, as it was lived by the FTM TSs who participated in this research, was (and presumably still is) a process, not an essential and unchanging characteristic.

The material presented in this article only weakly supported the contention that most pretransition FTM TSs see themselves as straight men in their relations with women. Some participants seemed to take the evidence of their physical selves as the most influential factor in their SOID forma-

TABLE 16.3. Sexual-Orientation Identities of Female-to-Male Transsexuals

Sexual-orientation identity	n Before	n After
Straight man	23	30
Lesbian woman	20	00
Straight woman	05	00
Bisexual man	04	05
Gay man	03	04
Gay	03	00
Bisexual woman	02	00
Lesbian man	00	01
None	01	03
Straight man only	13	26
Lesbian woman only	10	00
Both straight man & lesbian woman	10	00
Both straight man & bisexual man	03	03

Note: n Before = 41, n After = 39.

tion before beginning their transitions. In other words, for such persons, the fact that both they and their partners had female bodies was sufficient to cause them to name themselves as lesbian women. In instances in which the female partner of an FTM TS had a history of lesbian relations and a SOID as a lesbian woman, this tendency was reinforced. But eventually, even these participants became convinced that they were not really lesbian women. They concluded that, although their anatomy said that they were lesbian women, they were different from other lesbian women. Thus they came to give primacy to nonanatomical indicators of SOID. In some cases, this feeling was reinforced by the strictures of lesbian-feminist ideology concerning gender identity and sexual practices (Faderman, 1991). One person, who was active in a lesbian-feminist community, commented on this situation:

> There were a lot of needs that I could not express with lesbians, because the lesbians that I was having relationships with were not open to anything that had anything to do with males. For instance, they weren't interested in AIDS and all the variety of sexual things that go with that. I'm talking about dildos and vibrators and things like that.

For others, the evidence of their social relations and sexual practices were always the overriding factors in the establishment of their SOIDs. Their relationships with women were straight in all ways except for the shapes of their own physical bodies. These people discounted their corporal selves and privileged social and sexual practices to name themselves and their relationships as straight. In cases in which a partner had always been straight before becoming involved with an FTM TS, this tendency was reinforced and the impetus to achieve transition was that much greater. Consider the distinctions between lesbian and straight sexuality and relationships drawn by this participant:

> It also depends on whether you make love with a lesbian or a heterosexual woman. There is a different approach from a woman to her man than the approach from one woman to another woman who are lovers. It's just that it comes out in power differences. The areas of openness are different ones . . . the areas of allegiance are different ones. . . . A heterosexual relationship can never match a homosexual relationship because there is so much . . . depth and understanding of the psyche and of the heart and of the sexuality. In a heterosexual relationship, you also have . . . unknown factors that kind of demand a stretch, a greater give.

After the participants had begun their transitions, the situation became more clear cut. All but one of the people who called themselves straight men or lesbian women before beginning their transitions identified themselves as straight men afterward. (One person, reluctant to leave behind a well-loved place as a member of a lesbian community, called himself a lesbian man. I have recently observed an increasing number of FTM TSs with lesbian-feminist backgrounds who similarly continue to identify socially and politically with the gay or lesbian-feminist community. This phenomenon seems to be currently most common in, but not restricted to, the western USA.)

As soon as they had begun their transformational process, they had increased access to the usual markers of SOID—by way of recourse to a medical explanation. They could claim to be men with a medical condition which they were in the process of correcting. One participant talked about how he saw it:

> If anything I thought it would make it better. That we could be normal. . . . We don't have to pretend that we are lesbians. . . . We don't have to be on the fringes of society. We can be perfectly normal. We could have the house and the white picket fence, and we could get married. . . . People could be proud of us. We wouldn't have to slink around. We could just be proud to be in love and be a couple, and pay credit cards back, and barbecues in the back yard, and just all that stuff.

Unfortunately for the participants, the transformative technology available to FTM TSs is limited. The process usually takes at least 2 years, and considerably longer periods are common. Even for those who obtained phalloplasties, the results were such that they still required explanation in intimate sexual circumstances. But most participants had not taken this surgical step, and therefore were penisless men.

As a result, they were forced to either make use of the "sick role" to explain their embarrassing condition, or to be celibate until their bodies were more nearly complete. The "sick role" can be summarized as having four components: (a) Sick persons are not considered to be responsible for their condition; (b) While persons are sick they may be exempt from performing the roles that would normally be expected of them; (c) It is agreed that it is undesirable to be sick; (d) It is assumed that being sick is a temporary condition which sick persons are expected to seek help to eliminate as quickly as possible (Parsons, 1951).

Both FTM TSs and their partners routinely made use of this explanation in distinguishing their relationships as straight rather than lesbian ones. In all cases, the attributions of others were influential. Any sexual partner who concurred with a participant's self-image was a boon to his confidence in himself as a man. Those who had long-term partners who went through their transitions with them had access to the strongest confirmation that, even fully naked, they were men. As one man said: "If a person feels that they are a man, then they can be a man."

Certainly, sexual partners who believed them to be men must have contributed greatly to participants' feelings of being men. Despite the number of participants who did become sexually involved with men before they themselves became men, very few ever identified themselves as straight women. The few who did temporarily accept this SOID were entirely among those who had had long-term relationships with men. In those cases, it would seem that the confluence, over an extended period of time, of so many of the usual indicators of SOID were too powerful to ignore. All others who had sexual experience with men were able to write it off as a result of either having succumbed to social expectations or as youthful experimentation. In any event, they were able to minimize the importance of their heterosexual involvements by placing paramount importance on affectional preferences and by casting aside physical activity as inconsequential. They thus took a more feminine approach to questions of sexuality and love as they have been understood in the cultural context in which they functioned.

Three participants identified as gay men prior to beginning their transitions. One of them only flirted with this SOID. Another unswervingly identified as a gay man both before and after transition. The third was an individual who was in a 25-year relationship with a female woman partner, which both of them understood as a gay men's relationship. One posttransition FTM TS temporarily identified as a gay man on the basis of a one-year relationship with a gay man. One other person based his temporary identity as a gay man on a 3-year relationship with another FTM TS.

Theoretical Implications

Overall, it would seem that the participants in this study were reluctant to use their physical selves as the most important factor in selecting their SOIDs. Although they seemed to want to make their affectional preferences the pivotal point, the attributions (real or imagined) made by others seemed to weigh very heavily in the balance. Many vacillated between basing their SOIDs on their own heartfelt feelings and capitulating to the dictates of biologically based social conventions. Clearly, they could more easily claim manhood in everyday life than they could in intimate matters.

Gender, it would seem, can be entirely socially constructed. Love affairs may start with gender, but, if they are to become sexual, they must travel into the realm of sex. It was then that participants' incongruities between their genders and their sexes had to be managed. Some shied away from this challenge altogether. A few remained uncommitted to any SOID. Others based their identities on their affectional preferences but did not put them to the test by attempting sexual relations. A few circumvented the issue by having casual sexual affairs in which they kept their transsexual status hidden or by becoming involved with others like themselves. Those who successfully established relationships in the SOID they preferred did so with support of partners who shared their images of themselves as bona fide men with a physical problem which medical technology could fix.

My research indicated that FTM TSs are not always universally homosexually and heterogenderally oriented either before, or after, undertaking their transitions. What was most consistent in this sample was an enduring and a profoundly felt pattern of affectional preferences for women. But it is also significant to note that a large minority of FTM TS individuals also had sexual experience with men which they used as a basis for their SOIDS.

The processes that the FTM TSs in this study underwent, while searching for their SOIDs and ways to justify them, seem to be only a more stark version of what I would suggest that most members of society go through. Their SOIDs seem to have been based on (a) maintaining as socially correct as possible an alignment of a set of identities, attitudes, and behaviors which are popularly thought to be connected with genetic sex and (b) the reflexive confirmation gained from the SOIDs of, and the attributions made by, their sexual partners.

The FTM TSs in this study found that, at different times in their lives, they had to give greater weight to certain bases of SOID (e.g., sexual attractions and preferences) or to diminish the importance of others (e.g., physical body, actual sexual practices) in an attempt to achieve the status they desired. In attempting to make the whole picture as socially correct as possible, they had to remodel all aspects of their sexes and genders to be able to claim legitimately the SOIDs which best suited them. Perhaps the most delicate of all tasks they had to learn was how to perform sexually as men, which they largely had to learn through observation. Each of us must also learn the scripts of our sexes and SOIDs (Gagnon, 1990), but most members of society are fortunate enough to be able to learn their scripts using their own bodies as their test instruments.

Those FTM TSs who could find a validation of themselves, as sexed, gendered, and sexual persons, did so in the form of partners who would fully confirm their SOIDs. Those who could not find such partners were compelled to remain celibate. In this last regard, too, they were not so different from any other member of society.

For most members of society this whole process seems quite straightforward and unproblematic. We simply grow up into our socially expected and approved SOIDs. But if we were to look more closely at the lives of more typical members of society, we might find that each of us must search for our place within the gender schema of the society in which we live. Who among us have never wondered if they weren't somehow different from all the rest? Who among us have always felt so secure that they have never altered themselves to try better to live up to society's gender ideals?

Clothing, coiffures and cosmetics, bodybuilding, hair transplants, electrolysis, and surgeries are all used by transsexual and nontranssexual members of society to make ourselves more perfectly fit society's sex, gender, and sexual ideals. Perhaps, in the end, the biggest difference between FTM TSs and other members of society lies not so much in the nature of the identity-supporting processes they must pass through but in the anguish and consciousness with which they must negotiate them.

ACKNOWLEDGMENTS

Portions of this research were funded by the Social Science and Humanities Research Council of Canada and the University of Victoria.

My sincerest thanks go to the people who volunteered their time to become involved in this research project and to teach me something of their way of life. My thanks also go to Lin Fraser and Lynn Greenhough for helpful comments on earlier drafts of this paper and to my research assistants: Noreen Begoray, Bev Copes, Sheila Pedersen, and Sandra Winfield.

REFERENCES

American Psychiatric Association. (1987). *Diagnostic and statistical manual of mental disorders.* DSM III-R. Washington, DC: American Psychiatric Association.

Blanchard, R. (1985). Gender dysphoria and gender reorientation. In B. Steiner (Ed.), *Gender dysphoria: Development, research, management,* pp. 365–392. New York: Plenum.

Blanchard, R. (1989). The classification and labeling of nonhomosexual gender dysphorias. *Archives of Sexual Behavior, 18,* 315–334.

Blanchard, R. (1990). Gender identity disorders in adult women. In R. Blanchard & B. Steiner (Eds.), *The clinical management of gender identity disorders in children and adults,* pp. 77–97. Washington, DC: American Psychiatric Press.

Bolin, A. (1988). *In search of Eve: Transsexual rites of passage.* South Hadley, MA: Bergin & Garvey Publishers, Inc.

Bradley, S.J., Blanchard, R., Coates, S., Green, R., Levine, S., Meyer-Bahlburg, H.F.L., Pauly, I.B., & Zucker, K.J. (1991). Interim report of the DSM-IV subcommittee on gender disorders. *Archives of Sexual Behavior, 20,* 333–343.

Cass, V. (1984). Homosexual identity: A concept in need of definition. *Journal of Homosexuality, 9*(2/3), 105–126.

Clare, D., & Tully, B. (1989). Transhomosexuality, or the dissociation of sexual orientation and sex object choice. *Archives of Sexual Behavior, 18,* 531–536.

Coleman, E. (1987). Assessment of sexual orientation. *Journal of Homosexuality, 14*(1/2), 9–24.

Coleman, E., & Bockting, W. (1988). "Heterosexual" prior to sex reassignment—"homosexual" afterwards: A case study of a female-to-male transsexual. *Journal of Psychology & Human Sexuality, 1*(2), 69–82.

Coleman, E., Bockting, W., & Gooren, L. (1993). Homosexual and bisexual identity in sex-reassigned female-to-male transsexuals. *Archives of Sexual Behavior, 22,* 37–50.

De Cecco, J., & Shively, M. (1984). From sexual identity to sexual relationships: A contextual shift. *Journal of Homosexuality, 9*(2/3), 1–26.

Devor, H. (1990). A comparison of gender schema constructs and conformity among female-to-male transsexuals, lesbian and heterosexual women. Doctoral dissertation, University of Washington. *Dissertations Abstracts International, 51.*

Devor, H. (1993). Toward a taxonomy of gendered sexuality. *Journal of Psychology and Human Sexuality, 6*(1), 23–55.

Devor, H. (1994). Transsexualism, dissociation, and child abuse: An initial discussion based on nonclinical data. *Journal of Psychology and Human Sexuality, 6*(3), 49–72.

Devor, H. (1997). *FTM: Female-to-male transsexuals in society.* Bloomington: Indiana University Press.

Dixen, J.M., Maddever, H., Van Maasdam, J., & Edwards, P.W. (1984). Psychosocial characteristics of applicants evaluated for surgical gender reassignment. *Archives of Sexual Behavior, 13,* 269–276.

Faderman, L. (1991). *Odd girls and twilight lovers.* New York: Penguin Books.

Gagnon, J.H. (1990). Gender preference in erotic relations: The Kinsey scale and sexual scripts. In D.P. McWhirter, S.A. Sanders, & J.M. Reinisch (Eds.), *Homosexuality/heterosexuality: Concepts of sexual orientation,* pp. 177–207. New York: Oxford University Press.

Grimm, D. (1987). Toward a theory of gender: Transsexualism, gender, sexuality, and relationships. *American Behavioral Scientist, 31,* 66–85.

Huxley, P.J., Kenna, J.C., & Brandon, S.B. (1981). Partnership in transsexualism. Part II. The nature of the partnership. *Archives of Sexual Behavior, 10,* 143–160.

Kinsey, A.C., Pomeroy, W.B., & Martin, C.E. (1948). *Sexual behavior in the human male.* Philadelphia: W.B. Saunders.

Klein, F., Sepekoff, B., & Wolf, T. (1985). Sexual orientation: A multi-variable dynamic process. *Journal of Homosexuality, 11*(1/2), 35–49.

Lever, J., Kanouse, D.E., Rogers, W.H., Carson, S., & Hertz, R. (1992). Behavior patterns and sexual identity of bisexual males. *The Journal of Sex Research, 29*(2), 141–167.

Lothstein, L. (1983). *Female-to-male transsexualism: Historical, clinical and theoretical issues.* Boston: Routledge & Kegan Paul.

McCauley, E., & Ehrhardt, A. (1980). Sexual behavior in female transsexuals and lesbians. *The Journal of Sex Research, 16,* 202–211.

Money, J. (1988). *Gay, straight and in-between: The sexology of erotic orientation.* New York: Oxford University Press.

Parsons, T. (1951). *The social system.* New York: Free Press.

Paul, J. (1983). The bisexual identity: An idea without social recognition. *Journal of Homosexuality, 9*(2/3), 45–63.

Pauly, I. (1974). Female transsexualism: Part I. *Archives of Sexual Behavior, 3,* 487–507.

Pillard, R.C., & Weinrich, J.D. (1987). The periodic table model of the gender transpositions: Part I. A theory based on masculinization and defeminization of the brain. *The Journal of Sex Research, 23,* 425–454.

Shively, M., & De Cecco, J. (1977). Components of sexual identity. *Journal of Homosexuality, 3*(1), 41–48.

Steiner, B., & Bernstein, S.M. (1981). Female-to-male transsexuals and their partners. *Canadian Journal of Psychiatry, 26,* 178–182.

Stoller, R.J. (1972). Etiological factors in female transsexualism: A first approximation. *Archives of Sexual Behavior, 2,* 47–64.

Stuart, K.E. (1991). *The uninvited dilemma: A question of gender.* Portland, OR: Metamorphous Press.

Weeks, J. (1989). *Sex, politics and society: The regulation of sexuality since 1800.* New York: Longman.

Weinrich, J.D. (1988). The periodic table model of the gender transpositions: Part II. Limerent and lusty sexual attractions and the nature of bisexuality. *The Journal of Sex Research, 24,* 113–129.

17 Hormonal Therapy of Gender Dysphoria

The Male-to-Female Transsexual

Rosemary Basson

Jerilynn C. Prior

Fascination with cross-gender states appears to be intrinsic to being human. The "evidence" for the existence of a pope who appeared to be a man but was a fertile woman was recently the subject of the presidential address for the Endocrine Society (New & Ketzinger, 1993). Current medical understanding says that gender dysphoria or true transsexualism is a neuroendocrine condition of unknown cause, unknown inheritance, and has a prevalence of about 1:18,000 in the male population (Asscheman, 1989). Transsexualism has been shown to be poorly responsive to intense psychotherapy to change the identity disturbance. Therefore, treatment of a biological male with female hormones becomes the primary therapy followed by anatomical reassignment after a period of living as a woman.

The purpose of this chapter is to outline and review the more than 10-year experience of the clinical program at Vancouver Hospital (University of British Columbia) in treating men who are true transsexuals.

Overview of Hormonal Therapy

A review of the literature and communication with other centers reveals that the current standard therapy for male-to-female transsexuals (MTF) is 2.5 to 10 mg/d continuously of conjugated equine estrogen (Premarin®, CEE) or 0.1 to 1.0 mg/d of ethinyl estradiol (EE) (Meyer, Webb, Stuart, Finkelstein, et al., 1986; Asscheman, Gooren, & Eklund, 1989; Asscheman & Gooren, 1992). Similar doses of estrogen were in use when our clinic began (average dose of CEE was 3.9 ± 2.3 mg/d and of EE was 7.1 ± 7.2 mg/d) (Prior, Vigna, Watson, & Diewold, 1986; Prior, Vigna, & Watson, 1989). In addition, these men were commonly asking their family physicians for and receiving additional injected estrogen in their intense desire to become female (Prior, Vigna, Watson, & Diewold, 1986).

The differences in our approach to therapy are that we have added to estrogen therapy a nonandrogenic progesterone, medroxyprogesterone acetate (MPA). A progesterone is needed for two main reasons: feminization involves the action of both the estrogen and progesterone (secreted cyclically in the biological woman), and testosterone suppression is accompanied with lower estrogen doses. We also consistently prescribe a drug that competes with testosterone at its receptor. We began using spironolactone, a hypertension medication with which one of us (Prior) had experience during its initial clinical development to exploit its antiandrogenic properties (Prior, Vigna, & Watson, 1989). The concerns in this center, which has now had experience with over 238 male-to-female transsexuals, were to avoid the potential or documented complications of treatment with high doses of estrogens (thromboembolism, prolactinoma, myocardial infarction, breast cancer) (Asscheman, Gooren, & Eklund, 1989).

Men with gender-related concerns are not referred for endocrine treatment in the Centre for Sexuality, Gender Identity and Reproductive Health (formerly the Gender Dysphoria Programme) until they have been carefully screened and determined to have true transsexualism. They are initially interviewed by a psychiatric social worker, psychologist, or nurse clinician, and referred for two independent psychiatric assessments. Spironolactone may be given during the assessment and appears to help with the intense anxiety during the several-month process. Any men already on oral contraceptives or estrogen are told that they must discontinue current therapies and adopt those prescribed by this clinic at the time of endocrine assessment. Written information concerning this center's hormonal therapy program is provided ahead of the consultation. In this material and verbally, they are warned that estrogen therapy mandates discontinuation of cigarette smoking. Therefore the period of initial evaluation allows them to prepare for a new set of therapies.

OBJECTIVES FOR HORMONAL MANAGEMENT

Hormonal therapy for the man who feels he is, and wants to become more externally like, a woman, has several goals. These are summarized and then explained in detail below:

1. To reduce androgen activity through:
    a. decreased production of testosterone (T) and dihydrotestosterone (DHT)
    b. decreased effects of T and DHT
2. To promote estrogen and progesterone effects on secondary female sexual characteristics.

3. To prevent any negative effects of testosterone deprivation (such as accelerated bone loss or inadequate bone formation).
4. To provide adequate hormonal support prior to, during, and following recovery from sexual-reassignment surgery (SRS).
5. To minimize potential complications of exogenous hormone therapy (worsening of hypertension, diabetes, hyperlipidemia, or production of hyperprolactinemia, thromboembolic disease, or breast cancer).

Reduction of Androgen Activity

The first objective, decreasing androgen production and effects (Table 17.1), is met by combined therapy with an estrogen (CEE or transdermal estrogen [TDE]), a nonandrogenic progestin, MPA, and spironolactone as an antiandrogen. Figure 17.1 shows the actions of these different drugs to suppress the hormone levels and receptors. Estrogen and MPA feed back to the

---

TABLE 17.1. Actions of Testosterone and/or DHT

1. Sexual Function
Erection
Ejaculation
Time to Orgasm
Sexual Dominance

2. Cerebrum
Sexual Desire
Energy
Well-being

3. Metabolism
RBC Production
Anabolic to Muscle and Bone
Lipids—HDL Reduction
HbA1C ↑

4. Physical/Sexual Characteristics
Development of Male Genitalia and Prostate
Beard and Male-Pattern Body Hair
Skin Texture
Fat Distribution
Scalp-Hair Loss
Deepening of Voice
Skeletal Structure

---

pituitary and the hypothalamus to reduce luteinizing hormone (LH) production, decreasing the stimulation of testicular production of testosterone. This therapy has been shown, in a prospective but nonrandomized one-year study, to decrease testosterone levels into the female range in all of 50 MTF transsexuals (Prior, Vigna, & Watson, 1989).

The usual daily regime is:

1.   CEE 0.625 to 1.25 mg/d days 1–25 of the month or TDE 50–100 µg twice/week, with 7 patches/month
2.   MPA 20–50 mg/d

Medroxyprogesterone is given in low pharmacological doses. The latter medication is felt to be far safer (objective #5) than estrogen because it does not increase the risk for thrombosis or cancer (Clarke & Sutherland, 1990), lowers triglycerides and total cholesterol (Gallagher, Kable, & Goldgar, 1991) (although it may slightly decrease the HDL increase that occurs on oral estrogen [Writing Group for PEPI Trial, 1995], and has positive effects on bone formation (Prior, 1990; Prior, Vigna, Barr, Rexworthy, et al., 1994). Despite clinical reports, a double-blind, placebo-controlled trial showed no adverse effects to MPA therapy (Prior, Alojado, McKay, & Vigna, 1994). MPA in doses of 20–40 mg/d is needed to adequately suppress LH. MPA is a weak antiandrogen because it competes for the 5-alpha reductase enzyme that transforms testosterone into DHT, and thus is preferable to other available progestins, (e.g. norethindrone or norgestrol with androgenic effects), or the new progestins derived from norgestrol (desogestrel and norgestimate, which, although not androgenic, lack any antiandrogenic effect). However, because MPA may become androgenic at higher doses, oral micronized progesterone therapy has begun to be used, as it just became available in Canada. Progesterone activity also allows the full maturity of breast and nipple development (maturation to Tanner stage 5 requires progesterone [unpublished Prior, 1989]).

Spironolactone, which is commonly begun in a dose of 100 or 200 mg/day by the referring family physician or psychiatrist prior to our assessment, is increased to 300 or 400 mg/d in combination with the hormones listed above (Prior, Vigna, & Watson, 1989). It acts by at least three mechanisms to decrease the production and the effect of endogenous androgens (Corrol, Michaud, Menard, Freifeld, et al., 1975). First, it works through cytochrome P450 to decrease testosterone production by the gonad and adrenal glands. Secondly, it antagonizes testosterone or DHT effects at the intracellular nuclear receptor; and finally, spironolactone is a 5-alpha reductase inhibitor and interferes with the conversion of testosterone to DHT, its active intracellular form. It also may slightly reduce LH production (Prior, Vigna, & Watson, 1989).

Spironolactone, with which we have extensive experience (Prior, Vigna, & Watson, 1989), is an easy medication to administer, is not expensive in generic formulation, and has few and nonserious side effects. In our population, only two transsexuals have experienced a drug-related rash. Because spironolactone is an aldosterone antagonist and a mild diuretic, patients are always cautioned to drink plenty of fluids in the first several

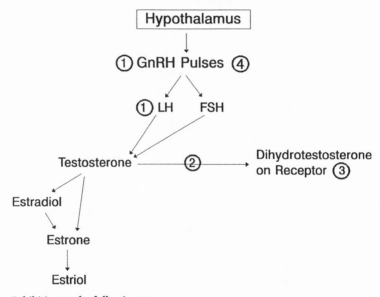

Inhibition at the following steps:

1. Progesterone—Provera
   Estrogen—Estradiol, Conjugated Estrogens
   Cyproterone Acetate
   Spironolactone

2. Progesterone—Provera
   Cyproterone Acetate
   Spironolactone
   Finasteride

3. Cyproterone Acetate
   Flutamide
   Spironolactone

4. GNRH Agonists

Figure 17.1. This diagram outlines the areas of the hypothalamic, pituitary gonadal axis at which the various gonadal steroid hormones, anti-androgens and other pharmacological agents act.

weeks of use and whenever they are exercising strenuously or in hot environments. The initial diuretic effect decreases in 1–4 months. Potassium levels do rise (usually to 4.8–5.2 mmol/L), but not significantly above normal if renal function is unimpaired and a potassium supplement or high fruit diet are not taken. We do not routinely measure serum potassium levels.

Alternative antiandrogenic drugs include cyproterone acetate, also a powerful antiandrogen and a progestagen, an antigonadotrophic agent which also competes with DHT binding to the receptor. Its use is limited by serious risks of interference with corticosteroid production, its high cost, and the common side effects of depression, fatigue, weight gain, and headaches (de Vries, Gooren, & van der Veen, 1986). Similarly, ketoconazole, which interferes with testosterone synthesis, is avoided because of possible hepatotoxicity and the same risk of interference with other steroid production rates. We have no experience using "pure antiandrogen" drugs such as flutamide; however, the secondary increase in LH and testosterone, the expense, and the short half-life would not be desirable. It may prove useful after SRS for persistent beard growth. Finasteride, as a 5-alpha reductase, is also a potential therapy, but it is expensive and would only oppose the formation of the DHT, and not of testosterone itself.

Spironolactone is often discontinued after SRS. However, for some, the sensitivity of the beard hair-cell receptors for testosterone is such that even normal adrenal androgen production appears sufficient to maintain beard growth. In these patients, spironolactone is continued, perhaps at a lower dose, until all male pattern hair is gone.

Promotion of Estrogen and Progesterone Effects

The second objective is to provide effective estrogen and progesterone actions. Estrogens, either CEE or TDE, are given in physiological doses (0.625–1.25 mg/d or 50–100 μg/d, respectively). In addition, we provide them cyclically days 1–25 or 26 of the month to mimic the time of low estrogen during the menstrual flow phase of the normal menstrual cycle. It is of note that the estrogen doses are in the physiological ranges for "hormonal replacement." Others (Asscheman, Gooren, & Eklund, 1989) have used ethinyl estradiol 100 μg (it is of note that this was the dosage used in the birth-control pills in the 1960s when they were documented to cause adverse cardiovascular effects), a dose that is approximately 15 times higher than physiological female levels. Doses ten times higher than this are also prescribed (Meyer, Finkelstein, Stuart, Webb, et al., 1981). The oral route of these high-dose estrogens leads to very altered liver metabolism with increased production of coagulation factors, triglycerides, and renin. High-dose estrogen is also a potent direct stimulant of pituitary prolactin production (Asscheman, Gooren, & Eklund, 1989; Goh & Ratnam, 1990; Goh, Li, & Ratnam, 1992; Kovacs, Stetaneanu, Ezzat, & Smyth, 1994). Pituitary prolactin-producing adenoma growth has been recorded in male-to-female transsexuals being treated with conventional high-dose estrogen therapy (Asscheman, Gooren, & Eklund, 1989; Kovacs, Stetaneanu, Ezzat, & Smyth, 1994). For this reason we routinely monitor prolactin levels, which serve as an indicator of high estrogen self-medication.

Prevention of Potential Adverse Bone Effects

The third objective is to prevent the negative effects of hypogonadism on bone metabolism (Orwoll & Klein, 1995). Men with anorexia, hyperprolactinemia, and congenital causes for low testosterone levels are known to have lower-than-normal bone-density levels and show increased rates of bone loss (Orwoll & Klein, 1995). Bone density has not been well studied in MTF transsexuals. A bone histomorphometry investigation studying specimens obtained during SRS at a time when these men had been off estrogen therapy for one month showed no consistent state of bone remodelling (Lips, Asscheman, Uitewall, Netelenbos, et al., 1989). At the Centre for Sexuality, Gender Identity and Reproductive Health, a prospective pilot study is in progress in which dual energy X-ray absorptiometry (DXA) of the spine and hip are measured at the time of enrollment in the program. Preliminary results show osteopenia in a higher-than-expected number of transsexual men prior to any hormonal or antiandrogen therapy (Personal communication, Prior, 1996). Negative life-styles (cigarette abuse and alcohol excess) and stress-induced delayed puberty may contribute to this observation. In addition, it is not currently known whether the combination of hormones and antiandrogen therapies can prevent the bone loss that would be expected following castration in SR surgery. Medroxyprogesterone therapy is used in addition to estrogen to stimulate bone formation (Prior, 1990).

To Provide Hormonal Support during and after Surgery

The fourth objective is to provide appropriate hormonal support through the presurgical, surgical, and post-reassignment periods if surgery is an option. Concern that estrogen therapy, especially in the high doses used in some centers, may increase the risk for thromboembolic events during and following surgery has led to the decision, both in Amsterdam (Lips, Asscheman, Uitewall, Netelenbos, et al., 1989) and in our center, to discontinue estrogen one month prior to hospital admission for surgery. In our experience, however, discontinuation of all medications, as sometimes recommended by the surgeon, is associated with a regrowth of beard hair that effectively obliterates months of progress toward feminization. Our recommendation is that both MPA and spironolactone be continued until the day of surgery and be restarted as soon as any oral therapy is possible postoperatively. Neither of these medications poses a risk for thrombosis, and this strategy appears to prevent rebound beard growth and may also help prevent increased bone turnover and potential bone loss that can occur with abrupt discontinuation of estrogen therapy (Lips, Asscheman, Uitewall, Netelenbos, et al., 1989). Estrogen is restarted when the person is fully ambulatory. Because surgeries for our patients are performed at other centers, and they experience, therefore, immobilization during long return flights, we do not resume estrogen therapy until the individual is home.

Sometimes vasomotor symptoms typical of menopause develop following surgery. Estrogen would not be appropriate initially, but medroxy-progesterone doses can be increased to treat these symptoms (Schiff, Tulchinsky, Cramer, & Ryan, 1980) until estrogen therapy is reinstituted.

There are no traditional guidelines for hormonal therapy following gender-reassignment surgery. Obviously there is decreased need for an antiandrogen once the primary source of androgens is removed. Our approach has been to gradually lower any previously pharmacologic doses of hormones into the physiological range and to discontinue spironolactone when beard growth is adequately eliminated. The plan is to continue the cyclic estrogen and continuous progestin therapy at least until the age of natural menopause in women (about 50 years). Bone density screening is appropriate prior to discontinuing hormonal therapy—if spinal bone density is low, hormonal or nonhormonal bone therapies would be needed. The long-term health risks of having neither ovarian nor testicular sex steroid production are not known.

To Prevent Complications of Estrogen Therapy

The final objective of the endocrine therapy of male-to-female transsexuals is to do no harm (Prior, Vigna, Watson, & Diewold, 1986; Prior, Vigna, & Watson, 1989). Prior to any hormonal prescription, therefore, the following health-related factors are considered:

CARDIOVASCULAR EFFECTS FROM SMOKING

Our guideline has been that smoking cigarettes precludes estrogen administration because both nicotine use and high-dose estrogen therapy in men increase risks for vascular disease (Coronary Drug Project Research Group, 1973). (It is simply not known whether "low-dose" estrogen increases the risk of heart disease in men.) This approach has provided the necessary motivation for smoking cessation for many of the transsexuals. In the occasional patient whose psychological problems are such that the nicotine addiction cannot be dealt with until the gender dysphoria is addressed, we would start transdermal estrogen in low doses (usually 25 µg).

GLUCOSE INTOLERANCE
Glycosylated hemoglobin (HbA1C) is monitored before therapy and every 6–12 months. We have only rarely seen a significant increase, and this has been associated with weight gain related to the stress of coping with the gender dysphoria itself, usually in association with a family diabetes mellitus history.

HYPERTENSION
Nine of 27 men assessed in the clinic, having previously been on pharmacological doses of estrogen, had elevated blood-pressure levels (Prior, Vigna, & Watson, 1989). However, because spironolactone is an antihypertensive and because we prescribe physiological doses of estrogen, we rarely create an increase in blood pressure. Those with initially elevated pressures usually become normal.

LACK OF EXERCISE
Encouragement of a more active lifestyle is a key part of our health education. Exercise is not only known to decrease risks for cardiovascular disease (Powell, Thompson, Caspersen, & Kendrick, 1987) and osteoporosis (Pate, Pratt, Blair, Haskell, et al., 1995), but may improve sleep and sense of well-being, and prevent depression. While male-to-female transsexuals are anatomically ambivalent, however, swimming and aerobics classes can be embarrassing and are not practical forms of activity.

HYPERLIPIDEMIA
Mild to moderate elevation of cholesterol will decrease during hormonal therapy. Unfortunately, reduced high-density lipoprotein cholesterol (HDL) levels tend to remain low. Those with abnormally low HDL levels will benefit from oral micronized progesterone therapy (300–400 mg at bedtime) rather than MPA because it has no negative HDL effect (Hargrove, Maxon, Wentz, & Burnett, 1989). To pharmacologically increase HDL, oral rather than transdermal estrogen would be most effective. Hypertriglyceridemia, by contrast, requires the use of transdermal rather than oral estrogen.

BREAST-CANCER FAMILY HISTORY
Although there are epidemiological data showing an increased risk for breast cancer in menopausal women treated with estrogen (Grady, Rubin, Petitti, Fox, et al., 1992), most of these women would have been exposed to 20 to 30 years of high endogenous estrogen. In contrast, the male-to-female transsexual will have an increased breast-cancer risk only with prolonged dura-

tion of therapy (Pritchard, Pankowsky, Crowe, & Abdul-Karim, 1988). Estrogen doses are kept in the low portion of the physiological range for the MTF transsexual who has a close relative with breast cancer. A pause in estrogen administration the last five or six days in each month is prescribed to mimic the low estrogen levels during normal menstrual flow. It may decrease breast tenderness symptoms. All MTF transsexuals are taught breast self-examination to learn their individual breast nodularity so that a change could be appreciated. After 10 years of exogenous estrogen use an initial and possibly yearly mammogram is recommended.

HISTORY OF THROMBOTIC COMPLICATIONS

A previous deep vein thrombosis (DVT) is not considered an absolute con-

TABLE 17.2. Comparison of Two Programs for Therapy of Male-to-Female Transsexuals

	Vancouver	Amsterdam*
Years studied	1985–1995	1980–1989
Number of male-to-females in active follow-up	196	303
Mean duration (in years) of hormone follow-up	5.5	4.4
Therapy		
Mean estrogen	CEE 0.9 mg cyclically	EE 100 µg daily
Antiandrogen	Spironolactone 300 mg daily	Cyproterone a. 100 mg daily
Progestin	Medroxyprogesterone 20 mg daily	—
Percentage of Complications		
Thrombotic	1.5%	6.3%
Prolactinomas**	0	1.7%
Hyperprolactinoma (>3 times upper female nl range)	<1%	21.4%
Clinical Depression	<1%	8.3%

*as reported in Asscheman, H., Gooren, L.J., & Eklund, P.L. (1989).
**All with higher-than-normal prolactin levels were followed. None have had persistent high levels or have been screened with pituitary imaging.

traindication to estrogen therapy unless it occurred during estrogen therapy. We would prescribe transdermal estradiol cautiously, in low doses, for a transsexual person with a history of thrombosis.

OUTCOME IN TERMS OF FEMINIZATION ACHIEVED
Observed Effects of Testosterone Antagonism

The degree to which the various actions of testosterone and DHT (Table 17.1) can be eliminated or antagonized is extremely variable. Bodily *bony structure* such as stature and the shoulder and chest widths cannot be al-

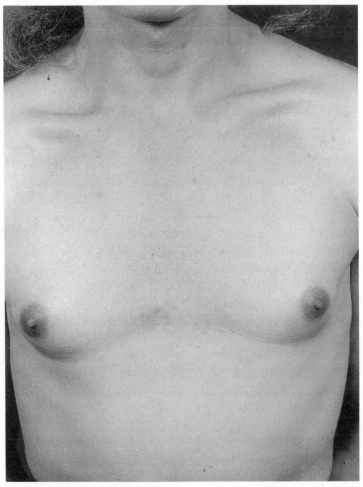

Figure 17.2. The broad chest, shoulders, and muscular neck of a biological male create a setting in which normal female breast enlargement and development may appear inadequate.

tered (Figure 17.2). Major clues to male biology may include the large sizes of hands and feet, prominence of the "Adam's apple" or laryngeal cartilage, and the angularity of nose and chin. Similarly, testosterone causes vocal-cord thickening, which leads to a *deeper voice*. This voice change is irreversible despite production of low levels of testosterone and increase in estrogen levels into the female range. Voice therapy is used in our clinic to train MTF individuals to speak with upper registers and to use female-like vocal patterns.

Fertility will be lost as sperm production ceases. The reversibility of azospermia has not been systematically assessed. Some patients may request that their semen be frozen and stored prior to beginning feminizing therapy. *Sexual function* will progressively change as the testosterone levels drop. Often desire or libido is reduced first, followed by an increased time to ejaculation, and a reduced ejaculate volume; eventually, ejaculate becomes absent. If orgasm can still be reached, it will be of reduced intensity. There is also progressive difficulty achieving and maintaining an erection. Sleep-induced erections are lost quickly, followed by the loss of sexual erections, even with self-stimulation or with partner stimulation. Some erectile capacity (usually insufficient for vaginal penetration) may persist despite low testosterone levels, especially with adequate visual stimulation, since visually induced erections are testosterone independent.

The positive early changes noticed with decreased production and ac-

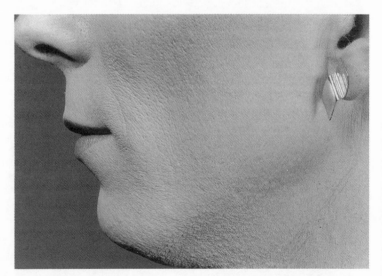

Figure 17.3. This male-to-female transsexual, who is now successfully living as a woman, had extensive electrolysis prior to the onset of anti-androgen and physiological hormonal therapy. Although beard growth is well controlled, she is left with scarring and skin changes that are difficult to cover up, even with makeup.

Figure 17.4. These three facial views are of the same individual in the process of gender reassignment. The high forehead with receding hairline is effectively covered by hair styling. Whether hormonal changes contribute to the subtle facial changes is unclear.

tion of testosterone are that hair softens, becomes pale, and disappears in male-pattern areas of trunk and pubic regions; and skin becomes smoother and less oily. The beard and head hair are more resistant to change. Beard hair was traditionally assumed to be nonresponsive to hormonal therapy; electrolysis alone was believed to be effective (Asscheman, 1989). When we first began the endocrine therapy of MTF transsexuals, most had undergone years of electrolysis with resulting facial scarring (Figure 17.3). However, with the combined estrogen, progestin, and antiandrogen therapy, gradually the hair is less coarse and less apparent high on the cheeks. The pattern of hair loss appears to reverse the pattern of acquisition of hair in puberty, with the last region of development being high on the cheeks. The hair on the upper lip and at the tip of the chin, which are the first hair seen during male puberty, may never disappear, even after castration. The high sensitivity of hair-cell receptors in certain regions to the little (adrenal) androgen that still circulates appears to explain the beard persistence.

Loss of hair on the temples and vertex of the scalp is only very partially reversible, perhaps because hair follicles in these regions become sclerosed or obliterated. Some soft, almost villous hair does grow back, but often the hair loss remains resistant to medical management (Figure 17.4). Styling of hair to cover a large forehead, or the use of light-weight, well-crafted hair pieces or wigs is usually effective.

Observed Effects of Estrogen & Progestin Therapy

Predicting the effects of the exogenous estrogen on sexual characteristics remains challenging. Estrogen and progesterone effect depends on appropriate suppression of androgen production and action. In addition, it is unclear which typical feminine characteristics are progesterone and which are estrogen effects, since both hormones work in the same tissues, often interact at receptor levels, and are synergistic.

Redistribution of *fat onto lower abdomen and thighs and buttocks* increases continually through the years. A degree of *breast development* may begin early, even with spironolactone alone, but often 4–6 years are needed for full maturation. Being underweight or smoking seems to often prevent full breast development. Progesterone appears to be necessary for maturation of the areolae and nipples to Tanner stage 5.

Sexual function changes appear to be predominantly related to the loss of testosterone rather than to the activity of estrogen and progesterone. However, some patients report experiencing a *need for intimacy,* as opposed to sexual activity per se, associated with female hormone therapies. Changes in mood with an apparent calmness and improved sleep are also reported. Some say they experience increased sensitivity of emotions, and feel more intuitive or tolerant.

PRINCIPLES OF THERAPY PUT INTO PRACTICE

To illustrate the principles outlined above, we will now illustrate with a typical story and hormonal profile, sexual function, and secondary sexual characteristics of one of our 238 evaluated persons with male-to-female gender dysphoria. "C.C." presented to the clinic in 1990 at age 40, and was diagnosed to be a high-intensity male-to-female transsexual by two psychiatrists. He had never previously received hormonal or antiandrogen therapy. He reported a life-long low sexual desire, with very few sexual thoughts or sexual fantasies, and minimal self-stimulation. He had never sought erotica (videos, magazines, etc.). His wife had been his sole sexual partner for the previous 17 years. Nocturnal erections were completely firm and lasted for several minutes. Self-stimulated erections, although rarely attempted, were also firm—ejaculation occurred after a few minutes, with a reasonable fluid volume. During intercourse with his wife, he experienced chronic and variable situational erectile dysfunction, often without orgasm or ejaculation.

Past history was normal. There was no family history of heart disease, diabetes, or osteoporosis. He lived with his wife, worked as a landscape gardener, used neither cigarettes nor alcohol, and had no regular recreational physical activity. On physical examination, he was a normal man who weighed 67 kg (148 lb.) and was 168 cm (5ft. 4 in.) tall, had minimal temporal balding, normal male-pattern body hair, and normal male genitalia.

There were no abnormalities of the respiratory, neurological, abdominal, or cardiovascular system. Blood pressure was 130/80.

At presentation, his hormonal profile was as follows:

Total testosterone	23.0	(10.4–34.7 nmol/L—male range)
FSH	8.4	(1.0–15.0 IU/L)
HDL	1.43	(0.9–1.94 mmol/L)
Total Cholesterol	7.4	(2.92–4.59 mmol/L)
Triglyceride	1.08	(0.5–2.4 mmol/L)
HbA1C	0.055	(0.043–0.062)
Prolactin	12.0	(3.0–18.0 µg/L)

Bone density of the spine was performed before hormones were given, and showed a value of 1.01 gram/cm², which was within one standard deviation of the young normal value. Therapy was begun with spironolactone in a dose of 300 mg/day, and later increased to 400 mg daily, CEE 0.625 mg days 1–25 of each month, and MPA 10 mg twice a day and later twice a day. During the therapy and before sex-reassignment surgery (SRS), typical values for her hormonal profile were:

Total testosterone	6.0	(0.5–3.1 nmol/L—female range)
Free testosterone	20.0	(2.5–12.0 pmol/L—female range)
HDL	1.3	(0.9–1.94 mmol/L)
Total cholesterol	5.05	(2.92–4.59 mmol/L)
Triglyceride	1.00	(0.5–2.4 mmol/L
HbA1C	0.052	(0.043–0.062)

Sexual function showed further reduction in the low sexual desire. However, she reported experiencing increased yearning to be physically intimate with a partner (but without genital stimulation or orgasm). Sexual thoughts included visualization of taking a female role in intercourse. Self-stimulation was rarely occurring. If she tried, she had difficulty reaching orgasm and the ejaculation volume was markedly diminished. In time, orgasms no longer occurred even in sleep, and the last few that occurred before self-stimulation stopped were reported as being of very low intensity. Sleep-induced erections stopped. Erections during sexual activity became soft.

Breast development gradually increased over the two and a half years of hormonal and antiandrogen therapy before surgery to Tanner stages III and IV, and bra with a B-cup. Body hair softened and was quite minimal within 1 year. Beard growth lessened significantly on the cheeks. Hair growth on chin and upper lip had never been particularly heavy, and after 1 year, with the help of weekly electrolysis for approximately six months, she could shave carefully once a day, apply makeup skillfully, and feel and look feminine. There was some redistribution of fat to the lower abdomen, thighs, and cheeks, as well as to the breasts. Her weight remained at 68–71 kg (150–156 lb.).

After SRS, spironolactone was reduced to 200 mg daily. She rarely uses electrolysis. CEE doses are still 0.625 mg cyclically and MPA is now prescribed at 10 mg b.i.d.. A repeat bone density study one year after surgery was unchanged and normal. Her hormonal profile post SRS revealed:

Total testosterone	<0.7	(0.5–3.1 nmol/L—female range)
Free testosterone	<2.2	(2.5–12.05 pmol/L—female range)
Prolactin	10.0	(3.0–18.0 µg/L)
Total cholesterol	4.9	(2.92–4.59 mmol/L)
HDL	1.21	(0.9–1.94 mmol/L)
HbA1C	0.057	(0.043–0.062)

Sexual function following SRS was characterized by an increasing sexual desire with more sexual thoughts and fantasies (in which she is exclusively the woman with a male partner). There has not yet been any sexual activity with a partner—nor has she had any relationship during the two postoperative years. There is still minimal sexual need for self-stimulation, but this has occurred as a process of discovery related to exploring her reactions after the surgery. There is pleasant sexual arousal from both stimulation within the new vagina and stimulation to the nipples and to the amputated portion of the dorsal nerve of the penis, which is covered by a crease of skin designed to resemble a clitoral hood. There has been no orgasmic experience, even in sleep. She reports a definite progressive return of sensation to the genital area—some areas, particularly around the posterior margin of the new introitus, had seemed totally anesthetic for the first six months. She was initially concerned that the spongy tissue left around the urethra became erect when she stimulated herself. This was distressing, as it reminded her of penile swelling. This seems to have lessened, and is no longer of concern.

Program Experience and Complications

The Gender Dysphoria Program, which officially began in 1986 within the Department of Psychiatry, has always been interdisciplinary, with co-leadership from endocrinology. Over the 10 years between 1986 and 1995, 238 male-to-female transsexuals have been evaluated and treated within the endocrine program of the center. There are 196 who continue to be in active therapy, of whom 55 have undergone sexual-reassignment surgery. (There are 42 who are inactive because they have moved away, have decided not to pursue transsexualism, were predominantly transvestitic, or had substance abuse preventing compliance with the program.) We have over 1,000 person-years of follow-up on these patients. Although this program is somewhat smaller than that reported from Amsterdam (Asscheman, Gooren, & Eklund, 1989), comparison of therapies and complications provides some assessment of the different approaches to feminization. Table 17.2 shows the characteristics of both programs. Notice that the incidence of thrombotic complications is significantly less in the Vancouver Centre. Both prolactin adenomas and hyperprolactinemia also appear to be less prevalent on the lower doses of estrogen. The apparently lower experience of depression may relate to the use of spironolactone rather than cyproterone acetate, which has depression as a potential side effect.

Thrombosis, a life-threatening complication of estrogen therapy in men (Coronary Drug Project Research Group, 1970, 1973), by inference, appears to be dose-related. Whether the incidence of thromboembolism can be lowered further by more universal use of transdermal rather than oral estrogen is worth study. None of the patients on the therapy we have outlined has experienced myocardial infarction (MI) during therapy. Over the 10 years, two patients have experienced MIs, but one was 67 years old, an alcoholic smoker with a positive family history of ischemic heart disease, and had previously received "standard" (i.e., high-dose) estrogen therapy. All estrogen was discontinued when he was first seen in the clinic in 1986. He remained on MPA and spironolactone alone, but had a fatal MI one year later. A second patient had a myocardial infarction some months after being started on spironolactone as the only medication because he was perceived to be at high risk of myocardial infarction.

The therapy we have used is effective in achieving feminization, decreasing male hormone effects, and appears to meet our goals of safety and improved quality of life. However, this report and those in the literature that have examined hormonal therapy in gender dysphoria are retrospective (except for our 1989 publication). Perhaps it is now appropriate to design and perform a multicenter, randomized, double-blind clinical trial in which feminization, hormonal levels, lipids, complications, and quality of life are prospectively and objectively documented.

SUMMARY

Men who are true transsexuals are intensely driven to become hormonally and physically female. Supraphysiological doses of estrogen have been traditionally given in an attempt to speed the external transformation of a man into a woman.

In contrast to the usual high-estrogen hormonal treatment, this center has used an antiandrogen and nonandrogenic progestin along with physiological levels of estrogen to meet the therapy goals for men with true transsexualism. Our retrospective 10-year review of 196 active male-to-female transsexuals shows a significantly lower incidence of thrombosis, hyperprolactinemia, and depression than reported from Amsterdam's large program (Asscheman, Gooren, & Eklund, 1989). Prior to any estrogen therapy, it is important to screen for any risk factors that are relative or absolute contraindications to estrogen therapy (such as cigarette use, hypertriglyceridemia, uncontrolled hypertension, active liver disease, or a history of thromboembolic disease).

The development of a female body habitus and breasts is similar in timing and progression to changes during normal puberty—the transition needs from 4 to 5 years. Beard and male-pattern body hair also respond (slowly) to hormonal therapy—the distribution of hair loss is in reverse to its acquisition during puberty.

At present, the therapy of male-to-female transsexualism is largely empirical. This chapter has presented a review of the current scientific literature, the clinical experience in our center, and a case history to provide the rationale for our center's modified, more physiological hormonal approach to the therapy of male-to-female transsexuals.

ACKNOWLEDGMENTS

This chapter is possible only through the support of all members of the clinic, especially Drs. Diane Watson and Oliver Robinow for psychiatric expertise, Dr. B. Anne Prestman for endocrinology, and Drs. Stacy Elliott and Marjorie Zapf-Gilje as family physician/sexual-medicine members of the endocrinology team. Special thanks to Teresa Janz for bibliographic work, to Teresa and also to Karen Smith for help with the database, to Alice Chan, RN, for dedication, conscientiousness, and support, and to Maureen Piper for her help in manuscript preparation.

REFERENCES

Asscheman, H. (1989). *Cross-gender hormone treatment, side effects and some metabolic aspects*. Ph.D. Thesis, Centrale Hussdrukkerij Vrije Lemierscteit, (Amsterdam), pp. 1–113.

Asscheman, H., & Gooren, L.J. (1992). Hormone treatment in transsexuals. *Journal of Psychology & Human Sexuality, 5,* 39–54.

Asscheman, H., Gooren, L.J., & Eklund, P.L. (1989). Mortality and morbidity in transsexual patients with cross-gender hormone treatment. *Metabolism, 38,* 869–873.

Clarke, C.L., & Sutherland, R.L. (1990). Progestin regulation of cellular proliferation. *Endocrine Review, 11*, 266–301.

Coronary Drug Project Research Group. (1970). Coronary drug project: Initial findings leading to modifications of its research protocol. *Journal of the American Medical Association, 214*, 1303–1313.

Coronary Drug Project Research Group. (1973). Coronary drug project: Findings leading to the discontinuation of the 2.5 mg/day estrogen group. *Journal of the American Medical Association, 226*, 652–657.

Corrol, P., Michaud, A., Menard, J., Freifeld, M., et al. (1975). Anti-androgenic effect of spironolactone: Mechanism of action. *Endocrinology, 97*, 52–58.

de Vries, C.P., Gooren, L.J., & van der Veen, E.A. (1986). The effect of cyproterone acetate alone and in combination with ethinylestradiol on the hypothalamic pituitary adrenal axis, prolactin and GH release in male-to-female transsexuals. *Hormones, Metabolism, and Research, 18*, 203–205.

Gallagher, J.C., Kable, W.T., & Goldgar, D. (1991). The effect of progestin therapy on cortical and trabecular bone: Comparison with estrogen. *American Journal of Medicine, 90*, 171–178.

Goh, H.H., Li, X.F., & Ratnam, S.S. (1992). Effects of cross-gender steroid hormone treatment on prolactin concentrations in humans. *Gynecology and Endocrinology, 6*, 113–117.

Goh, H.H., & Ratnam, S.S. (1990). Effect of estrogens on prolactin in secretion in transexual subjects. *Sex and Behavior, 19*, 507–516.

Grady, D., Rubin, S.M., Petitti, D.B., Fox, C.S., et al. (1992). Hormone therapy to prevent disease and prolong life in postmenopausal women. *Annals of Internal Medicine, 117*, 1016–1037.

Hargrove, J.T., Maxon, W.S., Wentz, A.C., & Burnett, A.L. (1989). Menopausal hormone replacement therapy with continuous daily oral micronized estradiol and progesterone. *Obstetrics & Gynecology, 73*, 606–612.

Kovacs, K., Stetaneanu, L., Ezzat, S.D., & Smyth, H.S. (1994). Prolactin-producing pituitary adenoma in a male-to-female transsexual patient with protracted estrogen administration: A morphological study. *Archives of Pathology and Laboratory Medicine, 118*, 562–565.

Lips, P., Asscheman, H., Uitewall, P., Netelenbos, J.C., et al. (1989). The effects of cross-gender hormonal treatment on bone metabolism in male-to-female transsexuals. *Journal of Bone Mineral Metabolism, 4*, 657–662.

Meyer, W.J., Finkelstein, J.W., Stuart, L.A., Webb, A., et al. (1981). Physical and hormonal evaluation of transsexual patients during hormonal therapy. *Archives of Sexual Behavior, 10*, 347.

Meyer, W.J., Webb, A., Stuart, C.A., Finkelstein, J.W., et al. (1986). Physical and hormonal evaluation of transsexual patients: A longitudinal study. *Archives of Sexual Behavior, 15*, 121–138.

New, M.I., & Ketzinger, E.S. (1993). Pope Joan: A recognizable syndrome. *Journal of Clinical Endocrinology and Metabolism, 76*, 3–13.

Orwoll, E.S., & Klein, R.F. (1995). Osteoporosis in men. *Endocrine Review, 16*, 87–116.

Pate, R.R., Pratt, M., Blair, S.N., Haskell, W.L., et al. 1995. Physical activity and public health: A recommendation from the Centers for Disease Control and Prevention and the American College of Sports Medicine. *Journal of the American Medical Association, 273*, 402–407.

Powell, K.E., Thompson, P.D., Caspersen, C.J., & Kendrick, J.S. (1987). Physical activity and the incidence of coronary heart disease. *Annual Review of Public Health, 8*, 253–287.

Prior, J.C. (1990). Progesterone as a bone-trophic hormone. *Endocrine Review, 11*, 386–398.

Prior, J.C., Alojado, N., McKay, D.W., & Vigna, Y.M. (1994). No adverse effects of medroxyprogesterone treatment without estrogen in postmenopausal women: Double-blind, placebo-controlled, cross-over trial. *Obstetrics & Gynecology, 83*, 24–28.

Prior, J.C., Vigna, Y.M., Barr, S.I., Rexworthy, C., et al. (1994). Cyclic medroxy-progesterone treatment increases bone density: A controlled trial in active women with menstrual cycle disturbances. *American Journal of Medicine, 96*, 521–530.

Prior, J.C., Vigna, Y.M., & Watson, D. (1989). Spironolactone with physiological female gonadal steroids in the presurgical therapy of male to female transsexuals: A new observation. *Archives of Sexual Behavior, 18*, 49–57.

Prior, J.C., Vigna, Y.M., Watson, D., & Diewold, P. (1986). Spironolactone in the presurgical therapy of male to female transsexuals: Philosophy and experience of the Vancouver Gender Dysphoria Clinic. *Journal of the Sex Information and Education Council of Canada, 1*, 1–7.

Pritchard, J.J., Pankowsky, D.A., Crowe, J.P., & Abdul-Karim, F.W. (1988). Breast cancer in a male-to-female transsexual. *Journal of the American Medical Association, 259*, 2278–2280.

Schiff, I., Tulchinsky, D., Cramer, D., & Ryan, K.J. (1980). Oral medroxyprogesterone in the treatment of postmenopausal symptoms. *Journal of the American Medical Association, 244*, 1443–1445.

Writing group for PEPI trial. (1995). Effects of estrogen and estrogen/progestin regimens on heart disease risk factors in postmenopausal women: The postmenopausal estrogen/progestin interventions (PEPI) trial. *Journal of the American Medical Association, 273*, 199–208.

18 HORMONAL THERAPY OF GENDER DYSPHORIA

THE FEMALE-TO-MALE TRANSSEXUAL

Jerilynn C. Prior

Stacy Elliott

Persons who were born into a female body who believe that they should have been men comprise approximately one-third of the transsexual population (Asscheman, Gooren, & Eklund, 1989). Prior to being referred for endocrinology assessment and treatment, all transsexuals are diagnosed as such by two independent psychiatrists and followed in the Gender Dysphoria Clinic (now called Centre for Sexuality, Gender Identity and Reproductive Health) of the University of British Columbia and Vancouver Hospital and Health Sciences Centre. In our center, we are actively following 36 female-to-male (FTM) transsexuals (of a total active transsexual population of 232); therefore, 16 percent of our clients are FTM transsexuals. Five have had genital-reassignment surgery. FTM transsexuals have been followed an average of 6.1 (range 1 to 10) years, while those who are postsurgery have a slightly longer follow-up of 6.8 years.

Female-to-male transsexuals commonly give a clear history of knowing they were different from other little girls, of preferring to play with boys rather than with girls, and of being upset at the onset of breast development and the first menstrual flow. In adolescence, many mistakenly assume their male persona to mean that they are gay or lesbian. By the time they recognize their transsexualism, they have commonly sought and found a job that is gender-neutral or more typical of a man. Often, dress is androgenous; some are accepted in an ambiguous male role prior to any therapy. (See below for a specific patient's history, therapy, and follow-up.)

The goals of hormonal therapy for women who want to become hormonally and phenotypically male are the attainment of male serum hormone levels and secondary sex characteristics, suppression of menstruation, and avoidance of adverse effects. In our center, the initial surgery, which is mastectomy, occurs after one year of hormonal therapy and cross-living (patients often choose to live with the discomfort of breast binding). Hysterectomy and ovariectomy tend to be performed after two or more years of therapy. No local or national (Canadian) surgeons are now doing phalloplasty; therefore few can afford to have genital-reassignment surgery.

PRE-THERAPY EVALUATION

After a diagnosis of true transsexualism is made, the patients are provided with informational material about transsexualism; are invited to informal weekly sessions with other transsexuals led by a psychiatric social worker, nurse clinician, or psychiatrist; and are provided with written information about hormone therapy. In this center, we emphasize that the course of physical change to full male characteristics takes three to ten years of androgen therapy, although most pass well as males within one year. Prior to treatment, clients are specifically asked to consider the risks for increased acne, male-pattern balding (if it is a family trait), and development of abnormal lipids that may increase coronary artery disease risk. As well, there is a theoretical increased risk for breast cancer (Coulam, Annegers, & Kranz, 1983), endometrial cancer (because of the aromatization of testosterone to estrogen), and significant weight gain (Asscheman, Gooren, & Eklund, 1989). All patients sign informed consent statements (Table 18.1) before starting therapy.

Prior to the initial testosterone therapy, screening tests are done which include fasting lipid levels, alkaline phosphatase (as assessment of liver function), LH, testosterone, and free testosterone levels, and assessment of glycosylated hemoglobin (to screen for diabetes mellitus risk). If the periods are predictable, a serum progesterone level is obtained the week before expected menstruation to determine whether ovulation has occurred in that cycle. For the last 2 years, as a pilot study, we have also systematically been ordering pretreatment bone-density determinations of the lumbar spine (dual energy x-ray absorptiometry, DXA) to assess whether these individuals are at risk for osteoporosis prior to beginning therapy.

The subsequent initial endocrine evaluations are performed by a team consisting of a psychiatric nurse practitioner, a sexual-medicine physician (a family physician with special interest and training in sexual dysfunction and transsexualism), and a reproductive endocrinologist. Each of the patients undergoes a full review by the nurse practitioner of past and present lifestyle (diet, exercise, vitamin use, and habits such as cigarette, alcohol, and caffeine use), social situation, and medical and surgical problems, as well as assessment of family, medical, and psychiatric history. The sexual-medicine physician then does a full medical history and physical examination, including careful weight and height measurements.

The patient who uses cigarettes is counselled about effective measures to reduce and stop smoking, and provided with prescriptions for transdermal or oral nicotine therapy, if necessary. Testosterone therapy is withheld until smoking has stopped because cigarette use lowers plasma HDL cholesterol levels, which predict increased risk for cardiovascular

---

TABLE 18.1. Consent to Hormonal Treatment of Female-to-Male Transsexualism

I understand that, although taking testosterone or male hormones causes my body to become more male, it also reduces my female hormones so that I will probably no longer have menstrual periods. I will probably become infertile for the duration of treatment and possibly for a longer period. I also understand that there are certain risks associated with this therapy that include, but are not limited to:

1. A reduction of the high density lipoprotein (HDL) cholesterol level. With a lower HDL (so called "good cholesterol" because it protects against heart disease), I may be at increased risk for heart attack. Therefore, I understand it is wise to lessen any other heart disease risks. For this reason I must discontinue cigarette use (if I am a current smoker) or must not begin to smoke. I also need to exercise regularly. Finally, I may need to follow a diet that will assist with other improvements in my lipid levels.

2. Some methods of giving testosterone may have adverse effects on the liver. I realize that giving testosterone by injection is believed to be safe for the liver, but other forms of male hormone (such as methyl-testosterone in a tablet) could cause jaundice and liver problems. For this reason, I understand that it is wise to be careful with other drugs or habits that may put increased demands on the liver. I will be asked to limit my alcohol intake to one drink a day or less.

3. I realize that taking testosterone may increase my sexual desire.

4. I realize that taking testosterone may cause acne.

5. I realize that taking testosterone may cause familial male-pattern balding.

---

disease in men (Stampfer, Sacks, Salvini, Willett, et al., 1991). Testosterone therapy itself decreases HDL cholesterol levels (Asscheman, Gooren, Megens, Nauta, et al., 1994). Therefore, there is real concern that the adverse lipid changes with androgen therapy and with cigarette use are additive and pose excess risk for heart disease (Stampfer, Sacks, Salvini, Willett, et al., 1991). Any patient with an abnormally elevated initial level of glycosylated hemoglobin will subsequently have fasting glucose measured and be referred to a dietician for instructions for a simple carbohydrate-restricted diet. The individual who meets criteria for diabetes mellitus (two fasting glucose values over 7 mmol/L, or a single random value over 11 mmol/L along with excessive thirst and urination) is referred to a diabetes education center for intensive instruction. Ideally, any transsexual would be proficient in glucose monitoring and compliant with diet and therapy before androgen therapy is begun because exogenous testosterone may be diabetogenic. The overweight or obese person will be referred for a dietary consultation and be given a specific physical-activity prescription because of the potential increased appetite and weight associated with testosterone therapy.

INITIAL THERAPY

An endocrinologist on the gender-dysphoria team reviews all of the gathered information and talks with and may re-examine the patient before making therapy decisions. A FTM transsexual with acne will often need systemic (tetracycline) and topical (peroxyl benzine with or without antibiotic) acne therapy begun at the same time as the testosterone. Those with obesity, pre-existing abnormal lipids, or hypertension will usually be prescribed testosterone at a reduced dose (for the psychological benefit of beginning therapy) while they concomitantly begin dietary and exercise modifications. Those on cigarettes are not prescribed testosterone until they have stopped smoking for a week and indicate they are motivated to continue the cessation.

Testosterone enanthate in a dose of 100–300 mg every two to four weeks i.m. is usually prescribed, depending on the size of the individual, individual risks related to therapy, intensity of transsexualism, and how frequently they are willing to have injections. A large majority of the transsexuals regularly receive injections from their family physicians. Approximately 20 percent of the patients (or their partners who are willing) have been taught by the nurse clinician to give their own injections. Intramuscular therapy is quite inexpensive; a vial containing 10 ml provides two months' worth of therapy and costs $12 (Canadian). Although syringes and needles are also purchased, the cost is low. An alternate, and probably preferable therapy, is testosterone undecanoate, a testosterone that is absorbed systemically through lymphatics, rather than being absorbed into the portal circulation, which first passes through the liver. However, this oral medication comes in 40 mg capsules costing over one dollar (Canadian) each. The usual dose is two tablets twice/day (160 mg), therefore, 2 months of therapy would cost approximately $250 (Canadian), or over 20 times more than injection therapy.

MONITORING OF THERAPY

After several months of testosterone injections, serum free and total testosterone and alkaline phosphatase levels will be obtained just before the next injection. This "trough level" of testosterone is used to judge the adequacy of the exogenous dose. The aim is to achieve a trough level of free testosterone in the lower range of normal male levels.

The patient will typically return after 6 months of therapy for review of masculinizing changes, including menstrual cessation, growth of facial and male-pattern body hair, redistribution of body fat, increase in muscle bulk, voice deepening, acne, clitoromegaly, and more masculine sexual functioning. In one study, the clitoris enlarged during the first year of androgen therapy from a pretreatment average of 1.4 cm to an average of almost 4.5 cm (Meyer, Webb, Stuart, Finkelstein, et al., 1986). Menstrual flow will have decreased in volume in the first two months and stopped entirely by six months. Weight and blood pressure are recorded. An assessment of the alkaline phosphatase level (to monitor for the potential development of obstructive liver disease), and a trough free testosterone level (for dosage adjustment) are obtained. Breast self-examination is demonstrated and retaught. The rationale for reinforcing breast self-examination is that androgen therapy, like endogenous androgen excess (Coulam, Annegers, & Kranz, 1983) may increase the risk for breast cancer. If the transsexuals are familiar with their normal breast tissue, they will be able to detect a change. The transsexual's birth date can become the day for this self-exam each month. A yearly screening mammogram will be suggested for those over forty years old prior to mastectomy.

In general, if the 6-month review goes well, the patient will be followed on a yearly basis, provided the initial lipids and glycosylated hemoglobin levels are normal. If these screens were initially abnormal, the patient will be reviewed more frequently. Should alcohol, drug, cigarette, or other social behaviors change, medications may need to be adjusted.

It is our experience that most FTM transsexuals have been sexually involved with partners, often women (as this commonly represents their true "heterosexual" orientation). Some have been married and had children; however, their sexual fantasy life consists of them playing the male role. As a group, they tend to divide themselves into two subgroups when it comes to sexual experience with their genitalia. Either they have been sexually active with either male or female partners and feel comfortable with self-stimulation, or they are extremely reluctant to touch their clitoral and vaginal areas or have a partner do so. In either case, use of exogenous androgen invariably increases their fantasy life, resulting in more, and sometimes intrusive, sexual thoughts and sexual dreams. For those FTM transsexuals who are comfortable with self-stimulation, a definite increase in masturbatory practices is seen. Also, orgasmic frequency and intensity increases. Partners often comment on this increase in libido and practices. Clitoromegaly occurs over time, and with initial enlargement, the clitoris may protrude through the labia, causing irritation. This discomfort resolves after a short time.

The enlarged clitoris is not satisfactory for intercourse. Most prefer not to have any vaginal entry or stimulation, and once androgen therapy is started, such stimulation is not a source of orgasm (even if it previously had been with a male partner). It appears that any function reminding them of their biological background as a woman (vaginal penetration, spotting, or bleeding) is particularly uncomfortable.

CHARACTERISTICS OF SEXUAL RESPONSE

Of particular interest is the need for phalloplasty and its result in sexual satisfaction. While our patients feel that the expense, pain, and surgical complications are ultimately worth it, the cosmetic and functional result of the phalloplasty is valued in terms of partner acceptability and satisfaction, and sexual self-image, versus enhanced sexual feelings from the phalloplasty per se. FTM transsexuals in committed relationships, especially ones that existed prior to hormonal treatment, often forego the phalloplasty. However, those who undergo phalloplasty feel more secure in the male role (for example, they are able to enter a men's washroom with the assurance there is something in the genital area). While the various procedures for phalloplasty involve taking tissue from other areas of the body, some FTM transsexuals comment that with time the phalloplasty itself begins to feel like a sexual organ in terms of genital sensation. One patient was able to achieve orgasm through intercourse or other direct stimulation of the phalloplasty.

The question of resecting, relocating, or amputating the clitoral body is still highly controversial; much more work is needed to understand the dimensions and limits of sexual satisfaction.

The Clinical History and Progress of One FTM Transsexual

This 28-year-old FTM transsexual presented to the Gender Dysphoria Clinic when he was 17 years old. He expressed wishes to be a boy even in the childhood journals that he kept as a young girl. As a 3- and 4-year-old, he would fly into a temper tantrum if he was required to wear a dress. He described his menarche at 14 years of age, as a "cruel joke." Menstrual cycles were unpredictable for many years, and flow was associated with severe cramps requiring antiprostaglandin medications. Because these episodes were a constant reminder that he had female anatomy, he felt miserable. Breast development was embarrassing and humiliating. Loose androgenous clothing was worn, and the patient used cubicles to change in female locker rooms. He shunned any sexual experiences in high school, was a "loner," and never acted on "crushes" with females lest "she" be considered a lesbian. As a 15-year-old, he became aware that sex reassignment existed, and finally confided in a school counselor about his gender confusion. The crisis that was precipitated at graduation by the social convention that "she" must wear a dress was accommodated by his choice to wear a white tuxedo.

The initial psychiatric assessments resulted in his being classified as having "high-intensity transsexualism," and an endocrine investigation was begun. The patient had a family history of hypercholesterolemia, hypertension, and early heart disease, as well as male-pattern balding.

The patient was slim, attractive, and androgenous in appearance with a height of 153 cm. (5 ft.), weight of 44 kg (97 lb.), and a blood pressure of 120/90. When initially examined, breast development was only at Tanner stage IV (ballooning areola and underdeveloped nipples). He had no acne or male-pattern facial or body hair, suggesting absence of endogenous androgen excess accompanying his clinically anovulatory cycles. Because the patient had never had anything enter the vagina and had not been involved sexually with a partner, even noncoitally, no PAP smear or pelvic examination was performed.

It was recommended by the clinical team that 200 mg of depotestosterone every two weeks be initiated, as well as an aerobic exercise and a weight-training program. A cholesterol- and salt-restricted diet was advised and taught. Masculine social support was also provided. Six months later, while taking 200 mg of depotestosterone every two weeks, his weight had increased by 5 kg (11 lb.), his voice was deepening, and he had follicular acne on his face and back, as well as small amounts of upper-lip hair growth. Table 18.2 shows the progress of changes in therapy and laboratory values.

Within a year of beginning therapy, the patient was fully cross-living as a man. He had not experienced any vaginal bleeding since the beginning of testosterone therapy. He was now shaving his upper lip, had some growth of sideburn hair, and had further voice deepening, but no thinning of head hair. His back acne was slower than his facial acne to respond to topical medications, so systemic tetracycline was added to his regime. Male-pattern body hair increased during the same time that he noted an increase in libido and some clitoromegaly. He was not bothered by these changes and he did not pursue partners. By 18 months, he had undergone bilateral peri-areolar subcutaneous mastectomy, with good cosmetic results. Prior to surgery, his rather small breasts had decreased during androgen therapy.

This man was not seen again until he had been on androgen therapy for three years. At that time he had developed a full pattern of male hair growth, was shaved daily, and had noticeable temple hairline recession. He appeared unequivocally male. While he reported masturbating regularly, he did not become involved with his first female partner until another year of therapy had passed. At that time, although both he and she were orgasmic with their sexual practices, and despite his partner's objections, the patient wanted to pursue phalloplasty so he "could tell there was something between my legs." Because of slowly increasing serum testosterone trough levels, his depotestosterone injections were reduced from 200 to 150 mg every two weeks.

Within the following year, the patient became highly motivated to seek genital surgery. He went to the United States and had a nonrigid phallus formed from lower abdominal skin flaps and testicular implants placed in the labia. After phalloplasty, a total abdominal hysterectomy and bilateral salpingo-oophorectomy were performed, using a lower transverse scar kept well above the presumed subcutaneous blood supply to the phallus. He had no wish to remove the vagina or clitoris. Pathology reported a uterus with transitional metaplasia and endometrial atrophy, polycystic ovaries, and unremarkable tubes.

To date, the patient has not pursued further surgery, including rod placement. Because he travels frequently, he has also undergone the expense of the use of testosterone undecanoate at a dose of 120 mg/day to maintain his serum trough testosterone levels in the range of 10–15 nmol/L.

This FTM transsexual has been followed for over ten years. He is quite successful as a man and reports an excellent quality of life.

TABLE 18.2. Time Course of Changes in Hormonal Levels During Therapy in One Female-to-Male Transsexual

Years Post-Therapy	Depotestosterone Dose	Testosterone (10–35 nmol/L)	Free Testosterone (30–160 pmol/L)	Cholesterol (CH)	HDL	CH/HDL Ratio	Alkaline Phosphatase	HbA1C (0.052–0.078)
Year 1: 1985	200 mg q 2 wks			5.7	0.7	5.3		0.048
Year 3: 1987		21.4		6.03	0.95	6.3		0.049
Year 5: 1990		25	74	5.8	1.05		62	0.048
Year 6: 1991		22	68	5.89	0.88		54	0.061
Year 7: 1992								
1st test		35	140	5.2	0.73	7.1		0.065
2nd test		27	79					
3rd test		14.5	58					
Year 8: 1993	150 mg q 2 wks	10.0	28	6.51	1.09	6.0	62	0.067
Year 9: 1994		6.6	22					
Year 10: 1995		11.6	42	5.56	0.87	6.4	62	0.075

There are several issues that have been reviewed in the literature concerning the endocrinology, therapy, and changes during androgen treatment of the FTM transsexual. These studies will be briefly reviewed.

The Prevalence of Anovulatory Androgen Excess

Women who believe they should be men often have signs and symptoms of male-hormone excess prior to therapy. The endogenous androgen excess, often clinically characterized as "polycystic ovary syndrome," arises from delayed maturation of the reproductive system with nonovulatory cycles associated with high LH levels and regular flow. Ovarian testosterone and androstenedione are produced in excess. The observation that this syndrome is associated with FTM transsexualism has been made several times from different centers, beginning as early as 1977 (Spiova & Starka, 1977; Kula, Dulko, Pawlikowski, Imielinski, et al., 1986). Spiova and Starka reported that 50 transsexual women randomly selected from a population of 97 FTM transsexuals and compared cross-sectionally with 50 regularly cycling women had higher testosterone values and slightly longer cycles, and were less likely to have cramps (Spiova & Starka, 1977). However, the prevalence of anovulation over a period of six to twelve months has not been documented. The pretherapy presence of significant acne is also unknown.

In this center, systematic longitudinal screening for ovulation disturbances (as we have previously done in healthy populations without gender issues [Prior, Vigna, Schechter, & Burgess, 1990; Barr, Janelle, & Prior, 1994]) is a research plan that we have not yet begun. Based on our previous work in women who seem to have less fundamental stressors in their lives, we anticipate that anovulation and luteal-phase disturbances will be prevalent (Prior, Vigna, Schechter, & Burgess, 1990; Barr, Janelle, & Prior, 1994).

Using the "molimina question" ("Can you tell, by the way you feel, that your period is coming?" [Prior & Vigna, 1987]), we have documented that disturbed ovulation is the rule rather than the exception in the FTM transsexuals who are usually unable to predict the start of flow. Androgen excess, rather than hypogonadotrophic ovulation disturbances, which are more common, may occur in over half of these nonovulatory FTM transsexuals, for reasons that are not clear. FTM transsexuals presenting with symptoms or signs of androgen excess (acne, hirsutism, oily skin, temporal head-hair recession; see Figure 18.1), appear to be protected against the osteopenia (Dixon, Rodin, Murby, & Chapman, et al., 1989) that is otherwise associated with anovulation (Prior, Vigna, Schechter, & Burgess, 1990).

Acne may be present before beginning androgen therapy. In our ex-

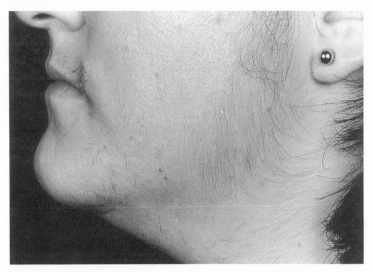

Figure 18.1. This biological female, who eventually discovered she was a transsexual, developed regular periods at puberty, but had persistent acne on her back and increasing facial hair. She was always surprised by her period and unable to tell, by the way she felt, that her period was coming. The facial hair and her history suggest that she had pre-existing anovulatory androgen excess before beginning testosterone therapy.

perience, if this is the case, the resulting skin problem during androgen therapy is likely to be severe. Approximately one-third of our patients have had moderate acne during therapy, with a further 7 percent having mild acne. This incidence, however, appears to be somewhat less than FTM transsexuals treated in Amsterdam, where 50–60 percent of the population developed acne (Asscheman & Gooren, 1992).

In the past, acne was treated with oral tetracycline in our center. Currently topical antibiotic and desquamation-producing therapies are used.

ADVERSE CHANGES IN LIPIDS DURING ANDROGEN THERAPY

It is well understood that premenopausal women are relatively protected from cardiovascular disease. This protection has been ascribed to prevention of low levels of high-density cholesterol (HDL), which are understood to result from the higher estradiol levels in women. Although a significant adverse effect of androgen therapy on HDL and its associated lipoproteins has clearly been documented (Asscheman, Gooren, Megens, Nauta, et al., 1994), no increased cardiovascular morbidity or mortality has been documented in a retrospective review of 122 FTM transsexuals in Amsterdam followed for a mean of 3.6 years (Asscheman, Gooren, & Eklund, 1989).

The oral testosterone, testosterone undecanoate, was the predominate therapy in this population. As mentioned previously, testosterone undecanoate is absorbed through the lymphatics rather than being processed through the portal system. It has been postulated that some forms of testosterone, such as testosterone enanthate or cypionate that can be aromatized to estrogen, will cause less depression in HDL levels (Asscheman, Gooren, Megens, Nauta, et al., 1994). The decrease in HDL cholesterol, therefore, may depend in part on whether estradiol levels increase during therapy. Because of the potential adverse coronary artery disease risk created by androgen therapy, the Amsterdam clinic advises their patients "not to smoke, to exercise moderately and to prevent excessive weight gain and high blood pressure" (Asscheman & Gooren, 1992).

ANDROGEN THERAPY AND BREAST CHANGES

Because testosterone is converted either to estradiol (by aromatization) or to dihydrotestosterone (DHT) by 5-alpha reductase, there is concern that long-term therapy before surgery may increase the risk for breast cancer. In a cohort study from the Mayo Clinic, premenopausal anovulatory androgen excess has been associated with a 3.6 times increased risk for postmenopausal breast cancer (Coulam, Annegers, & Kranz, 1983). However, there have been no reports of any FTM transsexuals who have developed breast cancer. The standard follow-up of FTM transsexuals in other programs does not include any screening for a potential risk of breast cancer (Meyer, Finkelstein, Stuart, Webb, et al., 1981; Asscheman, Gooren, & Eklund, 1989). In Vancouver, we recommend a monthly breast self-exam and yearly mammogram screening of those over age forty or who have had ten years of androgen therapy, and who have not had mastectomy. Our rationale is that these risks have not been evaluated properly to date.

One study analyzed breast histology in a blinded fashion in 12 patients who had been treated for several years with testosterone propionate in a dose of 400 mg every 3–4 weeks (Futterweit & Schwartz, 1988). Decreased breast lobules were shown in six FTM transsexuals, increased intralobular stroma in seven, and increased extralobular fibrous stroma in six. It is of interest that they did not find epithelial hyperplasia, the breast histology typically present when men experience breast enlargement (which is called gynecomastia) (Futterweit & Schwartz, 1988).

ANDROGEN THERAPY AND THE RISK FOR ENDOMETRIAL CANCER

The potential risk for endometrial hyperplasia, a precursor to endometrial cancer, is another concern during prolonged testosterone therapy in FTM transsexuals before they have undergone a hysterectomy. In each of these individuals, the uterus is exposed to persistent estrogen (in part because of inadequate suppression of pre-existing ovarian secretion and also the aromatization of exogenous testosterone into estrogen). There is also a strong tendency for these individuals to ignore symptoms related to the female anatomy with which they are uncomfortable. For this reason, the routine review should inquire about vaginal flow or spotting. If menstrual flow persists beyond three months for the FTM transsexuals in the Netherlands, an oral androgenic progestin in relatively high doses (e.g., lynestrol 5 mg/d) is routinely given (Asscheman, 1989).

Ten of 36 FTM transsexuals in our center have experienced persistent spotting or bleeding despite long-term androgen therapy sufficient to produce male-range trough levels of free testosterone. This incidence appears to be higher than in Amsterdam, where they reported progestin therapy in only 3 of 122 FTM transsexuals (Asscheman, Gooren, & Eklund, 1989). In our experience, spotting tends to occur if there is too long an interval between testosterone injections. This longer interval may produce a higher peak testosterone dose and perhaps even more aromatization to estradiol. In our center, we shorten the interval between injections and lower the dose. If spotting persists, we treat the FTM transsexual with 10–20 mg/d of medroxyprogesterone acetate to prevent endometrial hyperplasia. One patient with persistent abnormal bleeding had dilatation and curettage surgery and was found to have an endometrial polyp. (FTM transsexual patients are very reluctant to have gynecological assessments or procedures because they have often never used a tampon or had vaginal intercourse.) Should bleeding persist, an androgenic, 19–nor testosterone-derived progestin, such as norethisterone, would be preferable to medroxyprogesterone because the former would promote maleness.

IMPLICATIONS FOR CARE AND RESEARCH

A more systematic study of the facial and body hair in the FTM transsexual would be helpful. For example, a systematic study of the patterns of hair development may show that it is similar or different from that occurring in boys during puberty. It is not clear from the present literature what proportion of the FTM transsexual population will have significant difficulty with acne, and whether difficulties with acne in adolescence or pregnancy will predict the occurrence of similar problems after exogenous testosterone treatment is begun.

Prospective studies of bone density would be useful in the FTM transsexual who has not had androgen excess prior to beginning therapy. One of the questions in the bone-metabolism literature is whether androgens function to decrease bone resorption or whether they primarily promote new bone formation (Kasperk, Wergedal, Farley, Linkhart, et al. 1989). A recent study of bone histomorphometry in 15 FTM individuals after a mean of 39 months on therapy showed both decreased resorption and decreased formation (Lips, Van Kesteren, Asscheman, & Gooren, 1996). Therefore, it would be interesting to prospectively document bone-marker levels of resorption and formation in this population and observe serial changes in bone density.

The variability in timing of the development of a deeper voice is puzzling. For some FTM transsexuals the changes occur rapidly, and for others they appear to be delayed. The effects of androgen therapy on muscle mass and distribution of body fat are also worth systematic study.

The risks for breast cancer need to be better understood. If there are those transsexuals who have been functioning as men but who have not had breast-reduction surgery, they would be useful to survey both mammographically and histologically following eventual surgery (Futterweit & Schwartz, 1988).

The potential for endometrial cancer in this population is also important. It would be interesting to study the endometria from those FTM transsexuals who have been on testosterone therapy for varying periods of time, and subsequently have hysterectomy and ovariectomy. In particular, the question should be asked: would histological differences be observable in those with persistent flow versus those with no further bleeding after testosterone therapy is initiated?

Although a histopathological study of the ovaries from 14 FTM transsexuals was performed (Pache, Hop, de Jong, Leerentveld, et al., 1992), more data are needed on the effects on the ovary of therapy duration, type, and dosage. It is intriguing that one transsexual on very high doses of testosterone (400 mg i.m. every 2 weeks) developed hemorrhagic urethritis and was found to have a polyp that histologically resembled prostate tissue (Cohen & Sanchez, 1987).

Long-term studies of the risk for coronary artery disease are important. This population needs to be studied for twenty or thirty years. Sophisticated studies of endothelial and platelet function might elucidate mechanisms leading to coronary artery disease. Will these biologically female but hormonally male individuals have diagnostic electrocardiographic stress tests when they develop angina, or will they have the misleading and nonspecific tests typically found in women?

The characteristics of sexual response have been studied in the male-to-female transsexuals (Kwan, Van Maasdam, & Davidson, 1985). Similar studies of the sexual responses, fantasies, spontaneous lubrication, and frequency of sexual feelings have not to our knowledge been performed in the FTM transsexual population. Monitoring of hormonal changes over time would be important in these studies, because female cyclic estrogen production may not be fully suppressed.

A final area of research is to study the changes in feelings experienced by these biologically female people during testosterone therapy. Do frustration, depression, anxiety, or alternately, increased self-worth and energy and other physiological changes occur during placebo as well as actual testosterone therapy? A potential investigation could best be done with the oral preparation of testosterone undecanoate. In other words, how much of the early positive response in moods and self-worth is a matter of expectation, and how much is an effect of the change in testosterone levels?

Therapy of FTM transsexuals is rewarding, as clinicians can readily observe these patients' improved quality of life. Much remains to be learned about the effects of exogenous testosterone on the hormonal, sexual, and psychosocial functioning of these individuals.

Summary

Biological women who believe that they should be men are less prevalent than male-to-female transsexuals, but have unique characteristics that create challenges when deciding what treatment strategies to use. The purpose of this review is to provide a clinically relevant approach to the evaluation and therapy of this condition, review the existing literature, relate the experience in our center, and suggest areas for further research.

The female-to-male (FTM) transsexual, like her male counterpart, usually recognizes she is different from her peers at an early age. Major emotional trauma occurs with the onset of breast development and menstruation. Cycles may be regular, but anovulation is common and frequently associated with androgen excess (the so-called polycystic ovary syndrome). Clinically, it is important to determine if cycles are ovulatory or not because FTM transsexuals with past or present acne and male-pattern facial hair are at less risk for osteopenia, but other FTM transsexuals may need bone-density screening. Furthermore, breast-cancer risk is probably increased with a higher incidence of anovulatory cycles (Coulam, Annegers, & Kranz, 1983), and this risk persists until mastectomy. Therefore, breast self-exam must be taught and reinforced. Informed consent is needed prior to starting androgen therapy and should state that balding, acne, weight gain, and changes in lipids that may increase coronary artery disease risk are likely to develop.

Goals of therapy are the disappearance of cyclic flow, and masculinization of voice, muscularity, and hair patterns. Breast size rarely regresses and clitoromegaly is insufficient to create a functional phallus. Therapy requires testosterone, usually by injection at two-week intervals. Newer options are testosterone undecanoate, an oral form of which is absorbed through the lymphatics, or transdermal testosterone. Both are expensive.

Hormonal therapy for the FTM transsexual is rewarding. Clitoromegaly, increased libido, and voice deepening occur within a few months. Menstrual flow usually stops after a month or two of androgen therapy. Increased muscularity and male body habitus can be significantly enhanced by weight and endurance training over months. Male-pattern facial and body-hair growth are progressive and occur over several years. The significant long-term risks are excessive weight gain, abnormal lipids, and an increased potential for premature coronary artery disease, all of which can be countered by life-style measures.

ACKNOWLEDGMENTS

This chapter is possible only through the support of all members of the clinic, especially Drs. Diane Watson and Oliver Robinow, for psychiatric expertise; Drs. Rosemary Basson and Marjorie Zapf-Gilje as family physician/sexual-medicine members of the endocrinology team. Special thanks to Teresa Janz for bibliographic work, to Teresa and also to Karen Smith for help with the database, and to Alice Chan, R.N., for dedication, conscientiousness, and support.

REFERENCES

Asscheman, H. (1989). *Cross-gender hormone treatment, side effects and some metabolic aspects.* Ph.D. Thesis, Centrale Hussdrukkerij Vrije Lemierscteit, (Amsterdam), pp. 1–113.

Asscheman, H., & Gooren, L.J. (1992). Hormone treatment in transsexuals. *Journal of Psychology & Human Sexuality, 5,* 39–54.

Asscheman, H., Gooren, L.J., & Eklund, P.L. (1989). Mortality and morbidity in transsexual patients with cross-gender hormone treatment. *Metabolism, 38,* 869–873.

Asscheman, H., Gooren, L.J., Megens, J.A., Nauta, H.J., et al. (1994). Serum testosterone level is the major determinant of the male-female differences in serum levels of high-density lipoprotein (HDL) cholesterol and HDL2 cholesterol. *Metabolism, 43,* 935–939.

Barr, S.I., Janelle, K.C., & Prior, J.C. (1994). Vegetarian versus nonvegetarian diets, dietary restraint, and subclinical ovulatory disturbances: Prospective six month study. *American Journal of Clinical Nutrition, 60,* 887–894.

Cohen, M.S., & Sanchez, R.L. 1987. Hemorrhagic urethritis in a female-to-male transsexual. *Uropathology, 3,* 583–585.

Coulam, C.B., Annegers, J.F., & Kranz, J.S. (1983). Chronic anovulation syndrome and associated neoplasia. *Obstetrics & Gynecology, 61,* 403–407.

Dixon, J.E., Rodin, A., Murby, B., Chapman, M.G., et al. (1989). Bone mass in hirsute women with androgen excess. *Clinical Endocrinology, 30,* 271–277.

Futterweit, W., & Schwartz, I.S. (1988). Histopathology of the breasts of 12 women receiving long-term exogenous androgen therapy. *Mt. Sinai Journal of Medicine, 55,* 309–312.

Kasperk, C.H., Wergedal, J.E., Farley, J.R., Linkhart, T.A., et al. (1989). Androgens directly stimulate proliferation of bone cells in vitro. *Endocrinology, 124,* 1576–1578.

Kula, K., Dulko, S., Pawlikowski, M., Imielinski, K., et al. (1986). A nonspecific disturbance of the gonadostat in women with transsexualism and isolated hypergonadotropism in the male-to-female disturbance of gender identity. *Experimental Clinical Endocrinology, 87,* 8–14.

Kwan, M., Van Maasdam, J., & Davidson, J.M. (1985). Effects of estrogen treatment on sexual behaviour in male-to-female transsexuals: Experimental and clinical observations. *Archives of Sexual Behavior, 14,* 29–40.

Lips, P., Van Kesteren, P.J.M., Asscheman, H., & Gooren, L.J.G. (1996) The effect of androgen treatment on bone metabolism in female-to-male transsexuals. *Journal of Bone & Mineral Research, 11,* 1769–1773.

Meyer, W.J., Finkelstein, J.W., Stuart, L.A., Webb, A., et al. (1981). Physical and hormonal evaluation of transsexual patients during hormonal therapy. *Archives of Sexual Behavior, 10,* 347.

Meyer, W.J., Webb, A., Stuart, C.A., Finkelstein, J.W., et al. (1986). Physical and hormonal evaluation of transsexual patients: A longitudinal study. *Archives of Sexual Behavior, 15,* 121–138.

Pache, T.D., Hop, W.C., de Jong, F.H., Leerentveld, R.A., et al. (1992). 17B-oestradiol, androstendione and inhibin levels in fluid from individual follicles of normal and polycystic ovaries, and in ovaries from androgen treated female to male transsexuals. *Clinical Endocrinology, 36,* 565–571.

Prior, J.C., & Vigna, Y.M. (1987, June). Absence of molimina: The clinical or self-diagnosis of anovulation. *Society of Menstrual Cycle Research,* Abstract.

Prior, J.C., Vigna, Y.M., Schechter, M.T., & Burgess, A.E. (1990). Spinal bone loss and ovulatory disturbances. *New England Journal of Medicine, 323,* 1221–1227.

Spiova, I., & Starka, L. (1977). Plasma testosterone values in transsexual women. *Archives of Sexual Behavior, 6,* 477–481.

Stampfer, M.J., Sacks, F.M., Salvini, S., Willett, W.C., et al. (1991). A prospective study of cholesterol, apolipoproteins and the risk of myocardial infarction. *New England Journal of Medicine, 325,* 373–381.

Eugene A. Schrang

Gender dysphoria, or "psychosexual inversion," so characterized by Benjamin (1966), is a distinct and separate entity from any other psychological sexual disorder. It is irreversible, lasting and immutable. To think otherwise would be denying the facts as they are known, and until scientific research and discovery determines that the mind's gender can, indeed, be changed by predictable and reproducible means—something never accomplished throughout human history—the problem must be dealt with surgically in selected cases (Edgerton, 1973, 1983).

HISTORY

Historically, there is a long tradition of self-castration and self-emasculation, often associated with certain religious beliefs and ceremonies (Roscoe, 1994). However, there are reports of self-inflicted castrations and penile amputations from the 1600s, which were done for personal reasons, to give desperate people subjective relief. Self-mutilation in transsexual persons is not uncommon today, especially among those who are incarcerated, or otherwise feel hopeless (Brown, 1995; Farmer, 1994; Krieger, McAninch, & Weimer, 1982).

In 1931, Abraham reported the first modern sex-reassignment procedures on transsexual patients. In 1952, Paul Fogh-Anderson caused a sensation throughout the world by doing a simple penectomy and orchiectomy on Christine Jorgensen (Fogh-Anderson, 1969). Soon the procedure was being done in such cities as Paris, Vienna, and Casablanca (Burou, 1973; Sorensen & Hertoft, 1980). But it was Dr. Harry Benjamin who gave us, in the 1960s, the first real understanding of the problem; this, in turn, allowed serious interest to develop in all areas, especially surgery (Benjamin, 1966). Gender-identity clinics appeared, most notably at the Johns Hopkins Hospital, with such talent as Milton T. Edgerton, M.D., and John Money, Ph.D., (Hastings, 1969). The use of a free, split-thickness skin graft as described by McIndoe (1944) was replaced by the penile inversion flap technique described by Edgerton and Bull in 1970. Further development saw the use of a combination of these techniques.

As transsexualism became less of an anathema, more and more afflicted individuals appeared for counseling and help. This resulted in greater numbers of patients undergoing technically advanced surgical procedures, most notably by Stanley Biber, M.D., who has performed several thousand successful operations.

At the present time, the operation for sex reassignment is undergoing a high degree of development, with contributions coming from many sources. Any number of good methods are available, all being performed by capable, dedicated professionals throughout the world (for some descriptions of surgical technique, see Bouman, 1988; Crichton, 1993; Eldh, 1993; Glenn, 1980; Laub, Laub, & Biber, 1988; Jones, Schirmer, & Hoopes, 1968; Malloy, Noone, & Morgan, 1976; Meyer & Kesselring, 1980; Pandya & Stuteville, 1973; and Small, 1987).

PATIENT SELECTION

Without exception, every patient who presents to the operating surgeon should be properly referred by a psychologist, psychiatrist, or other licensed mental-health professional who is familiar with transgendered people and gender problems. Not every person who has gender dysphoria is a candidate for sex-reassignment surgery. Those who are schizophrenic or suffer from some other type of psychosis must be diagnosed as such and refused surgery until the psychosis is under control. The operation is irreversible, and for this reason alone, great care must be exercised in patient selection so that no one makes a terrible mistake that can never be rectified. Years of preparation by way of hormone therapy, psychological counseling, electrolysis, legal maneuvering, and living "full time" are necessary before the actual surgery can be performed. Thus, it is imperative that some standard of care be followed by all care providers to make absolutely certain that those selected for this highly technical procedure are prepared and ready, so as to ensure that their future lives will be enhanced by surgery.

A description of the operative technique I use follows.

PREOPERATIVE PREPARATION

Before surgery, some preparation is necessary. Patients who have a great deal of hair growth on the penis and surrounding pubic skin should have as much hair as possible removed by electrolysis prior to sex-reassignment surgery (SRS), as hair from these areas can grow inside the neovagina, causing embarrassment and making dilation and sexual intercourse difficult and painful ("AEGIS Suggests Electrolysis to Avoid Problem of Hair in Vagina," 1995; Aspen, 1995). Electrolysis should be concentrated on the shaft of the penis and the lower pubic area just above the base of the penile shaft. If this hair growth is removed, the final result will not only be more comfortable, but will appear more feminine as well.

Nature has provided the genetic female with protective mechanisms against thrombotic emboli that are not found in the genetic male taking female hormones; therefore, all ingestion or injections of hormones should be stopped 3 weeks prior to surgery and not resumed until 3 weeks after the operation so as to help avoid these potentially deadly emboli. Withdrawal symptoms are uncomfortable, but temporary, and are much better than the dreaded possibility of dying. To further aid in the prevention of thrombotic emboli, knee-high TEDS are worn to the operating room, where intermittent pressure stockings (sequential TEDS) are applied and worn on a continuous basis until the patient is ambulated 6 days following the procedure.

The patient must be admitted the day prior to surgery to give the nursing staff sufficient time to finish all the required work necessary to properly prepare the patient for the operation. Cleanliness is of paramount importance; this includes the skin around the operative area, as well as the gastrointestinal tract. After a bath and shampoo, a perineal and perianal prep is followed by painting the body with Betadine from the umbilicus to the mid-thighs. The G.I. tract is also prepared by having the patient take Reglan 10 mg orally, followed by the ingestion of 6 oz. of Nulytely every ten minutes until four liters have been consumed. Thirty cc of 50 percent magnesium sulfate is taken every hour for three doses after the Nulytely. One gram of Neomycin and one gram of Erythromycin base is then given to sterilize the gastrointestinal tract. Should the rectum be inadvertently entered during dissection of the neovagina, the possibility of this accident resulting in a recto-vaginal fistula is now minimized if the opening into the rectum is properly and securely closed with fine catgut sutures which do not pass through the rectal mucosa.

Minimal laboratory tests are done, which consist of a Hemogram and Rapid HIV determination. Other studies such as blood chemistries, chest film, EKG, etc., are run on an individual basis. Excessive blood loss during surgery is not common; therefore, it is not necessary to routinely type and crossmatch the patient in anticipation of replacing what will be lost. Concerned patients will on occasion donate one or two units of autologous blood, which is always returned to them during or after the procedure.

The proper consent form is signed by the patient to include not only the reassignment procedure, but any other operation to be done at the same time—for example, augmentation mammoplasty, tracheal shave, or facelift (cf., Creighton & Goulian, 1973).

A liquid supper is served, with the patient being allowed nothing by mouth after 10:00 P.M. Flurazepam 30 mg is given at the hour of sleep, and is repeated one time if necessary. In the morning, one hour before surgery, preoperative medications consisting of Demerol 75 mg, Atropine 0.4 mg, and Vistaril 50 mg are given.

OBJECTIVES AND GOALS

Regardless of which procedure or variation thereof is used, it is important to make every effort to achieve three goals:

1. An aesthetically acceptable result which resembles as closely as possible the genetic female.

2. A neovagina which is functional from the standpoint of adequate width and depth.

3. The preservation of sufficient nerve and erectile tissue to give the patient orgasmic capability.

If these objectives are met, all concerned can feel confident that the operative procedure has indeed been successful—but success will come only when there has been great attention to detail and the operation has been done with a sense of artistry and craftsmanship.

ANESTHESIA, POSITION, PREPARATION, AND DRAPE

A general anesthetic is most commonly used, but occasionally an epidural block can be administered if the operation is expected to be relatively short and the patient desires it.

The supine position with the arms on armboards is assumed for the administration of the anesthetic. If a split-thickness skin graft is required, the operating table is placed in extension to bring the lower abdominal area into maximum relief. This position is satisfactory for the taking of full-thickness grafts, as well; however, if no grafts are required, the patient is placed in lithotomy and Trendelenburg positions, at which time the rectum is emptied of any residual contents and the perineum washed with soap and water. The patient is now draped in whatever manner is suitable to the surgeon, leaving the perineal and perianal areas exposed. Utilization of as much Trendelenburg as possible brings the operative site into greater relief, while the intra-abdominal contents gravitate away when dissecting the neovagina.

STAGE I (SRS)
Procedure

Realistically, close to 80 percent of transsexual patients need a graft to achieve the necessary vaginal depth for comfortable intercourse. Two types of grafts are available: the split-thickness and the full-thickness graft. If a split-thickness graft is to be used (which is indicated only if the abdominal skin is too tight for easy removal of full-thickness grafts from the flank areas), it is best taken with a Paget-Hood or similar dermatome. The thickness should be set at seventeen-thousandths of an inch and the graft removed from the lower abdomen between the umbilicus and the pubic hair. This site is preferable because the location is most convenient for the surgeon. All Betadine must be removed from the donor-site skin; otherwise, the graft may not adhere to the dermatome drum.

After removing the split graft, glycerin-impregnated fine mesh gauze is placed over the donor site and is allowed to remain there until it rejects about three weeks later, leaving pink, healing epithelium. The resulting scar is a square patch which involutes with the passage of time until it becomes mature. Any resulting noticeable scar can oftentimes, but not always, be concealed with brief swimming attire. Although many donor sites heal well, they are virtually all more or less conspicuous. The degree of noticeability of the scar varies from patient to patient; in some it is not obvious, while in others, it can remain as a raised, thickened area which can oftentimes be treated successfully by the application of silicone gel sheets over a period of 6 months. Occasionally, it can be totally or partially excised by staged surgical resections. Another alternative would be a split-thickness graft taken with an air-driven dermatome. These grafts can be harvested from almost any part of the body, but ordinarily they are taken from the thighs or buttocks. The donor sites are treated in the same fashion as the abdominal donor sites, and they too leave noticeable scars.

Full thickness skin grafts are superior to split thickness grafts because a more durable lining of the neo-vagina results when they are used. Full thickness grafts do not "take" as well but when done properly, i.e., the graft is adequately defatted and the principle of good hemostasis is adhered to, rarely do these grafts not "take" in the neo-vagina. Provided that the donor sites are hairless or have been properly depilated by either electrolysis or laser technique, a number of areas can be used—the scrotum being by far the first area of choice. It is readily available being right there in the operative field and by using it, no telltale scars are left anywhere on the body. The volume, in many cases, may seem inadequate but, unlike skin from other places, the skin of the scrotum is very distensible and goes a long way. Still, however, a scrotal graft may be contraindicated if the penis is small and very little scrotal skin is present. The next area of choice is the lower abdomen if sufficient, hairless skin is present. This can be an excellent choice because the resulting transverse scar could be explained as a hysterectomy scar. The graft can be 2 in. wide by as much as 12 in. long. The last donor area of choice would be the bilateral flanks where the oblique donor sites can be 2 in. by no more than 7 in. in length. Two grafts are ordinarily needed and the flank sites do leave somewhat objectionable oblique scars which can be hidden by the straps of brief bathing attire. They are usually indicated when, for whatever reason, scrotal or lower abdominal skin cannot be used. After the lower abdominal or flank grafts are removed, they are carefully defatted and thinned. The open wounds are closed with three layers of deep running, buried 2-0 Mononcryl sutures and the wound edges reinforced with 1-inch steristrips to minimize the resultant scars. It must be kept in mind that the final cosmetic result of any skin-graft scar can never be predicted.

The initial genital incision contributes a great deal to the final appearance of the vulva and in part determines the degree of comfort the patient will have during intercourse later. A midline incision is made in the median raphe of the scrotum, extending from the base of the penis to a point 1.5 in. anterior to the anus, where a one-centimeter posteriorly based flap is formed. It is this small flap which will make future dilating and intercourse more comfortable, because the posterior vaginal entrance will be made of skin, and not scar tissue. This incision is carried down to the corpora spongiosum, where the loose areolar tissue is dissected bluntly from around the penis base at the level of Buck's fascia, and subsequently stripped distally to the glans penis. At this point some sharp dissection to free a few remaining bands of fascia may be necessary.

A Kocher clamp is placed across the distal penis, but proximal to the glans, to avoid cutting an opening in the skin when the glans penis is amputated with a large scalpel blade.

A small but adequate incision is made in the distal urethra just proximal to the Kocher clamp, into which is introduced the largest 30 cc Foley catheter that the patient can accommodate. If this incision is made carelessly or unnecessarily large, persistent bleeding throughout the operation will likely occur.

The testicles are grasped with towel clips, and by blunt and sharp dissection all loose areolar tissue along with the tunica albuginea are removed proximally to the external inguinal rings. If a hydrocele or hernia are encountered, they can be dealt with at this time. High ligation and amputation of the spermatic cords is mandatory to obviate the formation of painful neuromas, which can cause great distress, especially during intercourse. Great care must be taken to secure the spermatic cord stump prior to amputation with both a free tie of O-Monocryl and two suture ligatures of O-Monocryl to prevent postoperative bleeding from the spermatic blood vessels. The spermatic cords and accompanying vessels are amputated, with the stumps being allowed to retract within the external inguinal rings. Again, it is very important that they actually do lie within the external rings to obviate the formation of painful neuromas.

Attention is next directed to the formation of the neovagina. With fingers in the rectum as a guide, blunt and sharp dissection are used to develop the neovagina as far posteriorly as Denonvillier's fascia. Realizing that width is as important as depth, medial fibers of the levator ani muscle must be divided to give sufficient width to the vagina so that future intercourse will be comfortable. Brisk bleeding may be encountered. This can be controlled by electrocoagulation, but care should be taken not to cauterize a hole in the rectal mucosa. The plane of dissection is kept between the longitudinal fibers of the rectum and the capsule of the prostate gland. Entrance into the urethra and prostatic capsule must be avoided. If the urethra is inadvertently opened, it should be meticulously closed over the previously placed Foley catheter with 4–0 Monocryl sutures. Once the region of the urinary bladder and seminal vesicles is reached, the white, gossamer fibers of Denonvillier's fascia are encountered. These can be dissected easily with a peanut dissector.

Adequate width and depth are most important and must not be compromised for any reason unless it is the wish of the patient. For example, if a patient has a relatively small phallus and does not intend to develop any future intimate relationships, or does not desire penetration, it will not be necessary to dissect a deep neovagina—primarily, because the patient will not utilize it, and secondly, insufficient phallic skin will be present to line a deeply dissected neovagina. In the event that adequate penile skin is available in the patient who does not desire future intercourse, the neovagina should be made deep enough to accommodate the available skin. The greatest preponderance of patients wish future intercourse; therefore, it is mandatory that functional width and depth be achieved by not only careful surgical dissection but by lining the neovagina with inverted penile skin, a skin graft, or a combination of the two. After its formation, the neovagina is packed temporarily with saline-impregnated Kerlix gauze.

Attention can now be directed to the penile skin, which is inverted on a 60-cc plastic syringe. All extraneous tissue on the under surface of the penile skin is removed, preserving any obvious nerve tissue. The skin graft will be an extension of whatever phallic skin is available; therefore, a 180–degree incision is made on the ventral side of the base of the glans penis, and what little remains of the intact distal urethral tube is opened. In order for the glans to have the best chance to become vascularized, the excessive tissue on its undersurface is removed by sharp dissection. To this opening, the skin graft is sutured with continuous and interrupted 3-0 Monocryl sutures.

There is no standard technique which can be described for suturing the two grafts together; the surgeon must depend on his ability to improvise, since no two procedures will ever be the same, but the goal is as much depth as possible without compromising width. Great care must be taken while suturing the graft, because any "weak spots" could result in tearing later, when the neovagina is packed with Furacin gauze.

If no skin graft has been used, it will sometimes be necessary to mobilize the lower abdominal skin to allow greater mobility of the inverted penile skin when it is inserted into the neovagina. With the aid of a wide retractor and good light, the skin of the lower abdominal wall is elevated by sharp dissection from the fascia of the abdominal musculature as high as the umbilicus. Good hemostasis is essential to prevent hematoma later. This cavity should be irrigated thoroughly with saline and packed loosely with wet sponges until the penile skin is inserted into the neovagina later in the operation. If a skin graft is used, mobilization of the abdominal skin is usually not necessary, but partial mobilization may be appropriate in selected cases.

After all loose areolar tissue has been removed from the sulcus between the corpora spongiosum and the corpora cavernosa, the two are divided almost to the pubic bone by sharp dissection utilizing a scalpel rather than scissors for better control. Any corpora cavernosum left on the corpora spongiosum should be trimmed away with a sharp scissors.

The excessive corpora cavernosum is now removed. This is best accomplished by having the assistant place slight traction on the previously placed Kocher clamp while the left hand of the operating surgeon grasps and puts traction on an Allis clamp attached to the distal, ventral portion of the corpora cavernosa. With great care and using a #20 scalpel blade, the corpora cavernosa are divided approximately in half in a horizontal direction proximally to the divergence of the crura. The ventral portion is discarded. Some brisk bleeding will be encountered which can be controlled with electrocautery but most of the blood supply will be intact within the dorsal or remaining corpora cavernosa. All excessive corpora cavernosum tissue in the dorsal portion should be removed by scissors dissection; the amount to be trimmed away being a matter of judgement. Keep in mind that this remaining tissue is used to construct the clitoris and *most importantly* it contains the right and left dorsal nerves of the penis which are continuations of the pudendal nerves as they course to the tip of the newly created clitoris. It will be these nerves, if left intact, that will enable future orgasmic function.

The urethra must be carefully opened proximally to the bulb of the penis or where the urethra emerges from behind the pubic bone. This cut must be made proximally enough to ensure that the future urine stream will point downward, and not forward. The maneuver is best accomplished by having the assistant put gentle traction on the Foley catheter while the urethra is opened along its inferior side with a blunt-nosed scissors which will minimize damage to the urethral lining. The brisk bleeding encountered at this point subsides quickly, and no attempt should be made to control it. The Foley catheter is allowed to fall forward and downward so as to be out of the way of the next step.

In order to ensure excellence in construction of the urethral opening, the urethral lining, where it emerges from the pubic bone, should be sutured bilaterally to the crura of the corpora cavernosa. The opened urethra and corpora spongiosum are sutured to the corpora cavernosa from this point distally using continuous 4-0 Monocryl sutures with any knots buried. This approximates and closes the raw surface of both and in essence forms a flat, tube-like structure. The length of the "tube" is a matter of judgement but must be long enough to accurately construct the new clitoris, which should lie in a normal anatomical position.

Attention can now be directed to bringing the clitoral tissue to its finished shape. The corpora cavernosa part of the tube is grasped at its end with an Allis clamp. Using a slightly curved scissors, the end is cut off by aiming the points of the scissors distally at a 45 degree angle on both the right and left sides so that the two cuts meet its midline. This creates a beveled end to the clitoris which can be further shaped as the surgeon wishes. The open area is best closed by elevating the very tip with a skin hook and suturing the tip closed with 4–0 Monocryl sutures with the knots buried. Do this in such a way so as to make the tip point forward. The urethral mucosa is now draped around this "clitoral tip," trimmed of any excess tissue and also sutured with 4–0 Monocryl sutures. The whole concept is to form a structure whose end resembles a clitoris, which should be three to four times as large as one would ordinarily expect it to be because in several months it shrinks in size. If the clitoris does not shrink sufficiently, it can be surgically reduced at the time of the labiaplasty by removing an anterior ellipse of tissue and closing in the midline.

After the loose packing is removed from the cavity between the abdominal muscles and skin, the cavity should be irrigated with copious amounts of saline, and any bleeding points electrocoagulated to avoid hematoma formation. With traction applied downward, the abdominal skin is secured to the periosteum of the pubic bone with a single #5 Ethibond suture tied over a cotton bolster.

With continued downward traction on the penile skin, the neoclitoral and neo-urethral openings are made at the appropriate levels. If too much traction is exerted on the penile skin while making the incisions, the entire area can eventually retract superiorly, taking with it the neo-urethral opening, resulting in a urine stream that will point more forward than downward. The preferable way to make the two incisions is with a #20 scalpel blade, keeping the cuts vertical and exactly in the midline. Both openings should measure about 20 mm. These apertures should lie directly over the end of the clitoris and the visible orifice of the urethra. As far as the urethral incision is concerned, it is best to err more posteriorly than anteriorly. The neoclitoral orifice can be adjusted by extending the incision either way and suturing the opposite end closed. Generally speaking, the two incisions are about 15 mm to 18 mm apart. The bridge of skin between the two is the tissue that is divided at the time of labiaplasty. It is this division that results in the creation of the labia minora and exposure of the pink mucosa so characteristic of the female vulva. The neoclitoris is now passed through the neoclitoral opening and sutured to the skin from within with 4-0 Monocryl sutures so that any knots are buried. The Foley catheter is passed through the neo-urethral opening.

Few situations are more distressing to a woman than a urine stream which is neither straight nor focused. The "sprinkling can" effect is messy and frankly annoying; this is a condition which must be avoided. The problem can be circumvented at the time of surgery if the neo-urethral meatus is sutured so as to prevent the problem in the first place. This is quite simply done by suturing the skin of the neo-urethra to the mucosa of the urethra in such a way that the knots are buried rather than exposed where uneven healing and scar will inevitably occur. With gentle, upward traction on the Foley catheter, the first ligature, utilizing a 3-0 Monocryl suture, is placed carefully at the lower and posterior apex of the new urethra. A generous bite of corpora spongiosum *and* mucosal lining is taken. The needle is then passed through the neo-urethral opening in the skin to come back through the skin to the raw side where the knot is carefully tied *after* the two surfaces have been approximated. This is friable tissue and can easily be torn unless there is absolutely no tension present. The short end of the suture is cut off and the remaining suture is used as an over and over stitch taking an ample amount of corpora spongiosum and mucosal lining followed by a bite of neo-urethral skin. Proceed up one side placing the sutures until tension between the skin and mucosa is too great to comfortably place any more. The same is repeated on the other side. Note that the two rows will be going further and further apart and under no circumstance should the anterior/superior area be sutured. This opening forms the lower end of the urethro-clitoral fistula, which is opened at the time of labiaplasty. In some patients, urine can continue to pass through the fistula, making it appear as though the individual is urinating from the clitoris, a phenomenon which stops after labiaplasty. When suturing has been completed, the external orifice should be inspected for errant sutures which, if present, should be replaced.

The temporary Kerlix pack is removed from the neovagina, which is again irrigated with copious amounts of saline; all bleeding should be controlled at this time. The inverted penile skin with its skin-graft extension, if present, are slipped over a Deaver retractor moistened with mineral oil and together are inserted into the neovagina. There is no need to secure the inverted skin within the neovagina with sutures or by any other means, since the Furacin packing is more than capable of anchoring this tube of skin until healing has taken place. The opening of the skin tube is now adjusted to fit comfortably within the opening of the raw surface of the neovagina by simply cutting distally along the ventral surface of the inverted penile skin shaft until the two openings fit without tension. The perineal skin is sutured to the penile skin or skin graft, whichever may be the case, laterally for about 4–5 cm. The use of continuous 3-0 Monocryl sutures doubled back creates a strong junction in an area where it is important that the suture line be secure. This last maneuver not only ensures a resilient and durable perineal area, but begins construction of the lower labia majora.

With the Deaver retractor still in place, the neovagina, now lined with epithelium, is packed with up to 10 yards of 3-in., fine-mesh gauze impregnated thoroughly with Furacin. This packing, if done gently but firmly, will conform to the general shape of the new vagina and will allow the raw side of the skin tube to be pressed against the raw surface of the newly created vagina while they heal together over the next 8 days. The packing process is facilitated by leaving the retractor in place and slowly withdrawing it while the Furacin gauze is inserted with long bayonet packing forceps.

The labia majora are best formed by excising the excessive scrotal skin with a large, heavy curved scissors. Care and judgement must be exercised during the excision, so that all cuts are made as symmetrically as possible, while at the same time making sure that the blood supply of the penile skin flap is not compromised. This can be made easier by first outlining the cuts with a methylene blue pen.

Should the blood supply be interfered with, part or all of the neovaginal lining could be lost to necrosis, especially if the patient has a smoking habit or is diabetic; therefore, it is imperative that the final vertical incision not lie too far medially. On the other hand, it must not be located too far laterally as, in that position, the mature scar would be visible when wearing brief bathing attire. The amount of underlying fat to be removed before closure is again a matter of judgement, keeping in mind that most labia majora are relatively flat and not heavy or excessively large. After removal of skin and fat, meticulous attention is paid to hemostasis, since a hematoma can readily form in this area.

Closure is accomplished with continuous 3-0 Monocryl sutures over small penrose drains placed deep within the wound and brought out through the lower portion of the labia wound just above the point where the perineal sutures ended; here they are secured to the skin with 3-0 Monocryl sutures. Occasionally, "dog ears" form at the superior ends of the labial closures, which must be adjusted.

Following removal of all surgical drapes, the operative area is washed with saline and dried. Thrombin 30 cc is injected behind the penile skin flap through the neoclitoral opening. All suture lines are covered with a copious amount of Furacin, over which is laid fine-mesh gauze impregnated with Furacin. The Foley catheter is brought anteriorly over the thigh, where it is secured to the thigh with tape to prevent pressure necrosis of the bladder trigone from the catheter bulb.

A final rectal exam is done to determine the integrity of the rectal mucosa and tissue between the neovagina and rectum. An ABD pad and ice pack secured with a perineal binder finishes the dressing.

The patient spends about one hour in the recovery room, where vital signs are monitored and the perineal area is watched for any postoperative bleeding. Additional ice packs to the groin and perineum usually obviate any tendency to bleed. These are kept in place for 6 days until the patient is ambulated.

Postoperative Care

Once the patient has been returned from the recovery area to her own room, she is in the hands of professional nurses who specialize in the care of postoperative male-to-female patients. Complete bed rest for 6 days is mandatory, since ambulation could result in total or partial loss of the neovaginal lining. During this time, the patient receives physical and psychological support. Pain, interestingly enough, is rarely complained of if no split-thickness graft has been taken; what pain or discomfort there might be is well controlled by the use of a PCA, a device which automatically gives the patient 10 mg of Demerol every hour. The patient can supplement this by the simple press of a button if she desires more. Continuous ice packs applied to the groin area not only help control pain, but obviate bleeding as well.

Boredom during this period is not uncommon, so it is recommended that the patient bring materials to occupy her mind; the nursing staff can supply only so many VCR movies. A low-residue diet, along with DSS Plus 100 mg per day is suggested to prevent constipation and facilitate bowel movements while the vaginal pack is in place. To help avoid ileus, 20 mEq KCL in the IV solution run at 150 cc/hour is of value until the oral intake has been established. Should ileus occur, an N/G tube to relieve gastric distention is used. Supplemental vitamins and minerals are given along with antibiotics, usually Cephalexin 500 mg p.o. qid.

On the sixth postoperative day, the IV's, Foley catheter, drains, and wire suture are removed. If an augmentation mammaplasty was done, that dressing is removed as well. The patient is ambulated to the shower with specific instructions to bathe herself thoroughly and to gently "pat" the operated areas with copious amounts of soap and water; vigorous rubbing must be discouraged so as not to disrupt any suture lines. An attempt can be made to urinate in the shower, but if there is difficulty in this regard, the patient is catheterized until she can void on her own. Voiding problems usually stop once the vaginal pack has been removed.

At the end of the seventh or on the eighth postoperative day, the vaginal pack is removed. The patient is given instructions about how to dilate her neovagina with any well-lubricated dildo or dilator that conforms to the size and shape of the vagina. This must be done on a regular basis until the new vagina no longer has the propensity to contract or stenose. Dilation up to six times a day for one-half hour at a time is recommended in the beginning; the amount of dilating time can be reduced as inflammation subsides and healing progresses. Some patients can eventually stop dilating altogether, but most probably need some dilation all their lives.

Every patient is sent home with antibiotics for 10 days, ferrous sulfate for one month, and oral analgesics. Topical A & D ointment is recommended for the entire perineum until the self-dissolving sutures are no longer present and all areas are well healed.

No sexual intercourse is suggested for 6 weeks. If the patient so wishes, she may have a labiaplasty in 3 months.

Complications

Without argument, the death of the patient from thrombotic emboli secondary to deep vein phlebitis is the most devastating complication one could possibly have. Although rare, it can in most cases be totally avoided by having all patients stop taking female hormones 3 weeks prior to surgery and not resuming them for several weeks after surgery has been completed. The use of ordinary TED stockings together with sequential TED support stockings during the operation and for 6 days after also helps obviate the problem.

The most serious intraoperative problem is the surgeon's inadvertent entry into the rectum while dissecting the neovagina. If the patient has been well-prepped internally as well as externally, the opening through the rectal wall and mucosa can and should be repaired with fine (5-0 or 6-0 Monocryl) sutures without passing the needle and suture through the rectal mucosa itself. The operation should be continued with the expectation that the wound will heal without misadventure and that no future recto-vaginal fistula will occur.

Postoperative bleeding from the incision sites can in some cases warrant the need for blood transfusions. This should be monitored by judicially checking the patient's hemoglobin and hematocrit. Control of hemorrhage is best done by ice and pressure; rarely must a patient be returned to the operating suite for surgical control of bleeding.

Occasionally, ileus will result in gastric retention of air, which causes uncomfortable bloating. This is best relieved with a nasogastric tube, which, in some cases, must stay in place for several days. Supplemental potassium is administered as needed.

Once the patient has been sent home, vaginal stenosis can and occasionally does happen if the patient does not fastidiously dilate the neovagina. The importance of frequent dilation cannot be stressed enough. Should the patient find that the dilating maneuver is becoming more difficult, the frequency of dilation must be increased, or the entire vaginal canal could be lost. If this eventuality occurs, restoration of vaginal size will require a costly secondary and far more difficult operation to open and line the vagina with epithelium. These secondary procedures are not always successful.

STAGE II (LABIAPLASTY)
Procedure

Since vital blood supply would be cut off from the inverted penile skin, the reassignment procedure, as described here, unfortunately cannot be done in one stage. Therefore, it is common to do a second stage called labiaplasty in those patients who feel that they would like to have a more feminine-appearing vulva. It is estimated that about 60 percent of patients elect to undergo labiaplasty, which is done no sooner that 3 months after the SRS operation. It is performed on an out-patient basis unless the patient wishes to have a great deal more in the way of cosmetic surgery, in which case, an overnight stay would be appropriate. Either general anesthesia or epidural block can be used if no ancillary procedures are done in conjunction with labiaplasty.

The simple goal of labiaplasty is to make the perineum appear more feminine than can be accomplished at SRS. Basically, there are two surgical maneuvers. First, with scissors or scalpel, the urethro-clitoral fistula is opened in the midline, revealing the pink mucosa which was once the lining of the urethra. This also creates the labia minora after the wound edges are approximated with 5-0 Monocryl sutures. Second, by elevating and transposing double Z-plasties, the superior portions of the labia majora are approximated in the midline to form a hood over the clitoris.

Any adjustments deemed necessary to any part of the vulva can be done at this time, such as reduction of an oversized clitoris or labium. Examination of the neovagina will reveal depth and patency. Should any stenosis or fibrous bands be apparent, they can be cut at this time. Occasionally, raw granulation tissue is found, which should be cauterized with a silver nitrate stick. In general, any appropriate procedure which will enhance the feminine appearance and function of the perineum is performed during labiaplasty.

Postoperatively, the patient is placed on antibiotics and an effective analgesic drug for 10 days. A & D ointment on the perineal suture lines keeps them soft; panty-liner pads afford protection from clothing. Ice packs in the immediate postoperative period help control bleeding and give the patient a great deal of comfort.

Vaginal dilating and douching can be resumed immediately, but intercourse should not be resumed for at least 4 weeks or until healing is complete. Suture removal is not necessary when Monocryl material is used.

Discussion
Aesthetics

A perineum that closely resembles that of the genetic female is the obvious cosmetic objective when doing male-to-female SRS. The standard of excellence achieved depends on a number of things: for example, as with any surgery, the better the material the surgeon has to work with, the more likely the final result will be a good one. If, on the other hand, the patient is diabetic, malnourished, or has some systemic disease, the outcome may be compromised. The degree of difficulty has great bearing on the end product. Some patients, because of superior anatomy and physiology, are simply easier to do than others.

Furthermore, the patient herself must follow instructions and take proper care so that the healing process can proceed to its final conclusion without misadventure. The newly created genitalia must be kept clean and free of any excessive trauma. These tissues are delicate and need time to adjust to their new locations; therefore, the patient's motivation and desire to cooperate will be instrumental in whether or not the end result will live up to her expectations. Interestingly enough, excessively high patient expectations can also be detrimental, because when anyone expects more than can be delivered, that person will naturally be disappointed if the outcome is substandard in his or her eyes. And lastly, the skill and sense of craftsmanship of the operating surgeon will in all likelihood determine whether there will be a consistent reproduction of high-quality results.

Neovaginal Depth and Function

Adequate neovaginal depth is essential for successful, trouble-free intercourse, and depends on both the extent of the original dissection and the subsequent lining technique. If the initial dissection is not carried beyond the capsule of the prostate gland, there is little chance that satisfactory intercourse will be possible in most cases. The dissection must reach as far back as Denonvillier's fascia between the seminal vesicles and beneath the urinary bladder. Regardless of how much depth is obtained, the neovagina must be lined completely with epithelium from either the inverted penile skin or a combination of penile skin and skin graft. Without this complete lining, the neovagina will most certainly close from stenosis.

Ancillary maneuvers such as elevation of the abdominal skin from the underlying abdominal musculature in order to advance the lower abdominal skin toward the neovaginal opening is of some, but limited, value. It is unnecessary to suture the lining penile skin and/or graft to the deep tissues of the neovagina, as this only adds time to the procedure and causes needless trauma. The epithelial lining can be held in place by proper packing with fine-mesh gauze impregnated with Furacin. When the pack is removed in 8 days, the epithelial lining is sufficiently adherent to the walls of the new vagina.

Lubrication for intercourse must oftentimes be artificially supplied, but in some cases enough comes from the vaginal area itself, making this unnecessary. The most likely source of this lubrication material is the secretions from the prostate gland and Cowper's glands, which are left intact. If a mucosal flap, which is a portion of the distal urethra, is incorporated into the skin-graft extension of the neo-urethral lining, there may be some lubrication from this structure.

As long as there is inflammation in the depths of the neovagina, and until this inflammation has run its course, the neovagina will have the propensity to contract and stenose. Since this is the case, diligent dilating must be done on the part of the patient until the need to do so no longer exists. In some cases this need may last for a year or more, but generally it does not last as long when full-thickness grafts are used, as they have less tendency to contract.

Orgasm

One of the most important, if not *the* most important external structure of the female genitalia is the clitoris. Under no circumstance should SRS be undertaken without the formation and construction of this highly significant anatomic modality, because if omitted, the overall appearance of the external genitalia is visually and functionally incomplete. Indeed, there are a number of ways that this can be accomplished; but whatever method is used, some attempt must be made to build one, not only for the sake of orgasm, but for aesthetics.

Two studies, one qualitative (Walworth, 1994), and one quantitative (Lief & Hubschman, 1993), have shown relatively low rates of orgasm in postoperative male-to-female transsexuals, although some SRS surgeons (Biber, 1995; and Wilson, 1993) have claimed very high rates of orgasm in their patients. It is doubtful that a surgeon, no matter how well-meaning he may be, can implement orgasm by the manipulation of tissue. He can, on the other hand, do careful surgery. By not sacrificing more tissue than is necessary, he will preserve important nerve trunks which in turn will facilitate later orgasm. Studies have shown that more than one-half of genetic females, who for the most part have intact, unoperated genitalia, do not climax; therefore, how can we expect male-to-female transsexual individuals to do any better after their genitals have been surgically altered? Some postoperative male-to-female transsexuals report multiple and "explosive" orgasms, while others state that they have virtually no feeling whatsoever.

It has often been said that the human brain is the most important sex organ. Since this is the case, the most likely explanation would be that a sensuous patient will climax regardless of what is done surgically, provided that she receives quality surgery. If important anatomic structures are preserved and the surgery is trauma free—a sine qua non of transsexual surgery— orgasmic capability will be maximized.

Conclusion

The surgical aspect of gender reassignment is in a high state of evolution. New and exciting ideas are coming from many sources, and although the procedures performed to date are excellent, many more will be developed in the next few years to simplify and standardize the operation. Add to this the fact that because the entire concept of transsexualism is becoming better understood and less taboo, more interest by the university systems should stimulate research and teaching.

It has long been known by plastic surgeons that even a seemingly insignificant alteration in a patient's physical deformity can result in a profound improvement in self-esteem and well-being. One can only imagine the amount of happiness and sense of fulfillment that the successfully managed and operated transgendered individual must experience.

References

Abraham, F. (1931). Genitalunwandlung an zwei maennlichen transvestiten (Genital alteration in two male transvestites). *Zeitschrift Sexualwissenschaft, 18,* 223–226.

AEGIS suggests electrolysis to avoid problem of hair in vagina. (1995). Decatur, GA: American Educational Gender Information Service, Inc.

Aspen, B. (1995, February). Electrolysis for transgendered clients. *International Hair Route,* 11, 13, 46.

Benjamin, H. (1966). *The transsexual phenomenon.* New York: The Julian Press.

Biber, S. (1995). Sex reassignment surgery: An overview. Paper presented at the First International Congress on Gender, Cross Dressing, and Sex Issues, Van Nuys, CA, 23–26 February, 1995.

Bouman, F.G. (1988). Sex reassignment surgery in male-to-female transsexuals. *Annals of Plastic Surgery, 21*(6), 526–531.

Brown, G. (1995). Letter to the editor. *Chrysalis: The Journal of Transgressive Gender Identities, 2*(1), 8, 34.

Burou, G. (1973). Male-to-female transformation. In D. Laub & P. Gandy (Eds.), *Proceedings of the Second Interdisciplinary Symposium on Gender Dysphoria Syndrome,* pp. 188–194. Palo Alto, CA: Stanford University Medical Center.

Creighton, G.B., & Goulian, D. (1973). Secondary surgery in transsexuals. *Plastic and Reconstructive Surgery, 51*(6), 628–631.

Crichton, D. (1993, May). *SAMJ,* #83.

Edgerton, M.T. (1973). Introduction. In D. Laub & P. Gandy (Eds.), *Proceedings of the Second Interdisciplinary Symposium on Gender Dysphoria Syndrome,* pp. 1–4. Palo Alto, CA: Stanford University Medical Center.

Edgerton, M.T. (1983). The role of surgery in the treatment of transsexualism. In *Proceedings of the 9th International Gender Dysphoria Association.* Bordeaux, France.

Edgerton, M.T., & Bull, J. (1970). Surgical construction of the vagina and labia in male transsexuals. *Plastic and Reconstructive Surgery, 46*(6), 529–539.

Eldh, J. (1993). Construction of a neovagina with preservation of the glans Penis as a clitoris in male transsexuals. *Plastic and Reconstructive Surgery, 91*(5),895–903.

Farmer, D. (1994). Propelled to self-mutilation. *Chrysalis Quarterly, 1*(7), 9–10.

Fogh-Andersen, P. (1969). Transsexualism: An attempt at surgical management. *Scandinavian Journal of Plastic and Reconstructive Surgery, 3,* 61–64.

Glenn, J.F. (1980). One-stage operation for male transsexuals. *Journal of Urology,* *123*(3), 396–398.

Hastings, D.W. (1969). Inauguration of a research project on transsexualism in a university medical center. In R. Green & J. Money (Eds.), *Transsexualism and sex reassignment,* pp. 243–251. Baltimore, MD: Johns Hopkins University Press.

Jones, H.W., Schirmer, H.K.A., & Hoopes, J.E. (1968). A sex conversion operation for males with transsexualism. *American Journal of Obstetrics and Gynecology,* *100*(1), 101–109.

Krieger, M.J., McAninch, J.W., & Weimer, S.R. (1982) Self-performed bilateral orchiectomy in transsexuals. *Journal of Clinical Psychiatry,* *43*(7), 292–293.

Laub, D.R., Laub, D.R., II, & Biber, S. (1988). Vaginoplasty for gender confirmation. *Clinics in Plastic Surgery,* *15*(3), 463–470.

Lief, H.I., & Hubschman, L. (1993). Orgasm in the postoperative transsexual. *Archives of Sexual Behavior,* *22*(2), 145–155.

Malloy, T.R., Noone, R.B., & Morgan, A.J. (1976). Experience with the 1–stage surgical approach for constructing female genitalia in male transsexuals. *Journal of Urology,* *116*(3), 335–337.

McIndoe, A. (1944). Techniques for vaginoplasty. *Journal of Obstetrics & Gynaecology of the British Empire,* *51*: 24.

Meyer, R., & Kesselring, K. (1980). One stage reconstruction of the vagina with penile skin as an island flap in male transsexuals. *Plastic and Reconstructive Surgery,* *66*(3), 401–406.

Pandya, N.J., & Stuteville, O.H. (1973). A one-stage technique for constructing female external genitalia in male transsexuals. *British Journal of Plastic Surgery,* *26*(3), 277–282.

Roscoe, W. (1994). Priests of the goddess: Gender transgression in the Ancient World. Presented at the 109th Annual Meeting of the American Historical Association, San Francisco, CA.

Small, M.P. (1987). Penile and scrotal vaginoplasty for male-to-female transsexuals. *Urology,* *29*(6), 593–597.

Sorensen, T., & Hertoft, P. (1980). Sexmodifying operations on transsexuals in Denmark in the period 1950–1977. *Acta Psychiatrica Scandinavica,* *61*(1), 56–66.

Walworth, J. (1994). Sex reassignment surgery in male-to-female transsexuals: Client satisfaction in relation to selection criteria. Unpublished ms.

Wilson, N. (1993). Aesthetic reconstruction of the vulva with sensate clitoral reconstruction. Paper presented at the 13th International Symposium on Gender Dysphoria, New York City, 21–24 October.

20 ELECTROLYSIS IN TRANSSEXUAL WOMEN

A RETROSPECTIVE LOOK AT FREQUENCY OF TREATMENT IN FOUR CASES

Dallas Denny

Ahoova Mishael

The role of the electrologist is, of course, to permanently remove unwanted hair from the face and body. Many electrologists treat only females, but males frequently seek treatment as well. Men may desire to be rid of hair for any number of reasons: because they dislike shaving or have sensitive skin which makes shaving painful or difficult, because they are bothered by ingrown hairs, because they wish to have an even beard or hair line, because hair grows in unwanted areas like the back, or more thickly than wanted, or simply because hair on certain parts of their bodies just does not fit their self-image. Into the latter category fall males with transgender feelings—men who wish to become women, or more like women.[1]

Transgendered people are of both sexes, but the electrology needs of the genetic female who is moving in the masculine direction are quite limited, whereas the postpubertal genetic male will almost always need extensive facial electrolysis in order to achieve a suitably feminine appearance. In the remainder of this paper, we will use the words "transsexual woman" to refer to the male who is becoming or who has become a woman. We will address the special needs of the female-to-male transsexual (transsexual man) and the male cross-dresser in the discussion section.

ELECTROLYSIS NEEDS OF TRANSSEXUAL WOMEN

Despite an internal identity as females, transsexual women, before transition, find themselves with unremarkably male bodies. This means that in the absence of intervention with opposite-sex hormones, their facial, body, and head hair will follow the normal male pattern, with a diamond-shaped pubic patch which extends upward towards the navel, increased axillary hair, a heavy growth of facial hair, and thick dark hairs on the arms, legs, and torso (Dupertuis, Atkinson, & Elftman, 1945; Montagna, 1976).

Baldness, heavy body hair, and beard growth can be very ego-dystonic in transsexual women, who desire to pass in society as nontranssexual (Finifter, 1969) (But see again note 1). Bringing body and facial hair under control is critically important for the individual who plans to live as a woman, for the male beard can be concealed only by ingenuity and hard work, and even then not with complete success.[2] The transsexual client will in fact have the same distress about facial hair as the genetic female with hirsutism, especially if living as a woman.

Hormonal therapy, which is an essential part of the process of sex reassignment, will generally cause body hair patterns to change in the female direction (especially when antiandrogens are used; see Prior, Vigna, & Watson, 1989), but depending on the level of hirsutism of the individual, electrolysis on the torso, neck, legs, and arms may be necessary. With estrogen and progesterone, facial hair growth will slow, and with antiandrogens such as spironolactone, there may actually be some thinning of facial hair (Prior, Vigna, & Watson, 1989; Basson & Prior, in this volume), but unless the masculinization process is arrested early in puberty (which rarely occurs) or the individual naturally has sparse beard growth, extensive facial electrolysis is usually necessary (Finifter, 1969).

Sex reassignment is a process of physical and social change that takes place over a number of years, cumulating, in some cases, in genital surgery, which is a *confirmation* of the new gender, rather than the cause of it (Laub, Laub, & Biber, 1988). Living and working in the new gender role is in fact a prior requirement for surgery, as outlined in the Standards of Care of the Harry Benjamin International Gender Dysphoria Association (Walker, et al., 1990), the guidelines which are consensually used by health-care professionals. The individual must have proven competence in handling herself in the new gender before undergoing irreversible surgery; this is called the real-life test.

As it is very difficult to begin this period of cross-living while there is still heavy facial hair, electrolysis is best done early in the transition phase, while the individual is still living in the male role. Facial hair growth on a man will not ordinarily cause undue comment or ridicule, but the same growth on a woman, transsexual or otherwise, can be highly stigmatizing and very embarrassing. Consequently, the individual in real-life test may have scheduling difficulties caused by the need for seclusion while allowing the hair to grow for a day or two before treatment. A busy schedule may make it difficult to allow the hair to grow to a suitable length for treatment, and the individual may not be willing to show herself in public during the time necessary for growth.[3] However, by careful juggling of the schedule (e.g., treatment on Saturdays or evenings), it is possible for the transsexual individual to have electrolysis while in real-life test.

Removal of facial hair can require many hours of treatment. Anne Bolin, in her book, *In Search of Eve* (1988), estimates that an average of 200 hours of electrolysis are needed to completely clear the average male face. We have seen similar estimates in the magazines and newsletters of the transgender community. As in all electrolysis, it is critical that the hair root be killed. It is not unusual for a transsexual woman to undergo hundreds of hours of electrolysis with no significant reduction of beard density. Bolin gives an example of an individual who, after more than 300 hours of treatment, was still able to grow a beard. We have known individuals who have said they spent over ten-thousand dollars in a fruitless attempt to rid themselves of facial hair.

As the plans for the future of the transsexual woman may depend to a great extent upon having the facial hair under control, it is critical that she find an electrologist who is capable of removing her facial hair with a minimum of treatment, but without causing unsightly scarring, pitting, or discoloration of skin. Because the facial hair of the male is more difficult to remove than the thinner hair of the female, it is important that the transsexual woman seek an electrologist with experience with hair removal in males, and preferably one who has worked extensively with transsexual women. This is not always possible, however, because of geographic limitations.

It is important that electrologists who are treating transsexual women be aware that they may need to modify their techniques somewhat for these clients. Aspen (1995) noted that she has had success with the manual blend method, using dual foot pedals, using as a base rate (which is modified, as needed) a galvanic current ranging from 4 to 7 milliamperes, and high frequency ranging from 1.2 to 2.5 (low intensity). Aspen varies her timing according to the thickness of the hair: "Sometimes 8 seconds or less of dual currents is sufficient, and at other times it is necessary to lead with galvanic, for say 5 seconds, adding high frequency for another 5 seconds. Be consistent with the count . . . and use larger needles for the beard, whenever possible" (pp. 11, 13).

Some electrologists have reported success with insulated probes; current is delivered only at the tip of the probe. This theoretically causes less damage to the skin, although we are unaware of any data to support this.

A few electrologists advertise marathon electrolysis sessions in the magazines and newsletters of the transgender community; it is not unheard of for an individual to fly or drive to another state and have 40 or more hours of electrolysis in a 5- or 6-day period. While this certainly is much less expensive, both travel-wise (fewer trips are necessary) and treatment-wise (there is generally a discount for booking multiple-hour sessions), it seems reason-

337

able to assume that even with an insulated probe, this poses greater risk for damage to the skin than the same amount of treatment stretched over weeks or months.

As we prepare to go to press, there has been a great deal of speculation in the transgender community about electrolysis delivered via laser. Although lasers promise the development of an effective, rapid, and inexpensive way of getting rid of facial hair, we are reminded of the many past methods of electrolysis which were unproven and ultimately abandoned. The individual anxious to transition might well be better served by opting for proven methods than by waiting for technological breakthroughs which might or might not happen.

Thermolysis, galvanic electrolysis, and the blend all have their proponents, both within the transsexual community and within the community of electrologists, and both authors have heard reports of successful and unsuccessful treatment using all of these methods. *We believe that the technique (level of expertise) of the electrologist is the most critical factor in clearing the face and other areas of hair, whether in transsexual or nontranssexual women.* Unfortunately, it is sometimes difficult for the transsexual woman to judge the efficacy of electrolysis, for with treatment the hair will be removed, even if the root has not been destroyed. What seems to be a successful course of treatment will not be revealed to be unsuccessful until circumstances prevent the individual from seeing the electrologist for several months. Suddenly, it may become apparent that there has not been any appreciable reduction in beard growth. It goes without saying that any patient would find this highly distressing.

From conversations with many transsexual women, we have discovered that Bolin's estimate of 200 hours may be a reasonable estimate of the time required to "clear" a genetic male's face. However, our examination of the second author's treatment data shows that she has been successful in clearing the faces of the majority of her transsexual clients with far fewer hours of treatment, using the thermolysis method. Moreover, many of her clients have made dramatic personal changes as a result of combined electrolysis and hormonal treatment.

While our data are not as rigorous as we would have liked (i.e., we were unable to do actual hair-density counts or strictly control for previous electrolysis), our subjective impressions of the individuals before treatment were "Yes, she has a beard within normal male limits," and afterwards that their facial skin was free of large, thick hairs, as is the case with most genetic females; and that their facial skin did appear much more feminine. Progress of treatment was usually coincident with the beginning of life in

the feminine role, and it is our opinion that the electrolysis made a significant contribution to successful full-time cross-living. We believe our data,
limited as they are, are the first such ever presented.

METHOD

Subjects

Subjects were four adult transsexual women retroactively selected as representative from a pool of more than 20 transsexual women who had seen
the second author for treatment. Their ages ranged from the early thirties
to the mid-forties. Selection was dependent upon (1) initial presentation
with a significant amount of facial hair, which, in the opinion of both the
subject and the second author, was within the normal male range and
would have made living as a woman difficult; (2) a stated history of little
or no previous electrolysis (10 hours maximum); and (3) regular and continued treatment, until the second author and the subject reached a consensus that continuing electrolysis was not (or was only rarely) needed. We
found four subjects who clearly met these criteria. Three had transitioned,
and were living as women before the end of treatment. The fourth was living as a woman (with considerable harassment from her co-workers) when
she entered treatment.

Treatment

Treatment was by thermolysis, using an Instantron Model SS69 machine.
Time and intensity settings were adjusted according to the individual needs
of each subject. Subjects were encouraged to come weekly or biweekly for
treatment, as their finances permitted, but this was not always possible.

    All treatment was given by the second author or occasionally by
Hanna Dalal, using the same equipment. Typically, she would work in a

Table 20.1. Total Hours of Thermolysis by Subject

Subject	Total Hours	Months Elapsed between First and Last Treatments
Ann	48.5	18
Rachel	54.75	28
Candace	60.75	17
Marti	105.25	14

Mean Hours Per Subject: 67.3
Mean Time in Months Between First and Last Treatment: 19.25

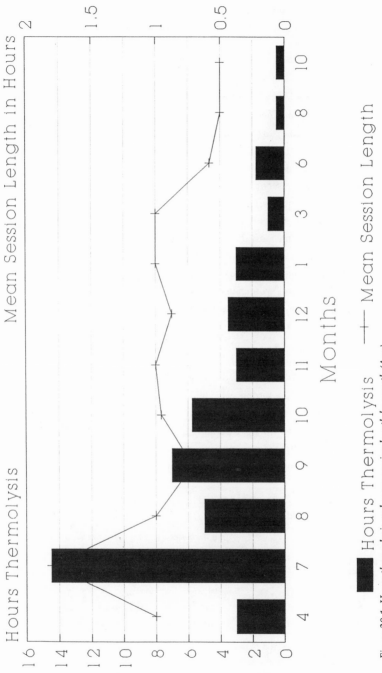

Figure 20.1. Hours thermolysis and mean session length by month (Ann).

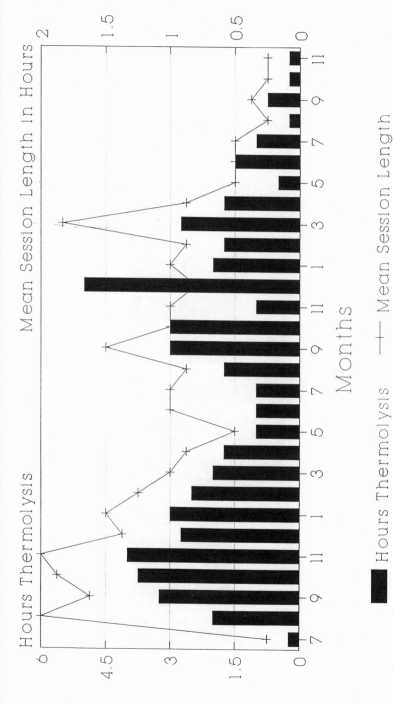

Figure 20.2. Hours thermolysis and mean session length by month (Rachel).

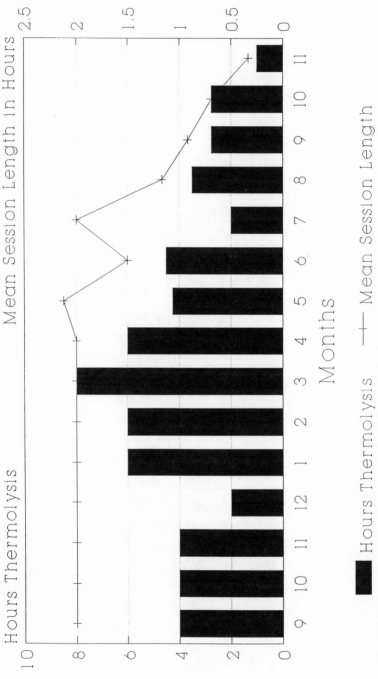

Figure 20.3. Hours thermolysis and mean session length by month (Candace).

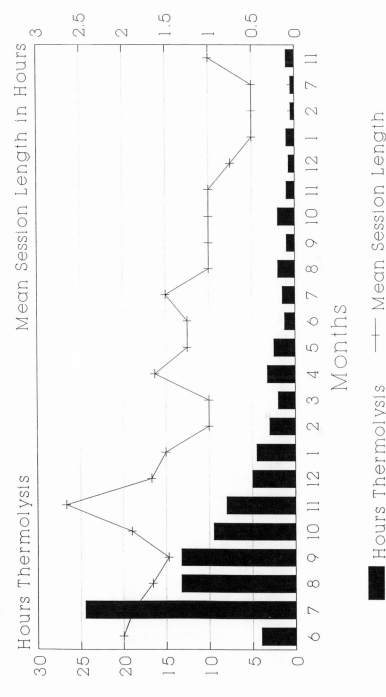

Figure 20.4. Hours thermolysis and mean session length by month (Marti).

specific area of the face, and would in subsequent sessions clear that area before moving into untreated areas. Thus, it was not necessary for the subject to shave the treated areas, so long as she was having weekly treatments.[4]

Usually, treatment would start with the cheek or lower neck area, but the site of initial treatment varied with the wishes of the subject. Subjects were urged not to shave or pluck areas which had been cleared, although they sometimes did, especially when extended time elapsed between treatments.

RESULTS

The hours in treatment ranged from 48.5 hours for Ann, whose facial hair was relatively sparse, to 105.25 hours for Marti, who presented with an exceptionally heavy beard. The mean was 67.3 hours. Total hours of thermolysis for each subject are shown in Table 20.1.

Ann's 48.5 hours of treatment took place over 18 months. Initially, she came frequently for treatment, and then less often, as regrowth decreased. Figure 20.1 shows a frequency distribution for Ann's treatment. We noted a similar tendency for the other three subjects (Figure 20.1).

Length of sessions gradually decreased for all four subjects. Early in treatment, most session lengths were one hour or more. Towards the end of treatment, three of the four subjects (Ann, Rachel, and Candace) had a mean session length of 30 minutes or less. Marti's session length increased from thirty minutes to one hour near the end of the treatment period, but she was coming only two or three times a year at that point.

It is worth noting that during her second month in treatment, Marti had 25 hours of thermolysis. This was at her insistence, for she was cross-living full-time and was ordinarily unwilling to grow her facial hair. She was on leave for a number of weeks following surgery (castration), and wanted to have as much electrolysis as was possible before going back to work. The second author had concerns about such an intensive schedule, but as Marti was already living as a woman and was unwilling to begin electrolysis except on her schedule, the second author acceded to her wishes.

Initially, all four subjects had facial hair growth which visually appeared to be within the normal male range. Afterwards, none of them shaved, which allowed for the growth of vellus hairs, giving their facial skin a feminine appearance. There was no visible scarring, pitting, or discoloration from electrolysis.

Subjects have continued to schedule treatment on an intermittent basis, but sessions are typically short, and regrowth is sparse.

Our experience suggests that if electrolysis is ongoing for more than about 20 hours without significant reduction of beard growth (and specifically, if the length of the session necessary to clear the face or certain sections of it has not become shorter than earlier in treatment), there should, if the individual's life circumstances permit, be a treatment holiday during which progress is evaluated. If treatment is judged to be ineffective, then a change should be made either in electrologist or in the method of treatment (e.g., blend instead of thermolysis, or a significant change in the intensity and/or duration of the current).

Future research should attempt to establish an objective method of effectiveness of electrolysis (e.g., density counts before and after treatment).

We cannot overemphasize the importance of facial electrolysis in transsexual women. The presence of heavy facial hair requires frequent shaving, with subsequent skin irritation, and no matter how closely the individual shaves, no matter how blonde the facial hair, no matter how much makeup is applied, no matter how much the transsexual woman insists that her beard doesn't show, the sophisticated observer will make assumptions that what is being covered up on the face relates to what is being covered up by the clothing.

Male cross-dressers—that is, men who dress as women, typically take two or more hours to ready themselves for public outings. Most of this time is spent in trying, with varying degrees of success, to control unwanted hair growth. Until her hair growth is brought under control, the transsexual woman must undergo the same sort of rigorous preparation for even the most simple excursion—that, or risk being perceived as a man. Wearing heavy makeup, wigs, and prosthetic devices is more akin to cross-dressing than transsexualism, which is a process of *becoming,* rather than simply dressing up. Control of unwanted hair is an integral part of that becoming. Few women have the luxury of a two-hour grooming process every day, and, if the transsexual woman is successful in her new role, neither will she.

A smooth face is a strong feminine signal, but even more so is a face which has the same amount of vellus hairs as is found in nontranssexual women. A face with these fine, light hairs will provide feminine gender cues which may not be consciously recognized, but which will nevertheless affect the overall perception of the individual. Shaving removes these vellus hairs as well as the thicker beard hairs.

Before treatment, when presenting as female, the four subjects and many other transsexual clients of the second author wore heavy foundation with beard cover, which they said they hated, but which they felt was nec-

Figure 20.5. The first author at 24 years of age, before hormonal therapy and electrolysis.

Figure 20.6. The first author at age 41, after ten years of hormonal therapy and approximately 110 hours of electrolysis (which in her case did not leave visible scars or skin texture changes, as happened with the individual in Figure 17.3).

essary. Afterwards, they wore little or no foundation, remarking that they didn't feel the need for it. They were thrilled that they no longer had to shave, as not having to do so reinforced their private views of themselves as women. Several stated that the morning shaving routine had always reminded them of their maleness.

With the loss of the facial hair came changes in hairstyle, clothing, comportment, and speech patterns, movement into full-time living (except for Marti, who had already—prematurely, in the view of her support group— moved into the female role), change of name, job changes, new relationships, and a gradual move into a new life. All of the subjects have since had genital surgery, although we point out that genital surgery is not necessary in order to lead a successful and productive life in the new gender role.

While electrolysis was certainly not the only factor which facilitated the change of role for these subjects, it was a critical one, for without it, they would have retained the strong secondary sex characteristic of beard growth, which would have strongly proclaimed them to be male and would probably have had a deleterious effect on their ability to find and maintain employment.

An example of the dramatic difference hormonal therapy and electrolysis can make in a transsexual woman can be seen in Figures 20.5 and 20.6. Figure 20.5 shows the first author at 24 years of age, before treatment. Figure 20.6 shows her at age 41, after 10 years of hormonal therapy and approximately 110 hours of electrolysis.

Male Cross-Dressers and Female Impersonators

Male cross-dressers dress as women for social reasons. Many are heterosexual, some are bisexual, and some are homosexual. Many cross-dressers experience sexual arousal from cross-dressing in puberty and young adulthood. This may persist, but in many men who cross-dress, there comes to be some degree of identification with women, and they develop a desire to look as much like women as possible on those occasions when they do cross-dress (Prince, 1976). Female impersonators, who make their livelihood by dressing as woman, have a similar desire. Some of these men will modify their bodies in an attempt to appear more feminine. Unfortunately, many turn to female hormones, which have global effects on body shape, emotional state, and sexuality, rather than to facial electrolysis, which has only local effects and which may actually be more helpful in allowing them to pass as women than will a year or two on hormones. However, many cross-dressers and female impersonators do approach electrologists for removal of unwanted hair. Total removal of male facial hair via electrolysis may result in a somewhat boyish appearance, but in the absence of other feminization will not have a great effect on the ability of a man to perform as a man, as will happen with a large enough dosage of female hormones taken for a long enough time. Partial removal of facial hair can result in improved appearance as a woman, but allow a convincing stubble when the individual does not shave.

Cross-dressers and female impersonators can make good clients, as they often desire not only facial electrolysis, but electrolysis on their bodies as well. It should be noted that for individuals not on female hormones, androgens will continually stimulate new hair growth, requiring ongoing electrolysis; transsexual people, on the other hand, frequently "finish" treatment. The second author has had no electrolysis for five years, with no regrowth of facial hair.

The Transgenderist

The transgenderist falls somewhere between the cross-dresser and the transsexual person. By some definitions, the individual who wishes to live full-time in the other gender but does not desire genital surgery is a transgenderist.

By others, the transgenderist is an individual who pursues characteristics of both sexes, who walks the middle line of androgyny. In either case, the electrology needs of the male-to-female transgenderist will be similar to that of transsexual women.

Transsexual Men

A significant minority, and perhaps as many as half of all transsexual people, are genetic females who wish to live as males. With the introduction of androgens, they will develop facial and body hair which is not distinguishably different from other men. Their electrology needs will for the most part be the same as those for other men, consisting primarily of treatment to reduce *pseudofolliculitis barbae,* to trim up beard lines, or to remove hair from unwanted areas like the back; however, there is a special consideration regarding phalloplasty.

Phalloplasty, the surgical technique whereby the male sexual organ is created in transsexual men, requires grafting of skin tissue from other areas of the body. This tissue can be taken from the torso, thigh, leg, or inner arm. Because some of this skin may wind up inside the phallus, providing a conduit for urine, it is important that it not be hair-bearing, as calcification tends to occur around hair in the path of the urine (Hage, 1992). Any hair in the donor areas should be removed. Obviously, this will be much easier before the surgery than afterwards.

Because phalloplasty is expensive (transsexual surgeries are almost never covered by medical insurance), and because of aesthetic and functional limitations of this surgery, most transsexual men opt either to forego "bottom surgery," or to have metadoioplasty (Laub, 1985), a surgical procedure which produces a small phallus from the testosterone-enlarged clitoris. In this case, electrolysis is generally not needed.

Vaginal Hair

In transsexual women, surgeons use penile and/or scrotal tissue and sometimes a flap of skin from the perineal area or a skin graft to line the neovagina. Because this is often hair-bearing tissue, it is important to remove any growth from the areas which will wind up inside the vagina. Otherwise, the vagina can become congested with hair, making dilation (a procedure necessary to keep the vagina open) and sexual intercourse uncomfortable and embarrassing (Farrar, 1994). Removal of these hairs is very difficult (and reportedly, painful) after surgery. Unfortunately, surgeons have been remiss in alerting their patients to the need for this. One surgeon, whom we shall not name, remarked in his presentation at the 13th International Symposium on Gender Dysphoria (New York City, October, 1993) that his transsexual patients were so grateful at having surgery that they did not mind having hair in their vaginas. Transsexual women assure us, however, that they *do* mind (Farrar, 1994).

Because many transsexual women are unaware of the problem of hair-bearing vagina, the American Educational Gender Information Service (AE-GIS), released an advisory bulletin in early 1995, designed to educate surgeons, electrologists, and transsexual women about the importance of electrolysis in the pelvic area.

It should be noted that electrolysis in this region is not needed until surgery is on the immediate horizon, by which time most of the facial hair should be removed and the individual should be living and working as a woman. Some individuals will not have hair in the target area, or their hair growth will be so light as to make electrolysis unnecessary. However, because electrolysis is an ongoing procedure, it is important that those with thick hair growth allow sufficient time for clearing the area before the date of surgery. In some cases, this may mean that it is appropriate to start treatment before the advent of full-time cross-living.

The individual who is presenting male with no facial electrolysis or other signs of feminization but insisting on electrolysis in this area should be treated with the same caution as would any male client requesting electrolysis in the genital area. However, the electrologist should keep in mind that many transsexual women do not pass particularly well as women, even after extensive hormonal therapy and electrolysis. Personal knowledge of the individual's life situation can be helpful to the electrologist in making a decision about treatment in the genital area. If in doubt, the electrologist might ask for a letter or phone call from the individual's therapist or support group as a confirmation that the request is genuine.

Many transsexual people are ill-at-ease about their condition, and this can cause apprehension in the electrologist. Such clients may schedule appointments and not show, or, more commonly, may dissemble about their real reasons for having electrolysis. The electrologist may be able to ease the client's apprehension by flatly stating that she treats a number of transsexual clients. This is generally more effective than revealing this information via hints.

The transsexual client may present for treatment looking like any other woman, or looking like an ill-at-ease man in women's clothing, or in male clothing, looking indistinguishable from other men. The electrologist should remember that the distinguishing characteristic in male-to-female transsexualism is not the individual's ability to pass convincingly as a woman, but rather her private view of herself as a woman.

While this study is flawed by lack of objective measurement of hair density in the treated areas, by the fact that some of the subjects had had previous electrolysis, and by our retroactive selection of test subjects, we are happy to present these data. Hopefully, future studies will provide better subject selection and more objective measures of the effectiveness of electrolysis.

SUMMARY

The condition called transsexualism is characterized by the persistent desire to change the primary and secondary sex characteristics to resemble those of the other sex. In sex reassignment, the individual actually does this via a series of procedures which may include electrolysis, hormonal therapy, plastic surgery, voice training, and resocialization. In postpubertal males, facial hair must be removed to facilitate successfully passing as female. This requires the transsexual woman to seek an electrologist. We present data from four male-to-female transsexual subjects, showing the number of hours of treatment across time. Time spent in treatment ranged from 48.5 hours to 105.25 hours (Mean = 67.3 hours, and the time between first and last treatments ranged from 14 to 28 months [Mean = 19.25 months]). Our results suggest that when electrolysis is ongoing for more than 20 hours without significant reduction of the time necessary to clear the face, there should, if the individual's life circumstances permit, be a 2- to 3-month treatment holiday during which progress is evaluated. If treatment is judged to be ineffective, then a change should be made either in electrologist or in the method of treatment. We were unable to obtain an objective measure of hair growth from our clients (e.g., beard-density count). Future studies should include objective measures of effectiveness of electrolysis.

NOTES

1. Many individuals wish to live as members of the sex other than that assigned at birth, but without genital surgery. The lack of a desire to modify the genitals should not be taken as a counterindication for electrolysis or other body-modifying procedures. Nor should an identity not as a woman or man, but as both, or neither, or as a blend of the two be seen as a counterindication for treatment. Also, some individuals have little or no desire to "pass" in society as members of the biological other sex, even though they live their lives in the clothing of that sex. Many postoperative transsexual women have had little or no electrolysis.

2. The lack of the thin, light vellus hairs which women have on their faces and other subtle cues will alert the sophisticated observer.

3. The differential in salaries between males and females can make it difficult for the transsexual woman to afford electrolysis in the new role. Discrimination frequently forces talented and qualified individuals out of their pretransition careers, and makes it difficult for them to find new jobs. The individual whose facial hair or other characteristics makes it difficult to "pass" frequently faces even more discrimination than those who do "pass." Finding themselves unable to get any job whatsoever and

unable to afford electrolysis, even talented and well-educated individuals sometimes find themselves in a downward financial spiral which leaves only sex work as an alternative to homelessness.

4. Aspen (1995) recommends working on the entire face of transsexual clients, clearing beard growth gradually, so that it is not apparent to observers who see hairless patches that the client is having electrolysis. If cost and speed are not a factor, or if security is an issue, this is certainly advisable. However, it is our experience that the kill rate for hairs in the anagen (early growth) phase is markedly higher than for older, more established hairs. The second author's clients are often anxious to be rid of facial hair as rapidly as possible, and have been able to explain the cleared areas without undue difficulty.

REFERENCES

American Psychiatric Association. (1987). *Diagnostic and statistical manual of mental disorders*. DSM III-R. Washington, DC: American Psychiatric Association.

Aspen, B. (1995, February). Electrolysis for transgendered clients. *International Hair Route*, 11, 13, 46.

Bolin, A. (1988). *In search of Eve: Transsexual rites of passage*. South Hadley, MA: Bergin & Garvey Publishers, Inc.

Dupertuis, C.W., Atkinson, W.B., & Elftman, H. (1945). Sex differences in pubic hair distribution. *Human Biology, 17*, 137–142.

Farrar, J. (1994). Letter to the editor. *Chrysalis Quarterly, 1*(7), 7.

Finifter, M.B. (1969). Facial hair: Permanent epilation with respect to the male transsexual. In R. Green & J. Money (Eds.), *Transsexualism and sex reassignment*, pp. 309–312. Baltimore, MD: Johns Hopkins University Press.

Hage, J.J. (1992). *From peniplastica totalis to reassignment surgery of the external genitalia in female-to-male transsexuals*. Amsterdam: Vrieji Universiteit Press.

Laub, D.R. (1985). Metadoioplasty for female-to-male gender dysphorics. Paper presented at the 9th International Symposium on Gender Dysphoria, Minneapolis, MN, September, 1985.

Laub, D.R., Laub, D.R., II, & Biber, S. (1988). Vaginoplasty for gender confirmation. *Clinics in Plastic Surgery, 15*(3), 463–470.

Montagna, W. (1976). General review of the anatomy, growth, and development of hair in Man. In K. Toda, Y. Ishibashi, Y. Hori, & F. Morikawa (Eds.), *Biology and diseases of the hair*. Baltimore, MD: University Park Press.

Prince, V. (1976). *Understanding crossdressing*. Los Angeles: Chevalier Publications.

Prior, J.C., Vigna, Y.M., & Watson, D. (1989). Spironolactone with physiological female steroids for presurgical therapy of male-to-female transsexualism. *Archives of Sexual Behavior, 18*(1), 49–57.

Walker, P.A., Berger, J.C., Green, R., Laub, D.R., Reynolds, C.L., & Wollman, L. (1990). *Standards of care: The hormonal and surgical sex reassignment of gender dysphoric persons*. (1990 Revision). Available from AEGIS, P.O. Box 33724, Decatur, GA 30033.

RELATIONSHIPS WITH TRANSGENDERED MEN

George R. Brown

Over the last 11 years, I have had the privilege of being welcomed into the transgender community in spite of my status as a psychiatrist. I say in spite of, not because of, largely as a result of the grave injustices many transgendered persons have suffered at the hands of some of my ill-informed and, at times, harshly judgmental colleagues. I'm disheartened to say that most of these self-identified patients would have been better served if they had been referred to someone with appropriate knowledge and training in this highly specialized area of human behavior. It was clear from my very first foray into the transgender community (the "CrossPort" support group in Cincinnati, Ohio, in 1985) that cross-dressing men and their spouses (I will use the shorthand notation "spouse" for all women in emotionally committed relationships with a transgendered man) were hungry for knowledge and for legitimate, open-minded inquiry into the phenomenon of cross-dressing. What they usually found when they went to a library was anything but open-minded and was often written by "researchers" who had never spent so much as one evening with a support group anywhere in the country, in spite of the fact that hundreds exist (see Appendix I for a listing of sources for information and support). Papers were written from the perspective of a treating health-care professional sitting behind a desk talking to a self-identified patient. Information was then generalized to the population of cross-dressers and their spouses at large, even though the majority of such individuals never seek psychiatric assistance or identify themselves as patients (Brown, 1995).

I approached the subject of cross-dressers and the women who love them from the entirely naive perspective of an upstate New York suburbanite of the pre-Oprah media era, without preconceived notions of who these people were or what "they" were like. That approach, combined with the inquisitiveness of an unbiased researcher, was appreciated by those in the transgender community and opened many doors for conjoint explora-tion. I took my lead in this endeavor by following the early work of Neil Buhrich, who worked closely with the Seahorse Club in Australia (Buhrich, 1976, 1978). As ground-breaking as Buhrich's work was, however, it was unfortunately limited to men who cross-dressed and largely ignored the spouses in these couples. What was apparent to me, and to most cross-dressers I had met, was that there was nothing in the research literature that valued representativeness as a guiding principle in understanding any-thing about women who choose cross-dressers as mates (or choose to stay with a man they later discover is a cross-dresser). Those who turned to the literature for guidance were treated to tales of women described as "mali-cious male haters" and "succorers" who later married transgendered men (Stoller, 1967). They read about these women's "moral masochism" (Stoller, 1967) and how these women had such low self-esteem that they had no choice but to "settle for a transvestite" mate in lieu of lifelong lone-liness (Wise, Dupkin, & Meyer, 1981). Talking with spouses in nonclinical, nonthreatening settings was all that was required to see that the literature was highly skewed in the direction of psychopathology and did little jus-tice to the majority of women in such relationships, who appeared much healthier than the literature would suggest and were eager to learn about themselves. In short, my nonclinical experiences with women associated with cross-dressing men stood in sharp contrast to what was published and I was dismayed by the lack of even one basic, descriptive study of a large group of women in such relationships. One could also make a case that the existing literature was potentially damaging to these couples in its in-appropriate generalizations and unsupported conclusions and did nothing to facilitate the process of communication and self-disclosure so vital to these relationships.

Just as transsexualism cannot be fully addressed without an intimate understanding of transvestism and other forms of transgenderism, men who cross-dress cannot be understood in any three-dimensional way without appreciating their relationships with women. Women are a central focus in both fantasy and reality, hence "femmiphilia" (Prince, 1967).[1] As in other areas of scientific inquiry (e.g., women infected with HIV; Brown, 1993), the genetic female half of a couple with a societally designated male "pa-tient" has been largely ignored in most research efforts. As transgendered men continue to "come out" in greater numbers, their spouses have gener-ally been left behind to keep the closet warm.

Legitimate, population-based research into a controversial life-style plays a critical role in the eventual societal acceptance (or tolerance) of a stigmatized population. Clearly, women who choose to remain in relationships with transgendered men are the subject of derision from many fronts, not the least of which includes women in relationships with "normal" men. The overriding question posed by many women I met in transgender support groups was "Who are we? Are there others like us?"

TABLE 21.1. Top Twenty Concerns Expressed by Women in Relationships with Cross-Dressing Men

I. Meaning for (or impact on) her:

1. Am I a lesbian?
2. What's wrong with *me* that he would have these wishes to dress as a woman?
3. Am I going to lose my mate (to sex change) if I accept this, or if I don't accept this (through divorce)?
4. I'm jealous of what "she" gets (time, clothes, makeup, etc.).
5. Who can I share my feelings with? I must be the only one!

II. Meaning for (or impact on) the family:

6. What should we tell the kids about this?
7. If our sons know about this, will they grow up the same?
8. Money and time spent on "her" is lost to the family.
9. What will happen to us if he is discovered/caught?
10. What will my parents and friends think if they find out?

III. Meaning for my husband:

11. Is he gay/bisexual?
12. Will this behavior progress to sex-change surgery?
13. If I encourage him to explore femininity, will he get out of control? Are support groups dangerous because they allow self-indulgence?
14. Does this urge to cross-dress ever go away? (Is there a cure?)

IV. Meaning for (impact on) our relationship:

15. He can't be trusted—he hid this from me for years.
16. If he hid this, what else has he lied about?
17. What other "perverted" things is he interested in?
18. How will this affect our sexual relationship?
19. Will our relationship become centered around cross-dressing activities (do I have to shop with/for "her")?
20. I married a *man*—I didn't get what I bargained for!

Table 21.1 describes the "Top Twenty" concerns expressed by women spontaneously and repeatedly during informal discussion groups throughout the country. Indeed, the first step in the research process seeking to learn about any population (and to develop answers for these questions and concerns) is descriptive in nature and must precede any conclusions that seek to answer "why?"

In the remainder of this chapter, I will present data from the largest and most representative descriptive study completed to date on women in relationships with transgendered men. Prior studies have derived from second-hand reports from cross-dressers themselves (Prince & Bentler, 1972; Bullough & Weinberg, 1988), or from clinical samples where one or both partners were identified as psychiatric patients (Stoller, 1967; Calogeras, 1987; Wise & Meyer, 1980; Wise, Dupkin, & Meyer, 1981; Wise, 1985). The few published studies that have sought to more adequately characterize women partners (most of whom are believed to never assume the role of "patient"; Woodhouse, 1985) have been limited by small sample size (Docter, 1988; Brown & Collier, 1989) or a lack of interview data to supplement self-report questionnaire data (Weinberg & Bullough, 1988; Bullough & Weinberg, 1988). The study that follows addresses the limitations of small sample size, "patient status" bias, and the lack of interview data in previous studies. Such information should add to understanding the phenomena of "stigma management" (Goffman, 1963) in the context of nonnormative dyadic relationships (Bullough & Weinberg, 1988). The data are also of potential value for the clinician who may be called upon to provide psychoeducational support, marital therapy, or individual counseling for such women (Brown, 1990, 1995).

Over a 6-year period, 106 women completed a 4-page, open-ended questionnaire regarding various aspects of their lives in a committed or exclusive relationship with a heterosexual, cross-dressing male (Brown, 1994). Participants were assured of confidentiality in their responses. No respondents were approached in a clinical setting, and none were receiving treatment in my clinical practice. Recruitment for this study came from two general settings:

1. Confidential monthly discussion groups for spouses or girlfriends affiliated with a support/social club for transgendered males (CrossPort, Cincinnati, OH: N = 7; Boulton and Park Society, San Antonio, TX: N = 25)

2. National conventions for transgendered men and their partners. I attended these events as an invited speaker and I was granted permission to both address the group and meet with wives for the purposes

of recruitment (Fantasia Fair, Provincetown, MA, 1990, N = 4; Texas "T" Party, San Antonio, TX, 1990–1992, N = 44)

I also distributed materials to the CD partners of women not in attendance at several conventions so that they could return their responses by mail (N = 26). Thus, 25 percent of the total sample did not have a personal interview and presumably sampled the population of women who would not appear publicly with their CD mate. The return rate of usable responses was 100 percent for women attending the discussion groups, as completing the forms was incorporated into the structure and discussions taking place during such informal meetings. Approximately 50 percent of the questionnaires otherwise distributed were completed; one was rejected for the purposes of this study because the respondent's partner was described as a postoperative female-to-male transsexual.

After basic descriptive information was obtained, the four-page questionnaire pursued preliminary findings and hypotheses raised by other investigators in this area: e.g., are women associated with cross-dressing mates more likely to have had homosexual experiences than other demographically similar American women? Are women in such relationships supportive of their cross-dressing partners if they choose somatic treatments associated with gender dysphoria? Are these women more likely to forgo childbearing than other age-matched American women? In addition to forced-choice questions, participants were afforded the opportunity to respond in an open-ended fashion, supplementing the questionnaire with lengthy additional responses and extensive elaboration.

The data collected were analyzed in a variety of ways. Where possible, cumulative responses were compared to published data from cross-sectional or large population surveys of American women using age-matched data when available. T-tests of proportions were conducted, two-tailed, with the acceptable Type I error rate set at $p = 0.05$. A RIDIT analysis (Fleiss, 1981; "relative to an identified distribution") was conducted to compare participant's birth-order data to that of the American population.

The demographic characteristics of the women in this study are recorded in Table 22.2. Marital status is divided into seven mutually exclusive categories that more adequately characterize the current status of their relationships than the traditional four categories. Nearly three-quarters of the women were married to their cross-dressing mate at the time of their participation in this study. Those in the divorced and separated categories were dating cross-dressing men who had never been their husbands; "widowed" refers to women whose previous non–cross-dressing spouse had died.

357

Variable	Value	%	n	Range
Age	40 years (avg.)			19–69
Height	64 inches (avg.)			54–72
Weight	142 pounds (avg.)			90–280
Years education	15 years (avg.) (58%>2-year degree)			8–21
Marriage number	1			0–4
Race/Ethnicity	Caucasian	97	103	
	Hispanic	3	3	
Religion	Protestant	42	45	
	Catholic	23	23	
	Christian	5	5	
	Jewish	5	5	
	Other	1	1	
	None	26	27	
Marital Status (mutually exclusive categories)				
	Married	74	78	
	Single	8	8	
	Divorced	5	5	
	Cohabitating	6	6	
	Engaged	3	3	
	Separated	2	2	
	Widowed	4	4	
Birth Order	1	54	57	
	2	25	27	
	3	10	11	
	≥4	10	11	
Number of Children	0	44	47	
	1	14	15	
	2	27	29	
	3	11	12	
	≥4	3	3	

TABLE 21.2. Sociodemographic Characteristics: (n = 106) Cross-Dressers' Partners

"Single" refers to never-married women in committed relationships with cross-dressing men.

The distribution of birth order in Table 21.2 is listed for natural sibships (born to same mother). As noted, these data appear to be skewed to the firstborn position. Therefore, this hypothesis was tested by comparing this distribution to birth-order data for white women delivering live infants in 1989, using the same four sibship categories (first, second, third, and fourth or higher). RIDIT analysis resulted in a mean RIDIT of 0.44 (z = 2.143; p = 0.03, two-tailed), indicating that women in this study were more likely to be firstborn than randomly selected individuals in the US. If birth data for 1950 were utilized, the predominance of firstborn women would be even more pronounced due to the much larger sibships of American families at that time, especially in the "four or more" category (*Monthly Vital Statistics Report*, 1991).

Respondents hailed from 25 different states and one Canadian province. The middle Southwest (all major Texas cities, Arizona, Louisiana), the Midwest, and the Northeast regions of the United States were broadly represented. The overrepresentation of Texas (38 percent of the group) is accounted for by the recruitment procedure, relying heavily upon the Texas "T" Party, the largest worldwide event for transgendered men and their spouses, held yearly in San Antonio. Forty percent (N = 42) of the women knew of their partner's cross-dressing before describing their relationship as "committed." The average duration of the relationships was 13.1 years (range 2 weeks to 46 years; only three women reported relationships of less than 1 year), while the average length of knowledge of their partner's cross-dressing was 8.9 years (range 2 weeks to 38 years). Cross-dressing in the woman's presence was reported by 94 percent (N = 100), with a wide frequency range ("daily" to "rarely"). An average frequency of once per week or more was reported by 50 percent (N = 53).

Limited personal and family psychiatric history data were obtained. Formal psychiatric treatment was received by one or more first-degree family members in 57 percent of participants' families (N = 60). Twenty-three percent (N = 24) of women reported their parents divorced while they were young. A small minority of participants (12 percent; N = 13) or their cross-dressing mates (17 percent; N = 18) were currently involved in mental-health treatment. However, 38 percent (N = 40) of women had received such treatment at some time during their lives. Regarding lifetime history of substance-use disorders, 6 percent (N = 6) of women self-reported problems with alcohol and/or drugs. Eighteen percent (N = 19) indicated that their cross-dressing mate had had such problem(s) during his lifetime. By way of comparison, the Epidemiologic Catchment Area surveys of the 1980s (Robbins & Regier, 1991) revealed that 16.5 percent of American men in the 18–44-year-old group (N = 5, 119) met Diagnostic Interview Schedule criteria for alcohol-use disorders. No statistical difference exists between these lifetime preva-lences and the present sample (z = .004; p = .99).

Nearly half of the women (48 percent; N = 51) reported that their part-ner had cross-dressed for at least one sexual encounter during their relation-ship. Of these, 39 percent (N = 20) reported that they were at least sometimes sexually aroused by their partner's cross-dressing. This was an unexpected find-ing and has not been mentioned in any prior research into this subject. Inter-estingly, 26 percent (N = 7) of the women who reported sexual arousal (N = 27) did *not* indicate that their partner ever cross-dressed for lovemaking.

Twelve women (11 percent) reported one or more homosexual expe-riences in their lifetime. Large surveys of the sexual behavior of American women (Kinsey, et al., 1953, N = 5940; Davis, 1929, N = 2200) were used for comparison to determine if this figure represented a significant departure from population norms. Kinsey, et al. reported that 19 percent of all adult women in their survey had had at least one episode of physical contact with a female which was "deliberately and consciously . . . intended to be sexual" (p. 453). By age 40, 12 percent (N = 33) of the subgroup of white women with 13–16 years of education (N = 272) reported one or more homosexual experiences culminating in orgasm (Kinsey, et al., 1953). This subgroup ap-proximates the demographic characteristics of the women in this study. No significant difference was noted in this comparison (z = 0.276, p = .78). Simi-larly, Davis found that 20 percent of women surveyed reported at least one same-sex experience by the age of 36, a finding also consistent with the re-sults of this study.

Participants reported that 21 percent (N = 22) of their cross-dress-ing partners experienced erectile dysfunction on at least an occasional basis during sexual encounters. Anonymous surveys of men regarding their sexu-ality indicate that at least 64 percent respond that they have experienced erectile difficulty during their lifetimes (Hite, 1981). Differences in method-ologies do not allow for direct comparisons of these data.

Regarding other partner behaviors, the women indicated that 17 per-cent (N = 18) of their partners had had one or more extrarelationship sexual encounters ("affairs") known to them. This result is not statistically differ-ent from that reported in anonymous surveys of male sexuality (22 percent; Hite, 1981; z = 1.35, p = .17).

For women who had seen their partners cross-dressed (94 percent; N = 100), 45 percent (N = 45) subjectively felt that he spent an inordinate amount of time in front of the mirror while cross-dressed.

Forty-four percent of the women in this study (N = 47) reported that they had never had children. The average age of childless women was 37.8 years (37 percent were less than 40 years old; 11 percent were less than 30 years old). Comparable data for white adult women up to age 35 in the United States for 1989 (N = 1,461,126), the midpoint of this study's data collection period, was 20 percent (*Monthly Vital Statistics Report*, 1991). Even if we assume that none of the American-population women had children after age 35 (an unrealistic assumption made simply to maximize the potential size of the American childless group), the women in relationships with cross-dressers are significantly less likely to have had children during their lifetimes (z = 3.52; p < .001).

Thirty-six percent (N = 38) of couples had one or more of their children under the age of 25 living at home. One-third of women (34 percent; N = 34) reported that their children (or their partner's children) were aware of their partner's cross-dressing activities, most often by being told about this and not by inadvertent discovery.

Few participants (13 percent; N = 14) reported they had ever dressed a boy in female attire; the majority of these occasions were related to Halloween parties. Three mothers, all of whom had told their children about their father's cross-dressing, reported that their young sons spontaneously cross-dressed on more than one occasion without assistance or overt encouragement from either parent. This question was asked because of the often-quoted, but rarely encountered, "petticoat punishment" of young males by adult women in an attempt to humiliate them for a childhood indiscretion, touted by Stoller as an important etiological consideration in the development of transvestism (Stoller, 1966).

The participants were extensively queried regarding their acceptance of their partners' crossgender interests and activities. Early after discovery, 25 percent (N = 27) believed that a "cure" could be found for cross-dressing interests. However, a current belief in a cure was reported by only two women (2 percent); they had known of their partner's cross-dressing behaviors for 10 and 3 years, respectively.

Thirty-two percent of participants (N = 34) indicated they had "seriously considered" either divorce or separation from their partners based wholly, or substantially, on his crossgender interests/activities. A minority (22 percent; N = 23) would support their partner if he chose to pursue feminizing somatic treatments (estrogen treatments or sex-reassignment surgery [SRS]); 15 percent (N = 16) were undecided on this issue. Twenty-five percent (N = 27) of the men had expressed a wish for such treatment(s) to their wives (often a transient wish with no intentions of actually seeking treatment). Fewer still were those women who believed their partners would ever pursue SRS (4 percent; N = 4), whether or not they were still together in the future.

Finally, women were asked to summarize their own overall level of acceptance of their partner's cross-dressing activities. Forty-four percent (N = 47) thought they should be more accepting, 8 percent (N = 9) rated themselves as "too accepting," and 42 percent (N = 44) believed no change was indicated (6 percent, N = 6, were "undecided").

Three levels of acceptance (low, moderate, high) of cross-dressing activities were determined by responses to two key questions: (1) "Did you ever *seriously consider* divorce or separation from your partner *because of his cross-dressing?* and (2) the global self-rating of tolerance/acceptance described above, focusing on *current* self-assessment of her partner's cross-dressing activities.

Those who considered divorce/separation *and* who evaluated themselves as less tolerant/accepting were rated as "low acceptors" (N = 20). Those who never considered divorce/separation and who provided self-ratings of "accepting" or "over-indulgent" were considered "high acceptors" (N = 41). "Moderate acceptors" comprised those who had never considered divorce/separation but indicated a desire to be more tolerant/accepting (N = 26). The following seven dichotomous variables were hypothesized to be associated with level of acceptance and tested against the overall sample proportions: being firstborn, having no children, knowing about cross-dressing before feeling "committed," high exposure to cross-dressing (at least once per week), presence of sexual arousal to cross-dressing, cross-dressing for lovemaking, and having a cross-dressing mate who spends a lot of time admiring himself in the mirror while cross-dressed (high "mirror time" vs. low mirror time).

Low acceptors, compared to other women in the sample, were characterized by a lack of sexual arousal to cross-dressing (5 percent; $z = 3.11$, $p = .002$), learning of her mate's cross-dressing after establishing a committed relationship (80 percent; $z = 1.974$, $p = .04$), and the absence of cross-dressing for lovemaking (10 percent; $z = 7.11$, $p < .0001$). Moderate acceptors were far more likely to report sexual arousal to cross-dressing (50 percent; $z = 2.343$, $p = .02$) and the presence of cross-dressing activities during lovemaking (69 percent; $z = 2.041$, $p = .04$). High acceptors, the largest subgroup, were not more likely to be characterized by any of the seven variables than the group as a whole, indicating that this subgroup's characteristics closely tracked those of the entire population.

Having been firstborn, reporting high exposure to cross-dressing activities, high mirror time, and never having had children were not factors that were statistically associated with level of acceptance, although a trend was noted for moderate acceptors to be firstborn (73 percent; $z = 1.907$, $p = .056$).

To place these results on women into context, it is helpful to know something about the sociodemographics of their cross-dressing mates. For example, Steiner & Bernstein (1981) have previously described a group of women married to female-to-male transsexuals, reporting very different results from those described herein. The vast majority of the male partners of women in this study are heterosexual cross-dressers and not men with fixed gender-identity disorders or those living full-time in a female gender role (transgenderists). Evidence to support this contention can be found in the responses to questions regarding desire for somatic treatments for gender dysphoria and the assessment by 96 percent of the women that they did not believe their mate would ever request SRS, even if she did not present an obstacle to this treatment path. Further, this study's recruitment settings specifically catered to the needs of heterosexual cross-dressers and offered relatively fewer activities for transsexuals. A parallel study of cross-dressing men, in preparation, including most of the partners of the women in this study and conducted during a similar time frame (from the same nonclinical settings) indicates that the following demographic characteristics applied to the men: average age was 43.7 years (s.d. = 10.9); 13 percent were currently in mental-health treatment; 53 percent were Protestant, 30 percent Catholic, 4 percent Jewish; average educational attainment was 15.4 years (median = 16.0).

DISCUSSION

Participants in this nonclinical study were likely to be 40–year-old, once-married white women with some college education who were slightly overweight for their average height of 5 ft. 4 in. They were more likely than other American women to be both firstborn and childless, but no more likely to have had lesbian experiences or substance-use disorders than comparably aged American women.

Like Docter's sample of 35 women (Docter, 1988), this description could be criticized as being more representative of partners who are positively disposed to their mates' cross-dressing activities. Intuitively, one would expect that women who appear with their cross-dressed partner in public to attend a cross-dressing social function would be accepting of this behavior and that recruitment for participation in this study would necessarily be biased. However, attendance at a monthly cross-dressing social gathering or an occasional multiday convention in a distant city is not always associated with high, or even moderate, acceptance. Some women attend the functions largely to participate in the "parallel track" limited to wives and female partners and specifically designed for mutual support, "ventilation," and education about cross-dressing issues. Heavy reliance on data gathered from open-ended discussion groups actually could have resulted in an oversampling of angry, hostile, and misinformed women, rather than those who have incorporated this activity into their life-style and experience no need to attend such groups or "parallel tracks." We are also reminded that nearly one-quarter of the responses came from women who did not appear in public with their husbands cross-dressed. Given that a great many women in relationships with cross-dressers neither seek psychiatric care nor participate in any activities related to cross-dressing (including anonymous survey research), any discussion of the sociodemographic representativeness of this group remains speculative. What seems likely, however, is that in comparison to any other published study of spouses, this approach yielded the widest cross-section of this population to date. I would hope that future attempts go beyond what was possible in this work and use methods that further reach those deepest in the closet.

Furthermore, a large subgroup of the subjects were "newcomers" to the cross-dressing subculture and sought out the discussion groups (as advertised in local newspapers and national newsletters catering to transgendered men or their female partners, e.g., *Gender Euphoria* and *Partner's* newsletter [Boulton and Park Society, San Antonio]) for the purposes of mutual support, information, and airing of negative feelings regarding cross-dressing. Many of these women participated in the study while distressed, confused, or angry. Subsequent follow-up in discussion groups over the ensuing 4–6 years clearly indicated that most women developed very different views/attitudes towards cross-dressing, due in part to the dispelling of myths and misinformation, reassessment of the relationship, and broader participation in cross-dressing social activities. Discussion groups often focused on one or more of the concerns listed in Table 21.1, with significant input by women in the group and not just by the facilitator. The overall trend observed was for greater acceptance over time, assuming that the woman obtained accurate information and access to other women living in similar circumstances. The moderate-acceptance group appears to include a number of such women "in transition" from a previous position of low acceptance. There was no attempt to readminister the questionnaire prospectively; therefore some of the cross-sectional data presented should be considered state, rather than trait, information.

The finding that 44 percent of women had never had children confirms previous reports (e.g., Talamini, 1982: 41 percent of 50 women). The specific reasons for choosing, or not being able, to conceive were not systematically addressed in this study. However, many women indicated that they made a conscious decision not to have children because of the complexity of their relationship with a cross-dressing mate and a desire to avoid having to keep cross-dressing activities hidden from children within their own homes. Others noted that there are no sources of information or studies that address the impact of cross-dressing activities on children, and they felt "lost" without some guidance on this issue (about one-half of those with children chose to tell them).

Decrying the absence of data, Docter has speculated that the "risk of giving young children information about the cross-dressing of the father seems to be far greater than any good which could be served by being 'open and honest'" (Docter, 1988, p.175). Based on anecdotal reports from 13 couples who had chosen to inform their children, Talamini concluded that no harm was apparent and that no cross-dressing by sons was reported. In contrast, three women in the present study reported spontaneous cross-dressing in latency-age boys who were aware of their father's cross-dressing activities. Such behavior could represent the onset of gender-identity disorder of childhood, early transvestism, or the first manifestations of a homosexual sexual identity (Zuger, 1988, 1989), or simply parental identification and modeling. In the absence of any other symptoms of gender-identity disorder or gender nonconformity, it is likely that such behavior represents a short-lived identification phase. Longitudinal studies have explored adolescent and early adulthood outcomes of childhood gender nonconformity in families without transgendered fathers (Green, 1985, 1987; Zuger, 1989). Although there are some case reports of transvestism occurring in families across generational lines (e.g., Buhrich, 1977), there is no convincing statistical evidence that it "runs in families" at rates that exceed what would be expected by chance alone.

Prospective studies of the adult outcomes of children with cross-dressing fathers are essential to help women in such relationships make informed reproductive decisions. These long-term studies are obviously difficult to accomplish.

It has been previously hypothesized that women who marry transvestites suffer from markedly low self-esteem (Feinbloom, 1976) and "moral masochism" (Stoller, 1967). Further, they have been described as having character styles "rich in dependency," choosing to settle for, and stay with, a cross-dressing mate as preferable to painful loss and loneliness (Wise,

Dupkin, & Meyer, 1981). Although this hypothesis has been challenged by work conducted in nonclinical settings (Docter, 1988; Brown & Collier, 1989), no direct assessment of self-esteem (e.g., the Tennessee Self Concept Scale, Roid & Fitts, 1988) in female partners of cross-dressing men has been completed. The data in this study, coupled with many years of contact with spouses, suggests to me that inadequate self-esteem and overwhelming dependency are not general characteristics of such women. The women in this study were far more likely to be firstborn than other American cohorts. Being firstborn in a sibship in Western culture has been associated with a number of characteristics, including higher educational and occupational achievement (Fullerton, et al., 1989; Marjoribanks, 1987), independent approach to problems (Hardman, Hoopes, & Harper, 1987), and adequate to enhanced self-esteem compared to later-born siblings (Falbo, 1981; Heer, 1986). Strachan (1980) studied ordinal position specifically in women and provided support for the notion that firstborn status is associated with more negative reactions to personal failure than younger female siblings. Aversion to failure may provide additional motivation to succeed or excel.

In addition to birth-order data, high average educational and occupational attainment and low lifetime prevalence of substance-use disorders (often associated with demoralization and negative self-concept) together lend little support to the speculation that these women, as a group, have poor self-esteem or must "settle" for a cross-dressing mate. Additionally, at least one study has demonstrated that low self-esteem and low contraceptive use by women are highly correlated (Hayes, 1987). The finding of a high proportion of childless women in the sample is presumptive evidence that these women have engaged in sustained, effective contraception. Last, observations made during extended interviews with a subset of this group do not indicate a preponderance of dependency, overtly apparent inadequate self-esteem, or generalized self-defeating behavior similar to that discussed for small clinical samples (Stoller, 1967; Wise, Dupkin, & Meyer, 1981). It is reasonable to tentatively conclude that inadequate self-esteem, although inevitably present in some of the women in this group (as in virtually any other group this large), is not a construct that generally describes women associated with cross-dressing mates when such individuals are observed in the nonclinical setting. It remains possible that the observations of impaired self-esteem noted by Stoller, Wise, and others are applicable to the minority of women in such relationships who seek psychiatric care.

An alternative explanation to deficient self-esteem would be that these women have high levels of openness, a personality trait that fosters novel ideas and rejection of rigid stereotypes. Openness is one of the five factors in a comprehensive trait taxonomy of personality (Costa & McCrae, 1985) and merits study as a nonpsychopathological element inherent in such relationships.

The birth-order data reported above may also be relevant in addressing the question of why such women choose a cross-dressing mate, whether or not they are consciously aware of the presence of this behavior. As noted, 60 percent of the women did not know that their partner engaged in cross-dressing activities at the time they considered themselves to be emotionally committed to the relationship. One woman, at two different times in her life, unknowingly married two transvestites, neither of whom informed her of their cross-dressing until many years into the relationships. Sutton and McIntire (1977), using the Eysenck Personality Inventory, reported that firstborn females scored high in neuroticism. Schachter (1959) similarly reported that young adult firstborn females are more anxious, neurotic, and stressed than their siblings. These women may therefore be attracted to partners who have increased capacities for soothing and other "traditionally feminine" interpersonal characteristics, e.g., warmth, tenderness, understanding, and empathy. Women married to cross-dressing mates often report that those features are very attractive to them and are present in their husbands, at least during the time they engage in cross-dressing activities (Docter, 1988). An obvious, but untested, hypothesis is that some of these women are unconsciously selecting a transgendered partner (even in the absence of knowledge of this status) because he has the tender interpersonal qualities that complement her needs. This could hardly be viewed as a psychopathological consideration in the vast majority of women who are attracted to these characteristics in a partner.

One of the notable findings of this study is that women who are in long-term relationships with cross-dressing mates display a wide range of acceptance of such behaviors, and that certain identifiable characteristics are associated with the degree of acceptance. A previous report detailing the first seven consecutive participants in this study (Brown & Collier, 1989) suggested that learning of her mate's CD interests after feeling committed in the relationship was associated with significant difficulties in accepting, or even tolerating, such behaviors. Talamini's group of 50 wives comprised 40 percent who did not accept this behavior; not surprisingly, 69 percent did not know they had married a cross-dressing man until after the wedding (Talamini, 1982). The finding that 80 percent of the low acceptors were not told (or did not discover) that their mate cross-dressed is strong support for the critical role such information plays in these relationships. The issues of betrayal and lost trust ("What else hasn't he told me?") were recurrent themes that were major obstacles to intimacy in relationships between low acceptors and cross-dressing men.

Previous work with partners of cross-dressing men has suggested that narcissism and self-centeredness, not cross-dressing per se, are often important determinants of stability in some of these relationships (Wise, Dupkin, & Meyer, 1981; Docter, 1988). Excessive self-admiration, in the mirror and otherwise, was cited by Talamini as a major problem for nonaccepting wives. As a surrogate marker of narcissism in men not interviewed for this study, 45 percent of the women indicated that their mate spent an inordinate amount of time "primping" and admiring himself in the mirror while cross-dressed. As noted, this behavior was not associated with level of acceptance in this study, and may not be an adequately sensitive probe for self-centeredness. However, individual interviews frequently revealed the importance of narcissism (e.g., wanting the glamour of femininity and not the work or responsibilities associated with the gender role; excessive purchases of clothes, makeup, accessories for "her" at the expense of family, etc.) as an important factor in their overall acceptance of, and participation in, cross-dressing activities.

Sexual arousal by her mate's cross-dressing, at least occasionally, was reported by a quarter of these women. As noted, this finding has not been previously reported, as all other studies have focused on the majority of women who are "typically turned off in the presence of a cross-dressed husband" (Docter, 1988, p.176). It is not surprising that arousal to cross-dressing was reported by only one of the low acceptors, whereas 36 percent of those rated as moderate or high acceptors reported arousal. Docter (1988) aptly noted that attention to sexuality and the sexual adjustment of women in relationships with transgendered men has been minimal. He further hypothesized that women who choose cross-dressing mates are likely to be sexually reserved, conventional, "attentive mothering types" who are unlikely to entertain the thought of including cross-dressing activities as part of their sexual repertoire (Docter, 1988). Although this description may be applicable to those women in this study considered low acceptors, the finding that nearly one-third of the others (26 of 86; 30 percent) report arousal and a majority of both moderate and high acceptors (61 percent of 67) have engaged in sexual activity while their mate was cross-dressed, broadens our understanding of the sexual openness, resiliency, and diversity presented by many women. A future study involving a subset of this population seeks to further understand their sexual functioning by examining their responses on the Derogatis Sexual Functioning Inventory (Derogatis & Melisaretas, 1979).

CONCLUSION

This report about women recruited from nonclinical settings involved in committed relationships with predominantly heterosexual cross-dressers yields results quite different from studies conducted with patient samples. It was undertaken to address the descriptive questions ("Who are they?") that had never been systematically addressed in a manner approaching representativeness. Since only a small minority of cross-dressing men or their partners seek mental-health treatment, this study group may approximate the sociodemographic features of most women involved in committed relationships with cross-dressing men (nontranssexual cross-dressers/transvestites).

In my many years of contact with the transgendered subculture, I have been struck by the tenacity and longevity of these unconventional relationships and the fact that over two-thirds of the women never seriously considered divorce or separation because of their partner's cross-dressing (in spite of receiving strong advice from family and/or friends to do so). In fact, I have encountered very few women who have divorced cross-dressers, and this subgroup of women is entirely undescribed in either the lay or professional literature. Docter concluded that the women in his study were "an unremarkable group of women who unexpectedly found themselves in a marriage with a transvestite husband" (Docter, 1988, p.192). Although a similar conclusion cannot be reached from this descriptive study alone, a follow-up study of a subset of this group will address both psychometric properties and global sexual functioning as compared to "unremarkable" age- and education-matched women. This work has already been completed for their cross-dressing mates (Brown, Wise, Costa, et al., 1996). My impression as a long-term student of transgender phenomena is consistent with Docter's comment—however, with the exception that I often found such women remarkable for their warmth, openness, and caring attitude towards others. They have welcomed me into the most intimate recesses of their lives, in nonclinical contexts, in an attempt to understand themselves and to help others in similar life situations. Their contribution has been important, and many women and clinicians in the future will benefit from their generosity.

NOTES

1. Prince (1967) coined the term "femmiphilia" to describe the love for women and all things feminine, which characterizes many cross-dressing men.

REFERENCES

American Psychiatric Association. (1987). *Diagnostic and statistical manual of mental disorders*. DSM III-R. Washington, DC: American Psychiatric Association.

Brown, G.R. (1990). The transvestite husband. *Medical Aspects of Human Sexuality*, 24, 35–42.

Brown, G.R. (1993). A prospective study of psychiatric aspects of early HIV disease in women. *General Hospital Psychiatry*, 15, 139–147.

Brown, G.R. (1994). 106 women in relationships with cross-dressing men: A descriptive study from a nonclinical setting. *Archives of Sexual Behavior*, 23, 515–530.

Brown, G.R. (1995). Transvestism. In G.O. Gabbard (Ed.), *Treatments of psychiatric disorders: The DSM-IV edition*. Washington, DC: American Psychiatric Press.

Brown, G.R., & Collier L. (1989). Transvestites' women revisited: A nonpatient sample. *Archives of Sexual Behavior, 18*, 73–83.

Brown, G.R., Wise, T., Costa, P., Herbst, J., Fagan, P., & Schmidt, C. (1996). Personality characteristics and sexual functioning of 188 cross-dressing men. *Journal of Nervous and Mental Disease, 184*, 265–273.

Buhrich, N. (1976). A heterosexual transvestite club: Psychiatric aspects. *Australian and New Zealand Journal of Psychiatry, 10*(4), 331–335.

Buhrich, N. (1977b). A case of familial heterosexual transvestism. *Acta Psychiatrica Scandinavica, 55*(3), 199–201.

Buhrich, N. (1978). Motivation for cross-dressing in heterosexual transvestism. *Acta Psychiatrica Scandinavica, 57*(2), 145–152.

Bullough, V.L., & Weinberg, T.S. (1988). Women married to transvestites: Problems and adjustments. *Journal of Psychology and Human Sexuality, 1*(2), 83–104.

Calogeras, R.C. (1987). The transvestite and his wife. *Psychoanalytic Review, 74*(4), 517–535.

Costa, P., & McCrae, R. (1985). *The NEO Personality Inventory manual*. Odessa, FL: Psychological Assessment Resources.

Davis, K.B. (1929). *Factors in the sex life of twenty-two hundred women*. New York: Harper & Brothers.

Derogatis, L., & Melisaretas, N. (1979). The DSFI: A multidimensional measure of sexual functioning. *Journal of Sex and Marital Therapy, 5*, 244–281.

Docter, R. (1988). *Transvestites and transsexuals: Toward a theory of cross-gender behavior*. New York: Plenum Press.

Falbo, T. (1981). Relationships between birth category, achievement, and interpersonal orientation. *Journal of Personality and Social Psychology, 41*(1), 121–131.

Feinbloom, D. (1976). *Transvestites and transsexuals: Mixed views*. New York: Delacorte Press.

Fleiss, J. (1981). *Statistical methods for rates and proportions*, 2nd ed. New York: Wiley & Sons.

Fullerton, C., Ursano, R., Wetzler, H., & Slusarcick, A. (1989). Birth order, psychological well-being, and social supports in young adults. *Journal of Nervous and Mental Disease, 177*(9), 556–559.

Goffman, E. (1963). *Stigma: Notes on the management of spoiled identity*. Englewood Cliffs, NJ: Prentice-Hall.

Green, R. (1985). Gender identity in childhood and later sexual orientation: Follow-up of 78 males. *American Journal of Psychiatry, 142*(3), 339–341.

Green, R. (1987). *The "sissy boy syndrome" and the development of homosexuality*. New Haven, CT: Yale University Press.

Hardman, R., Hoopes, M., & Harper, J. (1987). Verbal interaction styles of two marital combinations: Based on a systems approach to sibling positions. *American Journal of Family Therapy, 15*(2), 131–144.

Hayes, C.D. (1987). *Risking the future: Adolescent sexuality, pregnancy, and childbearing*. Washington, DC: National Academy Press.

Heer, D. (1986). Effect of number, order, and spacing of siblings on child and adult outcomes: An overview of current research. *Sociology and Biology, 33*, 1–4.

Hite, S. (1976). *The Hite report*. New York: Dell.

Hite, S. (1981). *The Hite report on male sexuality*. New York: Alfred A. Knopf.

Kinsey, A., Pomeroy, W., Martin, C., & Gebhard, P. (1953). *Sexual behavior in the human female*. Philadelphia: W.B. Saunders.

Marjoribanks, K. (1987). Birth order and sibsize correlates of educational attainment and occupational status. *Psychological Reports, 61*, 147–150.

McConaghy, N. (1982). Sexual deviation. In A. Bellack, M. Hersen, & A. Kazdin

(Eds.). *International handbook of behavior modification and therapy*. New York: Plenum Press.

National Center for Health Statistics. (1991). *Monthly vital statistics report: Advance report of final natality statistics, 1989, 40*(8), 4.

Prince, C.V. (1967). *The transvestite and his wife*. Los Angeles: Argyle Books.

Prince, C.V., & Bentler, P.M. (1972). Survey of 504 cases of transvestism. *Psychological Reports, 31*(3), 903–917.

Robbins, L.N., & Regier, D.A. (Eds.). (1991). *Psychiatric disorders in America: The epidemiologic catchment area study*. New York: The Free Press.

Roid, G., & Fitts, W. (1988). *Manual for the Tennessee Self Concept Scale*. Los Angeles, CA: Western Psychological Services.

Schacter, S. (1959). *The psychology of affiliation: Experimental studies of the sources of gregariousness*. Palo Alto, CA: Stanford University Press.

Steiner, B., & Bernstein, S. (1981). Female-to-male transsexuals and their partners. *Canadian Journal of Psychiatry, 26*, 178–182.

Stoller, R. (1966). The mother's contribution to infantile transvestic behavior. *International Journal of Psychoanalysis, 47*, 384–395.

Stoller, R. (1967). Transvestites' women. *American Journal of Psychiatry, 124*, 89–95.

Strachan, N. (1980). The relationship between ordinal position, reaction to failure, and anger toward mother among first and second-born females. *Dissertation Abstractions International, 42/03-B*, 1194.

Sutton, J., & McIntire, W. (1977). Relationship of ordinal position and sex in neuroticism in adults. *Psychological Reports, 41*, 843–846.

Talamini, J.T. (1982). *Boys will be girls: The hidden world of the heterosexual male transvestite*. Lanham, MD: University Press of America, Inc.

U.S. Bureau of the Census. (1989). Fertility of American women, June 1988. *Current population reports*, Series P-20, no. 436. Washington, DC: U.S. Department of Commerce.

Weinberg, T., & Bullough, V. (1988). Alienation, self-image, and the importance of support groups for the wives of transvestites. *Journal of Sex Research, 24*, 262–268.

Wise, T.N. (1985). Coping with a transvestite mate: Clinical implications. *Journal of Sex and Marital Therapy, 11*, 293–300.

Wise, T.N., Dupkin, C., and Meyer, J.K. (1981). Partners of distressed transvestites. *American Journal of Psychiatry, 138*, 1221–1224.

Wise, T.N., & Meyer, J.K. (1980). Transvestites who become gender dysphoric. *Archives of Sexual Behavior, 9*, 323–337.

Women associated with crossdressers support group newsletter, Spring, 1992. Bulverde, Texas.

Woodhouse, A. (1985). Forgotten women: Transvestism and marriage. *Women's Studies International Forum, 8*, 583–592.

Zuger, B. (1988). Is early effeminate behavior in boys early homosexuality? *Comprehensive Psychiatry, 29*(5), 509–519.

Zuger, B. (1989). Homosexuality in families of boys with early effeminate behavior: An epidemiological study. *Archives of Sexual Behavior, 18*(2), 155–166.

22 THE FEMALE EXPERIENCE OF THE FEMME

A TRANSGENDER CHALLENGE

Sandra S. Cole

THE COMPLEX MATRIX

As recently as five years ago, the word "transgender" began to emerge as an accepted term to describe the wide variety of individuals with gender-identity and cross-dressing concerns and the community they created. A new category was created to describe those whose identities lay "somewhere in-between" the already-defined categories of cross-dresser and transsexual. In this newly designated category, many individuals identify themselves as "transgenderists"—that is, bigendered, androgynous, or two-spirited. Some transgenderists live equally comfortably as female or male, some live androgynously, some cross-live full-time, some have feminizing or masculinizing procedures for personal enrichment, and many take hormones. None have genital surgery. The literature has only just begun to address this expanded definition of gender identity. What has been written has been primarily in the community's own newsletters and other publications.

Most cross-dressing and transgendered males in the transgender community identify themselves as heterosexual and seek relationships with female partners. It is my perception and experience that the primary focus of attention and concern of this community, and of helping professionals as well, is the transgendered partner. Attention needs to be directed to the nontransgendered partner, who is immersed not only in her partner's ever-changing, complicated, challenging, and complex journey, but her own as well.

The pivotal point for the female which dramatically influences *how* she experiences and learns to accommodate the gender uniqueness of her partner lies clearly in the manner of her discovery. More than anything else, *when, how,* and *from whom* the female learns of her partner's transgender status is of fundamental importance. These factors strongly influence her ability to understand, respond, and integrate the reality of transgender presence, which she may initially experience as emotional trauma. The discovery is compounded by her own sexual history.

Over the past twelve years, I have conducted scores of interpersonal discussion groups with couples, wives, or committed female partners, participated in hundreds of individual conversations at regional and national transgender conferences and conventions, and corresponded with transgendered individuals.

My work with support groups of wives and partners in intensive small-group discussion has revealed critical indicators of outcome and viability of relationships, as well as some indicative qualifiers of happiness, trust, respect, and longevity for the couple. This perspective has been repeatedly sustained in my work with couples' groups, where the quality of the relationship is distinctly influenced by the issues around discovery for the female partner.

The female is challenged by the conflict between her role as partner, helpmate, wife, and/or mother, and her discovery of the heretofore undisclosed aspect of her partner's transgendered persona. If she remains in the relationship, she will usually assume the largest, most comprehensive responsibility for managing the "secret" (his, hers, and theirs). This additional task is not always easily accommodated by her. She predictably will experience a wide range of emotions which may go unnoticed by both her and her partner, who is primarily focused on his own gender complexities.

She may be so diligent that she neglects her own health, including her sexual health. She may become chronically tired or sexually dysfunctional. The most common sexual dysfunction described in personal anecdotes in the womens' groups is secondary anorgasmia.

Contrary to some published self-reports of wives/partners and their perceptions of satisfaction with their relationships, which sometimes read as well-adjusted and near perfect, I have witnessed the testimonies of women which reveal an arduous journey toward acceptance of self and accommodation of the transgender "secret." There are enormous challenges to understand, retain, and potentially enjoy the relationship with her gender-shifting partner.

Supportive counseling for the individuals and the couple can help them to assess their strengths, communication styles, and skills. It can also help them perceive and identify problems which could negatively impact on the stability of their relationship.

DISCOVERY AT THE BEGINNING OF THE RELATIONSHIP

Of course, there is no definitive way to predict the impact of transgender issues on the relationship and personal experience of the female partner.

However, when the male partner's gender issues are identified in the early stages of the relationship and the transgendered male has told his partner himself, the couple can experience the intimate and erotic dynamics of building the relationship together to include the transgender component with openness, mutual respect, and mutual learning. If the two individuals have previous experience in marriage or commitment, their potential for building a strong new relationship is even greater.

Even when the transgender issues are known at the beginning of the relationship, management is more complex if there are children in the home. Optimally, in the case of a couple experienced in previous relationships, where the children are grown and gone from the home and the partner's transgender identity is known from the beginning, the transgender component can become a solid building block of their new and long-lasting union.

DISCOVERY AFTER THE RELATIONSHIP HAS BEEN ESTABLISHED

When the relationship has already been established and the presence of the transgender issues of the male partner have not been revealed from the beginning, there is another set of variables to consider: the duration of the relationship, how discovery was made, and the presence of children in the family.

DURATION OF THE RELATIONSHIP

It is realistic to anticipate that the reaction to discovery by the female partner will depend on how long the relationship has existed. If she learns early on, she will have opportunity to familiarize herself with transgender issues as the relationship develops. However, if the discovery is made after the establishment of habits, patterns, and traditions, such discovery can be understandably problematic. The female is naturally a candidate for feelings of extreme betrayal and anxiety, paranoia about what else she might not have been told, and erosion of trust in her partner. For example, she may be concerned that he is having an affair or engaged in other clandestine activities.

Interestingly, if discovery is made *long* after the relationship has been established and children are older and have left the home, discovery may be slightly less traumatic to the female. Women in such relationships have discussed the circumstances which influence their reactions: the children are gone, mothering tasks have diminished, the couple has aged together, and the extreme need for secrecy when children were in the home is removed. These women may be a little more receptive to these new and "strange" transgender issues.

There are also significant differences, depending on *how* the female partner has learned. If she has been told directly and honestly by her partner, meaningful and honest dialogue can usually occur, even if her partner has "accidentally" left signals that have increased her curiosity and caused her to initiate an inquiry. The relationship has a stronger chance of continuing if the male partner remains honest and truthful. The female will usually recognize that his truthful effort has been made at extreme risk to him losing her. Both are vulnerable and anxious. He may be "scared to death," and she may be "initially repulsed," yet they continue to discuss the revelation.

Commonly, after disclosure, the male may pressure his partner to comply: "Now that you know, let's get dressed and go to the mall." "Now that you know, I want to take hormones." She may be anxious and frightened, not knowing how far he may want to go with his transgender activities. He may be anxious to try everything more openly now that she "knows," and he truly may not know how far he will finally go himself. It is important for the couple to seek supportive counseling at this time. Again, the presence of children will directly affect the female partner's reaction—no matter how she learns.

If the female discovers her partner's transgendered persona herself or is told by a person other than her partner, the situation is usually quite different. She may overhear a conversation, see a photograph of him *en femme*, watch a television talk show on which her partner appears cross-dressed, or see her partner referenced in a newspaper or magazine article. There are far too many anecdotes of this nature. This manner of discovery commonly increases her experience of betrayal and generates tremendous feelings of humiliation, prejudice, and revulsion.

She may fear exposure and loss of control of her private life. Lack of trust and paranoia about the possibility of other unknown characteristics or activities of her partner predictably can increase her resistance to learn—let alone understand—what is going on with her partner. She feels deceived. Counseling intervention by a sensitive therapist can be extremely beneficial in assisting such couples in acute distress.

Discovery may also be made when the female partner is suspicious that something "funny" is going on in the relationship. Even though there may be no tangible clues, she becomes suspicious of her partner's activities, secretiveness, and unusual behavior. She may become very watchful. Subsequently, in pursuit of answers, she may discover a hidden bag or trunk of clothing, photographs of him *en femme*, a wig, female garments tucked in the back of a drawer or hidden in the trunk of his car, a newsletter from a support group, or matchbooks from a gay or "gender-friendly" bar. Feelings of fear, anxiety, shame, betrayal, rejection, violation, and extreme vulnerability are likely. In addition, she is apt to experience rage and react with threats to her partner. She may have a desire to flee, or actually may flee for a time, and may view herself as being at extreme risk of violence.

All of these reactions are further compounded by the presence of children, especially if she suddenly feels confronted with managing all this new information, and her own fears and feelings, in addition to being the primary nurturer and caretaker of the children. Both partners would be well advised to seek counseling at this juncture in the relationship.

Children

The presence and age of children will directly influence the female partner's ability to explore and integrate transgender expression into the relationship. There can be tremendous concern about the children. Should they be told? What if they suspect? What if they "catch him doing it?" What about their families and friends? What about the neighbors? She is likely to experience feelings of anxiety, fear, and shame because what she has learned about her partner is labeled deviant by society. What is she to do? She is reluctant to be a part of the societal rejection and stigma, yet she will feel extremely protective of her children and their emotional safety. She may be so aghast at the discovery that she resists the suggestion of supportive and crisis counseling. However, I strongly recommend that counseling be offered to her, to him, and to them as a couple. Family counseling may be necessary if the children have been made aware of the transgender issues.

It has been my privilege to become acquainted with and observe families who have made the decision to tell their young children about the transgender issues. These families have raised their children in the presence of a transgendered father and have assimilated transgender into the family life-style. They have been consistent throughout the entire child-rearing process in providing information, education, support, and practical family experiences to their children. Many of these families find comfort in creative, imaginative ways to cope with society's rigid reluctance to acknowledge persons who are transgendered.

Not surprisingly, there are more challenges as children enter adolescence. There tends to be more reluctance on the part of the mother to expose the adolescent to anything that might cause gender confusion for the child at the time when he/she is experiencing his or her own gender-identity awareness—the awakening of hormones, sexuality, and sexual orientation. Due to their own surging hormones and the rapid approach of adulthood, adolescents are highly curious and exploratory and unpredictable at this time in their lives. Pubescent and adolescent children are generally viewed as more vulnerable to emotional trauma of this nature because their own lives can be quite tumultuous. They have entered a challenging time in their own lives and need parents to be strong, stable, and reliable so they can feel somewhat secure in their own intense growth journey. Therefore, many parents choose not to disclose to their children during these years, but wait until early adulthood.

As children reach adulthood, families seem better able to disclose the transgender "secret" with honesty and information, encouraging the older children to integrate this with their own thinking and values. In many cases there have been remarkable accomplishments, and families have stayed together, with the transgendered component being an integral part of the family dynamics. Honest communication among the family members, respect for each others' uniqueness, trust, and unflagging love are essential ingredients for successful family transition and growth in these circumstances.

There are no specific recommendations or guidelines to families facing a member's transgender disclosure. Parents are quick to realize that each family is unique and that decisions must be made according to the needs, nature, and values of each family. Counseling is important to assist the couple in attaining the best possible outcome for themselves and their children.

Extended Families

Once immediate family concerns have been identified and addressed, the next most pressing issues will be disclosure to others. If the extended family lives in the community, there may be excessive tension regarding keeping the "secret" because of geographic proximity. However, some couples describe decisions to tell their extended families and how those concerned then have worked positively, though cautiously, together. Telling relatives and close friends is a choice for the couple. The decision will probably be based directly on the couple's perception of their vulnerability and the invasion of their personal privacy. Frequently, the female partner is more cautious about telling others. Once her partner has "come out," he may be less discriminating about his boundaries with others and may inadvertently put her and the family at risk by being increasingly casual or careless about his public transgendered appearances. Again, counseling and supportive peer advocacy can be beneficial to couples assessing these options and making decisions. Most transgender organizations have outreach programs for those in such situations.

Position in the Community

The public positions and community responsibilities of each partner and the couple together will influence whether the transgender issues are made private or kept secret. It must be recognized that stigma related to gender variation, a rigid and unforgiving society or social code, and community bias can have a negative impact on marriages and relationships which otherwise might be able to manage quite well. The couple will need to consider their social and public position and anticipated community reaction if the secret becomes known.

Presenting *en femme* publicly creates the possibility of serious consequences for the individual and family, particularly if the secret is disclosed without consent. Such possibilities often create fear of loss of employment and rejection by the church and/or social group.

The coming-out process has many variables, which influence individuals in profound and unique ways. *When* the female partner learns, *how* she learns and *whether* or not the safety of the family is emotionally or economically threatened are all considerations for anticipating and facilitating the female's ability to navigate in her "new world."

Potential Emotional Reactions and Responses of the Female Partner

The female partner's reaction to the news of her partner's gender issues can include a profound sense of betrayal, violation of trust, fear, competition with this "new female," shame, curiosity, anxiety, repulsion, embarrassment, fear, isolation, challenge, sexual arousal, eroticism, desire to be supportive, sexual dysfunction, aversion, increased self-imposed responsibility to the family, cooperative determination, and feelings of abandonment ("You never really loved me or you wouldn't have done this to me"). She may believe that she wasn't "woman enough" and be overcome with self-blame. She may also have childhood experiences and memories of having been abandoned physically or emotionally and may fear abandonment once this new "secret" is disclosed to her. Her own history may dramatically increase her vulnerability and fearfulness. She may, for example, come from a dysfunctional or divorced family. If she has been sexually exploited, raped, or abused, her reaction will be influenced and her vulnerability compounded by these early life experiences. Additionally, she may feel a challenge to her femininity. How would/could/should she compete with the "femme" person in his mirror? She may reduce her grooming efforts because of decreased self-esteem or body image, or she may compete and try to outdo this "new woman."

The female partner may privately self-identify as lesbian or bisexual, or she may realize she has an undiscovered and perhaps alarmingly uncomfortable emotional/sexual attraction to this "new woman," without having a previous positive concept of same-sex attraction. She may never have addressed, openly acknowledged, or been aware of this possible aspect of her sexual orientation. She may be fearful of her sexuality and the reactions a "lesbian" relationship will cause in others.

She may be anxious and challenged because of traditional sexual norms, and yet reluctantly find herself sensuously/sexually attracted to the femme persona of her male transgendered partner. She may not understand these new sexual, erotic stirrings. Moreover, she has been socialized to be feminine and attractive to men. This new phenomenon may threaten her and make her question her own gender identity. She may consider herself unable to keep her male partner attracted to her as she has learned she is supposed to do, and may thus regard herself as a failure.

It is likely that she has been socialized to accommodate her male partner's nature and personality, perhaps more than her own. However, she may or may not feel she is able to accommodate this new gender situation, and can easily feel overwhelmed. To protect herself, her partner, and the family, she will usually assume the greatest and more comprehensive responsibility for management of his secret, as she is fearful that he will not monitor and protect the integrity of the family. In an attempt to make the relationship work, particularly if the discovery occurs after marriage, she may "join up" and actively participate in his grooming, dressing, club attendance, and gender excursions. If so, she also will probably do whatever seems necessary to keep the relationship intact and to protect the rest of the family. If, after all this, her efforts do not work, she can easily blame herself or fearfully anticipate that others, unfamiliar with transgender issues, may blame her or her inability to "stop" her partner's behavior. Conversely, other partners of transgendered men may criticize her for her unwillingness and inability to "join the program" and "accept" her partner's transgenderism. Either way, she anticipates that she cannot "win" and may just become numb and resolute, overwhelmed with it all.

It is likely that she will experience mixed messages from her male partner, who may secretly want the world to see his whole persona and who may make unfortunate judgments about when to be *en femme*. She may feel resentful with this further imposition on couple boundaries; and, as stated before, she may also experience fear and anxiety regarding her need to protect her position in the community. Many women express concern about their church community. Her religion may be conservative or fundamental, with sanctions on sexual behavior, gender identity, or life-style conduct. She may fear abandonment from church, family, or supportive community, perceiving herself to be left isolated from that which she knows best and which comforts her. At this juncture, she may feel emotionally exhausted and dysfunctional. Professionals offering counseling will be well-advised to be particularly sensitive to these vulnerabilities.

A common question of most of these women is whether or not their partners are homosexual or "perverts." They also frequently wonder how far all of this will go. Will her partner become a woman? Will she, therefore, become a lesbian? Anxiety, grief, and fear can be natural reactions. The therapist will find it helpful and advisable to discuss such perceptions with her and the couple and to provide information and education. The couple needs to learn to fully and honestly communicate their thoughts and feelings to each other and to the therapist in an effort to achieve mutual understanding and arrive at acceptable plans and goals.

Also to be considered are her own special life dreams and concepts of marriage, partnering, love, intimacy, and parenting. They may have been shattered by her new discoveries. Perhaps her fantasies and realistic ideas of what "life is supposed to be like" are no longer available to her under these circumstances. She is likely to experience significant emotional trauma for these reasons alone.

She will spend an enormous amount of time guarding and maintaining the privacy, dignity, and integrity of her family. As a consequence, she may be delinquent about her own mental and physical health. It is not unlikely that she will become chronically fatigued and depressed. She may experience a variety of physiological limitations or inconveniences such as headache, chronic backache, chronic pain, or general malaise. In addition, she may have a lack of sexual desire or develop an aversion to sexual activity. Women in confidential small-group discussions tell of the distress of experiencing secondary anorgasmia, and, most severely, dyspareunia (painful intercourse) or vaginismus (painful vaginal contractions which prohibit intercourse). She may or may not recognize the relationship of these symptoms to fatigue, stress, energy spent focusing on managing "the secret," disrupted values, and her current struggles with transgender. Professional counseling will assist her in the recovery of her own sexual satisfaction.

Power struggles, which commonly take place in the sexual behavior of couples, can easily contribute to the vulnerability, anxiety, or anger in the female. When she is threatened in her own feminine and sexual security because of her partner's transgendered identity, her feelings can easily be expressed in angry, manipulative power struggles or in clearly defined sexual dysfunction. Role-entitlement expectations, particularly of the male, are often experienced or expressed sexually; and, because of the ways in which females are socialized about their own sexuality in our culture, there can be confusion over her surrender and resignation or giving in to sexual advances when she simultaneously feels conflicted. Many women will participate in sexual intimacy, including intercourse, even when they experience lack of desire, having competently learned to fake orgasm and to pretend that everything is fine. They thus add one more burden of deception to their already challenging role.

It could be anticipated that the female might only enjoy sex with her transgendered partner if she could find other ways to control her partner outside of the bed, considering that the only power she perceives she has is the power to say "no" to her partners' femme-related desires and requests. She may choose to use this power in nonintimate ways, restricting the frequency, nature, time, and place that dressing *en femme* will occur, how much she will participate in it, and so on. She may limit body shaving or other feminizing procedures which are serious desires of her partner. She may set conditions under which she will "allow" or "permit" his dressing. He will refer to these circumstances with the same descriptive language, such as "I am allowed," "She permits me." They appear to have agreed that she is responsible and has the power to determine such things. And yet, a common complaint of the female is that she resents the burden and responsibility of having to set all of the boundaries; and a common complaint for the transgendered man is that she appears to be inconsistent and too restrictive about the rules. The couple may reveal that they have never actually negotiated this arrangement, even though they feel very angry and conflicted with each other.

A sensitive clinician will focus on sexual health and happiness within the couple, and on understanding and evaluating the impact of discovery, the presence of children, and how the couple manages conflict and friction while trying to maintain intimacy.

BOUNDARIES

Once he discloses his transgender issues, the couple enters into negotiation around boundaries of the relationship and "how far" this newly discovered "she" will go. Common boundary issues include: how much dressing is tolerated, when is it OK, can it be done in the home, can it be done in public, can it be done in the presence of the partner. Do they shop at the mall together? If not, does he understand why not? If dressing is allowed in the home, is he restricted to wearing only his femme clothes, can he wear her clothes, will they share clothes? Regarding intimacy in the bed: is his dressing tolerated or not, his lingerie, her lingerie on him, or both, with makeup or not? How much of her partner's body hair is to be preserved and not removed? Is body shaving tolerated? Where, how much: legs, bikini line, arms? Is electrolysis acceptable? If so, how much? What about added expenses for clothing, electrolysis, hormones, or other feminizing procedures?

Largely due to lack of adequate medical information, taking feminizing hormones remains the biggest challenge for most couples. Does he tell her whether he is taking hormones or not? Does he/she fully understand the risks and possible side effects or limitations of a hormonal regime? Is fertility affected? Is libido affected temporarily? Irreversibly? If he takes hormones and does not tell his partner, what happens if she discovers this? What is the dosage? How far will it go? Probably the most common question I have heard in regard to hormones is, "Does this mean he is going to have surgery and become a woman?"

Taking hormones under medical supervision after comprehensive and careful evaluation and assessment of family history and current medical status is, without a doubt, the absolute safest method. However, many transgendered men obtain hormonal drugs from various sources: relatives, partners, friends, uninformed physicians with unsatisfactory standards of care, and, of course, covertly, on the street. Some take greater dosages of hormones than would otherwise be prescribed—which can lead to illness or death. Realistic concerns for obtaining hormones on the street are that administration is usually with dirty "works," risk of AIDS is increased, and purity, dosage, and reliability are questionable.

Faced with inadequate medical resources, or driven to have the optimum female experience as quickly as possible, many transgendered men foolishly risk their health and medical safety by taking enormous and dangerous doses of hormones—sometimes in secret. The fears of wives and partners are often acute, not just because of their concern about his becoming "too feminine," but also for his safety. It is essential to seek knowledgeable medical care for any kind of hormones. Mental-health professionals are well advised to be sure that the transgendered client consults knowledgeable physicians and that the partners are included in the process. Accurate medical information must be provided when determining hormonal regimens so that both the partner and the transgendered male have the opportunity to be educated.

For those on a regulated program of hormones, the results are not only safe but pleasing to the individual, who frequently states that he definitely physically feels more feminine. Many wives and partners talk about the noticeable comfort of their partners. The women whose partners are on hormones may be cautious about the whole experience; however, in group discussions, they seem more at ease and supportive as they become more knowledgeable about what to expect, what amounts of hormones are safe, and when they are included in the medical experience.

One might ask whether it is possible for the female partner to take care of herself, honor herself, celebrate her own sexuality, and ask for relationship attention without feeling that she is competing or fighting with her partner and his femme self every step of the way. Certainly, with informational resources, peer support and advocacy, and competent professional support, a woman partnered with a transgendered male can be provided with ongoing opportunity to learn, understand, process, and integrate accurate and honest information—thereby enabling her to participate in a more rational and informed manner. Most importantly, she needs time, respect, and support to put her own femininity and personal values into perspective with this new transgender phenomenon. Her partner may well have spent most of his life dealing with his transgender feelings—perhaps in secret—and has experienced many things along the way. She, however, has not shared this journey, nor had such a journey herself, and so, for her, this is sudden and foreign. She needs time to learn, consider, and accommodate. Her needs are to be respected. She is beginning her own journey.

THE CONTROVERSY OF FEMALE SEXUAL AROUSAL TO HER PARTNER'S FEMININE SELF

In safe, supportive, and respectful group sessions or private conversations, female partners of transgendered males will cautiously but honestly speak about their own feelings and sexual intimacies. It is important to listen carefully to these women and their perceptions of intimacy between themselves and their partners. A commonly recognized belief of some professionals who serve the gender community, and an equally common belief among wives and significant others, is that women stay in relationships with their transgendered partners with varying degrees of reluctance and resignation and are simply "going along for the ride" in order to keep the family together. Although this sentiment is present among many wives and partners, there is clearly another perspective which is rarely discussed, but which needs careful and respectful acknowledgement. The experience of being partnered with a transgendered male is positively experienced and enjoyed erotically, sensuously, and sexually by many wives and significant others. Although cautious to speak about such private matters and give truthful testimony regarding sexual intimacies, many of the women reveal that they are more sexually and emotionally satisfied and that their partners are better lovers when they are *en femme*.

A small proportion of cross-dressing and transgendered men take hormones to experience further feminization. A carefully managed hormonal regimen will decrease male libido somewhat; and many of the women in confidential and private group discussions report that their partner's somewhat reduced libido allows the couple more time for romance and increased attention to attentive communication and highly satisfying intimacy with one another. When the couple, particularly the male, reduces the focus on performance of coitus and achievement of orgasm, the female partner relates that she feels more relaxed and able to respond more to tenderness, intimacy, romance, and emotions shown by her partner. Being *en femme* increases communication between the couple; and the gentle, affective emotional qualities of the male partner are dramatically increased and satisfying to both as he manifests his feminine spirit.

Of interest also are the many reports from women partners in such discussion groups who state that they truly enjoy the increased adventure of transgender sexuality and actively become participants in creative romance and intimacy. However, it is my impression from interactions with these women that their level of sexual satisfaction does not seem to be directly or exclusively influenced by whether or not their partner is on a hormonal regime.

Specific masculine or feminine gender rehearsal for all persons occurs from puberty to late adolescence and is a critical component of adult gender identity and behavior. Cross-gender rehearsal is not a part of traditional gender socialization. Frequently, supportive wives and significant others enjoy trying to enhance the feminine aspects of their partners and voluntarily advise and teach women's skills and feminine ways never learned by their male partners when they were growing up.

A great deal can be learned from discussions with these women as they become increasingly aware of their own gender expression which, at times, is compatible and symbiotic to their partner's gender expression. Many women relate joy, arousal, and sexual satisfaction in discovering and embracing the presence of the masculine components of their own gender. They acknowledge how rewarding and enriching this experience is and how compatible it can be with their male partner's feminine aspects. They also describe feelings of intrigue and heightened arousal when their partners are *en femme,* as well as their ongoing pleasure and attraction to his masculinity. They speak of experiencing mutual tenderness, eroticism, and sexual satisfaction. They speak of developing expanded sexual repertoire, including fantasy and fantasy behavior as an active and exciting ingredient to the relationship.

It can be conjectured that a bisexual women might be particularly suited to be paired with a bigendered, androgynous male partner. It is also entirely possible that, prior to the knowledge of her partner's transgender issues, the female partner may not have been aware of the presence and potential of her own masculine elements of gender. Sharing mutually in the personal and private exploration of all of their gender capacities seems to increase the pair bonding and allows the couple to enjoy the fluidity of one another's gender potential while comfortably staying within their established committed partnership. This experience is commonly and affectionately mentioned by such women as "the best of both worlds for each of us."

These gender/relationship concepts and scenarios need to be more fully considered, discussed, and explored when offering professional outreach, therapy, support, recommendations, and intervention with women and their transgendered partners.

How Can the Medical or Mental Health Care Professional Be of Assistance?

There are some basic concepts that are helpful and useful to consider when providing services or interacting with transgendered individuals and their partners or families. Professionals are advised to:

1. Encourage women to strengthen recognition of their own sexuality, relationship needs, and personal health responsibilities. Too often, they focus disproportionately on their partners' concerns.

2. Reinforce among other professionals the importance of recognizing and understanding the impact of her partner's transgender identity on the female as changes in relationship dynamics emerge.

3. Be sensitive to the significance and symbolism each member of the couple has placed on their relationship, helping them to identify what cannot change, what does not have to change, what is desired that can be changed, and what is to be kept, nurtured, honored, and protected.

4. Facilitate an increase in the couple's ability to learn to *anticipate* problems, a form of mental rehearsal which increases preparedness to change, integrate or accommodate. Many times, the female partner will correctly anticipate risky situations and may fear the outcome, while her partner will seem to be unaware or uncaring about the results. This can lead to her increased anxiety, frustration, and rage as she fears that some situations may lead to unwanted discovery and damage which cannot be undone. Too often, the burden of management of risk is put on, or assumed by her when optimally *both* partners should be working on these issues together.

5. Assist in developing creative mechanisms to *accommodate* necessary changes and to mentally rehearse possible responses. Once situations

and problem areas are identified and rehearsed, the actual experience may have a decreased impact, and the potential for the female partner's own risk-taking abilities and curiosity are recognized in less threatening ways (i.e., excursions to public places with her partner. Would she be comfortable wearing a wig herself to avoid discovery?). Rehearsals reduce the element of surprise and vulnerability.

6. Address the issue of betrayal, remembering that possibly both persons are extremely vulnerable. When the male partner risks telling or being discovered by the female, he can experience extreme fear and anxiety, particularly concerning the possibility of being abandoned. The female partner needs to learn and understand that he probably withheld telling her for his own self-perceived logical reasons ("It will go away," "I can manage it privately"). He probably saw himself at being at extreme risk if the "secret" were known, fearing she would flee. This awareness will not immediately reduce her fear, rage, or anxiety; but it will be very helpful over the long term as she learns more.

Women in peer support groups openly discuss how they have modified their various initial reactions to discovery as they have learned to understand and believe their partners never intended to deceive them in order to manipulate, hurt, or betray; but that, most likely, they were extremely anxious that the women would leave them if they found out.

PROFESSIONAL COMPETENCE

The helping professional will:

1. Be able to give unconditional attention to the broad issues affecting the female partner and will not just concentrate on the male partner's transgender issues.

2. Be supportive and provide helpful services to the dyad and not just to the individual. If it is not possible to see the couple conjointly, then recommendation for counseling assistance should be offered to the partner.

3. Provide care which is sensitive, respectful, and nonjudgmental regarding transgender issues.

4. Pay respectful attention to the manner in which the female partner learned of her partner's transgender identity. The professional must never try to deny the importance of the disclosure experience and the way in which the discovery was made.

5. Provide support for emotional trauma and subsequent behaviors which may evolve into compounded post-traumatic stress disorder if discovery reactivates old unresolved issues for her.

6. Acknowledge and respect the validity of their transgender concerns.

7. Use supportive, proactive language. Avoid pathologic language such as *dys*phoria and *dys*function. It tends to negatively reinforce the dilemma. Also, avoid medical jargon.

8. Provide emotional guidance for the individual or couple and help them gain skills to set realistic expectations for themselves and each other.

9. Avoid predicting the future. Help them set their own goals through this challenging journey.

10. Recognize that many relationships do not last. There may be underlying pathology which the transgender issues amplified.

11. Avoid stereotyping transgender concerns into a sick or medicalized mode.

12. Avoid permanently classifying the client into one or more TV, TS, TG categories and further stigmatizing the couple. The transgender experience is fluid and can evolve, fluctuate, and/or change in relationship to the couple, family situation, work, and community environment. The female partner may need/want assurance of his stability. ("How far will this go?")

13. Encourage the couple to focus on the strengths and dynamics of the present relationship.

14. Educate the couple regarding the availability of local support groups for wives, partners, and couples. These can be extremely effective where professional services are limited or scarce, and peer advocacy can be a powerful therapeutic tool. Couple support groups are most effective when facilitated by a trained leader. Support groups should not be viewed as substitutes for counseling or therapy, but they provide a special opportunity to discuss personal transgender issues with peers who share similar experiences.

15. Be influential in assisting women partners and couples as they work toward balance around such issues as family, children, discovery, disclosure of transgender desires and expression, competition, femininity and masculinity, sexual health, trust, betrayal, and most importantly, management of the "secret."

16. Be sensitive in regarding the complex nature of the female in relationship to the complex nature of the transgendered partner and how all of this is played out in the couple relationship.

The purpose of therapy is to assist with the healing process and to assist the individual or couple in finding their own personal relationship, intimacy, and sexual harmony and happiness, despite the risks. In essence, the professional has a unique opportunity to be a supportive facilitator through their journey. It is a trusted privilege.

RISK

To laugh . . . is to risk appearing a fool.

To weep . . . is to risk appearing sentimental.

To reach out to others . . . is to risk involvement.

To expose feelings . . . is to risk exposing your true self.

To place your ideas and dreams before a crowd . . . is to risk their loss.

To love . . . is to risk not being loved in return.

To live . . . is to risk dying.

To hope . . . is to risk despair.

To try . . . is to risk failure.

But risks must be taken.

Because the greatest hazard in life is to risk nothing.

For the person who risks nothing, does nothing, has nothing . . .

They may avoid suffering and sorrow, but they cannot learn or feel or change, grow, love, or live.

Chained by their attitude, they are a slave. They have forfeited their freedom, for only a person who risks is free.

If you cannot risk, you cannot grow.

If you cannot grow, you cannot become your best self.

And, if you cannot become your best self, you cannot be happy.

And, if you cannot be happy, what else matters?

—Linda Peacock (Wife of a transgendered male), 1994
Printed with permission of the author.

We, as helping professionals, must diligently avoid adding to the transgendered person/couple's experience of pain, shame, guilt, and fear because of our own lack of training, basic information, or understanding. We must not be distracted by our own discomfort and possible reactions to the visuals of dressing *en femme*, artificiality, costumes, plumage and theatrics. These real-life situations can present dilemmas; and these very real individuals and couples deserve respect, understanding, and facilitative support and assistance.

In addition to visual signals of cross-dressers, transgendered persons, or transsexuals, much of the stigma surrounding transgender concepts lies within the rigid restrictions of gender definition in our society and within the strict limitations of language expression. Unfortunately, the burden of societal ignorance falls on the transgendered individual and family, resulting in unnecessary and insensitive disenfranchisement.

23 A PROCESS MODEL OF SUPPORTIVE THERAPY FOR FAMILIES OF TRANSGENDER INDIVIDUALS*

Carole Rosenfeld

Shirley Emerson

The psychotherapy literature is replete with descriptions of parents, partners, and other family members of the full spectrum of transgender individuals. The articles reviewed offer little help to therapists working with either the transgender person or the family. Psychodynamic explanations implicating the role of the mother's pathology, along with a colluding father, are offered as theories of the etiology of transsexualism (Lothstein, 1979; Stoller, 1985). Other discussions in the literature include male-to-female transsexuals' perceptions of their parents (Parker & Barr, 1982), female-to-male transsexuals' perceptions of their parents (Cohen-Kettenis & Arrindell, 1990), treatment for parents (Newman, 1976), a comparison of parental and interpersonal relationships between transsexual and homosexual men (Šípová & Brzek, 1983), and the role of maternal grandmothers in early childhood (Halle, Schmidt, & Meyer, 1980).

Steiner (1985) offered several vignettes in discussing marital and partnership issues. Peo (1988) discussed the accommodation and integration of cross-dressing within relationships. Stoller (1967) derisively classified women who become involved with transvestic men as malicious male-haters, succorers, or symbiotes. Also derogatory, Wise, Dupkin, and Meyer (1981) believed these women are "moral masochists." While noting indicators of low self-esteem in a nonpatient sample of women involved with transvestic men, Brown and Collier (1989) commented on such pejorative statements and pointed to their likelihood of biasing therapists against these women. Huxley, Kenna, and Brandon (1981a) compared partnered transsexuals with a nonpaired group and concluded that those without partners were more often without their fathers in the first decade of life and tended to fall into a

---

*This paper was presented by the authors at the International Congress on Gender, Cross Dressing, and Sex Issues, Center for Sex Research, Institute of Social and Behavioral Sciences, California State, Northridge, 24 February 1995.

narrower social-class distribution. In a second article, Huxley, Kenna, and Brandon (1981b) compared the transsexual partnership to a *folie à deux* based on the extent to which both parties support and share a delusion, for example, that the transsexual male-to-female is a biological woman. One must be a discriminating consumer of the clinical literature regarding transgender individuals and their families.

While there is much in the literature describing various family dynamics and characteristics, valid or otherwise, these are not systemic descriptions. Our search revealed only two systemically oriented articles related to transgenderism. One approach sought to prevent adolescent transsexualism (Wrate & Gulens, 1986), and the other posited an interactional explanation based on parental reactions with a view toward the prevention of transgender behavior (Jones & Tinker, 1982).

The family-therapy literature appears to lack a systemic model that is useful in guiding therapists in their efforts to assist all family members of transgender individuals. Therapists need a nonpathological, systemic conceptual framework for cross-gender behavior. This framework should acknowledge the reactions of family members to transgender behavior within the context of our gender-dichotomous society and, at the same time, allow for a multitude of transgender identities and behavior.

We assume the position of "what is," rather than "why?" The attribution of "cause" of transgender identification and behavior is beyond the scope of this article. We, as family therapists, suggest that persons are members of families, no matter with whom they reside. Helping the individual demands a consideration of his/her family system. The transgender individual has many hurdles and obstacles in the way of emotional health and productive life, and we maintain that the members of his/her family also have large adjustments to make when a family member is transgendered. Our focus is on the entire family system, with respect and caring extended to all members. The model presented here derives from interviews with family members of transgender individuals as well as from counseling transgender persons both individually and in group.

An Overview of Systems Theory

A family system may be defined as two or more persons who interact in relatively stable and consistent repetitive sequences over time. A systemic approach to family therapy considers relationships between family members as the focus of intervention, rather than individual intrapsychic processes. The perspective of a family-systems therapist is holistic, and focuses on the processes or context that give meaning to events instead of on the individuals or the events themselves (Becvar & Becvar, 1993). Family rules, usually implicit, govern what behaviors are tolerated within the system. Systems are self-regulating entities, and when behaviors deviate beyond an acceptable range, family members will attempt to restore a stable environment, usually referred to as homeostatic balance (Goldenberg & Goldenberg, 1991). While the family system is embedded within larger culturally defined suprasystems, such as employment, religious, and educational systems, the family system is itself comprised of various functionally defined subsystems. For example, in a traditional family, the parental subsystem acts as the executive arm of the system with each partner assuming functional roles or behaviors, however defined, to carry out the parenting function. Subsystems are also arranged hierarchically. The parental subsystem is at a higher level (in terms of authority and responsibility) in the structural hierarchy than the sibling subsystem (Becvar & Becvar, 1993).

Systems, subsystems, and individuals are defined and distinguished from outside surroundings by invisible lines of demarcation known as boundaries (Goldenberg & Goldenberg, 1991). Boundaries define who participates within a system or subsystem and who does not. Ideally, boundaries should be clear, yet flexible (Piercy & Sprenkle, 1986). Boundaries may become too rigid and reduce or preclude contact and support between family members. Alternatively, weak boundaries beg for violations such that privacy may be ignored as subsystems are not clearly defined (Becvar & Becvar, 1993). When intergenerational boundaries are weak, the line between parents and children becomes blurred. Emotional incest may occur when children assume the parental role. Whenever sexual abuse occurs between an adult and child, both intergenerational and individual boundaries have been crossed (Boszormenyi-Nagy & Spark, 1984).

Like individuals, family systems are dynamic entities with their own life cycle and developmental tasks. All families encounter expected developmental issues (Carter & McGoldrick, 1989). Changes and transition points in the life cycle produce anxiety with which the family must learn to cope. So while the system seeks to maintain homeostasis, the system's equilibrium is repeatedly disrupted as the family moves through its life cycle. What is important is how the family mobilizes to deal with the stressors encountered. The goal of the therapeutic process is to help the system stabilize at a functional level that supports all members and that will enable the family to deal more effectively with future developmental tasks.

Stages of a Treatment Model

While transgender individuals experience their process of transitioning and adjusting, family members also go through their unique process of "coming out" (Bockting & Coleman, 1992). Each individual's experience impacts the family system, and the family system affects each individual's private experience in a reciprocal and dynamic fashion (Becvar & Becvar, 1993).

Borrowing from Kubler-Ross (1969), after becoming aware of the transgender identity or behavior of a family member, others in the family appear to progress through overlapping, nondiscrete stages, depending on their relationship with the transgender individual. We believe the process that family members experience is an expected reaction to the culturally defined dichotomy of gender. While individual family members may need information to aid in the adoption of a more flexible view of gender, therapists must take the family as they are. This includes the family's cultural context with its accompanying beliefs. Approaching the family as an interlocking interactive system does not preclude therapists from becoming advocates for the transgender individual.

The stages presented, like the stages of grief suggested by Kubler-Ross (1969), are seldom progressed through cleanly or in a linear manner. One does not have to finish one stage to find oneself in another stage and may return to an earlier stage, back and forth, over time. The general direction of the stages is suggested here, with the understanding that some stages take longer for some individuals, and some are shorter or seemingly skipped. It is a highly individual process as well as a family-system process, and the family as a whole will experience stages which may be similar to or different from each individual's experience.

Denial Stage

Individual members may experience shock and denial upon learning of a relative's cross-gender identity. They may effectively put the issue out of their minds or assume the relative is going through a phase that will pass. Family members may be successful in maintaining their denial for extended periods of time if the transgender individual only assumes the role episodically and keeps the cross-gender identity secret. If the individual has cut off from the family while transitioning to a full-time cross-gender role, the family members are assisted in maintaining their denial by the individual's absence. Also, when family members are at different points in their own process of acceptance, and disagree due to disparate degrees of support of the transgender individual's process, the absence of the individual may allow harmonious relationships among the rest of the family to be restored.

Certain events may serve to break denial. We interviewed the sister of a female-to-male individual who stated she always believed his "problem" would pass until they parted ways when making a restroom stop at a mall. She had no idea he had been using the men's restroom and was shocked by her discovery. Even relatives who appear supportive and accepting may actually be in denial, believing the transgender individual will change. However, as noted by Bockting and Coleman (1992), that support may end upon the pursuit of sex reassignment.

The therapist's work at this stage may be mostly giving information, suggesting readings, and gently helping relatives realize that their transgender person is not sick or crazy or going through a phase, and that he/she will not "get over" the gender that he/she is.

Anger Stage

Once denial has diminished or been refuted, family members often realize that their predominant feeling is anger, surrounded by frustration. Scapegoating is likely at this point, and family members may state that everything would be fine in the family except for the transgender individual's crazy notions or behavior. The transgender family member may be blamed for all the problems in the family. Wives of cross-dressers may feel angry and betrayed; they may wonder what other secrets are yet to be discovered.

For the therapist working with the family system (no matter how many members come or do not come to therapy), the focus should be away from any identified patient and placed on the total system, on the relationships among the members. Care must be taken, however, not to alienate the family members and invalidate their experience. Particularly when working with parents, it may be helpful to allow them to focus on their son or daughter for several sessions before gently shifting to the dynamics of the marital relationship. Comments such as the following may be appropriate: "You have both been speaking of your son/daughter for several sessions and appear to discuss and perhaps argue about this at home. I am wondering what you do to relieve the stress you are experiencing." The focus may then center on how the couple deals with other stresses. Unfortunately, in some situations, the couple has little between them except the "problem" that may function to keep them together. Healthier avenues of focus that will serve the same function as the "problem" can be explored. At the same time, education about transgender individuals may need to continue, with a therapeutic goal of normalizing the couple's view of cross-gender behavior.

Bargaining Stage

During the bargaining stage, family members may make threats or promises to the transgender relative. On the negative side, in an attempt to stop transgender behavior, family members may threaten their transgender relative. A wife may threaten to leave a transvestic husband if he does not stop or restrict cross-dressing. Parents may threaten to disown and disinherit their child. Family members may form alliances and shun or ostracize the transgender individual. On the other hand, promises may be made. They may offer the transgender individual money to return to college or to start a business if he/she abandons all plans to pursue sex reassignment and "start behaving normally."

In their attempts to bargain with the transgender relative, family members are actively seeking to prevent or restrict the transgender individual's process and eliminate what they still perceive as a problem. The perception of transgender as a "problem" brings up many issues of concealment for the family. Families who have kept many secrets in the past may bargain with the transgender member to keep his/her identity, behavior, or planned surgery a secret.

Depression Stage

As the reality of the transgender experience becomes more definite, family members frequently lapse into depression. This may take many forms, from weeping and grief-type expression, to physical complaints, both minor and severe. This somatic embodiment of strong negative emotions may result in physical illness. If such disability is severe enough, it can take the focus or "heat" off the transgender person temporarily, thus engaging the family system in a realignment of loyalties, dependencies, and caretaking. Sometimes the transgender person becomes physically ill as a way of shifting the attention away from gender. Individuals may act out inappropriately with withdrawal, abuse of substances, loss of employment, and divorce. Suicide is always a possibility in an extremely dysfunctional system, not only for the transgender individual, but for other family members as well.

Guilt and blame are common in this stage. The fraternal twin of a female-to-male stated she would feel better if she could attribute the transsexualism to something beyond anybody's control. She said she would be relieved of guilt if she could find evidence of a hormonal imbalance resulting from their being twins. One mother of a male-to-female transsexual expressed guilt over what she did or did not do that could have caused her child to "become this way."

Acceptance Stage

Family members have come to an acceptance of reality when they no longer are determined to change the transgender relative. It is important to note that acceptance does not mean that the family member necessarily agrees with the transgender relative. Rather, it means the individual does not dwell on how things could be different. Most importantly, there is a realization of loss. One mother stated that she experienced a distinct feeling of loss for her son. She says she views her child's reassignment as the death of her son and the birth of her daughter. Her therapy included time to grieve that "death," after which she could celebrate having a daughter.

Some of the younger siblings of transsexual individuals we interviewed said they did not remember their brother or sister as being otherwise, so there were no feelings of loss. Younger siblings, therefore, may not progress through a grieving process. Older siblings, however, expressed the experience of loss.

Feelings of loss may also occur in family members of transgender individuals who are not living full-time in the cross-gender role. Acceptance of any transgender behavior, episodically or partially assumed, may evoke feelings of loss of the person one thought one knew.

At this point, family members may begin to express concern for the individual's welfare. Many who had achieved a degree of acceptance of their transsexual family member expressed concern over various issues they perceived as difficult for their relative. Several individuals expressed concern that hormones would adversely affect their relative's health or that there would be complications from reassignment surgery. Some expressed concern over their transgender relative's ability to maintain employment, maintain love relationships, and assimilate. While assimilation is not necesssarily the goal, the integration of one's transgendered status into one's self-identity should be an important objective for the transgender individual (Denny, 1995). It may be necessary for family members to be further educated in this regard.

ACKNOWLEDGMENT OR CONCEALMENT

The subject of sex can raise emotional issues in most families—traditional ones especially—and families may attempt to conceal gender-related concerns just as they would sexual problems. Among the most difficult, and often experienced as shameful, are problems related to gender identity (Money, Clarke, & Mazur, 1975). The fear, and indeed reality, of stigmatization can be felt as severe enough to pose a difficult dilemma for families with a transgender member. Money, Clarke, and Mazur (1975) state that the transsexualism of a family member is not easily concealed, even if the family resorts to disowning or disinheriting the individual.

The early study of Money, Clarke, and Mazur (1975) discussed in some depth the adjustments and acceptances, on follow-up after five to seven years, of seven families of male-to-female, surgically reassigned individuals.

They concluded that the differences between families who accepted the changed member and those who did not seemed to depend upon how open or concealed the fact of the change was to extended and immediate family, friends, and neighbors. When family members could be open, announce the change, and model their acceptance of the "new" family member, friends and neighbors accepted it also, and everyone got on with daily life. When the "secret" had to be maintained, contact, sociability, and relationships between the transgender member and the rest of the family were limited and strained.

A Family Ceremony

The experience for the family of reassigning the sex of one of its members is difficult and socially threatening. There is no routine formula, ceremony, or social institution to which the family can resort. There are no firm legal precedents and procedures. Instead, there is the stigma of deviating from one of society's most deeply ingrained beliefs, the absoluteness of two, and only two, distinct genders (Money, Clarke, & Mazur, 1975).

With this in mind, the family therapist may want to include in the therapy process a ceremony for all the family which would mark the life-cycle transition. Many rites of passage and acknowledgments of transition such as graduations, birthdays, bar mitzvahs, and citizenship change mark normative points in family life. The entrance into the family of the "new" gender person could be cause for a celebration similar to a wedding, where reunion of family members from far and wide might use this "occasion" to renew ties ar. bonds that are often neglected due to busy schedules and distance. Since, according to Imber-Black (1989), rituals make change manageable, family members can experience change as part of their system rather than as a threat to it. "A sense of self and a sense of family and group membership are enabled through rituals. Emotional and physical well-being may be promoted during times of intense relationship change" (Imber-Black, 1989, p. 149).

Presenting to the world the family member in the new gender role seems to constitute a time of intense relationship change, so a family-constructed ceremony could help all members to accept the change. Family members, working with the therapist in a creative session, can create a ritual that signifies rebirth and a new beginning for the whole family.

Conclusion

To many, the very idea of someone feeling totally compelled to change identity to the opposite gender, or even to assume the opposite gender role episodically, is foreign and bewildering. We fear what we do not understand.

As knowledge increases and more transgender individuals are speaking out, understanding is growing, albeit slowly. Families of transgender persons have not only the confusion and fear of what is happening in their family, but also the concern for what others will think.

Family therapists are in perhaps a unique role to assist in the process of adjustment to change, normalizing behavior previously incomprehensible because of misunderstanding, and establishing or re-establishing communication among family members who might otherwise remain estranged indefinitely. Therapists must examine their prejudices and remedy their ignorance in order to understand a family's process, and from that understanding, model acceptance of "what is" while working with all family members toward a harmonious future.

REFERENCES

Becvar, D., & Becvar, R. (1993). *Family therapy.* Boston: Allyn & Bacon.

Bockting, W.O., & Coleman, E. (1992). A comprehensive approach to the treatment of gender dysphoria. In W.O. Bockting & E. Coleman (Eds.), *Gender dysphoria: Interdisciplinary approaches in clinical management,* pp. 131–155. New York: The Haworth Press, Inc.

Boszormenyi-Nagy, I., & Spark, G. (1984). *Invisible loyalties.* New York: Brunner/ Mazel.

Brown, G.R., & Collier, L. (1989). Transvestites' women revisited: A nonpatient sample. *Archives of Sexual Behavior, 18,* 73–83.

Carter, B., & McGoldrick, M. (1989). Overview: The changing family life cycle. In B. Carter & M. McGoldrick (Eds.), *The changing family life cycle: A framework for family therapy,* pp. 3–28. Boston: Allyn & Bacon.

Cohen-Kettenis, P.T., & Arrindell, W.A. (1990). Perceived parental rearing style, parental divorce and transsexualism: A controlled study. *Psychological Medicine, 20,* 613–620.

Denny, D. (1995, February). Past, present, and future models of treatment. Paper presented at the First International Congress on Gender, Cross Dressing and Sex Issues, Center for Sex Research, Institute for Social and Behavioral Sciences, California State University, Northridge.

Goldenberg, I., & Goldenberg, H. (1991). *Family therapy: An overview.* Pacific Grove: Brooks/Cole Publishing Company.

Halle, E., Schmidt, C.W., & Meyer, J.K. (1980). The role of grandmothers in transsexualism. *American Journal of Psychiatry, 134(4),* 497–498.

Huxley, P.J., Kenna, J.C., & Brandon, S. (1981a). Partnership in transsexualism. Part I. Paired and nonpaired groups. *Archives of Sexual Behavior, 10,* 133–141.

Huxley, P.J., Kenna, J.C., & Brandon, S.B. (1981b). Partnership in transsexualism. Part II: The nature of the partnership. *Archives of Sexual Behavior, 10,* 143–160.

Imber-Black, E. (1989). Idiosyncratic life cycle transitions and therapeutic rituals. In B. Carter & M. McGoldrick (Eds.), *The changing family life cycle, a framework for family therapy,* pp. 149–163. Boston: Allyn & Bacon.

Jones, S.L., & Tinker, D. (1982). Transsexualism and the family: An interactional explanation. *Journal of Family Therapy, 4,* 1–14.

Kubler-Ross, E. (1969). *On death and dying.* London: The Macmillan Company.

Lothstein, L.M. (1979). Psychodynamics and sociodynamics of gender-dysphoric states. *American Journal of Psychotherapy, 32(2),* 214–239.

Money, J., Clarke, F., & Mazur, T. (1975). Families of seven male-to-female transsexuals after 5–7 years: Sociological sexology. *Archives of Sexual Behavior,* *4,* 187–197.

Newman, L.E. (1976). Treatment for the parents of feminine boys. *American Journal of Psychiatry, 133*(6), 683–687.

Parker, G., & Barr, R. (1982). Parental representations of transsexuals. *Journal of Sexual Behavior, 2*(3), 221–230.

Peo, R.E. (1988). Transvestism. *Journal of Social Work and Human Sexuality, 7*(1), 57–75.

Piercy, F., & Sprenkle, F. (1986). *Family therapy sourcebook.* New York: The Guilford Press.

Šípová, I., & Brzek, A. (1983). Parental and interpersonal relationships of transsexual and masculine and feminine homosexual men. *Journal of Homosexuality, 9*(1), 75–85.

Steiner, B.W. (1985). Transsexuals, transvestites, and their partners. In B.W. Steiner (Ed.), *Gender dysphoria: Development, research, management,* pp. 351–364. New York: Plenum Press.

Stoller, R.J. (1967). Transvestites' women. *American Journal of Psychiatry, 124*(3), 333–339.

Stoller, R.J. (1985). *Presentations of gender.* New Haven: Yale University Press.

Wise, T.N., Dupkin, C., & Meyer, J.K. (1981). Partners of distressed transvestites. *American Journal of Psychiatry, 138,* 1221–1224.

Wrate, R.M., & Gulens, V. (1986). A systems approach to child effeminacy and the prevention of adolescent transsexualism. *Journal of Adolescence, 9,* 215–229.

24 GYNEMIMESIS AND GYNEMIMETOPHILIA

INDIVIDUAL AND CROSS-CULTURAL MANIFESTATIONS OF A GENDER-COPING STRATEGY HITHERTO UNNAMED*

John Money

Margaret Lamacz

In the popular as well as the professional sexological literature there has been and continues to be uncertainty regarding the nomenclature and the classification of the different types of gender transposition or gender dysphoria. This uncertainty is especially evident with respect to the phenomenon of the person who has the anatomy and morphology of one sex, and who lives in society as one who has the gender identity and gender role—that is the gender-identity/role, or G-I/R (Money & Wiedeking, 1980)—of the other sex.

In the vernacular, such a person has been variously known as a drag queen, fairy, faggot, or effeminate homosexual, if morphologically a male; and as a bull dyke or butch, if morphologically a female. In the language of the popular stage, both have been known, respectively, as female or male impersonators or transvestites (in Europe, as travesties). Legally and morally, both have been classified as perverts or deviants. Scientifically and medically they have been diagnostically innominate, except for being misassigned in an oversimplified way to the diagnosis of homosexual, transvestite, or transsexual.

Such people do not belong exclusively in any one of these three categories, but to a partial degree in each. They are homosexual insofar as they fall in love with and/or have genitosexual relations with someone of their own morphologic sex. They are transvestite insofar as they cross-dress and present themselves in public permanently as a member of the sex to which they do not belong morphologically; however, they are not fetishistically attached to clothing for erotosexual arousal and orgasm, as in the manner of the paraphilic transvestite. They are transsexual insofar as they may

*This chapter was previously published in *Comprehensive Psychiatry,* 25(4), 1984, and was supported by USPHS Grant #HD 00325 and Grant #83086900, William T. Grant, Jr., Foundation. Copyright © 1984 by Grune & Stratton, Inc. Used with permission.

change their body morphology by taking the hormones of the other sex. But they are not transsexual insofar as they live continuously with the genitalia with which they were born, rather than claim the right to genital surgical sex reassignment—even though they may claim the right to cosmetic transformation of other secondary-sexual parts of the body by plastic surgery.

There are no epidemiological statistics as to the incidence or prevalence of this phenomenon. The available clinical evidence indicates that its prevalence is greater in those born with the male than the female genital morphology. For these individuals, it may be called the lady-with-a-penis syndrome.

Using Greek etymology, the name herein proposed for the syndrome is "gynemimesis" (woman-miming; Money, 1980). Its counterpart is "andromimesis" (man-miming).

The person who falls in love with a gynemimetic is a gynemimetophiliac. Gynemimetophilia is the erotosexual phenomenon of being attracted toward a gynemimetic lover explicitly and not inadvertently by misattribution of the gynemimetic as a regular female. The counterpart terms are "andromimetophiliac" and "andromimetophilia."

The purpose of this paper is to present an illustrative case of gynemimesis followed for a period of 10 years, from 16 to 26 years of age; and to discuss gynemimesis in the local community in cross-cultural comparison with the hijras of India and the xanith of Oman.

Case Report

Referral

At the age of 16 years, 10 months, this patient was referred for evaluation in the Psychohormonal Research Unit by a Juvenile Services caseworker in the urban division of Social Services. At the time, the patient was registered as a boy, Gerald, who dressed in girls' clothes under the name of Geraldine, also known on the street as Regina. The patient claimed the right to be officially recognized as a female, to live full-time as a female, and, like some of her cross-dressing companions, to be authorized to take female hormones in order to have a more feminine-appearing body.

Juvenile Services Biography

The patient was born to unwed parents too young for parental responsibilities. The maternal grandparents took on the responsibility of their grandson's rearing. Contact with the parents of birth ultimately was lost. At age 3, because of his grandparents' illness, the patient and his sister, 20 months older, were transferred to the permanent foster care of a distant female cousin, in accordance with the tradition of the black community in which they lived (Money, 1977). He established with her a bond of mother-child dependency that, with the knowledge of hindsight, appears to have been pathologically close to child abuse. The foster father was alleged to beat him and his sister injuriously. This man died of a heart attack two days after the two children had been transferred to another foster home. In this new placement, the boy became enuretic, argumentative, and defiant, and ran away, back to his first foster mother. It required another 18 months, however, before he was permitted to return to her permanently. Soon he was joined by his sister.

By the time he was 11 and the sister was 13, the sister's behavioral pathology led her into trouble with the juvenile authorities on charges of sexual promiscuity. She was put in juvenile detention.

It was while she was away that her brother began locking himself away in his room. He did not know that his foster mother would peep through a crack in the door and observe him primping in the mirror while wearing a woman's wig and clothing. Prior to this time, the foster mother recalled, she had not been aware of any cross-gender signs in the boy's thoughts or behavior. Nor had she been aware of any juvenile sexual play. She considered herself a very religious person, averse to children's exposing their own nudity and to learning about sex.

At the time he began cross-dressing, the patient also spent many hours occupying himself in feminine domesticities, helping his foster mother. Eventually, other children called him a fag and a punk, and there were complaints about him "fooling around" with other boys.

Shortly before his fourteenth birthday, he had six psychiatric appointments, without effect. The following month, he was brought home by the police wrapped in only a sheet. His alibi was that he had been abducted by a man and raped. Then he admitted that he had been visiting the man regularly.

He was 16 when his sister was released from detention. The two of them sometimes cooperated and sometimes feuded over his wearing of her clothes, for example, or seducing her boyfriends. He regularly wore unisex styles or cross-dressed, with feminine accessories and cosmetics. In his girl's outfit, he was considered by some to be more femininely attractive than was his sister. He kept very late hours, and often did not come home at all. He was rebellious if censured or restricted. His poor school record made him ineligible for training in cosmetology. He had a short live-in relationship with at least one "husband." He had a record of arrest and detention for an "indecent sex act" in the men's room of a bus station, and was released under the continued supervision of Juvenile Services.

The caseworker, recognizing the central role of the problem of gender identity, initiated the psychohormonal referral. The request was for evaluation with respect to hormonal sex reassignment, with or without a later possibility of surgical sex reassignment. The patient's own concern was specifically to grow breasts, not to undergo genital surgery.

Hormonal and Physical History

At the age of 17, and as a candidate for estrogen therapy, the patient was given a standard physical examination. The appearance was healthy. The height was 172 cm (5 ft. 8 in.), and the weight 71 kg (157 lb.). The body build and proportions were normal. Puberty, on the criterion of sparse pubic-hair growth was at Tanner stage V (adult). The growth of facial hair was sparse. The penis was uncircumcised and 12 cm (4.75 in.) in length, flaccid. The testes were within normal adult limits in size (10 on the Prader scale). They were soft. This finding, together with that of a nubbin of breast tissue, bilaterally, and everted, prominent nipples, was attributed to an undisclosed, probably prior use of a small amount of estrogen. Otherwise, the physical examination was unremarkable.

Serum FSH (follicle-stimulating hormone) was 177 ng/ml (normal range 150–300); and serum LH (luteinizing hormone) was 102 ng/ml (normal range 30–75).

The consensus of opinion among endocrine, psychiatric, and sexological consultants was for hormonal sex reassignment as a transsexual, but with surgical reassignment indefinitely deferred. The Juvenile Services supervisor, the foster mother, the birth mother, and the patient signed their informed consent. The patient was begun on Premarin 2.5 mg once a day, for both its antiandrogenic behavioral effects and its feminizing body effects.

After 8 weeks, Premarin was changed to Depo-Estradiol, 1 mg each week intramuscularly, for 10 more weeks. At the end of this time, the visible evidence of bodily feminization was negligible, and testosterone (normal range 425–725 ng/dl) was incompletely suppressed from 579 to 231 ng/dl. Depo-Estradiol was increased to 1.5 mg a week. Six months later, the breasts had attained the size of Tanner stage IV puberty, with 10–11 cm of breast tissue bilaterally. In the next six months they did not enlarge further, nor did they after the addition of 10 mg daily of the synthetic progestin, Provera, to the hormonal prescription. They remain rather nonprotuberant. The nipples and areolae are small.

Subsequently, the same two hormones were prescribed on a maintenance daily dosage of Premarin, 5 mg, and Provera, 5 mg, both by mouth. Compliance has been unpredictable, with at least two periods of several months of being off treatment, ostensibly for financial reasons. At the present time, the hormonal dosage is being reevaluated.

The patient is able to pass as a female in appearance, despite the small size of the breasts. Facial hair is scant and cosmetically controlled by shaving twice a week. The voice has a tenor quality and does not contradict the overall impression of femininity.

Body-Image Dimorphism

Throughout the ten–week period of follow-up, the patient's most consistent self-image has been that of an androgyne. At age 17, the androgynous balance was in favor of a "guy with tits," rather than "a girl with a dick." Whereas she said she wanted to "get titties on my chest," she disclaimed wanting to get genital surgery. Her ambition to have larger breasts has been consistent. She still would like silicone injections, or augmentation mammoplasty, but has not made a concerted effort to obtain the funds to pay for either procedure.

Over the years, her position on genital surgery has wavered from time to time, chiefly as a function of her resentment of financial hardship and abandonment by those on whom she depended for support. Once, when she was 17, out of money, and not yet reconciled with her foster mother, she conjectured the possibility of deciding to live again as a man—though not for another 15 years. More recently, at the age of 26, in another crisis of abandonment, this time by a live-in boyfriend and provider, she resentfully blamed her fate on her boyfriend's discovery of her genital status, and on an economic system that failed to provide her with transsexual surgery. In actual fact, there was documented evidence that the boyfriend had always known of her genital status, and found it acceptable. When the crisis resolved, her resentment at not having had the surgery faded and disappeared.

She was again able to be content with herself "as a woman with everything," as opposed to a man with breasts or a woman with a penis. At age 18, she made the following statement: "I'm making good money now. It's fun to freak out the straights, by pulling out my dick when I want to. I can tuck it in to dance, and fool everybody that way, too."

In an interview at age 24, she was queried specifically about her self-image. "I could put myself into the category of transsexual," she said, "or it could be bisexual. . . . I don't consider myself as a drag queen. . . . I still consider myself as a woman with ability to please everyone."

Projecting herself into the role of writing an autobiography, and selecting a title, she mused, ". . . the woman behind the man, or the woman in front of the man . . . and all the time you're writing about this woman, but in reality it's still a man. Let me see—He/She."

With respect to surgery, she said, "I don't want to be a woman. I just want to look like one. . . . There are some things I want, some things I don't want. Like, I want bigger boobs. Nice big plush hips. I notice, as I've gotten older, my hips have sunken in, taken on that male form. And the buttocks, I want to fill them out. I would like to go through the whole process of electrolysis. And just be castrated, for the time being. . . . After the castration, you know, you take on a more feminine form. . . . You have to be castrated before the operation, anyhow."[1]

When keeping a hospital appointment, the patient was groomed and dressed sometimes informally, sometimes formally, following the fashions of the day. One observational note, written by a female medical student when the patient was 21, reads as follows: "Looking very well. Neat and sedate appearance. Minimal makeup. Nails polished. Perfumed. Very convincing. Very feminine. Not overdone. Weight 165 pounds. Height 5 ft. 8 in."

Gynemimetic Community

At the time of her first interview, while still not quite 17, the patient had established contact with people like herself in the historic port area of the city. They worked as impersonators—nightclub entertainers and hostesses, or bar girls, alongside regular hostesses, earning a living chiefly on a commission basis. Their impersonator status was traditionally one of the attractions of the bars where they were employed. In many instances, customers would patronize such a bar because of their presence. They were not, however, standard gay bars, but bars of mixed clientele where impersonators were to be found.

Despite changes of management and site, bars frequented by impersonators continue to operate in the city, catering to their particular clientele. There are also bars in which impersonators are not hostesses or entertainers, but patrons on the lookout for a pick-up.

Currently, some of the impersonators in these bars identify themselves as preoperative transsexuals. Those who have had sex-reassignment surgery and still participate in the bar scene are referred to by nontranssexuals, somewhat disparagingly, as "sex changes." Impersonators of the same type as the patient have no definitive name for themselves. They do not use the term "cross-dresser," nor "transvestite," in self-reference.

There is no name by which to differentiate the men with a proclivity for impersonators from those without. In fact, an integral part of the credo of impersonation is not to make the distinction, the ideal of the impersonator being to attract ordinary heterosexual male partners.

A majority of the patrons at the bar are transients, interested in a casual relationship or one-night stand. Some, however, are regulars, and some maintain repeat engagements with the same impersonator. Rarely, a patron might establish a live-in relationship with a particular impersonator as a boyfriend and household provider.

Such a couple might break with the bar scene. More likely, the impersonator would regularly return, if not accompanied, then alone, drawn by her fascination for participating in the sexual life-style of the bars.

This life-style included a loose-knit friendship or neighborhood network of impersonators. In the present instance, the patient participates in such a network. Several of them rent apartments in the same building. When times are hard, they share accommodations and help one another.

Though they socialize together, members of the network work independently. The patient, for example, has been solo when seen "working the bars" or "turning a trick" on the street. So engaged, she might signal one of her friends that she did not want to be recognized, lest it destroy her image of herself as a real lady. If she and her friends should meet together at the same bar, it would be for purposes of socializing, not picking up a partner.

The patient does not have a generic term with which to identify the network that constitutes her gynemimetic community. Their work might be "hustling," but they are not hustlers. Their female wardrobes might be referred to as "drag," but they do not qualify as "drag queens." The patient disdainfully rejects this latter term as not having self-application.

For the most part, the gynemimetic community or friendship network is parochial. It has no organizational relationship with similar groups within the city, state, or region. They do not participate in the regional Gay Community Center, nor in the politics of gay liberation. They have no organization for defense against periodic police harassment, nor for the male sexual status accorded to them should they be held in jail for soliciting.

On the basis of individual contacts, the patient has known about the impersonator scene in other big cities. She has lived out of state twice—once for a few weeks with a friend in South Carolina and once for a few months in New Jersey with her live-in partner whose job had taken him there. Her knowledge of impersonation and impersonators in other countries was fragmentary.

Partner Affiliations

It became evident with the passage of time that there were two themes in the patient's sexual life. They corresponded to the familiar split between the madonna and the whore, and its reciprocal, the provider and the playboy (Money, 1980). On the madonna side of the split, the patient romanticized the idea of having an enduring partnership with a boyfriend who would be a husband-equivalent. He would be her provider, and would support her. She would delight in pleasing him. Erotosexually, her satisfaction would be achieved in satisfying him. He was idealized as being exclusively heterosexual in proclivity, blue-eyed, blonde, and totally accepting of her as a woman, despite his knowledge of her genital status.

Romantic idealization of the partnership as a heterosexual one imposed a veto on permitting the partner to have a homosexual interest in the patient's own penis. Thus the sexual history, as reported in the patient's interviews over the years, tends toward being prudish with respect to genitosexual participation and erotic technique.

In the course of the decade under review, there was no period longer than a few weeks when the patient failed to have an affiliation with a boyfriend who was a provider. Whereas some of the affiliations lasted only a few weeks or months, two had a longer history. The first of these longer affairs began shortly before the patient was 18. The boyfriend was 33. They lived together for 18 months. Then the patient was arrested for soliciting, and the boyfriend, a diabetic, left town for job retraining. Eighteen months later they resumed contact but did not begin living together for another year or more. They then shared an apartment in a distant city for nine months, after which they went their separate ways.

The patient spoke endearingly of this partner. There was no evidence, however, that either of them had undergone the complete pair-bonding experience of falling in love. In fact this type of experience appears not to have been included in the patient's erotosexual repertory. Her partner affiliations have resembled rather the convenience of an arranged marriage. Each affiliation was not without fondness and affection, but it did not include the excitement of being love-smitten. Excitement belonged less to the madonna and more to the whore in her clandestine encounter with a playboy, or the call girl with her client. No matter how well the provider provided, he would not compete with the challenge of "turning a trick" on the side, irrespective of its monetary return, or the danger involved.

The home visit made by two members of the Psychohormonal Research Unit for the purpose of meeting the first long-term partner did not succeed. It was the second such partner who gave an interview. He was a man in his late forties when the patient was 23. He had been married for 25 years, and separated for four. His four children were young adults. He and the patient had known each other casually for several years before they started living together as a couple.

It was fairly well known that the patient's partner was attracted exclusively to black transvestites and transsexuals, one of whom had previously lived with him for a time. He himself was white. He had no attraction to gay men in male clothing. Though he rated himself as bisexual, he said, "I play the man's role only, and I got that straight with each of the girls before I started living with her—that I would not play the feminine part. I would never dress up . . ." He said that he hadn't even heard the term, "drag queen," until he was 40 and first met the one he eventually began to live with.

Of his partners' male genitals, he said, "I don't know. I don't think that really matters. The anatomy, it doesn't phase me at all—period. It's just the feelings that I have for her, mainly . . ."

"I had more sex with my wife," he said, "than with the transsexuals I've lived with. . . . [W]ith my wife, we were having a lot more sex, and our sex life was great, and [we] never had any problems." He could not explain why he had left his wife, apart from his fascination with the gynemimetics whom he referred to as transsexuals. There was nothing unmasculine in his lean, gnarled, farm-worker appearance and manner.

Queried about love, romance, and sex in her relationship with this man, the patient said, "I don't know if it's love I feel for him, or just friendship, but I would say it's love. . . . It seems to me that it's something I can't do without. The feeling of being lonely . . . I'm sure everybody has experienced that feeling of being with someone. In my situation, I hate being alone. Just for him to call me on the phone from work, and say that he loves me . . . that makes me feel good all inside . . ."

"Romantic," she said, "to me is being in a little boat, just the two of you fishing with a bottle of Chablis and Galiano, and just sit there, and look out into the water, and tell each other your thoughts. That's romantic to me."

Sex, with body contact, was more elusive and problematic for her to define. "Sex is something that you would really like to have, to get into it, you know, heavily, emotionally, and you have to put all your feelings into it. You just do it, get it over with, and go to sleep." The playing around she referred to was having her breasts sucked, and her flaccid penis perhaps played with, as she played with her partner's penis until he ejaculated.

Genital-Erotic History

Inconstancy of memory and recall was characteristically typical of the patient's attempt to retrieve biographical information on different occasions. Thus it is not possible to give a juvenile erotosexual history with consistency or precision.

From puberty until the present, there has been no evidence that the wearing of female clothing served a paraphilic and fetishistic function in promoting erotic arousal and the achievement of orgasm.

409

The history of masturbation dated from about age 14. At that time, as a boy, he had become involved in gay life at school. While masturbating he would sometimes "concentrate on feelings," and sometimes on a boy who had been a sexual partner—"trying to reach the stage where I would be what I always want to be, a woman."

There was no early history of difficulty with erection or ejaculation when masturbating. In the role of a woman, in order to suppress erection so as to be more womanly with a male partner, she would think distracting thoughts. The idea of using her own penis for anal penetration of a partner was offensive to her.

A detailed inquiry into erotic practices took place in a recorded interview when the patient was 24 years old. At that time, she had recently resumed regular treatment with estrogen and progestin, with a resultant antiandrogenic effect on the genitalia, namely reduction of erection and ejaculation. "The last time I can remember getting an erection," she said, "was about a month ago. It was a very settled, cold feeling, not the way it used to be, real warm and cheerful. . . . It was like, after I was done, I couldn't be bothered . . . don't touch me; leave me alone. . . . So I just said, forget it . . . My penis doesn't really bother me . . . It's not even there . . . I'm just as happy now as I ever was."

At this time, she down-played having sex with anyone other than her regular boyfriend. "The only time I go to bed with another man," she said, "is when he's paying me some money. Other than that, I can't be bothered."

Of her own sexual feeling, she said, "It's in my tits . . . only when Albert (my boyfriend) does it. It feels great when he does it, but when somebody else does it, it doesn't feel the same. . . . It doesn't make my penis hard, or nothing like that, but it just feels good . . ." Albert himself reported more varied sexual activity, including anal intercourse with himself as inserter.

Referring back to her previous boyfriend, and a period when she was not taking hormones, the patient said of orgasm, "Now that was a feeling I could say really went over the top, the whole bit, because he made me feel . . . well, you have to understand, at that point in my life, I was feeling unwanted, really down . . . and he brought back all these feelings I thought were never there." Their activities included sixty-nine, "and I always played the role of the woman . . . or I would be very upset. . . . I wouldn't fuck him in his ass; so that brought along some difficulty in the relationship. . . ."

For paying clients, the patient had perfected her own technique for concealing her male genitalia. Eventually, in response to professional skepticism, she documented this technique, photographically. It entailed first pushing each testicle up through the inguinal ring so that it would not descend. Then the uncircumsized penis was stretched over the empty scrotum, backwards to the anus, and entrapped there, between the legs, by the tight clamping of the gluteal musculature. It was so firmly gripped that it would stay in position irrespective of vigorous movement, as in dancing or sexual intercourse. It was released by relaxation of the muscular grip, while in the squatting position—a trick which the patient had, on occasion, performed while showering postcoitally, as a joke, to surprise and dumbfound her unsuspecting customer. Previously, while having sexual intercourse, the customer's penis would have been thrusting, usually on the right side, deeply into a suitably lubricated pouch of scrotal skin, high into the cavity of the inguinal canal. To guarantee the complete success of this method, it was necessary that a client be sufficiently inebriated, and not too diligent in his pursuit of cunnilingus or digital-vulval activity.

Some clients did not require direct genital activity, but a paraphilic substitute. For example, one man regularly paid the patient to slowly chew dry hamburgers, which he provided. That was his erotic turn-on, until one day he discovered that the cook had put relish on the hamburgers. He left, and never returned.

Behavioral Health and Psychology

As a teenager known as a boy and named Gerald, the patient lived in an era when he might well have been given a diagnosis of juvenile deviancy or antisocial personality disorder. The evidence adduced would have been: dressing as a girl, soliciting homosexual sex, having sex with an older male partner, not returning home at night, confabulating or lying about these activities, and underachieving at school.

A preteenaged diagnosis of the syndrome of child abuse or the battered-child syndrome would probably not have been given because, at that time, these diagnoses were not yet in vogue.

Nonetheless, it is correct that, as a juvenile, the patient did have an undiagnosed case of child abuse. Thus, it now becomes possible to reconceptualize the subsequent behavioral development of puberty and the teenage years as the outcome of a developmental strategy for coping with the stress of child abuse. This strategy can thus be construed as a strategy of self-rehabilitation or self-healing. As a strategy, it needs a name for easy reference. Hence the term, "gynemimesis."

Whether or not a strategy of self-rehabilitation or self-healing (Money, 1971) should or should not be equated with pathology is a matter of officially endorsed nosological policy. In the present instance, those responsible for case management, especially the administration of hormones, did in fact need the support of a diagnosis to justify giving treatment. In the absence of the contemporary, generic terms, "gender dysphoria," or "gender transposition" (Money & Wiedeking, 1980), they fell back on the term "transsexualism." Transsexualism, however, falls short of being precisely accurate. Hence the new term, "gynemimesis." Gynemimesis is not by definition a pathology, but the term can be applied nosologically and diagnostically, as necessity dictates.

If that is done in the present instance, then the patient qualifies for only one diagnosis, namely gynemimesis. She has no other history of psychopathology, despite the fact that the law has disapproved of her sexual method of earning a living. Recently, even the latter has changed. Through the help of a friend, the patient has become employed as a female security officer.

DISCUSSION

In the foregoing, the duality of Gerald and Geraldine may be considered in the context of the dual principles of identification and complementation (Money & Ehrhardt, 1972). These are the two principles according to which G-I/R differentiates in its postnatal, socialization phase. Under ordinary circumstances, identification is with persons of the same sex as that in which the child is assigned, and complementation is to the other sex. Parents usually occupy an initial role in identification and complementation, but they are not the exclusive representatives of their sex in a child's G-I/R differentiation. Eventually, age mates assume a key position, also.

Analogously with the way that native language becomes implanted as a schema in the brain, so also do identification and complementation implant their gender schemas in the brain. Regardless of genital sexual status, everyone's brain carries a socialized implant of the gender schema of each sex, one by identification, and one by complementation. The identification schema carries the label, "this is me." The complementation schema carries the label "this is not me, it is with whom I interact." Ordinarily, the identification schema, which is postnatally implanted in the brain, makes a conjunction with the erotosexual schema of the genitalia that precedes it, prenatally, and is phyletically preplanted in the brain.

Phenomenologically, it is the disjunction instead of the ordinarily expected conjunction of the phyletically preplanted and the socially implanted aspects of the identification gender schema which constitute the fundamental anomaly in the gender-transposition syndromes, gynemimesis included.

One consequence of this disjunction is that the observer frequently recognizes an element of theatrical play-acting in the gynemimetic, and of being on stage (Green & Money, 1966). Being on stage as an exotic dancer or entertainer is, indeed, a career favored by gynemimetics. The zenith is to seduce a man and entertain him erotically and sexually without being discovered. Multiply the number of men, addictively, and this strategy becomes synonymous with promiscuity.

As in all the gender-transposition syndromes, the etiology of gynemimesis remains obscure. In this present case, there were no retrievable prenatal hormonal or pharmacological data that may have been significant with respect to subsequent vulnerability to an anomaly of postnatal differentiation of gender-identity/role (G-I/R). The retrievable data on childhood experiences relative to G-I/R differentiation are scanty. Nonetheless, these data do include evidence of child abuse which could be etiologically important. It is not uncommon to find such evidence in the history of a child with a G-I/R transposition. Abuse and neglect dislocate the parent-child alignments that affect the early differentiation of G-I/R as masculine or feminine. In the present instance, the child became pathologically aligned with the foster mother, though it was the older sister whom the brother emulated as he became increasingly effeminate at puberty and thereafter.

The only information on the child's sexual learning, which affects G-I/R differentiation in childhood, was that it had been prohibited. As an adult, the patient had negligible recall of erotosexual play in childhood, and referred to a childhood sexual experience only once—in an outburst of anger, she claimed to have been raped by an older man at the age of eight.

In the course of Geraldine's long follow-up, Gerald did not ever appear in toto. If he had ever alternated with Geraldine, in the manner of a patient with two names, two wardrobes, and two personalities (Money, 1974), then that alternation had long since ceased. Geraldine had center stage, and Gerald was incognito.

Only when Geraldine underwent a crisis of feeling that her status was being thwarted or destroyed, by the police, for example, or by the abandonment of a lover, might Gerald threaten to materialize. Then in a mood of depressive anger, Geraldine might make a reference to her penis, either to reinstate it, or to repudiate it completely by considering sex reassignment.

Irrespective of etiology, duality in the G-I/R differentiation of Gerald/Geraldine might be ascribed technically to the phenomenon of splitting, if one uses psychoanalytic terminology; or to dissociation, if the terminology is that of Pierre Janet or Morton Prince. That which is split off, or disassociated, is that which pertains to masculinity and its stereotypes.

The two components of the split or dissociation may or may not have equal status. The syndrome in which their status is more or less equal is the syndrome of episodic transvestism, already referred to as two names, two wardrobes, and two personalities. This syndrome may be lifelong, or it may metamorphose into full-blown transsexualism. When the two personalities alternate, they typically represent extreme exaggerations or travesties of the stereotypes of masculinity and femininity, respectively. To be gentle, tender, or erotic, and to perform sexually, the episodic transvestite man has to become a woman by proxy, that is by wearing a woman's clothes. In men's clothes, he is domineering and aggressive even to the point of treachery and violence.

In the syndrome of cross-dressing or transvestism that is not episodic, or that changes from episodic to continuous, the biography is one in which the split or dissociation becomes lopsided, so that one part of the split predominates at the expense of the other. Thus, the boy who grows up to live and cross-dress full-time as a girl and woman becomes increasingly convincing as a gynemimetic. He is able to give a well-rounded impression of femininity that does not seem exaggerated or grotesquely stereotyped. Conversely, he becomes increasingly unable to give a convincing impression of a man.

In some cases, gynemimesis becomes attached to an abiding obsession to demasculinize the body by castration, by hormonal feminization, or by hormonal and surgical sex reassignment. The latter has become known as the syndrome of transsexualism, though, more accurately, transsexualism names the method of treatment and rehabilitation, not the syndrome.

The syndrome of gynemimesis without transsexualism is probably the same as what sexologists earlier in the twentieth century called passive or effeminate male homosexuality, or in some instances, male transvestism. However, gynemimesis is not a synonym for male homosexuality, nor for transvestism, per se. By far the vast majority of males who are defined as homosexual are not gynemimetic, and are not transvestic.

Some males are defined as homosexual erotosexually only. They are able to fall in love only with other men. Otherwise their G-I/R is masculine. They may have been able to copulate with a female and may have produced offspring.

Other males who are defined as homosexual should more properly be defined as partly bisexual. They are males whose love affairs are, or have been, exclusively with women. Situationally, as in prison (Money & Bohmer, 1980), they have proved capable of relating genitally to a male whom they cast in the role of female.

There are some 50/50 bisexuals. However, most people who have had bisexual experiences are more likely to fall in love with only a man, or only a woman, not both.

For most of the general public, gynemimesis may be construed as a medical or psychiatric condition, though more likely as an egregious insult to common sense, a defiance of the social definition of male and female, a conspiracy against sexual morality, or a criminal offense to be apprehended and punished. Conversely, the general public also condones gynemimesis provided it is institutionalized within the entertainment industry on stage, in the movies, or on television, where the impersonation does not need to be unmasked because it is advertised in advance.

Gynemimesis has been differently institutionalized in other societies. In India, for example, gynemimetics become members of what is in effect partly a special caste and partly a religious order. They are the "hijras," recently well-documented by Nanda (1984). Traditionally, hijras did not, of course, have sex hormones available to feminize the body. They did, however, have the age-old ability to become demasculinized by becoming eunuchs. The caste has its own traditional specialists in castration, which includes removal of the penis as well as the testicles and scrotum. Not all members undergo this operation. Those who do serve a prolonged novitiate as members of the caste beforehand. The operation is done without anesthetic.

Hijras have a national organization in India which resembles that of a religious order, with allegiance to a hierarchy of gurus. At the local level, they live in small households, their relationships patterned after those of mother, daughters, and sisters. In their families of origin, they may have been either Hindu, Muslim, or Christian. As hijras, they venerate Bahuchara Mata, a mother goddess sometimes represented as a yantra, the conventional symbol of the vulva.

A hijra typically has a history of gynemimesis in childhood and early adolescence. While still living with his family, he will recognize the affinity that exists between him and the local or visiting hijras who sing and dance at public festivals. When he leaves home to join the hijras, it may be to escape defamation and abuse, or to relieve his parents of the embarrassment of his presence, and his brothers of the duty to postpone their own marriages while he remains single.

As the new member of a hijra household, his eligibility for membership will be on trial before he is initiated into having a female name and clothing. He is required to earn a living. The least desirable option is begging for alms. Hijras are also, by tradition, the keepers of public bathhouses, used by those who lack domestic hot water for bathing. By tradition, they are also singers and dancers who have the right to demand money from the wealthy for performing at their marriages, when a son is born, or on the occasion of other celebrations. Some hijras achieve fame as entertainers, and may get parts in films. Hijras are also renowned for their careers as prostitutes, which may be either full-time or part-time, and as kept concubines. They engage in anal, oral, and interfemoral intercourse. Some hijras have no sexual interests at all, and others are sexual enthusiasts who enjoy being in the role of women servicing men.

The members of a hijra household are not cut off from contacts with their families of origin, nor from helping them financially. Those are matters of individual option.

Another recent ethnographic study of gynemimesis was done in Oman by Wikan (1977). In Oman, a gynemimetic is known as a "xanith" (pronounced "hanith"), a term that is also more widely used in Arabic as the translation of the English "homosexual." Xanith is applied in Oman only to the gynemimetic partner in a homosexual coupling—that is, to the one who consistently performs as if in the sexual role of a woman with a man. It does not apply to the partner who, when having sex with a xanith, consistently performs as if in the role of a man with a woman.

In Oman, the xanith may gain public status as a man instead of a xanith, provided he enters into marriage arranged by his family and produces the public evidence of successful vaginal penetration of the virgin bride, namely a blood-stained cloth. He gains this status despite the persistence of his feminine demeanor in facial expressions, voice, laughter, and movements. He may relinquish his male status and revert to that of xanith.

> The xanith always retains his male given name. He is not allowed to wear the face mask of purdah, nor other female clothing. His clothes are intermediate between male and female: he wears the ankle-length tunic of the male, but with the tight waist of the female dress. Male clothing is white. Females wear patterned cloth in bright colours, and xanith wear unpatterned coloured clothes. Men cut their hair short, women wear theirs long, the xanith medium long. Men comb their hair backward away from the face, women comb theirs diagonally forward from a central parting, xanith comb theirs forward from a side parting, and they oil it heavily in the style of women. Both men and women cover their head, xanith go bareheaded. Perfume is used by both sexes, especially at festive occasions and during intercourse. The xanith is generally heavily perfumed, and uses much make-up to draw attention to himself. This is also achieved by his affected swaying gait, emphasised by the close-fitting garments. His sweet falsetto voice and facial expressions and movements also closely mimic those of women. If he wore female clothes, it would in many instances not be possible to see him to be, anatomically speaking, male and not female.

—Wikan, 1977, p. 307

Nonetheless, the xanith has no tradition of feminizing the body either by becoming a eunuch, or by the contemporary method of taking sex hormones.

The xanith is publicly recognizable in Oman as having the status of neither male nor female, but of xanith. Like his clothing, his role in society resembles that of women, but does not replicate it. Unlike men, he is permitted to move freely among women behind purdah, and to share their social life, intimate gossip, domesticity, and activities. At a wedding, whereas musical instruments are played by men, the xanith joins the women singers. Unlike women, the xanith is not ruled under the power and dominion of a man. Like men, he has the right to go about in public unaccompanied. He also has the right, exclusive to the role of xanith, to live alone, to be hired as a house servant, and to be hired by men as a prostitute. Female prostitution is outlawed, and, like adultery, is subject to severe punishment.

Wikan estimated the prevalence of xanith in the small town of her study as 2 percent of the 3,000 adult males.

Contemporary groups of xanith in Oman, hijras of India, and gynemimetic ladies with a penis in American urban society historically have not been exposed to cultural borrowing from one another. The congruency in their traditions may, therefore, be presumed to be a feature of the gynemimetic syndrome itself, in accommodation to society. Thus it is that gynemimesis, being itself a feminine identification, manifests itself as an impersonation of women in cosmetics, dress, and mannerisms. Being a manifestation of acting, it lends itself to musical, theatrical, film, or television entertainment as an occupation. Being also a manifestation of falling in love with men, it lends itself to prostitution or multiple partnering with men as an affirmation of excellence in the ultimate test of femininity, namely being the sexual partner of a man.

Society at large in India and Oman institutionalized gynemimesis without exactly endorsing it, but also without persecuting and criminalizing it. Boys confronted with recognizing the syndrome in themselves at puberty could find a place of belonging in society instead of being alienated from it. By contrast, their counterparts in America are confronted with being stigmatized as criminals, unless they enter into complicity with the social system by pretending that they cross-dress optionally, voluntarily, and only for the purpose of earning a living, and not because that is, indeed, their very way of being.

SUMMARY

"Gynemimesis" is a subtype of gender transposition or gender dysphoria in which a person with male anatomy and morphology lives as a woman without genital sex-reassignment surgery, and with or without taking female sex-hormone therapy. The lover of such a person is a "gynemimetophile." The corresponding terms that apply to the female are "andromimesis" and "andromimetophile." In most large cities in the West there exists an unnamed gynemimetic community that corresponds to the social institution of the hijras in India and xanith in Oman. Clinicians can contribute to the rehabilitation and welfare of gynemimetic youth in society by providing health care, including endocrine treatment and mental-health counseling.

NOTE

1. Geraldine was in error about this. Prior castration is not a requirement for vaginoplasty; in fact, some surgeons prefer that it not have been done previously.

REFERENCES

Green, R., & Money, J. (1966). Stage acting, role-taking and effeminate impersonation during boyhood. *Archives of General Psychiatry, 15, 535–538.*

Money, J. (1971). Transsexualism and the philosophy of healing. *Journal of the American Society of Psychosomatic Dentistry and Medicine, 18, 25–26.*

Money, J. (1974). Two names, two wardrobes, two personalities. *Journal of Homosexuality, 1, 65–70.*

Money, J. (1977). The American heritage of three traditions of pair bonding: Mediterranean, Nordic, and Slave. In J. Money & H. Musaph (Eds.), *Handbook of Sexology.* New York: Excerpta Medica.

Money, J. (1980). *Love and love sickness: The science of sex, gender difference, and pair-bonding.* Baltimore, MD: Johns Hopkins University Press.

Money, J., & Bohmer, C. (1980). Prison sexology: Two personal accounts of masturbation, homosexuality, and rape. *Journal of Sex Research, 16, 258–266.*

Money, J., & Ehrhardt, A.A. (1972). *Man and woman, boy and girl: The differentiation and dimorphism of gender identity from conception to maturity.* Baltimore, MD: Johns Hopkins University Press. [Also, Northvale, NJ: Jason Aronson. (1996).]

Money, J., & Wiedeking, C. (1980). Gender identity/role: Normal differentiation and its transpositions. In B.B. Wolman & J. Money (Eds.), *Handbook of human sexuality.* Englewood Cliffs, NJ: Prentice Hall.

Nanda, S. (1984). The hijras of India: A preliminary report. *Medicine and Law, 3, 59–75.*

Wikan, U. (1977). Man becomes woman: Transsexualism in Oman as a key to gender roles. *Man, 12, 304–319.*

CONCLUSION TO *TRANSSEXUALISM AND SEX REASSIGNMENT*

REFLECTIONS AT 25 YEARS

Richard Green

Startling as it is for me to think it, I wrote the conclusion to *Transsexualism and Sex Reassignment* about 25 years ago. It's been a long time since I re-read it. As I write my reflections, I am struck at the outset that the biggest change with this new text may be that it is edited by a transsexual.

In retrospect, it was a groundbreaking work. Published only three years after Harry Benjamin's pioneering *The Transsexual Phenomenon*, it was the first interdisciplinary professional text. Its legitimacy was promoted as "consistent with the tradition of scientific inquiry and medicine," examining "deviations from the norm in the hope of better understanding normal processes." In part to justify serious professional attention, transsexualism was packaged in time-honored wrapping.

The subject was exotic and esoteric. In the 1960s and 1970s, professional papers on transsexualism needed to define the term at the outset. Now children know it. They have seen transsexuals on television talk shows.

Does transsexualism still pose the most controversial subject in medicine? Although transsexualism is still a contentious issue, other topics such as abortion and euthanasia also exercise emotions. But they do not challenge psychodynamic theories or learning paradigms as does transsexualism.

In the intervening quarter century, research on the origins of transsexualism has not evolved all that much. It remains true that "no one now, be he psychoanalyst or neuroendocrinologist or expert in any other science, can claim to have the complete explanation of transsexualism."* "Much (still) remains to be discovered about how masculinity and femininity develop." And the "eventual availability of measures of circulating gonadal hormones during prenatal development" to help explain the neuroendocrine origins of gender identity remains that—a potential. However,

---

*Quotations not otherwise cited are from my original "Conclusion" (Green, 1969b).

advances in neuroscience offer promise. This year's excitement is about a brain nucleus that may characterize transsexuals and supports the century-old speculation/explanation—"a female mind trapped in a male body." If the finding holds, will it medically legitimize Harry Benjamin's "transsexual phenomenon" more than the past 25 years of professional energy?

We can still clarify the nature of the transsexual's statement, "I feel like a (person of the opposite sex)." To what extent do "cross-gender iden-tifications reflect a distorted or accurate perception of the other gender . . . (Are transsexuals) in greater consonance (cognitively) with their anatomic or their preferred physiologic sex?" Will that "prove to be modifiable through hormonal or experiential manipulation?"

Not all personal research potentials I addressed in the 1969 text have been realized. However, I did follow a sample of boys whose behaviors ap-proximated those retrospectively reported by adult male transsexuals. But 15 years on, most were homosexual or bisexual, not transsexual. Much re-mains to be learned.

Transsexualism was characterized in *Transsexualism and Sex Reas-signment* as the most atypical pattern of psychosexual development, with all three components of gender identity being atypical. The transsexual was atypical on basic identity as male or female, for behaviors as masculine or feminine, for sexual orientation as homosexual or heterosexual. Today the relation between components one and two versus three is being refined. We have considerable experience with lesbian male transsexuals and limited experience with gay female transsexuals. But it remains true that "the vari-ables on which transsexualism, transvestism, and homosexuality overlap and on which they are separate are not entirely clear."

In the intervening years, surgeons have harnessed the transsexual's re-quest as technological challenge. To some, vaginoplasty refinement has been likened to the quest for "building a better mousetrap." Phalloplasty is also evolving. But the surgical adage of the 1960s remains "It's easier to build a hole than a pole."

The prevalence of transsexuals appears higher than previously thought, perhaps double. Probably this is not a true increase, but rather an expression of patient optimism that coming forward for help will be re-spected by the healing professionals.

Very early follow-up data available in the late 1960s "support(ed) the contention that in the majority of persons in whom cross-gender iden-tity is extensive and of longstanding duration—conflict can be significantly lessened by sex reassignment." This remains true. But follow-up data re-main elusive. When I reviewed the 1980–1990 English-language reports of transsexual follow-up, I found that most patients operated on during those years were not reported, although at least 90 percent of reported patients appeared to have benefitted from reassignment (Green & Fleming, 1990).

The methodologically silly Johns Hopkins study of 1979 (Meyer & Reter, 1979) questioning benefits of sex reassignment surgery was an excuse for discontinuing that hospital's pioneering program. But it made only a dent in the worldwide professional recognition of the legitimacy of sex change. The methodologically serious study from London's Charing Cross of 1990 clearly demonstrated the benefits (Mate-Kole, Freschi, & Rubin, 1990).

Attitudes have changed. In contrast to the figures cited in 1969, when most doctors would permit a transsexual to commit suicide before granting a sex-change, today most of the public, professional and lay, would not likely oppose sex reassignment (Green, 1969a).

Some professionals do remain opposed to hormonal or surgical reassignment, retreating into psychodynamic formulations of pathology, falsely equating insight with change, reminiscing about a poorly adjusted postoperative patient they once saw, indicting the follow-up literature as methodologically flawed. But when pressed to recount their personal success rate in modifying gender identity or to cite substantial follow-up reports of psychiatrically treated successes, they retreat to their armchairs, where they reign.

It remains a truism that "the law must share with medicine responsibility for some of the transsexual's plight. . . . The problem remains . . . whether what has been granted medically will be acknowledged legally." Partly in response to the perseverance of legal discrimination in the interim 25 years, I have also obtained a degree in law.

Cross-gender living prior to surgery, the "real-life test," as coined by my co-editor John Money, has proven to be the critical rite de passage. But clinical management of the real-life test is obstructed by employment discrimination. The *Ulane* case, where I was an unsuccessful expert witness, was the death knell for protecting transsexuals in the U.S. under federal anti-gender discrimination law. Eastern Airlines (now defunct) successfully prevented a previously male pilot with an impeccable record from continuing to fly as a woman. Lawsuits in the United Kingdom and Europe are moving toward a more successful outcome, particularly in the European Court of Human Rights, the latter only a dream in 1969.

Unhappily, other legal issues also remain topical. The debate continues over "whether it should be the rightful concern of the law to deny one the right to dress as one wishes, conduct one's life in a preferred gender role, privately conduct one's sexual relationship as preferred by oneself and one's partner, and even to marry in the preferred sexual role." Not only does U.S. fair employment law neglect the transsexual, but half the states still criminalize same-sex genital contact, and in the U.K. post-operative transsexuals cannot marry.

Allocating resources for transsexual treatment is the new discrimination. Transsexuals are marginalized by government funding agencies and insurance companies. They are an easy target: a small constituency.

The newer adversary is the Bottom Line Bandit, the MBA or accountant who runs the business of medicine. Third-party payers argue that transsexual treatment is still experimental—after three decades. Is sex change more experimental than heart change or liver change? Another hollow utterance, ignoring the cry for help, labels the procedures "cosmetic," trivializing the pain of the transsexual, revealing a vacuous absence of empathy for human distress.

Risks of medical negligence suits for facilitating sex reassignment have been substantially reduced, when standards adopted by the professional community are followed. The "Harry Benjamin Guidelines" are in effect, at least for the adult. But with adolescents, similar concerns for medical negligence confront us as previously existed for adults. What is (will be) the standard for accepted practice? Should the physical changes of puberty that handicap later cross-gender passing be interrupted? Will research reveal that benefits to most young patients outweigh the risks that some will regret the intervention?

Newer ethical concerns have also evolved from whether clinicians should grant a request for sex reassignment, to the question, are clinicians necessary? Unfettered self-determination by gender-dysphoric patients is upon us. Should sex change be available on demand? That was hardly the issue in 1969, as the nearly insurmountable professional hurdle then was professionally sanctioned sex reassignment. If gender patients can procure surgeons who do not require psychiatric or psychological referral, research should address outcome for those who are professionally referred versus the self-referred. Then an ethical issue could be, if success is less (or failure greater) among the self-referred, should otherwise competent adults nevertheless have that autonomy of self-determination? And what should be the medical responsibility for the growing number of persons who do not want a "complete" sex change, but "only" gynecomastia, if male, or mastectomy, if female?

On examination and reflection, the 1969 chapter has aged well. Some progress has been made, but much remains to be examined, to be learned, and to be taught.

REFERENCES

Benjamin, H. (1966). *The transsexual phenomenon: A scientific report on trans-sexualism and sex conversion in the human male and female.* New York: Julian Press.

Green, R. (1969a). Attitudes toward transsexualism and sex-reassignment surgery. In R. Green & J. Money (Eds.), *Transsexualism and sex reassignment,* pp. 13-22. Baltimore: Johns Hopkins University Press.

Green, R. (1969b). Conclusion. In R. Green & J. Money (Eds.), *Transsexualism and sex reassignment.* Baltimore: Johns Hopkins Press.

Green, R. (1987). *The "sissy boy syndrome" and the development of homosexuality.* New Haven, CT: Yale University Press.

Green, R., & Fleming, D.T. (1990). Transsexual surgery follow-up: Status in the 1990s. In J. Bancroft, C.M. Davis, & D. Weinstein (Eds.), *Annual Review of Sex Research,* pp. 163-174. Mount Vernon, IA: Society for the Scientific Study of Sex.

Green, R., & Money, J. (Eds.). (1969). *Transsexualism and sex reassignment.* Baltimore: The Johns Hopkins University Press.

Mate-Kole, C., Freschi, M., & Rubin, A. (1990). A controlled study of psychological and social change after surgical gender reassignment in selected male trans-sexuals. *British Journal of Psychiatry, 157,* 261–264.

Meyer, J.K., & Reter, D. (1979). Sex reassignment: Follow-up. *Archives of General Psychiatry, 36*(9), 1010-1015.

Ulane v. Eastern Airlines, Inc., et al. (1984). 581 F. Supp. 821, 35 Fair Empl. Prac. Cas. (BNA) 1332; 34 Empl. Prac. Dec. (CCH) P34,334, 28 December, 1983; 8 February, 1984; and 6 March, 1984. 742 F. 2d 1081 (7th Cir. 1984).

Afterword

During the several years that have elapsed since work began on this book, the gender revolution has been taking place. The political awakening of the transgender community has given me new ways of looking at transsexualism and cross-dressing and caused me to reassess much of what I thought I knew.

As my thinking has evolved, the assumptions and biases of much of the existing literature has become more apparent. I find myself looking at old studies in a new way. Consider, for instance, the much-researched question of whether transsexuals are more likely to have psychiatric disturbances than nontranssexuals. Previously, such studies have tended to assume that transsexuals are inherently unstable, completely overlooking the fact that being transsexual is likely to lead to a lifetime of abuse and discrimination. The important questions then, become not "Do transsexuals exhibit significantly more psychopathology than nontranssexuals, and, if so, what is it about them that makes them so?" but "What environmental stresses do transsexuals encounter, how does this affect them, and how can we ensure that they are treated better?" The locus of the problem changes: it is externalized, no longer within the transsexual. It is not the transsexual or transsexualism that is at fault; the problem is an intolerant and violent society.

When such a shift of viewpoint takes place, much of the existing literature immediately becomes irrelevant. It no longer tells us anything very useful.

This does not mean that the existing research was unimportant or trivial. Indeed, it was essential, for without it, we would never have found ourselves in this place of changing perspectives. This is how science works. Our old models topple, and we are off on a new quest, asking new questions which will themselves one day seem quaint and limited.

Not everyone "gets it" at once. Some take a while longer than others—and a few diehards will refuse to acknowledge the validity of the new order. But the paradigm shift is a juggernaut, impossible to resist. It changes things, and it changes them forever.

I'm very excited to be around while all this is happening.

Dallas Denny

Appendix

The Empowerment of a Community

Rosalyne Blumenstein

Barbara E. Warren

Lynn E. Walker

It is now over forty years since Christine Jorgensen's surgery reintroduced transsexualism to the modern world. As more and more people have undergone the process of gender reassignment, men and women of transsexual and transgender experience have begun to develop more awareness, not just as individuals, but as members of a common group. Rather than turning only to psychiatrists, physicians, and plastic surgeons to define and describe our identities and experiences, we have begun to look to each other for support, affirmation, healing, and self-definition. The expression of individually developed gender identity within an atmosphere of nonconformity and unconditional positive regard is supplanting the (increasingly unfashionable) psychopathological view.

The Lesbian and Gay Community Service Center's Gender Identity Project (GIP) in New York City is at the forefront of the movement to empower the community and its members, so that each member of the community has the inner resources to make decisions and prepare the way for future generations of transpeople.

Six years ago, the organized gender community had very little visibility. The trans population, along with other sexual minorities, was (and still is) at high risk for alcohol and substance abuse and HIV infection. At that time, the level of services available to this community was limited. Barbara Warren was then Director of the Lesbian and Gay Community Service Center's alcohol and drug intervention program, Project Connect. Several people of transsexual experience came to her for help through this service because it was a place in which they thought they might be safe. Barbara responded, and through doing work with transpeople in Project Connect, met Riki Anne Wilchins and Kathy Ottersten. In time, Riki Anne approached Barbara about providing a setting where people of transsexual experience might be able to gather together to work on issues specific to them. In short order, the Gender Identity Project was inaugurated, with a core volunteer staff composed of Yvonne Ritter, Rachel Pollack, Riki Anne Wilchins, Toni Gilligan, Christian O'Neal, and Kathy Ottersten. Day-to-day administration and supervision fell to Barbara Warren, who is now the Center's Director of Mental Health and Social Services. Six years later, the GIP now has a salaried coordinator, a community advisory council, and two dozen peer counselors from all walks of life.

The basic mission of the GIP has been to create a nonjudgmental atmosphere in which transpeople can grow at their own pace. Our great success is largely due to the fact that ours is a peer-driven program with an approach that depathologizes and normalizes the process of transition. In addition to one-on-one peer counseling, we offer professionally and peer-facilitated groups for women and men of transsexual experience, and for parents, family, and friends of transpeople. These groups generally meet weekly throughout the year. Those involved with the GIP also have access to the Center's other mental health and social service programs, which provide a variety of services focused on bereavement and grief, "coming out" issues, recovery, and HIV/AIDS-related services to the lesbian, gay, bisexual, and trans communities.

We offer orientation in the form of public forums, and in-service training to social-service agencies, youth organizations, schools, universities, the court system, and the police. This training is tailored to the needs of the agency, and normally takes the form of sensitivity training, cultural diversity orientation, and basic information on the characteristics and issues related to transsexualism and transgenderism. In April 1995, with the co-sponsorship of the International Foundation for Gender Education and the Greater New York Gender Alliance, the GIP presented its first Transsexual and Transgender Health Empowerment Conference at the Center. The conference attracted over one hundred health providers and consumers. A significant feature of this conference (which had the themes of partnership and empowerment) was that the presentations and most of the breakout sessions were led by transpeople and service providers together. Our perspective demystified the topic, dislodged some of the ignorance, and introduced the audience to the notion of an empowered community working together in partnership with service providers.

The discovery and development of trans-friendly and trans-knowledgeable health care providers is a major function of the GIP, and is closely linked to our efforts to reach out to caregivers to provide information and to develop a genuine sense of partnership. Many people in our society, including those in the health professions, regard transpeople as abnormal, sick, deviant, or perverted. This leads many of our people to shame, depression, and fear, and can lead to compulsive behavior, exploitation, rage, guilt, addictions, and suicide. By developing a positive and viable working relationship with these professionals, we can significantly impact the quality of care provided to our community.

Medical care is often costly. That isn't a problem if the consumer is wealthy or well insured. However, many of us are not able to afford such necessities. The HBIGDA Standards of Care are not easily met by those who are economically disadvantaged or economically oppressed. Two years ago, sensing that some work needed to be done in this area to alleviate this very significant problem, Barbara Warren, along with three of our peer counselors (Yvonne Ritter, Carla Roidos, and Philip Roemer) got involved with the Community Health Project (CHP), an agency with offices in the Center. The persistence and collaborative efforts of the CHP and the GIP came to fruition in May of 1995 with the opening of the THE (Transgender Health and Education) Clinic. Open once a month, the THE Clinic has a host of dedicated and enthusiastic trans volunteers (several of whom are GIP peer counselors), who provide medical, nursing, counseling, and administrative staff. Through the THE Clinic, trans people have access to health care in a trans-friendly atmosphere, as well as the opportunity to see firsthand what happens when an empowered community, their own trans brothers and sisters, develops a working and productive partnership with service providers.

A key to the ongoing success of the GIP has been the diversity of our peer counselors. They encompass a spectrum of lifestyles and provide role models from nearly every socio-economic, ethnic, and cultural category. Our participants include cross-dressers, transsexuals (pre-, post-, and non-operative), transgenderists, and nearly every other aspect of our community. The appreciation and celebration of our diversity encourages the development of an open-minded attitude. By building solidarity within our community, we can develop the strength to face the discrimination and prejudice without guilt, fear, or shame. Perhaps particularly for those who are HIV-positive or have AIDS, or are sex-industry workers, the experience of prejudice, violence, and internal and external transphobia is not new. In our groups, we seek to assist individuals to overcome the shame and guilt associated with gender-based oppression so that each of them can build a life which will promote growth, development, and freedom.

Our Gender Identity Project is one of New York's success stories—not only as a resource for advice, information, and assistance (telephone and written requests for information are received daily from across the country, as well as from the New York area), but also as a demonstration of community solidarity. We are, by our presence in the Lesbian and Gay Community Services Center, the nexus of that demonstration, showing that the categories themselves are far from rigid, and that they shift and overlap. Viewed only as trans folk, we are most certainly a minority. However, some of us also identify as members of the lesbian, gay, bisexual, drag, or leather communities. The acceptance and celebration of each other's uniqueness, along with these overlapping categories, constitutes the strength that builds a strong community. And it is our charter, the GIP's charter, to work together to overcome gender-based oppression, to break down the barriers and build community, not merely to build thicker sheaths of armor or stronger walls of protection.

CONTRIBUTORS

BARBARA F. ANDERSON, M.S.W., PH.D. maintains a private practice limited to sex therapy and provision of consultation to colleagues in the areas of gender counseling and ethical professional practice. She works in the Gender Program at the Center for Special Problems, and serves on the Transgender Task Force of the Human Rights Commission of San Francisco and on the ethics committees of the American Association of Sex Educators, Counselors and Therapists and of the Society for the Scientific Study of Sexuality. She is currently pursuing California licensure as a Clinical Social Worker.

ROSEMARY BASSON, B.B.B.S., M.R.C.P. is a sexual medicine consultant specializing in the management of sexual difficulties of men and women associated with medical and surgical disease and transgender conditions, and the teaching of sexual medicine. She is a member of the clinical faculty of the University of British Columbia within the Department of Psychiatry and the Department of Obstetrics and Gynecology.

ROSALYNE BLUMENSTEIN is the coordinator of the Gender Identity Project of the Gay and Lesbian Community Services Center of New York. Prior to coming on staff, she worked for the Project as an intern and volunteer. Her work at the center has included the development and implementation of the first support-group services for New York City transgender youth. She is currently studying the psychology of addictions at the City University of New York, where she was the first woman of transgender experience to receive the prestigious Belle Zeller Scholarship for community service and the Thomas W. Smith Academic Fellowship. Recently, she was invited to present on transgender issues as the first openly transgender psychology student at the American Psychological Association Annual Conference in New York City.

ANNE BOLIN, PH.D. received her Ph.D. in cultural anthropology from the University of Colorado. She is an associate professor of anthropology in the Department of Sociology at Elon College in Elon College, North Carolina. Her book, *In Search of Eve: Transsexual Rites of Passage* (Amherst, MA: Bergin & Garvey, 1988) received a CHOICE Magazine Award for an Outstanding Academic Book for 1988–1989. She has co-authored an anthropology of human sexuality text, *Bicultural Perspectives in Human Sexuality* (Albany, NY: SUNY Press, 1996), a multidiscliplinary and multicultural human sexuality textbook including primatology, the evolutionary record, cross-cultural and contemporary issues. She is co-editor and contributor to an anthology, *Athletics Intruders: Women, Culture, and Exercise* (Albany, NY: SUNY Press, 1996). Her current ethnographic research is with competitive women bodybuilders for a book entitled *Elegant Ironworkers: Beauties and Breasts in Bodybuilding*. She is an active competitor in amateur women's bodybuilding and continues her research with the transgender community. She is author of numerous articles on gender and the body, sexuality, gender theory, transgenderism, and gender variance.

HOLLY BOSWELL is the founding director of Phoenix Transgender Support in Asheville, NC. She is a pioneer with the transgender movement, who has always actively promoted a free range of gender expression through her essays, public speaking, and by developing educational programs. She has been centrally involved with the International Foundation for Gender Education, the Southern Comfort Conference, and was an editor of the journal *Chrysalis*.

Boswell has also been a primary initiator of Transgender Spirituality Awareness and circle gatherings. She is currently working to establish Kindred Spirits, a year-round "Transcend-Gender" retreat center in the Asheville area.

GEORGE R. BROWN, M.D. is chief of psychiatry and director of psychiatric research at Mountain Home VA Medical Center in Johnson City, Tennessee, and associate chairman, East Tennessee State University. He is a member of the Board of Directors of Harry Benjamin International Gender Dysphoria Association, and a member of the Board of Advisors of American Educational Gender Information Service, Inc., and a medical and psychiatric consultant to Boulton & Park Society. He was Boulton & Park Health Professional of the Year for 1993.

BONNIE BULLOUGH, R.N., PH.D. AND VERN L. BULLOUGH, R.N., PH.D. Together or individually, Vern and Bonnie Bullough have written extensively on prostitution, contraception, fertility, homosexuality, lesbianism, marriage and family, transgender and transsexual issues, and, in fact, on almost all aspects of human sexuality. Recent books they have authored include *Sexual Attitudes: Myths and Realities* (Amherst, NY: Prometheus Books, 1995), *Handbook on Medieval Sexuality* (in press), *Human Sexuality: An Encyclopedia* (New York: Garland, 1994), and *Cross Dressing, Sex, and Gender* (Philadelphia: University of PA Press, 1993).

Bonnie, who passed away in April 1996, was both a sociologist and a nurse, as well as a former dean at SUNY Buffalo. She was professor of nursing at the University of Southern California.

Vern is both a SUNY distinguished professor emeritus and dean emeritus at SUNY College in Buffalo. His primary field is history, but he has also taught sociology and is also a nurse. Currently, he is a visiting professor of nursing at the University of Southern California.

COLLIER M. COLE, PH.D. is a clinical psychologist practicing at the Rosenberg Clinic in Galveston. (This clinic is an outpatient psychiatric facility dealing with a wide spectrum of mental and emotional problems. Several "specialty" programs are housed there that specifically address various psychosexual disorders.) In addition to being a member of the American Psychological Association and Texas Psychological Association, Dr. Cole is a member of the Harry Benjamin International Gender Dysphoria Association and is a certified sex therapist and sex educator with the American Association of Sex Educators, Counselors, and Therapists. Additionally, he is an associate professor at the University of Texas Medical Branch in Galveston, holding appointments in the School of Allied Health Sciences and in the School of Medicine, where he teaches courses in psychiatry and human sexuality. He serves also as director for an interdisciplinary gender treatment program which has provided professional services to the transgender community throughout the Southern United States since the mid-1970s. He has lectured extensively on the subject of gender dysphoria and has published numerous articles in the area of human sexuality.

SANDRA S. COLE, PH.D. is a professor at the University of Michigan Medical School. She is a sexologist and is certified as a sex educator and counselor by AASECT (The American Association of Sex Educators, Counselors, and Therapists). For twenty-five years, she has taught sex education to medical students, physicians, and other health-care professionals. She has done pioneering work since 1968 in sexual health concerns in rehabilitation medicine, working with persons with physical disabilities.

For the past twelve years, Dr. Cole has affiliated with the transgender community—working with wives and partners on the topics of sexual health, intimacy, and relationships. She has been a consultant or participant at most of the national gender conferences and many regional chapters as well. Her extensive contributions to the community have included day-long workshops for women, workshops for couples, presentations on sexual development, and workshops on community outreach to professionals. Dr. Cole is the acting director and founder of the University of Michigan Medical Center Comprehensive Gender Services Program.

Dr. Cole has served for over ten years on the National Board of AASECT and served as its president from 1989 to 1994. She is also an elected fellow of the Society for the Scientific Study of Sexuality.

JASON CROMWELL, PH.D. is a doctoral student in anthropology at the University of Washington. He is past president of Ingersoll Gender Center, and a member of the Board of Directors of American Educational Gender Information Service, Inc. and the International Foundation for Gender Education. With Jamison Green, he revised and expanded the late Lou Sullivan's *Information for the Female-to-Male Transsexual and Crossdresser* (Seattle, WA: Ingersol Gender Center, 1990).

DALLAS DENNY, M.A. is founder and executive director of the American Educational Gender Information Service, a 501(c)(3) nonprofit clearinghouse for information about transgender and transsexual issues, and publisher of *Chrysalis: The Journal of Transgressive Gender Identities*. She holds a master's degree from the University of Tennessee and is a Licensed Psychological Examiner with more than twenty years of experience as a mental-health professional. Her books *Gender Dysphoria: A Guide to Research* and *Identity Management in Transsexualism* were published in 1994.

HOLLY DEVOR, PH.D. is associate professor of sociology at the University of Victoria, Canada. She is the author of *Gender Blending: Confronting the Limits of Duality* (Bloomington: University of Indiana Press, 1997), *FTM: Female-to-Male Transsexuals in Society*, and numerous scholarly articles.

RICHARD EKINS, PH.D. is director of the Trans-Gender Archive and Senior Lecturer in Social Psychology and Psychoanalysis at the University of Ulster of Coleraine. He has published widely on various aspects of transgender and is co-editor of *Centres and Peripheries of Psychoanalysis* (Karnac Books, 1994) and *Blending Genders* (New York: Routledge, 1996). His book *Male Femaling* was published by Routledge in 1996.

STACY ELLIOTT, M.D. graduated from the University of British Columbia Medical School in 1985 and went on to do a two-year clinical fellowship in sexual medicine in Vancouver, B.C., Canada. She now specializes in male sexual dysfunction, gender dysphoria, and the sexual and fertility rehabilitation of persons with traumatic injury or illness.

SHIRLEY EMERSON, PH.D. is an associate professor of counseling at the University of Nevada, Las Vegas. She is the president of the Nevada Board of Marriage and Family Therapist Examiners.

JAMISON GREEN M.D., J.D., M.F.A. is the director of FTM International, the world's largest information and networking group for female-to-male transgendered people and transsexual men. He is a writer of both fiction and nonfiction, and until recently served as editor of the *FTM Newsletter*. As a gender-diversity consultant, Mr. Green provides academic lectures, organizational sensitivity training, and transgender advocacy services to groups, institutions, and corporations. He is a member of the board of directors of the International Foundation for Gender Education, and his work with the San Francisco Human Rights was instrumental in the 1995 implementation of legislation to protect transgendered people in the City and County of San Francisco. He holds a master of fine arts degree in English/creative writing, and has published several short stories, one of which was nominated for the 1984 Pushcart Prize. He is also a technical communications consultant for high technology medical, electronics, and financial corporations.

RICHARD GREEN, M.D., JD.S. co-edited the first interdisciplinary text on transsexualism in 1969, *Transsexualism and Sex Reassignment*, published by the Johns Hopkins Press. His continued focus on transsexualism is illustrated by his 1995 co-authored chapter "Gender Identity Disorder" (the new diagnostic term for transsexualism), published in the *Comprehensive Textbook of Psychiatry*. Dr. Green is both a psychiatrist and an attorney, having graduated from the Johns Hopkins Medical School and the Yale Law School. He is professor emeritus of psychiatry at the University of California, Los Angeles, visiting professor of psychiatry, Charing Cross and Westminster Medical School, and consultant psychiatrist and research director, Gender Identity Clinic, as well as senior research fellow, Institute of Criminology, University of Cambridge. He has been editor of *Archives of Sexual Behavior* since 1971 and has authored, co-authored, or edited over 150 professional journal articles, textbook chapters, and books.

WILLIAM A. HENKIN, PH.D. is a licensed marital and family therapist who practices in San Francisco, California. He is a board-certified sex therapist, a member of the American Educational Gender Information Service, Inc., Harry Benjamin International Gender Dysphoria Association, and the International Foundation for Gender Education. He is author or co-author of more than a dozen books, including *Bodywise* (with Joseph Heller), *The Psychic Healing Book* (with Amy Wallace), and *Consensual Sadomasochism: How to Talk About It, and How to Do It Safely* (with Sybil Holiday).

RUTH HUBBARD, PH.D. is professor emerita of biology at Harvard University. She spent many years doing research in biology and has been a health activist, involved primarily in women's health issues. She also has thought and taught about how the society in which scientists work influences the questions they ask in their research and the answers they find acceptable and true. She has written articles and books on these various subjects, many of them with colleagues and students.

DAVE KING, PH.D. is a lecturer in the Department of Sociology, Social Policy and Social Work at the University of Liverpool, England. He has been researching and writing in the area now known as transgenderism for a number of years. In addition to several articles, he has written *The Transvestite and the Transsexual: Public Categories and Private Identities* (Brookfield, VT: Avebury, 1993) and has edited (with Richard Ekins) *Blending Genders: Social Aspects of Cross-dressing and Sex-changing* (New York: Routledge, 1996).

MARGARET LAMACZ, PH.D. is staff psychologist, clinical research in family study of obsessive compulsive disorder, Johns Hopkins University School of Medicine, Department of Psychiatry. She is co-author, with Dr. John Money, of *Vandalized Lovemaps*, and has seventeen scientific papers published in the field of sexology, psychoendocrinology, and genetic psychiatry.

WALTER J. MEYER III, M.D. is board-certified in pediatrics, pedi-endocrinology, general psychiatry, and child psychiatry. He is a professor in the departments of Psychiatry and Behavioral Sciences, Pediatrics, and Human Biological Chemistry and Genetics; director of the Psychiatric Clinical Research Center; Gladys Kemptner and R. Lee Kemptner Professor in Child Psychiatry, Department of Psychiatry and Behavioral Science; and vice dean of the School of Medicine at University of Texas Medicine Branch in Galveston. He is also a child psychiatrist at Shrine Burns Institute. He is the author of more than 120 articles and book chapters.

AHOOVA MISHAEL, C.P.E. is a certified professional electrologist with over 18 years of experience. She has treated more than 150 transsexual women and crossdressers in a respectful, caring, and supportive environment. She takes pride and joy in the practice of electrology. Her practice is located in Atlanta, Georgia.

JOHN MONEY, PH.D. is internationally known for his work in psychoendocrinology and the new and growing science of developmental sexology. He introduced the now universally accepted idea that there is not one single criterion of sex, but several, ranging from genetic sex through morphologic sex to gender role as male or female. In 1955 he formulated, defined, and coined the term "gender role," and later expanded it to "gender-identity/role" (G-I/R). In 1961, he proposed the hypothesis that androgen is the libido hormone in both sexes.

An indexed bibliography of Dr. Money's publications, 1948–1995, was published by Haworth Press in *John Money: A Tribute*, edited by Eli Coleman (1991). It contains 34 books authored, co-authored, edited, or co-edited by Dr. Money; 346 scientific papers; 87 scholarly review and book chapters; and many short communications, comments, and book reviews.

Dr. Money continues to publish prolifically. His most recent book, *Reinterpreting the Unspeakable: Human Sexuality 2000* (New York: Continuum Publishing Group, 1995) is about the philosophy and methodology of science in the practice of clinical psychoendocrinology and sexology.

IRA B. PAULY, M.D. received his M.D. from UCLA Medical School in 1958. He trained in psychiatry at New York Hospital, Cornell Medical Center from 1959 to 1962. He was on the faculty of the Department of Psychiatry at the University of Oregon from 1962 to 1974. He moved to Nevada in 1978 to chair a new department of psychiatry at the School of Medicine at the University of Nevada at Reno. He remained chairman and professor of psychiatry from 1978 to 1994.

While Dr. Pauly was in medical education and teaching throughout his career, he has remained active in clinical work, both as a general psychiatrist and as a specialist in human sexual concerns. He became interested in gender identity disorder in 1961 when he saw his first transsexual patient while still a resident in psychiatry. He began seeing Dr. Harry Benjamin's patients in his office in New York City. He published his first paper on treatment in 1965 in *The Archives of General Psychiatry*. Over a 30-year period, he published approximately 100 journal articles, book chapters, abstracts, films, and videotapes, most of which deal with sexual and gender issues.

He is a founding member of the Harry Benjamin International Gender Dysphoria Association, and was president from 1975 to 1987.

Currently, Dr. Pauly spends half of his time in Reno, and half in the northern part of New Zealand, where he is a psychiatric consultant in a small mental-health clinic.

JERILYNN C. PRIOR, M.D., F.R.C.P.C., professor of medicine in endocrinology at the University of British Columbia, is fascinated by and has studied many of the diverse effects of female hormones, especially progesterone's effect on bone formation. She was a founding member and co-chair of the Vancouver Hospital Gender Dysphoria Clinic, beginning in 1984.

CAROLE ROSENFELD, M.S. has counseled transgender clients individually and has facilitated a transgender support group for two years. She is a marriage and family therapist intern.

EUGENE A. SCHRANG, M.D. has been in medical practice since 1965; his professional interests are cosmetic and reconstructive plastic surgery and male-to-female transgender surgery. He is board-certified by the American Board of Plastic Surgery, and is an active member of both the American Society and International Congress of Plastic and Reconstructive Surgeons. He presently practices and resides in Neenah, Wisconsin.

LYNN E. WALKER holds graduate degrees in Medieval English, Education, Counseling, and Theology, and has served actively as an ordained minister of the Christian clergy. She is co-founder of Metropolitan Gender Network, of which she was chair from 1991 until 1994. She is vice-chair of the Congress of Transgender Organizations, co-founder and chair, GenderPAC, and co-founder, Transsexual Menace. She is a peer counselor at the Gender Identity Project of the Gay and Lesbian Community Services Center of New York City.

BARBARA E. WARREN, PSY.D., CAC is Director of Mental Health and Social Service Programs for the Lesbian and Gay Community Services Center of New York. She holds a doctorate in counseling psychology from the Florida Institute of Technology's School of Psychology and is a credentialed addictions counselor in New York State and a faculty member of the New York State Academy of Addiction Studies. She has years of experience in the development and implementation of addiction recovery services in community-based settings. In 1988, she was the founding director of the Center's Project Connect, one of the U.S.'s first gay-identified programs for prevention of abuse of alcohol and other drugs. As a consultant on policy and program development, she has worked with a number of city, state, and federal agencies, including the New York State Department of Health, the New York State Office of Alcoholism and Substance Abuse Services, the Federal Centers for Substance Abuse Prevention and Substance Abuse Treatment. She is currently Community Co-Chair of New York City's HIV Prevention Planning Group, with the Centers for Disease Control. Dr. Warren has taught in the graduate programs of Fordham, Hunter, Yeshiva, and Columbia universities, and has developed and taught courses for alcohol and drug counselors locally and nationally and provided diversity training to human services organizations and treatment facilities. As part of her special interest in the transgender communities, Dr. Warren developed the Gender Identity Project, the Lesbian and Gay Community Services Center's peer empowerment program for transgender and transsexual people. She is the author of several articles on community approaches to gender-identity resolution and a noted speaker and trainer in this area.

Index of Names

A., Johnny, 151
Abbe de Choisy (François Timoleon), 6
L'Abbe d'Etragues, 7
Abdul-Karim, F.W., 286
Abraham, F., 42, 43, 315
Abrams, P., 100
Ackinson, W.B., 325
AEGIS. *See* American Educational Gender
    Information Service, Inc.
"Agnes," 52
Agnew, Spiro, 43
Alice, 198
Allen, Carolyn, 141
Allen, Edgar, 19
Allen, William A., 19
Alojado, N., 280
American Educational Gender Information
    Service, Inc. (AEGIS), 24, 30, 31,
    80, 224, 317, 349
American Psychiatric Association, 22, 27,
    31, 74, 80, 130, 137, 138, 163,
    164, 169, 176, 215, 216, 217, 222,
    223, 228, 229, 230, 232, 237, 238,
    239, 240, 243, 244, 252-253
Annegers, J.F., 298, 301, 308, 311
Anzaldua, Gloria, 140, 141
Arana, Marcus, 154
Armstrong, D., 104
Arrindel, W.A., 391
Ashley, April, 101
Aspen, Bina, 317, 337, 351
Assagioli, Roberto, 169, 170, 171, 174
Asscheman, Henk, 277, 282, 283, 284, 286,
    289, 293, 294, 297, 298, 300, 307,
    308, 309, 310
Attis, 4
Auge, Rebecca, 177

Baldwin, L., 171, 172
Barbie, 88
Barr, S.I., 280
Barreto-Neto, Tony, 154
Bart, R., 391
Bart, S.I., 306
Basson, Rosemary, 336
Bateson, Gregory, 173
Bateson, Mary Catherine, 63
Beach, Frank, 11,
Bean, Babe. *See* Garland, Jack Bee
Beatty, Christine, 157
Beaumont Society, 110, 181, 198, 199
Beaumont Trust, 181
Becarelli, 7
Bechtel, S., 164
Becvar, D., 393, 394
Becvar, R., 393, 394
Bem, Sandra, 56, 57, 60
Benjamin, Harry, xix, xxi, 3, 5, 13, 17-20,
    31, 69, 70, 92, 163, 209, 237, 239,
    243, 315, 419, 420
Bentler, Peter, 21, 31, 356
Berdache Society, 65, 65-67, 70, 74, 75, 79,
    80, 81
Berger, Jack, 33, 92
Berger, Peter, 98, 105
Berger, R., 183, 184
Berne, Eric, 173
Bernstein, P., 185
Bernstein, S., 137, 363
Berry, L., 171
Berti, Allesandro, 171
Besnier, 58, 60
Biber, Stanley, 24, 25, 316, 331, 336
Bigus, O., 182
Billings, D.B., 23, 29, 31, 106, 108, 185

David, King, 97, 98, 103, 106, 108, 110, 187, 202
Davidson, J.M., 310
Davis, Aaron, 155
Davis, K.B., 360
D'Eon, Chevalier, 6-7
de Cecco, J., 189, 251
de Jong, F.H., 310
de Lange, Jenny Savalette, 7
De Lauretis, Teresa, 118
De Magalhaens, G.P., 11, 13
De Savitsch, E., 6, 7, 13
De Vaca, Cabeza, 85
De Vries, C.P., 282
Dekker, Rudolph, 42, 43, 136, 141
Denny, Dallas, 22, 30, 32, 59, 60, 68, 75, 76, 79, 80, 224, 397
Derogatis, L.R., 21, 32, 368
Devereux, G., 9, 13
Devor, Holly, 29, 30, 32, 92, 102, 137, 250, 251, 255, 256, 257, 268
Devor, Howard, 177
Diagnostic and Statistical Manual of Mental Disorders (DSM). *See* American Psychiatric Association
Dickey, Richard, 224, 243
Dietrich, Marlene, 50
Diewold, P., 277, 284
Dillon, Michael, 158, 159
Dixen, J.M., 254
Dixon, J.E., 306
Djerassi, Carl, 20
Docter, Richard, 25, 32, 169, 231, 363, 366, 367, 368, 369, 365
Doisy, Edward, A., 19
Douglas, Mary, 139
Dragoin, William, 57,58, 60
Draper, A., 121
Driscoll, J.P., 103
DSM. *See* American Psychiatric Association
Duff, R.W., 87
Dulko, S., 306
Dupertuis, C.W., 325
Dupkin, C., 354, 356, 366, 368, 391

Eastwood, Clint, 43
Edgerton, Milton, 20, 33, 237, 315, 316
Educational TV channel (ETVC), 160, 163
Edwards, P.W., 254
Ehrhardt, Anke, 21, 33, 45, 46, 54, 68, 183, 237, 254, 412
Eichler, M., 106
Ekins, Richard, 98, 99, 100, 103, 181-182, 193
Eklund, P.I., 278, 282, 283, 286, 293, 294, 297, 298, 300, 307, 308, 309

Elbe, Lili, 15, 42, 43, 69
Eldh, J., 316
Elftman, 325
Ellenberger, H., 170
Ellis, Havelock, 237
Eltinge, Julian, 86
Emergence, 147
Emory, Lee, 231, 232
"Ephemeral Center," 81, 82
Epstein, J., xix, xxi, 54
Erdoes, R., 58, 60
Erickson, Reed, 20, 147
Erickson Educational Foundation, 20, 29, 147
European Court of Human Rights, 421
Everson, Cory, 87-88
Evert, Chris, 152
Ezzat, S.D., 283

Faculty of Social and Health Sciences Research Committee, University of Ulster, 202
Faderman, L., 124, 125, 269
Fagan, Peter J., 149
Fagot, Beverly, 237
Falbo, T., 366
Fallowell, D., 101
Fantasia Fair, 65, 86, 93, 357
Farley, J.R., 310
Farmer, Dee, 315
Farrar, Jennifer, 348, 349
Farrer, Peter, 100, 105
Fausto-Sterling, Anne, 46, 47, 54, 107
FDA, 233
Feinberg, Leslie, 57, 60, 156
Feinbloom, Deborah, 104, 137, 138, 187, 216, 237
Finifter, M.B., 325-326
Finklestein, J., 233, 277, 282, 301, 308
Finque, S., 123
Fire, J., 58, 60
Firestein, Beth, 160
Fisher, M.M., 86, 92
Fisk, Norman, 97, 98, 183, 237
Fitts, W., 366
Fleiss, J., 357
Fleming, Davis, 27, 32, 421
Fleming, M., 25, 32, 130, 131, 132, 240
Fogh-Andersen, Paul, 315
Food and Drug Administration, 233
Ford, C., 8, 11, 13
Foucault, Michel, 67
Foundation for the Advancement of Canadian Transsexuals, 147
Foundation for Full Personality Expression (FPE), 110

443

Fox, C.S., 285
FPE. (Foundation for Full Personality Expression), 110
Fraser, L., 169
Frazer, Sir James, 11, 12, 13
Freifeld, M., 280
Freud, Sigmund, 170, 171, 173
Freund, K., 21, 32
Fried, B., 45, 54
Friedreich, J., 237
FTM (Female-to-Male)
    FTM, The Newsletter of FTM International, 118, 141, 146, 148, 149, 160
    FTM Conference of the Americas, 158
    FTM International, 118, 158
Fullerton, C., 366
Fuss, Diane, 128
Futterweit, Walter, 308, 310

G., Julie, 123
Gabriel, Davina, 60
Gagnon, J.H., 272
Gallagher, C., 67
Gallagher, J.C., 280
Gamson, J., 230
Gandy, P., xix, xxi
Garber, Marjorie, 109, 111, 128, 133, 134, 137, 138, 139, 140, 141
Garbo, Greta, 50
Garfinkel, Harold, 52, 54, 105, 188
Garland, Jack Bee, 122, 124, 125, 160
Gay and Lesbian March on Washington, 155
Gay Liberation Front, 109
Geertz, C., 92
Gender Dysphoria Trust International, 181
Gender Identity Project (of Lesbian and Gay Community Service Center of New York), 427-429
Gender Networker, 147
Gender Review: The FACTual Journal
Gender Trust, 181, 183
Gender Worker, 147
Gifford, E., 8, 13
Gilbert, O.P., 6, 7, 13
Gilligan, Toni, 428
Gillmor, M.H., 31
Ginger, 193
Glaser, B., 100, 182, 184, 186, 187, 188, 189, 194
Glenn, J.F., 316
Goddell, Charles E., Senator, 43
Goffman, Irving, 55, 57, 60, 83, 99, 100, 187, 194, 196, 356

Goh, H.H., 283
Goldenberg, H., 393
Goldenberg, J., 393
Goldgar, D., 280
Goldin, N., 104
Goodheart, S.P., 171
Goodrum, Alexander, 154
Gooren, Louis, 278, 282, 283, 286, 293, 294, 297, 298, 300, 307, 308, 309, 310
Gorney, Cynthia, 153
Gossett, H., 141
Gould, M., 189
Goulian, D., 318
Grady, D., 285
Gravel, Thalia, 158
Graves, Robert, 12-13
Greater New York Gender Alliance, 428
Green, Jamison, 148, 159, 160
Green, Richard, xix, xxi, 27, 31-33, 70, 149, 183, 185, 209, 227, 243-244, 36, 412, 421
Grimm, D., 252
Gulens, V., 392
Gurdjieff, G.I., 172

Hadden, S., 182
Hage, J. Joris, 348
Hale, Jacob, 154, 155
Haley, Jay, 173
Halle, E., 391
Hamburger, Christian, 15, 16, 17, 28, 32, 36, 37, 43, 69
Hammond, W., 4, 10, 13
Hardman, R., 366
Hargrove, J.T., 285
Harper, J., 366
Harrison, David, 157
Harry Benjamin International Gender Dysphoria Association (HBIGDA), 23, 24, 92, 97, 216, 227, 234, 237, 240, 243, 348-349
Haskell, W.L., 285
HBIGDA. *See* Harry Benjamin International Gender Dysphoria Association
Hayes, C.D., 366
Head, Henry, 207
Heap, J., 188
Heer, D., 366
Heliogabalus, 5
Henry III, king of France, 6
Herdt, Gilbert, xix, xxi, 48, 54, 63, 92, 99, 202
Hermaphrodites with Attitude, 54
Hernandez, Michael, 155, 157

Leo IV, Pope, 5
Lesbian and Gay Community Service Center
    of New York, 427, 428, 429
Lever, J., 251
Levine, Richard M., 153
Levine, Steven B., 31, 232
Lewis, Yosenio, 154
Li, X.F., 283
Lief, Harold, 331
Linda/Les and Annie, 151
Lindemalm, G., 26, 32
Lindgren, T.W., 22, 33
Linkhart, T.A., 310
Lips, P., 283, 284, 310
Lorenz, Konrad, 18, 33
Lothstein, Leslie, 132, 133, 134, 242, 254, 391
Louis XIV, king of France, 6
Louis XV, king of France, 6
Luckmann, 105, 183-184
Lukas, M.J., 190
Lukianowicz, N., 243
Lundström, B., 21, 26, 33, 237
Lynn, Merissa Sherrill, 78

MacCormack, C.P., 121
Mackenzie, Gordene, 57, 60, 104, 105
Maddever, H., 254
Madonna, 50, 170
The Mahabharata, 4
*Malleus Maleficarum ("Hammer Against
    Witches")*, 4
Malloy, Terrence R., 316
Manilus, 5
Marcus, G.E., 86, 92
Marjoribanks, K., 366
Marker, Russel, 19
Martin, C.E., 251
Martin, E., 70
Martin, M.K., 91
Martindale, L., 92
Martino, Mario (pseudonym), 145, 147
Mary Elizabeth, Sister, 147
Masters, Robert E.L., 4, 5, 7, 12, 13, 14
Maxon, W.S., 285
Mazur, T., 397, 398
McAninch, J.W., 315
McCauley, E., 21, 33, 254
McCulloch, H., 23, 33
McDougal, William, 171
McGoldrick, M., 393
McGowan, B., 130, 131, 132
McIndoe, A., 315-316
McIntire, W., 367
McKay, D.W., 280
McKee, E., 33

McKenna, Wendy, 45, 50, 54, 68, 69, 99,
    105, 183, 184
McLish, Rachel, 87
McRae, R., 367
Meerloo, Joost, A.M., 28, 33
Megens, J.A., 307, 308
Melisaretas, N., 368
Menard, J., 280
Metamorphosis Medical Research Founda-
    tion, 147
    Metamorphosis Magazine, 147
Meyer, Jon K., 21, 25, 33, 237, 354, 356,
    366, 368, 391, 420, 421
Meyer, Walter J., 70, 230, 233, 277, 282,
    301, 308
Meyer-Bahlburg, Heino F.L., 31
Michaud, A., 280
Milligan, Billy, 176
Money, John, 3, 21, 22, 33, 45, 46, 54, 68,
    70, 183, 185, 190, 209, 217, 227,
    237, 315, 397, 398, 401, 402, 403,
    407, 411, 412, 414, 421
Montagna, W., 325
Monthly Vital Statistics Report, 357, 361
More, Kate, 160
Moreno, Jacob, 172, 174
Morgan, A.J., 316
Morris, Jan, 51
Morris, Ken, 154
Morton, Shadow, 154, 157
Murby, B., 306
Myers, P.S., 231

Nanda, Serena, 58, 60, 85, 415
National Institutes of Mental Health, 231
"National Transgender Annual Meetings",
    65, 85
Nauta, H.J., 307, 308
Navratilova, Martina, 151-152
Nero, 5
Nestle, Joan, 141
Netelenbos, J.C., 283, 284
Netherlands Gender Center Foundation, 26
New, M.I., 277
Newman, L.E., 391
Newton, Esther, 66, 103, 122, 187
New Woman's Conference, 84
New Woman's Caucus, 84
Nichols, Les, 151
NIMH, (National Institutes of Mental
    Health), 231
Noone, R.B., 316

O'Boyle, M., 231, 232
O'Neal, Christian, 428

Schminke, Thurin, 155
Schneider, J.W., 105
Schreiber, F.R., 164, 171
Schulter, M.P., 140
Schwartz, H., 181
Schwartz, I.S., 308, 310
Seahorse Club, 110, 354
Seeley, J., 186
Segal, L., 111-112
Shapiro, Judith, 98, 125, 126
Sheiner, Marcie, 151, 155
Shively, M.G., 189, 251
Siddigui, T., 12, 14
Sidis, Boris, 171
Signer, S.F., 297
Silverstone, R., 100
Simmel, G., 200
Simpson, O.J., 170
Singer, Ben, 154
Sipova, I., 306, 391, 306
Sliker, G., 167, 171
Small, Michael, 316
Smith, Karen, 312
Smith, Terry, 123
Smith-Rosenberg, Carol, 119, 139
Smyth, H.S., 283
Socarides, Charles, 28, 33, 106
Society for the Scientific Study of Sex, 17
Society for the Second Sex, 168, 170
Sontag, Susan, 66, 93
Sorensen, T., 315
Southern Comfort, 59
Southern Janus Alliance, 81
Spark, G., 393
Sparrer, Andreas, 15, 42, 43, 69
Spencer, R., 4, 14
Spier, L., 8, 14
Sporus, 5
Sprenkle, F., 393
Sprinkle, Annie, 151
Stall, B., 25, 33
Stampfer, M.J., 300
Stanislavski, Constantin, 172
Starka, L., 306
Steiner, Betty, xix, xxi, 21, 24, 32, 33, 117, 130-132, 137, 141, 237, 240, 363, 391
Steinman, C., 25, 31
Stephens, J., 243
Stetaneanu, L., 283
Stinson, B., 21, 33
Stone, Hal, 174
Stone, M., 56, 58, 60
Stone, Sandy, 51, 52, 54, 117, 118, 123, 125, 126, 138, 149

Stone, Sidra, 174
Stone Butch Blues, 156
Stoller, Robert, 117, 132, 135-139, 141, 183, 185, 188, 219, 237, 239, 253, 354, 356, 361, 366, 391
Strachan, N., 366
Strassberg, D.S., 21, 33
Strassberg, Lee, 172
Straub, K., xix, xxi, 54
Strauss, Anselm, 97, 182, 186, 187, 189, 198
Stryker, Susan, 157, 158
Stuart, C.A., 233, 254, 255, 277, 282, 301, 308
Stuart, Kim, 277
Sturup, G.K., 15, 32, 43, 69
Stuteville, O.H., 316
Sullivan, Louis G., 122, 124, 131, 145-149, 160, 170
Sun, Midnight, 86
Susie Homemaker, 88
Sutherland, R.L., 280
Sutton, J., 367
Swifthawk, Rena, 58, 60
Sybil, 176
Syntex Company, 20
Szasz, Thomas, 106

Talamini, John, 104, 187, 365, 367, 368
Taylor, John, 129, 230, 234
Teena, Brandon, 159-160
Thigpen, Corbett, 171
Thomas, W., 183
Thompson, P.D., 285
Thorne, Stephan, 153, 155
Thuwe, I., 21, 33, 237
Tipton, Billy, 109, 123-125, 141, 145, 152, 158-160
Tiresias, 3
T.O.P.S. (Transgendered Officers Protect and Serve), 154
Transactional Analysis, 173
Transexual Menace Men, 154
Transexual and Transgender Health Empowerment Conference, 428
Trans-Gender Archive, 181
Transgender Academic Network, 148
Transgender Health and Education Clinic, 429
Transgender Warriors, 156
Transgendered Officers Protect and Serve, 154
Transsexual People, 157
The Transsexual Phenomenon, xix, 3, 237, 419

Index of Subjects

GARLAND GAY AND LESBIAN STUDIES

WAYNE R. DYNES, *Series Editor*

FORMS OF DESIRE
*Sexual Orientation and Social
Constructionist Controversy*
Edited by Edward D. Stein

GENDER DYSPHORIA
A Guide to Research
by Dallas Denny

CURRENT CONCEPTS IN
TRANSGENDER IDENTITY
Edited by Dallas Denny